EUROPEAN POPULATION
DEMOGRAPHIE EUROPEENNE

Vol. 1 : Country Analysis/ Analyse par pays

Edited by/Edité par : Jean Louis RALLU et Alain BLUM

British Library Cataloguing in Publication Data
Rallu, Jean-Louis
European population.
Vol. 1. Country analysis.
I. Title II, Blum, Alain
304.6094

ISBN 0-86196-336-9
ISSN - INED 1144 - 7648

Éditions John Libbey Eurotext
6, rue Blanche, 92120 Montrouge, France.
Tél. : (1) 47.35.85.52 - Fax : (1) 46.57.10.09

John Libbey and Company Ltd
13, Smith Yard Summerley Street, London SW18 4HR, England
Tél. : (81) 947.27.77

John Libbey CIC
Via L. Spallanzani, 11
00161 Rome, Italy
Tél. : (06) 862.289

© 1991, Paris

Il est interdit de reproduire intégralement ou partiellement le présent ouvrage — Loi du 11 mars 1957 — sans autorisation de l'éditeur ou du Centre Français du Copyright, 6 bis, rue Gabriel-Laumain, 75010 Paris, France.

EUROPEAN POPULATION
DEMOGRAPHIE EUROPEENNE

Vol. 1 : Country Analysis/ Analyse par pays

Edited by/Edité par : Jean Louis RALLU et Alain BLUM

Published for the European Population Conference
Paris - October 21 - 25, 1991

Publié à l'occasion du Congrès Européen de Démographie
Paris - 21-25 Octobre 1991

Le Congrès est placé sous le haut patronage de
Monsieur François MITTERRAND
Président de la République

Sponsored by/ Organisé par

The European Association for Population Studies/ L'Association Européenne pour l'Etude de la Population (EAPS)

The International Union for the Scientific Study of Population / L'Union Internationale pour L'Etude Scientifique de la Population (IUSSP/UIESP)

L'Institut National d'Etudes Démographiques (INED - Paris)

REMERCIEMENTS/ACKNOWLEDGMENTS

Le Comité d'organisation remercie les organisations suivantes pour leur assistance financière/The Organizing Committee gratefully acknowledges the support of the following organizations:

Commission des Communautés Européennes
Office Statistique des Communautés Européennes (OSCE)
Ministère français de la Recherche et de la Technologie
Ministère français des Affaires Sociales et de l'Intégration
Mairie de Paris
Fonds des Nations Unies pour la Population (FNUAP/UNFPA)
United Nations Educational, Scientific and Cultural Organization (UNESCO)
Agence de Coopération Culturelle et Technique (ACCT)
The Population Council
Association Générale des Institutions de Retraites des Cadres (AGIRC)
Caisse Nationale d'Assurance Vieillesse des Travailleurs Salariés (CNAVTS)
Fédération Française des Sociétés d'Assurances (FFSA)
Union des Assurances de Paris (UAP)

L'organisation du colloque a, en outre, bénéficié des conseils de Bruno Remiche et de l'assistance scientifique de Thomas Frejka (Population Council)/The Organizing Committee has also been helped by Bruno Remiche and has received the scientific assistance of Thomas Frejka (Population Council).

Nous remercions d'autre part tout particuliérement Mmes Dany Faugère, Jacqueline Le Gourierec et Françoise Milan qui, par leur travail de dactylographie, mise en page et d'organisation ont permis la réalisation de cet ouvrage dans les délais voulus.

Comité d'Organisation/Organizing Committee:
Président : Gérard CALOT, Institut National d'Etudes Démographiques (INED)

Membres : Charlotte HÖHN, Bundesinstitut für Bevölkerungsforschung. Massimo LIVI-BACCI, Università degli Studi di Firenze, Dipartimento Statistico. Mohammed MAZOUZ, UNFPA/CIDEP. Nico VAN NIMWEGEN, Nederlands Interdisciplinair Demograpisch Instituut (NIDI). Guillaume WUNSCH, Institut de démographie, Univ. Catholique de Louvain.
Secrétaire Général : Alain BLUM - INED

CONTENTS/SOMMAIRE

VII. List of authors/Liste des Auteurs
IX. List of Countries/Liste des pays

XI.   **PREFACE/FOREWORD**
          Gérard CALOT

XIX   **AVANT PROPOS/PREFACE**
          Jean Louis RALLU

1.   **LA GRANDE-BRETAGNE/GREAT BRITAIN**
          Kathleen KIERNAM et Michael MURPHY

19.   **LA FRANCE/FRANCE**
          Roland PRESSAT

41.   **LA BELGIQUE/BELGIUM**
          Paul WILLEMS et Christine WATTELAR

63.   **LES PAYS-BAS/THE NETHERLANDS**
          Dirk VAN DE KAA et Yves DE ROO

83.   **L'ALLEMAGNE/GERMANY**
          Charlotte HÖHN

113.   **LE DANEMARK/DENMARK**
          Otto ANDERSEN

129.   **LA NORVEGE/NORWAY**
          Lars OSTBY et Inger TEXMON

151.   **LA FINLANDE/FINLAND**
          Mauri NIEMINEN

165.   **L'URSS/THE USSR**
          Anatole VICHNEVSKI

177.   **LA POLOGNE/POLAND**
          Jerzy HÖLZER

191.   **LA TCHECOSLOVAQUIE/CZEKOSLOVAKIA**
          Zdenek PAVLIK

209. **LA HONGRIE/HUNGARY**
 Andras KLINGER

225. **L'AUTRICHE/AUSTRIA**
 Peter FINDL

237. **LA SUISSE/SWITZERLAND**
 Hermann - Michel HAGMANN

257. **LA BULGARIE/BULGARIA**
 Kiril DONKOV

277. **CHYPRE/CYPRUS**
 Ionna CHAPPA

289. **LA GRECE/GREECE**
 Georges SIAMPOS

311. **L'ALBANIE/ALBANIA**
 Piro DISHNICA et Emira GALANXHI

325. **LA YOUGOSLAVIE/YUGOSLAVIA**
 Dragana AVRAMOV

347. **MALTE/MALTA**
 Reno CAMILLERI

355. **L'ITALIE/ITALY**
 Antonio GOLINI et Annunziata NOBILE

379. **L'ESPAGNE/SPAIN**
 Juan FERNANDEZ CORDON

393. **LE PORTUGAL/PORTUGAL**
 Maria José CARRILHO et João PEIXOTO

411. **LE LUXEMBOURG/LUXEMBOURG**
 Jean LANGERS

429. **LA SUEDE/SWEDEN**
 Peter SPRINGFELD

LISTE DES AUTEURS / LIST OF AUTHORS

Otto ANDERSEN, Danmarks Statistik, Sejrogade 11, 2100 COPENHAGUE (DANEMARK).

Dragana AVRAMOV, Institute of Social Sciences, Demographic Research Centre, Narodnog Fronta 45, 11000 - BELGRADE (YOUGOSLAVIE).

Reno CAMILLERI, Ministry for Eco. Affairs, Auberge d'Aragon, VALLETTA (MALTE).

Maria-José CARRILHO & Joäo PEIXOTO, Instituto Nacional de Estatistica, Gabinete de Estudos Demogràficos, 1078 - LISBOA CODEX (PORTUGAL).

Ionna CHAPPA, Ministry of Finance, Department of Statistics, Demographic and Social Division, NICOSIA (CHYPRE).

Piro DISHNICA & Emira GALANXHI, Direction de la Statistique, Secteur Démographie, Commission d'Etat du Plan, TIRANA (ALBANIE).

Kiril DONKOV, Office Central de Statistique, 2 rue Volov, 1592 - SOFIA (BULGARIE).

Juan FERNANDEZ CORDON, Institut de Démographie, Calle Amaniel 2, 28015 - MADRID (ESPAGNE).

Peter FINDL, Austrian Central Statistical Office, Population Division, Hintere Zollamtsstrasse 2B, A-1033 WIEN (AUTRICHE).

Antonio GOLINI, Istituto di Richerche sulla Popolazione, Viale Beethoven 56, 00144 ROMA (ITALIE).

Hermann - Michel HAGMANN, Université de Genève, Laboratoire de Démographie économique et Sociale, 7 rte de Drize, Case postale 266, CH-1227 CAROUGE, GENEVE (SUISSE).

Charlotte HÖHN, Bundesinstitut für Bevölkerungs-forschung, Postfach 5528, 6200 - WIESBADEN 1 (ALLEMAGNE).

Jerzy HÖLZER, Mazowiecka 11 m. 143, 00-052 WARSZAWA (POLOGNE).

Kathleen KIERNAN & Michael MURPHY, The London School of Economics and Political Science, Houghton Street, LONDON WC2A 2AE (ANGLETERRE).

Andràs KLINGER, Hungarian Central Statistical Office, II, Keleti kàroly utca 5/7, 1525 - BUDAPEST (HONGRIE).

Jean LANGERS, Service Central de la Statistique et des Etudes Economiques, Statistiques Sociales, 19 - 21 Boulevard Royal, BP 304, L-2013 (LUXEMBOURG).

Annunziata NOBILE, Universita degli Studi di Roma "La Sapienza", Dipartimento di Scienze Demografiche, Via Nomentana 41, 00161 - ROMA (ITALIE).

Mauri NIEMINEN, Central Statistical Office, Population Statistics Division, P.O BOX 770, 00101 - HELSINKI (FINLANDE).

Lars OSTBY & Inger TEXMON, Section for Analysis of Demography, Central Bureau of Statistics, P.O BOX 8131, Dep. 0033 OSLO 1 (NORVEGE).

Zdenek PAVLIK, Charles University, Faculty of Sciences, Dept. of Demo. and Geodemography, Albertov 6, 12843 - PRAGUE (TCHECOSLOVAQUIE).

Roland PRESSAT, Institut National d'Etudes Démographiques, 27 rue du Commandeur, 75014 - PARIS (FRANCE).

George SIAMPOS, Athens Univ. of Eco. and Business, Dept. of Statistics, 76 Patission St., ATHENS 10434 (GRECE).

Peter SPRINGFELD, Section for Demographic Analysis, Statistics Sweden, S-115 81 STOCKOLM (SUEDE).

Dirk VAN DE KAA & Y. de ROO, NIAS, Meijboomlaan 1, 2242 PR WASSENAAR (PAYS-BAS).

Anatole VICHNEVSKI, Institut des Problèmes socio-Economiques de la Population, ul. Krassikova 27, 117218 - MOSCOU (URSS).

Christine WATTELAR, Institut de Démographie, Université Catholique de Louvain, Place Montesquieu 1, Boîte 17, 1348 - LOUVAIN-LA-NEUVE (BELGIQUE).

Paul WILLEMS, Centrum Voor Bevolkings en Gezinsstudieu, Markiesstraat 1, 1000 - BRUXELLES (BELGIQUE)

INDEX DES PAYS/COUNTRIES INDEX

ALBANIE/ALBANIA	*311.*
ALLEMAGNE/GERMANY	*83.*
AUTRICHE/AUSTRIA	*225.*
BELGIQUE/BELGIUM	*41.*
BULGARIE/BULGARIA	*257.*
CHYPRE/CYPRUS	*277.*
DANEMARK/DENMARK	*113.*
ESPAGNE/SPAIN	*379.*
FINLANDE/FINLAND	*151.*
FRANCE/FRANCE	*19.*
GRANDE-BRETAGNE/GREAT BRITAIN	*1.*
GRECE/GREECE	*289.*
HONGRIE/HUNGARY	*209.*
ITALIE/ITALY	*355.*
LUXEMBOURG/LUXEMBOURG	*411.*
MALTE/MALTA	*347.*
NORVEGE/NORWAY	*129.*
PAYS-BAS/THE NETHERLANDS	*63.*
POLOGNE/POLAND	*177.*
PORTUGAL/PORTUGAL	*393.*
SUEDE/SWEDEN	*429.*
SUISSE/SWITZERLAND	*237.*
TCHECOSLOVAQUIE/CZEKOSLOVAKIA	*191.*
URSS/USSR	*165.*
YOUGOSLAVIE/YUGOSLAVIA	*325.*

Préface
Gérard CALOT
Président du Comité d'Organisation
Président de l'AEEP

C'est à la fois un honneur et une joie, pour les démographes français, d'accueillir dans leur pays le Congrès européen de démographie, organisé en commun par l'Association européenne pour l'étude de la population (AEEP), l'Union internationale pour l'étude scientifique de la population (UIESP) et l'Institut national d'études démographiques (INED).

A notre époque, où l'Europe a probablement les plus grandes chances de toute sa longue histoire de donner une signification politique concrète à ce qui fait son unité, il était bon que les scientifiques apportent leur contribution. Plus que d'autres, peut-être, cette rencontre à Paris des démographes de toute l'Europe constitue un symbole de cette volonté commune de mieux nous connaître, de confronter nos préoccupations et nos résultats, de porter ensemble notre regard sur l'avenir.

Notre plaisir est grand de voir aujourd'hui abolies les barrières qui entravaient, il y a peu de temps encore, la communication entre scientifiques européens. Nous sommes de ceux qui n'ont jamais cru à la pérennité de ces barrières et, en dépit des difficultés, nous avons toujours été convaincus de l'impérieuse nécessité de maintenir des relations entre les deux parties de l'Europe. Mais, comme bien d'autres, nous n'osions espérer que l'Histoire prendrait soudain une telle accélération ! C'est pourquoi nous adressons un message particulièrement chaleureux de bienvenue à nos collègues d'Europe de l'Est.

Nous ne manquerons pas d'évoquer, au cours de nos travaux, la communauté de destin qui, par-delà nos différences, nous unit. C'est en tout cas un des enseignements majeurs de la démographie contemporaine que l'étroite analogie des grandes pulsations qui impriment leur marque sur les courbes démographiques européennes, surtout en Europe occidentale. Non seulement nos pyramides d'âge portent à des degrés variables les traces des deux conflits qui ont embrasé notre continent, mais encore les courbes de fécondité et, dans une certaine mesure, celles de mortalité et même de migrations, témoignent, par leur convergence, de l'unité grandissante de notre culture et de notre civilisation. A coup sûr, c'est à un avenir de plus en plus commun, et aussi de plus en plus solidaire, que nous sommes promis.

Cette communauté de destin et cette solidarité croissante du "Vieux Continent" ne doivent pas pour autant nous faire oublier nos devoirs de solidarité à l'égard du Tiers Monde. L'Europe a tissé trop de liens avec l'ensemble du monde pour accepter que le fossé se creuse entre elle et les plus démunis. Le développement économique et social du Tiers Monde, dans le respect des cultures et des différences, doit demeurer parmi les préoccupations majeures des Européens.

La communauté des démographes français a été cruellement éprouvée l'année dernière par la disparition de deux personnes éminentes, qui auraient partagé notre joie à accueillir les démographes européens à Paris : Alfred Sauvy, il y a presque exactement un an, et Jean Bourgeois-Pichat, au printemps 1990. Nous saluons leur mémoire, avec reconnaissance pour ce qu'ils ont apporté à notre discipline. Le sourire, si pétillant, de l'un et de l'autre, nous manquera douloureusement à tous.

La tenue d'un tel congrès repose sur l'énergie et l'imagination de ses organisateurs, mais aussi sur la générosité des organismes qui sont en mesure de lui apporter leur contribution. En outre, une telle opération ne peut être réalisée sans le soutien des autorités politiques. Le haut patronage que le Président de la République française, Monsieur François Mitterrand, a bien voulu accorder à notre congrès témoigne de l'intérêt qui est porté au plus haut niveau de l'Etat à nos travaux et à notre discipline.

Les aides financières internationales qui ont permis de faire face aux dépenses entraînées par le Congrès de Paris proviennent de la Commission des Communautés Européennes, à qui nous devons rendre un hommage particulier pour l'assistance déterminante qu'elle a apportée, soit directement, soit par le canal de l'Office Statistique des Communautés Européennes (EUROSTAT), du Fonds des Nations Unies pour la Population, de l'UNESCO, du Population Council, de l'Agence de Coopération Culturelle et Technique. Les contributions françaises émanent du ministère de la Recherche et de la Technologie, du ministère des Affaires sociales et de l'Intégration, de l'INED, ainsi que de divers organismes publics et privés. A tous nous exprimons notre plus vive gratitude.

PREFACE

Je voudrais également remercier particulièrement le Comité d'organisation, constitué de Massimo Livi Bacci, président de l'UIESP, Mohammed Mazouz, membre de l'UIESP, Charlotte Höhn, Nico van Nimwegen et Guillaume Wunsch, membres du bureau de l'AEEP. Notre gratitude va également à Bruno Remiche, directeur de l'UIESP et Tomas Frejka, membre du Population Council, pour les conseils éclairés dont ils ont fait bénéficier les organisateurs.

La cheville ouvrière de la préparation de ce congrès a été Alain Blum, chargé de recherche à l'INED. Les efforts qu'il n'a cessé de déployer depuis deux ans vont trouver leur récompense dans le succès de ce congrès. Nous lui en exprimons toute notre reconnaissance.

Le présent ouvrage ambitionne de rester un souvenir tangible du Congrès de Paris : il contient un bref descriptif de la situation démographique contemporaine des divers pays d'Europe. Pour le préparer, Jean-Louis Rallu, chargé de recherche à l'INED, et Alain Blum ont fait appel à des collègues particulièrement bien informés sur les évolutions, notamment les plus récentes, observées dans leur pays. Aux uns et aux autres, nous adressons nos remerciements et nos félicitations.

Foreword
Gérard CALOT
Chairman of the Organizing Committee
President of EAPS

It is both an honour and a pleasure for French demographers to host the European Population Conference, jointly organized by the European Association for Population Studies (EAPS), the International Union for the Scientific Study of Population (IUSSP) and the French National Institute for Population Studies (INED).

At the present time, when Europe probably has the greatest chance, in her long history, of giving concrete political contents to her unity, it is well that scientists make their own contribution. More than others, maybe, this meeting in Paris of demographers from all over Europe is a symbol of this common will to know one another better, to compare our concerns and results, and to cast a joint glance at the Future.

It is with great pleasure that I see that those barriers which, not so long ago, still impeded communication among scientists, have been abolished. We never believed that they would stand for ever and, in spite of difficulties, we have always been convinced that relations between both parts of Europe should imperatively be maintained. But like many others, we dared not hope that History would suddenly race forward at such a pace ! For this reason, we extend a particularly warm welcome to our East European colleagues.

During our discussions, we shall probably evoke the community of destiny that, over and above our differences, unites us. One of the major lessons to be drawn from contemporary demography is the similarity of the currents which have marked European population curves, specially in Western Europe. Not only do our age-pyramids show the effects of the two conflicts which set fire to our continent, but fertility curves --- and, to a certain extent, mortality and even migration curves --- attest, by their convergences, the growing unity of our cultures and civilizations. Undoubtedly, we are set for a more or less common and mutually dependent Future.

This community of destiny and this growing solidarity within the ``Old Continent" should not, however, lead us to forget our commitment of solidarity with the Third World. Europe has woven too many ties with the rest of the world to accept that the gap between herself and the most deprived countries should enlarge. The economic and social development of the Third World, respecting cultures and differences, must remain one of the priority concerns of Europeans.

Last year, the community of French demographers was cruelly struck by the death of two outstanding persons, who would have shared our pleasure in welcoming European demographers to Paris: Alfred Sauvy, almost exactly a year ago, and Jean Bourgeois-Pichat, in spring 1990. We honour their memory, with gratitude for their contribution to our discipline. Their sparkle and their smiles will be painfully missed.

A conference of this dimension calls for many resources: the energy and imagination of its organizers, but also --- probably more --- the generosity of institutions that have the capacity to provide financial assistance. Moreover, such an operation cannot be undertaken without the support of political authorities. The patronage so kindly granted by the President of the French Republic, Mr. François Mitterrand, is proof of the interest taken in the highest spheres in our meeting and our science.

International financial aid that permitted to meet the expenses of the Paris Conference was provided by the European Community Commission - to which we owe special thanks for the efficient assistance provided both directly and through the Statistical Office of the European Communities (EUROSTAT) - , the United Nations Fund for Population Activities, UNESCO, the Population Council, and the Agence de Coopération Culturelle et Technique. French financial contributions were received from the Ministry of Research and Technology, the Ministry for Social Affairs and Integration, INED and various public and private institutions. To all of them, we express our gratitude.

I would like also to thank the Organizing Committee, composed of Massimo Livi Bacci, President of IUSSP, Mohammed Mazouz, IUSSP member, Charlotte Höhn, Nico van Nimwegen and Guillaume Wunsch, members of the EAPS Bureau. Our gratitude goes also to Bruno Remiche, Executive Secretary of IUSSP, and Tomas Frejka, member of the Population Council, for the instructive advice they gave the organizers.

The main bulk of the preparation of the conference has lain on the shoulders of Alain Blum, *chargé de recherche* at INED. The unflagging efforts he has made during the last

FOREWORD

two years will be rewarded by the success of the conference. We gratefully acknowledge the pains he has taken.

It is hoped that this volume will provide a concrete souvenir of the Paris Conference: it contains a brief description of the contemporary demographic situation in the various European countries. To prepare it, Jean-Louis Rallu, *chargé de recherche* at INED, and Alain Blum called on the participation of colleagues specially well informed on the evolutions, including the most recent ones, recorded in their countries. To all concerned, we express our thanks and congratulations.

Avant-Propos
Jean-Louis RALLU

Les caractères déterminants d'un siècle sont souvent annoncés dans les dernières années du précédent. Peu avant l'aube du XXIème siècle, l'Europe a connu des bouleversements décisifs pour son avenir, faisant suite à des évolutions démographiques plus anciennes mais qui furent également bouleversantes en leur temps.

Bien qu'appelée depuis longtemps outre-atlantique le "vieux continent", l'Europe reste - avant que commence un siècle qu'on qualifie déjà de "siècle du Pacifique" - un enjeu mondial au plan économique et géostratégique. Si, avec 790 millions d'habitants, y compris l'URSS (501 millions sans l'URSS), l'Europe est appelée à voir sa part dans la population mondiale diminuer - à partir d'environ 15% actuellement -, une grande partie de l'idéologie s'y crée encore et l'avenir des relations nord-sud, imposées par la démographie du siècle prochain, passe en partie par l'Europe. Deux guerres mondiales à un quart de siècle de distance ont montré que l'équilibre du monde dépend pour beaucoup de la situation de l'Europe. Après cinquante ans de paix en Europe, de semblables conflits mondiaux (même dans un cadre européen "élargi") ne paraissent plus guère possibles à l'avenir. Si un tel malheur devait se produire à nouveau, il renverrait le monde à un état antérieur et signerait probablement la fin prématurée de l'"ère occidentale". En effet, presque tous les pays européens ont subi, à des degrés divers, des pertes sévères lors des deux guerres mondiales, comme l'attestent les rapports nationaux présentés ici.

Cet ouvrage va permettre de faire le point des situations démographiques nationales en Europe et d'envisager les conditions d'une stabilité démographique européenne dans l'avenir.

L'Europe a connu au XIXème siècle et jusqu'au XXème siècle des transitions de la fécondité et de la mortalité dans le cadre de différences nationales et régionales très marquées. La baisse de la fécondité fut plus précoce à l'ouest et au nord qu'à l'est et au sud, selon l'histoire du peuplement de chaque région, la composition de la population et la rapidité du développement économique. La transition épidémiologique a été également très diversifiée dans sa chronologie selon les régions.

Le XIXème siècle et le début du XXème siècle virent des migrations très importantes en Europe et au départ d'Europe vers l'Amérique du nord. C'est à cette époque que s'est constituée la mosaïque des nationalités d'origine des Américains, à partir des populations des Iles Britanniques, de Scandinavie, d'Europe centrale et du sud. Cette migration s'est aussi dirigée vers l'Amérique du sud et l'Australie.

Les importantes différences observées dans la fécondité et la mortalité dans la première moitié du XXème siècle résultent largement de ces divers états d'avancement dans la transition démographique. Cette période fut aussi celle, dans les années 1920 et 1930, du premier choc économique moderne se répercutant à grande échelle sur la démographie.

De nombreux changements démographiques fondamentaux sont survenus au cours des dernières décennies. En premier lieu, la fécondité est retombée au-dessous du remplacement des générations de manière durable dès les années 1960 ou même 1950 en Europe de l'est, à partir de la fin des années 1960 ou des années 1970 en Europe de l'ouest et du nord et au cours des années 1980 dans l'Europe du sud, à l'exception de quelques rares pays. Bien que la fécondité se soit plus ou moins stabilisée à ces bas niveaux, souvent depuis plus d'une décennie, ces changements ne sont pas nécessairement irréversibles. Plusieurs auteurs dans cet ouvrage estiment que la fécondité pourrait remonter dans les années 1990, et les évolutions les plus récentes dans un certain nombre de pays - certes encore peu nombreux - vont dans ce sens. A notre avis, il semble cependant exclu qu'on retrouve dans un futur proche les niveaux de fécondité de la période du baby-boom qui, outre les variations de calendrier, reflétaient un modèle de fécondité où la part des familles de trois enfants et plus était encore élevée. Les conditions économiques qui prévalent actuellement, la nécessité d'une scolarité de plus en plus longue - allongée encore par la crise de l'emploi - ont pour corollaire un coût élevé de l'enfant, très dissuasif de la constitution de familles nombreuses. On peut ajouter que, jusqu'à présent, les craintes concernant l'avenir démographique et notamment l'équilibre futur des systèmes de retraites n'ont pas fait remonter la fécondité ni guère conduit les gouvernements à envisager de la relancer ; il est vrai que la solution du problème des retraites tel qu'il va se poser dans les deux ou trois prochaines décennies ne résulte pas de l'évolution de la fécondité future mais de l'évolution de la fécondité passée,

AVANT-PROPOS

conjuguée à celle de la mortalité. Il faudra donc trouver des solutions économiques au second problème démographique récent qu'est le vieillissement de la population, phénomène où l'allongement de l'espérance de vie, notamment aux âges élevés, joue un rôle important, en liaison avec les progrès de la médecine et les conditions économiques permettant les nouvelles découvertes et leur application à grande échelle.

Les changements récents de la nuptialité et de la divortialité, avec éventuellement leur corollaire qu'est l'augmentation de la fécondité hors mariage, s'ils ne marquent pas dans l'absolu la fin du mariage en tant qu'institution sociale, encore moins celle de la vie en couple, n'en posent pas moins des problèmes pour l'étude des phénomènes démographiques, nécessitant l'élaboration de méthodes nouvelles et d'études particulières qui sont un des sujets du second volume de la conférence.

Nous espérons que les changements politiques récents en Europe de l'est sont, quant à eux, globalement irréversibles. La constitution progressive d'une Europe de l'Atlantique à l'Oural - ou au Pacifique - va probablement s'accompagner de mouvements migratoires intra-européens - en Europe centrale et du sud - nouveaux non pas tant dans leur direction (car les migrations clandestines ont existé depuis longtemps) que dans leur possible importance numérique. Ces migrations peuvent être localement bénéfiques et leur importance économique et sociale pourrait être considérable. Cependant elles ne changeront rien à la structure par âge de la population européenne dans son ensemble et aux conditions économiques globales qui lui sont liées. Tous les équilibres régionaux (à l'échelle des nations d'aujourd'hui) peuvent être à repenser dans un futur proche. Le développement égal des régions d'Europe est une tâche prioritaire pour les toutes prochaines années.

Cette étape acquise, se reposera, s'il doit jamais cesser de se poser, le problème des migrations trans-méditerranéennes. C'est dans ce domaine que l'Europe peut assurer un équilibre mondial englobant les trois continents qu'aucune mer ne sépare complètement. L'avenir de ces migrations est étroitement lié à l'évolution démographique future des pays d'origine des migrants, dont la relation avec le développement économique a été mainte fois abordée et qui dépasse le cadre de cet ouvrage, sans, pour autant, devoir sortir de notre esprit. Cependant la situation économique et politique des pays d'accueil a aussi son importance dans la direction et l'importance numérique de ces mouvements. C'est la raison pour laquelle la plupart des rapports, notamment ceux des pays d'Europe de l'ouest, consacrent une place significative aux migrations et à leurs effets sur la population.

Des législations à caractère démographique ont été adoptées par plusieurs pays dans des domaines aussi divers que la nuptialité, le divorce, la fécondité, l'avortement et les migrations. Chaque pays passe ici en revue les grandes étapes de sa politique démographique et des politiques sociales en relation plus ou moins étroite avec la population. Si les effets à long terme des politiques démographiques sur la fécondité sont toujours l'objet de débats, les législations ont, dans le domaine des migrations, des conséquences beaucoup plus rapides et mesurables, même s'il existe une immigration clandestine. C'est aussi dans ce domaine que l'harmonisation des législations au niveau régional est sans doute la plus nécessaire.

Nous regrettons l'absence de quelques pays dans cet ouvrage: Islande, Irlande, Turquie, Roumanie. Des contraintes de délai ne nous ont pas permis de les insérer dans ce volume. Enfin, pour éviter l'arbitraire de l'ordre alphabétique juxtaposant l'Albanie et l'Allemagne, la Grande-Bretagne et la Grèce, Malte et la Norvège, la Pologne et le Portugal..., nous avons retenu une présentation qui devrait faciliter la lecture et qui consiste à faire le tour de l'Europe à partir du nord-ouest dans le sens des aiguilles d'une montre[1]. Les unités et les différences régionales et intra-régionales devraient ainsi être mieux mises en évidence.

---

[1] Les analyses du Luxembourg et de la Suède, parvenues tardivement, ont été placées à la fin du volume.

Preface
Jean-Louis RALLU

The particular characteristics of a century often begin to appear in the last years of the preceding one. As the 21st century dawns, Europe is witnessing upheavals of fundamental importance for her future, which themselves succeed earlier, though equally fundamental, demographic transformations.

Although long since dubbed "the old continent" by her transatlantic neighbours, Europe remains - even at the dawn of a century already termed the "century of the Pacific" - centre stage in economic and geostrategical terms. It is true that in demographic terms, with a population of 790 million including the Soviet Union and 501 excluding it, Europe's share of world population is declining from its present day figure of 15%; yet she still forms much of world ideology, and the future of north-south relations, which will depend on the demography of the next century, will partly be determined in Europe. Two world wars within one quarter-century have shown that to a great extent world stability depends on the situation in Europe. Such world conflicts (with their origins in Europe in its broadest sense) no longer seem possible. If by some misfortune such an event was to re-occur, it would set the world back to an earlier age and would probably mean the premature end of the "Western era". It is the case that almost all European countries suffered losses to a greater or lesser extent in the two world wars, as the national accounts presented here witness.

This collection of papers makes it possible to assess current national demographic situations within Europe and to consider the conditions necessary for future stabilisation of those situations.

In the last two centuries Europe has witnessed transitions in natality and mortality within a context marked by important regional and national differences. The drop in birth rate occurred earlier in the West and the North than in the East and the South, depending on the history and composition of the population of each region and on the speed of economic development. The epidemiological transition had an equally varied history from one region to another. The 19th century and the beginning of the 20th century were also a period of migration within Europe and from Europe to North America. It saw the creation of the wealth of national origins evident in America based on the populations of the British Isles, Scandinavia, Central and Southern Europe. Migration also took place towards South America and Australia.

The marked differences obvious in natality and mortality in the first half of the 20th century result in general terms from the different stages reached in the process of demographic transition. It was during this period - in the 1920s and the 1930s - that there occurred the first modern economic shock to have a major impact on demography.

Numerous fundamental demographic changes have taken place in recent decades. First, fertility fell below replacement level and remained there from the 1960s or even the 1950s on in Eastern Europe; from the late 1960s or the 1970s on in Western and Northern Europe; and in the 1980s in Southern Europe - with the exception of a few countries. Although fertility has often remained stable at these low levels for more than a decade, this trend is not necessarily irreversible. Several of the authors in this volume show how fertility could rise again in the 1990s, and the most recent developments in a number of countries - admittedly only a few - are in this direction. However we do not believe that in the immediate future we will see the type of fertility levels which characterised the baby boom, which besides changes in the timing of births, reflected a model with a high number of families with three or more children. Today's economic conditions; lengthening scolarity, prolonged yet further by the employment crisis, mean that children are expensive and discourage the formation of large families. It is worth adding that so far fears about future population decline and low levels of retirement pensions have neither pushed up natality figures nor governments to consider much population policies, and it is true that the solution to the kind of pension problems we will have over the next two or three decades will not lie in increased natality - being a result of former natality and of mortality. We will therefore need to find solutions to the second recent demographic problem, that of an ageing population, a phenomenon in which increased life expectancy plays an important role along with medical progress and an economic situation which favours new discoveries and their application on a large scale. The recent changes in marriage and divorce rates, and perhaps the accompanying rise in the rate of birth outside marriage, may not mean the final end of marriage as a social institution and even less so of life in couples, but they do raise certain problems for the study of demographic phenomena, and make necessary the development of new methods and the use of the type of individual case studies which are the subject of the second volume of the conference.

PREFACE

As for recent political developments within Europe, we hope that they shall not be reversed. The gradual creation of a Europe stretching from the Atlantic to the Urals - or indeed to the Pacific - will probably be accompanied by internal migration within Europe - in Central and Southern Europe - the importance of which will lie less in its direction (clandestine migration has existed for a long time) than in its volume. This type of migration may be beneficial in local terms, while its economic and social importance may be considerable. However it will neither alter the age structure of the population of Europe as a whole, nor the general economic conditions related to it. In the not too distant future we may have to rethink all the regional balances (in terms of present day nations). The equal development of the different European regions must be a priority in the coming years.

If we manage this, we will again be confronted - if indeed we ever cease to be confronted - by the problem of trans-Mediterranean migration. It is in this context that Europe will have the oppotunity to create a world balance which will encompass the three adjacent land continents. The future of these migrations is closely linked to the future demographic development of the countries of origin. The relation of this demographic development to economic progress has often been considered and goes beyond the subject of this volume - although of course we must bear it in mind. However the economic and political situation in the receiving country also plays an important role in determining the direction and volume of this type of migration. This is why most of the papers, especially those from Eastern Europe, discuss migration and its effects on the population in some depth.

Legislation of a demographic nature has been passed in several countries, covering such diverse topics as marriage, divorce, fertility, abortion and migration. Here each country takes a look at the major phases in its demographic policy and in its social policy in relation to population. Although the long term effects of demographic policy on fertility are still debated, legislation in relation to migration has much more rapid and more quantifiable consequences, even if clandestine immigration continues. It is no doubt in this context that regional harmonisation is most necessary.

We regret the absence of several countries from this volume - Iceland, Ireland, Turkey, Rumania. Deadlines would not permit their inclusion. Finally, to avoid the arbitrary nature of alphabetical order which would juxtapose Albania and Austria; Great Britain and Greece; Malta and Norway; Poland and Portugal, we have chosen an order which we hope will facilitate reading and which, grosso modo, starts in the North-West and moves clockwise round Europe[1]. In this way similarities and differences within and between regions should become obvious.

---

[1] The country studies of Luxembourg and Sweden were received late and have been inserted at the end of the volume.

COUNTRY ANALYSIS
ANALYSE PAR PAYS

Great Britain/La Grande Bretagne
Kathleen E. KIERNAN and Michael J. MURPHY

INTRODUCTION

This report on Britain highlights the main demographic changes that have occurred since the 1950s with a particular focus on the 1970s and 1980s. The Population of Great Britain (England, Wales and Scotland) was estimated to be 55.7 million in 1989 (50.6 million in England and Wales) compared with 48.9 million in 1951 and 54.4 million in 1971. In 1951 the expectation of life at birth (in England and Wales) was 66.5 years for men and 71.5 years for women, by 1971 the corresponding figures were 69.0 and 75.2 years, whilst in the period 1986-88 the values were 72.4 years for men and 78.1 years for women. In 1951 the Total Period Fertility Rate (England and Wales) was 2.14, in 1971 it stood at 2.37 and in 1989 at 1.80. Many of the data we present is derived from vital registration statistics and refers to England and Wales only; they are collected by the Office of Population Censuses and Surveys (OPCS) from whose publications all of the data presented here are derived, unless otherwise noted. Data for Scotland are collected separately, and combined data are not readily available for many of the topics that we discuss, although some are published both by OPCS and the Central Statistical Office (CSO).

Acknowledgement: Part of the funding for this paper is due to the Economic and Social Research Council under a grant on the Changing Demography of Families and Households (Grant number R000232161).

I. POPULATION SIZE AND STRUCTURE

The population of Great Britain rose from 37.00 million in 1901 to 44.80 million in 1931 and then growth was lower so that the population was 51.28 million in 1961. In the 1970s population growth slowed significantly but overall numbers still rose over that decade even though population actually declined in some years. The trend of population growth over the last two decades has been of a modest growth which is expected to continue for a similar period ahead, although this outcome will depend largely on the accuracy of fertility forecasts (Table 1).

TABLE 1: POPULATION SIZE AND STRUCTURE, GREAT BRITAIN 1951-2011 (MILLIONS)

Year	Age group						
	0-14	15-29	30-44	45-64	65-74	75 & over	Total
1951	10.95	10.02	10.85	11.71	3.60	1.73	48.85
1961	11.92	9.96	10.26	13.09	3.88	2.17	51.28
1971	12.93	11.36	9.51	13.07	4.61	2.54	53.98
1981	11.04	12.04	10.49	12.00	4.89	3.05	53.56
1991	10.66	12.57	11.80	12.08	4.91	3.93	55.94
2001	11.63	10.54	12.88	13.51	4.68	4.31	57.55
2011	10.89	11.43	11.15	15.42	5.05	4.37	58.32

Note: 1951 to 1971 data are census estimates, 1981 is resident population.
Source: Census reports, Official Population Projections, CSO Annual Abstract of Statistics 1991, Tables 2.4 & 2.5.

Turning to the age structure of the population, the main determinant is the previous trend of births, except at the oldest ages where mortality improvements have also had substantial effects. The most important aspect of fertility trends for current and future population age structure is the post-war baby boom and bust. Thus the birth peak in the early 1960s, followed by the subsequent trough around the middle 1970s, has progressively affected the educational, employment and housing sectors as these birth cohorts move through the relevant age-groups. The numbers of children peaked in the early 1970s; the numbers of young adults entering the labour force and forming new households (15 to 29) peaked in the late 1980s. The number of children was at a minimum in the late 1980s and young adults will be in this situation in the early years of the next century respectively. The other major change in age structure is in the numbers of elderly people - this topic will be covered in a separate section. Future population projections are based on a long-term assumption of around 2 births per woman, slightly above the estimate for the achieved fertility of women now finishing their childbearing.

The main determinant of population change has been annual fluctuations in the numbers of births; deaths have remained relatively constant and net migration has been both erratic, generally negative in magnitude and small when compared with natural change (Table 2).

TABLE 2.- CHANGE IN TOTAL POPULATION, GREAT BRITAIN 1946-89 (000s)

Period (mid-year to mid-year)	Population at start of period	Total change	Births	Deaths	Natural increase	Migration and other[1]
1946-51	47,867	262	876	576	300	-38
1951-56	49,176	166	768	568	200	-35
1956-61	50,004	304	849	588	261	+43
1961-66	51,380	358	954	617	337	+21
1966-71	53,168	244	904	628	276	-32
1971-76	54,388	61	738	653	85	-25
1976-81	54,693	24	678	646	32	-7
1981-86	54,815	76	705	646	59	+17
1986-89	55,196	152	749	626	123	+29

[1] 'Other' includes adjustments for armed forces and balancing items.
Source: Demographic Review 1977, Table 1.2 and Population Trends 63, Table 5.

II. FERTILITY TRENDS

There have been marked changes in the fertility patterns in the post-war period. In common with many other western societies, fertility reached its zenith in the early 1960s, peaking in 1964. From then there was a consistent decline until 1977, to a low-point of 1.66. The TPFR has remained below 2.1, replacement level, since 1973 (Table 3). During the 1980s it has oscillated around a level of 1.8. As yet there is little sign of a rise in fertility in Britain as has occurred recently in such countries as Sweden, Norway, USA and the former West Germany.

TABLE 3.- ENGLAND AND WALES TOTAL PERIOD FERTILITY RATES 1950-1989

Year	TPFR	Year	TPFR	Year	TPFR	Year	TPFR
1950	2.18	1960	2.68	1970	2.40	1980	1.88
1951	2.14	1961	2.77	1971	2.37	1981	1.80
1952	2.16	1962	2.85	1972	2.17	1982	1.76
1953	2.22	1963	2.88	1973	2.00	1983	1.76
1954	2.21	1964	2.93	1974	1.89	1984	1.75
1955	2.22	1965	2.85	1975	1.78	1985	1.78
1956	2.35	1966	2.75	1976	1.71	1986	1.77
1957	2.45	1967	2.65	1977	1.66	1987	1.81
1958	2.52	1968	2.57	1978	1.73	1988	1.82
1959	2.56	1969	2.47	1979	1.84	1989	1.80

Source: Birth Statistics Series, FM1.

TABLE 4.- AVERAGE NUMBER OF LIVEBORN CHILDREN BY AGE 40 (OR 1988 FOR THOSE NOT YET ATTAINED 40)

Year of Birth	Average Family Size	Year of Birth	Average Family Size	Year of Birth	Average Family Size
1931	2.32	1939	2.35	1947	2.06
1932	2.32	1940	2.35	1948	2.09
1933	2.37	1941	2.32	1949 (39)	2.05
1934	2.41	1942	2.27	1950 (38)	2.02
1935	2.40	1943	2.23	1951 (37)	1.98
1936	2.39	1944	2.20	1952 (36)	1.95
1937	2.37	1945	2.18	1953 (35)	1.91
1938	2.37	1946	2.17	1954 (34)	1.83

Source: Birth Statistics 1988, Table 10.2.

The TPFR is sensitive to short-term changes in the timing of having children, which may affect the number of births in a particular year. The average completed size of birth cohorts provides a more tempered measure of fertility (Table 4). Much of the 1940s generation, like their predecessors born in the 1920s and 1930s, achieved replacement level fertility. It is unlikely that the 1950s generation will do so unless they were to exhibit very high fertility rates in their late thirties. The partially-projected average family size for women born during the early 1960s (currently passing through their peak childbearing years) is just below two children per women (1.95) which is slightly above the current period rate of 1.8.

TABLE 5.- KEY STATISTICS ON FERTILITY 1964-1988, ENGLAND AND WALES

Year	1964	1978	1988
Live births (000s)	876.0	596.4	693.6
Crude birth rate	18.5	12.1	13.8
General Fertility Rate	92.9	60.1	63.0
Mean childbearing age			
All births	27.2	26.6	27.2
First births	24.0	24.5	25.1
Births outside marriage (%)	7.2	10.2	25.6
Births to non-UK born mothers (%)	n.a.	13.1	11.7
Source: Birth Statistics.			

A recent dramatic change in fertility behaviour is the growth in the proportions of births outside marriage (table 5). For much of this century up to the 1960s, apart from the periods covering the two World Wars, the illegitimacy ratio, i.e. the proportion of births born outside marriage was of the order 4-5 per cent. The ratio increased during the 1960s to a level of 8 per cent, fluctuated around 8-9 per cent during the 1970s, but since the late 1970s it has increased dramatically; reaching a level of 27 per cent in 1989. Half of these births are likely to be to couples who are cohabiting, in that they are living at the same address at the time the birth is registered.

III. FIRST MARRIAGE

Since the beginning of the 1970s young people have been marrying at increasingly older ages, and fewer of them are marrying (Table 6).

In 1961 the median age at first marriage amongst women was 21.6 years; by 1980 it had increased slightly to 21.8; but by 1989 it had risen sharply to 23.9. Teenage marriages have declined significantly in recent years and there has been a noticeable growth in the proportions of single women in the population. If present marriage rates continue, then the expected proportions of men and women married by age 50 derived from gross nuptiality tables, would be of the order of 78 per cent for men and 83 per cent for women compared with 92 per cent of women and 87 per cent of men in 1980.

TABLE 6.- KEY STATISTICS ON MARRIAGE 1971-1988, ENGLAND AND WALES

Year	1971	1980	1988
Number of marriages (thousands)	405	370	349
Median age at first marriage:			
Men	23.4	24.0	25.6
Women	21.4	21.8	23.6
Percentage of spinster brides:			
aged under 20	31	26	11
aged 30 or over	6	7	10
Percentage never-married:			
Men aged 20-24	63	73	85
25-29	26	32	50
30-34	14	15	23
Women aged 20-24	40	51	69
25-29	13	17	33
30-34	8	8	14
Estimated percentage married by age (Gross Nuptiality):			
Men aged 30	84	72	54
aged 50	93	87	78
Women aged 30	92	83	66
aged 50	96	92	83

Source: Marriage and Divorce Statistics Series FM2.

IV.- COHABITATION

Marriage rates began to fall in the early 1970s and have continued to fall throughout the 1980s. These sharp falls have been accompanied by a rise in the proportions of young people in cohabiting unions (Table 7). An increase in the proportions who cohabit or a lengthening of the time spent in such unions or both would tend to account for some of the fall in marriage rates.

During the 1980s the proportions of single women cohabiting has increased, from 8 per cent in 1981 to 20 per cent in 1988 (Table 7). Estimates show a three fold increase (from 185,000 to 617,000) in the number of single women cohabiting between 1979 and 1987. However, the duration of cohabitation amongst single women has changed very little: the median duration stood at 18 months in 1979; the corresponding figure in 1987 was 19 months.

TABLE 7.- WOMEN AGED 18-49: PERCENTAGE COHABITING BY LEGAL MARRIED STATUS: GREAT BRITAIN 1979 TO 1988

Legal married status	1979	1981	1982	1984	1985	1986	1987	1988
Single	8	9	10	12	14	15	17	20
Widowed	nil	6	3	4	5	3	11	5
Divorced	20	20	21	20	21	27	27	28
Separated	17	19	18	17	20	7	15	16
All never married	11	12	13	14	16	17	19	21
All women	3	3	4	4	5	6	6	8

Source: General Household Survey Report 1988.

To what extent does cohabitation compensate for the reduction in the proportions married? We estimate that, for the 1980s, around a half of the reduction in the proportions of women ever-married at ages 20-24 and one third of the decline at ages 25-29 years could be accounted for by the increased propensity to cohabit. Thus cohabitation is not the whole story in the decline of marriage rates. Young people are spending longer periods of time as solos than in the recent past; living with their parents, on their own, or sharing with others. Young people's formal marriage behaviour in the mid-1980s most closely resembles the marriage patterns prevailing during the 1940s.

Nowadays it is a virtually a majority practice to cohabit before marrying. For example, amongst never-married women marrying in 1987, 48 per cent had cohabited prior to marriage as compared with 19 per cent for women marrying in the late 1970s and 7 per cent of women marrying at the beginning of the 1970s. Cohabiting between marriages is virtually the norm: around 7 out of 10 second marriages are preceded by a period of cohabitation. In contrast to the position of single women where there has been apparently little change in the duration of cohabitation, the length of time that divorced women have been cohabiting has increased noticeably. For example, the median duration in 1979 was 28 months whilst amongst those cohabiting in 1987 it was 34 months. Part of the explanation for the declines in re-marriage rates observed throughout the 1980s (see Table 9 later) is likely to be that not only have divorced people continued to cohabit extensively but they also have been cohabiting for longer periods.

V.- DIVORCE TRENDS

Death still terminates the majority of marriages. However, marriages are increasingly being dissolved by divorce at a stage in marriage before one of the partners has died. Divorce has increased since the beginning of the 1970s and Britain has one of the highest divorce rates in Western Europe. Some key statistics are shown in Table 8.

The speed of change is most clearly seen when one considers the divorce behaviour of people married in the same year. For example, 10 per cent of couples who married in 1951 had divorced by their 25th wedding anniversary. However, amongst those marrying in 1961, 10 per cent had divorced by their 12th wedding anniversary, whilst amongst those marrying in 1971 and 1981 the corresponding durations of marriage were 6 and 4.5 years. There has also been a significant increase in the proportion of divorces where one or both partners had been previously divorced; 24 per cent of couples who divorced in 1988 in England and Wales fell into this category, compared with 9 per cent in 1971 and 17 per cent in 1981.

TABLE 8.- KEY STATISTICS ON DIVORCE, 1951-1988, ENGLAND AND WALES

Year	1951	1961	1971	1981	1988
Number of divorces (000s)	29	25	74	146	153
Divorce rate (per 1000 married couples)	2.6	2.1	5.9	11.9	12.8
Percent of divorced partners aged under 35 at divorce:					
Husbands	41	38	45	49	44
Wives	52	49	54	58	53
Percent ever-divorced by age 50:					
Men	n.a.	n.a.	7	13	n.a.
Women	n.a.	n.a.	8	12	n.a.
Percent of divorcing couples with both partners married:					
Once only	n.a.	88	89	81	75
Both more than once	n.a.	1	1	5	8
Percentage divorces granted to wives	55	55	60	71	71
Number of children aged under 16 of divorcing couples (000s)	35[1]	35[1]	81	159	150

[1] Children of all ages
Source: Population Trends 54, and Marriage and Divorce Statistics 1988, FM2 No 15.

VI.- RE-MARRIAGE

Marriages involving previously married partners now form a substantial minority of all marriages. Prior to 1972 about 80 per cent of marriages were first marriages for both parties, in 1988 the corresponding figure was 63 per cent and it is has been around about the two-thirds level for most of the 1980s (Table 9).

TABLE 9.- KEY STATISTICS ON REMARRIAGE 1971-1988, ENGLAND AND WALES

	Year		
	1971	1980	1988
Percent of all marriages: bachelors with spinsters	79	65	63
at least one partner divorced	16	32	33
Annual remarriage rate per 1000 Divorced people:			
Men aged			
25-29	504	299	144
30-34	396	231	130
35-44	254	157	97
Women aged			
25-29	364	228	147
30-34	237	161	108
35-44	141	105	70
Source: Marriage and Divorce Statistics Series FM2.			

How common is re-marriage after divorce and how soon after a marriage breaks down do the partners re-marry? A substantial proportion of divorced people eventually re-marry. Combined data from the 1987/8 General Household Surveys show that 29 per cent of women who divorced during the period 1981-1984 had re-married within two years and that 52 per cent of those divorced during the period 1977-1980 had re-married within six years.

Re-marriage rates for both men and women have been in decline since 1972. Much of the decline during the 1970s was probably related to the dramatic growth in the divorced population, the denominator of the rate, rather than a reduced propensity to re-marry. The declines during the 1980s are probably more associated with lower propensities to re-marry which may in turn be related to changes in cohabitation behaviour: as we noted earlier around 7 out of 10 second marriages are preceded by a period of cohabitation and the duration of cohabitation has been rising.

VII.- MORTALITY

Mortality improved substantially over the century from an expectation of life of around 45 years at birth at the turn of the century to 75 years now (Table 10). Most of the improvement took place in the early decades, but in the post-war period, improvement was relatively less in the 1960s than in surrounding epochs. It appears that mortality in the 1980s has been improving at a similar rapid rate to the 1970s.

TABLE 10.- EXPECTATION OF LIFE AT SELECTED AGES, ENGLAND AND WALES

	Birth			Age 15			Age 65		
Period	Male	Female	Ratio M:F	Male	Female	Ratio M:F	Male	Female	Ratio M:F
1891-00	44.1	47.8	0.92	45.2	47.6	0.95	10.3	11.3	0.92
1950-52	66.5	71.5	0.93	54.4	58.9	0.92	11.7	14.3	0.82
1974-76	69.6	75.8	0.92	56.2	62.1	0.91	12.4	16.4	0.76
1980-82	71.1	77.1	0.92	57.3	63.1	0.91	13.1	17.1	0.77
1986-88	72.4	78.1	0.93	58.4	63.9	0.91	13.7	17.6	0.78

Source: Demographic Review 1977 Table 2.5 and CSO Annual Abstract of Statistics.

These declines in mortality have meant that the age pattern of deaths has altered so that in 1901, 37 per cent of deaths were to children under 5, and 24 per cent to those aged 65 and over. By 1988 the figures were one per cent and 80 per cent respectively. In the 1980s particularly impressive falls in mortality among the elderly have been recorded, in contrast to the 1970s, where infant mortality exhibited the greatest improvements (Table 11).

Considerable attention has been given to socio-economic differentials in mortality. The most recent data for the 1970s, however, suggest that mortality inequalities widened rather than decreased in the recent past.

Among causes of death, circulatory system deaths fell below half of all deaths in the late 1970s, and respiratory diseases also became less prominent. However, neoplasms increased, together with a variety of other causes such as diabetes not shown in Table 12. In terms of the age pattern by cause, during the 1980s the main causes within ages have remained the same, with accidents being the main cause for ages one to 34; cancers for 35 to 54; and heart diseases for older ages.

GREAT BRITAIN/ LA GRANDE BRETAGNE

TABLE 11.- MORTALITY RATES (PER 000) IN SELECTED AGE GROUPS, ENGLAND AND WALES

	Age group						
	Infant mortality rate	1-4	25-34	45-54	65-74	85 & over	All ages
	Males						
1971	19.8	0.76	0.97	7.07	50.5	231.8	12.1
1981	12.6	0.53	0.89	6.11	45.6	226.5	12.0
1989	9.6	0.44	0.88	4.73	39.5	195.7	11.4
	Females						
1971	15.1	0.63	0.60	4.32	26.1	185.7	11.0
1981	9.4	0.46	0.52	3.80	24.1	178.2	11.3
1989	7.3	0.36	0.45	2.98	22.6	162.4	11.4

Source: Population Trends 63 Table 13.

TABLE 12.- DISTRIBUTION OF DEATHS (PER 000) BY SELECTED MAIN CAUSES OF DEATH, GREAT BRITAIN

	1971	1989
Infectious and parasitic	6	4
Neoplasms	209	250
Circulatory system	521	461
Respiratory system	127	117
Accidents and violence	41	32
All other causes	96	136
Total number of deaths (1000)	628,876	641,889

Source: CSO Annual Abstract of Statistics.

VIII.- INTERNATIONAL MIGRATION

In general, Britain has been a net exporter of population. Except for the decade mid-1956 to mid-1966, when there was an annual average net inflow of 21 thousand people, in the other decades since the war from 1946 to 1986, there was a net outflow, with the largest being between 1966 and 1976 when the annual figure was 46 thousand people. However, for most of the 1980s, there has been a positive inflow. In most years, there are gross flows of around 200 thousand migrants in both directions and migrants now form the highest number and proportion of the population since records began. In the 1981 Census of Great Britain, 3.36 million (6.3 per cent of the population) were born outside the United Kingdom, compared with 1.58 million in 1951 (3.2 per cent).

Of those born outside the UK in 1981, the largest number, 607 thousand were born in the Irish Republic, 625 thousand in other parts of Europe, 1,513 thousand in the 'New Commonwealth', mainly India, Pakistan, Bangladesh and the West Indies, who form the majority of Britain's 'ethnic minority' populations. For many purposes, such as the assessment of racial discrimination, information is required on ethnic groups rather than immigrants per se. In the mid-1980s, there were 2.5 million people classified in this way (Table 13). Because of their young age-structures, ethnic minorities will comprise a larger proportion of the population in years to come although the numbers will depend on the speed with which fertility differentials converge towards that of the indigenous population (which has already happened for some groups).

TABLE 13.- POPULATION BY ETHNIC GROUP AND COUNTRY OF BIRTH, GREAT BRITAIN 1985-87

Ethnic group	Numbers (000s)	Percent of pop.	Percent UK-born
White	51,333	94.4	96
Ethnic minorities	2,473	4.6	43
West Indian (including Guyana)	521	1.0	53
African	105	0.2	37
Indian	745	1.4	37
Pakistani/ Bangladeshi	515	0.9	40
Chinese	120	0.2	26
Arab	71	0.1	13
Other	141	0.3	31
Mixed	255	0.5	76
Not stated	570	1.0	70

Source: J. Haskey in Population Trends 54 (Labour Force Survey: 1985-87)

IX.- THE ELDERLY

The numbers of 'younger' elderly people will actually decline in the next decade as the low birth cohorts of the 1930s reach 65. However, the numbers of the 'old' old group (aged 85 and over) are expected to double between 1981 and 2501 (Table 14). There will therefore be a shift within the elderly population, a trend which is likely to continue into the next century although there have been problems in forecasting mortality at older ages (for example, the 1989 official population projections for people aged 85 and over for 2001 were 56 per cent higher than the comparable 1981 projection). Although the female advantage in mortality leads to increasingly larger proportions of women at older ages, it is anticipated that the sex ratios will become less extreme over time.

TABLE 14.- THE ELDERLY POPULATION (000s), ENGLAND AND WALES 1981-2001

Year	Males	Females	Persons	% of pop.	Sex ratio (m/f %)
65-74 years					
1981	2020	2599	4619	9.3	78
1991	2021	2549	4570	9.0	79
2001	1994	2272	4266	8.1	88
75-84 years					
1981	825	1564	2389	4.8	53
1991	1027	1759	2786	5.5	58
2001	1149	1759	2908	5.5	65
85 and over					
1981	126	415	541	1.1	30
1991	204	603	807	1.6	34
2001	290	770	1060	2.0	38

Sources: OPCS population estimates and mid-1989 based projections

X.- POPULATION POLICY

Unlike other countries in Western Europe, Great Britain has had no explicit population policy or family policies. However a wide range of British social and public policies affect the family in a variety of ways. From the perspective of the impact of policies on fertility and family size one might conclude that the effects are broadly neutral. There are policies which, on the one hand support families with children, while there are other provisions and services which enable couples to control their fertility.

1) Divorce

Before 1857, divorce could only be obtained by a private Act of Parliament and so was only available to the very wealthy. In 1857 an Act was passed which enabled divorce to be granted in a civil court. Divorce was only allowed on the sole ground of adultery. The first radical change to divorce law this century, occurred with the Matrimonial Causes Act of 1937. This Act extended the grounds on which divorce was admissible to include desertion, cruelty and incurable insanity. The second major piece of legislation of this century was the 1969 Divorce Reform Act, which came into effect on January 1st 1971 in England and Wales. This Act introduced a solitary ground for divorce of the 'irretrievable breakdown of marriage' which can be established by proving one or more of five 'facts'. The 'facts' are unreasonable behaviour, adultery, desertion, having been separated for two years if both parties agree and separated for five years is there is not mutual consent. The Matrimonial and Family Proceedings Act of 1984 included two main changes. One related to the minimum interval between date of marriage and being able to file for divorce. Prior to this Act the interval was three years, with some exceptions, afterwards it was one year. The second change was that the Act removed the previous and largely unworkable requirement that the Court should place the parties in the financial position in which they would have been in the marriage had it not broken down. Few people in Britain earn enough to be able to support two households. Now the court has to give first consideration to any children of the family and place greater emphasis on the desirability of the parties becoming self-sufficient so far as possible and empowers the court to dismiss outright an application for maintenance (alimony) payments. The Scottish Law Commission went a stage further in the principle of self-sufficiency and actually put a maximum of three years on the award of maintenance payments, except in exceptional circumstances.

2) Contraception and Abortion

The development of family planning in 20th century Britain arose from a concern about depopulation and the implications of differential fertility decline. The 1920s witnessed the expansion of voluntary birth control clinics. With the threat of war and depopulation in the 1930s, birth control clinics changed their emphasis from family limitation to the positive side of planned parenthood and promoted birth spacing as means of improving the health of women and children. A desire to tackle social problems after the Second World War led to the development of a comprehensive National Health Service (NHS) in 1946. Family planning however, was not incorporated into the NHS proposals. Central and Local government viewed birth control as a non-priority, in part because the issue was still strongly objected to on moral and religious grounds. Until the advent of the contraceptive pill the medical profession had chosen to largely ignore the issue of birth control. Specific legislation relating to the provision of family planning came into effect with 1967 National Health Service (Family Planning) Act which was facilitated by the passing of the Abortion act in the same year. The Family Planning Act allowed the provision of contraceptive advice regardless of marital status on social as well as medical grounds. Thus, family planning provision was extended in the late 1960s to the unmarried and the young. The 1973 National Health Service Reorganisation Bill led to further expansion by making contraception free of charge through clinics in 1974, and through community doctors in 1975. Vasectomy services were also provided free from around the early part of the 1970s.

Patterns of contraceptive use have changed markedly since the 1960s. Nowadays the most popular methods of contraception are the oral contraceptive and sterilisation. The former is declining somewhat in popularity.

Abortion became legal with the introduction of the 1967 Abortion Act but it continues to be a controversial issue. Various attempts have been made to restrict the conditions under which a women may terminate her pregnancy. The most recent attempt in 1990 has reduced the legal time limit for an abortion from 28 to 24 weeks. The numbers of abortions rose sharply in the years immediately following the 1967 Act from 54 thousand in 1969 to 119 thousand in 1973. The corresponding figures in 1980 and 1989 were 129 thousand and 171 thousand respectively. The rise in abortion rates during the 1970s occurred across all age groups; during the 1980s abortion rates at younger ages have continued to increase whilst those at older ages, beyond 30 years, have declined.

3) Immigration Policy

Immigration policy is not part of an explicit population policy, although successive attempts to restrict immigration, especially for those who are non-white, has been partially prompted by quasi-demographic concerns about 'swamping' of the native population. Moreover, patterns of immigration have been substantially affected by actual or proposed legalisation. Until 1961, Commonwealth citizens were allowed unrestricted right of entry, but Immigration Acts in 1961 and 1966 removed these rights. EC citizens became eligible for free right of entry following accession in 1973. The Nationality Act 1981 took away the right of abode for those born in the UK to non-UK citizens, and to certain other UK citizens deemed not to be 'closely connected with Britain'. Restrictions have also been placed on the entry of husbands of UK citizens. In addition, Britain has accepted many fewer refugees than comparable European countries, for example, by imposing substantial fines on carriers who bring refugee applicants to Britain without valid visas.

La France/France
Roland PRESSAT

I.- LA POPULATION DE LA FRANCE JUSQU'A LA DEUXIEME GUERRE MONDIALE

1) Aspect spécifique de l'évolution démographique passée

Certains aspects de la situation démographique actuelle de la France ne se comprennent bien que si on retrace l'évolution de cette situation au cours des deux derniers siècles.

Le trait marquant est la baisse précoce de la fécondité : amorcée à la fin du XVIIIème siècle, cette baisse ne connaîtra son terme qu'à la veille de la deuxième guerre mondiale.

L'évolution du taux de natalité en France et dans quelques pays voisins (tableau 1) montre qu'il y a eu baisse continue tout au long de la période en France tandis que dans les trois autres pays, la chute a été à la fois beaucoup plus tardive (dans la seconde moitié du XIXème siècle) et plus vive, en sorte que les situations étaient comparables à la veille de la dernière guerre.

TABLEAU 1.- TAUX DE NATALITE (POUR 1000 HABITANTS)

Période	France	Allemagne	Angleterre-Galles	Suède
1780-1789	38,3			
1790-99	36,9			
1801-10	32,0			30,9
1811-20	31,9			33,4
1821-30	31,0			34,6
1831-40	29,0			31,5
1841-50	27,4	36,1	32,6	31,1
1851-60	26,3	35,3	34,1	32,8
1861-70	26,4	37,2	35,2	31,4
1871-80	25,4	39,1	35,4	30,5
1881-90	23,9	36,8	32,5	29,1
1891-1900	22,1	36,1	29,9	27,1
1901-10	20,6	32,9	27,2	25,8
1920-24	19,8	23,1	21,3	20,3
1925-29	18,4	19,1	17,1	16,3
1930-34	17,0	16,3	15,3	14,4
1935-39	14,8	19,4	14,9	14,5

Source : 1780-1799 - L. Henry et Y. BLayo.- "La population de la France de 1740 à 1860", *Population*, numéro spécial, nov. 1975.
1801-1939 - INSEE.- *Annuaire statistique de la France*. Résumé rétrospectif 1966. Pour La France, jusqu'en 1860 non compris la Savoie, La Haute-Savoie et une partie des Alpes-Maritimes et de 1871 à 1910 non compris la Moselle, le Bas-Rhin. Pour l'Allemagne, jusqu'en 1910 territoire de l'Empire allemand de 1910 et, à partir de 1920, territoire de 1937.

C'est cette disparité des taux de natalité entre la France d'une part, et la plupart des pays européens voisins d'autre part, qui est, pour l'essentiel, à l'origine de la disparité des taux de croissance des populations correspondantes (tableau 2), alors même que l'émigration, insignifiante en France (et nettement inférieure à l'immigration) pesait d'un grand poids en Allemagne, en Angleterre et en Suède.

Finalement, le bilan démographique de la période allant de 1800 à 1936 peut être dressé ainsi que l'indique le tableau 3. L'immigration nette y est estimée par différence entre l'accroissement naturel (excèdent des naissances sur les décès, connu avec beaucoup de précision), et l'accroissement total (qui souffre de l'imprécision des recensements).

TABLEAU 2.- EVOLUTION COMPAREE DES POPULATIONS

Période	France	Allemagne	Angleterre-Galles	Suède
1800	100	100	100	100
1850	129	145	202	146
1910	147	262	407	229
1938	148	312	468	263

Source : INSEE.- *Annuaire statistique de la France.* Résumé rétrospectif 1966, sauf pour la France, "La population française", Tome I - France métropolitaine. *La Documentation Française,* 1955.
Note : Les données de la France se rapportent au territoire actuel, celles de l'Allemagne au territoire de 1870-1914.

TABLEAU 3.- ACCROISSEMENT DE LA POPULATION LORS DE DIVERSES PERIODES INTERCENSITAIRES (CHIFFRES EN MILLIERS)

Période	Accroissement de la population	Accroissement naturel	Immigration nette	Immigration nette cumulée
1801-1821	3 113	2 942	171	171
1821-1841	3 768	3 208	560	731
1841-1861	2 487	2 433	54	785
1861-1872	267	575	- 308	477
1872-1891	2 240	1 685	555	1 032
1891-1911	1 262	689	571	1 603
1911-1921	- 2 307	2 600	293	1 896
1921-1931	2 416	672	1 744	3 640
1931-1936	- 22	177	- 199	3 441

Source : "La population française", Tome I - France métropolitaine. *La Documentation Française,* 1955.
Note : Lors des périodes où il y a eu changement de territoire (1861-1872 ; 1911-1921), le bilan a été établi par référence au territoire actuel. Les accroissements de la période 1911-1936 ont été modifiés par rapport aux données figurant dans le tableau d'origine pour tenir compte de la surévaluation de la population de Lyon (de 1911 à 1936) et de Marseille (de 1921 à 1936).

Pour l'ensemble de la période 1801-1936, le chiffre cumulé de 3.441.000 immigrants nets donne une idée acceptable de l'apport net qu'a constitué le solde des mouvements migratoires en 135 ans, mais il faut remarquer que la moitié de cet apport a eu lieu dans la décennie 1921-1931. Ainsi, à la différence de la plupart des pays voisins dont la croissance démographique a été freinée par une émigration nette importante, la France a bénéficié d'un apport migratoire non négligeable et, malgré tout, l'accroissement de population y a été beaucoup plus faible qu'ailleurs.

Si la baisse précoce de la fécondité en France explique le moindre développement de la population au cours du XIXème et du début du XXème siècle, ce phénomène est aussi à l'origine d'un vieillissement de la population plus prononcé que dans les autres pays (Tableau 4).

TABLEAU 4.- POURCENTAGE DE PERSONNE DE 60 ANS OU PLUS

Date	France	Angleterre-Galles	Suède
1801	8,9		8,4
1851	10,2	7,3	7,7
1901	12,7	7,4	11,9
1936	14,9	11,6*	13,2
* année 1931 ; en 1951 la proportion s'élève à 15,9 (16,7 en France)			

2) Les étapes de la baisse de la fécondité et de la mortalité

On peut suivre de façon convenable l'évolution de la fécondité depuis le milieu du 19ème siècle, en se référant à l'indice synthétique de fécondité (tableau 5).

TABLEAU 5.- FRANCE. INDICE SYNTHETIQUE DE FECONDITE (EN NOMBRE MOYEN D'ENFANTS PAR FEMME)

1851-1855	*3,38*	1881-1885	*3,38*	1911-1915	2,25
1856-1960	*3,46*	1886-1890	*3,12*	1916-1920	1,65
1861-1865	*3,50*	1891-1895	2,97	1921-1925	2,42
1866-1870	*3,50*	1896-1900	2,90	1926-1930	2,30
1871-1875	*3,42*	1901-1905	2,79	1931-1935	2,16
1876-1880	*3,45*	1906-1910	2,60	1936-1940	2,07

Source : P. Festy.- "La fécondité des pays occidentaux de 1870 à 1970", INED Cahier de *Travaux et Documents*, n° 86, Paris, 1979.
Note : Les valeurs en italique reposent sur des estimations.

Dès le milieu du siècle la fécondité a atteint un niveau relativement bas (3,38), plus bas qu'en Suède (4,22), qu'en Angleterre-Galles (4,47), qu'en Allemagne (4,67). La situation est à peu près stable ensuite et ce jusque vers 1885 après quoi il y a chute régulière, marquée par l'accroc de la première guerre mondiale (déficit durant la période 1915-1919 et légère récupération ensuite).

Mesurée par la vie moyenne et le taux de mortalité infantile (tableau 6), la mortalité apparaît comme ayant sensiblement régressé à la charnière des XVIIIème et XIXème siècles ; les progrès stagneront un peu ensuite pour reprendre à la fin du XIXème siècle (les aggravations provisoires liées aux guerres de 1870 et 1914-1918 n'apparaissent pas dans le tableau 6 ; en se référant à J. Vallin[1] on peut avancer pour les années 1914-1918

---

[1] "La mortalité par génération en France, depuis 1899", Cahier de *Travaux et Documents* de l'INED, n° 63, Paris, 1973.

une vie moyenne masculine de l'ordre de 30 ans contre une valeur attendue un peu supérieure à 50 ans).

TABLEAU 6.- FRANCE. EVOLUTION DE LA MORTALITE

Période	Vie moyenne		Taux de mortalité infantile
	Sexe masculin	Sexe féminin	p.1000
1780-1789	27,5 ans	37,5 ans	278
1820-1829	38,3 ans	39,3 ans	181
1840-1859	39,3 ans	41,0 ans	166
1861-1865	39,1 ans	40,6 ans	199
1877-1881	40,8 ans	43,4 ans	183
1898-1903	45,3 ans	48,7 ans	150
1908-1913	48,5 ans	52,4 ans	123
1920-1923	52,2 ans	55,9 ans	99
1928-1933	54,3 ans	59,0 ans	81
1933-1938	55,9 ans	61,6 ans	68

Sources : 1780-1829 - Y. Blayo.- "La mortalité en France de 1740 à 1829", *Population*, n° spécial, nov. 1975.
1840-1938 - *Annuaire statistique de la France*, résumé rétrospectif 1966.
Note : Les vies moyennes sont exprimées en années et dixièmes d'année. Les taux de mortalité infantile sont ceux découlant des tables de mortalité donnant les vies moyennes ; ces taux ne comprennent pas les faux mort-nés.

Aussi importants qu'ils puissent paraître sur la longue période, ces progrès n'en classent pas moins la France à une position médiocre à la veille du deuxième conflit mondial. On relevait en effet, au cours des années trente, les valeurs suivantes de l'espérance de vie à la naissance (tableau 7).

TABLEAU 7.- VIE MOYENNE (EN ANNEES ET DIXIEMES D'ANNEE)

	Période	Sexe masculin	Sexe féminin
Allemagne	1932-1934	59,9	62,8
Angleterre-Galles	1930-1932	58,7	62,9
Suède	1931-1940	63,8	66,1

Sources : INSEE. *Annuaire statistique de la France*, résumé rétrospectif 1966.

Sauf lors de quelques années isolées durant les périodes de conflit armé (1870-1871 ; 1914-1919) et, de façon durable après 1934, les naissances l'ont toujours emporté sur les décès tout au long du XIXème siècle et dans la première partie du XXème. Ce n'est pas dire que les générations assuraient intégralement leur remplacement. Nous allons voir ce qu'il en est.

3) *La reproduction de la population*

Nous avons à répondre à la question suivante : est-ce que 1.000 filles nées chacune des années considérées auront donné lieu, globalement, à 1.000 naissances de filles et, conjointement, à 1.050 naissances de garçons (intervient ici le rapport de masculinité des naissances qui varie peu autour de 1,05) ?

Une réponse partielle nous est donnée par l'examen des descendances finales des générations considérées : tant que cette descendance atteint au moins 2,05 naissances vivantes chez les femmes ayant atteint au moins l'âge de 50 ans (limite supérieure de la période de fécondité) celles-ci auront assuré leur propre remplacement. D'après le tableau 8, il en est toujours ainsi, génération 1895 exceptée. Mais il nous faut prendre en compte ce qu'aura été la reproduction des femmes décédées avant 50 ans ; pour ces femmes, les descendances n'auront pas été pleinement constituées et même, pour certaines, spécialement pour celles décédées très jeunes, cette descendance aura été nulle. Ainsi le rôle des femmes qui survivent jusqu'à 50 ans est d'assurer par leurs nouveau-nés, outre leur propre remplacement, celui des femmes qui n'ont pas pu ou n'ont pu que partiellement constituer leur descendance. Ces descendances finales nécessaires (3ème colonne du tableau 8) sont d'autant plus élevées que la mortalité est plus forte. Par confrontation avec les descendances finales effectives, on fait apparaître dans quelle mesure le remplacement à la naissance est réalisé : il apparaît qu'il n'a jamais été assuré intégralement avec un déficit croissant au fil des générations.

Il reste à se demander pourquoi malgré ces comportements procréateurs déficitaires la population française n'a pratiquement pas cessé de croître au cours du XIXème siècle et au début du XXème (périodes de guerre exclues). Deux facteurs interviennent ici :

- l'importance d'une génération dans la population ne tient pas seulement à son effectif à la naissance, mais encore à son temps moyen de présence, c'est-à-dire sa vie moyenne. Avec le recul de la mortalité au cours de la période étudiée, un même nombre de nouveau-nés a compté de plus en plus dans la population, ce qui a quelque peu freiné l'effet du déficit croissant à la naissance ;

- la répartition par âge a toujours été plus favorable que l'aurait voulu une répartition qui aurait répercuté strictement les effets du niveau de fécondité de l'époque.

TABLEAU 8.- FRANCE. REMPLACEMENT DES GENERATIONS A LA NAISSANCE

Génération née vers	Descendance finale effective	Descendance finale nécessaire	Remplacement assuré à concurrence de
1825	3,40	3,61	94 %
1830	3,40	3,60	94 %
1835	3,40	3,51	97 %
1840	3,39	3,48	97 %
1845	3,35	3,50	96 %
1850	3,28	3,48	94 %
1855	3,16	3,42	92 %
1860	3,05	3,38	90 %
1865	2,89	3,35	86 %
1870	2,70	3,31	82 %
1875	2,62	3,17	83 %
1880	2,41	3,12	77 %
1885	2,24	3,08	73 %
1890	2,07	3,03	68 %
1895	2,00	2,93	68 %
1900	2,10	2,83	74 %

4) Effets démographiques des deux guerres mondiales

L'effet le plus direct résulte des opérations militaires. Alors que l'on peut chiffrer les pertes de la guerre 1914-18 à plus de 1.300.000,, celles de la deuxième guerre s'élèvent à quelque 600.000 morts, les pertes militaires proprement dites comptant pour 250.000, les pertes civiles s'élevant à 350.000 résultat des opérations militaires sur le territoire national et des déportations. Dans les deux cas, à cette surmortalité liée directement à la guerre s'ajoute une surmortalité due aux conditions matérielles de vie de la population civile. Assez faible durant la première guerre, cette surmortalité n'a pas atteint au cours de la seconde guerre l'ampleur que les rigueurs de l'occupation militaire allemande pouvaient faire craindre. C'est qu'à côté des aspects néfastes des pénuries diverses, certaines de ces pénuries se sont révélées salutaires et tout principalement celles entraînant des restrictions dans la consommation d'alcool. Au total, on n'aura eu à déplorer qu'une régression moyenne de 2 ans de l'espérance de vie à la naissance.

Les pertes indirectes résultent des déficits de naissances dus aux couples provisoirement désunis et aux mariages empêchés ; on chiffre ainsi à quelque 1.250.000 le manque de naissances ainsi provoqués au cours des années 1915-1919, portant le coût démographique total de la première guerre à près de 3 millions. Fait étonnant, malgré l'absence prolongée de 2 millions de prisonniers et l'existence de conditions générales peu favorables à la constitution de nouvelles unions, le taux de natalité, au plus bas en 1941 (13,1 p.1000) remonta ensuite : 14,5 p.1000 en 1942, 15,7 p.1000 en 1943, 16,1 p.1000 en 1944, 16,2 p.1000 en 1945, dépassant alors son niveau de la fin des années trente (moyenne 14,7 p.1000 en 1936-1939). Cette reprise, mesurée en terme de fécondité, se traduit par le passage de l'indice synthétique annuel de 2,10 en moyenne pour la période 1936-1939 à 2,19 en 1943, 2,24 en 1944 et 2,30 en 1945.

II.- L'APRES-GUERRE ET LA PERIODE RECENTE

1) L'essor démographique de l'après-guerre

Estimée à 41.502.000 habitants au recensement de 1936 (le dernier avant la guerre), la population de la France régressait à 40.503.000 au recensement de 1946, le vieillissement s'étant accentué, la proportion des "60 ans ou plus" passant de 14,9 % à 16,0 %.

La reprise de la fécondité observée au cours des sombres années de guerre va se trouver amplifiée par le retour aux conditions normales de vie amenant une reconstitution des unions avec récupération, au moins partielle, des naissances empêchées, et la récupération conjointe de mariages différés. Finalement ce phénomène de récupération est apparu à terme comme un épiphénomène face à un changement fondamental du comportement fécond de la population : au plus fort de la récupération, l'indice synthétique de fécondité avoisinait les 3 enfants par femme (moyenne 1946-1949, cf tableau 9), l'indice se situant ensuite très peu en retrait oscillant, avec de faibles amplitudes, autour de 2,70 et cela pendant plus d'une décennie. Il y eut même après 1960 une hausse ayant son origine dans la venue de plus en plus précoce des naissances.

TABLEAU 9.- **FRANCE**. INDICE SYNTHETIQUE DE FECONDITE (EN NOMBRE MOYEN DE NAISSANCES VIVANTES PAR FEMME)

1946	2,99	1954	2,70	1962	2,79
1947	3,02	1955	2,67	1963	2,89
1948	3,01	1956	2,66	1964	2,91
1949	2,99	1957	2,68		
1950	2,93	1958	2,67		
1951	2,79	1959	2,74		
1952	2,76	1960	2,73		
1953	2,69	1961	2,81		

Source : Calculs INED

Dans le même temps, la mortalité recule très sensiblement : la baisse de la vie moyenne durant les années 1940-1945 sera vite effacée et ensuite la hausse s'inscrira dans une ligne de tendance qui ignorera cet accroc des années de guerre (tableau 10). Le recul de la mortalité infantile est particulièrement spectaculaire.

TABLEAU 10.- **FRANCE**. EVOLUTION DE LA MORTALITE

Année	q_0	e_0 SM	e_0 SF	Année	q_0	e_0 SM	e_0 SF	Année	q_0	e_0 SM	e_0 SF
1946	77,8			1952	45,1			1960	27,4		
1947	71,1			1953	41,7			1961	25,7		
1948	55,9	61,56	67,19	1954	40,8	64,71	70,89	1962	25,7	67,20	74,16
1949	60,3			1955	38,6			1963	25,6		
1950	51,9			1956	36,2			1964	23,4		
1951	50,2			1957	33,8						
				1958	31,4						
				1959	29,6						

Source : INSEE
q_0 : Taux de mortalité infantile (pour 1000 naissnces vivantes)
e_0: vie moyenne en années et dixièmes d'année
SM : sexe masculin ; SF : sexe féminin

2) Evolution récente de la fécondité

Si l'on excepte les cinq premières années de l'immédiat après-guerre, 1964 marque le point haut de la fécondité en France après le deuxième conflit mondial. Après quoi, comme dans nombre de pays européens, une baisse à peu près continue sera enregistrée, faisant chuter l'indice synthétique jusqu'à un niveau inconnu jusqu'alors (sauf en 1915-1919 et en 1941)

TABLEAU 11.- **FRANCE**. EVOLUTION DE L'INDICE SYNTHETIQUE DE FECONDITE

1964	2,91	1971	2,49	1978	1,82	1985	1,82
1965	2,84	1972	2,41	1979	1,86	1986	1,84
1966	2,79	1973	2,30	1980	1,95	1987	1,82
1967	2,66	1974	2,11	1981	1,95	1988	1,82
1968	2,58	1975	1,93	1982	1,91	1989	1,81*
1969	2,53	1976	1,83	1983	1,78		
1970	2,47	1977	1,86	1984	1,81		

* Résultats provisoires

A quelques à-coups près, l'indice synthétique est stabilisé depuis 1978. Est-ce dire que nous sommes entrés dans un régime permanent de fécondité à ce bas niveau qui ne permet pas d'assurer le strict remplacement des générations ? Cette question conduit à analyser l'évolution de la fécondité selon l'âge de la femme et de préciser ainsi par quel mécanisme l'indice synthétique demeure à peu près stable.

- Le fait le plus frappant est la forte baisse pour ne pas dire l'effondrement de la fécondité aux jeunes âges. Ainsi, on relève à 19 ans et 24 ans révolus les descendances atteintes suivantes (pour 10.000 femmes).

	à 19 ans		à 24 ans	
Génération 1955 :	1412	*100*	7693	*100*
Génération 1960 :	979	*69*	6637	*86*
Génération 1965 :	677	*48*	(5 000)	*65*
Génération 1970 :	(480)	*34*		

- Parallèlement, à partir de l'année 1983, et à partir de 26 ans et plus nettement à partir de 28 ans, il y a hausse régulière des taux de fécondité (p. 10.000) :

	Taux le plus faible		Taux observé le plus récent		Pourcentage de hausse
	Génération	Valeur	Génération	Valeur	
28 ans	1955	1 277	1960	1 433	12 %
29 ans	1954	1 143	1959	1 312	15 %
30 ans	1953	1 000	1958	1 174	17 %
31 ans	1952	855	1957	1 028	20 %
32 ans	1951	708	1956	884	25 %
33 ans	1951	605	1955	739	22 %
34 ans	1949	473	1954	621	31 %
35 ans	1948	387	1953	511	32 %
36 ans	1947	305	1952	418	37 %
37 ans	1947	246	1951	321	30 %
38 ans	1946	183	1950	247	35 %
39 ans	1945	143	1949	178	24 %

C'est par un jeu de compensations entre taux en baisse (aux jeunes âges) et taux en hausse (à des âges assez avancés) que l'indice synthétique de fécondité se maintient à un niveau peu variable depuis 1978. Il y a remodelage de l'histoire génésique des générations féminines dans le sens d'une élévation de l'âge à la maternité.

Au terme de ce remodelage, à quel niveau s'établira la descendance finale ? C'est là la question essentielle dès lors que l'on s'interroge sur la manière dont s'effectuera le remplacement des générations : remplacement déficitaire, remplacement assurant la stationnarité de la population ou entraînant une croissance ?

Ce que l'on sait des descendances finales déjà acquises ne permet évidemment pas de répondre à cette question, puisqu'il s'agit de résultats nous renvoyant à des périodes anciennes. Si l'on admet que la connaissance de la descendance acquise à 35 ans permet de se prononcer sur ce que sera la descendance finale, on peut, au mieux, avec la connaissance des données de 1989 avancer ce que sera la descendance finale jusqu'à la génération 1954.

TABLEAU 12.- **FRANCE**. DESCENDANCE FINALE DES GENERATIONS

Génération	Descendance finale	Génération	Descendance finale	Génération	Descendance finale
1931	2,61	1939	2,44	1947	2,13
1932	2,62	1940	2,41	1948	2,11
1933	2,61	1941	2,37	1949	2,10
1934	2,59	1942	2,31	1950	2,11
1935	2,58	1943	2,29	1951	2,10
1936	2,54	1944	2,26	1952	2,11
1937	2,52	1945	2,22	1953	2,10
1938	2,48	1946	2,17	1954	2,10

A la stabilisation de l'indice synthétique correspond la stabilisation de la descendance finale, mais cette fois à un niveau plus élevé (2,10), niveau assurant le remplacement strict des générations.

A terme les courbes de ces deux indices finiront par se rencontrer puisque résultant de l'addition des mêmes éléments constitutifs (les taux par âge), la différence provenant d'un agencement différent de ces éléments. L'avenir est donc largement ouvert d'autant que le témoignage le plus récent fourni par la descendance finale est celui de la génération 1954, laquelle n'a pas connu avant 25 ans l'effondrement de la fécondité des jeunes femmes (générations nées depuis 1960) ; de plus cette génération était en pleine période de fécondité entre 25 et 30 ans, ce qui nous reporte aux années 1979 à 1984, marquées par un relèvement de l'indice synthétique. Ce qui peut faire douter d'une stabilisation quelque peu durable de la descendance finale à 2,10, c'est que le déficit des naissances chez les jeunes femme continu à croître de manière qu'il semble peu probable qu'il puisse y avoir pleine compensation en fin de vie féconde.

3) Nuptialité et cohabitation juvénile

La nuptialité connaîtra elle aussi une inversion dans son évolution : à la tendance à des mariages de plus en plus précoces mais conduisant à des proportions finales d'hommes et de femmes finissant par conclure un premier mariage peu varaibles, fera suite, à partir de 1972, un mouvement dans le sens de mariages de plus en plus tardifs et de moins en moins fréquents.

Cette désaffection vis-à-vis de l'union légale trouvera une compensation dans l'apparition puis l'extension très sensible de la cohabitation juvénile. Au total, ainsi que le montre le tableau 13, la nuptialité de fait qui se traduit par une situation de marié ou de cohabitant, aura peu varié, sauf avant 25 ans.

TABLEAU 13.- PROPORTIONS POUR 100 PERSONNES DE CHAQUE GROUPE D'AGE, DE CELLES MARIEES (1970) ET DE CELLES VIVANT EN UNION (MARIEES OU COHABITANTES,1986)

Ages	1er janvier 1970	1er janvier 1986		
	mariés	mariés*	cohabitants**	ensemble
		Sexe masculin		
21-24 ans	36,5	17,1	12,7	29,8
25-29 ans	69,7	54,1	16,9	71,0
30-34 ans	79,1	70,0	9,5	79,5
35-39 ans	83,0	81,2	6,6	87,8
40-44 ans	84,3	86,6	3,4	90,0
		Sexe féminin		
21-24 ans	59,4	34,6	19,3	53,9
25-29 ans	81,3	69,2	11,3	80,5
30-34 ans	87,9	75,5	8,5	84,0
35-39 ans	86,5	81,0	5,2	86,2
40-44 ans	85,0	79,6	4,0	83,6

Sources : 1970, INSEE ; 1986, INED
* : Ne concerne que les marié(e)s vivant avec leur conjoint légal.
** : Comprend des personnes mariées vivant en cohabitation.

Cette modification des comportements aura un retentissement important sur les manifestations de la fécondité en occasionnant en premier lieu une montée extrêmement forte des naissances hors mariage lesquelles, pour ne retenir que quelques chiffres, ont évolué comme suit :

En 1970 : 6,8 % du total des naissances
En 1975 : 8,5 % du total des naissances
En 1980 : 11,4 % du total des naissances
En 1985 : 19,6 du total des naissances
En 1988 : 26,3 du total des naissances

Le retentissement sur le niveau d'ensemble de la fécondité est plus difficile à déterminer, la pratique de la cohabitation pouvant très justement apparaître comme liée à un type de comportement vis-à-vis de la fécondité et non comme la cause directe déterminant ce comportement. Il reste qu'en période de cohabitation, la fécondité ne tient pas la place qu'elle occupe dans le mariage.

4) Baisse récente de la mortalité et vieillissement de la population

Jusque vers le début des années soixante le recul de la mortalité concernait essentiellement les enfants et les jeunes adultes. A ces âges, les progrès se sont poursuivis jusqu'à nos jours au point que parfois les taux sont devenus si faibles qu'il y a peu à attendre en gains en vies humaines d'une continuation de la baisse. Le recul de la mortalité infantile est à cet égard exemplaire (tableau 14)

TABLEAU 14.- **FRANCE**. EVOLUTION DE LA MORTALITE

Année	q_0	e_0 SM	e_0 SF	Année	q_0	e_0 SM	e_0 SF	Année	q_0	e_0 SM	e_0 SF
1965	21,9			1973	15,4			1981	9,7		
1966	21,7			1974	14,6			1982	9,5		
1967	20,7	67,69	75,20	1975	13,8	69,10	77,00	1983	9,1	71,04	79,19
1968	20,4			1976	12,5			1984	8,3		
1969	19,6			1977	11,4			1985	8,3		
1970	18,2			1978	10,7			1986	8,0		
1971	17,2			1979	10,0	70,05	78,20	1987	7,8	71,96	80,14
1972	16,0			1980	10,0			1988	7,8		
								1989	7,5		

Source : INSEE
q_0 : taux de mortalité infantile (pour 1000 naissances vivantes)
e_0 : vie moyenne en années et dixièmes d'année
SM : sexe masculin ; SF : sexe féminin

Mais le trait saillant de l'évolution récente est la baisse de la mortalité chez les gens âgés. Mettons en relief cet aspect nouveau de l'évolution en examinant comment les espérances de vie à 60 ans et à 85 ans ont progressé (tableau 15). Le tournant est pris vers 1970 : les progrès durant la période de 18 années allant de 1970 à 1988 sont nettement supérieurs à ceux de la période de 24 ans qui précède (qui va de 1946 à 1970). Le changement est particulièrement sensible chez les hommes. Il n'empêche que la surmortalité masculine est toujours allée en s'accentuant avec toutefois une tendance à un net ralentissement au cours des toutes dernières années.

TABLEAU 15.- ESPERANCE DE VIE A 60 ANS ET A 85 ANS (EN ANNEES)

Période	Sexe masculin				Sexe féminin			
1946-49	15,31		3,59		18,13		4,24	
1952-56	15,24	+0,52	3,44	+0,44	18,54	+2,28	4,12	+0,64
1960-64	15,78		3,85		19,82		4,57	
1966-70	15,83		4,03		20,41		4,88	
1978-80	17,14		4,46		22,21		5,41	
		+2,55		+0,69		+3,17		+0,93
1983-85	17,76		4,45		22,84		5,16	
1986-88	18,38		4,72		23,58		5,81	

Source : INSEE

Mais la conséquence la plus importante de ce changement d'évolution est d'avoir fait de la mortalité un facteur de vieillissement de la population, ce que montre bien les données du tableau 16 : à mortalité invariable au niveau de la période 1950-1952, les "60 ans ou plus" auraient constitué en 1985 15,9 % de la population et non la valeur observée de 18,1 % ; et l'on voit que l'amplification du processus de vieillissement dû au recul de la mortalité aux âges élevés est particulièrement sensible après 1970.

TABLEAU 16.- **FRANCE**. POURCENTAGE DE LA POPULATION DE 60 ANS OU PLUS

Pourcentage	1950	1955	1960	1965	1970	1975	1980	1985
- à mortalité constante*	16,2	16,2	16,4	16,9	17,1	17,2	15,3	15,9
- tel qu'observé	16,2	16,3	16,7	17,4	18,0	18,4	17,0	18,1

Source : Calculs INED
* : au niveau 1950-1952

5) Mouvement de la population depuis la dernière guerre

Avec le tableau 17 nous récapitulons ce qu'a été l'évolution de la population par grandes périodes depuis la fin de la guerre, chaque période étant délimitée en raison des caractéristiques particulières des modalités d'accroissement de la population :

1946-1953 : natalité et mortalité relativement fortes, faible migration nette ;
1954-1965 : natalité encore assez forte et forte migration nette où les rapatriés, essentiellement d'Algérie, comptent environ pour moitié
1966-1973 : natalité en baisse, migration nette encore forte

1974-1989 : poursuite de la baisse de la natalité et migration nette sensiblement ralentie (encore que la comptabilité du phénomène étant assez imprécise, on ne saurait prendre les données du tableau comme donnant un reflet exact de la migration nette).

TABLEAU 17.- **FRANCE**. MOUVEMENT DE LA POPULATION

Date	Population	Naissances	Décès	Accroissement naturel	Migration nette	Accroissement total
1.1.1946	40 125					
		6 744	4 322	2 422	338	2 760
		20,3	13,0	7,3	1,0	8,3
1.1.1954	42 885					
		9 941	6 274	3 667	2 402*	6 069
		18,1	11,5	6,6	4,3	10,9
1.1.1966	48 954					
		6 840	4 396	2 444	923	3 367
		16,9	10,9	6,0	2,3	8,3
1.1.1974	52 321					
		12 264	8 719	3 545	417	3 962
		14,1	10,0	4,1	0,5	4,6
1.1.1990**	56 304					

Source : INSEE ; les nombres absolus sont exprimés en milliers; les taux (en "pour 1000") sont respectivement les taux moyens annuels de natalité, de mortalité, etc.
* : dont 1 147 000 rapatriés
** : donnée provisoire

III.- ASPECTS DE LA POLITIQUE DE POPULATION

1) Politique profamiliale et nataliste

Un aspect important de la politique de population en France concerne les mesures en faveur de la famille et de la natalité.

La prise de conscience à la fin du XIXème siècle du déclin démographique du pays a donné naissance à diverses ligues ou associations à but nataliste ; au premier rang de ces associations on trouve l'*Alliance nationale pour l'accroissement de la population française*, fondée en 1896 avec J. Bertillon comme président.

Dans un premier temps les mesures profamiliales que l'action de ces groupements a pu inspirer avaient un caractère ponctuel ; si, entre les deux guerres, les progrès de la législation profamiliale seront plus conséquents, il faudra attendre 1939 avec la promulgation du décret-loi du 29 juillet, dénommé *Code de la famille*, élaboré par le *Haut Comité de la Population*, organisme consultatif créé quelques mois plus tôt, pour qu'un programme cohérent de mesures voit le jour.

La politique profamiliale française s'inspire encore actuellement dans ses grandes lignes des principes contenus dans le Code de la famille et cela après les très nombreuses retouches et compléments apportés aux premières dispositions prises pendant la guerre. Le principe de l'octroi de diverses prestations en espèces est au coeur du dispositif : allocations prénatales, de maternité, allocations familiales à partir du 2ème enfant,.... Par ailleurs, le principe du quotient familial, disposition originale, propre au système français, vise à alléger les charges fiscales des familles : le revenu du ménage est divisé en un certain nombre de parts (1 part pour chacun des parents, 1/2 part par enfant - actuellement 1 part pour chaque enfant à partir du 3ème) et la progressivité de l'impôt s'applique à chaque part et non au montant global du revenu.

Au total un ensemble de dispositions très complet sera mis en application à la suite des recommandations contenues dans le Code de la famille, ce qui n'avait de précédent dans aucun pays ; et certaines analyses suggèrent que la législation qui vit ainsi le jour a une responsabilité dans le relèvement de la fécondité dès les mariages conclus en 1941. Avec le temps, le poids relatif (c'est-à-dire par rapport aux revenus des ménages), des diverses dispositions financières au coeur de cette nouvelle politique, a perdu sensiblement de son importance tout en maintenant la France au plus haut niveau quant à l'aide apportée aux familles.

2) Contraception et avortement

Ce sont probablement les lourdes pertes de la guerre de 1914-1918 qui ont inspiré la loi du 31 juillet 1920 réprimant la provocation à l'avortement et à la propagande anticonceptionnelle.

Seuls étaient autorisés la vente du préservatif masculin en raison de son rôle prophylactique dans les maladies vénériennes et le recours à l'avortement thérapeutique lorsque la vie de la mère était en danger. Ajoutons que pour éviter qu'une trop grande indulgence se manifeste de la part de jurys populaires ayant à juger d'affaires d'avortements, ces derniers relèveront à partir de 1923 de tribunaux correctionnels. Enfin la loi de 1920 s'est trouvée renforcée sur certains points par un article du Code de la Famille de 1939 et la répression se fit particulièrement rigoureuse au cours de la guerre de 1939-1945, ce qui ira même jusqu'à l'exécution d'une avorteuse en 1943.

On a épilogué pendant longtemps sur les effets démographiques de cette loi. A-t-elle constitué un frein à la baisse de la natalité ? A-t-elle entraîné l'apparition d'un nombre important d'avortements clandestins ? Ces avortements sont-ils à l'origine de nombreux décès ? Il n'a jamais pu être apporté de réponses précises à ces questions.

En 1967 (Loi du 28 décembre dite loi relative à la régulation des naissances) les dispositions de la loi de 1920 relatives à la propagande anticonceptionnelle ont été abrogées. Cette nouvelle loi interviendra après que des associations aient vu le jour qui violeront ouvertement la loi répressive en vigueur. La délivrance des produits contraceptifs était subordonnée à une prescription médicale, la création de centres de planification et d'éducation familiale était prévue, et la propagande antinataliste restait interdite.

La crainte que de telles dispositions libérales fassent chuter la natalité a conduit le législateur à prévoir explicitement qu'"un rapport rendant compte de l'évolution démographique du pays" soit publié chaque année.

Les dispositions de la loi de 1920 relatives à l'avortement seront abolies par une loi du 17 janvier 1975, et l'avortement autorisé dans de larges conditions. Mais, ici encore, les dispositions législatives ont obéi aux pressions d'une large partie de l'opinion et entériné des pratiques se réfugiant de moins en moins dans la clandestinité. Et cette fois encore quelque peu inquiet par les conséquences possibles de son acte, le législateur, fait insolite, a assigné aux termes de la présente loi une durée de 5 ans, délai permettant de dresser un premier bilan de ses effets. C'est finalement une loi du 31 décembre 1979 qui entérina définitivement les dispositions de la loi de 1975. Toute femme enceinte de moins de 10 semaines qui en fait la demande peut avoir recours à l'avortement - sous réserve de l'autorisation parentale si elle est mineure -, celui-ci étant pratiqué par un médecin dans un établissement public ou privé.

Les craintes de ceux qui voyaient dans cette loi le risque d'une épidémie d'avortement ont été démenties. Sur la base des déclarations d'opérations pratiquées, lesquelles pêchent très probablement par défaut, et en ayant recours à des redressements, on peut avancer un chiffre annuel d'avortements de l'ordre de 200.000 à 250.000.

3) *Le divorce*

Institué en France par une loi du 20 septembre 1792, le divorce, qui pouvait dans un premier temps être prononcé dans des conditions très larges, fut supprimé en 1816 et à nouveau rendu possible par la loi du 27 juillet 1884. Si différentes modifications furent apportées aux dispositions de cette loi, les contours de cette dernière restèrent inchangées jusqu'à la loi du 11 juillet 1975 : le principe essentiel était celui exclusif, du divorce par faute d'un des deux conjoints.

Désormais, avec la loi de 1975, à côté du divorce pour faute, coexisteront le divorce par consentement mutuel et le divorce pour rupture de la vie commune (lorsque les époux vivent séparés de fait depuis six ans).

Cette modification profonde de la législation n'a pas entraîné une flambée de divorces ; c'est que, dans la pratique, depuis longtemps déjà des ruptures camouflées sous des motifs légalement recevables relevaient en fait du libre accord des deux conjoints. On observera en France une montée régulière de la fréquence des divorces dès la fin des années 1960 sans que la loi de 1975 ait introduit une rupture dans les séries statistiques (tableau 18).

TABLEAU 18 : **FRANCE**. DIVORCES ET INDICE SYNTHETIQUE DE DIVORTIALITE
(NOMBRE DE DIVORCES POUR 100 MARIAGES)

Année	Divorces	Indice synthétique	Année	Divorces	Indice synthétique	Année	Divorces	Indice synthétique
1970	38 949	11,8	1976	60 490	16,9	1982	93 892	26,0
1971	41 628	12,4	1977	71 319	19,8	1983	98 730	27,5
1972	44 738	13,2	1978	74 416	20,6	1984	104 012	29,2
1973	47 319	13,7	1979	78 571	21,5	1985	107 505	30,4
1974	53 106	15,2	1980	81 156	22,3	1986	108 380	31,0
1975	55 612	15,7	1981	87 615	24,1	1987	106 527	30,8
						1988	106 096	31,2

Sources : INSEE, INED

4) *Immigration et acquisition de nationalité*

Jusqu'à la première guerre mondiale l'immigration en France, motivée pour des raisons économiques, découle d'initiatives individuelles, sans entraves particulières des Pouvoirs publics.

Ce n'est que pendant la guerre que l'Etat interviendra dans le recrutement des travailleurs migrants ; à cette époque (1917) est créé la Carte de séjour. Toutefois, et jusqu'à la crise de 1931, un certain partage des rôles a lieu entre l'administration qui procède à différentes opérations de contrôle et les associations professionnelles qui pourvoient au recrutement. Des dispositions restrictives entreront en vigueur en 1932 afin de protéger la main d'oeuvre nationale gravement atteinte par le chômage.

Au lendemain de la seconde guerre mondiale, les exigences de la reconstruction créeront des besoins de main-d'oeuvre. Est créé alors *l'Office national d'immigration* (ONI, le 2 novembre 1945) qui se substitue aux organisations patronales dans les opérations de recrutement ; la délivrance de la carte de séjour sera désormais conditionnée par l'obtention préalable d'un contrat de travail. Par la suite, l'ONI aura aussi comme mission l'introduction des familles des travailleurs.

L'immigration ne connaîtra un véritable essor qu'à partir du milieu des années cinquante, cette reprise s'accompagnant d'une perte de contrôle de l'Etat, les lois du marché jouant un rôle prépondérant : l'ONI n'interviendra plus qu'a posteriori à des fins de régularisation de la situation des entrants.

LA FRANCE/FRANCE

La détérioration de la situation économique et le développement du chômage conduiront les Pouvoirs publics à prendre en juillet 1974 une série de mesures prescrivant "l'arrêt provisoire de l'introduction des travailleurs étrangers" tout comme "l'introduction des familles étrangères". Si certains assouplissements ont pu être apportés à ces mesures, tels ceux visant les regroupements familiaux et, en 1981, l'application d'une procédure de régularisation exceptionnelle des travailleurs étrangers entrés en France clandestinement avant le 1er janvier 1980, le principe d'un arrêt de l'immigration étrangère reste en vigueur (ne sont naturellement pas concernés les ressortissants de la Communauté économique européenne).

L'acquisition de la nationalité française est régie par le *Code de la nationalité*. Promulgué par une ordonnance du 19 octobre 1945, complété par la suite, ce Code définit les différents modes d'obtention de la nationalité qu'on peut définir comme un droit du sol. En s'en tenant aux possibilités les plus courantes, on devient Français

- si l'on est immigré
    - du fait du mariage avec un conjoint français (sur déclaration)
    - si l'on obtient la naturalisation

- si l'on est né en France
    - de deux parents étrangers
        - automatiquement à la majorité, sauf refus explicite
        - avant la majorité sur déclaration

    - de parents naturalisés ou de couple mixte
        - automatiquement.

A noter que la naturalisation, qui n'est pas un droit, est accordée par décret et suppose, en général, la justification de 5 ans de séjour en France. Voici, à titre indicatif, l'importance qu'ont prises récemment les dispositions actuellement en vigueur permettant l'entrée dans la communauté française (tableau 19).

TABLEAU 19.- ACQUISITIONS DE LA NATIONALITE FRANÇAISE (EN FRANCE METROPOLITAINE ET DANS D'AUTRES PAYS DE RESIDENCE)

Mode d'acquisition	1979	1980	1981	1982	1983
Naturalisation	20 164	20 203	21 541	18 073	13 213
Réintégration	1 562	1 977	2 811	2 349	1 557
Mineurs*	9 256	9 324	10 048	8 037	5 220
	30 982	31 504	34 400	28 459	19 990
Déclaration acquisitive	15 808	20 619	19 615	20 369	19 705
Ensemble des acquisitions	46 790	52 123	54 015	48 828	39 695

Mode d'acquisition	1984	1985	1986	1987	1988
Naturalisation	13 635	26 902	21 072	16 205	16 762
Réintégration	1 599	2 708	1 986	1 649	2 251
Mineurs*	4 822	11 978	10 344	7 848	7 948
	20 956	41 588	33 402	25 702	26 961
Déclaration acquisitive	15 517	19 089	22 566	16 052	27 328
Ensemble des acquisitions	35 573	60 677	55 968	41 754	54 299

Source : Rapport statistique annuel. Sous-Direction des naturalisations. Ministère de la solidarité, de la santé et de la protection sociale.
* Compris dans le décret de naturalisation de leurs parents.

ANNEXE.- POPULATION DE LA FRANCE AUX RECENSEMENTS (EN MILLIERS D'HABITANTS)

Date	Frontières			Taux annuels d'accroissement intercensitaire (1)
	de 1815 (538 000 km2)	de 1871 (536 000 km2)	Actuelles (551 000 km2	
1801	27 349		28 250	0,49
1821	30 462		31 161	0,64
1831	32 569		33 218	0,61
1836	33 541		34 240	0,39
1841	34 230		34 911	0,67
1846	35 402		36 097	0,21
1851	35 783		36 472	0,13
1856	36 039		36 714	0,36
1861	36 717		37 386	0,36
1866			38 067	- 0,18
1872		36 103	37 653	0,52
1876		36 906	38 438	0,41
1881		37 672	39 239	0,28
1886		38 219	39 783	0,08
1891		38 343	39 946	0,11
1896		38 517	40 158	0,26
1901		38 962	40 681	0,19
1906		39 252	41 067	0,17
1911		39 605	41 415	- 0,57
1921		37 500	39 108	0,74
1926			40 581	0,46
1931			41 524	- 0,01
1936			41 502	

Source : INSEE. Annuaire statistique de la France. Résumé rétrospectif 1966.
Pour la définition des territoires se référer au tableau 2.
Les chiffres de 1911 à 1936 ont été rectifiés pour tenir compte de la surévaluation de la population de Lyon (de 1911 à 1936) et de Marseille (de 1921 à 1936).
(1) Taux calculés dans les frontières actuelles (en "pour cent).

Belgium/La Belgique[1]
Paul WILLEMS and Christine WATTELAR

I. INTRODUCTION.

The core of this text is a longitudinal analysis of fertility by birth order covering approximately the last 40 years. However, as an introduction and in order to broaden the perspective, crude rates for a period covering the last 90 years are also presented. Despite the subtitle of this contribution, data for 1990 are not available yet at the time of writing: in the field of fertility data are available up to 1987. As for marriages and divorces data are available up to 1989. We will also formulate our expectations about future developments.

II. POPULATION MOVEMENT 1900-1990.

Figure 1 presents the evolution of crude birth and death rates and hardly needs any comment.

As in most West European countries the last half of the previous century is a period of rapid population growth. Except for a few mortality peaks the relatively low death rates

---

[1] The authors thank Martine CORIJN for her careful reading of several drafts of this text.

are combined with high birth rates, hence large growth rates. Besides the interruption caused by the first World War, growth gradually declines during the first half of the twentieth century to reach a minimum towards the end of the thirties. After the second World War and until 1964, the crude birth and death rates remain quite stable, leading once again to substantial levels of natural increase in the population. After 1964 the birth rate falls rapidly and natural increase is almost reduced to zero since 1975. However, from 1985 onwards the crude birth rate is rising again.

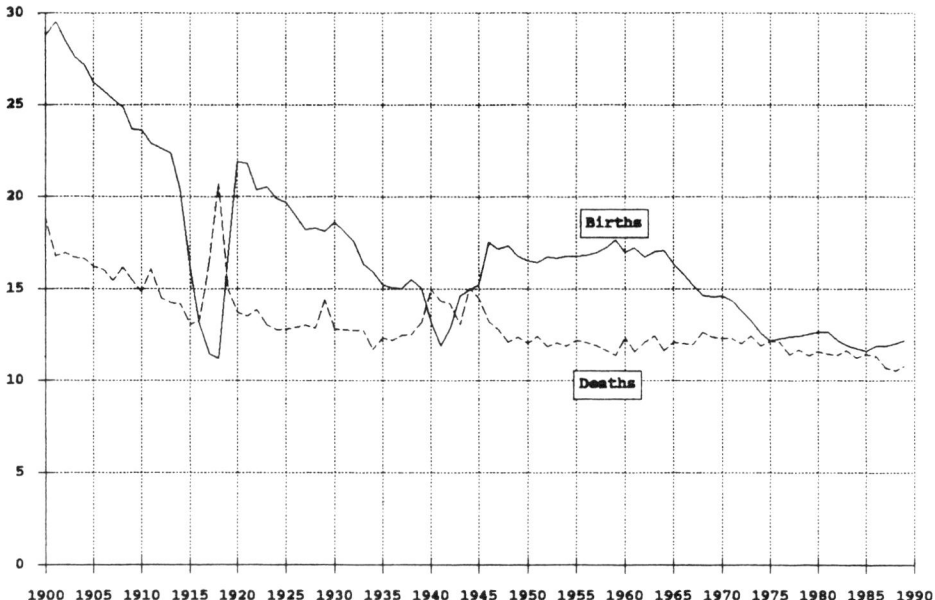

Figure 1.- Evolution of births and deaths per 1000 population. Belgium 1900-1990

The interesting question is of course if this situation will last and if this is a sign announcing a fundamental reversal of trends? These questions will be addressed in paragraph IV where fertility will be discussed.

In it's history, Belgium was often at the heart of massive migratory movements. Today, approx. 9% of the population is non-Belgian (870,000 inhabitants). Since it is a small, densily populated country, also internal migration is quite important. The statistics collected in the Population Register enable to study migratory movements by age and sex.

The immigration waves, especially the ones of 1948, 1957 and 1964, are due to the massive arrival of Italians, Hungarians, Turcs and Moroccans. As far as foreigners are concerned there is net immigration. As far as the population of Belgian nationality is concerned, emigration exceeds immigration. As in most industrialised countries, immigration slowed down towards the middle of the 70s, but it never stopped. Today, net migration oscillates close to zero.

More than 60% of the foreign inhabitants are Europeans, (approx. 20% coming from neighbouring countries: the U.K., the Netherlands, Germany, Luxembourg and France) while slightly more than 20% are Turcs and Maghrebians. Political refugees account for 2.6% of the foreign population in Belgium.

TABLE 1.- DISTRIBUTION OF THE FOREIGN POPULATION

Nationality	Number	Percent
EUROPA	555.370	63.93
CEE	536.665	61.77
Other	18.705	2.15
AFRICA	172.913	19.90
Maghreb	152.355	17.54
Zaire	10.871	1.25
Other	9.687	1.12
AMERICA	18.085	2.08
North Am.	13.150	1.51
Latin Am.	4.935	0.57
ASIA	99.135	11.41
Turkey	79.460	9.15
Japan	2.731	0.31
Israel	1.726	0.20
China	1.784	0.21
Other	13.434	0.21
OCEANIA	443	0.05
REF./APATR.	22.811	2.63
TOTAL	868.757	100.00

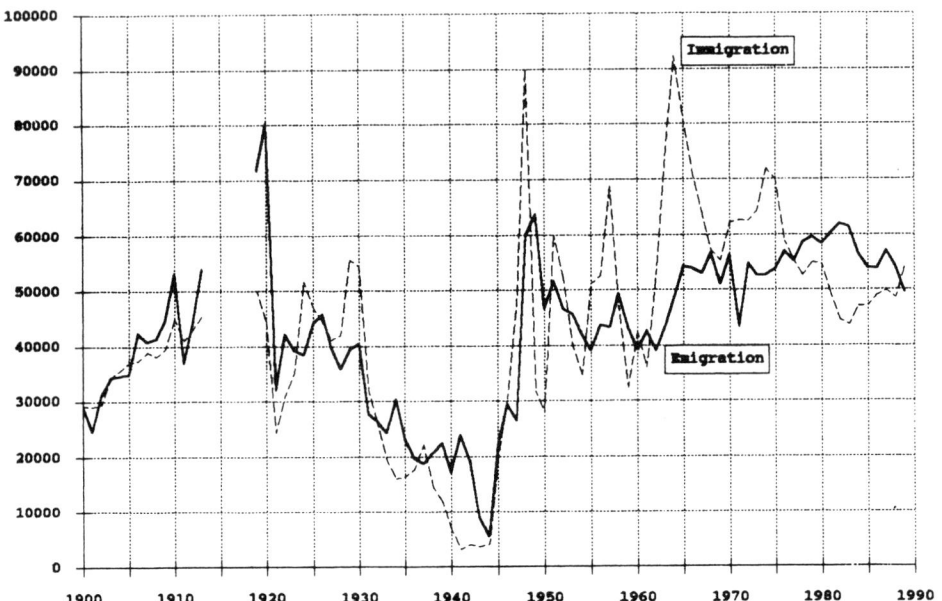

Figure 2.- International migration. Belgium 1900-1990

III. AGE-COMPOSITION OF THE POPULATION

Since this report limits itself to what happened between 1950 and 1989, it is only natural to start with a presentation of the age-composition of the population at both dates.

In the 1950 population (and to a lesser extent also in the 1989 one) the deficit of births during the wars produces troughs around ages 7 and 30 in the 1950 population. 40 years later these troughs have shifted to ages 47 and 70 in the 1989 population. Likewise, the baby-boom generations (aged approx. 27-35 in 1989) will produce a bulge in the 2030 population at ages 65 to 75.

In the oldest age segment of the population there is not only the remarkable difference between the two sexes within each population, but above all the substantial growth in absolute numbers since 1950. In less than 40 years, the female population aged 75 and above almost doubled from 220,000 to 434,000. In the male population the increase is less spectacular. Changes in mortality are an important element in changes in this age-segment. This issue will be dealt with in paragraph VI.

If one speaks about ageing of the population, one must bear in mind that there are two components in this ageing process. One component has to do with the evolution of the number of births, and instead of ageing one might follow the way of speech in the Netherlands and call the fall in the number of births a process of 'de-juvenation'. The other component (ageing sensu strictu) has to do with mortality and the number of deaths. Let us first focus on dejuvenation and the evolution of fertility.

IV. FERTILITY

1) Total fertility rate

There are many ways to look at the data concerning fertility. The most classical way to describe how fertility changes over time is to present a series of Total Fertility Rates (TFR's), i.e. the sum of age specific fertility rates observed in a given year. An age specific fertility rate is the ratio of births born to women of a given age to the total number of women at that age. As in most West European countries the Belgian TFR values fell from a maximum attained in the mid sixties to a minimum in 1975. The TFR remained at a low level since that time.

As a summary index the TFR gives the number of children a woman would have if age specific
fertility rates observed in a given year would remain unchanged in the next 35 years. Because of this "ceteris-paribus"-clause, the TFR is to some extent a very defective instrument to describe fertility changes over time. If one adds to this the deplorable habit to label the TFR as merely "the average number of children per woman", all conditions are fulfilled to produce misunderstandings.

Consider the following situation[2]. If, at a certain point in time, ever growing numbers of older women decide to stop childbearing, e.g. because they have already two children, then the total number of births starts to decrease due to the loss of third and higher order births. If at the same time ever growing numbers of young women decide to postpone the arrival of a first and/or second child to a later age, then the total number of births falls further due to the loss of first and/or second order births. In other words: these conditions are sufficient to produce a drastic drop in the number of births at all ages and consequently a drop in all the age specific period fertility rates. Summing up these age specific rates gives very low TFR values.

---

[2] A similar example is recently given by Lévy (1990)

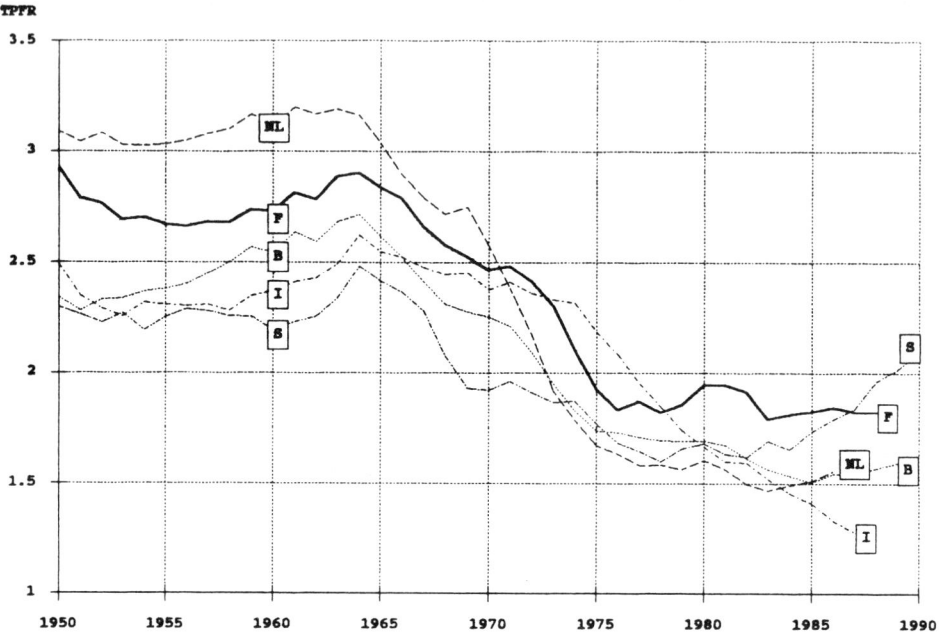

Figure 3.- Total Period Fertility Rates for Belgium (B), France (F), the Netherlands (NL), Italy (I) and Sweden (S)

After a number of years the tide might turn. The women who postponed childbearing have grown older and decide to have their first and/or second child now, i.e. at age 27, 30 or even later. In that case the fertility rates at these ages would start rising again. Suppose also that at the same time the youngest generations have changed their mind and prefer to have their first and/or second child at young ages again, then fertility rates at these ages start rising also. At all ages fertility rates increase, and their sum, the TFR ends up at a high level again.

According to this scenario replacement was never endangered, although TFR values well below replacement level may have been recorded. Nevertheless, the birthstream got upset and consequently the relative weight of certain age-groups within a population got disturbed. This certainly creates a number of problems at a societal level. However, the diagnosis that these problems are caused by below replacement level fertility (indicated as period TFR values less than 2.1) is wrong. Consequently, these problems do not get solved by a policy aimed at increasing fertility levels. If the birthstream and the age structure get upset due to changes in the timing of births in one's life, one would need a policy aimed at influencing the timing of fertility. It is hard to imagine how such a policy would look like and the question remains if such a policy would be desirable.

BELGIUM/LA BELGIQUE

It might be that Belgian fertility follows the scenario just described or a very similar one. In the next few paragraphs some elements are brought together to support this view. In order to do so fertility rates have been rearranged longitudinally by year of birth of the mother. Only then it is possible to follow a generation through its childbearing period and to calculate a generation's average number of children per woman. For Belgium data are available up to 1987 which allows to determine the average number of children of the cohorts born towards the end of the forties.

Instead of TFR-maxima and minima of 2.7 and 1.5 respectively, the gap in fertility between successive generations is rather small. From an average of about 2.3 children per woman for the women born in the thirties, fertility dropped to about 1.8 children per woman for the women born towards the end of the forties. Any attempt at predicting the average number of children of the women born in the sixties is a risky enterprise, because nobody knows to what extent fertility will be rescheduled.

2) Fertility by birth order

An average number of children per woman is only a final result. A more detailed analysis takes also birth-orders into account so that all intermediate steps leading to the average number of children are revealed. However, one should note that in Belgium the birth-order of a child is defined as the ranknumber within the current marriage. Therefore, each study of fertility by birth-order is limited to legitimate fertility. As long as the number of illegitimate births is rather small there is no harm, but recently illegitimate births make up approx. 10 % of all births. To tackle this problem it will be assumed first that none, and secondly, that all illegitimate births are births of rank one, the 'truth' being closer to the last assumption.

Figure 4.1 gives age specific first birth rates for a selection of generations born since 1940, assuming that all illegitimate births are first order births. Figure 4.2 is identical, except that illegitimate births are excluded. Altough there is some difference between the generations born between 1940 and 1950, these generations behave more or less in the same way: the great majority has a first child at age 22 or 23. In the younger cohorts however, the rates at young ages have fallen to very low levels. However, in order to see to what extent it might be possible for these generations to compensate at later ages for fertility "lost" at young ages, it makes quite a difference if one includes illegitimate births or not. If one excludes illegitimate births, it seems as if all first births lost at young ages are lost forever (figure 4.2). If they are included however, first birth rates at ages around 30 are quite high so that in the end there might be no loss whatsoever.

If one cumulates the first birth rates one gets the proportion women having at least one child. The reciprocal values give proportions childless women at each age (see fig 6.3). The estimate given by the thick line rests on the assumption that all illegitimate births are first-order births. The dotted line gives proportions childlessness if none of the illegitimate births would be first order births. The "real world"-value lies somewhere in between, but probably closer to the thick line. It is clear from figure 4.3 that at most one out of ten women born between 1940 and 1947 will remain childless at age 45. Or putting it the other way round: nine out of ten women have at least one child.

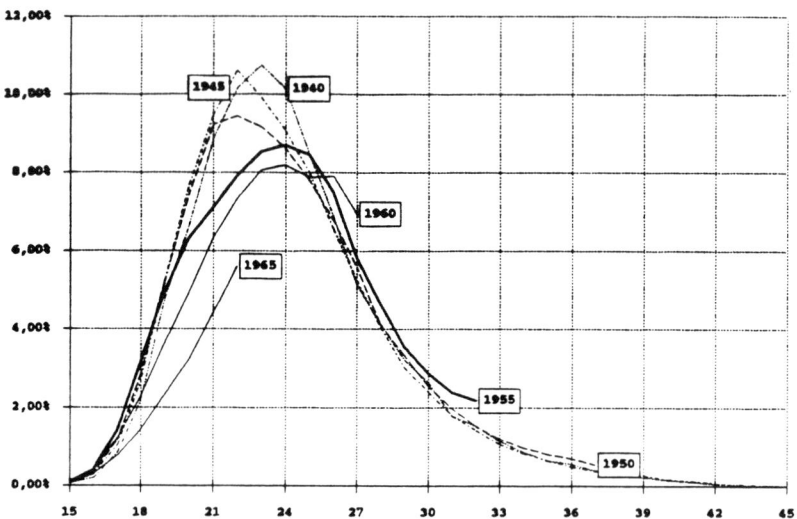

Figure 4.1.- Proportions women giving birth to a first child. Belgium, a selection of generations born after 1940 (All illegitimate births included)

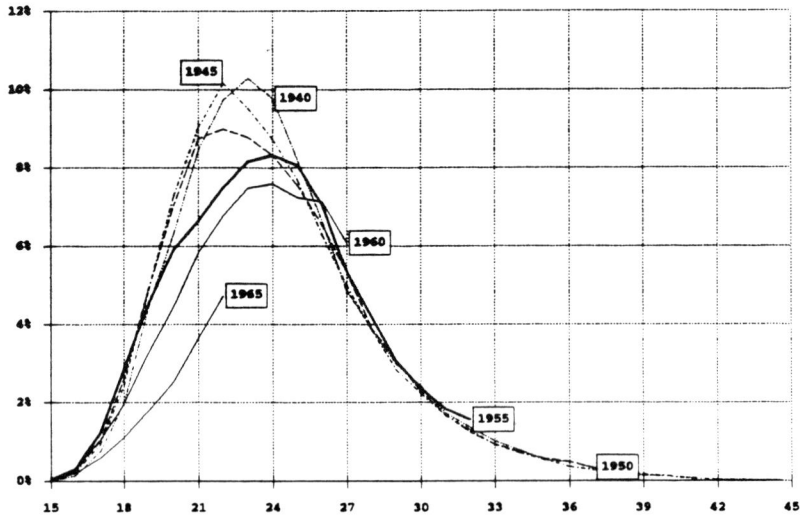

Figure 4.2.- Proportions women giving birth to a first child. Belgium, a selection of generations born after 1940 (All illegitimate births excluded)

BELGIUM/LA BELGIQUE

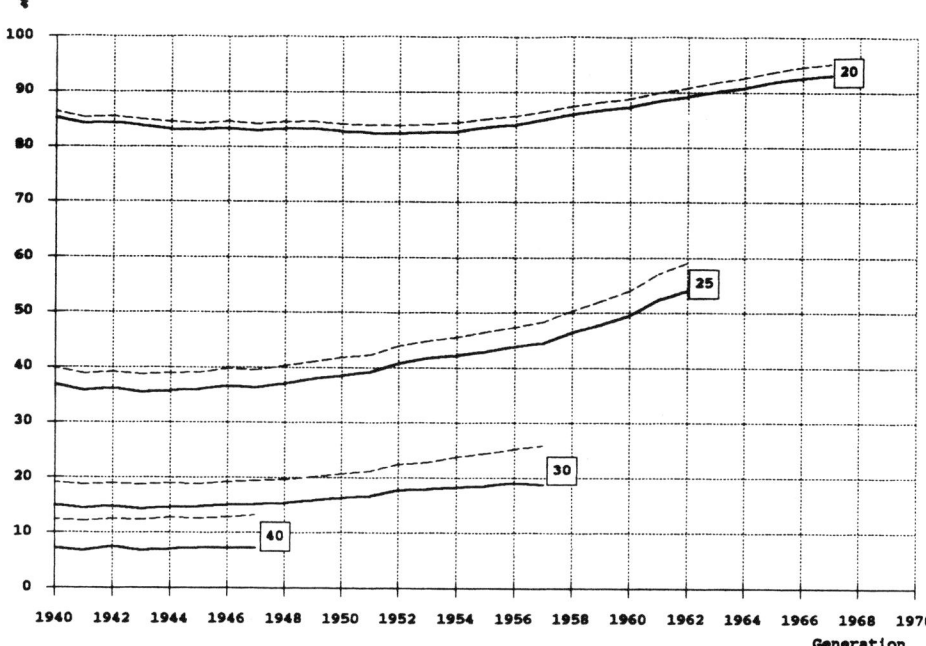

Fig 4.3.- Proportions childless women, Belgium, generations born between 1940 and 1970

It is clear how dangerous it is to predict future levels of proportions childless women, because these predictions by necessity imply predicting shifts in the timing of first births. There is a large increase in proportions childless woman at age 25, but due to the rescheduling of fertility these changes won't get reflected in similar shifts in the proportions childless at ages 30 and 40. It needs only a small proportion of the women born between 1947 and 1957 that plans the arrival of a first child after age 30 to keep the proportion childless women at age 40 constant at about 10%. This scenario (i.e. complete compensation at older ages of first births 'lost' at young ages) certainly holds for the generations born between 1947 and 1957. Is it too bold to predict that childlessness will remain close to 10 percent, even for the generations born in the early sixties? In our view it is much more likely than predicting some 20%, i.e. the outcome of a scenario without compensation at all.

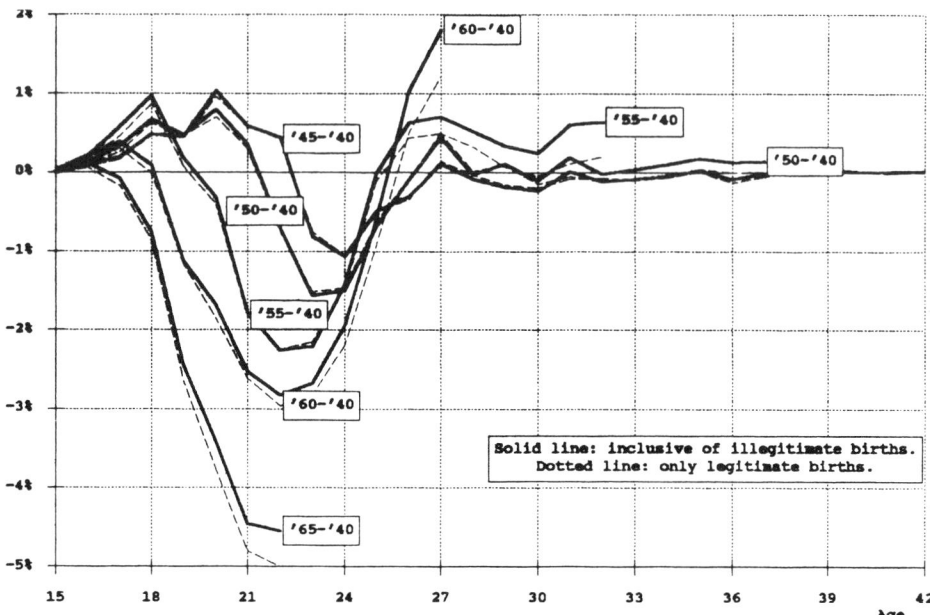

Figure 5.1- Proportions women giving birth to a first child. The generations born between '45 and '65 compared with the generation of 1940

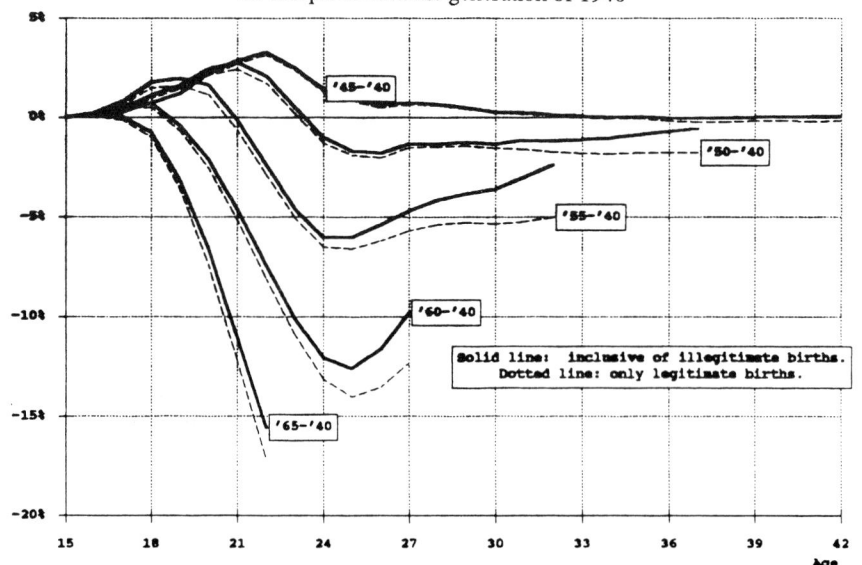

Figure 5.2- Proportions women having a first child. The generations born between '45 and '65 compared with the generation of 1940

A more telling representation of first birth fertility is given in figures 5.1 and 5.2. In figure 5.1 the age-specific first birth rates of the generations born since 1945 are compared, taking the 1940 generation as reference. Figure 5.2 contains the cumulated rates. The shift in the timing of first births and its effect on proportions childlessness at different ages emerges very clearly. As in figure 4.3 two estimates of first birth fertility are given: the solid thick line is based on the assumption that all illegitimate births are first order births, while illegitimate births are excluded in the dotted line[3].

These figures make clear to what extent the youngest cohorts have postponed first births, and how rapidly they are making up arrears in their late twenties. First birth fertility is rescheduled very radically.

It is illuminating to contrast these developments with third order births (see figures 6.1 and 6.2). One should note two things about figures 6: first there is the difference in scale in comparison with figures 5, and secondly, one should take into account that these figures underestimate third birth fertility since the calculations were restricted to legitimate third births. A proportion of the illegitimate births belongs to rank 3, as well as a proportion of first and second order births[4]. Yet, it is clear that third birth fertility rates as observed in the 1940 generation - leading to 32% having at least three children (see the right hand scale of figure 6.2) - are beyond reach for the more recent generations. Even taking the underestimation due to misclassifications into account, it seems as if at most 22% of the younger generations will have (at least) three children.

It is very unfortunate that data for 1988, 1989 and 1990 are not available yet at the time of writing. The last year for which detailed data are available is 1987 and this was the second year that the absolute number of births was rising again. Moreover the rise in number of births between 1986 and 1987 was only a very modest one compared to what happened since 1987. In 1987 approx. 117,400 births were recorded and this increased with 5.8% to 124,200 in 1990. This recent upswing is probably not only due to first births but to increasing numbers of second or third order births as well.

What about second order births? The data are summarised in figures 7.1 and 7.2. As could be expected, these figures take up an intermediate position between first and third order births. Up to 1987 at least, there are no clear signs of any recovery at later ages of second order births that were 'lost' at young ages. However, it should be stressed once again that figures 7.1 and 7.2 underestimate second order birth rates because illegitimate

---

[3] The solid line marks off an absolute maximum number of first births not only because all illegitimate births are assumed to be first order births, but also because a woman's second or third birth *which is the first one in a second marriage* is classified as a first order birth.

[4] The overestimation due to assigning rank 3 to a third birth in a second marriage whereas it is a 4th or 5th in a woman's life, is probably negligible.

births are left out and because a proportion of first order births (in the current marriage) are second order births (in a woman's life).

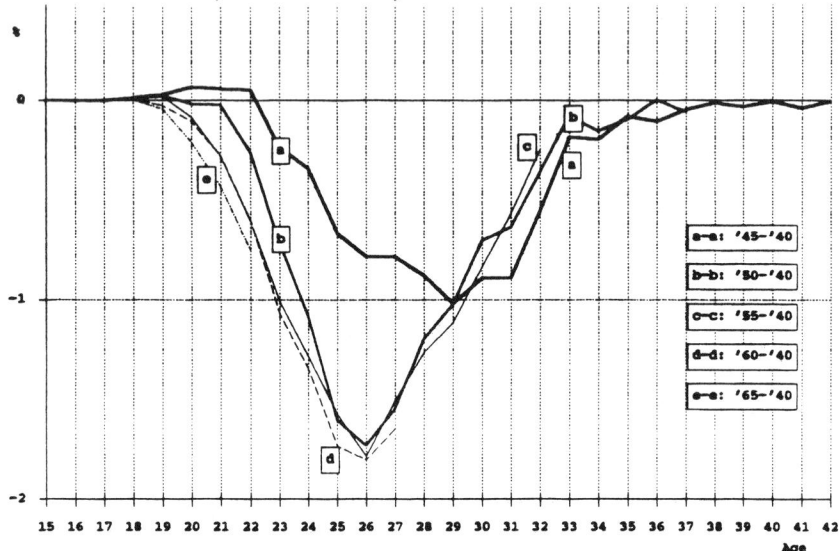

Figure 6.1- Proportions women giving birth to a third child. The generations born between '45 and '65 compared with the generation of 1940.

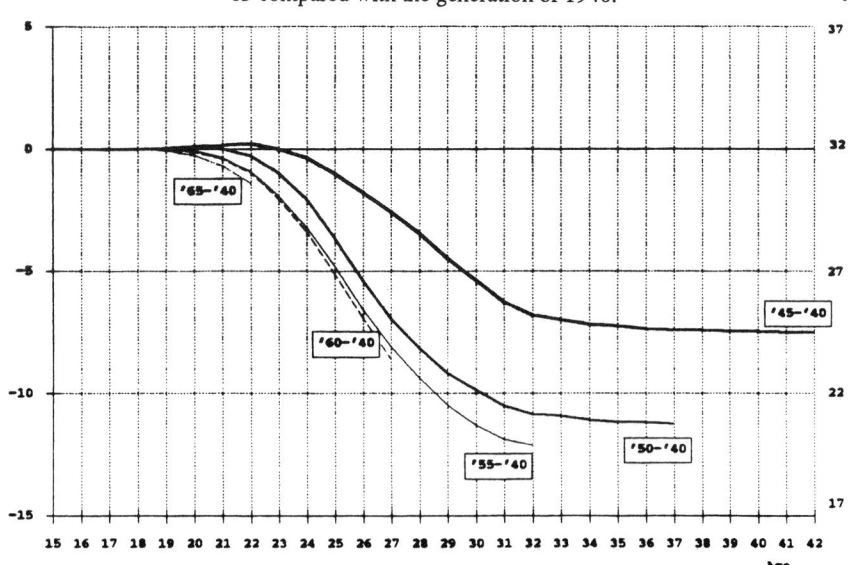

Figure 6.2- Proportions women having a third child. The generations born between '45 and '65 compared with the generation of 1940.

BELGIUM/LA BELGIQUE

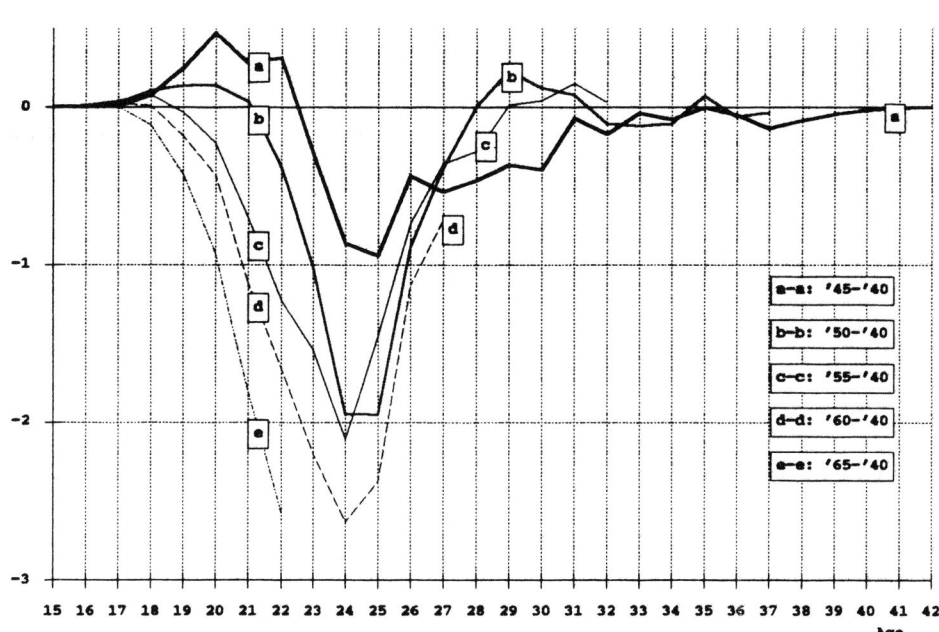

Figure 7.1.- Proportions women giving birth to a second child. The generations born between '45 and '65 compared with the generation of 1940.

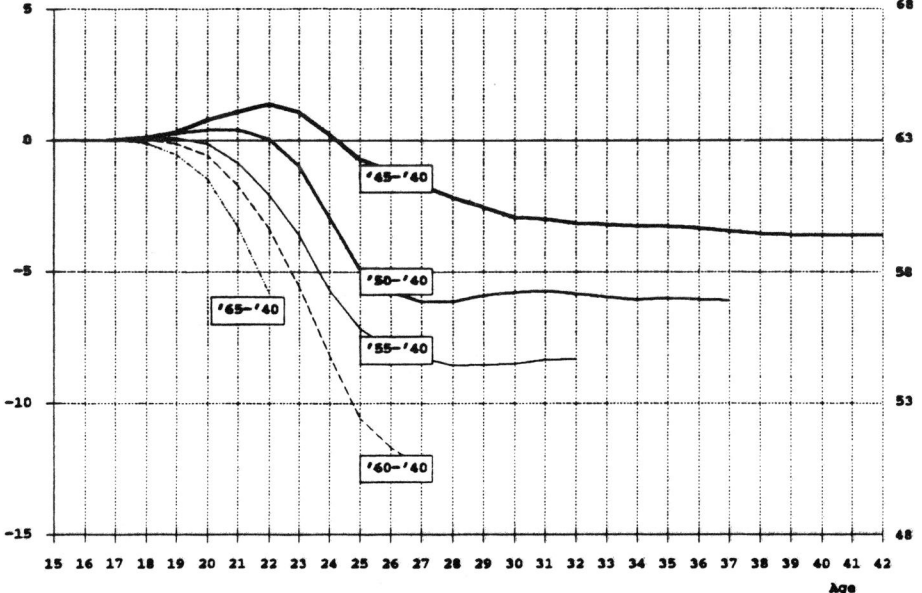

Figure 7.2.- Proportions women having a second child. The generations born between '45 and '65 compared with the generation of 1940

Moreover, given the fact that the youngest generations postponed the arrival of a first child to their late twenties or even early thirties, it is only natural that the second birth (and a fortiori the third one), comes much later. Therefore, the pictures as they appear in 1987, are not final ones, and given the major upswing in the total number of births since 1987, they might have changed quite drastically by 1991.

How are all these shifts in timing reflected in period age specific fertility rates and what will be the effect on future TFR levels? Figures 8.1 and 8.2 give the evolution of period age specific fertility rates (all births). The overall picture is quite clear: the decline at older ages (>26) stopped and the net result of all the shifts in timing is a clearly upward trend.

In a cross-sectional analysis one confounds the experience of different cohorts. Consequently, in summing up the rates one finds since 1985 a TFR that no longer declines but starts increasing again. The increasing rates at ages beyond 26 (older cohorts having not only higher order births but also first and second order births at later ages) more than compensate the declining rates before that age. If the decline at young ages stops, and this soon might be the case, TFR values might temporarily rise to values above 2 (as in the case of Sweden with an estimated TFR of 2.14 in 1990).

This whole discussion merely proofs a long known fact: the TFR is a fanciful thing. If the timing of a phenomenon changes quite fundamentally, this gets reflected in a distortion of a summary period measure such as the TFR. "Period synthetic measures of intensity, which summarize the behavior of many cohorts, usually do not adequately reflect the true cohort intensity, as the period measures are also dependent on the tempo of events in the cohorts considered. Conversely, synthetic period tempo measures do not usually correspond to true cohort measures, as they are also influenced by cohort intensities.... Ryder (1956)... called this bias 'distributional distortion'." (Wunsch and Termote, 1978). Sometimes, one gets the impression that people forget about these things.

It is clear from the above discussion that distributional distortion is not limited to the study of fertility but is also present in the study of nuptiality.

BELGIUM/LA BELGIQUE

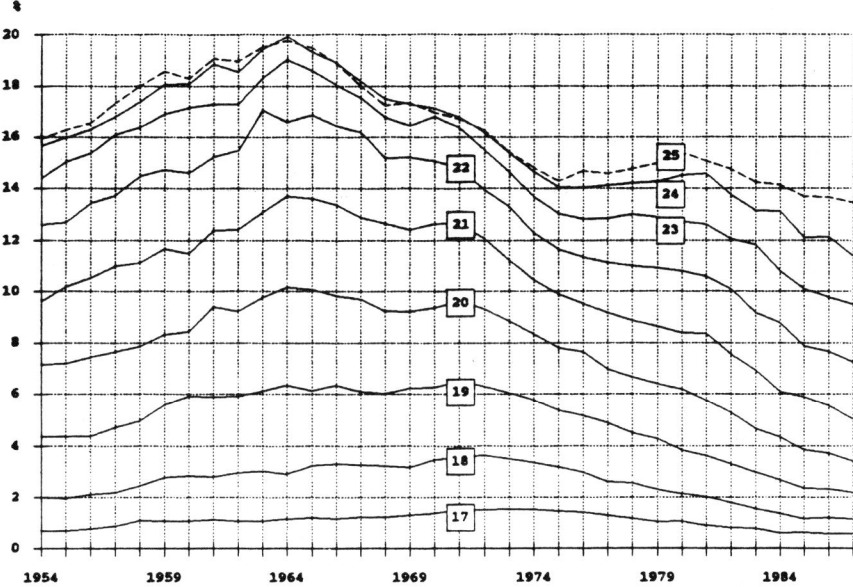

Figure 8.1.- Proportions women giving birth at selected ages. Belgium, years 1954-1987

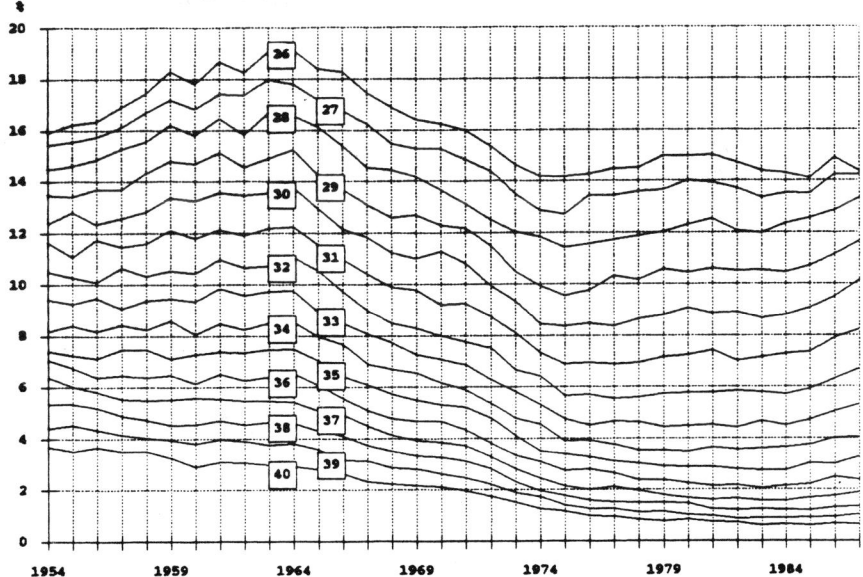

Figure 8.2.- Proportions women giving birth at selected ages. Belgium, years 1954-1987

V. NUPTIALITY

As in the case of fertility, the sum of the age-specific first marriage rates (of women) is a summary index (the total period first marriage rate) giving the proportion of a (fictitious) female generation that would marry if the current age specific first marriage rates would prevail unchanged in the future. As in the case of fertility, distributional distortion might seriously limit the value of this index.

Austria is a case in point. The Austrian total period first marriage rate for females jumped from 0.61 in 1986 to 1.07 in 1987 and fell to 0.44 in 1988. The upswing in 1986 is entirely due to fiscal measures. Sweden is another example: more than 64,000 marriages were recorded in december 1989 alone against annual totals close to 40,000 in the previous years. Both examples indicate also to what extent the content of marriage has changed. These 64,000 Swedish couples marrying in december 1989 were living together without having done the necessary paper-work to make it a formal marriage (Hoem, 1990). The fact that fertility was well increasing before december 1989 also proofs that the effect of the formal structure of cohabitation (married or unmarried) is rather limited. Put into other words, even without formal marriage, fertility was increasing again.

The methodological drawbacks of a cross-sectional analysis are easily overcome by presenting a longitudinal analysis. But even then the value of such a nuptiality analysis is limited since it is by necessity limited to formal 'paperwork' marriages. One should keep this in mind when reading the following paragraphs.

The generations born between 1940 and 1960 married extremely early so that already one third of them was married by the age of twenty. Very suddenly things started to change drastically. In the generation born in 1969 only ten percent was married by the age of twenty!

It is very clear from figure 9 that for women a marriage at young ages lost its popularity. Nevertheless, compensation of first marriages that were "lost" at young ages is well under way as can be seen from figures 9. Once more the key question is to what extent early marriages will be replaced by late ones. The answer is again: only time can tell. It is thus too early to come up with the conclusion that marriage was dead and is now rising again from its ashes. It looks as if a great number of successive generations merely has postponed the necessary paperwork to make a stable partnership into a formal marriage. Instead of translating a stable relationship immediately into a marriage, the younger cohorts preferred a period of unmarried cohabitation as an alternative for marriage.

Falling marriage rates suggested that marriage had been done with. This idea got also fuelled by the increasing numbers of divorce since the seventies. Figure 10.1 gives at each marriage duration the proportion of the initial size of the marriage cohort that got a divorce. Unlike the familiar bell shaped curves of age specific fertility (or marriage) rates, divorce rates rise steeply to a maximum value at marriage duration 6, 7 or 8 and more or less stay at the same level for the remainder of the marriage durations.

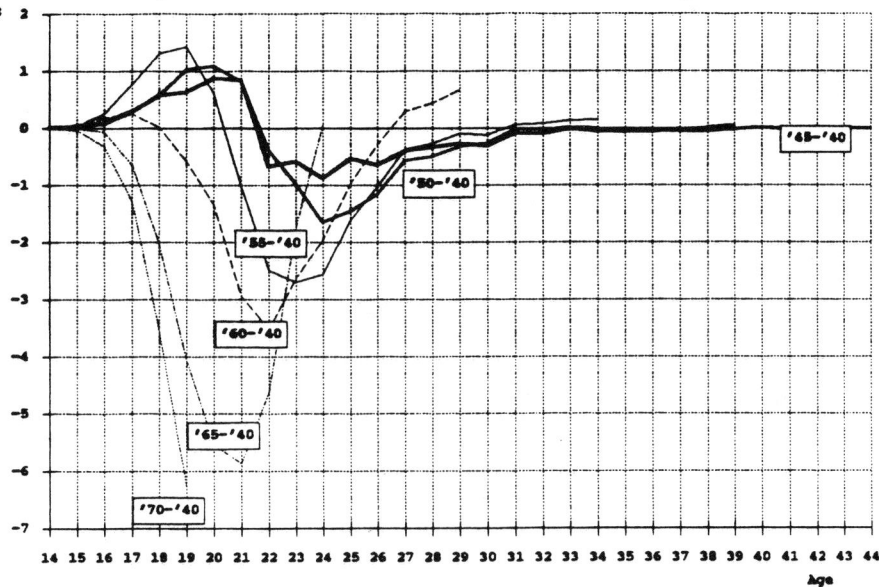

Figure 9.1- Proportions women marrying for the first time. The generations born between '45 and '70 compared with the generation of '40

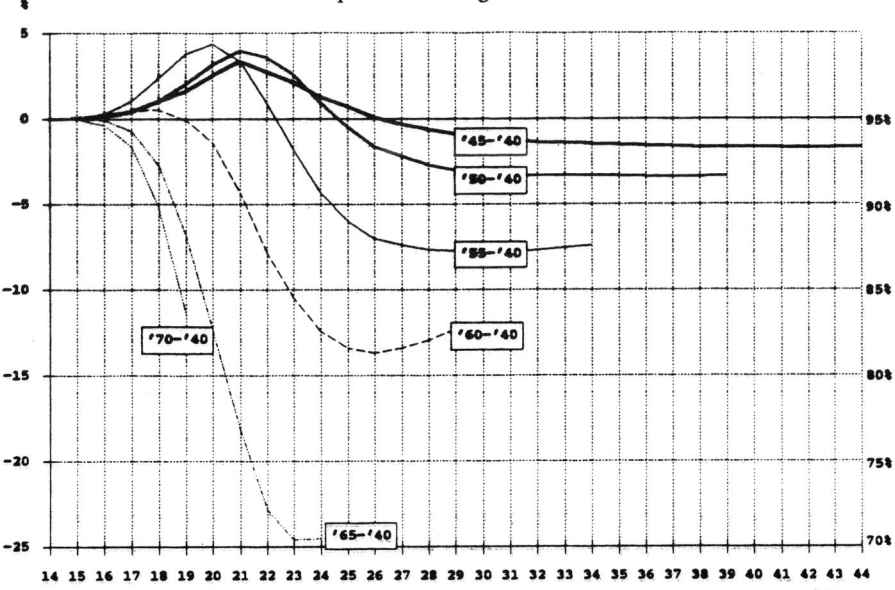

Figure 9.2- Proportions of married women. The generations born between '45 and '70 compared with the generation of '40

It is not certain at all if this pattern will also hold for the most recent marriage cohorts. Suppose it holds for those who married in 1980. After 9 years of marriage 11% got divorced. If, on average, each year an additional 1.5% gets a divorce (a), then one third (33.5%) of all marriages would be broken before reaching their 25th marriage-anniversary. The corresponding percentages in the marriage cohorts of 1955 and 1965 are 8 and 16. If the number of dissolved marriages would increase annually with only 1.1% on average (b) - but then the divorce rates would display a bell-shaped curve - this would bring the proportion divorces to 27% after 24 years of marriage. Given the large number of divorces it is no surprise to find increasing numbers of remarriages.

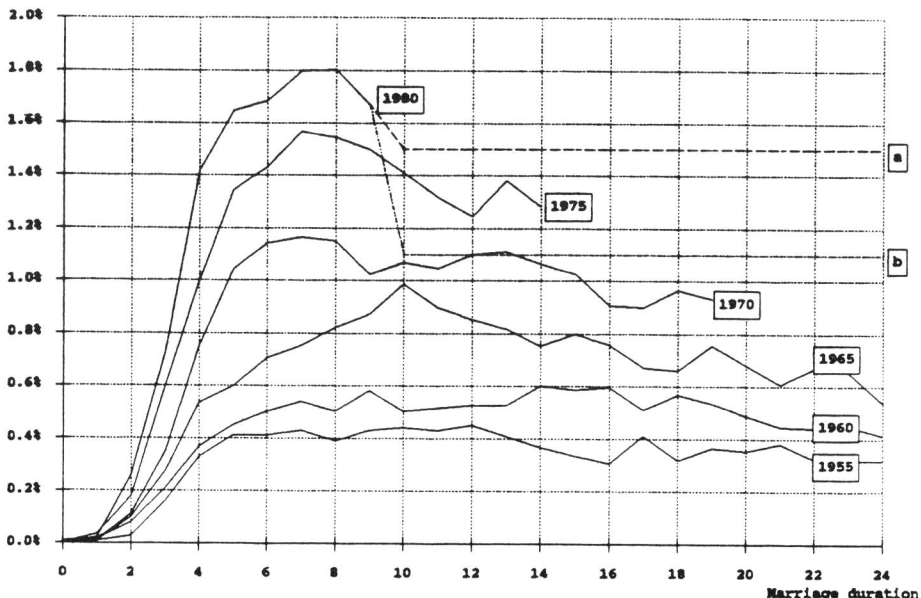

Figure 10 - Divorce per 100 marriages by duration of marriage. Belgium, selected marriage cohorts

VI. MORTALITY AND AGEING

One way to document the progress in the field of mortality is to give the l(80) values from the lifetable, i.e. the proportion of a fictitious generation that would survive until age eighty. Almost 59% of a female birth cohort would survive till 80 if it would experience the mortality conditions of 1988/89. It was 42% given the mortality conditions of 1970, only 22% according to the lifetable of 1928-32 and 13% around 1885. This is a very substantial progress in 100 years. Progress was less spectacular for males with 9% surviving until age 80 according to the 1885 life table, 16% in 1930, 23% in 1970 and 34% in 1988/89. At this age the gap between the two sexes increases rather rapidly.

BELGIUM/LA BELGIQUE

At the other end of the age-scale the l(1) value gives the proportion newborn babies surviving a full year. According to the 1880/90 lifetable 82.78% males and 85.45% females survived till their first birthday i.e. an infant mortality rate of 172 per thousand for males and 145 for females. A century later less than 8 per 1,000 newborn boys and slightly more than 6 per 1,000 newborn girls die in the course of their first year. Again, this is a very substantial change.

This progress at both ends of the age scale is of course reflected in the life expectancy at birth. During the last century life expectancy at birth increased from 43.6 to 72.5 years for males and from 46.6 to 79.2 for females. On average, this is a gain of more than 1 season each year or more than one year of life per 4 calender years.

Whatever the future sequence of births shall be, it is clear that the problem of "ageing" remains, at least if one restricts it to the context of social-security systems, i.e. defined as proportions aged 60 (or 65) and over. If the current rate of improvement in the field of mortality holds in the next 30 to 40 years, this would add about 8 years to the life expectancy at birth and bring it to over 80 for males and 87 for females. This development stretches the survivorship function towards the upper right. Not only the absolute number of people above age 60 or 65 will increase (the babyboom will be aged 60 to 70) it is likely that they will live longer. Given these developments, would it not be wise to follow Norman Ryder's advise and use a new index of old age and to determine at what age the expectation of life is e.g. 10 years, "that age to be considered the point of entry into old age" (Ryder, 1975).

DEMOGRAPHIE EUROPEENNE

Table 2.1 Life tables Belgium 1890-1990 (females)

	l(1)	l(25)	l(60)	l(80)	%80+	e(0)	e(60)	e(80)
1880/90	85.446	69.388	47.359	13.174	-	46,63	14,77	4,80
1928/32	92.145	85.026	65.982	21.548	-	59,79	15,93	5,20
1946/49	95.073	91.913	77.173	31.048	-	67,26	17,45	5,79
1959/63	98.134	96.931	86.829	40.004	-	73,51	18,69	6,07
1979/82	98.940	97.990	89.483	51.156	-	76,79	20,93	7,11
1969/70	98.203	97.060	87.214	41.659	3,6	73,99	19,03	6,32
1970/71	98.193	97.110	87.449	43.448	3,7	74,38	19,37	6,36
1971/72	98.351	97.223	87.706	43.275	3,7	74,48	19,31	6,35
1972/73	98.342	97.213	87.798	44.266	3,8	74,69	19,53	6,39
1973/74	98.457	97.413	88.207	45.553	4,0	75,17	19,84	6,60
1974/75	98.577	97.583	88.113	44.714	3,9	75,09	19,68	6,49
1975/76	98.556	97.604	88.408	45.719	3,9	75,28	19,80	6,45
1976/77	98.725	97.780	88.705	47.606	4,3	75,87	20,28	6,86
1977/78	98.840	97.847	88.770	47.827	4,3	75,93	20,28	6,81
1978/79	98.873	97.793	89.168	49.464	4,6	76,37	20,69	7,06
1979/80	98.867	97.880	89.356	50.600	4,6	76,60	20,81	7,01
1980/81	99.002	98.041	89.662	51.038	4,7	76,82	20,88	7,10
1981/82	99.033	98.205	89.800	51.781	4,8	77,08	21,04	7,17
1982/83	99.079	98.238	90.039	52.070	4,8	77,19	21,05	7,11
1983/84	99.108	98.287	90.072	53.065	5,0	77,41	21,29	7,25
1984/85	99.158	98.426	90.670	54.216	5,2	77,90	21,55	7,45
1985/86	99.161	98.444	90.746	54.419	5,2	77,95	21,56	7,41
1986/87	99.278	98.545	91.051	56.458	5,6	78,61	22,14	7,86
1987/88	99.194	98.494	91.168	57.672	5,8	78,85	22,37	7,92
1988/89	99.379	98.663	91.569	58.631	5,9	79,18	22,53	7,97

Tabel 2.2 Lifetables Belgium 1890-1990 (males)

	l(1)	l(25)	l(60)	l(80)	%80+	e(0)	e(60)	e(80)
1880/90	82.783	67.280	41.521	9.464	-	43,59	13,53	4,42
1928/32	89.925	82.367	59.650	15.638	-	56,02	14,53	4,65
1946/49	93.597	89.501	67.302	20.936	-	62,04	15,45	5,18
1959/63	97.586	95.429	76.938	24.573	-	67,73	15,52	5,29
1979/82	98.655	96.837	81.178	27.759	-	70,04	16,26	5,74
1969/70	97.447	95.274	77.411	22.669	1,8	67,44	15,09	5,46
1970/71	97.629	95.482	78.169	24.424	2,0	68,02	15,44	5,46
1971/72	97.736	95.694	78.211	23.315	1,9	67,94	15,22	5,47
1972/73	97.946	95.701	78.295	23.972	1,9	68,11	15,38	5,43
1973/74	98.061	96.051	79.464	25.521	2,1	68,79	15,68	5,58
1974/75	98.067	96.001	79.227	24.138	1,9	68,54	15,43	5,45
1975/76	98.220	96.224	80.105	24.695	1,9	68,91	15,49	5,31
1976/77	98.236	96.281	79.815	26.119	2,2	69,21	15,91	5,78
1977/78	98.455	96.503	80.164	25.851	2,2	69,36	15,88	5,79
1978/79	98.507	96.574	80.613	27.096	2,3	69,70	16,12	5,93
1979/80	98.633	96.837	81.011	27.214	2,3	69,90	16,15	5,88
1980/81	98.637	96.809	81.239	27.472	2,3	70,04	16,23	5,87
1981/82	98.655	96.914	81.834	28.650	2,4	70,40	16,44	5,80
1982/83	98.782	97.133	81.748	28.941	2,3	70,52	16,51	5,70
1983/84	98.753	97.121	82.139	29.576	2,4	70,66	16,60	5,76
1984/85	98.877	97.461	82.893	29.971	2,5	71,13	16,74	6,02
1985/86	98.895	97.371	83.248	30.331	2,5	71,18	16,74	5,83
1986/87	98.874	97.412	83.795	33.028	2,9	71,92	17,34	6,40
1987/88	98.904	97.405	83.659	33.327	2,9	71,90	17,45	6,28
1988/89	99.204	97.597	84.730	34.476	3,0	72,45	17,64	6,26

References:

HOEM, J.M.,Änkepensionen och giftermalen i december 1989: Att gifta sig om utifall att..., Välfärds Bulletinen, 1990, 4, p.18-20.

LEVY, M.L., Le calendrier de la fécondité., Population & Sociétés, 249, 1990, INED.

RYDER, N.B., Notes on stationary populations., Population Index, 41, 3, 1975.

WUNSCH, G.J. and M.G. TERMOTE, Introduction to Demographic Analysis. Principles and Methods. Plenum Press, New York, 1987.

Les Pays-Bas/ The Netherlands
Dirk J. Van de KAA et Yves de ROO

I. LA PERIODE ANTERIEURE AUX RECENSEMENTS (1500-1795)

Dans le parcours de l'histoire démographique des Pays-Bas l'année 1795 présente une transition importante. Avant cette date il n'était guère question d'un réel gouvernement central. Chacune des provinces composant l'ensemble de la République des Provinces Unies disposait d'un pouvoir propre et d'une administration autonome. Il s'agissait en fait d'une fédération. Le changement intervint en 1795 lorsqu'avec l'appui de troupes françaises la révolution conduisit à l'établissement d'une République Batave, qui comme on peut le concevoir aisément, subissant la forte empreinte française, ne fut que de courte durée. En 1806 déjà, elle devint Royaume de Hollande pour être gouvernée par le Roi Louis Napoléon, frère de Bonaparte. L'influence française s'accrut et culmina en 1810 avec l'incorporation à la France. La 'Période Française' dura de 1810 à 1813 et se termina par la défaite de Napoléon. Le Congrès de Vienne réunit les Pays-Bas du Nord et du Sud en un royaume.

Du point de vue démographique, l'année 1795 et les années suivantes ont une signification particulière car elles sont marquées par l'introduction de l'état civil, du mariage civil, d'un nouveau système fiscal, du droit successoral et d'un nouveau cadastre. C'est pourquoi nous sommes beaucoup mieux informés sur le plan démographique à partir de 1800 qu'auparavant. La création de la République Batave fut accompagnée d'un recensement destiné à servir à l'élaboration d'une constitution, et ce recensement fournit pour la première fois dans l'histoire des données quantitatives nationales concernant la population. Les statistiques établies pour les périodes antérieures furent obtenues à partir d'estimations empruntées à des recensements partiels et composées à partir de sources diverses usuelles dans le cadre de l'analyse démographique historique (par exemple, les registres de baptêmes et d'enterrements, les comptes d'imposition fiscale et les listes des hommes aptes au service militaire).

L'effectif de la population antérieure a pu être établi rétrospectivement jusqu'en 1500 (Slicher van Bath, 1986) à partir d'extrapolations de données connues pour cinq régions couvrant 60 à 65 % du territoire national actuel. La population double presque de 1500 à 1650 puis augmente de seulement 11% de 1650 à 1795. La stagnation de la croissance durant la deuxième période ne s'explique pas par les épidémies, pourtant nombreuses, car la période 1500-1650 fut bien autant touchée, mais elle est essentiellement attribuée aux guerres, aux inondations deux fois plus fréquentes et surtout à divers cycles successifs de récession économique.

II. LA PERIODE 1800-1935

A la fin de la période française le tracé des frontières n'avait pas encore atteint sa forme définitive. En 1831 les provinces du sud se séparèrent des provinces du nord. Cet événement eut aux Pays-Bas un retentissement démographique plus important qu'en Belgique, comme Hofstee l'a démontré de manière fort convaincante. De toute manière, par la suite les tendances démographiques divergentes ont persisté pour les deux Pays. Une explication de ce phénomène, par ailleurs extrêmement intéressant, n'a toujours pas été fournie.

Le tableau 1 donne un aperçu de l'évolution de la population totale des Pays-Bas avec l'accroissement de la période et l'accroissement cumulatif. Les valeurs d'avant 1830 sont empruntées à Hofstee, tandis que celles de l'année 1830 et des années suivantes proviennent des recensements tenus aux Pays-Bas entre 1830 et 1971, environ tous les dix ans. Après 1971, les recensements furent abandonnés suite aux vives protestations de la part du public. La popoulation passa, en 135 ans environ, de 2,08 à 7,94 millions, soit un accroissement de 382%. Jusqu'en 1870 on constate une croissance uniformément distribuée pour les provinces. Après cette date, l'Est du pays l'emporte de manière significative. Ainsi, la croissance cumulative atteignit respectivement 507, 370 et 419% entre 1795 et 1830 pour la Hollande Méridionale, la Hollande Septentrionale et Utrecht, tandis qu'on observe 216% pour la Zélande et 247% pour la Frise.

1) Natalité, mortalité et accroissement naturel

Grâce aux travaux détaillés et minutieux de Hofstee consistant en l'examen d'archives et de reconstitution des statistiques, nous disposons de données fiables concernant la fécondité, la mortalité et la croissance naturelle depuis 1806, pour chacune des provinces des Pays-Bas. Les chiffres montrent que la période de stagnation démographique qui débuta aux alentours de 1650 se maintint environ jusqu'en 1815. Un accroissement - à peu près exceptionnel pour l'Europe entière - de la fécondité débuta en 1815. Aussi les taux de natalité ne furent, durant le 19e siècle, quasiment jamais inférieurs à 33 pour mille, nonobstant la légère baisse qui se manifesta à partir de 1881-85. Durant le 19e siècle les taux de mortalité chutèrent de 30,9 en 1806/10 à 14,4 en 1906/10 avec pour conséquence un accroissement naturel notable. A partir de 1861, le taux d'accroissement dépassa constamment les 1,0%, pour atteindre le sommet de 15,6 pour mille en 1901/05 (tableaux 1 et 2). La constatation la plus nette est le caractère tardif de la fécondité conjugale aux Pays-Bas. Il en résulte, par exemple, que la transition démographique néerlandaise n'est observée qu'à peu près cinquante ans après la transition française. Même si le nombre d'enfants nés pour mille femmes mariées baisse entre 1861-65 et 1891-95, cette baisse reste fort modeste. Néanmoins, pour les Pays-Bas l'année 1875 est considérée généralement comme le point de départ de la baisse structurelle de la fécondité et on doit certainement admettre que le contrôle volontaire des naissances à l'intérieur du mariage entre en pratique dans les provinces les plus modernisées.

TABLEAU 1.- POPULATION DES PAYS-BAS (1795-1930)

Période	Effectifs	Acc^t.	Acc^t. cumulé
1795	2078487		100,0
1815	2202191	1,06	106,0
1830	2613487	1,19	125,7
1839	2860559	1,09	137,6
1849	3056879	1,07	147,1
1859	3309128	1,08	159,2
1869	3579529	1,08	172,2
1879	4012693	1,12	193,1
1889	4511415	1,12	217,1
1899	5104137	1,13	245,6
1909	5858175	1,15	281,8
1920	6865314	1,17	330,3
1930	7935565	1,16	381,8
Source: Hofstee, 1981			

Pour la période considérée les fluctuations non négligeables de la natalité et de la mortalité sont corrélées de manière certaine aux guerres et aux avatars régulièrement encourus par l'agriculture. Les épidémies (choléra) et les maladies endémiques (malaria) jouent un rôle important. Des différences régionales notables sont également observées, marquant non seulement une opposition nord-sud, mais aussi des tendances opposées et des différences écologiques qui au cours de la période s'orientent lentement vers la moyenne nationale.

TABLEAU 2.- DIVERS INDICATEURS DEMOGRAPHIQUES (PAYS-BAS; 1806-1930)

Période	(1)	(2)	(3)	(4)	(5)
1806-10	31.0		31.9		0.1
1811-15	33.8		29.8		4.0
1816-20	35.3		27.0		8.3
1821-25	38.3		25.7		12.5
1826-30	36.2		30.1		6.2
1831-35	34.3	340.0	28.0		6.3
1841-44	36.1	367.0	25.6	177	10.5
1851-55	33.7	356.4	24.9	195	8.8
1861-65	35.1	359.5	24.8	204	10.3
1871-75	35.9	355.3	25.5	198	10.4
1881-85	35.0	354.4	21.6	181	13.4
1891-95	33.2	341.3	19.7	165	13.5
1901-05	31.8	315.1	16.2	136	15.6
1911-15	28.0	261.5	12.9	99	15.0
1921-25	25.9	231.9	10.4	62	15.4
1931-35	21.3	183.1	8.9	44	12.3

Source: Hofstee (1981), van der Woude (1985)
(1) Taux de natalité; (2) Taux de fécondité (pour 1000 femmes mariées de 15 à 44 ans; (3) Taux de mortalité; (4) Taux de mortalité infantile; (5) Accroissement naturel.

2) Etat civil et nuptialité

Van der Woude (1985) insiste sur l'impact des valeurs de la tradition occidentale (liées aux facteurs de subsistance autonome) sur la fécondité conjugale et naturellement sur la fréquence des mariages et sur l'âge au mariage qui a pesé de tout son poids aux Pays-Bas durant le 19ème siècle, à l'opposé de certains pays où l'on ne compte quasiment pas de célibataires à certaines périodes et où l'âge au mariage est parfois fort bas. L'âge au mariage se maintient de manière stable jusqu'en 1875, dans la fourchette de 26,6 à 27,5 ans pour les femmes, et de 28,0 à 29,0 ans pour les hommes. Pour la génération née cette même année il fut constaté par la suite que 13% des hommes restèrent finalement célibataires, contre 14 à 15% des femmes.

Comme cela a déjà été mentionné auparavant, la baisse de la fécondité conjugale se manifesta aux alentours du dernier quart du 19e siècle. Jusqu'à cette période également, la proportion de gens mariés était en relation directe avec le nombre de naissances annuelles.

3) Mouvement de la population

Les calculs de Stokvis synthétisés dans le tableau 5 indiquent un solde migratoire positif pour les années 1820-29 et dans une moindre mesure pour les années 1830-39. Un solde négatif avant 1820 est attribué au rapatriement des Français et au départ de fonctionnaires et de militaires vers les provinces du sud récemment conquises, ainsi que vers les colonies restituées. A partir de 1840 (tableau 3) le solde devint durablement négatif jusqu'à la première guerre mondiale. Pendant vingt ans on constate un équilibre entre l'émigration outre-mer et l'immigration des pays avoisinants, mais par la suite le départ vers les pays lointains, l'emportera largement. Selon l'auteur, les Pays-Bas perdirent ainsi au moins 343000 personnes entre 1840 et 1904, sans compter les départs compensés. Les statistiques relatives aux allochtones dans les pays de destination confirment largement cette thèse.

TABLEAU 3.- LA MIGRATION AUX PAYS-BAS ENTRE 1820 ET 1920

Période	(1)	(2)	(3)	(4)	(5)	(6)
1815	-13					
1820-29	+90					
1830-39	+22					
1840-49	-6	55.2	9.8			68.5
1850-59	-9	61.5	28.3			89.8
1860-69	-75	65.0	46.8			111.8
1870-79	-16	70.1	58.1			128.2
1880-89	-68	100.4	81.9		0.9	183.3
1890-99	-82	156.3	95.4		1.9	253.6
1909-09	-87	222.6	123.8	0.7	5.4	352.2
1920		142.8	137.6	1.5	5.4	287.2

Sources: P.R.D. Stokvis, 1985

(1): Solde migratoire, (2): pays limitrophes, (3): Amérique du Nord, (4): Austr. N. Zélande, (5): Afrique du Sud, (6) Total

La dernière grande épidémie qui frappa les Pays-Bas fut celle qu'on appela la "grippe espagnole" de 1918. Par la suite, il y eut encore quelques épidémies de moindre envergure, qui, bien qu'affectant encore la mortalité, n'eurent plus les effets considérables si caractéristiques du dix-neuvième siècle où sévissent le choléra en 1849, la variole en 1859, à nouveau le choléra en 1865 et encore la variole en 1870, tandis que les famines dues à la destruction du produit de l'agriculture n'avaient pas complètement disparu. Ainsi l'espérance de vie à la naissance se maintint à un niveau relativement bas avec en 1850, 36 ans pour les hommes et 38 ans pour les femmes. A la fin du dix-neuvième siècle une espérance moyenne de vie de 50 ans n'est pas encore réalisée. Mais on atteint 55,6 ans pour les hommes et 57,7 ans pour les femmes au début de la première guerre mondiale.

III. LES DEUX GUERRES MONDIALES

Paradoxalement la deuxième guerre mondiale ne semble pas avoir affecté considérablement l'effectif de la population, mais à l'instar de la première guerre mondiale, à laquelle les Pays-Bas n'ont pas participé, c'est une baisse de l'accroissement net de la population qui se remarque en premier lieu (tableau 4). L'année 1943 présente même un taux de fécondité accru. Bien entendu, c'est du côté des décès qu'il faut chercher la baisse de l'accroissement auquel contribue une mortalité infantile dont l'accroissement dès le milieu de la deuxième guerre mondiale s'avère relativement plus élevé que pendant la première guerre mondiale.

TABLEAU 4 - INDICATEURS DEMOGRAPHIQUES ENTRE LES DEUX-GUERRES

Année	(1)	(2)	(3)	(4)	(5)
1915	6340	167	3.6	80	14.3
1916	6433	173	3.6	84	14.6
1917	6527	173	3.6	87	15.1
1918	6618	168	3.5	115	17.4
1919	6675	164	3.4	90	15.5
1920	6754	193	3.9	82	16.1
1921	6865	190	3.8	77	16.3
1935	8392	170	2.6	74	6.8
1942	9002	190	2.7	86	7.5
1943	9076	209	3.0	91	8.4
1944	9129	220	3.1	108	10.2
1945	9220	210	3.0	141	16.7
1946	9304	284	4.0	80	11.0
1947	9543	267	3.7	78	9.0

LES PAYS-BAS/ THE NETHERLANDS

Année	(6)	(7)	(8)
1915	110	88	21
1916	134	89	45
1917	142	86	51
1918	54	52	-2
1919	53	75	-22
1920	34	111	-21
1921	112	113	-5
1935	82	97	-14
1942	69	104	-34
1943	52	118	-62
1944	92	112	-19
1945	84	68	13
1946	238	204	41
1947	173	190	-11

Source: CBS, 1989
(1) Population (en milliers); (2) Naissances (en milliers); (3) Indice synthétique de fécondité; (4) Décès (en milliers); (5) Décès infantiles (en milliers).(6) Accroissement de la population; (7) Solde naturel; (8) Solde migratoire) (en milliers)

Paradoxalement, également, on notera des renversements de la tendance du solde migratoire, passant d'une valeur négative à une valeur positive en 1945, à l'opposé de 1918. Beaucoup de Néerlandais résidant ailleurs en Europe rejoignirent les Pays-Bas, pays neutre, durant la première guerre mondiale, tandis que l'hospitalité fut accordée à des réfugiés, provenant, par exemple, de la Belgique. Durant la deuxième guerre mondiale, les rôles furent inversés. De plus, 100 000 juifs environ, inclus dans le total des migrants, moururent en déportation.

IV. LA PERIODE 1945-1990

1) Taille et croissance de la population

Lors du dernier recensement précédant la deuxième guerre mondiale, environ huit millions d'habitants furent comptés aux Pays-Bas. Un recensement préparé pour l'année 1940 dut être reporté jusqu'en 1947. A cette date les Pays-Bas comptaient 9,5 millions d'âmes. Les chiffres 'magiques' de 10 et 15 millions furent respectivement atteints en 1949 et 1990. Jusqu'au milieu des années soixante la natalité ne fut jamais inférieure 20 pour mille, taux fort inusité en Europe. Parallèlement on observe une mortalité en baisse constante, tout ceci pour aboutir à une croissance naturelle élevée. Jusqu'à la deuxième guerre mondiale, c'est essentiellement l'excédant de naissances qui contribua à l'accroissement de la population. Par la suite, l'émigration et l'immigration jouèrent un rôle non négligeable. Pour des raisons multiples, l'année 1965 présente une nouvelle transition dans l'histoire démographique des Pays-Bas. Dans un premier temps, une baisse dramatique de la natalité et une hausse de l'immigration se manifestèrent, d'abord de manière officielle et planifiée, plus tard de manière beaucoup plus spontanée et incontrôlée. Le tableau 5 montre l'importance de la migration et du solde des naissances par rapport aux décès dans l'accroissement de la population néerlandaise. Il illustre non seulement clairement l'effet de la baisse du taux de natalité, mais souligne également l'effet accentué de la migration internationale compensatoire.

TABLEAU 5.- ACCROISSEMENT DE LA POPULATION DE 1950 A 1989 (EN MILLIERS)

Année	Tx. Nat. (p. 1000)	Tx Mort. (p. 1000)	Tx. Mort. infant.	Solde naturel	Solde migratoire	Acct. total*
1950	22.7	7.5	26.7	154	20	174
1955	21.3	7.6	12.6	148	-5	142
1960	20.8	7.6	17.9	151	-13	138
1965	19.9	8.0	14.4	147	19	166
1970	18.3	8.4	12.7	129	34	163
1975	13.0	8.3	10.6	64	72	136
1980	12.8	8.1	8.6	67	54	121
1985	12.3	8.5	8.0	55	24	79
1986	12.7	8.6	7.7	60	32	92
1987	12.7	8.3	7.6	65	44	109
1988	12.6	8.4	6.8	63	35	98
1989	12.7	8.7	6.8	60	39	99
1990	13.2	8.7	-	69	60	129

Source: CBS, 1989. * Corrections administratives exclues.

2) Nuptialité et natalité

Durant la période 1950 - 1990, les courbes de la fécondité et de la nuptialité sont affectées aux Pays-Bas par une série de modifications fort remarquables. L'impression se dégage que la nuptialité a joué durant les années soixante un rôle moteur à cet égard pour ensuite voir ses effets s'atténuer. Le nombre de naissances vivantes connut un accroissement appréciable jusqu'en 1965, première année où une baisse est constatée. La chute dramatique d'un niveau de 248000 naissances en 1969 à 177000 en 1976 fut une surprise pour l'ensemble des observateurs. A partir de 1984, une légère reprise fait remonter les naissances vivantes pour aboutir au total actuel de 187000 (1988).

TABLEAU 6.- EVOLUTION DE LA FECONDITE (1950-1990)

Année	ISF	Naissances vivantes pour 1000 femmes dans le groupe d'âge				% de naiss. hors mar.
		15-19	20-24	25-29	30-44	
1950	3.10	12.5	93.9	181.6	110.4	1.5
1955	3.03	13.6	103.2	189.8	101.7	1.2
1960	3.12	16.3	120.3	208.4	93.5	1.4
1965	3.04	21.0	140.3	207.2	77.9	1.8
1970	2.57	22.6	136.8	185.0	57.6	2.1
1975	1.66	12.6	97.9	137.6	30.0	2.1
1980	1.60	9.2	80.1	142.6	33.8	4.1
1985	1.51	6.8	60.6	131.4	36.5	8.3
1986	1.63	6.8	58.0	134.0	39.0	8.7
1987	1.56	6.7	54.3	132.1	41.0	9.3
1988	1.54	7.2	51.3	127.7	42.2	10.1
1989	1.55					10.6
1990	1.63					11.2
Source: CBS, 1991						

L'examen des taux de fécondité générale, révèle une évolution analogue : une tendance ascendante jusqu'au milieu des années soixante, ensuite une chute considérable, finalement une relative stabilité. L'accroissement des naissances jusqu'au milieu des années soixante s'accompagne simultanément d'une baisse des naissances de rang supérieur à 3. Et c'est précisément le nombre croissant d'enfants de rang 1 et 2 qui compense la perte encourue par les naissances de rang supérieur. Dans une certaine mesure la chute abrupte est également compensée (alors que le nombre de premiers-nés augmente d'abord et baisse ensuite durant cette période) par un accroissement de femmes ayant leur premier enfant à un âge plus jeune (tableau 6). Ces mouvements compensatoires font ressortir à l'évidence ici des déplacements importants du calendrier. Ensuite, la hausse légère du taux de natalité après 1984 n'est pas causée par un accroissement des familles nombreuses, mais parce qu'un certain nombre de femmes décidèrent à un âge plus avancé de mettre au monde un premier ou un deuxième enfant. Durant cette même période, le nombre de femmes (volontairement) sans enfant continue à croître. Ce pourcentage pourrait bien atteindre 20% à 25% pour les femmes de la génération 1960-65 (figure 1).

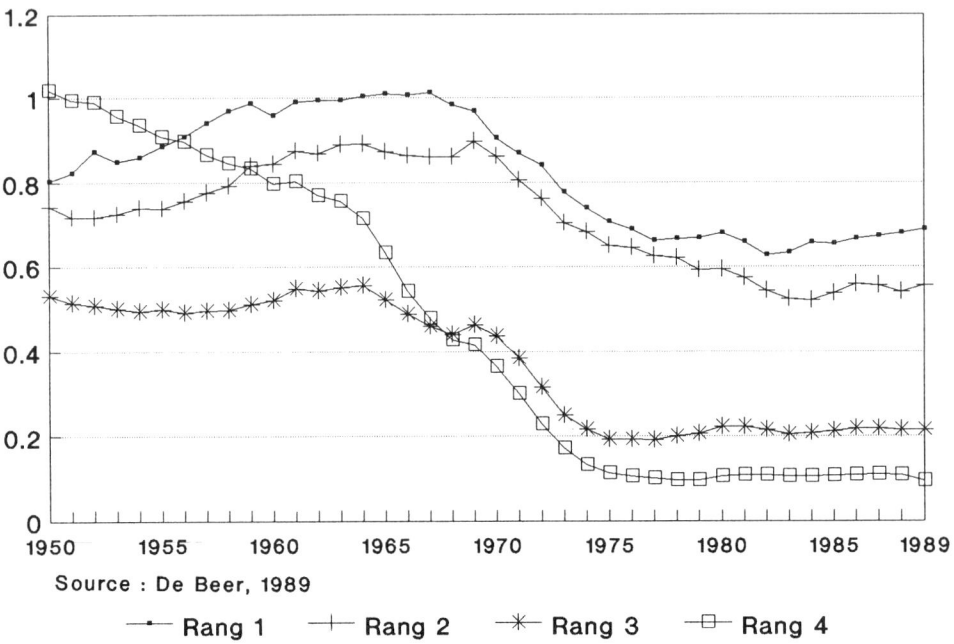

Figure 1.- Taux de fécondité selon le rang

Comme cela a été montré plus haut, c'est après 1950 que la relation entre la nuptialité et la fécondité subit une modification cruciale. Entre 1950 et le milieu des années soixante-dix l'âge médian au mariage baissa de trois ans, tant pour les hommes que pour les femmes. Au début de cette phase ceux qui entreprirent de se marier se trouvaient dans une position d'aptitude matérielle et mentale favorable pour fonder une famille. Le mariage aboutit souvent à la naissance rapide d'un premier enfant, généralement suivie à court intervalle, d'une deuxième naissance.

Dès lors, la fécondité des couples jeunes présente un taux en hausse (tableau 6). Après 1965, la situation se modifie. Les moyens contraceptifs et leur application sont rapidement adoptés; dès le début des années soixante-dix, l'interruption volontaire de grossesse est de fait rendue possible. Ce qui conduit à une régulation minutieuse de la procréation à l'intérieur du mariage. Pour ceux qui ne désirent pas d'enfant ou ne peuvent, pour une quelconque raison, s'en occuper ou les entretenir, il devient facile d'empêcher une naissance à l'intérieur du mariage. Ceci rend possible une baisse de l'âge au mariage. Entre 1965 et 1970 la part de jeunes, tant garçons que filles, aptes au mariage augmente davantage encore le nombre de mariages réalisés (tableau 7).

LES PAYS-BAS/ THE NETHERLANDS

TABLEAU 7.- INDICATEURS DE NUPTIALITE ET DIVORTIALITE (1950-1990)

Année	(1)	(2)	(3)	(4)	(5)
1950	83	8.2	6.5	3.0	11.2
1955	89	8.3	5.5	2.3	11.4
1960	89	7.8	5.7	2.2	11.1
1965	109	8.8	6.2	2.2	11.5
1970	124	9.5	10.3	3.3	11.8
1975	100	7.3	20.1	6.0	12.5
1980	90	6.4	25.7	7.5	11.9
1985	83	5.7	34.0	9.9	12.8
1986	87	5.7	29.8	8.7	12.9
1987	87	6.0	27.7	8.1	13.1
1988	88	6.0	27.8	8.0	12.9
1989	90	6.1	28.3	-	-
1990	-	6.5	-	-	-

Source: CBS, 1991.
(1) nombre de mariages (en milliers); (2) Mariages pour 1000; (3) nombre de divorces (en milliers); (4) divorces (pour 1000 couples); (5) Durée moyenne du mariage lors du divorce.

A l'évidence, après que l'option "se marier jeune, sans immédiatement avoir d'enfants" fut introduite, une nouvelle option se présente avec l'alternative de la cohabitation. Après 1970, le nombre de mariages diminue et le taux de primo-nuptialité baisse rapidement tandis que l'âge au premier mariage s'élève à nouveau. On observe un retournement de situation où le facteur "nuptialité" devient une dérivée du facteur "fécondité". Il semble finalement que la relation n'est officialisée par le mariage que dès que l'enfant est souhaité ou s'annonce. Ce processus conduit ensuite à une situation où le mariage lui-même est considéré comme totalement inutile. Le tracé de la courbe du pourcentage de jeunes mariées enceintes montre que si la contraception efficace conduit d'abord à une baisse des mariages forcés, elle induit par la suite une augmentation de mariées enceintes, et finalement un accroissement significatif du pourcentage des naissances hors mariage. En 1988, ce pourcentage dépasse même le niveau de 10%, tandis le pourcentage de premiers-nés hors mariage atteint 15%. Un bon nombre d'enfants finissent par voir leurs parents se marier ultérieurement. La présence d'une part importante de femmes non néerlandaises dans la population contribue à l'accroissement de la fécondité durant cette période. Mais l'effet final reste modéré. Ainsi, de Beer (1989) rapporte que seulement 10% de l'accroissement du nombre de naissances depuis 1983 peut être attribué aux mères turques et marocaines. La hausse du nombre de mariages vers la fin des années 1980, de même que la hausse légère de la fécondité parmi les femmes plus âgées indique qu'une opération de 'rattrapage' est en cours parmi les femmes néerlandaises.

Comme c'est le cas dans beaucoup de pays européens, les années 1970 marquent le changement de la législation à l'égard du divorce. Le divorce obtenu par consentement mutuel, motivé exclusivement par une "désorientation conjugale sans issue", l'emporte sur les autres causes. La stabilisation du nombre de divorces vers la moitié des années 1980 frappe néanmoins et une explication claire pour ce phénomène fait encore défaut. Des facteurs économiques pourraient en être à l'origine, comme par exemple la prise de conscience du coût d'un divorce, ou dans une autre perspective la tendance à la cohabitation. Il apparaît qu'après un divorce la durée moyenne de la période vécue "conjugalement" est légèrement plus longue que pour les célibataires et que le nombre de divorcés présente une hausse continue, inversement à la propension à se remarier.

3) Mortalité

L'espérance de vie à la naissance est en hausse régulière et continue avec une interruption unique durant la seconde guerre mondiale (figure 2). En 1989, les Pays-Bas appartiennent au petit groupe exceptionnel de pays où les femmes atteignent 80 ans et les hommes 73,7 ans. Une autre caractéristique se développe de manière analogue : l'écart entre l'espérance de vie des hommes et des femmes s'est accru depuis 1960. Le taux de mortalité a grimpé légèrement durant les 30 dernières années ; ceci est dû au vieillissement de la population. Mais cette hausse est restée fort modérée. La forte baisse de la mortalité infantile y a contribué très largement. Dans la répartition des décès par cause, d'importants déplacements eurent lieu. Beets (1989,17) signale qu'en 1987, 44,4% des décès sont dus aux maladies cardio-vasculaires et 23,5% aux cancers tandis que pour l'intervalle 1905/09 ces proportions sont respectivement 12,4% et 7,0%.

4) Migration

Les Pays-Bas sont traditionnellement un pays d'émigration. Après la deuxième guerre mondiale beaucoup de citoyens quittèrent le pays vers l'Australie, la Nouvelle-Zélande, l'Afrique du Sud, le Canada ou les USA. Cet "exodus contrarié" atteint, par exemple, en 1952 le nombre de 51700 personnes.

Durant cette période, le gouvernement néerlandais favorisa l'émigration et signa plusieurs accords avec les pays d'adoption. Ce flux considérable de migrants s'arrêta au début des années 1960 (tableau 8). L'essor économique qui s'amplifia après la guerre provoqua une demande sur le marché de l'emploi et l'amélioration des dispositions sociales rendirent l'émigration moins attrayante.

LES PAYS-BAS/ THE NETHERLANDS

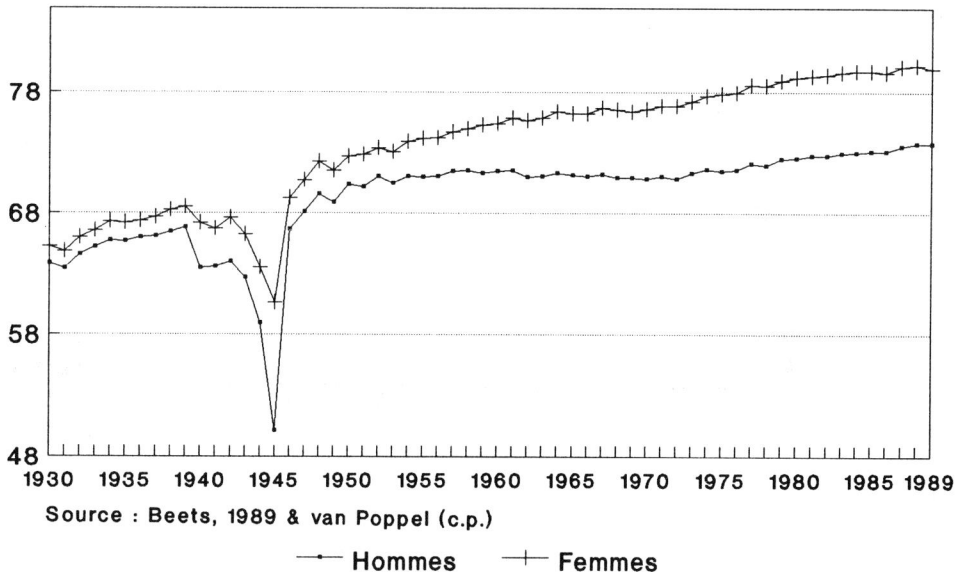

Figure 2.- Espérance de vie à la naissance

TABLEAU 8: L'EMIGRATION VERS QUELQUES PAYS SPECIFIQUES ET L'EMIGRATION TOTALE 1945-1959 (EN MILLIERS).

Période	Indonésie	Surinam	Antilles	**	Total
1945-49	90.5		13.4*	-	273
1950-54	43.5	3.3	10.6	190.4	327
1955-59	25.9	4.3	12.4	152.3	293

Source: CBS, 1989
* Surinam inclus
** Australie, Canada, Nouvelle-Zélande, Afrique du Sud, USA

Le refroidissement des relations avec l'Indonésie suite à l'acquisition de l'indépendance de ce pays en 1949, eut pour effet d'atténuer considérablement l'émigration vers ce pays. L'immigration après la deuxième guerre mondiale se développe principalement selon quatre phases (tableau 9). La première phase intervient directement après la guerre lorsque de nombreux réfugiés rentrèrent au pays et lorsque de nombreux Hollandais

(181400) quittèrent les Indes, anciennement néerlandaises. Parmi les rapatriés des Indes se trouvèrent à peu près 17000 militaires moluquois, membres de leurs familles inclus, qui selon toute prévision, retourneraient rapidement en Indonésie. Ceci ne fut finalement pas réalisé et conduisit indirectement à des frustrations culminant notamment dans la célèbre prise d'otages du train de Wijster. L'intégration des autres rapatriés d'Indonésie se fit de manière fort harmonieuse. La seconde phase concerne l'entrée sollicitée des travailleurs étrangers de, par exemple, la Turquie et le Maroc. Le recrutement de ces immigrés avait pour but de maintenir la capacité de la production à un niveau salarial optimisé dans le cadre d'un marché de l'emploi demandeur. Cette phase débuta en 1963. En 1973 la crise pétrolière eut pour conséquence un affaiblissement de ce flux d'immigrés, mais le processus relativement important du regroupement des familles maintient cette immigration. La troisième phase se situe dans la perspective de l'Indépendance de la colonie du Surinam. Les ressortissants de ce pays, ayant jusqu'à leur indépendance la nationalité néerlandaise en profitèrent juste avant 1975 pour s'installer définitivement aux Pays-Bas. Un renforcement des restrictions légales, convenues et annoncées pour 1980, conduisit à un nouveau flux vers les Pays-Bas en 1979/80. La quatrième phase, actuellement en cours, est celle où les Pays-Bas, qui ne se considèrent pas comme un pays d'immigration, connaissent un solde migratoire positif d'environ 45000 personnes par an. Parmi celles-ci se trouve un grand nombre de réfugiés politiques du tiers monde et d'autres personnes qui cherchent à s'installer en terre d'asile néerlandaise pour des motifs humanitaires ou dans le cadre de conventions internationales.

TABLEAU 9: NOMBRE TOTAL D'IMMIGRES DE QUELQUES PAYS (1946-88).

Période	Indonésie	Surinam	Antilles	Maroc	Turquie	Tous pays
1946-50	181.4	11.4	1.2			314
1951-55	108.8	3.5	11.5			208
1956-60	92.8	6.1	13.8			252
1961-65	40.7	11.9	16.0	4.1	7.3	320
1966-70	10.7	25.8	17.4	18.4	26.5	369
1971-75	8.9	86.7	18.2	19.5	49.8	482
1976-80	11.9	55.2	22.9	36.8	63.8	474
1981-85	8.8	21.8	22.8	30.5	27.5	364
1986-88	4.5	15.9	23.2	22.0	28.6	274

Source: CBS, 1989

LES PAYS-BAS/ THE NETHERLANDS

L'arrivée continuelle de migrants a provoqué la mise en oeuvre d'une politique compliquée envers les groupes minoritaires, une politique qui confronte les responsables à des difficultés certaines. De plus, parmi les 641.918 habitants, non directement d'origine néerlandaise se trouvent 381.687 personnes provenant d'un autre pays européen. Parmi eux, les Turcs forment le plus grand groupe avec 171000 personnes. Le continent africain est le lieu d'origine de 170.647 personnes, dont 147.975 ressortissants provenant du Maroc. Les plus petits groupes viennent d'Asie (46920), et d'Amérique (34529), tandis que quelque 6000 personnes ont le statut d'apatride.

Le tableau 10 donne un aperçu des immigrants par région d'origine au 1/1/90 pour autant que leur nombre dépasse 10000 unités. Pour ce qui concerne les personnes provenant du Surinam et des Antilles néerlandaises, le tableau inclut celles qui disposent de la nationalité néerlandaise. Parmi l'ensemble des 15 millions d'habitants que comptent les Pays-Bas, 8% est né en dehors des frontières. Ce qui présente un accroissement important par rapport à 1920 (2.8%) ou 1971 (4.5%) (Van Poppel, 1992). Il est à signaler que le nombre de personnes d'origine néerlandaise vivant à l'étranger équivaut à celui des étrangers qui habitent aux Pays-Bas. La majorité d'entre eux réside en Belgique (75000) et en RFA (115000). Hors d'Europe, c'est dans les pays d'émigration traditionnelle qu'on trouve la plupart des Néerlandais émigrés.

TABLEAU 10: ETRANGERS RESIDENTS AUX PAYS-BAS ENTRE 1970 ET 1990.

Origine	1970	1975	1980	1985	1990
Belgique	20.2	20.7	23.0	23.6	23.3
RFA	31.3	40.1	42.7	44.8	41.8
Italie	16.3	19.7	20.9	20.3	16.7
Yougos.	4.3	12.9	13.7	12.2	12.8
Maroc	17.4	33.2	71.8	111.3	147.9
Espagne	22.6	31.3	23.5	20.7	17.4
Turquie	23.6	62.6	119.6	155.6	191.4
G.-B.	9.8	19.5	35.4	40.7	37.5
USA	7.4	9.6	10.7	10.4	10.5
Surinam*	38.1**	79.2	145.7	181.4	203.0***
Antilles Néerland.*	18.2**	23.9	36.2	46.2	60.8***

Source: CBS
* y compris la nationalité acquise; ** 1971; *** 1989.

5) *Composition de la population et perspectives*

La structure par âge de la population néerlandaise porte encore clairement le sceau d'une fécondité longtemps élevée. Un léger rétrécissement de la base de la pyramide des âges n'apparaît qu'à partir des groupes d'âge inférieurs à vingt ans. Le "baby bust" d'après 1964 qui reçut au début des années 1970 une accentuation supplémentaire a sérieusement influencé la forme de la pyramide. Les effets sur le marché de l'offre de l'emploi se feront sans aucun doute sentir durant les années 1990. Les conséquences des deux guerres mondiales sont également encore visibles. Le 'baby boom' qui se manifesta durant les premières années après la deuxième guerre mondiale est un cas de figure caractéristique à cet égard. Les prévisions obtenues par les projections démographiques réalisées annuellement par le Bureau National Néerlandais de Statistiques (CBS) ont systématiquement du être actualisées à la baisse pour les années 1960 et 1970. Durant la seconde moitié des années 1980, une adaptation dans le sens de la hausse s'avéra cette fois-ci nécessaire. Une migration sans cesse croissante, une fécondité plus élevée que prévue, et des décès en deça des prévisions, en furent les causes principales. Dans les projections de 1990 (variante moyenne) un solde migratoire positif de 25000 personnes est avancé pour l'an 2020, ainsi qu'une espérance de vie moyenne de 81,5 ans pour les femmes, et de 75 ans pour les hommes. Selon ces mêmes calculs les femmes de la génération 1985 auront une descendance moyenne de 1,65 enfants. Dans ces conditions et sous quelques hypothèses moins solidement fondées la population des Pays-Bas augmentera d'abord quelque peu pour ensuite baisser réellement. Le niveau de population le plus élevé se réaliserait en 2025 avec quelque 16,5 millions d'habitants. Pour 2050, il faudrait compter néanmoins sur une population plus réduite de 15,3 millions.

Des projections ont été réalisées pour diverses sous-populations. Ainsi, van Imhoff, Keilman et Wolff (1990) élaborent un scénario réaliste des types de ménages selon leurs caractéristiques. Ils aboutissent a un accroissement gigantesque du nombre des personnes vivant seules - par exemple, s'ils dénombraient en 1975 880000 femmes isolées, ce nombre devrait atteindre 2.3 millions en 2035. Ils obtiennent également une hausse considérable de femmes cohabitantes (un niveau de 573000 en 2035, dont 159000 avec des enfants) ainsi qu'une diminution considérable de femmes mariées avec enfant(s) (un passage de 2.182 millions en 1985 a 1.365 millions en 2035). Actuellement, en 1988, parmi toutes les femmes âgées entre 20-24 ans aux Pays-Bas, 19% cohabitent et ce pourcentage atteint 16% pour celles du groupe 25-29 ans. Il est sûr que ces pourcentages s'élèveront encore dans le futur. Pour ce qui concerne l'accroissement de la population dite 'allochtone', des chercheurs du NIDI ont également réalisé quelques estimations prédictives (Nusselder, Schoorl, Berkien, 1990). Pour une période couvrant dix ans, à savoir de 1989 à 1999 ils avancent un accroissement de quelque 285000 personnes. Mises à part 100.000 personnes, de nationalités les plus diverses, ce sont surtout les minorités turques et marocaines qui interviendront dans l'accroissement. Le nombre d'habitants provenant des autres pays de l'Europe est évalué aux alentours de 180000.

Finalement, le groupe provenant de divers autres pays du tiers-monde s'élèvera à plusieurs dizaines de milliers de personnes.

6) *Politiques démographiques*

Les Pays-Bas n'ont jamais à proprement parler connu de politique démographique active. A l'heure actuelle le gouvernement se déclare non appelé à diriger de manière directe les développements démographiques du pays - en particulier la natalité et la nuptialité. Une telle attitude est d'une certaine manière compréhensible mais cache en fait une partie de la réalité. Ainsi il est évident que l'émigration après la deuxième guerre mondiale a bénéficié des encouragements d'une politique adoptée sciemment. Bien entendu l'excuse de la promesse d'un avenir meilleur permit de faire passer l'aspect démographique au second plan. Dans le même registre, afin de ne pas devoir s'aventurer dans le domaine contestable du contrôle des naissances, le gouvernement fournit un support indéniable à l'émigration. A d'autres périodes, certaines mesures dont l'effet démographique n'était pas ignoré furent introduites. Ainsi par exemple, les allocations familiales en 1920 et la mise en place d'une ordonnance en 1924, renvoyant au foyer les femmes fonctionnaires qui se mariaient avant l'âge de 45 ans (van Praag, 1976). Ce n'est qu'en 1965, lorsque le CBS publia ses premières perspectives de population, prédisant pour l'an 2000 une population de 21 millions, que l'attitude officielle envers cette évolution se manifesta. Un symposium organisé par le Conseil Social et Economique appartenant à l'Académie Royale Néerlandaise des Sciences (fondée en 1808!) attira l'attention publique par le titre "L'homme entassé" et contribua à la prise de conscience. L'opinion selon laquelle les Pays-Bas auraient de grosses difficultés à endiguer une croissance débridée de la population se développa. Les enquêtes publiques révélèrent que la majorité de la population considérait les Pays-Bas comme "surpeuplés" et dans les cercles gouvernementaux, une certaine inquiétude non simulée se développa. Finalement, une Commission Royale ayant pour objet la "Question de la population" fut instaurée avec pour mission d'étudier les développements démographiques et les conséquences attendues. Les résultats obtenus étaient censés présenter une plateforme pour des mesures éventuelles à considérer. La Commission publia un rapport intermédiaire en 1973, et la version définitive du rapport parut en 1977. Dans une certaine mesure les événements qui survinrent entretemps rendirent le rapport partiellement caduc. La fécondité avait baissé de manière spectaculaire et les prévisions démographiques furent adaptées en conséquence. Dans son rapport final, la commission accueillit favorablement ces développements. Parmi les 66 recommandations présentées, la commission en retint 3 ayant un caractère spécifiquement démographique (Van de Kaa et van de Windt, 1979, p. 254) L'étendue de celles-ci avait une double dimension: d'une part le gouvernement fut invité à obtenir l'arrêt de l'accroissement naturel de la population le plus rapidement possible pour arriver à une population stationnaire; à moyen terme un niveau de fécondité en dessous de 15% à 30% du taux de remplacement des générations était requis. Le gouvernement reçut également l'avis que la migration ne devrait pas affecter l'évolution démographique de manière trop prononcée. Dans un nombre de prises de positions officielles (1979, 1983, 1988), le gouvernement inclut ces propositions. Une population stationnaire de 14 millions y fut présentée comme expressément souhaitable, et un frein à l'accroissement naturel fut demandé de manière explicite. Une réorientation non négligeable eut lieu en 1988. Le gouvernement décréta alors qu'aucune mesure ne devait être introduite, qui puisse conduire à une perception négative des frais occasionés par les enfants pour un couple. Une certaine inquiétude occasionnée par la baisse de la population et par le vieillissement de celle-ci se fait néanmoins sentir. Nonobstant tout ceci le point de vue officiel reste en vigueur et en accord avec les recommandations de la Commission. Ceci n'implique pas nécessairement qu'une politique active soit menée pour réaliser certains buts prédéterminés. C'est principalement, et par exception, à l'égard de l'immigration et de l'accueil des étrangers, qu'une politique active est menée. Pour une grande partie, celle-ci s'exerce dans le cadre des conventions internationales et des accords de l'Europe Nouvelle, comme les accords de Schengen.

Bibliographie

Beer, J. de, Jaren tachtig : ombuiging of voortzetting van demografische trends? Maandstatistiek van de bevolking, 37(1989)12, pp 16-35.

Beets, G.C.N., Sterfte, Maandstatistiek van de bevolking, 37(1989)10, pp 16-17.

CBS, Negentig jaren statistiek in tijdreeksen, Voorburg, 1989.

CBS, Maandstatistiek van de bevolking, Voorburg, série 1989/1990.

Hofstee, E.W., Demografische ontwikkeling van de Noordelijke Nederlanden, circa 1800-

circa 1975, in : Algemene Geschiedenis der Nederlanden, Unieboek, Bussum 1981, vol. 10, pp. 63-93.

Imhoff, E. van, N. Keilman et S. Wolff, Huishoudens en uitkeringen in de 21e eeuw,

NIDI, report nr. 18, Den Haag, 1990, 166 pp.

Kaa, D.J. van de et K. van der Windt, Minder mensen, meer welzijn, Aula-boeken 615,

Uitgeverij het Spectrum, Utrecht etc., 1979, 284 pp.

LES PAYS-BAS/ THE NETHERLANDS

Nusselder, W. J. Schoorl et J.Berkien, Bevolkingsvooruitberekening allochtonen in Nederland naar nationaliteit 1989-1999, NIDI, report nr 16, Den Haag, 1990, 179 p.

Poppel, F.W.A. van, Les Pays-Bas, dans : Histoire de la population Européenne, J. Dupâquier et J.P.Baudet (ed.), Paris, Fayard (1992), vol. iii (à paraître).

Praag, Ph. van, Het bevolkingsvraagstuk in Nederland, van Loghum Slaterus, Deventer, 1976.

Slicher van Bath, B.H., Historical Demography and the Social and Economic Development of the Netherlands, in: Daedalus, 97(1986)2, pp 604-622.

Sardon, J.P., Le rempacement des générations en Europe, in: Population, déc. 1990, pp. 962-963.

Stokvis, P. R. D., Nederland en de internationale migratie, 1815-1960, in: De Nederlandse samenleving sinds 1815 : wording en samenhang, F.L. Holthoon (ed.), Assen, Van Gorcum, 1985, pp. 71-113.

Woude, A.M. van der, Bevolking en gezin in Nederland, in: De Nederlandse samenleving sinds 1815 : wording en samenhang, F. L. van Holthoon (ed.), Assen, Van Gorcum, 1985, pp. 19-70.

Germany/ L'Allemagne
Charlotte HÖHN

FROM ONE TO TWO TO ONE GERMANY

This report deals with Germany, which was divided into two countries and unexpectedly became one again. The first part highlights the common population history up to World War II. The second part outlines the main demographic trends in the former German Democratic Republic (GDR) and in the Federal Republic of Germany while the third part gives an overview of the population-relevant policies in the two Germanies. A final part will summarize the demographic lessons to be drawn from the past for the future.

I. THE DEMOGRAPHIC SITUATION FROM 1871 TO THE END OF WORLD WAR II

a) Demographic transition in Germany

This period from the foundation of the German Empire in 1871 which ended with World War I over the Weimar Republic to the Third Reich and World War II comprises the period of demographic transition in Germany. The many dramatic and historical events in these troubled years reflected in the birth and death rate make it difficult to determine the true point where demographic transition in the classical sense was over and progressed (or transformed) into the so-called second demographic transition (Van de Kaa, 1987). Here we deem it more important to point out that in Germany cohort replacement fertility was reached as early as in the twenties of this century, never attaining cohort replacement again.

The onset of the secular fertility decline in Germany more or less precisely coincides with the foundation of the German Empire. In the decades between 1870 and 1910 the economic and social transformations of unprecedented dimensions, the strong industrialisation, the urbanisation but also the establishment of a welfare state have to be located.

The economic transformation (table 1) together with the introduction of a compulsory old age pension system (in 1889 by Bismarck) and a compulsory general schooling scheme reduced the value of children (the birth rate fell) and enhanced medical progress (the death rate fell too).

We all know that crude demographic rates for good reasons are labeled "crude", since they, inter alia, reflect all kinds of special fluctuations. We therefore will analyse fertility and mortality in a more appropriate way, i.e. if possible with period and cohort measures.

TABLE 1.- GERMANY. BIRTH AND DEATH RATE, ECONOMIC STRUCTURE AND AVERAGE HOUSEHOLD SIZE, 1870 - 1939

Year	Births per 1000 inhabitants	Deaths	% of economically active persons in			Average number of persons per household
			agriculture	industry	trade, transport and other services	
1871	34.5	24.6	-	-	-	4.64
1882	37.2	25.7	43.4	33.7	22.9	4.60 (1880)
1895	36.1	22.1	37.5	37.5	25.0	4.53
1907	32.3	18.0	35.2	40.1	24.7	4.45 (1905)
1913	27.5	15.0	-	-	-	4.40 (1910)
1925	20.7	11.9	30.5	41.4	28.1	3.98
1933	14.7	11.2	28.9	40.4	30.7	3.61
1939	20.4	12.3	25.0	40.8	34.2	3.27
Source: Federal Statistical Office						

b) Fertility transition

The myth of the German family insists on the conception of the extended family with many children. Historical evidence for Western Europe does not support this idea (Laslett and Wall, 1972; Wall, Robin and Laslett, 1983). In Germany, people married late and illegitimate fertility was to a large degree avoided (see table 4). Marital fertility was relatively low; the family formation in general was neolocal. We find this lack of large households reflected in the small average household size of 4.64 persons already in 1871, dropping to 3.27 in 1939 (see table 1).

More pertinent to fertility are informations on the average number of children per marriage cohort (table 2).

TABLE 2.- GERMANY*. FINAL FAMILY SIZE OF MARRIAGE COHORTS 1900 - 1974

Years of marriage	Of 100 marriages had					children on average
	no child	1 child	2	3	4+	
1900-1904	9	12	16	15	47	393
1905-1909	10	15	20	17	38	335
1910-1912	12	17	22	17	32	294
1913-1918	14	20	24	17	25	252
1919-1921	16	23	24	15	21	234
1922-1925	18	24	24	15	20	222
1926-1930	17	23	25	15	20	223
1931-1935	16	22	27	17	18	218
1936-1940	14	25	31	17	14	205
1941-1945	13	25	31	17	14	205
1946-1950	13	26	30	17	14	207
1951-1955	13	25	31	17	14	205
1958-1962	13	22	36	19	10	200
1961-1965	14	24	40	16	6	180
1965-1969	16	29	40	12	3	159
1970-1974	19	29	40	10	2	148

* Since 1949 Federal Republic of Germany
Source: Bundestags-Drucksache 10/863; 132 und BIB-Mitteilungen, 8. Jg. 3/87; 11

The estimate for marriages contracted around 1870 is 5 children per marriage. Marriages contracted in 1900 to 1904 on average had 3.93 children with 47 percent having 4 and more children and - remarkable for that early period - 9 percent remaining childless.

The decisive and dramatic fertility decline in Germany occured within few decades. Already marriages contracted in 1922 to 1925 eventually had only 2.22 children on average. The percentage of childless marriages doubled from 9 to 18 percent. We may conjecture that in the Weimar Republic methods of birth control were known and applied

(David, Fleischhacker and HOhn, 1988) to avoid unwanted offspring in a period of economic hardship (big inflation in 1923-25 and world economic crisis in 1931) and of social upheaval (dramatic value change in a young democracy already threatened by new autoritarian forces).

It should be noted that final family size of marriages contracted in 1931 to 1935 did not increase, though these couples were fully exposed to the aggressive "population" policy of the Nazis. It is obvious when comparing cohort and period measures for the thirties and forties that the Nazi policy (a racist and imperialistic pronatalist policy) did increase the birth rate but not cohort fertility. The explanation of this phenomenon is simple: postponed fertility decisions and births planned for later were realized at the same time. It was a situation of changed timing of births under the possibilities of making windfall profits.

c) *Mortality transition*

There are four life tables available for the period under consideration which have been calculated on the basis of population census results (table 3).

In 1871/81 male newborn could expect to live 35.6 years and females 38.5 years (i. e. 2.9 years longer). The remarkable mortality decline manifests itself in a rising life expectancy with the strongest acceleration between 1901/10 and 1924/26. In the 30 years between the first two life tables of 1871/81 and 1901/10 males (females) gained 9.2 (9.8) years of life expectancy, but in the app. 25 years from 1901/10 to 1924/26 the increase was bigger with 11.2 years (males) resp. 10.5 years for the female newborn.

To assess the weight of infant and child mortality in the level of life expectancy at that time it should be noted that the further life expectancy of 15 year old persons of either sex was higher than that of newborn children according to the two life tables of 1871/81 and 1901/1910.

Indeed, infant mortality was high. In 1871/81, out of 100 newborn 24.2 male and 20.7 female children died before completing their first year of life (table 3).

Also the decline of infant mortality was big. The rate per 1 000 male/female newborn fell from 241.7/207 in 1871/81 to 202.3/170.5 in 1901/10 by 16/18 percent and to 85.4/68.4 in 1939. Again we notice an acceleration in the reduction of infant mortality after 1901/10.

The development of life expectancies at various completed ages, as shown in table 3, indicates that the gain in life expectancy at birth is mainly due to a successful reduction of infant mortality and, to a smaller degree, to a moderately declining young adult mortality. The latter trend can be deduced from the increase of life expectancy of the 15 year old persons by 10 years between 1871/81 and 1932/34. Old age mortality improved however only relatively little in the period under consideration. Life expectancy of 60 year old men increased by three years, those of women by 3.4 years. Even smaller was the increase for the 80 year old (plus 0.7 year for men and one year for women).

TABLE 3.- GERMANY. LIFE EXPECTANCY (IN YEARS) AND INFANT MORTALITY (PER 1000 NEWBORN), 1871/81 - 1932/34

	1871-81	1901-10	1924-26	1932-34
	Males			
Infant mortality	241.7	202.3	115.4	85.4
Life expectancy at age				
0	35.6	44.8	56.0	59.9
15	42.4	46.7	51.0	52.6
60	12.1	13.1	14.6	15.1
80	4.1	4.4	4.8	4.8
	Females			
Infant mortality	207.0	170.5	93.9	68.4
Life expectancy at age				
0	38.5	48.3	58.8	62.8
15	44.2	49.0	52.4	54.4
60	12.7	14.2	15.5	16.1
80	4.2	4.7	5.1	5.2

Source: Federal Statistical Office

d) Marriage and divorce

We already mentioned a few characteristics of German family formation. As table 4 illustrates, single men and women married relatively late (unfortunately data before 1911 could not be found) with an even slightly rising trend towards 1939.

In the crude marriage rates we see reflected the after-war marriage booms, here in 1872 and 1920 as examples, but also the incentives-supported increase of marrying under Nazi rule (see 1939).

Children born out of wedlock were undesired despite of late marriage. The illegitimacy ratio remained low and virtually constant at 9 percent up to World War I though urbanisation (with its alleged vices) was progressing rapidly during the German Empire.

TABLE 4.- GERMANY. ILLEGITIMACY RATIO, AGE AT FIRST MARRIAGE, MARRIAGE, DIVORCE AND EMIGRATION RATE, 1872 - 1939

Year	Illegitimate births per 1000 births	Marriages per 1000 inhab.	Average age at 1st marriage		Divorces per 10.000 inh.	Emigrants per 100.000 inh.
			men	women		
1872	88	10.3	..	..	..	311
1875	86	9.1	..	..	..	76
1880	89	7.5	..	..	..	260
1885	94	7.9	..	..	1.4^1	236
1890	..	8.0	..	..	1.3	197
1895	90	8.0	..	..	1.6	72
1900	86	8.5	..	..	1.4	40
1905	84	8.1	..	..	1.9	47
1910	90	7.7	27.4^2	24.8^2	2.3	40
1920	112	14.5	28.6	25.7	5.9	14
1923	103	9.4	27.6	25.1	5.5	185
1930	120	8.8	27.5	25.3	6.3	57
1933	107	9.7	27.5	25.4	6.5	19
1939	76^3	11.2	28.8^3	26.2^3	8.9	37

Source: Federal Statistical Office; ^{1}=1888; ^{2}=1911; ^{3}=1938

During the Weimar Republic (1919-1932) modernization and social upheaval in the big cities did cause a temporary increase of fertility out of wedlock. This "immoral" behaviour was drastically changed under the Nazis: the ratio fell to a historical low of 7.6 percent children born out of wedlock in 1938.

There remains, however, one unbroken demographic indicator of modernization, the ever increasing divorce rate. Though on a very low level, the trend is remarkably strong. The divorce rate quadruples from 1888 to 1920, with the second doubling between the beginning and end of World War I. Since then, it keeps increasing both during the Weimar Republic and the Nazi period, adding 50 percent from the end of World War I to the beginning of World War II.

e) International migration

There are very few migration statistics before 1950. We have included the emigration rate in table 4. Germany was an emigration country until the middle of the 20th century. Particularly the 19th century can be characterized by a number of emigration waves to overseas countries. Let us note that settlement in (emigration to) Eastern Europe is the older chapter of international migration of Germans starting in the 14th century with bigger intensity in the 18th century.

Without historical events like the big inflation in 1923 emigration of Germans would have come to an end with World War I. In the twenties Polish workers were even recruited for the Ruhr mining area to overcome labour shortage. The expanding economy transformed Germany from an emigration to an immigration country.

f) Population growth and demographic ageing

In 1871, the German Empire had a population size of 41.1 million of which 4.6 percent were aged 65 and over (table 5). The age structure had the shape of a pyramid and hence ressembled that of Third World countries of today.

Since the territory changed several times during the whole period under consideration we will also present some data relating to the constant territory of the Federal Republic of Germany (before reunificaton). On that territory, in 1871, lived 20.4 million inhabitants.

Due to demographic momentum of a young age structure the population in West Germany from 1871 to 1939 more than doubled to 43 million inhabitants. Population growth in Germany in its respective borders only seems to be smaller because the territory became smaller after World War I by some 13 percent (The data of 1939 are for the territory as of 1937).

What really matters is the ageing process of the population. Here we have the data only for Germany on its changing territory, but we assume that these structures, grosso modo, also apply to the population on the constant territory of the (old) Federal Republic of Germany.

The pronounced fertility decline which brought down fertility to replacement level in the twenties initiated the demographic ageing process in Germany. Already in 1939 7.8 percent of Germany's population were over 65 years old. This heritage of early demographic ageing was conveyed to the two Germanies after the end of World War II.

TABLE 5.- GERMANY. POPULATION DEVELOPMENT, 1871 - 1939

Year (Census)	Population on the territory of Germany(1)			F. R. G.(2)	
	in million	per km2	percent aged 65 and over	in million	per km2
1871	41.1	76	4.6	20.4	82
1880	45.2	84	4.7	22.8	92
1890	49.4	91	5.1	25.4	102
1900	56.4	104	4.9	29.8	120
1910	65.0	120	5.0	35.6	143
1925	62.4	133	5.8	39.0	157
1933	65.4	139	7.1	41.0	165
1939	69.3	147	7.8	43.0	173

(1) Territory between 1871 and 1910 app. 540.000 km2; 1925 and 1933 468.700 km2; 1939 470.400 km2; (2) 248.600 km2
Source: Federal Statistical Office

II. THE DEMOGRAPHIC SITUATION IN THE TWO GERMANIES FROM 1950 UP TO 1989

In 1949, as the consequence of total capitulation of Germany to the four allies and the subsequent occupation, the three Western zones (American, English and French) formed the Federal Republic of Germany while the Soviet zone became the German Democratic Republic (GDR). 40 years later, on 9 November 1989 the wall and the iron curtain opened. Less than one year later on 3 October 1990 the five states (Länder) created on GDR territory acceded to the Federal Republic of Germany. The Federal Republic of Germany became larger and more populous but retained its name. In order to avoid confusion we will call it just Germany.

In this chapter we will try to show the common trend of demographic ageing and how it was shaped after World War II. And we will also point out a few divergent demographic trends and will try to provide some explanations for it (Höhn, Mammey, Wendt, 1990).

a) Fertility trends in the two Germanies

From 1950 to 1956 the total fertility rate in GDR (with 2.4 in the early fifties versus 2.1 in the Federal Republic of Germany) was higher. Then, for 17 years, from 1957 to 1975, the total fertility rates followed a nearly identical course. This fact, however, should not be interpreted as the result of common German culture. There are indeed numerous demographic differences concealed behind the summary indicator of TFR. What is more decisive are the quite different socio-economic backgrounds. I just mention the high level of female economic participation ratio in GDR versus the moderate one in the Federal Republic of Germany, the protestant or denomination-free GDR versus the 50:50 protestant and catholic West German population, the booming economy of the Federal Republic of Germany with ever increasing consumption and leisure facilities versus a modest standard of living in GDR with highly restricted leisure and travel possibilities. From figure 1 we nevertheless notice a nearly parallel increase of the TFR up to the mid-sixties followed by a sharp decline until 1975. The two Germanies display a pattern very similar to other Central and Northern European countries during the same period.

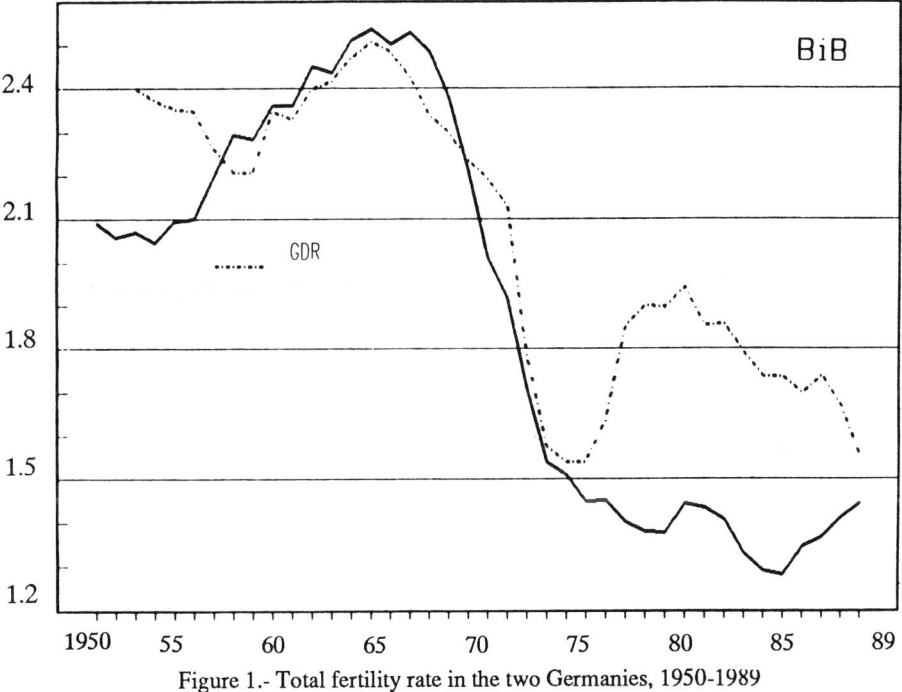

Figure 1.- Total fertility rate in the two Germanies, 1950-1989

After 1976 when GDR launched a comprehensive pronatalist policy (see III. for details) the TFRs diverge. While in the Federal Republic of Germany the fertility level continued to fall (with a small fluctuation around 1980) to a low of 1.28 in 1985, TFR rose in GDR to a relative maximum of 1.94 in 1980. The objective of GDR policy to reach replacement level was never again achieved. On the contrary: after 1980 the TFR resumed its decrease. Already in 1989, the TFRs in the two Germanies have become quite close again.

Before we turn our attention to cohort fertility in the two Germanies we would like to demonstrate a few differences in procreative behaviour (table 6).

TABLE 6.- INDICATORS OF FERTILITY IN THE TWO GERMANIES, 1950 - 1989

Year	Age at birth		Age at 1st birth[1]		Illegitimacy ratio (%)	
	FRG	GDR	FRG	GDR	FRG	GDR
1950	28.3[2]	27.2[3]	25.2[2]	24.0[3]	9.7	12.8
1960	27.9	26.4	24.8	23.0	6.3	11.6
1970	27.4	25.4	24.3	22.5	5.5	13.3
1975	27.0	24.6	24.8	22.5	6.1	16.1
1980	27.0	24.6	25.2	22.3	7.6	22.8
1981	27.1	24.6	25.3	22.3	7.9	25.6
1982	27.2	24.6	25.5	22.3	8.5	29.3
1983	27.3	24.7	25.7	22.3	8.8	32.0
1984	27.5	24.7	26.0	22.3	9.1	33.6
1985	27.7	24.8	26.2	22.3	9.4	33.8
1986	27.9	24.9	26.4	22.4	9.6	34.4
1987	28.0	25.1	26.5	22.5	9.7	32.8
1988	28.1	25.2	26.7	22.6	10.0	33.4
1989	28.2	-	26.8	-	10.2	33.6

([1] Age at first legitimate birth in FR Germany, at first biological birth in GDR
[2] 1951
[3] 1952
Source: Höhn; Mammey; Wendt, 1990 and BIB/INED

It is worth to note that age at birth was one year lower in GDR already in the early fifties, that it continued to fall until the early eighties, and that since 1975 age at all births in GDR is lower than age at first birth in the Federal Republic of Germany. Women in GDR formed their family much earlier and spaced closer than women in the Federal Republic of Germany.

While women in the Federal Republic of Germany started to postpone their first birth already since 1970 showing a clear increase in age at first birth this indicator remained low from the sixties to the mid eighties in GRD.

Even bigger differences existed concerning the percentage of children born out of wedlock. In the historical overview we noted that illegitimacy traditionally was low in Germany. Of course, under the turmoil of postwar conditions the illegitimacy ratio was high. But while it returned to low values in the Federal Republic it never really fell in GDR. Already in 1970 the illegitimacy ratio in GDR was more than double of the equivalent rate in the Federal Republic of Germany.

And while there was only a moderate increase there up to present the increase in GDR was most unusual. In the eighties one third of GDR babies were born to unmarried mothers.

TABLE 7.- COMPLETED FERTILITY OF FEMALE GENERATIONS IN THE TWO GERMANIES

Generation	FRG	GDR	Generation	FRG	GDR
1931	2.20	2.22	1946	1.78	1.87
1932	2.21	2.21	1947	1.75	1.84
1933	2.23	2.19	1948	1.73	1.83
1934	2.20	2.15	1949	1.71	1.80
1935	2.17	2.12	1950	1.70	1.79
1936	2.13	2.09	1951	1.66	1.80
1937	2.11	2.08	1952	1.64	1.81
1938	2.07	2.05	1953	1.62	1.82
1939	2.02	2.02	1954	1.60	1.82
1940	1.97	1.98	1955	1.61	1.84
1941	1.90	1.95	1956	1.60	1.84
1942	1.85	1.90	1957	1.58	1.86
1943	1.81	1.89	1958	..	1.87
1944	1.78	1.87	1959	..	1.88
1945	1.77	1.86	1960	..	1.87

Source: BIB/INED

If we look at completed fertility of female generations in the two Germanies (table 7) we observe a parallel gradual decline for the generations born 1931 to 1940. Starting with the generation born in 1941 women in the Federal Republic of Germany have less births from generation to generation with a much faster speed of decline than in GDR. There the lowest completed fertility is achieved for women born in 1950 followed by a moderate increase (plus 0.09 children per woman).

The interesting fact is that only those women born after 1950 have been affected by the pronatalist policy in GDR, giving due consideration to average age at birth. Earlier differences in completed fertility of West and East German female cohorts (namely for the generations born between 1941 and 1950) very likely go to the account of earlier and more rapid family formation in GDR, or, in other word, cannot be attributed to direct pronatalist incentives which massively started in 1976.

b) Marriage and divorce

We have noted that age at first marriage in prewar Germany was relatively high, 28.8 years for bachelors and 26.2 years for spinsters in 1938 (see table 4). In the Federal Republic of Germany this was still true for men in 1950 while women married 0.8 years earlier (table 8).

In table 8 we also find that marriage intensity (total first marriage rate) of West German men was extremely high in 1950 due to the effects of World War II on the marriage market. The appropriate male cohorts were reduced by war losses, and also postponed marriages could then be contracted. The latter effect also concerns single women. In addition, the tendency to marry earlier began in the fifties.

TABLE 8.- INDICATORS OF NUPTIALITY IN THE TWO GERMANIES, 1950 - 1989

Year	Total first marriage rate				Age at first marriage				Total divorce rate	
	men		women		men		women			
	FRG	GDR	FRG	GDR	FRG	GDR	FRG	GDR	FRG	GDR
1950	135	-	112	-	28.1	26.1	25.4	24.0	-	-
1955	106	105	105	96	27.0	24.6	24.4	23.2	-	-
1960	106	103	106	105	25.9	23.9	23.7	22.5	-	-
1965	91	86	110	105	26.0	24.2	23.7	22.9	12.2	-
1970	90	101	97	98	25.6	24.0	23.0	21.9	25.9	26.0
1975	73	88	76	92	25.3	23.2	22.7	21.3	23.4	37.8
1980	64	79	66	81	26.1	23.4	23.4	21.3	22.7	38.6
1985	58	70	59	74	27.2	24.3	24.6	22.2	30.2	42.9
1986	60	73	61	78	27.5	24.6	24.9	22.5	29.2	47.0
1987	59	74	61	81	27.7	24.8	25.2	22.7	30.8	45.3
1988	-	71	-	78	28.0	25.0	25.5	22.9	30.6	-
1989	-	-	-	-	28.2	-	25.7	-	-	-

Source: Höhn; Mammey; Wendt, 1990 and BIB/INED

In postwar GDR, men and women married much earlier than the Germans in prewar Germany. We find the same nuptiality pattern elsewhere in Eastern Europe, and we suspect that it spread as a "socialist" marriage model to a part of Europe that used to have other traditions.

In the Federal Republic of Germany, total first marriage rates remained high (above unity) for both sexes until the early sixties due to a high propensity to marry and a falling age at first marriage. After 1962, the total first marriage rate started to decline though age at marriage still fell (until app. 1975). After 1975 both marriage propensity declined and age at first marriage increased combining to a further drop of the total first marriage rates.

In GDR, marriage at an ever lower age was the generally preferred (and socially approved) behaviour. Only after 1985 age at first marriage slowly increased thus reducing the total first marriage rates. This nearly universal marriage pattern is particularly remarkable under the aspect of a fairly high incidence of illegitimate births. One of the consequences is that in GDR after 1986 age at first birth was lower than age at first marriage of women. The sequence of events was more and more often reversed: first a child, then marriage. The reason for this behaviour was that unmarried mothers were granted preference for a day care place. But in order to get a flat GDR couples had to be married.

We may conjecture that living together arrangements of unmarried couples were rather exceptional in GDR. The governing rules of behaviour together with a distinct shortage of housing did not permit unmarried cohabitation. Unfortunately there are so far no household statistics available for GDR.

Another effect of early marriage in GDR is the much higher divorce level as compared to the Federal Republic of Germany. While there the total divorce rate levels off at 30 percent, in GDR the percentage reached 40 to 50 out of hundred marriages in the late eighties.

The marriage and divorce patterns in the two Germanies are clearly different. One cannot abstain from assuming that these divergent styles of behaviour have developped because of the different social, political and economic conditions.

In table 9 we summarize the effects of nuptiality on the living arrangements of adult men and women. Since there are no comparable statistics for the GDR table 9 relates to the Federal Republic of Germany only. When comparing the situation in 1972 to 1988 we find that marriage has declined and cohabitation increased up to the age of 55 years. However, the increase in cohabitation did not fully compensate for the decrease in formal marriage. This is particularly true for men and women in the age bracket of 26 to 35 years but also for the "middle-aged" men of 36 to 55 years, and for young women aged 18 to 25 years.

TABLE 9.- FEDERAL REPUBLIC OF GERMANY. LIVING ARRANGEMENTS BY AGE (IN PERCENT OF AGE GROUP), 1972 AND 1988

Age	Of 100 persons were							
	married		cohabiting		living in a union		living alone	
	1972	1988	1972	1988	1972	1988	1972	1988
Men								
18 - 25	18.0	6.4	0.7	5.2	18.7	11.7	81.3	88.3
26 - 35	74.1	49.5	0.5	6.3	74.6	55.8	25.4	44.2
36 - 55	89.3	78.6	0.4	2.6	89.7	81.2	10.3	18.8
56 +	82.1	81.6	1.1	1.3	83.2	82.9	16.8	17.1
Women								
18 - 25	44.5	16.6	0.9	8.9	45.4	25.5	54.6	74.5
26 - 35	85.9	64.6	0.4	5.3	86.3	69.9	13.7	30.1
36 - 55	81.4	79.4	0.5	2.1	81.9	81.4	18.0	18.5
56 +	43.4	45.7	0.6	0.9	44.0	46.5	56.0	53.5

Source: Federal Statistical Office (Microcensus; figures for unmarried cohabitation are estimates)

The biggest increase in cohabitation can be observed for women aged 18 to 25 years, and yet they also experienced the biggest increase in living alone.

The trend to live together in an informal union is most pronounced among the younger people. In 1972, older men had the highest cohabitation rate which only modestly increased. Older women over 56 years are very often living alone, with many of them being widowed (and some of them cohabiting).

While young men (under 25 years) are to over 80 percent living alone (with increasing tendency), men over 36 years are to over 80 percent living in a union. Women at no age are living alone to the same degree as young men (but younger women seem to catch up).

Finally we should note that illegitimacy is still quite low in the Federal Republic of Germany though cohabitation spreads among the younger population. These unions of singles rarely have a baby out of wedlock. In the Federal Republic of Germany the traditional rule to give birth only in a marriage is still strong. It seems to have prevailed also in GDR despite of the high illegitimacy ratio. These children very soon were legitimized by a formal marriage. The rule was relaxed but not broken.

c) *Mortality*

Infant mortality was high in the two postwar Germanies. In 1950 over 55,3 per 1000 newborn babies died before completing their first year of life in the Federal Republic of Germany respectively 72,2 in GDR. The decline of infant mortality to a level of 7,6 resp. 8,1 in 1988 is a big success. It should be noted that infant mortality for some years (namely from 1966 to 1980) was reported to be lower in GDR than in the Federal Republic of Germany (table 10).

TABLE 10.- INFANT MORTALITY AND LIFE EXPACTANCY IN THE TWO GERMANIES, 1950-1988

		1950	1960	1970	1988
Infant mortality (per 1000 live births)					
	FRG	55.3	33.8	23.4	7.6
	GDR	72.2	38.8	18.5	8.1
Life expectancy at age					
Males					
0	FRG	64.56	66.86	67.41	72.21[2]
	GDR	63.90[1]	66.49	68.10	70.03[3]
60	FRG	16.20	15.49	15.31	17.55[2]
	GDR	15.91[1]	15.55	15.21	16.16[3]
Females					
0	FRG	68.48	72.39	73.83	78.68[2]
	GDR	67.96[1]	71.35	73.31	76.23[3]
60	FRG	17.46	18.48	19.12	21.95[2]
	GDR	17.62[1]	18.20	18.29	19.79[3]

[1] 1952; [2] 1986/88; [3] 1988/89
Source: Federal Statistical Office

Life expectancy at birth strongly increased between 1950 and 1960 and increased only moderately in the sixties. From 1965 to 1975 male life expectancy was higher in GDR than in the Federal Republic of Germany. But after 1975 GDR male life expectancy stagnated while West German males could clearly improve their expectation of life. The female life expectancy was always higher in the West. At the end of the eighties FRG males had the prospect to live 2.2 years longer than their GDR peers while FRG females enjoyed a plus of 2.45 years. The gap between life expectancies has widened. This is also true for the 60 years old though the differential is slightly smaller (1.4 years for men and 2.16 years for women aged 60).

d) Migration

The most pronounced demographical differences between the two Germanies, no doubt, relate to migration. While the GDR ever since its foundation in 1949 was an emigration country (with most emigrants going to West Germany) the Federal Republic of Germany (with only a few exceptional years) was an immigration country.

Table 11 reveals that immediately after World War II the Western zones of the divided Germany were the region of heavy immigration of German refugees and expelled persons. We do not know the exact number of arrivals in 1945, but an estimate is some 4 million. Not all Germans (immigrants and residents) stayed in the Western Zone. Indeed it was another period of emigration to overseas countries (therefore, from 1951 to 1956, the negative balance in relation to GDR is bigger than the positive balance.

With the erection of the Berlin Wall the exodus from GDR was abruptly stopped (see also figure 2). Until then GDR had lost 3.5 million inhabitants to the Federal Republic of Germany. The wall and the complete closure of the iron curtain perhaps was the most effective demographic measure ever known to prevent emigration.

Already in the late fifties, but more after German immigrants became few, the Federal Republic recruited foreign labourers. So the migration balance remained positive until 1973 (with exception of the economic recession year 1967). Then a recruitment stop became effective. From 1974 to 1976 and from 1982 to 1984 therefore the migration balance of the Federal Republic of Germany was negative. After the recruitment stop family reunion was admitted and turned the migration balance positive in the late seventies.

The high positive migration balance in 1979 and 1980 is to a large degree fueled by the arrival of asylum seekers. Many of them entered via the Berlin wall with the approval of GDR authorities. After useful negociations this undesirable gap in the iron curtain could be closed and the influx of asylum seekers temporarily stopped.

GERMANY/L'ALLEMAGNE

The next chapter of German migration history is due to Gorbatschev's reform policy. Ethnic German (whose ancestors had settled in Eastern Europe) were allowed to emigrate to the Federal Republic of Germany. Since 1986 sizeable numbers of ethnic Germans arrived from USSR, Poland and Romania. 80 percent, however, do not speak enough German to be easily integrated. Finally, and unexpectedly, in summer 1989 Germans left GDR in masses via Hungary and Austria and the German embassies in Poland and Czechoslovakia.

TABLE 11.- MIGRATION BALANCE OF THE TWO GERMANIES, 1946 - 1989 (000S)

Year	FRG	GDR(1)	Year	FRG	GDR(1)
1946-1950(2)	+921,2	-262,8(3)	1972	+330,5	- 18,0
1951-1955(2)	+276,9	-319,2	1973	+384,0	- 15,6
1956	+348,2	-407,7	1974	- 9,3	- 14,6
1957	+400,8	-371,6	1975	-199,4	- 18,9
1958	+305,8	-226,7	1976	- 72,3	- 15,8
1959	+170,9	-150,6	1977	+ 32,7	- 12,7
1960	+335,8	-222,3	1978	+115,4	- 13,2
1961	+419,2	-216,7	1979	+246,0	- 14,0
1962	+283,3	- 12,7	1980	+311,9	- 14,2
1963	+223,5	- 42,4	1981	+152,4	- 16,5
1964	+301,5	- 34,4	1982	- 71,9	- 14,0
1965	+343,8	- 23,9	1983	-115,3	- 12,1
1966	+131,6	- 20,1	1984	-145,7	- 40,7
1967	-176,9	- 17,0	1985	+ 89,4	- 26,4
1968	+278,3	- 15,7	1986	+195,9	- 26,8
1969	+572,0	- 18,1	1987	+220,0	- 20,4
1970	+575,2	- 18,6	1988	+485,6	- 40,8
1971	+430,3	- 18,0	1989	+977,2	-343,9(4)

(1) Only migration between the two Germanies; (2) Annual average; (3) 1950; (4) Arrivals in FRG only
Source: Federal Statistical Office

In figure 2 we see the immigration of Germans from GDR until 1961 and the dramatic upsurge since 1986 which explodes in 1989. In 1989 the Federal Republic of Germany has a migration surplus of 977.200 immigrants of whom one third comes from GDR in a few months only, one third are ethnic Germans and one third foreigners (mainly asylum seekers).

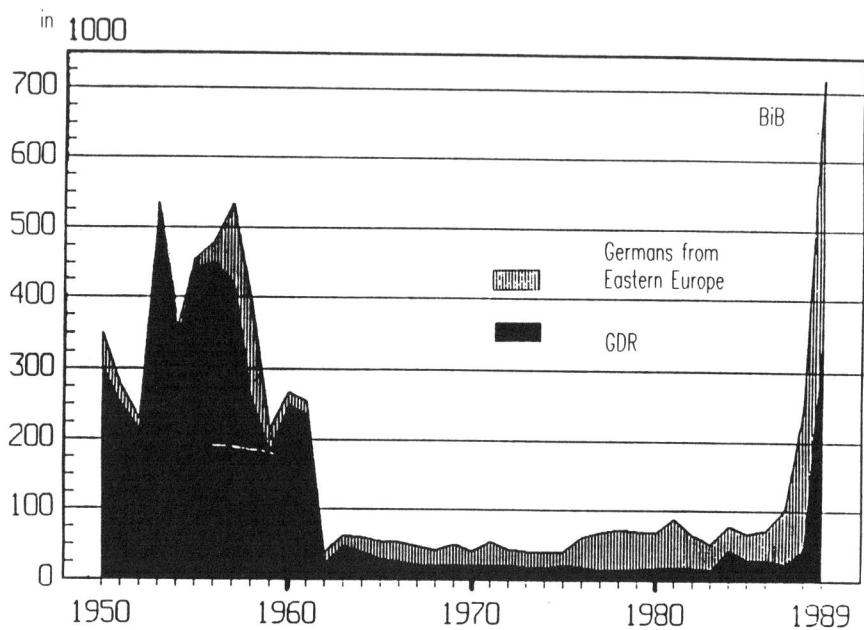

Figure 2.- Federal Republic of Germany. Immigration of Germans from GDR and from East European countries

Exodus of Germans from GDR continued in 1990 so that it was necessary to form an economic and social union of the two Germanies bringing the hard deutschmark to GDR already in July 1990. And on 3 October 1990 the new five states of the GDR acceded to the Federal Republic of Germany. With this, migration between the two Germanies became just internal migration again, dismanteled of drama.

GDR can be characterized as an emigration country. Emigration was massive in the postwar period until in August 1961 the wall was built to stop it. Nevertheless emigration with and without permission of GDR authorities never stopped. Between 1962 and 1988 12-40 thousand Germans annually on average left GDR. In 1989, in a peaceful revolution GDR population forced their obsolete government to open the wall and the borders and made the way free to unification.

e) Population trends and demographic ageing

On unification day 79.7 million inhabitants lived on the bigger territory of Germany.

Despite many different developments since the end of World War II the two Germanies have a common heritage from their population history. Since the secular fertility decline in Germany brought fertility to replacement level already in the twenties the demographic consequence of this fact should show some 50 years later. And indeed, in 1969 in GDR and in 1972 in the Federal Republic of Germany (there only the German population) an excess of deaths over births transformed natural increase into natural decrease. While in the Federal Republic of Germany this negative natural balance continued since 1972 (though melting together since 1986 due to an increase in births and decline in mortality) the GDR was able to redress the natural balance for a few years, namely from 1979 to 1988, as a result of short term increases in fertility under the influence of a massive population policy.

The age structure of the two Germanies before unification shows a remarkable similarity but the GDR age structure has less elderly persons. The reason is that since the seventies GDR pensioners were allowed to join their family members in the Federal Republic of Germany which (advantageous to GDR) payed the pensions. Part of the ageing problem hence migrated from East to West - but remained in Germany.

It is also easy to discern more children and youth at the bottom of the GDR age pyramid (the effect of the population policy). But given the fact that GDR population is only one fifth of the population of united Germany this juvenation has no major impact on the overall age structure.

In table 12 we give the population in the Federal Republic of Germany, in GDR and the sum from 1950 to 1985. 1990 is the first projection result from the UN population projection in its low variant. These projections ignore international migration. The effect of this neglect can easily be assessed when comparing the UN estimates for the mid-1990 populations with the actual figures for the unification day of 3 October 1990: the Federal Republic of Germany had gained 2.3 millions from international migration (in excess of the 2.5 millions the UN allows for the period 1985-90 !).

More important are the trends in demographic ageing. As we observe in table 12, the percent of persons older than 65 years increased steadily in the two Germanies from 1950 to 1980. Before World War II the percentage was 7.8 (see table 5), some 10 years later (1950) it amounted to 9.4 percent in the Federal Republic of Germany and to 10.6 percent in GDR.

We already explained why the percentage of seniors stagnated and even declined in GDR since the seventies. In addition to age-selective migration there was another special effect. Since the eighties the reduced male cohorts of war participants entered this age bracket. So, even in the Federal Republic of Germany, the percentage of persons aged 65 and more declined in the eighties. And for the combination of the two parts of Germany this ageing process will be retarded, because of this special historical reason, until 2000.

TABLE 12.- POPULATION TRENDS IN THE TWO GERMANIES, 1950-1990, AND UN-PROJECTION, 1995-2025

UN-population estimates							
	1950	1960	1970	1980	1985	1990	3/10/1990
Population (in million)							
FRG	50.0	55.4	60.7	61.6	61.0	61.3	63.6
GDR	18.4	17.2	17.1	16.7	16.6	16.2	16.1
Total	68.4	72.6	77.8	78.3	77.6	77.5	79.1
Percent 65 years and more							
FRG	9.4	10.8	13.2	15.5	14.8	15.4	
GDR	10.6	13.7	15.5	15.9	13.6	13.1	
Total	9.7	11.5	13.7	15.6	14.5	14.9	
UN-population projection (low variant)							
	1995	2000	2005	2010	2015	2020	2025
Population (in million) (FRG and GDR as before 03.10.1990)							
FRG	60.8	60.0	58.8	57.2	55.4	53.5	51.4
GDR	16.1	16.0	15.8	15.7	15.4	15.0	14.6
Germany	76.9	76.0	75.6	72.9	70.8	68.5	66.0
Percent 65 years and more (FRG and GDR as before 03.10.1990)							
FRG	14.7	15.5	15.9	16.1	18.2	20.3	22.2
GDR	13.5	14.5	16.7	17.9	17.7	19.6	21.7
Germany	14.4	15.3	16.1	16.5	18.1	20.1	22.1

Source: UN World Population Prospects 1990, New York 1991 (Mid-year population); 1990 also on 3 October 1990 as assessed by Federal Statistical Office

The low variant of the UN population projections has fairly appropriate fertility and mortality assumptions. Fertility will remain at 1.4 for the old Federal Republic of Germany and will fall from 1.6 to 1.5 in the former GDR (it might fall even more). Since there are no better projections available (relating to migration) and in order to show the effects of sustained low fertility and decreasing mortality the UN population projections are presented here.

Table 12, in its lower block, illustrates that, migration excluded, the population size of Germany and both its parts will decline and at the same time age. In 2025 the number of Germans would be slightly smaller than in 1950, but the number of seniors would more than double. We should also note that ageing accelerates (without and with unification) after the year 2000.

In 1990, 14.9 percent of the population of Germany were older than 65 years. But in 2025 very likely 22.1 percent will be seniors. We all know that international migration cannot reverse this process of ageing. Even under massive influx of half a million foreigners annually the ageing process only could be halted (Steinmann, 1991). The "price" would not only be a dramatic population growth but also an enormous increase in the percentage of foreigners. Steinmann's model calculations relate to the Federal Republic of Germany, where the population under these assumptions would grow from some 60 millions to 90 millions in 2033 and eventually 140 million inhabitants with an increase of the ratio of foreigners from 7 percent now to 46.19 percent in 2033 and 38.54 percent of the stationary 140 million (Steinmann, 1991). Even under such assumptions the percentage of seniors were 15 percent.

III. ASPECTS OF POPULATION-RELEVANT POLICIES

As I have argued elsewhere (Höhn 1990, 1991) population-relevant policies encompass three types of political action: (1) population policies proper; (2) indirect policies influencing demographic processes; and (3) adaptation policies.

Under population policies proper I here will discuss the family and population policies including contraception and abortion in the two Germanies. But I will embed these presentations by remarks on the influence of indirect policies. Finally I will report on the policies of adaptation in the Federal Republic of Germany.

a) Population-relevant policies in GDR

GDR in the early seventies started to worry about the very low fertility level and, in 1976, implemented a generous and comprehensive pronatalist policy. The core element was a family formation loan given to newly wed couples provided the wife was under 25 years of age. The loan was interest free and was to be paid back in small monthly amounts. It was released, however, by one third of the loan with the birth of a child provided that these (up to three) births would happen during the first eight years of marriage. With these two age limits, I believe, the concentration of marriage and births in the bracket between 20 and 30 years of the mother can be explained. One may conjecture, though I know of no official declaration, that low age at marriage and close spacing was intended to be maintained. In addition there were a birth grant of nearly one monthly income and monthly child allowances increasing with the rank of the child.

Contraception was free of charge and abortion in the first three months of pregnancy available upon request and costfree. When looking at abortion ratios by age of mother (in percent of known pregnancies) it is difficult to abstain from the impression that in GDR beyond the age of 30 years and under 18 years contraception was replaced by induced abortion. Particularly the abortion ratios for minors and women over 35 years are alarming (table 13).

TABLE 13.- ABORTION RATIOS IN THE TWO GERMANIES, 1989

Abortions per 100 pregnancies(1) by age of the pregnant woman							
	15-18	18-21	21-25	25-30	30-35	35-40	40-45
Federal Republic of Germany(2)							
Married	3,7	3,0	3,4	3,19	5,50	14,09	32,50
	(9,19)	(7,51)	(8,46)	(8,07)	(13,40)	(30,37)	(56,15)
Unmarried	43,2	33,9	35,5	34,22	31,16	36,69	48,85
	(66,92)	(57,68)	(59,43)	(58,02)	(54,63)	(60,65)	(71,75)
All	29,8	15,5	10,4	6,65	7,98	16,84	35,00
	(53,03)	(32,85)	(23,69)	(15,92)	(18,74)	(35,01)	(58,88)
GDR							
All	65,8	21,7	13,1	24,3	45,5	70,2	90,8

(1) Pregnancies are the sum of abortions and live births in GDR, and in the FR Germany they also include still births
(2) Ratios in brackets are estimates on the basis of 200 000 abortions instead of the statistically declared 75 297 abortions
Sources: Federal Statistical Office and Statistical Yearbook of GDR. Own calculations
*Schwangerschaften = Summe aus Schwangerschaftsabbrüche, Lebendgeborenen, Totgeborenen Quelle: StBA

In GDR, the pronatalist measures were supported by comprehensive child care provisions and facilities. After the birth of a child the mother could enjoy a paid maternity leave up to one year (since 1984 two years for the third child). Unmarried mothers could take a longer maternity leave if they did not find a place in a creche. They, however, had priority for a creche place. (This preferential treatment of unmarried mothers made the illegitimacy ratio skyrocket. It was not the new life style to have an emancipatory child out of wedlock).

In fairly good regional distribution the GDR established a plethora of child minding facilities. In the late eighties two thirds of the children 1-2 years old were in creches, 90 % went to kindergarden. During compulsory school enrolment children stayed in school the whole day with free meals. During holiday vacations there were numerous opportunities of a quasi cost-free stay for pupils and students.

Mothers also enjoyed a reduced working time, a free day per month for housework, longer holidays. They could take paid leave for caring ill children.

When looking on figure 1 we easily can discern an immediate rise in TFR from 1.5 in 1975 to 1.94 in 1980. While not denying this short-term effect, one has to admit that TFR never reached replacement level again and TFR has kept falling during the eighties down to 1.6 in 1989. A look at completed TFR, hence at a long-term effect, reveals that not more than 0.09 child was yielded (see table 7).

Why was not this generous pronatalist policy more successful? Some important indirect policies counterbalanced the population policy of East Germany. The low incomes required that both parents would have to be economically active. This put a double burden on mothers preventing to a degree a "large" family with three or more children. The time budget of mothers tightened by daily queuing too. On the other hand the low incentives in consumption and leisure possibilities and the financially low costs of children worked in favour of having at least two children and definitely against voluntary childlessness. The age limits of financial support in the most fertile period of women cemented low age at birth and marriage.

One also has to mention the chronic housing shortage and the small size and poor quality of flats to understand the negative impact of this underdeveloped indirect housing policy on fertility.

I do not believe that in GDR policies for the emancipation of women played a decisive role in respect of family formation. Certainly, a number of the measures mentioned were "sold" to reconciliate the female "needs" to have a job and a family. But women in GDR rarely made a professional career or obtained a top post in management, government or administration. Though very well educated and to 90 percent economically active women did not advance and also could not achieve what the West calls self-realization. The time budget of women was so much under stress that they could not "lobby" in the party which was decisive for a career in GDR.

In the context of the direct and indirect population-relevant policies spelled out for GDR one can also try to understand the high level of divorce. Certainly the retreat into private life of young couples was vulnerable. In the event of divorce spouses had to pay little or no maintenance or alimony because both spouses had an own income, and having children seemed to be costfree.

While the rearing of children seemed to be costfree from the individual point of view it, of course, was very expensive at the societal or rather state level. No adaptation policies to ageing could be financed. The pensions in the former GDR were low and the living conditions of the elderly very poor indeed. The only strategy was to "export" pensioners to the Federal Republic of Germany where they recevied a pension as if they had worked there all their life. This was good for the pensioners who very often joined family members that had fled earlier. On the societal level, however, young families, or rather demographic trends, were supported at the expense of the elderly.

b) Population-relevant policies in the Federal Republic of Germany

The official attitude of all the governments of the Federal Republic of Germany is that they do not persue a pronatalist policy. It is the right of couples to decide freely on the number and spacing of their children.

The Federal Republic of Germany, however, developed a family policy with a fairly low child allowance for the first child and moderately high child allowances for the second and further children. A rebate in income taxation has been considerably increased in 1986 while a monoparental tax rebate exists since the late seventies. There are additional tax rebates for students older than 18 or in vocational training. Though these financial alleviations have been increased they are far from covering the cost of rearing a child. But this never was the objective of family policy.

In 1986, a paid maternity leave was introduced. The allowance is means-tested after the child is 6 months old. The maternity leave was gradually extended from one year to 18 months. The mother (or father) may work part-time (up to 19 hours per week) while on leave. There are discussions to extend the leave further up to three years.

Since 1986 one year of rearing a child is considered like an economically active year for the calculation of the pension. For children born in 1992 and later three such years will be given credit for in the pension.

Very underdeveloped are the child-minding facilities in the Federal Republic of Germany as compared to GDR. There are virtually no creches (a few in West-Berlin and Hamburg) implying that working mothers after maternity leave will have to find private arrangements or interrupt their economically active life at least until the child is three years old. Kindergardens are in fairly good supply with certain regional shortages. But kindergardens rarely offer full day care. School also is only in the morning. The strategy for mothers therefore is to find a part-time job with a strong preference for the morning, something business and administration find increasingly difficult to accomodate.

With these new measures of family policy TFR in West Germany went up from 1.28 in 1985 to 1.43 in 1989. This might be a, however, very modest effect of the new measures on fertility.

Why is fertility so low in West Germany? Apart of the tradition of low fertility and socially accepted high childlessness I would like to draw attention to some of the indirect population-relevant policies namely to policies for economic growth and for the emancipation of women. The individual-centered employment strategy with a stress on performance and availability ignores the needs of parents and children. Some of the big corporations now offer an unpaid leave up to seven years, the state administration up to 12 years. More and more big firms and agencies entertain a kindergarden.

But in principle the problem remains that the economic world is blind to families. The independent childfree individual or couple can best compete for jobs, is regionally mobile and can afford the best appartments and housing. "Childfree" people can also better enjoy travel and leisure, sports and recreation because they have the money and the time. Families are relatively deprived as compared to the childless. It is hardly surprising that family formation is delayed and the number of children, if any, limited.

I am the last who would call for an old-fashioned policy for women back to children, kitchen and church. But it has to be stated that emancipation policies encourage women to achieve a good education and to find self-realization in a well-paid job and in career. In former times women wanted to have a family and (perhaps) a job too. Today many (not all) women have a job first and then contemplate whether and when to have a family too. Modern contraception, a main pillar of female emancipation I believe, allows for a prolonged decision making process.

Modern contraceptives have to be paid in the Federal Republic of Germany while the cost of a legal abortion is covered by general health insurance. Since 1977, an abortion can be obtained after compulsory counselling and on medical, eugenic, criminal and social ("other severe hardship") indication. As can be derived from table 13 unmarried pregnant women much more often than married women end their pregnancy by an induced abortion.

Different from the former GDR, the Federal Republic of Germany is a pioneer country in what concerns policies of adaptation to ageing. Early in the seventies, when the trend to population decline and inevitable demographic ageing was assessed by demographers, an interministerial working group on population matters was established. It produced a population report in two parts which were submitted to parliament. The first part deals with the demographic trends and projections and their determinants

(Bundestagsdrucksache 8/4437 published in 1980). The second part focusses on the consequences (mainly of population ageing) on the different fields of state and society (Bundestagsdrucksache 10/863 published in 1984).

In reaction to these reports administration and legislation prepared two major reforms. The 1992 reform of the pension system maintains the existing pay-as-you-go system with two major modifications. The first one is an adaptation of the pension level to the development of net incomes (instead of to the gross income) with the effect of slower increase of pensions. Pensions are also taxed now though with a sizeable old age rebate. Demographically more obvious is the gradual extension of age at retirement to 65 years abolishing many variants of early retirement. With this the nightmare model calculation presented in the population report that under status-quo conditions in 2030 either the pensions would have to be halfed or the contribution rates (at present 18 precent) doubled can be mitigated. Up to 2010 the contribution rates will increase to 22 percent only and pensions will continue to increase.

In the compulsory health insurance system pensioners have been gradually included and their contribution rate will reach the same percentage as that of the economically active population. Also a number of cost-intensive treatments and medication have to be partially covered by the patient.

As to economic policies the governments of the Federal Republic of Germany, advised by economists, hold the opinion that the social market economy is sufficiently flexible to adapt to changing age-specific patterns of consumption and to the ageing labour force without interventions. The German private economic sector already today is becoming more and more capital intensive, and it invests into their ageing human capital by training and qualification courses. Up to now there is no labour shortage but rather structural unemployment.

Finally, the Federal Republic of Germany has developped a policy of integration for foreigners which relates to access to education for the second and third generation and to housing. In the sixties and early seventies immigration policies were economically motivated. Since then it related to family reunion and recently to asylum-seekers. Though only a small percentage is granted the status of asylant the refused are tolerated to nearly 90 percent.

IV. OUTLOOK ON POPULATION-RELEVANT POLICIES OF GERMANY

As to the direct pronatalist policies of the former GDR it has to be said that the financial part has already been suspended in the five new states of Germany and replaced by the pertinent legislation of the Federal Republic of Germany. The child-minding facilities in the Eastern part will be maintained up to the end of 1991. The prize is of course very high. There is, however, the request from two advisory boards, on family matters and on female emancipation, to the government to redress the quality of creches and to establish creches in sufficient number in the Western part of Germany too. Very likely the high coverage rate of children under 3 years by creche places cannot be achieved. An alternative discussed in the Christian Democratic Party is to extend paid maternity leave until the child is 3 years old and eligible for kindergarden. The problem to reconciliate job and family aspirations of mothers and fathers has been recognized and requires an adequate solution.

The government still considers Germany not to be an immigration country and consequently has not developed a demographically motivated immigration policy. Indeed, the time of labour shortage has not yet come. Due to the hidden unemployement in the former GDR masses of people do seek a job, and this unpleasant situation might continue for some years. Model calculations for West Germany show that a shortage of labour will not occur before 2010 or so. An obvious need to recruit foreign labour does not yet materialize.

There is, however, the policy to integrate foreigners into the German society. This policy has to be extended to the new part of Germany where, so far, only few foreigners reside. With the influx of ethnic Germans from Poland, USSR and Romania a modified integration policy needs to be developed. Roughly 80 percent of these ethnic Germans do not speak sufficient German to find a job. They will have to be offered language courses first. It has to be seen how they will spread over the larger territory of Germany. The arrival of some 2 million ethnic Germans more is expected for the next years.

The most important population issue will remain increasing demographic ageing. Immigration of the dimension experienced so far (an annual average of plus 110.000 immigrants since 1953 in West Germany) does not stop ageing as model calculations show. The reason is that foreigners age too and that they, so far, adapt their fertility to the host country. Only under the heroic assumptions that foreigners of the first generation maintain fertility well above replacement and that there would be half a million of new arrivals annually the ageing process could be halted (Steinmann, 1991). Though such a nightmare scenario cannot be completely rejected it is neither very probable and certainly not a political strategy to overcome ageing.

Ageing remains the top issue. Therefore the reform of the pensions system implying increasing the age at retirement will have to be extended to the Eastern part of Germany. During the next years the elderly in the former GDR will also rightly demand an adaptation of their pensions and an improvement of their living conditions.

In the context of ageing demographers should inform their government that the elderly of tomorrow will be much different from the elderly today. They will be better educated, they will be more self-reliant, they will have better pension coverage. More and more women do not interrupt their professional career and need not rely on derived widow pensions. We only have to look at the middle-aged generations now to conjecture how the future elderly will be. Pertinent socio-economic projections are required.

However, the percentage of the old-old grows fastest. This raises the question of who is going to care for the old and frail. In addition to expanding institutional care the familial support has to be strengthened. Models of a long-term care insurance are discussed already now in Germany. I believe that we must financially recognize care provided by family members or friends in order not to weaken the family system as did the welfare state since 100 years.

References

Bundestagsdrucksache 10/863, Bericht über die Bevölkerungsentwicklung in der Bundesrepublik Deutschland, 2. Teil: Auswirkungen auf die verschiedenen Bereiche von Staat und Gesellschaft; Der Bundesminister des Innern (Hrsg.); Bonn, 1984

Bundestagsdrucksache 8/4437: Bericht über die Bevölkerungsentwicklung in der Bundesrepublik Deutschland, 1. Teil: Analyse der bisherigen Bevölkerungsentwicklung und Modellrechnungen zur künftigen Bevölkerungsentwicklung; Der Bundesminister des Innern (Hrsg.); Bonn, 1980

David, Henry P.; Fleischhacker, Jochen; Höhn, Charlotte: Abortion and eugenics in Nazi Germany; Population and Development Review, 14, 1, 1988. - pp. 81-112

Federal Statistical Office (Statistisches Bundesamt): Bevölkerung und Wirtschaft 1872-1972; Stuttgart und Mainz: Kohlhammer, 1972

Federal Statistical Office (Statistisches Bundesamt): Bevölkerung gestern, heute und morgen; Mainz: Kohlhammer, 1985

Federal Statistical Office (Statistisches Bundesamt): DDR 1990. Zahlen und Fakten; Stuttgart: Metzler-Poeschel, 1990

Federal Statistical Office (Statistisches Bundesamt): Fachserie 1, Reihe 1, Gebiet und Bevölkerung, Stuttgart: Metzler-Poeschel (diverse years)

Federal Statistical Office (Statistisches Bundesamt): Statistisches Jahrbuch, Stuttgart: Metzler-Poeschel (diverse years)

GERMANY/L'ALLEMAGNE

Höhn, Charlotte; Mammey, Ulrich; Wendt, Hartmut: Bericht 1990 zur demographischen Lage: Trends in beiden Teilen Deutschlands und Ausländer in der Bundesrepublik Deutschland; Zeitschrift für Bevölkerungswissenschaft, 16, 1990, 2. - pp. 135-205

Höhn, Charlotte: Population policies in advanced societies: pronatalist and migration strategies; European Journal of Population, 3, 1987. - pp. 211-220

Höhn, Charlotte: Country report Federal Republic of Germany, in: Dumon, Wilfried (ed.), Family Policy in EEC countries; Brussels/Luxembourg: Commission of the European Communities, 1990. - pp.79-102

Höhn, Charlotte: Policies relevant to fertility, in: Lutz, Wolfgang (ed.), Future Demographic Trends in Europe and North America. What Can We Assume Today?; London: Academic Press, 1991. - pp. 247-255

Laslett, Peter & Wall, Richard (eds.), Household and Family in Past Time, Cambridge University Press, 1972

Steinmann, Gunter: Immigration as a remedy for the birth dearth: The case of West Germany, in: Lutz, Wolfgang (ed.), Future Demographic Trends in Europe and North America. What Can We Assume Today?; London: Academic Press, 1991. - pp. 337-357

Van de Kaa, Dirk: Europe's Second Demographic Transition; Population Bulletin, 42, 1987, 1 (Population Reference Bureau, Washington)

Wall, Richard; Robin, Jean; Laslett, Peter (Hrsg.): Family Forms in Historic Europe; Cambridge: Cambridge University Press, 1983

Denmark/Le Danemark
Otto ANDERSEN

I. ASPECTS OF THE HISTORICAL DEMOGRAPHIC EVOLUTION IN DENMARK

1) Introduction

The evolution of the Danish population during the last 300 years has been the result of the very marked changes which have occured in the main demographic components, i.e. births, deaths and migration, during this period. Since the late 1700s Denmark has developed through, the main phases of the so-called demographic transition, and according to this, it has developed from a country with a high rate of mortality and fertility into a country where both of these components are at a much lower level. The transition itself was introduced by a fall in the rate of mortality. Only later, and after a comprehensive restructuring of the country - both economically and socially - did the rate of fertility start its decline.

Due to reports on the total number of births and deaths as far back as 1735 and to the early Danish population censuses held in 1769, 1787 and 1801, it has been possible to estimate the size of the Danish population to be approximately 718,000 persons in the year 1735.

Measured at each million the Danish population has developed as follows:

1811	1 million persons
1881	2 -
1918	3 -
1944	4 -
1972	5 -

As of January 1st, 1991 the Danish population numbered 5,146,469 persons of which 2,536,391 were males and 2,610,078 were females.

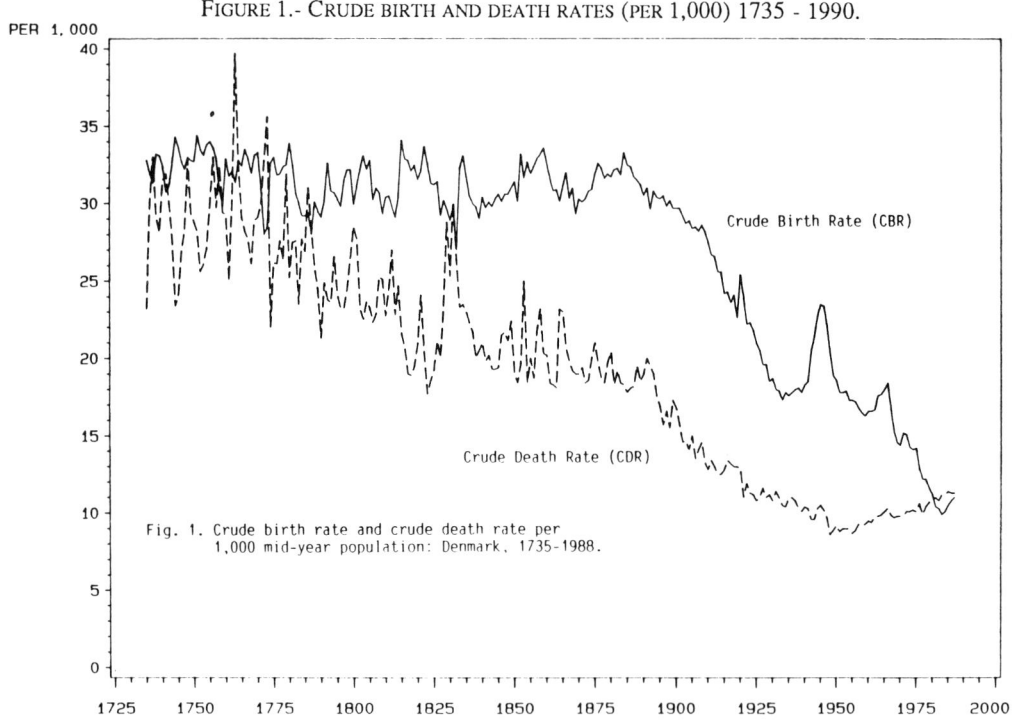

FIGURE 1.- CRUDE BIRTH AND DEATH RATES (PER 1,000) 1735 - 1990.

Fig. 1. Crude birth rate and crude death rate per 1,000 mid-year population: Denmark, 1735-1988.

In the following we will give an overview of the historical development behind these figures. We shall divide the periods according to the phases of the demographic transition, i.e.

1. A first, pre-transitional, phase were both mortality and fertility were at a relatively high level. In Denmark this period lasted until approx. 1785.

2. A second phase, were mortality declined while fertility remained high, a period approx. between 1785 - 1890.

3. A third phase, with a decline in mortality as well as in fertility, a period from 1890 until very recently.

4. A fourth phase, with a very low rate of mortality and fertility, characterizing the present period.

2) The Period from 1735 - 1785

Economically, Denmark was a very primitive country in the middle of the 18th century with a subsistance economy and a very low standard of living.

By far the largest occupational group were persons employed in agriculture counting for more than 60% of the total population. The level of production in agriculture was seldom larger than needed to cover the agricultural workers needs. At the same time, production in the cities was extremely modest. These conditions combined with poor understanding of hygiene and low medical knowledge can explain the high level of mortality in this period. Pronounced yearly variations in mortality, due to the influx of disease and starvation, were extremely typical at this time. These conditions seem often to be caused by wars and by war preparations in Europe.

The fact that years with high mortality rates were often followed by years with low mortality rates have been expressed as "death reaped also for the morrow". The feeble and the most exposed died under these epidemics. The strong and the less exposed survived.

Fertility had to be high in a community with a high rate of mortality, to insure the population against extinction. The crude birth rate was high and relatively constant in the 1700s, even though the level was not as high as that which is to be found in the developing countries of the world today. One of the reasons for this difference is that the age of marriage was markedly higher in Denmark in the 18th century, than it is in today's developing countries, partly because of the many restrictions which the community itself lay upon the act of marriage. It was common for a person to wait with his marriage until he had ensured himself a means of supporting his wife and children, either through an occupation in agriculture, or as a self-employed tradesman. Furthermore a smaller part of the women married in Denmark then, than is now the case in the developing countries.

3) The Period 1785 - 1890

Until the end of the 18th century the CDR was characterized by the large, yearly variations, typical of agricultural societies.

However, a marked decline in mortality occurred around 1800, increasing the difference between the CBR and the CDR significantly. At the same time, the yearly variations in the CDR became less pronounced as the epidemics was weakened during this period.

This relatively early decline in the rate of mortality cannot be explained by the general progress of medical science, as advancements in this field first occured much later in the 19th century. In the late 1700s, however, a series of agricultural reforms were inaugurated in Denmark, making it possible, among other things, for 2/3 of the agricultural workers to become owners of their own farm-steads. Agricultural production was re-organized, and production increased substantially. The reforms provided for a dispersing of the villages in the rural areas, and the distances between farms and houses were increased. This in itself probably did much to limit the spread of epidemics. An important medical advancement was taken in 1810, when smallpox vaccinations were made obligatory and free of charge in Denmark; but improved nutrition and a better understanding of the general principles of hygiene have also played an important role in the reduction of the rate of mortality.

The decline of mortality in Denmark is only once, in any serious way, disturbed, and this by an epidemic of malaria, which culminated in 1831. There is no doubt that malaria, or as it also was then called "cold fever", was a torment for the Danish population in the 19th century.

From 1840 it is possible to follow the development in mortality by more refined demographic measures (table 1). The infant mortality rate around 1840 was about 130 - 150 per thousand and the life expectancy at birth was about 44 years. From 1840 until 1900 only little progress is seen in the infant mortality rate but due to a decrease in mortality in other age groups life expectancy increases for both males and females by about 6 years. An important demographic event in this period must be mentioned, i.e. the importance of the international migration. From 1869 - 1913 more than 280,000 Danes migrated from Denmark, especially to North America.

TABLE 1: INFANT MORTALITY RATE PER 1,000 LIVE-BORN CHILDREN AND LIFE EXPECTANCY AT BIRTH (IN YEARS); DENMARK, 1840-1950.

Period	Males		Females	
	Infant mortality rate	Life expectancy at birth	Infant mortality rate	Life expectancy at birth
1840-49	155	42.9	132	45.0
1850-59	148	43.1	124	45.4
1860-69	145	43.7	124	45.6
1870-79	148	45.5	128	47.2
1880-89	149	46.8	125	48.9
1890-00	149	48.6	122	51.4
1901-10	126	53.9	101	57.1
1911-20	107	56.0	85	58.7
1921-30	93	60.6	72	62.3
1931-40	77	62.8	59	64.8
1941-50	50	66.7	39	68.9

Source: Det Statistiske Department, Befolkningsudvikling og Sundhedsforhold (Population Development and Health Conditions), Copenhagen 1966

The population growth rate was in the period 1850 - 1890 between 1 and 1.5% per years due to the increased difference between CBR and CDR.

4) *The period 1890 - 1950*

The decline in fertility had its start around 1890 and coincided with the development of the Danish industrial revolution (fig. 1). The changes which have occurred while the Danish community has gone from an agricultural to an industrial way of life, have clearly had an influence on the size of the Danish family. It is worth to mention that the decline of fertility had its start in a period, where contraceptives were as yet very incomplete. In spite of this, the pressures on the family were so expressed, that the family size had to be reduced.

The total fertility rate (table 2) has decreased from 4,608 in the period 1880-84 to 2,757 in the period 1946-50.

From fig. 1 is clearly seen the low fertility rate in the 1930s and the baby boom in the years after the Second World war.

TABLE 2.- TOTAL FERTILITY RATE (TFR) PER 1,000 FEMALES : DENMARK, 1860 - 1950

Year	TFR	Year	TFR	Year	TFR
1860-64	4,453	1890-94	4,364	1921-25	2,854
1865-69	4,438	1895-99	4,229	1926-30	2,409
1870-74	4,464	1901-05	4,001	1931-35	2,151
1875-79	4,563	1906-10	3,792	1936-40	2,170
1880-84	4,608	1911-15	3,450	1941-45	2,640
1885-89	4,521	1916-20	3,150	1946-50	2,757

Sources : 1860-1899, Hohn Umpagliazzo, Deterministic Aspects of Mathematical Demography, Springer Verlag. 1984.
1901-1950, Det Statistiske Department, Population Development and Health Conditions, Copenhagen 1966.

The life expectancy has increased with 11-12 years between 1900 and 1950 and the infant mortality rate has decreased significantly to a level of 40-50 per thousand in the period 1941-50. Except for the years during the First World War, Denmark had an almost constant negative rate of migration until around 1930. After this time there has been a fluctuation between net emigration and net-immigration.

Denmark was not directly involved in the two World Wars and its age structure, therefore, shows no sign of the wars as in many other European countries.

II.- ASPECTS OF THE DEMOGRAPHIC DEVELOPMENT AFTER THE SECOND WORLD WAR

The main feature of the development after the Second World War is the drastic decline in fertility since 1966. This development has altered the demographic situation in Denmark in a very important way.

1) *Fertility*

In 1946 Denmark experienced 96,111 live births, the largest number ever born in a specific year. The total fertility rate (TFR) corresponding to this figure was 3,016 per 1,000 women. After twenty years with fluctuations in the TFR between 2,500 and 2,600 the rate began to fall down to a level as low as 1,377 in 1983, (table 3).

LE DANEMARK/THE DENMARK

TABLE 3.- TOTAL FERTILITY RATE (TFR) PER 1,000 FEMALES : DENMARK, 1951 - 1988

Year	TFR	Year	TFR	Year	TFR
1951	2,502	1964	2,602	1977	1,660
1952	2,535	1965	2,610	1978	1,668
1953	2,595	1966	2,615	1979	1,602
1954	2,542	1967	2,350	1980	1,546
1955	2,576	1968	2,117	1981	1,437
1956	2,590	1969	2,000	1982	1,427
1977	2,556	1970	1,950	1983	1,377
1958	2,535	1971	2,043	1984	1,400
1959	2,494	1972	2,029	1985	1,447
1960	2,543	1973	1,917	1986	1,480
1961	2,547	1974	1,897	1987	1,496
1962	2,544	1975	1,919	1988	1,560
1963	2,642	1976	1,747		

Sources : Denmark Statistik, Vital Statistics, 1988

In the latest years from 1984, fertility has increased. In 1988 the TFR was 1,560 an increase of 13 per cent since 1983 (table 3).

From table 4 the age specific fertility rates show clearly the drastic decrease in fertility between 1966 and 1983 in all age groups but relatively most important in the youngest and oldest age groups. It is also clear that the increase in fertility since 1983 has happened among women above age 25 as a sign of an attempt to make up for the lost births.

For the youngest generations of women (table 5) the number of live births accumulated at the end of an age group is much lower than for the oldest generations. In the generations of women born in 1945 - who were 21 years old when fertility began to fall - 35% had already at least one child at this age. This proportion has fallen to 17% for the women born in 1960 (21 years old in 1981) and further to 9% for the 1967 birth cohort (21 years old in 1988).

The main characteristics of the decrease in fertility by birth order (table 6) is seen to be a) a larger number of women in the younger generations have remained childless compared to the older generations, and b) fewer women give birth to 3 or more children. Yet another point could be mentioned. The average age of mothers has increased. The average age at the first birth was 22.5 years in the mid 1960s and 26 years in the late 1980s. A number of factors must be held responsible for the decrease in fertility. Most important is probably that the role of women has changed in the Danish society. This new role has meant a higher level of education and a marked increase in the participation in the labour market. In the mid 1960s fewer than 50 per cent of the married women between age 20 and 50 were reported in the labour force, while the number is 90 per cent to day.

TABLE 4.- AGE SPECIFIC FERTILITY RATES PER 1,000 FEMALES : DENMARK, 1966, 1983 AND 1988

Age group (years)	1966	1983	1988	Index 1966 = 100	
				1983	1988
15-19	49.6	10.6	9.1	21	18
20-24	179.2	80.0	71.3	45	40
25-29	161.3	111.6	128.1	69	79
30-34	87.6	55.7	76.7	64	88
35-39	36.5	15.1	23.4	41	64
40-44	8.2	2.2	3.2	27	39
45-49	0.6	0.2	0.2	33	33
TFR	2,615	1,377	1,560	53	60

Sources : Denmark Statistik, Vital Statistics, 1988

TABLE 5.- LIVE BIRTHS PER 1,000 FEMALES, BORN 1935/36 - 1963/64 (CUMULATIVE FIGURES) : DENMARK

Generation	Age (years)						
	15-19	15-24	15-29	15-34	15-39	15-44	15-49
1935-36	210	1,064	1,858	2,227	2,338	2,353	2,353
1940-41	226	1,094	1,795	2,116	2,201	2,212	
1945-46	230	990	1,686	1,965	2,042		
1950-51	187	879	1,480	1,761			
1955-56	132	692	1,262				
1960-61	90	508					
1961-62	84	490					
1962-63	70	454					
1963-64	59	441					

Sources : Denmark Statistik, Vital Statistics, 1988

TABLE 6.- NUMBER OF FEMALES (PER 1,000) AT AGE 35 BY NUMBER OF CHILDREN EVER BORN ALIVE
DENMARK

Year of birth	Number of live births				Average number of children per women
	0	1	2	3 +	
1945	98	166	469	267	1,90
1946	93	178	477	252	1,89
1947	105	176	487	232	1,85
1948	110	185	480	225	1,82
1949	112	198	482	208	1,79
1950	126	200	482	192	1,74
1951	129	206	477	188	1,72
1952	144	208	465	182	1,69
1953	148	213	461	178	1,67

Sources : Denmark Statistik, Vital Statistics, 1988

It is most common that both parents are in the labour force, which means that it has been necessary for the families to reduce the number of children and to alter the fertility pattern. The limitation and the postponement of the births has been much easier with the introduction of the pill as well as the IUD, which were made free during the 1960s. Furthermore abortion was given free in 1973 and a law on sterilization was introduced. All men and women above 25 have the right to be sterilized.

2) *Abortions*

An important aspect of the fecundity in the Danish society is the level of abortions. The sudden increase in the number of abortions in the beginning of the 1970s (table 7) is due to the legalization of abortions within 12 weeks pregnancy. The legalization meant that the former large number of illegal abortions now became legal, with great improvement in health conditions. After a peak of 27,884 abortions in 1975 the amount has stabilized at approx. 21,000. This figure corresponds to one third of the live births.

TABLE 7.- LEGAL ABORTIONS AND GENERAL ABORTION RATE [1]: DENMARK, 1960 - 1988

Year	Legal abortions	Rate	Year	Legal abortions	Rate
1960	3,918	3.6	1975	27,884	23.7
1961	4,124	3.8	1976	26,842	22.7
1962	3,996	3.6	1977	25,662	21.6
1963	3,971	3.6	1978	23,699	19.7
1964	4,527	4.0	1979	23,193	19.1
1965	5,188	4.6	1980	23,334	19.0
1966	5,726	5.1	1981	22,779	18.4
1967	6,324	5.6	1982	21,462	17.2
1968	5,986	5.2	1983	20,791	16.5
1969	7,295	6.4	1984	20,742	16.4
1970	9,375	8.1	1985	19,919	15.6
1971	11,157	9.7	1986	20,067	15.6
1972	12,985	11.2	1987	20,830	16.1
1973	16,536	14.2	1988	21,199	16.3
1974	24,868	21,2			

(1) : Number of legal abortions per 1,000 females aged 15-49 years (per year)

Sources : Denmark Statistik, Vital Statistics, 1988

3) Nuptiality, cohabitation and divorce

In the 1950s and the first half of the 1960s the relative number of men and women who were married with a legal marriage certificate was almost the same in each generation. From 1965 until 1982, however, the number of yearly marriages went down from about 42,000 to 24,000.

As has happened for fertility, marriage has been postponed. From 1961/65 until 1988 the average age among the first time married men increased from 25.3 years to 29.6 years and for women from 22.5 years to 27.1 years.

The increase in the number of marriages contracted since 1982 is due to an attempt to catch up with the lost marriages, as it is almost only the men and women in the age groups 25 to 35 years old, who have contributed to the increase.

The number of divorces (table 8) has increased significantly from below 7,000 in the mid 1960s to 14-15,000. It is especially the marriages contracted since 1965, which have been dissolved.

TABLE 8.- NUMBER OF MARRIAGES CONTRACTED AND DISSOLVED : DENMARK 1960 - 1988

Year	Marriages contracted	Marriages dissolved by		Marriages at 1st January
		death of spouse	divorce	
1960	35,897	19,768	6,682	1,092,128
1965	41,693	22,025	6,527	1,145,227
1970	36,376	22,454	9,524	1,200,719
1975	31,782	23,028	13,264	1,196,795
1980	26,448	25,122	13,593	1,165,366
1985	29,332	24,804	14,385	1,103,782
1988	32,080	24,209	14,717	1,084,167

Sources : Denmark Statistik, Vital Statistics, 1988

The impact on the number of existing marriages of this development has been a decrease by about 125,500 from 1972 to 1988. The marital distribution has altered completely as a much lower proportion of the population below age 30 lives in a legal marriage. As an example two thirds of all women between age 20 and 30 were married in the mid 1960s, compared to one third of to day.

This changed marital distribution must be seen in connection with the number of men and women who cohabit, i.e. living together without a marriage certificate. The number of cohabitants relative to the number of married and cohabitants (table 9) is very high (75-85 per cent) among the youngest. More than one third of all couples who cohabit have at least one child. Is is common practice, that many who cohabit, later marry, especially after the birth of a child. The development in the nuptiality pattern has resulted in a situation where 45 per cent of all children are born out of a legal marriage. In the period 1961/65 the number was only 8.9 per cent. However, more than 90 per cent of all children are born in a family, where both parents live together. It is worth to mention, that the proportion of men and women living as pairs, with or without a marriage certificate is almost the same to day as the proportion of men and women who lived in a legal marriage in the mid 1960s.

4) *Mortality*

The infant mortality rate (table 10), has decreased significantly since 1950, and is to day below 10 per 1,000 live born children. This development is mainly a result of a reduced mortality from infectious diseases.

TABLE 9.- NUMBER (PER CENT) OF COHABITANT MALES AND FEMALES AMONG ALL MARRIED AND COHABITANT : DENMARK, 1976 - 1988

	Males			Females		
	20-24 years	25-29 years	30-34 years	20-24 years	25-29 years	30-34 years
	per cent					
1976-77	69	30	10	49	19	10
1978-79	73	38	15	56	26	12
1980-81	73	48	22	64	32	13
1982-83	79	54	24	68	38	18
1984-85	83	56	31	72	40	19
1986-88	85	61	34	77	44	21

Sources : Denmark Statistik, Vital Statistics, 1988

TABLE 10.- INFANT MORTALITY RATE PER 1,000 LIVE-BORN CHILDREN AND LIFE EXPECTANCY AT BIRTH (IN YEARS) : DENMARK, 1951 - 1988

	Males		Females	
Period	Infant mortality rate	Life expectancy at birth	Infant mortality rate	Life expectancy at birth
1951-1955	31.7	69.8	23.6	72.6
1956-1960	26.9	70.4	20.0	73.8
1961-1965	22.5	70.3	16.5	74.5
1966-1970	18.2	70.6	12.6	75.4
1971-1975	13.4	70.9	9.8	76.5
1976-1980	10.4	71.2	7.5	77.2
1981-1985	9.0	71.5	6.7	77.5
1985-1988	9.0	71.7	7.0	77.6

Sources : Denmark Statistik, Vital Statistics, 1988

As seen from table 10 and 11, the mortality has developed quite different for men and women. The life expectancy at birth for men has only increased by 1.9 years since 1950, while women have experienced an increase by 5 years.

The male population has especially had a stagnation and even an increase in mortality among the middle-aged, which is seen from the life expectancy at age 60 (table 11). Men have only had a small increase in life expectancy among the oldest, while women have had an increase at all ages.

TABLE 11.- LIFE EXPECTANCY (IN YEARS) AT AGE 60 AND 85 : DENMARK, 1951 - 1988

	Males		Females	
	60 years	85 years	60 years	85 years
1951-1955	17.4	4.2	18.4	4.3
1956-1960	17.3	4.2	19.0	4.4
1961-1965	16.9	4.1	19.4	4.5
1966-1970	16.9	4.3	20.2	4.8
1971-1975	17.1	4.5	20.9	5.2
1976-1980	17.1	4.6	21.4	5.4
1981-1985	17.2	4.7	21.6	5.6
1985-1988	17.5	4.8	21.7	5.8

Sources : Denmark Statistik, Vital Statistics, 1988

5) *Migration and the rate of growth*

The number of people who have migrated to and from Denmark since 1950, has varied between 20,000 and 40,000 per year, with only a minor netmigration as a result. 12 years have resulted in net-emigration and 26 years in net-immigration. Since 1960 as a whole the net migration has been positive and has amounted to about 84,000 people (table 12).

It is also seen, that netimigration now is more important for the overall population growth than earlier, as the natural increase has decreased together with the decrease in fertility.

During the years 1981-1984 the population growth rate has been negative for the first time since the 1830s.

Even if the Danish net migration is quite small compared to other European countries, it is worth to mention, that the migration pattern has altered completely during the 1970s. Until the late 1960s the immigrants to Denmark came mainly from Norway, Sweden, United Kingdom, West Germany and North America, and the main emigration went to the same countries. Most of the migration was only of temporarily nature and work related.

TABLE 12.- POPULATION GROWTH : DENMARK, 1951 - 1988

	Natural increase	Net migration	Population growth
1951-1955	189,816	- 21,241	168,575
1956-1960	167,957	- 21,119	146,838
1961-1965	176,700	8,949	185,649
1966-1970	145,739	18,318	164,057
1971-1975	113,796	5,765	119,561
1976-1980	37,995	20,328	58,323
1981-1985	- 22,252	13,250	- 9,002
1986-1988	- 4,843	17,684	12,841

Sources : Denmark Statistik, Vital Statistics, 1988

In the last half of the 1960s the situation has changed, as the immigration began to increase from other countries, especially Yugoslavia, Turkey and Pakistan. As of 1st, January 1990 there were approx. 151,000 persons living in Denmark with a foreign citizenship, i.e. 2.9 per cent of the total Danish population.

6) The age distribution

The demographic development and especially the development in fertility and mortality has altered the age distribution of the Danish population in a significant way. The relative number of children 0-6 years (table 13) old has decreased from 17.1 percent in 1901 to 7.6 per cent in 1990. The same pattern is seen among the children and young people attending schools or other teaching institutions. On the other hand, the relative number of senior citizen has increased. The increase in life expectancy - especially among women - has had an impact to increase the number of older and very old people. The population projected to 2030 (table 13) is based on a small increase in fertility, a small decrease in mortality above age 60 and a slightly positive net migration. Because of the TFR below the replacement level, the population is expected to decrease in number.

TABLE 13.- POPULATION BY FUNCTIONAL AGE GROUPS : DENMARK, 1901 - 2030

	1901	1950	1990	2030
	per cent			
0-6 years	17.1	13.9	7.6	7.8
7-16 years	21.0	15.3	12.3	11.0
17-24 years	14.0	11.0	12.2	8.8
25-66 years	42.4	52.3	54.2	53.8
67-79 years	4.6	6.3	10.0	12.3
80 + years	0.9	1.3	3.7	5.8
Total	100.0	100.0	100.0	100.0
Number	2,443,450	4,281,275	5,135,408	4,780,209

Sources : 1901 and 1950. Det Statistiske Department, Population development and Health Conditions, Copenhagen 1966.
1990 and 2030, Denmark Statistik, Population Projections 1990-2030, 1990.

III.- POPULATION POLICY

There has never been an attempt to formulate a population policy in the Danish Parliament with a specific goal for the size or composition of the Danish population. However, many laws and regulations have been carried through, with an impact on the number of births, deaths, migration etc. The Danish health system can be taken as an example. Every Danish citizen, regardless of income and property has the right to consult a doctor or a hospital without paying directly for the services received. It is only a few years ago that private hospitals were allowed to be established and it is still debated, whether it is right or wrong for wealthy people to be able to buy services from doctors or hospitals. The Danish health system is among the best in the World and must have been a vital element in the reduction of mortality and morbity. However, at the latest, some concern has been given to the fact, that the Danish population does not seem keep up with the improvement in life expectancy, as can be observed in surrounding countries.

The most important Danish legislation with an influence on fertility has been the law of free abortion within 12 weeks pregnancy. The law was carried through the Danish Parliament in October, 1973. The aim of the law was not to have an impact on fertility as such, but to prevent unwanted births and illegal abortions, which were of great threat to the women. At the same time a law of sterilization gave every man and woman above age 23 the right to be sterilized. The number of sterilizations is around 10-15,000 per year.

All contraceptions are available in the Danish society, at least after consulting a doctor or a family planning clinic and together with abortion and sterilization every Danish woman and man have the possibility to decide, when to have children, a possibility which have clearly been used to alter the pattern of fertility.

The Danish family policy allows maternal leave and child allowances, but the size of these benefits are not of such a magnitude, that the family policy could at all be characterized as pro natalistic. The parents have to pay for the day care of their children and are facing quite a waiting list problem. In one area the Danish Government has tried directly to control the development, i.e. within immigration. Late in the 1970s it was decided not to issue new work permits to migrant (guest) workers not covered by the special rules within the Nordic countries or EEC. Because of the rules, which allow migrant workers to bring their family to Denmark, the population with foreign citizenship has increased by about 50,000 people during the 1980s. The number of refugees with foreign citizenship and living in Denmark is about 25,000.

Norway /La Norvège
Lars ØSTBY and Inger TEXMON

I.- FROM PRE-TRANSITION TO POST-WORLD-WAR II

1) Introduction

At the dawn of the 19th century, Norway had been a "sleeping partner" in a union with Denmark for 400 years. Towards the end of the 18th century, national feelings were awakening, with more frequent expressions of patriotic attitudes. At that time, there were no real ideas of independence in Norway. As Denmark was involved on the losers side in the Napoleonic Wars, Norway was handed over to Sweden as a part of the peace treaty. Before this transfer, there was room for an independence movement in the year 1814, and we entered the union with Sweden with a modern constitution and with full rights to decide in internal questions.

In 1801, Norway had a total population of 883 603. That figure is taken from the population census of 1 February 1801, (Central Bureau of Statistics, 1980). That was our second census, and the first one on a nominative basis. The population history of Norway is well documented. Together with Denmark, we had a system for registering vital events

TABLE 1.- VITAL STATISTICS 1800 - 1900

Period	Mean population, 1000	Gross birth rate ⁰/₀₀	Gross death rate ⁰/₀₀	Net migration ⁰/₀₀	Population growth ⁰/₀₀	Infant mortality ⁰/₀₀	Age distribution		
							0-14 %	15-59 %	60+ %
1801-05	887	28.23	24.12		21.7		34	57	9
1806-10	905	26.80	26.25		-4.2				
1811-15	903	27.09	23.35		23.5		—		
1816-20	945	32.71	18.93		70.5				
1821-25	1013	33.68	18.71		79.1				
1826-30	1093	32.92	18.99		71.1				
1831-35	1163	31.18	20.10		57.1				
1836-40	1223	28.08	20.27	-0.20	43.2	139.8			
1841-45	1286	30.37	17.44	-0.77	65.6	118.1			
1846-50	1364	30.92	18.85	-1.75	54.0	111.6	34	58	9
1851-55	1442	32.51	17.31	-2.81	65.1	105.4			
1856-60	1546	33.34	16.85	-2.06	75.5	101.3			
1861-65	1649	31.86	18.55	-2.87	57.6	104.0			
1866-70	1722	29.88	17.44	-8.64	22.3	113.5	36	55	9
1871-75	1771	30.33	17.53	-5.12	48.1	107.2			
1876-80	1876	31.55	16.60	-4.25	51.4	101.0			
1881-85	1927	30.95	17.14	-10.98	18.4	98.6			
1886-90	1977	30.54	17.10	-8.20	27.7	96.4	35	54	11
1891-95	2043	30.14	16.91	-6.00	49.3	97.6			
1896-00	2172	29.99	15.69	-3.10	67.8	95.7			
1901-05	2285	28.54	14.56	-9.02	28.5	80.6			
1906-10	2349	26.39	13.85	-7.47	35.2	70.0	35	54	11
1911-15	2448	24.97	13.36	-3.65	50.6	66.3			
1916-20	2578	24.62	14.23	-1.32	57.8	61.9			
1921-25	2710	22.25	11.52	-3.31	35.7	51.7			
1926-30	2785	17.99	10.99	-3.00	22.0	49.5	30	59	11
1931-35	2857	15.17	10.35	-0.18	28.2	44.9			
1936-40	2937	15.38	10.31	-0.20	29.9	39.4			
1941-45	3037	18.44	10.45	0.00	45.7	37.3			
1946-50	3198	20.62	9.15	-0.61	54.0	31.1	23	63	13
1951-55	3361	18.59	8.50	-0.53	49.8	22.6			
1956-60	3522	17.90	8.89	-0.55	43.3	19.9			
1961-65	3667	17.45	9.54	-0.11	39.8	17.1			
1966-70	3817	17.48	9.83	0.22	39.8	13.9	25	58	18
1971-75	3958	15.52	10.00	1.22	31.5	11.6	24	57	19
1976-80	4057	12.75	10.04	1.02	18.3	9.0	23	57	20
1981-85	4127	12.28	10.30	1.22	16.5	8.1	21	58	21
1986-90	4206	13.52	10.70	1.51		8.0*	19*	60*	21*

* 1986-89

DIAGRAM 1.- LIVE BIRTHS, DEATHS AND EMIGRATION PER 1000 OF MEAN POPULATION. 1771 - 1989

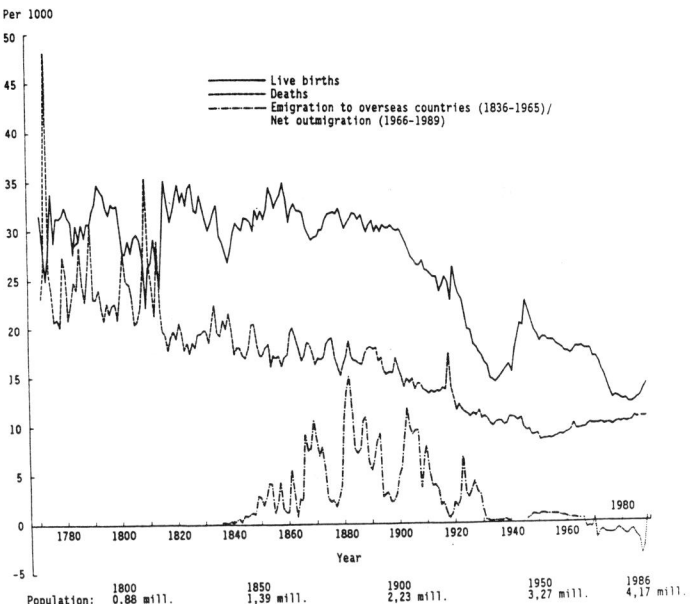

from 1735, and that system was further improved during the "Swedish period". Together with the Nordic neighbours, Norway has probably among the best population statistics in the world on the national level from the 18th and 19th century (see Drake, 1969 and Henry, 1970).

The population increase was very steady after 1800. We had a population decline around 1810 due to crop failure and blockade by the British during the Napoleonic Wars, and in 1880-81 due to very heavy emigration to the United States. As can be seen from diagram 1, taken from Kravdal (1991), the smooth curve for the total population growth do hide rather dramatic changes in the different population components. We shall go into some detail in commenting the varius growth components, based on diagram 1 and table 1.

2) Growth rate

Between 1815, when the mortality went under 20 per 1000, and 1865, when the overseas out-migration reached a high level, Norway had a yearly population growth of 1 - 1,5 per cent, almost doubling the population in 50 years. From then on, the emigration took away much of the birth excess. When the emigration to the United States came to an end, the country had entered the inter-war baby-bust.

Consequently, the population growth rate never came back to the level from the first part of the 19th century.

3) Fertility

The fertility of Norway and the rest of Scandinavia was never very high compared to the standards of contemporary Europe, and low compared to non-European pre-transitional societies. Diagram 1 shows the crude birth rate. Due to recent reconstructions of 19th century population data, we are also able to give total fertility rate (TFR) on period and cohort basis back to 1845 (Brunborg, 1988). Based on these calculations, diagram 2 shows that the TFR was very close to 4,5 for most cohorts born between 1820 and 1855, going down to less than 4,0 from the 1870-cohort. The period TFR varied on the yearly basis, but was never above 5,0. The decrease was very strong around the turn of the century. The decrease connected to the transitional process was reinforced by the interwar depression, and around 1935 the TFR was down to 1,78 before an increase towards World War II.

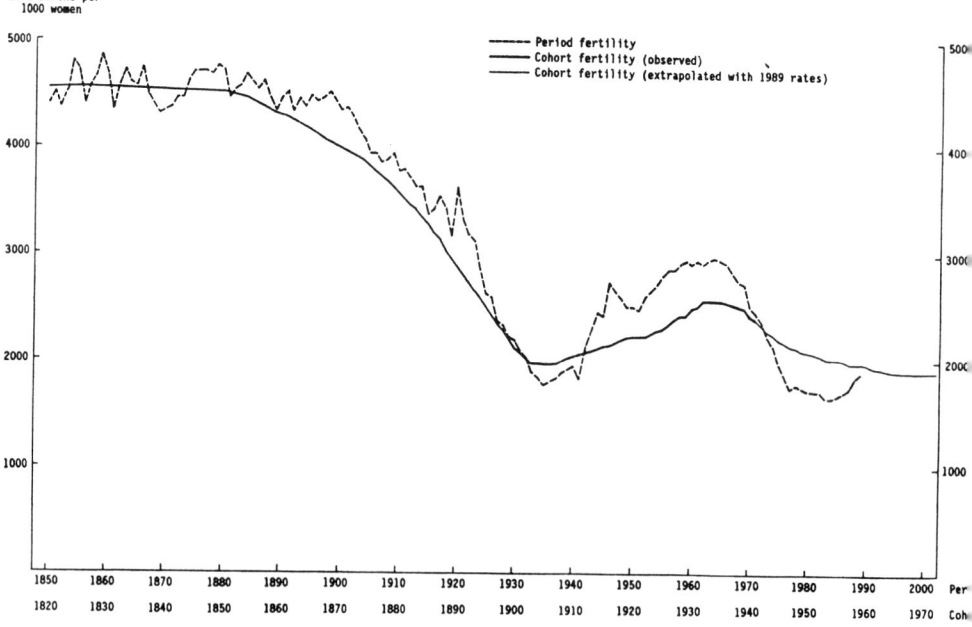

DIAGRAM 2.- TOTAL FERTILITY RATE FOR THE YEARS 1850 - 1989 AND THE COHORTS 1820 - 1973

The cohort TFR shows less dramatic changes in diagram 2, but the overall decline is of considerable magnitude. The cohorts born 1903-1908 had less than 2.0 children on average, less than half the level of those born one generation before. The cohorts born at the beginning of our century has the lowest completed cohort fertility registered in Norway. They may, of course, be surpassed by those born towards the end of the 1950s.

Although the period TFR was between 5 and 1,8 in the 19th and first part of the 20th century, the year to year variation was small (diagram 2). Diagram 3 shows also a rather smooth pattern. The year to year changes in the number of births have been important in periods. By and large, the number of births were doubled during the first 50 years of the 19th century. From then on, the number has been between 50 000 and 70 000, with the baby-bust 1928-1941 as the only lasting exception.

In diagram 2, the cohort reproduction level is also included. Among Norwegian cohorts, those born before 1890 and between 1920 and 1950 seems to have reproduced themselves. As a comparison, no Swedish cohorts born after about 1880 have reproduced themselves (Hofsten and Lundstrøm, 1976.)

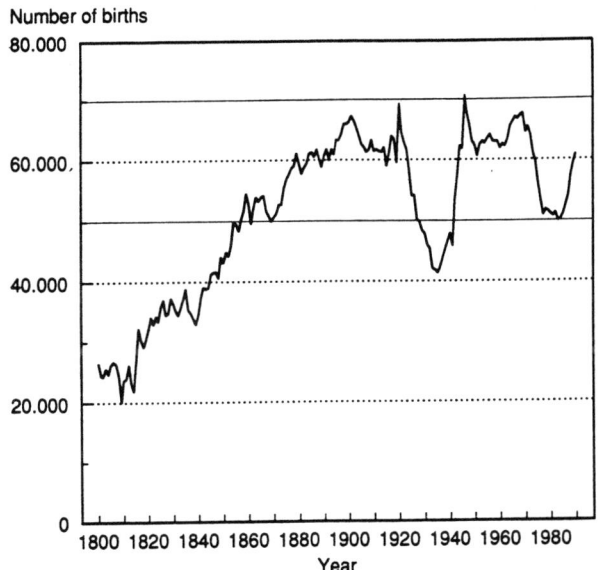

DIAGRAM 3.- YEARLY NUMBER OF BIRTHS 1800 - 1990

The comparatively low fertility in Norway and the rest of Scandinavia around 1800 should be seen in relation to the marital pattern (Hajnal, 1982, see also Sogner et. al., 1984). In most cases, a new household had to be able to support itself and be economically independent from the start. Very often, this caused high age at marriage, and the female exposure time for pregnancy was correspondingly low. Malthus noticed this under his visit to Norway, and recommended late marriages. On average, a man was around 30 before being able to established himself as a supporter of a family. The wife was normally a few years younger. This age at marriage (28-30 years for males, and 2-3 years younger for women) was the same until the end of World War II. Among cohorts with low fertility, there was in addition high proportion unmarried women, for women born 1900-1910 around 20 per cent. This was partly due to sex imbalances caused by selective out-migration, and partly due to problems for many youngsters to establish a basis for supporting a family during the inter-war economic recession.

4) Mortality

The crude mortality rate fell under 20 per 1000 in 1815, and reached that level again only for very short periods (see diagram 1). The decrease was very stable, with the Spanish influenza of 1918 as one prominent exception. The life expectancy at birth and at most ages were increasing. From the second half of the 19th century, Norway had among the highest life expectancies in the world, together with the Scandinavian neighbours and Belgium.

The life expectancy at selected age groups are shown in table 2. In the 19th century, the life expectancy at birth improved by 10 years, while the increase among children of age 5 was around 5 years, and less for adults. This means that the decrease in infant and child mortality was the most important factor in the mortality decline. In the first 50 years of our century, the life expectancy increased even faster than in the 19th century for children and young adults, but the increase was only one year at the age of 70.

TABLE 2 .- LIFE EXPECTANCY AT SELECTED AGES, 1846 - 1989

Period	Males					Females				
	0 year	5 years	30 years	50 years	70 years	0 year	5 years	30 years	50 years	70 years
1846-50	45.48	52.14	34.40	20.40	8.82	48.64	54.76	36.25	21.88	9.25
1866-70	47.31	53.13	35.66	21.40	9.35	50.65	55.84	37.43	22.89	10.00
1886-90	48.98	54.21	37.80	23.18	10.16	51.54	56.34	39.06	24.67	10.98
1906-10	55.64	57.27	39.04	24.02	10.56	58.40	59.31	40.37	25.34	11.21
1926-30	61.74	61.39	40.77	24.64	10.77	64.58	63.44	42.34	25.96	11.43
1946-50	69.09	67.22	44.20	26.43	11.44	72.40	69.87	46.21	27.92	12.04
1951-55	71.19	68.46	44.87	26.66	11.64	74.78	71.64	47.38	28.63	12.35
1956-60	71.39	68.35	44.62	26.24	11.40	75.62	72.21	47.78	28.87	12.38
1961-65	71.07	67.76	43.94	25.63	11.06	76.02	72.40	47.89	28.91	12.31
1966-70	71.16	67.54	43.63	25.35	10.90	76.90	73.02	48.51	29.48	12.84
1971-75	71.44	67.65	43.77	25.43	10.89	77.73	73.64	49.12	30.07	13.22
1976-80	72.24	68.14	44.14	25.71	11.13	78.70	74.46	49.91	30.77	13.90
1981-85	72.69	68.50	44.48	25.96	11.25	79.44	75.15	50.55	31.44	14.46
1989	73.34	69.13	44.49	26.46	11.48	79.85	75.51	50.87	31.76	14.77

Borgan (1983) has calculated the cohort mortality for all cohorts born after 1845, and the mortality based on deaths after 1845 for those born before. The survival curves for cohorts born after 1870, shows consistingly that every younger 5-years cohort have more survivors at each age than the preceding cohorts, for men and women. For cohorts born before 1870, the picture is not that clear.

As infant and child mortality is crucial, diagram 4 (based on Backer, 1961) with infant mortality rates 1836-1989 is included. For some decades after 1850, the rate was quite stable. In the rest of the period, it was declining, even during the war. In diagram 4, the infant mortality of some European countries for the period 1876-80 is shown. The relative rank was very much the same until World War II, with the Netherlands approaching the Scandinavian level.

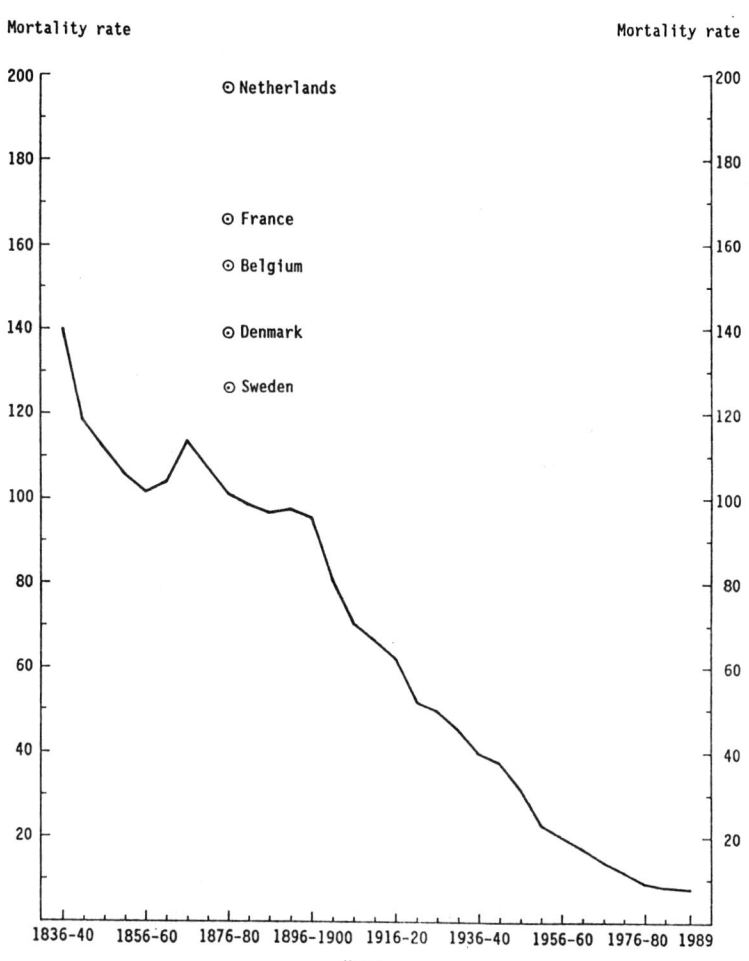

DIAGRAM 4.- INFANT MORTALITY RATE IN NORWAY, 1936 -1939.
SOME OTHER COUNTRIES 1876 - 1880

5) Migration[1]

As shown in diagram 1, the out-migration from Norway to overseas countries was of great importance between 1865 and 1930. Following some pioneers from the first half of the century, migration to the United States became increasingly common from 1850. The natural population growth had been between 1,2 and 1,5 per cent per year most of the period since 1815, and the modernizing agriculture or growing cities could no longer absorb the population surplus in the country. We had waves of out- migration, mainly following the economic cycles in the United States. At the beginning, the out- migrants were young men, later followed by single women and families as well. In some years the country lost more than 1 per cent of its population, with 1882 (1,5 per cent) as the peak year.

The relative out-migration from Norway was second only to Ireland in Europe. The total out-migration to overseas countries was 850 000 before 1930, or about 40 per cent of the birth surplus. That year, American quotas brought the out-migration from Norway to an end. The pre-war population statistics had no figures on return migration, but may be 1/4 of the emigrants did return to Norway.

In the pre-war period, it was no registration of migration other than to overseas. However, it can be made some estimates on the basis of the question on place of birth in the population censuses 1865-1960. Norway seems to have had a permanent immigration in the second half of the 19th century from Scandinavian countries. Many were recruited as construction workers for building railroads, factories etc. The immigration was never high enough to counterbalance the overseas emigration of Norwegians. In the year 1900, almost 3 per cent of the population was born abroad, 3/4 of them in Sweden. Even the immigration came to an end in the inter-war period. In 1950, only 1,4 per cent was born abroad, and 0,4 per cent were foreign citizens.

6) Age structure

Due to these population processes, Norway has had a rather old population compared to the rest of Europe, but not as old as the French one. In 1801, 34 per cent were less than 15 years of age, and 9 per cent above 60 (table 1). The percentage old persons was very stable in the 19th century, even though there were substantial demographic changes. The increasing number of births, increasing life expectancy and the out-migration among young adults counteracted each other as far as the age structure is concerned. In some periods, however, the out-migration was heavy enough to cause an increasing proportion aged.

---

[1] This section is based on Backer, 1965.

The survival percentages and the number of births in diagram 3 gives the main pattern of the aging in Norway. It has been stronger than in most other European countries, but at the end of World War II, the percentage above 60 was still only 13.

II.- THE POST-WORLD-WAR II EPOCH

1) *Norway after World War II*

The destructions of war in Norway was probably of lesser importance than in most other countries having been occupied by German troops, except from in the far north. The infrastructure was nevertheless run-down, and the reconstructions started in a very optimistic spirit. The post-war economic growth was very fast, among other things due to the Marshall plan. At the time the economic growth levelled off in other European countries, the North Sea oil was introduced in the Norwegian economy, keeping the growth rate among the highest in the industrialized world.

The settlement pattern of Norway is very dispersed, with single farms, small towns and no villages. At the moment 3/4 of the population lives in densely populated areas, but only three cities have more than 100 000 inhabitants. Much of the settlement follows the coast, and the rest is located in the valleys. Only three per cent of the land area is cultivated, 20 per cent is productive forest, and the rest is unproductive, mostly mountains, bare lands and bogs.

The population density is about 14 per square km. - the lowest in mainland Europe. In the period after World War II, there has been, and still is a significant population increase in the central parts of the country, within commuting distance from the bigger cities. The population is declining in many remote districts. Due to low density, the settlement pattern is vulnerable to decreasing population size and increasing centralization. The regional population processes, however, will not be addressed in this short paper.

After World War II, Norwegian population statistics are more and more based on our Population Register. It was established on the municipal level just after the war, and it became a centralized system in 1964. Based on the population census of 1960 and birth and migration records, everyone who lived in Norway at that time got a unique identification number. That number will follow a person throughout the life, and it is becoming increasingly used in contacts with governmental authorities etc. It is used for many statistical purposes, and it is the key when establishing individual demographic history files and in other kinds of record linkages.

2) Fertility

In diagram 3, we can see an extraordinary high births figure at the end of the war. 1946 had the maximum number of births ever recorded. This was partly due to the catching up of postponed births from the 1930s and the war period. The war effect was temporary, but every cohorts born 1908-1918 had higher birth rates in 1946 than in the preceding and following year. In addition, the number of women in fertile age was very high. The previous maximum number of births was in 1920.

Diagram 5 shows a general increase in the fertility to 1965, reaching a maximum of almost 3,0. At that time the post-war baby-boom came to its end in Norway as in many other countries. In the next 12 years, the period TFR came down to 1,75, and stayed around that level for 10 years. Diagram 5 illustrates also the changing age pattern of the fertility in the post-war period. During the increase of the fertility, it was a distinct shift towards younger mothers. The fertility was increasing for women in their twenties, most clearly for those younger than 25. Women above thirty had a slow fertility decrease before 1965, then accelerating.

DIAGRAM 5.- AGE SPECIFIC FERTILITY AND TOTAL FERTILITY RATE 1950 - 1989

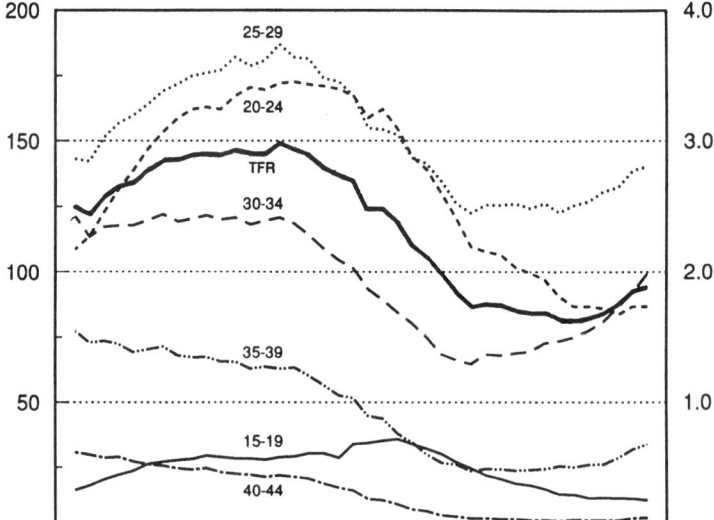

Many changes in the European societies contributed to the fertility decline from the 1960s, but this short note shall not address the causes of the process. We shall only give reference to our fertility surveys of 1977 and 1988 (Central Bureau of Statistics, 1981 and 1991).

The fertility of Norway reached the lowest level ever experienced in 1983, with a total fertility rate of 1,65. The number of births was equal to that of 1854, when the population was 1/3 of the size in 1983. From 1983, the fertility has been increasing. The total number of births were 22 per cent higher in 1990 than in 1983, the total fertility rate was about 16 per cent higher. In this period, there has been a substantial increase in the fertility among women of age 25-34 (diagram 5).

Even though the number of births are increasing, and we have some talk about a new baby-boom, the cohort fertility is still declining. The first cohort able to have as many children as their precursors, are born in 1954. There has to be a continued high fertility increase to bring this cohort to a TFR of 2,05.

The increase in the TFR is due to the fact that the decline in fertility among women younger than 25 is slowing down at the same time as women in the older half of their reproductive period is catching up parts of their lost fertility.

The fertility increase has been stronger in Sweden than in Norway, and it has been quite clear in Denmark as well. With a fertility level like the Scandinavian, the third births are considered to be crucial for the reproduction level. The population register system gives us a good basis for parity progression analyses. The tendency to have a third child, given that the family already had two, dropped steeply during the decline of the period fertility (Kravdal and Brunborg, 1988). The third birth intensity, however, has been increasing for some years now. This might indicate that the fertility increase is not only a temporary one. The forerunners in this process are those with higher education. In Norway (Kravdal, 1990) and Sweden (Hoem, 1990), women on the highest level of education have the highest third birth intensities.

3) Family formation

The number of births and the number of marriages shows the same pattern between 1945 and 1985, but we have not had any marriage boom in the late -80s. The maximum number of marriages was 30,000 in 1946 and 1969 and a temporary minimum of 23 000 around 1960. During the 1970s and early 1980s, the number decreased with 1/3, then stabilizing on 20 000. For the first 20 years after the war, the number of divorces were 2 000, then increasing to present day 9 000.

The marriage rates for women are shown in table 3, and the average age at first marriage in table 4. The age at first marriage was declining for both sexes between the war and the end of the 1960s, down to 23 years for women and 25 years for men. Due to high rates and declining age at marriage, the sum of the age specific marriage probabilities were above 1 for many years. In the cohorts born between 1934 and 1942, there are only 5 per cent never married women, and 10 per cent among men.

In the last 20 years, the family formation pattern has changed considerably. The age at marriage for never-married increased with fully three years. When accounting for the changes in the age distribution in the population, the increase will be 1,5-2 years higher. The marriage rates have decreased, most clearly pronounced among the younger age groups (table 3). In the last years, the decrease has levelled off among those above the age of 30, but there is only little compensation for the decline at younger ages. The marriage rates of 1989 point towards almost 1/3 never married among men and 1/4 among women.

TABLE 3.- FEMALE MARRIAGE RATES 1929 - 1989

Period	Age						
	15-19 years	20-24 years	25-29 years	30-34 years	35-39 years	40-44 years	45-49 years
1929-32	7.6	67.0	96.0	61.4	29.3	15.6	8.8
1945-48	15.3	108.1	162.5	111.3	57.8	29.1	14.0
1949-52	23.0	146.6	178.7	110.3	55.0	27.4	14.1
1955-56	33.4	193.1	197.3	107.3	53.7	27.5	14.9
1959-62	38.8	217.0	203.0	99.7	49.5	24.8	13.1
1961-65	42.9	206.8	182.4	85.6	44.3	22.6	12.1
1966-70	47.5	226.0	176.7	80.4	38.3	20.3	11.3
1971-75	44.5	208.0	163.7	70.4	36.3	16.2	10.1
1976-80	27.6	142.3	128.2	65.5	32.1	15.3	8.1
1981-85	14.3	95.1	106.2	58.5	27.6	13.1	8.2
1989	5.8	54.8	83.5	56.0	29.0	11.7	5.5

TABLE 4.- AVERAGE AGE AT FIRST MARRIAGE 1931 - 1989

Period	Males	Females
1931-35	29.11	26.27
1936-40	29.29	26.38
1941-45	29.15	26.35
1946-50	29.25	26.35
1951-55	28.45	25.53
1956-60	27.68	24.52
1961-65	26.45	23.38
1966-70	25.32	22.78
1971-75	25.2	22.8
1976-80	25.9	23.3
1981-85	26.8	24.2
1989	28.3	25.8

The weakening of the marriage is clearly illustrated by the percentage non-marital births. After the war, the percentage was down to under 4 per cent. The increase was very slow at the beginning, then steeper and steeper. Still, it is not as high as in Denmark, and well below Iceland and Sweden. The extra-marital fertility can no longer be taken as an indicator of percentage single mothers. Most of the increase from 4 per cent to 36 per cent, but not all of it, is due to births to cohabiting women.

Also the decrease in the marriages from 1970 is closely linked to the increase in cohabitation. Unfortunately, our Central Population Register do not have much information on unmarried cohabitation at the moment. Thus, we have to rely upon demographic sample surveys to estimate such cohabitations. In diagram 6, we give the estimates based on the fertility and family surveys of 1977 and 1988 (Central Bureau of Statistics, 1981 and 1991).

In 1988, the majority of women below the age of 25 living with a partner, was not married. There has been a substantial increase during the 1980s, but still the figures are well behind those of Sweden and Denmark. In spite of the increase, we still do not consider unmarried cohabitation as a permanent alternative to marriage. In most cases, cohabiting partners who never have been married, will marry after some time, if they do not move apart. The time of the marriage seems to be little influenced by the arrival of children.

DIAGRAM 6.- COHABITING* WOMEN AS PER CENT OF ALL WOMEN AND WOMEN LIVING IN A UNION. 1977 AND 1988

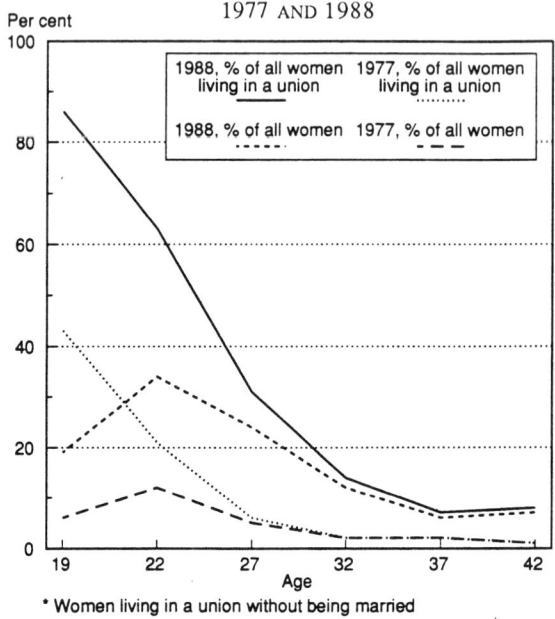

* Women living in a union without being married

The increase in age at first marriage has been clear (table 4), but when we see married and unmarried cohabitation together, there have been small changes among cohorts born after World War II. Among those born before the war, unmarried cohabitation was too uncommon to have any influence on the total cohabitational pattern. Those born just after the war, started to form couples at higher ages than their younger sisters. Among cohorts born after 1950, there seems to be small differences in age at starting living together. Unmarried cohabitation have a significant higher tendency than marriages to be dissolved, so at most ages the percentage living alone is higher in 1988 than in 1977.

The declining position of the family has also influenced the number of divorces. They started to increase at same time as two other indicators changed. Between 1960 and 1990, the age specific divorce rates increased by a factor of four. The divorce pattern of 1989 indicates that 40 per cent of the marriages will end in a divorce, around three times as many as 30 years ago. The divorce rates are on the same level in Finland, Norway and Sweden, Denmark is on a higher level.

The weakening of the family ties since 1965 is clearly illustrated in all indicators referred in this section. After World War II, the marriage rates were high and divorce rates low until 1965. Hitherto, changes in marital behaviour were clearly dependent on the economic conditions influencing the possibilities for young people to establish their own households. From 1965, the situation seems to be changing, with increasing unmarried cohabitation and divorce, and decreasing marriage rates. Unmarried cohabitation is not yet a significant alternative to marriage, but the importance is growing.

4) *Mortality*

World War II did not affect the overall mortality of Norway very much. The mortality rates were higher during the war than before for children and young men. After the war, the mortality for all females and males under the age of 50 improved. The life expectancy for men was decreasing towards the middle of the 1960s, while steadily increasing for women. After the 1960s, the life expectancy has improved year by year for most groups. The number of years to live is still lower in 1989 than in the beginning of the 1950s among men older than 50 (see table 2).

With the exception for boys born around 1960, the life expectancy at birth has been increasing throughout the post-war period. The decrease in the infant and child mortality (diagram 4) has been strong enough to counteract the unfavourable developments among adults.

At the moment, the infant mortality of Norway is much higher (20-30 per cent) than in the most favourable countries like Japan, Iceland, Sweden and Finland. At the end of World War II, only Sweden had lower infant mortality than Norway. The excess infant mortality in Norway has been addressed by the health authorities, who consider it possible to reduce the infant mortality by 1/3 with optimal perinatal care (Sosialdepartementet, 1984). The excess is located mostly in the post-neonatal period, and is partly due to diseases (cot death is one important cause), partly to accidents.

For at least 100 years up to 1970, Norway had among the highest life expectancies in the world. From then on, several industrial countries have challenged that position. Between 1980 and 1987, Norway had a slower increase in the life expectancy than any other country within the Council of Europe region (Council of Europe, 1990).

5) *International migration*

Emigration and immigration had a much stronger influence on the population development 1860-1930 than after World War II (see diagram 1). Still, in a permanent below-replacement situation, immigration is of demographic relevance. Up to 1967, Norway was a moderate net out-migration country. On the average, the country lost less than 2 000 inhabitants yearly, mostly to our Scandinavian neighbours. Towards the end of the 1960s, the demand for labour in Norway increased faster than the population in active ages. We received citizens from many European countries, the United States and some from Pakistan, Turkey, Yugoslavia and Morocco.

For 15 years after 1970, the net immigration was around 4 000, and even the numbers migrating in and out were stable (see diagram 7). In 1985, Norway was "discovered" by asylum seekers, taking the authorities by some surprise. The number of asylum seekers was more than 8 000 in 1987, as a per cent of the population, more than most Western European countries. The number went down to 4000 in 1989 and 1990, partly as a response to more restrictive handling of the asylum applications. Among those arriving in 1990, less than 50 per cent seems to be allowed to stay. The main countries for the asylum seekers have been Chile, Iran, Sri Lanka and Yugoslavia.

In addition, the Norwegian labour market's demand for workers 1985-1988, led to net immigration from most of our European neighbours as well. During most of the post-war period, it was a net emigration of 1-2 000 Norwegian citizens, increasing in the late 1980s.

DIAGRAM 7.- IMMIGRATION, EMIGRATION, ASYLUM SEEKERS AND POLITICAL REFUGEES (QUOTA).
1972 - 1990

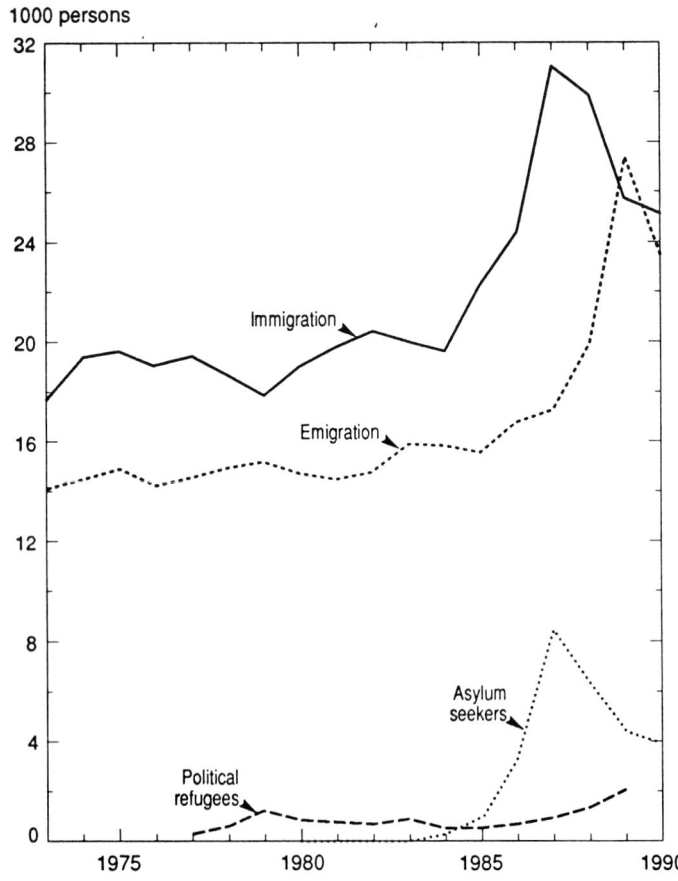

In 1989, the migrations changed significantly. This year, Norway experienced net out-migration. The main changes from the previous years were the following: the number of emigrating Norwegian citizens increased by 60 per cent, mainly due to economic recession in Norway and a very active labour market in Sweden. There was a small net out-migration of Norwegian citizens to most other countries as well. Norwxegians reacted more quickly to the changing labour market than foreigners in Norway did. The migration of third world citizens was not all influenced by the changes in the labour market.

The five Nordic countries have had a common labour market since 1954, probably with even fewer regulations than in the Single European Market from 1993. This has had a significant influence on the migration pattern for Norway only in shorter periods. When the differences in the labour market is increasing, there can be seen a response in the migration pattern. That was the case during the heavy migration from Finland to Sweden at the end of the 1960s, and during the smaller movements from Denmark to Sweden around 1975, from Sweden to Norway 1985 and from Norway to Sweden in 1989. The permanent effects for the population was important only in the first case. Stable differences in the unemployment level seems to have small effects on the inter-Nordic migrations.

Of course, the migrations have changed the population structure of Norway, but the influence have not yet been very important. All together, we have 3,3 per cent foreign citizens in Norway at the beginning of 1990. This is less than Sweden (5,3 per cent) and on the same level as Denmark. Most of the high Swedish figure is due to the immigration from Finland.

One forth of the foreigners in Norway are from another Nordic country, one forth from the rest of Europe and one forth from Asia. Altogether, 40 per cent came from a third world country. From 1975 to 1990, the total number of foreign citizens was more than doubled. The increase was moderate for Nordic citizens (from 24 000 to 36 000), and quite significant for third wold citizens (from 8 000 to 55 000).

6) Age structure

As a result of the processes described in this article, the age structure of the Norwegian population has changed considerably. We have until now had an aging population. During the 1980s, the proportion old in Norway was higher than in every other country except Sweden (OECD, 1988). Diagram 3 shows the variations in the number of birth, and there we can find the "age-boom" by adding 70 years. The improved survival probabilities have also been important. Among those born 100 years ago, 50 per cent of the men and 55 per cent of the women experienced their 67th anniversary. The same happened to 66 and 79 per cent respectively among those born 1920. The mortality of 1989 indicates that 75 and 87 per cent will live at least 67 years.

7) The future of the population

The picture we can give of the demographic future of Norway is to a great extent dependent upon what will happen to the fertility and migration. The mortality is in the population projections expected to continue the slow decline in the years to come. An increase in the life expectancy of 1,7 years for men and women is expected from 1989 to 2010.

The key question regarding fertility is to which extent the rise in the period TFR (see II.2) will continue. As there has been no traces of an increasing cohort fertility, the high alternative for the future TFR was set to 2,05, equal to the expected level of the early 1950-cohorts. TFR of 1,7, equal to the lowest level from the beginning of the 1980s was taken as the low alternative. In addition we used a reference alternative with constant fertility (1,89) throughout the period. For yearly net immigration we have high, medium and low alternatives of 10000, 5000 and 0, respectively.

Without net immigration, and fertility decreasing to 1,7 within 20 years, the population of Norway will reach its maximum before 2010. Due to the very low number of births in the inter-war period, Norway will very soon (1994) reach the maximum number of aged (over the age of 67, the limit for old age pensions). From then on, the number will decline as long as the old are recruited from small birth cohorts. In 2010, the population projection expects the number of aged to be 25 000 lower than in 1990, 13 per cent of the total population. Before 2050, that percentage will increase to 20.

With moderate net immigration and TFR on the 1989-level, the population will increase by 0,5 million before having its maximum around 2030. The combination of high net immigration and increasing fertility will give 30 per cent increase in population during the next 60 years. With these assumptions, the age structure will be changed only modestly from the age structure of today.

III.- ASPECTS OF POPULATION POLICY

Norway has never had any specific policy concerning the total population in the country, but two very different kinds policies have had demographic implications. The general social policy, including welfare policy, distributional policy, social security legislation, policy for the family and child, and policy for equal opportunities between the sexes do influence the demographic attitudes and behaviour of the population. There will, however, not be possible to describe these demography-related systems within the frame of this paper.

The other kind of policy is more specific, and its effects are easier to point out. Regional policy, and in that setting, the regional distribution of the population has been a central political issue in the post-war era. It is an important aim for our regional policy to make it possible to keep the settlement pattern as dispersed as possible. For many years, there has been an important aim in the regional policy that every region should keep its population figure, or even have population growth.

Nevertheless, during the last 5-8 years 50 per cent or more of the municipalities has every year had population decline. Regional questions lies outside the scope of this note, so we shall not go into details of our regional population policy.

There are some other laws and regulations with demographic consequences. At the moment, our immigration law is the most influential one. As mentioned in section II.5, from 1968 on labour migrants from third world countries arrived to Norway. From 1975, we introduced a temporary immigration ban, that later became permanent. The reason stated for the ban, was that foreigners already in the country should be given better living conditions before letting new ones in. Influence of the immigration ban is not reflected in the immigration figures in diagram 7, but the composition of the migrants changed from young male workers to women and children for family reunification as a consequence of the law.

There are many exceptions from the immigration ban, mainly for experts and for family members, and for refugees etc. The law had not very precise criteria for handling applications for political asylum. The first years after 1985, the applications were treated rather liberally, giving more than 50 per cent political asylum. Besides, a majority of the rest were allowed to stay on humanitarian reasons. In 1990, less than 5 per cent of the asylum seekers were given political asylum, and only 1/3 got permission to stay on humanitarian reasons. From 1991, there will be implemented new regulations to our aliens act, probably opening for more uniform decisions to the applications, and we also expect some liberalization. In 1988, the Parliament was given a report on our migration policy. The summary of this report is translated to English (Kommunal- og Arbeidsdepartementet, 1988).

Arguments concerning population questions were never used as reasons for the immigration policy. However, in 1988, when below-replacement fertility had lasted for more than 10 years, two governmental documents stated that we could have future population problems arising from decreasing population numbers together with a high percentage aged in the population. They indicated that these problems might make it necessary for Norway in the future to consider a more liberal immigration policy.

For 10-15 years before 1988, some 2000 foreigners changed into Norwegian citizenship every year. Adopted children from abroad (about 500 yearly) could be naturalised just after arrival, in normal cases a foreigner had to live in Norway for seven years before being entitled to Norwegian citizenship.In 1989-90, the number naturalised has doubled, the increase is mostly for refugees (see Ostby, 1990).

Some other laws have had an intention to regulate population relevant factors, but their influence have never been significant. From time to time, the norms for societal acceptable behaviour changed, leaving the laws as archaic rests of former norms. That was the case for the "concubine paragraph", not repealed before 1972. At that time, unmarried cohabitation had for a long time been common in some parts of the country, and it started to become rather universal.

The law against recommending publicly the use of contraception were also in force long time after the general introduction of contraception. Doctors were allowed to prescribe the pill for contraceptive purposes from 1965, and at the same time the IUD was introduced as well. During the later years, there have been public campaigns to promote the use of condoms to limit the spread of HIV-virus. The results of the campaigns can not be registered in the overall use of condoms, but the campaigns might still have had some effects in more selected groups exposed to the risk of acquiring the virus.

According to the existing divorce law, there is no major obstacles against obtaining a divorce in Norway, but it might take some time. There has not been any major change in this law since 1918, but the divorce rates have multiplied several times since then. In a proposed new act, the separation time before a divorce will be reduced.

The access to abortions was regulated in the general medical laws until 1964. Before that time, abortion could only be performed on medical reasons. The number of such abortions was estimated to be some 2-3000 yearly. The number of illegal abortions was may be three times as high. From 1964, every hospital had an abortion board, handling applications for abortion set forward by a doctor on behalf of the pregnant woman. The law now accepted medical and some socio-medical reasons for allowing abortions to be performed. The number of abortions accepted by the boards increased to about 15 000 in 1976, under an unchanged law. The illegal abortions must have disappeared. In 1976, social criteria were included, the boards were reorganised, and the woman was allowed to make an application herself. This was the last change before abortion was made the decision of the pregnant woman in 1979. The changes in 1976 and 1979 do not seem to have had any significant influence on the abortion figures. In 1990 the number of abortions was still 15 500, with more women in reproductive age than ever before, and the highest number of births since 1973.

REFERENCES:

Backer, J. (1961): Trends of mortality and causes of death in Norway 1856-1955. SØS 10. Central Bureau of Statistics (CBS), Oslo.

Backer, J. (1965): Marriages, births and migrations in Norway 1856-1960. SØS 13. CBS, Oslo.

Borgan, J.-K. (1983): Cohort mortality in Norway 1846-1980. Report 83/28, CBS, Oslo-Kongsvinger.

Brunborg, H. (1988): Cohort and period fertility for Norway 1845-1985. Report 88/4, CBS, Oslo-Kongsvinger.

Central Bureau of Statistics (1980): Population Census 1801, Reprocessed. NOS B 134, Oslo.

Central Bureau of Statistics (1981): Fertility Survey 1977. NOS B197, Oslo.

Central Bureau of Statistics (1991): Family- and Occupation Survey 1988. NOS B959, Oslo.

Council of Europe (1990): Recent Demographic developments in the Member States of the Council of Europe. CDPO, 4 September, Strasbourg.

Drake, M. (1969): Population and Society in Norway. Cambridge.

Hajnal, J. (1982): Household formation pattern in historical perspective. Population and Development review, 8.

Henry, L. (1969): La population de Norvege depuis deux siecles. Population, 25, p. 544-557.

Hoem, B. (1990): Alla goda ting är tre? (Do all good things come in three? Third births to Swedish women born 1936-1960. In Swedish only.) Stockholm Research Reports in Demography 45, Stockholms University, Section of Demography, Stockholm.

Hofsten, E and H. Lundstrøm (1976): Swedish Population History. Urval 8. National Central Bureau of Statistics, Stockholm.

Kommunal- og Arbeidsdepartementet (1988): Report no. 39 (1987-88) to the Storting on Immigration policy. English introduction and summary. Oslo.

Kravdal, Ø. (1990): Who has a third child in contemporary Norway? Report 90/8, CBS, Oslo-Kongsvinger.

Kravdal, Ø. (1991): Hvor mange barn? (How many children. In Norwegian only.) Universitetsforlaget, Oslo.

Kravdal, Ø. and H. Brunborg (1988): Recent fertility trends in Norway. Scandinavian Population Studies 8, p.55-72. Nordic Demographic Society, Copenhagen.

OECD (1988): Ageing populations. Paris.

Sogner, S. et. al. (1984): Fra stua full til tobarnskull. (In Norwegian only.) Universitetsforlaget, Oslo.

Sosialdepartementet (1984): Perinatal omsorg i Norge. (Perinatal care in Norway. In Norwegian only.) NOU 1984:17, Oslo.

Østby, L. (1990): International migration to Norway 1989. Report 90/24, CBS, Oslo-Kongsvinger.

Finland/La Finlande
Mauri NIEMINEN

I.- POPULATION HISTORY UP TO THE 1940'S

1) Population development in pre-industrial period

The population statistics of Finland give a very good picture of the population trends from the historical perspective. The development of population in Finland is characteristic of an industrialized country. Summary of the population development in the 18th and 19th century can be divided into two parts. Up to 1870 the urbanization was insignificant. The year 1870 can be regarded as the starting-point of industrialization in Finland, because before this year there was no considerable increase in the urban population.

In 1750 the population of Finland was 422,000. The limit of the first million was exceeded in 1811. The population had doubled in 60 years. Then it doubled in about 70 years from 1811 to 1873 and 1950. At the beginning of 1991 the population exceeded 5 million.

TABLE 1.- YEARS WHEN THE LIMIT OF MILLION WAS REACHED (1750-1991)

1750	422 000
1811	1 053 000
1879	2 033 000
1912	3 016 000
1950	4 030 000
1991	5 000 000

2) High fertility and mortality

In the 18th century both fertility and mortality were high. In the middle of the 18th century the crude birth rate remained above 40 per 1,000. There was no strong decline in the rate yet, although a slight decrease had started at the beginning of the pre-industrial period. During the 19th century the crude birth rate declined to almost 35 per 1,000.

The crude death rate did not decline as clearly as the birth rate. There was a significant decline only in the infant mortality rate.

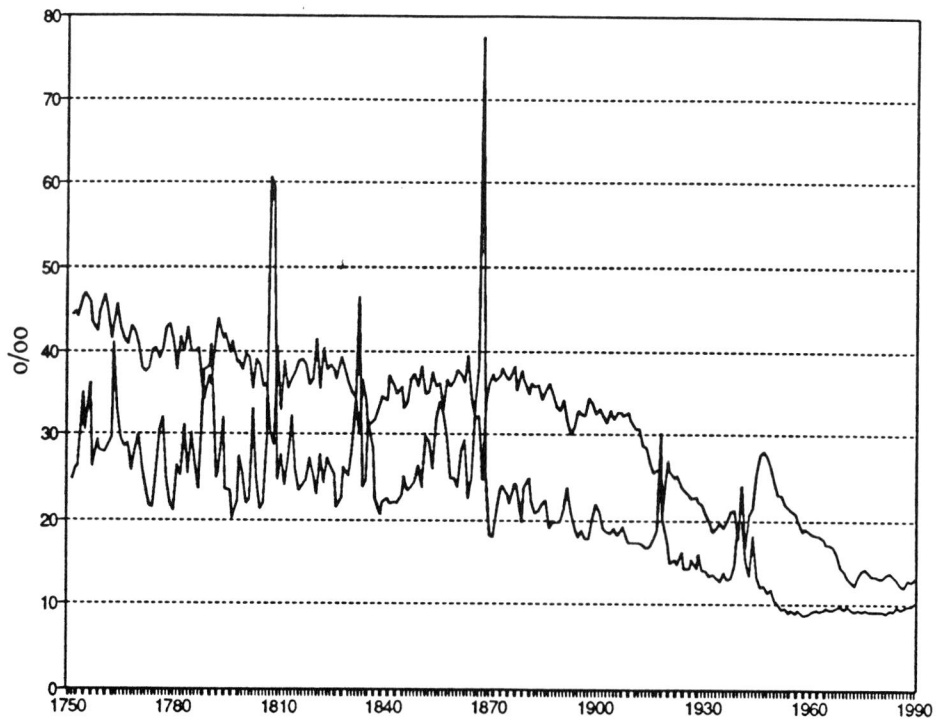

Figure 1.- Crude birth and death rates in 1751-1990

In the first half of the 19th century mortality declined slightly, and the crude death rate settled at 20-25 per 1,000. The strong fluctuations in mortality had a remarkable influence on the natural growth. During the years, when the living conditions were exceptional, mortality rose drastically.

Epidemics often raged simultaneously with wars, killing also part of the population which was not directly involved in the war operations. The worst death peak of the pre-industrial period occurred in 1868. A great famine killed about 8 per cent of the population during a single year.

3) Infant mortality from the 18th century onward

Infant mortality was relatively high in the 18th century. In the middle of the century approximately one third of all deaths was infants deaths and also the infant mortality rate remained high - about 250 deaths per 1,000 live births.

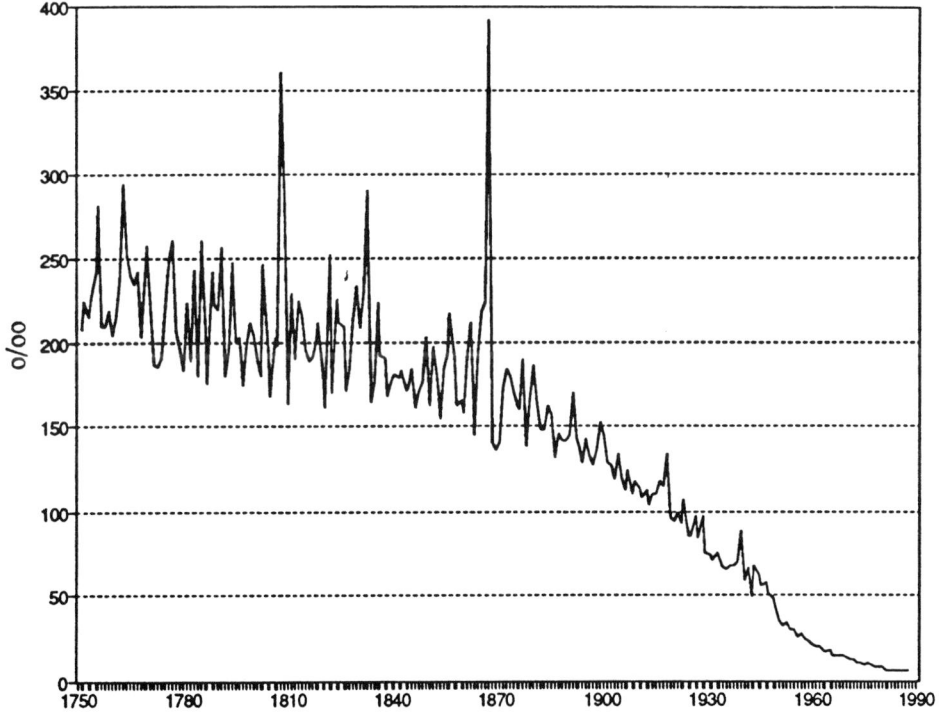

Figure 2.- Infant mortality rate in 1771-1990

The infant mortality rate decreased slowly, but the figure varied notably each year. In the years of famine and war infant mortality was high. At the end of the 19th century the infant mortality rate was about 100-150, after that it began to decrease quickly. By the eve of World War II the infant mortality rate fell to the level of 50 per 1,000.

4) Demographic transition

The overall picture of the demographic transition is similar in Finland to that in any industrialized western country. Mortality began to decrease slightly before the actual industrial breakthrough. At the beginning of the industrial period, in the 1870s, the crude death rate declined to 20 per 1,000 and the crude birth rate remained around 35 per 1,000. Towards the close of the 19th century both rates were on the decline. Because fertility was relatively high, it followed that natural growth was relatively high as well (over 1 per cent).

At the beginning of 1910, there was a distinct decline in the crude birth rate and the figure dropped below 30 per 1,000. After this the birth rate dropped drastically and was lowest (under 20 p. 1000) just before World War II.

5) Total fertility

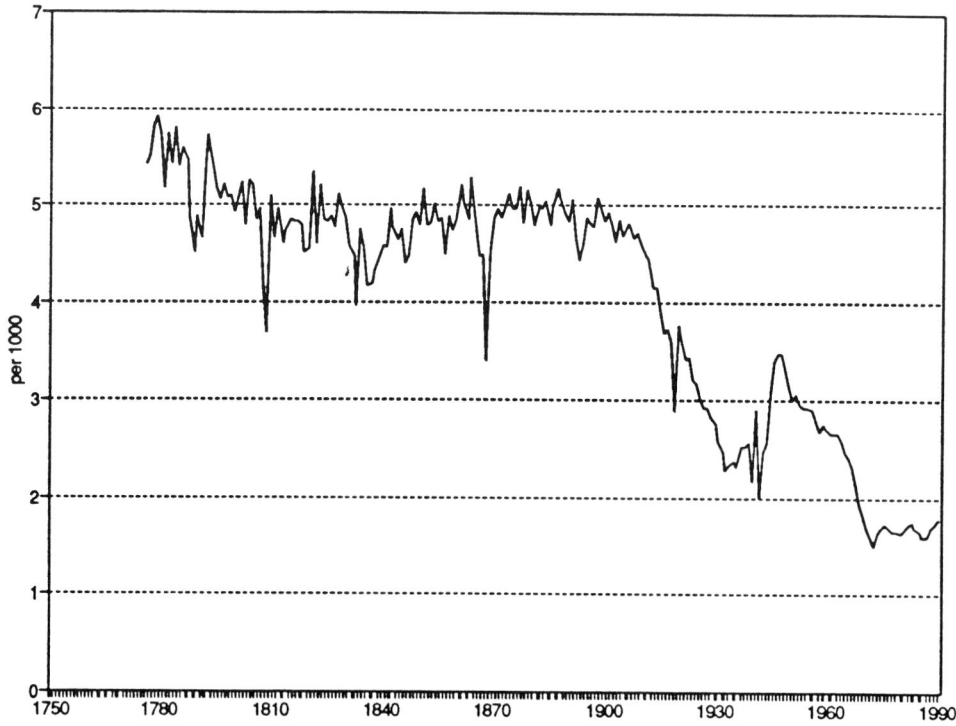

Figure 3.- Total fertility rates in 1771-1990

Figure 3 illustrates the total fertility rate from 1771 till 1990. In the 18th and 19th century total fertility was high.

Total fertility remained a long time near 5.0 and it varied yearly. A sharp decline began at the end of the 19th century and continued up to World War II. In the first decades of the XXth century fertility dropped very sharply. Just before the war the total fertility fell near replacement level (2.1). During World War II, it varied yearly.

6) Life expectancy up to World War II

At the beginning of the industrial period in the 1880s the life expectancy was 41.4 years for men and 44.2 years for women. The life expectancy increased year by year and it was 54.3 for men and 59.5 for women before World War II. The difference between the life expectancies for men and women also increased during this period and it was at the end of the 1930s over 5 years.

TABLE 2.- LIFE EXPECTANCY IN 1881-1988

Year	Male	Female
1881-1890	41,4	44,2
1901-1910	45,3	48,1
1921-1930	50,7	55,1
1941-1945	54,6	61,4
1951-1955	63,4	69,8
1961-1965	65,4	72,6
1971-1975	66,7	75,2
1981-1985	70,1	78,4
1988	70,9	78,6

II.- POPULATION HISTORY FROM 1940S ONWARDS

1) The baby boom

During World War II the population development was insignificant mainly because of the exceptional circumstances. Immediately after World War II, the crude birth rate began to climb and in 1947 it was almost as high as at the beginning of the century. The year 1947 was a record year with regard to the crude birth rate, which was 28 per 1,000. After 1947 the crude birth rate began to decline rapidly. Finland, as well as other industrialized countries, experienced a postwar baby boom. The baby boom age-groups of the late 1940s are visible for a long time in the shape of the age pyramid of Finland. At the turn of the 1950s the population of Finland reached 4 million.

After World War II fertility increased sharply and was highest in 1947 3,4. Just after the war the number of marriages increased and due to this fertility increased. Moreover parents postponed the enlarging of the family until the war was over. Furthermore, the shortened birth intervals effected on the cumulative fertility. At the same time the age at marriage went down and the childbearing women were younger than before. Without a doubt, the great baby boom was also the result of other factors, such as the general attitude after the war, the social policy favouring families with children and the rapid economic development.

2) *Declining fertility*

In the 1950s fertility decreased, more considerably from 1964. In 1973 the number of children was at its lowest and the total fertility rate (see Fig. 3) was 1,50. After that year the fertility increased slightly and the total fertility rate varied between 1.60 and 1.70 depending on the year. The net reproduction rate has been below one since the latter part of the 1960s; the generation born is approximately 15 to 20 per cent smaller than the generation bearing the children.

Older cohorts gave birth to more children than younger cohorts (Table 3). Birth cohort 1908/09 gave birth to about 2.4 children, whereas the figure for the 1948/49 cohort is only 1.8.

TABLE 3.- FERTILITY BY BIRTH COHORT IN 1908/09-1948/49

Birth cohort	Number of children
1908-09	2,44
1918/19	2,48
1928/29	2,53
1938/39	2,10
1948/49	1,83

The factors which have been given to explain the sharp decline in fertility during the last decades include for instance, the development of birth control methods, the longer education of women, the growing employment of women and the changes in the traditional role of women.

3) *High education - low fertility*

The downward trend of fertility was regionally similar. The high fertility in the northern part of Finland fell at the same time as in the south. Though the decline was faster in the north, because the level of fertility had originally been higher there. Nowadays there are clear regional differences in the fertility rates - in the north the total fertility rate is over 1.9, whereas in the south it is near 1.6.

According to the Family and Fertility Survey in 1989 there are clear differences in the fertility by education. High education means less children (Table 4).

TABLE 4.- NUMBER OF CHILDREN BY MOTHER'S EDUCATION

Birth cohort	Education level		
	Basic	Middle	High
1938-42	2,4	2,0	1,7
1943-47	2,1	1,9	1,7
1948-52	2,0	1,8	1,8
1953-57	1,9	1,7	1,5
1958-62	1,7	1,1	0,8

Fertility rates by education show that those who have only basic education have the highest number of children and those who have higher education have the lowest fertility in every birth-cohort.

4) Marriages and cohabitation

Before World War II the crude marriage rate (see Fig. 4) was rather stable and it began to grow during the war. Just after the war the number of marriages increased rapidly and after a sharp increase it levelled near 8 per 1,000. In the 1970s the number of marriages began to decrease slowly. One reason for this development was the growing number of consensual unions (figure 5).

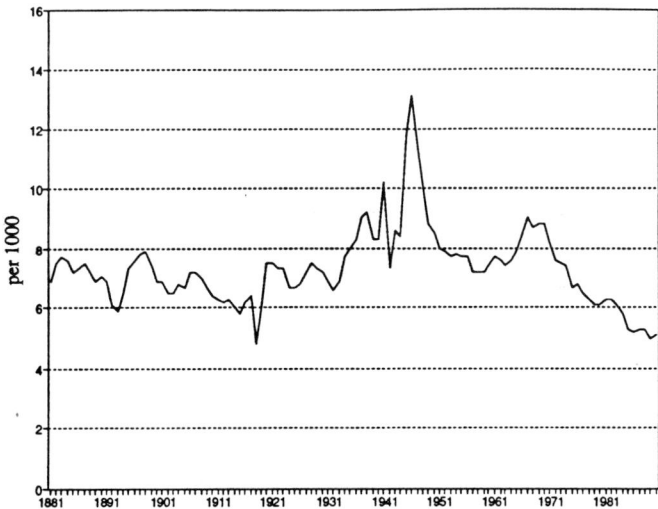

Figure 4.- Crude marriage rates in 1881-1990

In 1989 the percentage of cohabiting population was highest in the youngest age-groups. In the age-group 20-24 a large number of people living together are in a consensual union.

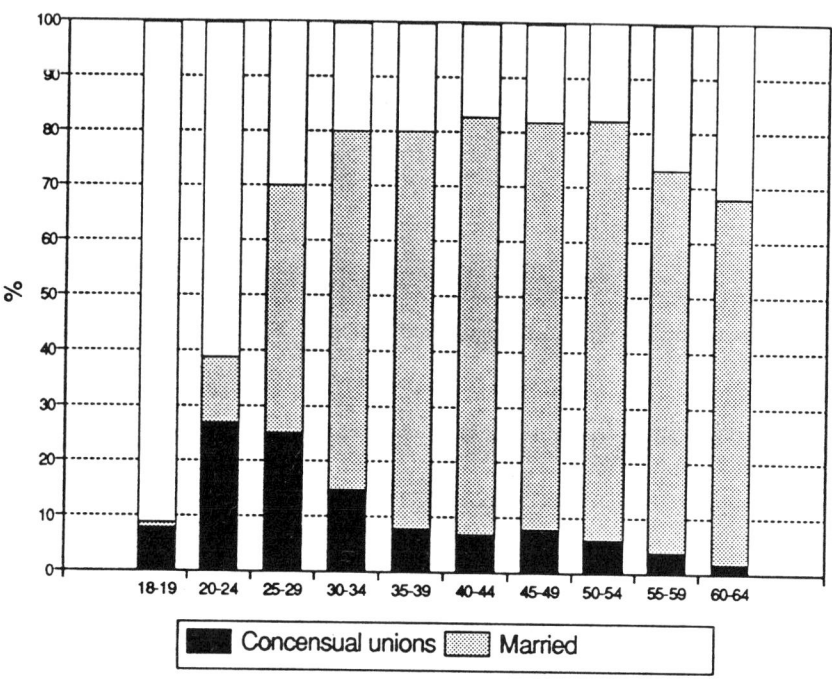

Figure 5.- Cohabiting by age-groups in 1989

5) Increasing number of divorces

Figure 6 illustrates the crude divorce rate in 1927-1990. It examines the divorces of three main periods. Before World War II the crude divorce rate increased slightly. During the war there was a sharp increase, which culminated to the high divorce rate of 1945-1946. Then the divorce rate stayed long at the same level until the 1960s when it began to increase. In the 1970s the crude divorce rate levelled off at 2 per 1,000 till the end of 1980s.

In 1988 the number of divorces increased sharply. This development was due to the New Marriage Act, which was reformed totally in 1988. According to the new law, spouses are entitled to get a divorce on demand after a waiting period of six months from the initation of the proceedings. Since the entry into force of the New Marriage Act it has been easier to get judgment for the divorce. It is supposed that the increase of divorces is a temporary phenomenon.

FINLAND/LA FINLANDE

When examining the divorce rates by length of marriage, we can say, that about one third of marriages ends in a divorce. Remarriages are quite common, as over 40 per cent of men and women get engaged after divorce.

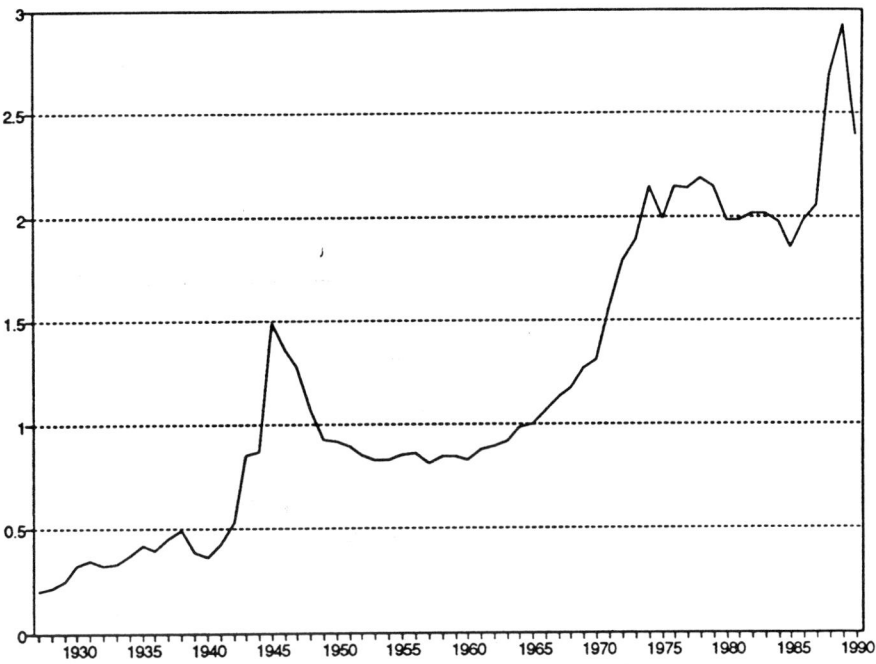

Figure 6.- Crude divorce rates in 1927-1990 (per 1000)

6) Life expectancy

Although the fell in mortality has followed the general trends of the industrialized countries over the past few decades, the Finnish mortality rate displays nevertheless certain features that differ from those in other countries. Life expectancy has increased since 1950 with 7 years for men and 9 years for women. At the same time the difference between male and female mortality has also increased. The difference in the life expectancy is now over 8 years - one of the highest in the western world. The excess mortality of Finnish men of working age is also high. In 1988 the male life expectancy was 70,9 years and the female 78,7.

Infant mortality rate is at present one of the lowest in the world. In the 1980s the figure was 6-7 per 1,000.

7) *International Migration*

After World War II, the net migration was fairly negative and the figures show a deficit of a few thousand reaching about 15,000 in 1950 and 1951 ; then deficit was smaller. The mid and late 1960s saw a marked increase in the international migration, especially to Sweden (see Fig. 7). At that time the large age-groups born after the war were entering into the Finnish labour market. Migration was further stimulated by the labour shortage in Sweden. Sweden was suffering from a shortage of labour, so the age-structure "surplus" of Finland filled the gap created by the age-structure "deficit" of Sweden. The higher wages, the higher standard of living and the shortage of labour encouraged Finns to migrate. Furthermore, the highly-automated industry in Sweden was able to offer employment even to those who hardly spoke the language.

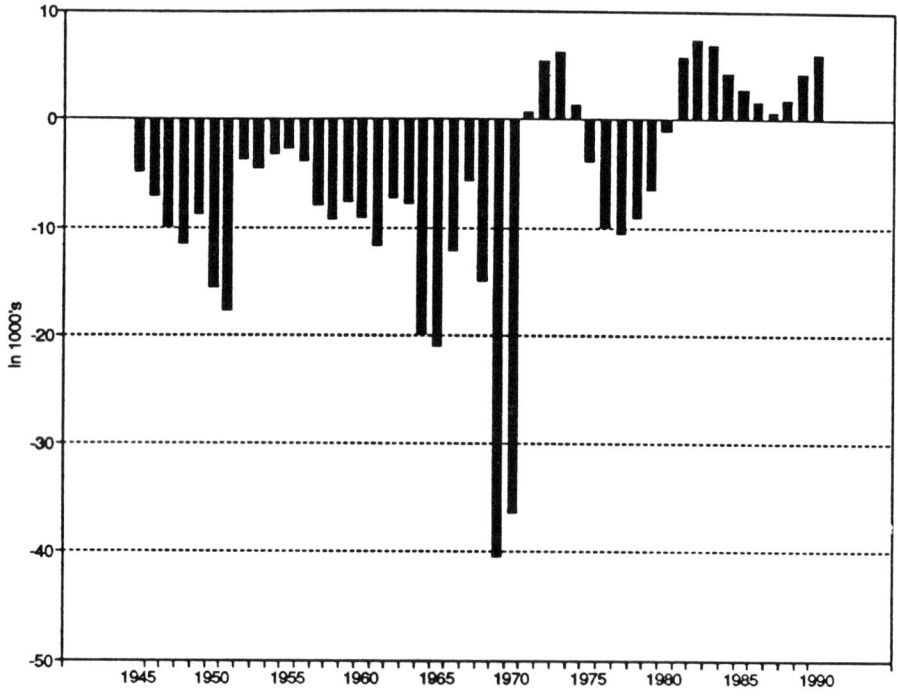

Figure 7.- Net-migration in 1945-1990

Migration to Sweden varied greatly in the 1960s and 1970s according to the employment situation there. As the number of vacancies increased, so did the number of people migrating from Finland to Sweden. When the large age-groups of Finland reached the working age in the late 1960s, nearly 10 per cent of them spent a few years in Sweden.

In the first half of the 1970s the net migration was positive ; but it was negative again in the second half of the decade. The net migration for the 1980s was in Finland's favour.

Migration to Finland has never been significant. The majority of the immigrants in Finland are in fact Finns who have returned after a few years stay in Sweden. Therefore, immigration has not added greatly to the Finnish labour force. Immigration proper, in other words the migration by citizens of other states, has not had notable influence on the population trend of Finland. At present, foreign citizens account for 0.4 per cent of the Finnish population, and even the number of people born abroad stands at just over 1 per cent. Again, some of these people are Finnish descendants born abroad, chiefly in Sweden.

8) Influence of baby boom age-groups

The age structure of the Finnish population is influenced most by the large age-groups born after the war. These groups are clearly larger than their predecessors, and nothing like it has been recorded since.

The large age-groups have had a complex influence on the development of the Finnish society. Some of the schools built for them have been subsequently closed because of the lack of pupils. This was followed by the increasing demand for housing, these age-groups were housed in the suburbs. The housing density in Finland is at present one of the highest in the western countries. In the early 1970s this age-group yielded a large surfeit of labour, some of which was channelled to Sweden. In the late 1970s there was a peak in unemployment.

One of the consequences of the decline in fertility is that for each age-group born today can be guaranteed at least a vocational education. The education level of the population has in fact risen considerably in the past few years. The marked economic upswing has been supported by the rise in the level of education among the whole population.

Although the age-groups approaching working age are becoming steadily more educated, one of the biggest challenges in the next few decades will - apart from the quantitative rise in the number of old people - be the changes taking place in the structure of the labour force itself. So far the population of working age has increased steadily, and this has furthered the favourable economic trend of today.

III.- FUTURE POPULATION

The present trend in the population clearly indicates the future prospects. Despite of the decline in fertility the percentage of working age population has remained one of the highest in the western countries. This trend has meant a slow but steady increase in the number of old people.

Changes in population trends are often slow and predictable. A good example of this is the effect which the large age-groups born in Finland after the war have on different sectors of society. When the fertility rate dropped, this age-group remained larger than any other and its influence will be felt for years to come - at the moment as an aging labour force and in the future as a rapid increase in the number of old people.

The growing number of old people is naturally being felt in several sectors of society. More services are needed for old people, more facilities for nursing them, and more staff to look after them. The training of new staff requires more resources. Wage policy and staff availability in general will be two of the major issues in the future. On the other hand, the planning for the future is to some extent made easier by the fact that the basic services have already been built in past decades: hospitals, health centres, dwellings, roads and railways. In the future it will only be a question of improving the quality of these services.

As a result of the decline in fertility, families have become smaller, which in turn has affected the life of individual families in many ways. In the old days, when there were lots of children in the family, the youngest child left home when the parents approached the age of 60. Nowadays, when there are only one or two children in each family, the parents are in their forties when their children leave home. Parents have more time for other things, and they begin at an increasingly early age to consume the services brought by the economic progress.

More and more people are living alone as a result of the reduction in the number of children, the growing incidence of divorce and the shorter male life expectancy. This has an effect on the services provided by the society. Financial support in the form of allowances for single persons have to be taken into account in future plans.

Possibly one of the biggest challenges facing the future society will be the need to adapt to an aging population. The higher life expectancy is accompanied by an increasing number of old people. People who are at present over the age of 65 account for 13 per cent of the population and will, depending on the population projection alternative used, account for 25 per cent by the year 2030. Even without a notable drop in mortality in the next few decades, there will be a clear increase in the number of old people.

The majority of the present population of working age is over the age of 40. During the next two decades the largest part of the working population will be in the oldest age-group. This will naturally reflect on the labour market. The oldest age-groups of the working population are not as highly educated as the younger, smaller age-groups. The changes in the working life are often first perceived as a need for new skills and education.

FINLAND/LA FINLANDE

IV.- POPULATION POLICY

The Finnish population policy does not comprise a separate sector in the area of the social development policy, for there has never existed a government organ especially for the affairs of the population policy. Several actions undertaken to improve living conditions have been performed by other sectors of the social development policy.

The industrial structure of Finland underwent a quick change from an agrarian society into an industrial and service society. In 1950 nearly half of the population earned its living from agriculture, today the proportion is only 10 per cent. In addition, Finland is a sparsely populated country, which has had effect on the decisions concerning social development policy.

Measures which clearly relate to the population policy are often connected to family policy, social policy, health policy and housing policy. In addition, various acts on regional policy have been issued in order to control migration.

No attempt has been made to influence fertility, i.e the population growth. On the other hand, several acts relating to the family policy favour families with children. These acts are assumed to affect indirectly the decisions which the parents make on the size of the family.

Maternity welfare and the child benefit system have existed for long in Finland. The rate of women in the labour force is the highest in the western world, but several new acts make it easier for women in the labour force to have children.

It is possible for families to get a housing loan with liberal conditions, the amount of the loan depends on the size of the family. Furthermore, the economic burdens of the families are eased with various taxation measures.

The reforming of the Abortion Act at the beginning of the 1970s abolished illegal abortions and liberalized the content of the act. Nevertheless, the number of abortions is not high, because the public health service provides instruction on birth control. At the beginning of the 1980s the maternity allowance was increased, which made fertility rise temporarily.

REFERENCES

Central Statistical Office.- *Vital Statistics 1750-1990.*

Central Statistical Office.- *Population in Finland : Past, Present, Future.* Helsinki, 1987.

Central Statistical Office.- "The Population Of Finland", *A World Population Year*, Monograph. Hameenlinna, 1975

L'URSS/The USSR
Anatole VICHNEVSKI

D'après le dernier recensement, l'URSS comptait au 12 janvier 1989, 286 700 000 d'habitants.

Des 15 républiques fédérées constituant à cette date l'URSS, 6 se trouvent en Europe (Ukraine, Biélorussie, Moldovie, Lituanie, Lettonie, Estonie), 8 en Asie (presque tout le Kazakhstan à l'est du fleuve Emba, 4 républiques de l'Asie Centrale, 3 républiques de Transcaucasie) et une, la R.S.F.S.R., couvrant de vastes étendues dans les parties européenne et asiatique de l'Eurasie. La partie européenne de l'URSS (à l'ouest du versant Est de l'Oural et au nord des fleuves Emba, Kouma et Manytch), couvre 24 % du territoire de l'URSS et 53 % du territoire de l'Europe. D'après le recensement de 1989, son territoire était peuplé de 189 millions d'habitants, soit 66 % de la population du pays et 28 % environ de la population d'Europe.

La population de l'URSS est extrêmement diversifiée dans sa composition nationale, linguistique et religieuse. Le pays compte plus de 100 nationalités dont l'effectif varie de plusieurs dizaines de millions à des milliers voire des centaines de personnes. Les Russes (145 200 000), un des groupes ethniques les plus importants de la planète, représentent la moitié de la population en URSS, les Ukrainiens (44 200 000) plus de 15 %. Les autres nationalités sont moins nombreuses mais il y en a plus de 20 qui comptent plus de 1 million de personnes. Au moment du recensement de 1989, les plus nombreux étaient les Ouzbeks (16 700 000) et les moins nombreux les Estoniens (un peu plus de 1 million).

Par sa langue, la majorité de la population appartient au groupes des langues slaves (70,3 %) et turques (17,3 %), mais il y a aussi plusieurs millions de représentants des langues balte, germanique, romane, arménienne, iranienne, finno-ougrienne, khartvélienne et daghestanaise.

Par leurs traditions religieuses les chrétiens dominent (orthodoxes pour l'essentiel mais il y a aussi des partisans du monophysisme, des catholiques et des protestants). Ensuite, viennent les musulmans à prédominance sunnite, une minorité des musulmans confesse le shiisme (les Azerbaïdjans, les Kurdes, les Talychs, les Tates). Il y a aussi des représentants du judaïsme et du bouddhisme.

L'immense diversité sociale et culturelle des peuples de l'URSS, les particularités de leur destin historique et la spécificité régionale des processus économiques et sociaux influent sur tous les aspects de la vie du pays y compris, bien sûr, son développement démographique. Les traits principaux de ce développement au XXème siècle sont déterminés par les processus de la modernisation de la société soviétique, qui se sont étalés sur des dizaines d'années. Les plus importants d'entre eux sont pour nous la transition démographique et épidémiologique ainsi que l'urbanisation. Leur évolution, le début et la rapidité avec lesquels ces étapes principales sont franchies, les mécanismes de comportement au moyen desquels se réalisent les transformations démographiques sont différents selon les peuples et les régions du pays.

Bien que les processus de modernisation essentiels se soient déployés pour la plus grande partie de la population de l'URSS dans la première moitié du XXème siècle, ils ont aussi connu un développement assez intensif dans la période de l'après-guerre. Ils ne sont pas encore achevés aujourd'hui et il est, apparemment, beaucoup plus important que pour la plupart des autres pays de les connaître pour comprendre les réalités démographiques de l'URSS de ces 40-50 dernières années.

I.- ACCROISSEMENT DE L'EFFECTIF DE LA POPULATION

Après la fin de la Seconde Guerre mondiale, la population de l'URSS a augmenté relativement vite mais dès les années 60 on observe un ralentissement de sa croissance. Ce ralentissement ne s'est stabilisé que dans les années 80 (tableau 1).

Dans l'ensemble, la population a augmenté de 62 % en 40 ans. Vu le peu d'importance de la migration extérieure, l'accroissement de la population est défini presque exclusivement par son accroissement naturel. Au cours de la période intensive de la transition démographique de la fin du XIXème siècle à la fin des années 1950, le rythme d'accroissement naturel était relativement élevé. Le taux d'accroissement dans les années "normales" de cette période dépassait, en règle générale 1,7 %, bien que pendant les années de guerre et de cataclysmes sociaux, il ait baissé brusquement réduisant même parfois l'effectif de la population.. Dès la fin des années 50, on observe une baisse rapide des taux d'accroissement naturel qui oscillent depuis vingt cinq ans entre 0,8 et 1 % par an (figure 1).

TABLEAU 1.- EFFECTIF DE LA POPULATION DE L'URSS ET SES CHANGEMENTS

Années	Effectif de la population à la fin de la période (millions)	Accroissement pour la période (millions)	Taux annuel moyen d'accroissement (p. mille)
1950	178,5		
1950-1960	212,4	33,9	17,5
1960-1970	241,7	29,3	13,0
1970-1980	264,5	22,8	9,1
1980-1990	288,6	24,1	8,8

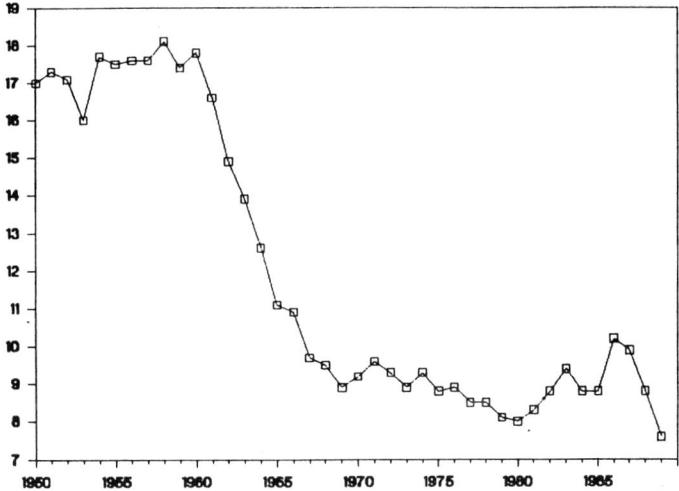

Figure 1.- Taux d'accroissement naturel de la population de l'URSS

Le taux net de reproduction de la population de l'URSS par rapport aux autres pays européens est relativement élevé. Au cours de la période de l'après-guerre, il n'a jamais été inférieur à 1 et n'a été inférieur à 1,1 que quelques années (à la fin des années 70 et au début des années 80). Toutefois cet indice moyen dissimule de grandes différences territoriales. Le taux net de reproduction de la population urbaine est inférieur à 1 depuis déjà 30 ans. Presque toutes les régions européennes (Ukraine, Biélorussie, Lituanie, Lettonie, Estonie), la RSFSR en entier se trouvent à la limite du remplacement des générations. Les taux moyens de l'Union se maintiennent relativement élevés grâce aux républiques asiatiques surtout les républiques d'Asie Centrale où le taux net approche 2 ou est supérieur à 2.

L'accroissement de la population par régions du pays est extrêmement inégal. La population de la plus grande république, la RSFSR a augmenté de près de 1,5 fois ; toutes les républiques européennes à l'exception de la Moldova présentent une croissance moindre. Par ailleurs, la population de toutes les républiques asiatiques, à l'exception de la Géorgie, a plus que doublé en 40 ans et celle de l'Ouzbékistan, du Tadjikistan et de la Turkménie a plus que triplé.

L'évolution de l'effectif de la population de l'Union et de ses parties dépend de l'accroissement naturel et de la migration. Ces deux processus se sont modifiés tout au long du XXème siècle et, notamment, dans la période de l'après-guerre.

II.- LA FECONDITE

Jusqu'au milieu des années 1920, l'URSS appartenait au nombre des pays à très haute fécondité. A la fin du siècle passé le taux de natalité dans la partie européenne de la Russie dépassait 50 pour mille ; il était de 44 pour mille à la veille de la Première Guerre mondiale, et ce niveau s'est rétabli en 1926 pour accuser une baisse régulière dès la seconde moitié des années 20. En 1950, le taux de natalité est passé à 26,7 pour mille et a continué à baisser. La baisse était due pour l'essentiel à la réduction de la fécondité légitime (figure 2) ; ce processus en URSS ne s'accompagnait pas, à l'encontre des autres pays européens, du perfectionnement des méthodes de planification de la famille. Encore aujourd'hui le nombre des avortements est très élevé chaque année ; il était de 7 millions en 1989 contre 5,1 millions de naissances).

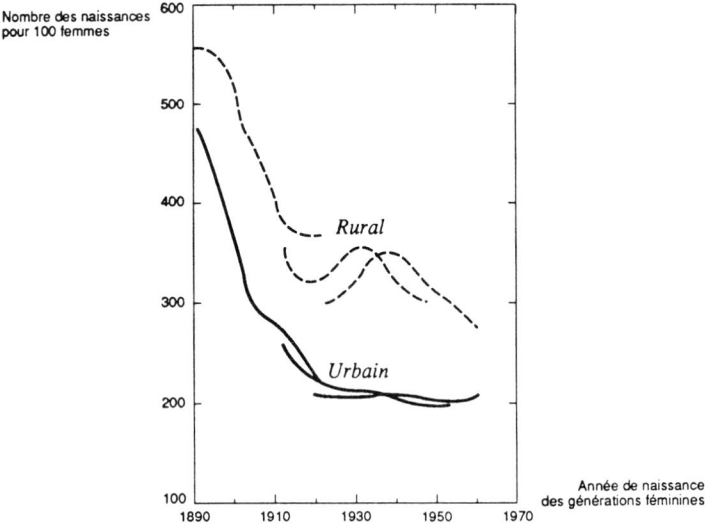

Figure 2.- Fécondité des femmes mariées selon la génération.

Les changements survenus au cours des 30 dernières années dans l'indice synthétique de fécondité montrent une stabilisation graduelle du niveau de fécondité dans l'ensemble de l'URSS. La baisse constante au milieu des années 60 a fait place à des oscillations autour d'un indice relativement stable - près de 2,4 naissances par femme (figure 3). N'oublions pas cependant que les indices moyens de l'Union sont constitués par les indices républicains entre lesquels existent des différences immenses - de l'ordre de 2 - 3. On ne peut parler d'une stabilisation relative du niveau de fécondité que dans le cas des républiques dont la transition démographique est déjà achevée pour l'essentiel. Mais là aussi, on ne peut exclure l'apparition d'une tendance à une nouvelle baisse de la fécondité. Dans les républiques où l'on n'observe pas encore une baisse de la fécondité ou bien où elle est en pleine expansion, on ne peut s'attendre, dans un avenir proche, qu'à une baisse considérable des indices.

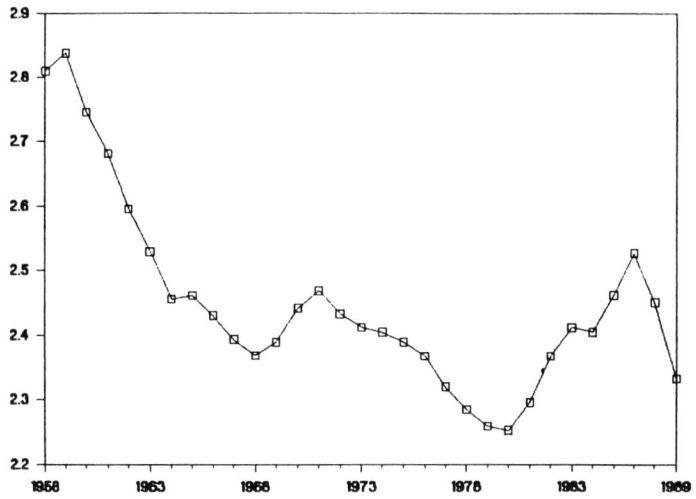

Figure 3.- Indice synthétique de fécondité

III.- LA MORTALITE

Les premières évaluations authentiques de l'espérance de vie (et encore seulement dans la partie européenne du pays) se rapportent à la fin du siècle dernier et montrent que la transition démographique en Russie n'en était qu'à ses débuts. Toutefois, au XXème siècle, surtout dans les années 20-50, les processus de transition connaissent un développement intense et, à la fin des années 50, l'espérance de vie par rapport à la fin du siècle passé, a doublé (tableau 2). Cela s'explique par la baisse de la mortalité à tous les âges, mais le rôle essentiel a été joué par la réduction de la mortalité infantile et jusqu'à l'âge de 5 ans. Dans les années 60, la réduction de la mortalité et l'élévation de l'espérance de vie a fait place à une stagnation et à l'apparition dans certains cas d'indices montrant des tendances opposées.

Les statistiques soviétiques de la mortalité surtout en Asie Centrale et dans certaines autres régions ne sont pas tout à fait fiables. Ce n'est pas un hasard si l'espérance de vie dans les républiques telles que le Tadjikistan ou l'Azerbaïdjan est plus élevée, selon les données officielles, que, par exemple, en Estonie, ce qui contraste avec le niveau de la mortalité infantile (cf. Annexe). La dynamique peu favorable de ces dernières décennies peut être liée à un enregistrement plus complet des décès. Néanmoins, les spécialistes estiment que dès le milieu des années 60, la situation réelle s'est aggravée, en particulier en ce qui concerne l'élévation de la mortalité infantile et de la mortalité dans d'autres groupes d'âges notamment chez les hommes à l'âge actif.

TABLEAU 2.- ESPERANCE DE VIE DE LA POPULATION DE L'URSS (EN ANNEES)

Années	Les deux sexes	Hommes	Femmes
1896-1897	32,3	31,3	33,4
1926-1927	44,4	41,9	46,8
1938-1939	46,9	44,0	49,7
1958-1959	68,6	64,4	71,7
1964-1965	70,4	66,1	73,8
1978-1979	67,9	62,5	72,6
1980-1981	67,7	62,3	72,5
1989	69,5	64,6	74,0

L'élévation de l'espérance de vie à la naissance ne s'est pas seulement arrêtée mais elle a fait place à une baisse qui a atteint son point le plus bas au début des années 80. Puis un changement de la situation s'est produit. En 1987, les indices se sont considérablement améliorés, l'espérance de vie a augmenté de plus de deux ans sans atteindre cependant le niveau du milieu des années 60 (qui est peut être, il est vrai, quelque peu exagéré, en raison d'un enregistrement incomplet). Après 1987, on observe une nouvelle baisse de l'espérance de vie.

Aujourd'hui, l'URSS accuse un retard sur les pays développés en ce qui concerne l'espérance de vie et présente des taux de mortalité moins favorables dans tous les groupes d'âge. On peut très bien voir les tendances décrites sur l'exemple de la mortalité infantile : d'une part, une baisse très forte au cours du XXème siècle, et de l'autre, une stagnation dans les années 70-80 ; le niveau actuel est de 3-4 fois supérieur à celui des pays à faible mortalité (figure 4).

La baisse de la mortalité et l'élévation de l'espérance de vie sont intimement liées à la transition épidémiologique, aux changements profonds, dans la structure de la pathologie médicale et des causes des décès. En URSS comme dans les autres pays, les causes d'origine exogène qui provoquent un grand nombre de décès à des âges plus jeunes, font place pour l'essentiel à des causes dépendant, en premier lieu, des facteurs endogènes et qui présentent, en règle générale, un danger pour les personnes âgées. Pour le moment, la transition épidémiologique n'est pas achevée en URSS, la structure des causes des décès reste archaïque. La probabilité pour un nouveau-né de mourir au cours de la vie d'un cancer, maladie typique pour les personnes âgées, est relativement basse en URSS alors qu'est élevée, au contraire, la probabilité de mourir de maladies infectieuses ou de l'appareil digestif, de traumatismes, qui sont moins liées à l'involution de l'organisme humain avec l'âge.

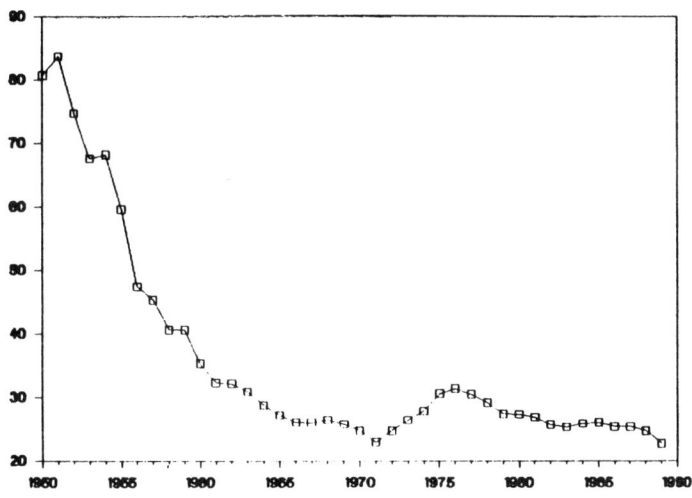

Figure 4.- Taux de mortalité infantile

Mais les différences essentielles se retrouvent dans les courbes par âge d'extinction de nombreuses causes importantes. En URSS les décès par suite de maladies infectieuses et de l'appareil digestif, de maladies de l'appareil respiratoire, de tumeurs, d'accidents, d'autres causes, sont concentrées, à la différence de la plupart des pays européens, dans les groupes d'âge plus jeunes, souvent même parmi les enfants, ce qui fait que l'âge moyen des décès dus à ces causes est plus bas.

IV.- STRUCTURE DE LA POPULATION PAR SEXE ET PAR AGE

La pyramide des âges de la population de l'URSS (figure 5) est marquée par les conséquences des événements catastrophiques de l'histoire soviétique au XXème siècle.

La déformation de la partie supérieure de la pyramide révèle la baisse brusque de la natalité et l'élévation de la mortalité au cours des deux dernières guerres mondiales - avec une rupture des proportions normales des sexes due aux pertes de guerre de la population masculine -, de la famine et des répressions des années 30. La partie inférieure de la pyramide parle en faveur d'une époque plus calme. Elle reflète nettement la baisse de la fécondité qui a suivi l'essor de l'après-guerre, ce que l'on peut considérer comme un résultat naturel de la transition démographique.

Le contour général de la pyramide montre que la population de l'URSS vieillit constamment en raison essentiellement de la baisse de la fécondité. Selon les données des recensements d'après-guerre, le rapport des trois grands groupes d'âge a beaucoup varié (tableau 3). Le processus du vieillissement a fait des progrès surtout dans la partie européenne de l'URSS, où la zone de fécondité faible s'est formée depuis assez longtemps. La part des personnes âgées de 60 ans et plus est supérieure à 14-16 %. Dans les républiques asiatiques où s'est maintenu jusqu'à ces derniers temps une fécondité élevée, la population reste pour le moment jeune, la part des personnes âgées ne dépassant pas 6-8 %.

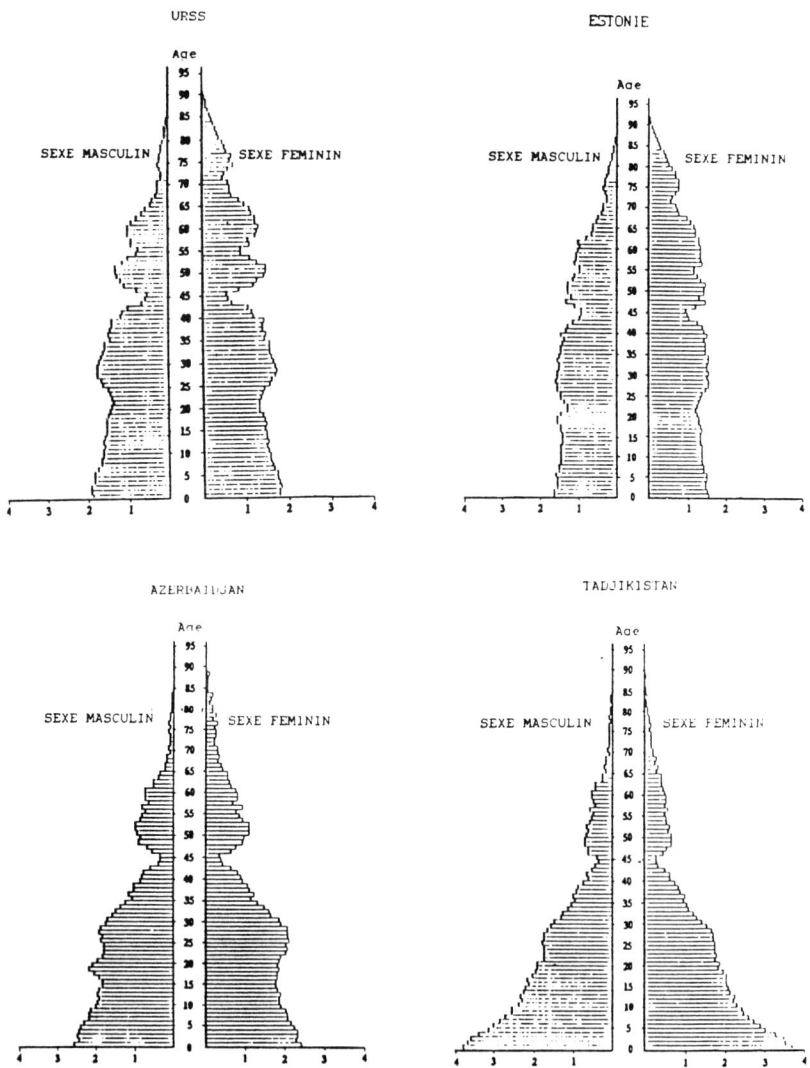

Figure 5.- 1989 Pyramide des âges de la population de diverses républiques d'URSS

TABLEAU 3.- STRUCTURE PAR AGE DE LA POPULATION DE L'URSS (%)

	1959	1970	1979	1989
0-19 ans	37,4	38,2	34,2	33,2
20-59 ans	53,1	50,0	52,9	52,6
60 ans et plus	9,4	11,9	12,9	14,2

V.- LA MIGRATION

La seconde Guerre mondiale a provoqué des déplacements de population en Europe ; les citoyens de l'URSS ont également participé par divers canaux à ce mouvement à travers les frontières de l'Etat. Toutefois, dans la période de l'après-guerre la participation de l'URSS aux migrations internationales a été minime ; c'étaient pour l'essentiel des immigrés, surtout Arméniens, qui se rapatriaient. L'émigration n'existait pour ainsi dire pas et ne joua pas de rôle important sur l'accroissement de la population du pays. La situation ne s'est modifiée qu'à la fin des années 80 avec un courant important d'émigration de l'URSS. En 1987 on comptait 39 000 départs, 108 000 en 1988 et 235 000 en 1989.

Par contre, la migration à l'intérieur du pays dans la période d'après-guerre a été très intense. Elle était formée de deux types de déplacement qui s'entrecroisaient - entre la ville et la campagne et entre les régions de l'URSS.

Les processus de l'urbanisation, qui ont connu des rythmes intenses, ont attiré un courant important de population dans les villes. Rien qu'en 1961-1990, l'accroissement de la population urbaine par migration, s'est élevé à près de 40 millions de personnes (tableau 4). La plus grande migration dans les villes en chiffres absolus se rapporte à la seconde moitié des années 70, et en chiffres relatifs à la seconde moitié des années 60. Le déplacement de la population vers les villes modifiait rapidement le rapport entre la population urbaine et rurale. Dès 1960, la population urbaine a augmenté de 2,7 fois alors que la population rurale s'est réduite de plus de 10 %. La réduction continue de la population rurale a commencé en 1964 et était surtout intense au début des années 70 (à cette période la population rurale se réduisait de 0,9 % par an). En conséquence la part de la population urbaine en URSS est passée de 39 % en 1950 à 66 % en 1990. C'était surtout la population des grandes villes qui augmentait très vite. Entre les recensements de 1959 et de 1989, le nombre des villes à population dépassant le million d'habitants est passé de 3 à 23 et le nombre de leurs habitants de 10,5 millions à 41,4 millions. Le potentiel de migration de la population rurale s'est peu à peu épuisé sur la plus grande partie du territoire de l'URSS et la migration vers les villes s'est arrêtée. C'est ce que l'on ne peut pas encore dire de l'Asie Centrale et de certaines autres régions où la transition démographique et l'urbanisation ont débuté plus tard et qui se trouvent actuellement à des stades antérieurs. Le potentiel de migration de la population rurale est ici immense et continue à grandir. Actuellement, il se réalise peu en raison de la faible mobilité de la population rurale et de la force d'attraction insuffisante des villes locales où la population elle-même connaît des rythmes élevés d'accroissement naturel. Mais cela ne durera pas. Une très forte migration vers les villes de la population autochtone de l'Asie Centrale, du Kazakhstan, de l'Azerbaïdjan, aura lieu dans un proche avenir.

TABLEAU 4.- ACCROISSEMENT MIGRATOIRE DE LA POPULATION URBAINE DE L'URSS

	1961-1965	1966-1970	1971-1975	1976-1980	1981-1988
En milliers de personnes	6 371	8 093	8 266	5 963	8 928
Sur 1 000habitants urbains (en moyenne par an)	11	12	11	7	5

De grandes modifications ont eu lieu ces 30 dernières années dans la migration interrégionale. A partir du milieu des années 50 et jusqu'au milieu des années 70 environ, toutes les républiques se divisaient nettement en deux groupes - pays de départ et pays d'accueil (tableau 5). Se rapportaient au premier groupe la RSFSR, la Biélorussie, la Géorgie et l'Azerbaïdjan (auxquels se sont joints dans la première moitié des années 70 le Kazakhstan et la Kirghizie) et au second - toutes les autres républiques. Le reflux de la population de la RSFSR a joué un grand rôle par son importance. En vingt ans - du milieu des années 50 au milieu des années 70 - le solde négatif de la migration était ici de 2,3 millions d'habitants, ce qui a conditionné dans une grande mesure le solde positif dans de nombreuses autres républiques. Le reflux de la population de la RSFSR s'effectuait, pour l'essentiel, vers les régions centrales de la Russie et de la Sibérie.

TABLEAU 5.- SOLDE MIGRATOIRE PAR GRANDES REGIONS DE L'URSS (EN MILLIERS DE PERSONNES)

	1951-55	1956-60	1961-65	1966-70	1971-75	1976-80	1979-88
RSFSR	160	- 1 015	- 522	- 598	- 195	725	1 767
Ukraine, Biélorussie, Moldovie	- 629	255	54	367	173	- 137	89
Pays baltes	- 15	60	136	152	130	101	248
Transcaucasie	65	- 14	- 28	- 21	- 23	- 166	- 639
Asie centrale	- 19	198	261	197	109	- 244	- 850
Kazakhstan	489	597	407	24	- 261	- 414	-784

On assiste au milieu des années 70 à un changement des tendances au niveau de la migration inter-républicaine. On voit apparaître et se développer, d'une part, un solde positif de la migration en RSFSR et, d'autre part, un solde négatif de la migration dans toutes les républiques de l'Asie Centrale et le Kazakhstan (au Kazakhstan et en Kirghizie dès la première moitié des années 70, comme nous l'avons déjà noté). On assiste également à un reflux brusque de la population de Transcaucasie. La plupart de ceux qui partaient étaient des représentants de la population non autochtone des régions citées alors que la population autochtone restait peu mobile.

ANNEXE

DIFFERENCIATION REGIONALE DES PROCESSUS DEMOGRAPHIQUES (URSS ET TROIS REPUBLIQUES TYPIQUES - POST-TRANSITOIRE, TRANSITOIRE ET PRE-TRANSITOIRE), 1989

	URSS	Estonie	Azerbaïdjan	Tadjikistan
Natalité				
Taux de natalité (pour mille)	17,6	15,4	26,4	38,7
Indice synthétique de fécondité	2,34	2,22	2,76	5,08
Part des naissances des trois premiers rangs dans le chiffre total des naissances (%)	88,0	92,8	86,1	62,2
Nombre d'enfants vers l'âge de 35 ans dans la cohorte des femmes nées en 1955	2,06	1,90	2,63	4,31
Mortalité et espérance de vie				
Espérance de vie				
Hommes	64,6	65,8	66,6	66,8
Femmes	74,0	75,0	74,2	71,7
Mortalité infantile	22,7	14,7	26,2	43,2
Reproduction de la population				
Taux d'accroissement naturel (pour mille)	7,6	3,7	20,0	32,3
Taux net de reproduction	1,096	1,047	1,267	2,290
Part de la population à l'âge de :				
0-19 ans	33,2	29,4	42,7	53,3
20-59 ans	52,6	53,8	49,5	40,6
60 ans et plus	14,2	16,8	7,9	6,1
Migration				
Solde migratoire interrépubliques sur 1 000 habitants de la république (1979-1988)	-	36	- 41	- 23
Solde migratoire dans les villes pour 1 000 habitants urbains (1979-1988)	5	5	- 6	- 2
Solde migratoire des campagnes pour 1 000 habitants ruraux (1979-1988)	- 9	- 9	- 3	1
Part de la population urbaine (1990, %)	66,0	71,6	53,8	32,2

Poland / La Pologne
Jerzy Z. HOLZER

I.-THE POPULATION OF POLAND UNTIL THE SECOND WORLD WAR

Poland regained independence in 1918 after 123 years (1795-1918) of captivity. Polish provinces were annexed by Prussia, Russia and Austria in 1795 and so the whole country was partitioned between the neighbouring powers. After 20 years of independence, Poland was invaded by Germany and the Soviet Union in 1939. The occupation of Poland lasted for five years and in 1945 the country once again regained its independence, within the now existing boundaries. Therefore Poland, or even more precisely the Polish territories, has frequently changed its territorial and even more distinctly its ethnic unity since the beginning of the XXth century. (graph 1.)

GRAPH 1.- POLISH TERRITORIES IN HISTORY

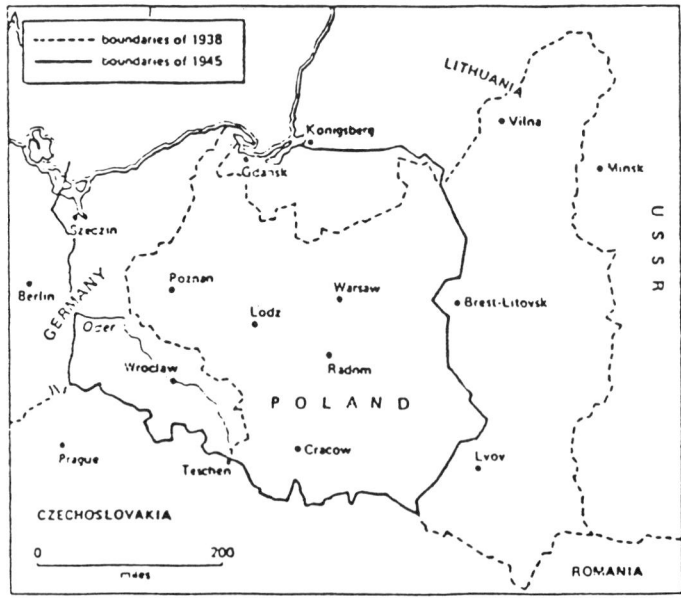

Poland. 1809-1918

Poland since 1945

POLAND / LA POLOGNE

It would be possible to trace the population changes by selected variables eg. ethnic or territorial definition. An alternate solution would be to seek the evaluation of the recorded change in terms of the actual population evolution irrespective of territorial and national shifts. The first approach would yield results more relevant to the question of the movement of the Polish population stricto sensu and the second in terms of change in the de facto population within the historically relevant Polish boundaries. This second alternative has been chosen in our presentation.

The description of demographic processes at the beginning of the XXth century in Poland has been estimated on the basis of the country's boundaries as of 1919, ie. after the First World War (Versailles Treaty).

The total population of Poland amounted to 25.1 million on the 1st of January 1919 and reached 35.3 million at the beginning of the Second World War in August 1939. Population increased by 10.2 million over almost 21 years with population density increasing from 70 inhabitants per square km in 1921 to 90 in 1939.

TABLE 1.- POPULATION, DENSITY, URBANISATION AND VITAL RATES IN THE POLISH TERRITORIES.

Year	Population (millions)	per sq. km.	Percent urban	Births	Deaths	Natural increase	Infant mortality
			Area 388.6 thousand square kilometers				
1900[a]	25106	65	19.6	44.0	25.5	18.5	210
1921	27177	70	24.6	32.8	20.9	11.9	*
1931	32107	83	27.4	30.2	15.5	14.7	142
1938	34849	90	30.0	24.6	13.9	10.7	140
			Area 311.7 thousand square kilometers				
1946	23640	76	34.0	26.2	10.2	16.0	119.8
1960	29795	95	48.3	22.6	7.6	15.0	54.8
1970	32658	105	52.3	16.6	8.1	8.5	33.4
1977	34850	111	57.4	19.1	9.0	10.1	24.5
1980	35735	115	58.7	19.5	9.9	9.6	21.3
1989	37963	122	61.4	14.8	10.0	4.8	15.9

a. rough estimate
Source: statistical and demographic yearbooks, CSO, Warsaw.

At the 1931 census 68.9% of the population declared Polish as their mother tongue, 10.1% Ukrainian, 8.6% Yiddish or Hebrew, 6.9% Russian or Bielorussian and 2.3% German. No differentiation of population processes among minorities has been reported; however some estimates give evidence that they existed. That is the reason why longitudinal analysis of demographic data in Poland is limited, due to territorial and national changes.

1) Fertility

At the beginning of the century a very high fertility was registered in the Polish territories. Fertility was highest in the 25-29 and 30-34 age groups but the 20-24 age group and the 35-39 group also showed very high levels. At the beginning of the century the TFR was 6.2 children per woman.

During the following 30 years a significant drop in fertility was observed in all age groups. At the beginning of the 1930s age-specific fertility rates were relatively low in the older age groups. The peak of fertility was still in the age group 25-29. The TFR was 3.5 children per woman (2.2 and 4.1 in urban and rural areas respectively).

TABLE 2.- AGE-SPECIFIC FERTILITY RATES AND TFRs OF WOMEN IN POLAND (POLISH TERRITORIES)

	Live births per 1000 women aged						TFR		
Years	15-19	20-24	25-29	30-34	35-39	40-44	45-49	T	U	R
1900-01	34	208	315	308	226	121	33	6.2	-	-
1931-32	25	145	189	164	118	53	10	3.5	2.2	4.1
1950-51	39	196	210	158	110	38	4	3.8	3.2	4.1
1960-61	45	198	162	100	56	21	2	2.9	2.3	3.6
1970-71	30	168	133	72	36	11	1	2.3	1.8	3.0
1980	33	180	136	69	29	8	1	2.3	1.9	2.9
1989	31	168	125	60	25	6	0	2.1	1.8	2.5

Source: Statistical Yearbooks CSO, Warsaw and authors calculations

2) Mortality

The crude death rate decreased from ca. 26 per 1000 at the beginning of the century to 13.7 in 1939. During this period infant mortality dropped by a third. Due to incomplete registration, infant mortality is underestimated prior to 1940 (table 1). However the presented changes may show the correct picture, assuming that incompleteness was the same throughout the period under consideration.

The only life tables calculated before the Second World War relate to the years 1931-1932 (table 3). Expectation of life at birth was 48.2 years for males and 51.4 years for females.

It is worth noting that the female expectation of life at age 30 was higher than for males by only 5.5%, whereas at age 0 it was higher by 6.6% and at age 60 by 10.2%. This indicates that mortality of females at childbearing age was high.

TABLE 3.- EXPECTATION OF LIFE IN 1931-1932

Age	Males			Females		
x	0	30	60	0	30	60
e_x	48.2	36.0	13.7	51.4	38.0	15.1

Source: 1931-1932 life tables, Statistical Yearbook 1939, p. 51

3) Migration

The period between the two world wars was characterised by relatively high seasonal immigration and emigration. Unfortunately data for the years 1919-1925 are not complete. It is however estimated that in the period 1927-1938 more than 0.8 million Poles left Poland as emigrants : around 380 000 to European countries (mainly France and Belgium) and around 400 000 to other parts of the world (mainly Argentina, Canada, Palestine and the USA).

4) Effects of the Second World War

Poland had relatively the highest war losses among the countries that took part in the anti-Nazi coalition in the Second World War (table 4).

TABLE 4.- LOSSES OF SELECTED EUROPEAN COUNTRIES

Country	in thousands	per 1000 pop.
U.S.S.R	20.000	103
Poland	6.028	220
Yugoslavia	1.706	108
Greece	558	70
The Netherlands	200	22
France	653	15
Great Britain	368	8

Source: Polska wsrod krajow europejskich 1950-1970, "Statystyka Miedzynarodowa", No. 7/1971, p. 166, GUS, Warsaw

It is worth emphasizing that 123 000 soldiers and 521 000 civilians were killed or died in military action. The rest of the 6 million losses was due to extermination (camps, prisons, ghettos, etc.). The cited data for Poland are currently under revision.

The population number of pre-war Poland in 1939 compared with the number in 1945 shows a difference of ca 16 million persons. This means that apart from the 6 million killed by the Nazis, around 10 million persons "disappeared" or changed country of residence. All these changes had an impact on the age-sex structure of the population.

II.- POPULATION OF POLAND FROM THE SECOND WORLD WAR

Data for the contemporary period refer to the borders that were established in 1945 ie. after the Second World War (figure 1). Poland became a one-nation country with a very low share of minorities (under 5%).

In 1977 population reached the pre-war size of 34.9 million inhabitants; it has been permanently growing since and has passed 38 millions in 1990. Poland is still the sixth country in terms of population in Europe and whichever variant of the available forecasts is taken, this position will be maintained in the logically predictable future.

1) Recent fertility trends

After the Second World War pre-war changes in the fertility age-pattern continued, leading to maximum fertility occurring in the 20-24 age group (table 2.). The 25-29 age group still had a relatively high age-specific fertility rate and other age groups presented low fertility. At the beginning of the 1950s the TFR was 3.8 children per woman (3.2 and 4.1 in urban and rural areas respectively).

The pattern of age-specific fertility rates is the same in 1989 as at the beginning of the 1960s, but at a much lower level. The TFR was equal to 2.1 children per woman (1.8 and 2.5 in urban and rural areas respectively). On the national scale the TFR reached the niveau below replacement level in 1989.

Since the beginning of the 1930s a systematic fall in fertility rates is observable - in urban as well as in rural areas. But since the mid 1960s TFR in urban areas has always been below replacement level. While in 1960 the TFR in urban areas was 2.4, in 1965 it was only 1.9 and in 1989 1.8 children per woman. TFR was at its lowest with 1.7 in 1970.

POLAND / LA POLOGNE

The fertility survey of females in Poland - Inquiry of Maternity 1984 - confirmed that for the procreational decisions in the period under study, emotional /subjective/ factors were of greater importance than economic ones. This statement is in agreement with the hypothesis that on the grounds of the existing socio-economic crisis and also with the prospects of long standing difficulties (particularly for young couples) the significance of a family as a basic social cell and a source of satisfaction increases.

The family formation process was subject to further changes, due to shifts in birth schedule and shortening of intervals between marriage and the first and successive births. Paid Maternity Leave was of considerable consequence at the beginning of the 1980s. As a result of devaluation of currency and a constant increase in living costs the importance of this stimulus declined with time.

For both rural and urban areas, the model of a family with two or three children became the decidedly dominating one. This is the result of long-term changes in the fertility model in Poland.

Responses of surveyed women did not enable a sole prevailing family pattern, common for all the country to be distinguished. About equal shares of women considered two and three children (respectively: 43.9% and 41.2%) to be the "ideal" number. Age, place of residence (urban/rural areas) and education were the main attributes differentiating the views.

Rural women preferred the family pattern with three and - to a lesser extent - with two children. Therefore, there is a tendency to reject the large family pattern, which was typical of the generation of mothers of the surveyed females.

Demometric analysis showed that the motivation factors were most distinctive for second and third birth. There the decisions were most rational, in the sense of definition and justification of the attitudes towards the pattern and process of family formation.

2) *Recent changes in mortality*

Crude death rate reached the lowest level of 7.3 per 1000 in 1966. Due to changes in age-specific mortality rates and mainly due to the ageing process of the population the rate reached 10 per thousand in 1989. Moreover, in recent years mortality has increased in the productive male population in urban areas.

The mortality pattern is typical of developed countries. The lowest level of mortality is around 10-11 years of age. The three main causes of death are: cardio circular diseases; neoplasms; accidents. However the level of age-specific mortality rates is much higher than in other developed countries. It is worth emphasizing that 11% of the Polish territory which is inhabited by 33% of the total population is situated in a polluted area.

Expectation of life at birth reached the highest value of 66.9 years at the beginning of the 1980s and decreased to 66.8 years in 1989 (table 5). At the beginning of the 1960s expectation of life at age 60 was 15.8 years; it decreased to 15.4 years in 1989.

Expectation of life for females reached 75.5 years at birth and 19.9 years at age 60. The decrease in male expectation of life at age 30 over recent years is a sign of deterioration in health conditions. Poland belongs to the few countries in Europe where one may observe a decrease in expectation of life.

TABLE 5.- EXPECTATION OF LIFE (1952-1989)

Period	Males at age			Females at age		
	0	30	60	0	30	60
1952-53	58.6	38.9	14.7	64.2	43.0	17.3
1960-61	64.8	41.1	15.8	70.1	45.5	18.6
1970-72	66.8	40.7	15.5	73.8	46.5	19.3
1980-81	66.9	40.1	15.7	75.4	47.6	20.3
1985-86	66.9	39.5	15.3	75.3	47.2	19.9
1987	66.8	39.4	15.3	75.2	46.9	19.8
1988	67.2	39.6	15.5	75.7	47.3	20.1
1989	66.8	39.3	15.4	75.5	47.1	19.9
urban	66.6	39.0	15.1	75.1	46.7	19.6
rural	67.0	39.8	15.9	76.1	47.8	20.4

Source: Statistical Yearbook 1990, p. 56, GUS, Warsaw, 1990.

The gap between age-specific mortality rates of the two sexes has continued to increase over time. Mortality is many folds higher for males than for females: 2-4 times for cardio-circular diseases in the age groups 20-70 years; 2 for cancer in age groups 50-80; 5-8 times for accidents in age groups 20-60.

A very important decrease in infant mortality occurred over the time under consideration (table 1). However, the value of the infant mortality rate in 1989 calculated according to WHO recommendations would be 19 per thousand (3 times as high as in the Scandinavian countries).

3) Recent migrations

The main migration streams up to 1990 were connected with settlement in the Western and Northern territories which were recovered after the Second World War and with the periods of high industralization and urbanization.

TABLE 6.- INTERNAL MIGRATION, 1951-1989

	1951-1955	1956-1960	1961-1965	1966-1970	1971-1975	1976-1980	1981-1985	1986-1989
Total in thousands	6905	6718	5031	4324	4271	4662	3661	2520
Inflow to :								
- Urban area	3793	3169	2433	2212	2465	2996	2270	1581
- Rural area	3112	3549	2598	2112	1806	1666	1391	939
Balance in migrations in urban area								
- in thousands	+628	+420	+503	+698	+938	+1067	+686	+546
- per 1000 pop.	+11.6	+6.3	+6.7	+8.5	+10.4	+10.6	+6.4	+6.0

Source: Statistical Yearbook of Poland

The periods 1951-1957 and 1966-1980 have witnessed the highest inflow to urban areas (table 6). The share of female inflow was 51-53% throughout the time under consideration. The current situation is characterized by a much lower number of persons taking part in the movement (in 1986-89 it was 2.7 times lower than in 1951-55) and a very low balance of inflow to urban areas, both in absolute and relative terms. The slow down in internal migration is due to the economic recession. At the beginning of the 1990s, 62% of the population lived in towns.

International migration was at an extremely low level until 1956 (table 7). The whole period after 1956 was characterised by a much higher emigration than immigration. Moreover, the existing data show only the number of persons who left the country with an immigration visa, yet after 1981 a significant proportion of the population (estimated around 0.8 million) left the country for a temporary stay abroad and have not, and probably will not, return. The growing unemployment in the country creates the need to seek jobs abroad.

TABLE 7.- IMMIGRATION TO AND EMIGRATION FROM POLAND IN 1951-1989

Years	Immigration	Emigration in thousands	Balance
1951-55	16.6	17.9	-1.3
1956-60	261.1	359.5	-98.4
1961-65	13.9	119.5	-105.6
1966-70	10.4	104.3	-93.9
1971-75	8.2	83.7	-75.5
1976-80	8.1	142.0	-133.9
1981-85	6.7	120.0	-113.3
1986-89	8.0	128.3	-120.3

Source: Own calculations on the basis of data from Demographic Yearbooks

4) *Some aspects of population reproduction*

Three aspects of population reproduction in Poland have to be taken into consideration when discussing the current situation. First, the age structure of population is characterised by serious irregularities (previous baby "booms" and "busts") and, secondly the population is undergoing rapid ageing. The population aged 60 years and over has grown from around 8% in 1950 to 14% in 1990, and is expected to reach 17% in the year 2000 and ca 22% in 2030. The population aged 70-79 and 80 and over will double in the next 40 years.

The expected increase in the number of aged persons calls for long term population policy goals, such as the creation of favorable conditions to induce fertility at replacement level and to keep in proportion the relations between the three basic age groups.

Special efforts should be undertaken by Government to reverse the declining fertility trend and make TFR reach replacement level. This problem refers to general economic conditions of the country and particulary to housing conditions and the standard of living.

Thirdly, special efforts have to be undertaken to reduce mortality. Positive results of those efforts would speed up the ageing process of population. This is yet another argument in favour of long term population policy goals. (Paragraph 3.1.) An alternative solution may be seen in the opening of boundaries for significant international migration connected with the creation of the common European labour market.

III.- SOME ASPECTS OF POPULATION POLICY

1) The concept of strategic population strategy

The present stage of demographic development, significant irregularities in the age-sex distribution, declining fertility and stagnant (or growing) mortality, high level of internal migration, call for a new concept of strategic goals in population policy. This has recently been formulated by demographers in four points:

a) To create favorable conditions for maintaining fertility at least at replacement level;

b) To ensure improvements in various qualitative features for the population, such as its living conditions, cultural and health levels, by various means, including a halt in the degradation of health, changes in diet, improved general education, promotion of health education;

c) To influence internal migrations, by not only stimulating the direction of inflows, but also the direction of outflows by making small investments in rural areas to give that population employment opportunities and to slow down the depopulation of rural areas; and

d) To organize a proportion of international migration, for instance, by making arrangements with foreign governments as to how and under what conditions Polish nationals can work in respective countries.

Strict population policy has never been introduced in Poland. Several social and economic policy measures promoted population growth. Five periods may be distinguished in post-war Poland, each with a different approach to population problems.

In the immediate post-war period population policy was based on:

- combating symptoms of extermination of population,

- pro-natalist attitudes,

- repatriation and re-emigration policy.

The second period started in 1956 with the changing climate of political and social aspects of life. The anti-natalist climate became predominant until the end of the 1960s. The third period started at the beginning of the 1970s, with the new pro-natalist climate and some measures, based on accelerated economic growth.

The fourth period began at the end of the 1970s and can be linked with a decline of economic growth. Social and economic aspects of population well-being became the only problem taken into consideration. Due to fund shortages, only special target groups were considered to be under the state umbrella (pensioners, single parents).

The most important economic measures directly connected with population policy might be summed up as follows. The monthly family allowance for children up to 19 years of age were stable for a long period of time, but in recent years due to inflation it has been raised several times. Family allowance reduces discrepancies in the standard of living between families with and without children; however the level of allowance is not adequate to needs. Disabled children and persons over 75 years of age or whose state of health calls for constant care are paid special nursing allowances.

Maternity leave was extended for the last time in the middle of 1972 to 112 days with the birth of the first child and to 126 days with the birth of the second or next child. Unpaid child-care leave (for mother or father) was extended from 1 to 3 years in 1972 and then changed in 1981 to leave with alimony benefits if the child was under four years of age.

M.Latuch and others (1989) wrote: "In addition to the child allowances, other important changes in the principles of child care leave were introduced in 1981. They consist, among other things, in:

- an extension of child care leave to include the child's father, if the mother cannot take leave and agrees to the father taking this leave,

- a reduction of the period of employment qualifying the parent for a child care leave from 12 to 6 months,

- the possibility of taking care of a sick or crippled child even if he is more than 4 years old but not more than 10 years of age,

- the obligation of a place of work to grant child care leave if it is divided in parts,

- the period of child care leave is not deducted from the years of continuous employment and does not affect seniority rights."

Finally it is worth mentioning the free system of education, from primary to university level.

2) Contraception and abortion

There are difficulties in estimating the contraceptive prevalence since only some results of sampling surveys exist. According to the 1972 and the 1977 surveys, the withdrawal and rhythm methods were most common (accordingly 38% and 33% in 1972 and 25% and 41% in 1977) as well as the condom (17% and 19%). Use of the pill showed an important increase from 4% to 10% among the respondents, use of the IUD only from 1% to 2%.

The 1984 sample survey covered 7161 women who had delivered a child in 1984. Among them 49% in urban areas and 60% in rural areas did not use contraceptives or any other method to prevent a pregnancy. The most common methods were withdrawal (27.5% in urban and 25.6% in rural areas), rhythm (27.6% and 21.4%), thermal method (11.6% and 5.0%). The condom was used by 8.3% of respondents in urban areas and 4.5 in rural. The pill was used by 4.7% of respondents in urban areas and 2.3% in rural.

To sum up, it is easy to state that the use of contraceptives, especially the modern ones, is not very widespread. The Catholic church permits only natural family planning methods and the Polish population is under the influence of the Church.

A law legalizing and liberalizing abortion was adopted in Poland in 1956. This law provided that a pregnancy at an early stage may be interrupted, free of charge in health facilities for women who are insured and thereby are entitled to free medical care. This provision was introduced in three cases:

   1) on medical recommendation,

   2) due to pregnant woman's difficult living conditions (social reasons),

   3) a well grounded suspicion that the pregnancy is an effect of rape (criminal offence).

Practically, in the case of social reasons an oral statement about the woman's living conditions justified medical interruption. The ratio of reported number of abortions to the number of live births has decreased from 1:2 to 1:3. The actual number of abortions was higher, due to unrecorded abortions treated outside the public health services (in private clinics).

The Minister of Health introduced in 1989 some restrictions to limit the number of abortions in the country. Three independent opinions (two medical doctors and one physiologist) are needed to obtain permision for abortion.

The Sejm (the lower chamber of the Polish Parliament) is currently (Spring 1991) discussing a new law which would severely restrict the availability of induced abortion. This law has already been approved by the Senat (the higher chamber of the Polish Parliament) in October 1990. This new proposal permits induced abortion only if the pregnant woman's life is threatend and if the pregnancy is the result of a crime, presumably rape or incest. In all other cases punishment of medical doctors inducing abortion is envisaged (up to 3 years imprisonment).

The project of the new law was introduced by the group of Catholic parliamentarists. There is a strong "pro-life" movement lobbying for the approval of the abortion restricting law. This movement is vocal with propaganda against the use of modern contraceptives, especially those which are considered to be abortefacients (IUD).

REFERENCES

Demographic and Statistical Yearbooks, CSO, Warsaw.

Holzer, Jerzy Z. (1980). Demografia. Warsaw, PWE.

--------- (1982). The Final Report from the Head of the Keynote Problem No.11.5 "Optimization of Demographic Structures and Processes in the Polish People's Republic, Monografie i Opracowania, ISiD SGPiS (Warsaw) No. 4/111.

--------- (1989) Czy w Polsce potrzebna jest polityka ludnosciowa, (Is a population policy needed in Poland?), Studia Demograficzne (Warsaw), No.1/83, pp3-11

--------- (1990) Perspektywy demograficzne Polski do roku 2030. (Demographic Perspectives of Poland till 2030). Monografie i Opracowania, ISiD SGPiS, (Warsaw) No.6/300.

Latuch M., Dzienio K., Drzewieniecka K., (1989). Poland's Poulation Policy, 1945-1988, Oeconomica Polona No.9, pp.253-277.

Okolski, Marek, (1988) Reprodukcja Ludnosci a Modernizacja Spoleczenstwa, Polski Syndrom. (Population Reproduction and Modernization of Society, Polish Syndrom). Warsaw, KIW

La Tchécoslovaquie/Czechoslovakia
Zdenek PAVLIK

I.- LA SITUATION DEMOGRAPHIQUE JUSQU'A 1950

1) Aspects spécifiques de l'évolution démographique passée avant 1918

La République Tchécoslovaque a été constituée après la première guerre mondiale ; elle a été formée de trois parties dont l'histoire était différente - les pays Tchèques, la Slovaquie et la Rhuténie - quoique leur langue soit similaire, spécialement la langue tchèque et la langue slovaque. La Ruthénie a appartenu à la Tchécoslovaquie seulement vingt ans ; pendant la deuxième guerre elle était occupée par la Hongrie et a été cédée à l'Union Soviétique. Elle ne sera pas traitée dans le cadre de la population Tchécoslovaque ci-dessous. La Ruthénie comptait 605 000 habitants en 1921 et 725 000 en 1930 sur un territoire de 12 617 km^2.

Des traditions différentes ont influencé l'histoire démographique des parties tchèque et slovaque de la Tchécoslovaquie et c'est pourquoi il est légitime de les traiter séparément. Les pays tchèques furent nettement plus proches de l'évolution démographique de l'Allemagne, et la Slovaquie, de la Hongrie et de la Pologne. Cette situation reflète des différences dans le développement économique. Dans les pays tchèques, la révolution démographique a suivi la révolution industrielle ; en Slovaquie, ces deux phénomènes ont eu lieu presque en même temps. Dans les pays tchèques, la révolution industrielle s'est étendue des années 1830 au tournant du 20ème siècle ; l'industrie était déjà largement développée. En Slovaquie, jusqu'à la deuxième guerre mondiale il existait seulement des manufactures d'importance limitée. Soixante-dix pour cent de la population active travaillait dans l'agriculture en Slovaquie contre 43 % dans les pays tchèques. La scolarisation universelle introduite dès le milieu du 18ème siècle par Marie-Thérèse devint obligatoire en 1869. Ce fait fut d'une importance primordiale pour le commencement de la révolution démographique. La situation en Slovaquie (partie intégrante de la Hongrie jusqu'en 1918) fut beaucoup moins favorable, surtout dans l'enseignement primaire (en langue maternelle). Il s'ensuit que le processus de l'urbanisation fut plus développé dans les pays tchèques pendant tout le 19ème siècle.

a) La transition démographique

Les changements dans le domaine de la mortalité précèdent souvent ceux dans le domaine de la fécondité. Le 19ème siècle se caractérise par une baisse de la mortalité dans la plupart des pays européens (tableau 1). L'Allemagne et les pays tchèques représentent l'Europe Centrale et la Slovaquie, l'Europe de l'Est et du Sud. Le taux brut de mortalité est un indice objectif de la mortalité au XIXème siècle, la structure par âge étant assez semblable dans les divers pays.

Le taux de mortalité infantile fut presque stable (autour de 250 à 265 %) dans les pays tchèques pendant le XIXème siècle (tableau 2).

Dans le cas des pays tchèques, ces taux semblent peu sous-estimés et sont bien au-dessus de ceux de la France ; des taux au-dessus de 250 % existèrent probablement au XVIIIème siècle en France. Les données pour la Slovaquie sont plutôt des estimations.

On estime l'espérance de vie à la naissance à près de 30 ans au début XIXème siècle. Ensuite, la mortalité a baissé (tableau 3) et cette baisse a continué pendant la première moitié du XXème siècle. L'espérance de vie a doublé dans les pays tchèques en l'espace de quatre générations féminines depuis la moitié du XIXème siècle.

La baisse de la natalité (tableau 4) est le second aspect de la transition démographique et cet indice distingue les pays tchèques et la Slovaquie en Europe.

Les indices synthétiques de fécondité confirment les tendances présentées ci-dessus et montrent une baisse de la fécondité dans les pays tchèques pendant la deuxième moitié du XIXème siècle, et leur décalage avec la France (tableau 5). La fécondité était plus élevée dans les pays tchèques en 1910-1911 qu'en France au milieu du siècle précédent.

LA TCHECOSLOVAQUIE/CZECHOSLOVAKIA

TABLEAU 1.- TAUX BRUT DE MORTALITE (POUR 1000 HABITANTS)

Période	Pays Tchèques	Slovaquie	Allemagne	France	Suède
1785-1790	31,9				
1791-1800	33,3				
1801-1810	37,7			27,8	28
1811-1820	32,4			26,1	26
1821-1830	28,3			25,2	24
1831-1840	30,8			24,8	23
1841-1850	30,3		27,5[a]	23,3	21
1851-1860	28,5			23,9	22
1861-1870	29,9			23,6	20
1871-1880	29,0	39,9	28,2[b]	23,7	18
1881-1890	28,9	34,1		22,1	17
1891-1900	25,8	29,6		21,5	16
1901-1910	22,3	25,1	19,9[c]	19,4	15
1911-1918	19,7	21,8		18,3[d]	15

a) 1841-1845
b) 1871-1875
c) 1901-1905
d) 1911-1913
Sources : "Demograficka prirucka", FSU, Praha, 1982.
"La population de la France", CICRED, Séries, 1974.
Z. Pavlik.- "Nastin populacniho vyvoje sveta", Praha, 1964.

TABLEAU 2.- TAUX DE MORTALITE INFANTILE (POUR 1000)

Période	Pays Tchèques	Slovaquie	France
1821-1830	254		188
1831-1840	261		174
1841-1850	258		159
1851-1860	251		172
1861-1870	264		177
1871-1880	261		177
1881-1890	264		166
1891-1900	249	259[a]	164
1901-1910	215	200	132
1911-1918	192	182[b]	124[c]

a) 1891-1892
b) 1910-1912
c) 1911-1913
Sources : voir tableau 1.
J. Sveton.- "Obyvatelstvo Slovenska za kapitalismu", Bratislava, 1958.

TABLEAU 3.- ESPERANCE DE VIE A LA NAISSANCE (EN ANNEES)

Période	Pays Tchèques		Slovaquie		Epoque	France	
	M	F	M	F		M	F
1869-1880	33,1	36,9	31,5	33,2	1817-1831	38,3	40,8
1899-1902	38,9	41,7	36,5a)	38,4	1840-1859	39,3	41,0
1909-1912	42,8	45,9	40,2b)	42,8b)	1861-1865	39,1	40,6
					1877-1881	40,8	43,4
Génération							
1875	36	40			1898-1903	45,3	48,7
1900	44	49			1908-1913	48,5	52,4
1910	49	54					

a) 1900-1901
b) 1910-1911
Sources : voir tableau 1.
Pour les générations, calculs au Département de démographie, Univ. Charles.

TABLEAU 4.- TAUX BRUT DE NATALITE (POUR 1 000)

Période	Pays Tchèques	Slovaquie	Allemagne	France	Suède
1785-1789	44,2			38,3b)	
1790-1799	43,3			36,9	
1800	42,1				
1801-1810	42,2			32,0	30,9
1811-1820	43,6			31,9	33,4
1821-1830	40,3			31,0	34,6
1831-1840	38,5			29,0	31,5
1841-1850	38,3		36,1	27,4	31,1
1851-1860	38,3		35,5	26,3	32,8
1861-1870	38,2		37,2	26,4	31,4
1871-1880	38,8	44,0a)	39,1	25,4	30,5
1881-1890	37,1	43,5	36,8	23,9	29,1
1891-1900	35,8	41,1	36,1	22,1	27,1
1901-1910	32,5	37,3	32,9	20,6	25,8
1911-1914	27,4	33,7			
1915-1918	14,2	18,1	14,0c)		22,0d)

a) 1870-1880
b) 1780-1789
c) 1917-1918
d) 1911-1920
Sources : Voir tableau 1.

LA TCHECOSLOVAQUIE/CZECHOSLOVAKIA

TABLEAU 5.- INDICES SYNTHETIQUES DE FECONDITE (NOMBRE MOYEN D'ENFANTS PAR FEMME)

Période	Pays Tchèques	Période	France
1857-1858	5,06	1856-1860	3,46
1869-1870	5,14	1866-1870	3,50
1880-1881	5,06	1876-1880	3,45
1890-1891	4,92	1886-1890	3,12
1900-1901	4,85	1896-1900	2,90
1910-1911	4,03	1906-1910	2,60

Sources : V. Srb et M. Kucera.- "Vyvoj obyvatelstva ceskych zemi" v XIX, stoleti, Statistika a demografie I, Praha, 1959.
P. Festy.- "La fécondité des pays occidentaux de 1870 à 1970", INED, Paris, 1979.

Les indices de fécondité de Coale montrent une évolution parallèle entre les pays tchèques et la Slovaquie, vis-à-vis de la fécondité générale (tableau 6). La fécondité illégitime était peu importante.

TABLEAU 6.- INDICES DE FECONDITE DE COALE

Année	Pays tchèques			Slovaquie		
	I_f	I_g	I_h	I_f	I_g	I_h
1857	0,400	0,720	0,114			
1869	0,406	0,713	0,100			
1880	0,404	0,699	0,093	0,453	0,613	0,097
1890	0,391	0,678	0,098	0,453	0,604	0,115
1900	0,393	0,655	0,096	0,456	0,627	0,102
1910	0,328	0,549	0,082	0,416	0,594	0,097

Notes : I_f = indice de fécondité générale ;
I_g = indice de fécondité légitime ;
I_h = indice de fécondité illégitime.
Sources : L. Fialova, Z. Pavlik et P. Veres.- "Fertility Decline in Czechoslovakia During the Last Two Centuries" Population Studies, 44, 1990, 89-106.

L'évolution de l'effectif de la population (tableau 7) est régulièrement croissante dans les pays tchèques. Il apparaît une relative stagnation en Slovaquie dans la deuxième moitié du XIXème siècle, mais les données pour la Slovaquie sont de moins bonne qualité jusqu'au milieu du XIXème siècle.

La comparaison des taux d'accroissement total et naturel (tableau 7) suggèrent une émigration importante pendant toute la période considérée. En pays tchèque, l'émigration a réduit d'un tiers l'accroissement naturel. La situation était encore plus grave en Slovaquie et certaines années, le taux d'émigration a dépassé 0,5 %.

TABLEAU 7.- POPULATION (EN MILLIERS) DES PAYS TCHEQUES ET DE LA SLOVAQUIE, ET TAUX D'ACCROISSEMENT TOTAL ET NATUREL (%)

Date	Pays tchèques			Slovaquie		
	Population	Total	Naturel	Population	Total	Naturel
1787	4 355			1 945		
1840	6 369	0,72	0,8	2 355	0,36	
1860	7 256	0,65	0,8	2 400	0,09	
1869[a]	7 617	0,54	0,83	2 482	0,37	
1880[a]	8 222	0,69	0,82	2 478	- 0,01	0,41
1890[a]	8 665	0,52	0,85	2 595	0,46	0,94
1900[a]	9 372	0,78	1,00	2 783	0,69	1,15
1910[a]	10 079	0,72	1,02	2 917	0,47	1,22

a) au 31 décembre
Notes : Données et taux pour les frontières actuelles ;
La République Tchèque = 78 861 km^2 ; La Slovaquie = 49 009 km^2.
Sources : Demograficka prirucka, 1982.

2) Les effets des deux guerres mondiales

Les pertes militaires totales de l'Autriche-Hongrie pendant la première guerre mondiale sont estimées à 1,1 million dont 30 % pour les pays tchèques et 8 % pour la Slovaquie ; soit environ 400 000 pour toute la Tchécoslovaquie, ce qui correspond assez bien aux estimations basées sur les résultats des recensements en 1910 et 1921.

Les pertes totales, en Europe pendant la deuxième guerre mondiale, furent beaucoup plus élevées que celles de la première guerre, mais pas pour la Tchécoslovaquie occupée par les Allemands. Les pertes militaires sont estimées à 46 000, mais il faut ajouter les pertes des Juifs presque totalement éliminés du territoire de la Tchécoslovaquie : ils étaient au nombre de 250 000 en 1930. Les Romanis (Tziganes) connurent le même destin, surtout dans les pays tchèques. Les pertes parmi les Allemands de Tchécoslovaquie furent aussi assez élevées ; on les a estimées à 200 000.

LA TCHECOSLOVAQUIE/CZECHOSLOVAKIA

a) L'entre-deux-guerres

Les années vingt ont vu la fin de la transition démographique (tableau 8) dans les pays tchèques. La Slovaquie a connu une fécondité assez élevée jusque dans les années cinquante. Cette situation est confirmée par les indices synthétiques de fécondité (tableau 11). Entre les deux guerres, la fécondité dans les pays tchèques fut plus basse qu'en France. On ne dit pas par hasard que le comportement démographique tchèque est similaire à celui de la France. L'indice synthétique de fécondité fut le plus bas dans les pays tchèques en 1936 (1,664) ; le plus bas niveau de cet indice en Slovaquie fut 2,796 en 1937. Le taux brut de natalité a commencé de se relever dès avant la deuxième guerre mondiale.

La mortalité enregistre une baisse continue pendant la période envisagée. Néanmoins, les taux de mortalité infantile (tableau 9) montrent une situation peu favorable surtout après la première guerre mondiale. Le retard de la Slovaquie en ce domaine est bien évident. L'espérance de vie à la naissance (tableau 10) a dépassé 60 ans pour les deux sexes seulement après la deuxième guerre mondiale dans les pays tchèques.

TABLEAU 8.- TAUX BRUTS DE MORTALITE ET NATALITE (POUR 1000)

Période	Pays Tchèques		Slovaquie	
	Natalité	Mortalité	Natalité	Mortalité
1920-24	24,1	15,6	35,4	19,5
1925-29	20,4	14,3	31,1	18,0
1930-34	17,5	13,2	26,7	15,4
1935-39	15,2	13,0	22,7	13,8
1940-44	19,5	13,9	24,9	15,4
1945-49	21,3	13,5	25,3	14,0
Sources : Demograficka prirucka, 1982.				

TABLEAU 9.- TAUX DE MORTALITE INFANTILE (POUR 1000)

Période	Pays Tchèques	Slovaquie
1920-24	154,3	173,0
1925-29	132,8	173,4
1930-34	114,1	158,6
1935-39	96,3	142,3
1940-44	89,2	145,8
1945-49	86,7	130,2

Sources : Demograficka prirucka, 1982.

TABLEAU 10.- ESPERANCE DE VIE A LA NAISSANCE (EN ANNEES)

Années	Pays Tchèques		Slovaquie	
	M	F	M	F
1920-22	47,6	50,8	43,4	45,1
1929-32	53,7	57,5	48,9	50,9
1937	56,6	60,5	51,8	54,7
1947	60,3	65,0		
1949-51	62,2	67,0	59,0	62,4
Générations				
1930	58	64		
1950	64	71		

Sources : Demograficka prirucka, 1982 ; pour les générations le calcul est fait au Département de démographie, Univ. Charles.

TABLEAU 11.- INDICES SYNTHETIQUES DE FECONDITE (NOMBRE MOYEN D'ENFANTS PAR FEMME)

Période	Pays Tchèques	Slovaquie	France
1920	2,96	4,28	
1921-1925	2,75	4,52	2,42
1926-1930	2,22	3,71	2,30
1931-1935	1,85	3,08	2,16
1936-1937	1,68	2,80	2,07[a]
1946-1949	2,98	3,21	3,00

Sources : Demograficka prirucka, 1982 ;
P. Festy.- "La fécondité des pays occidentaux de 1870 à 1970", INED, Paris, 1979.
Calculs : Département de démographie, Univ. Charles.

LA TCHECOSLOVAQUIE/CZECHOSLOVAKIA

L'évolution de l'effectif de la population témoigne de grandes perturbations avant et après la deuxième guerre mondiale (tableau 12). Après la première guerre mondiale, on a enregistré une émigration importante contrebalancée par un accroissement naturel élevé en Slovaquie. Les migrations internationales sont présentées dans le tableau 13.

TABLEAU 12.- POPULATION DES PAYS TCHEQUES ET DE SLOVAQUIE (EN MILLIERS)

Date	Pays Tchèques		Slovaquie	
Année	accroissement	%	accroissement	%
31.12.1910	10 079		2 917	
15.2.1921	10 010	- 0,07	2 994	0,26
1.12.1930	10 674	0,66	3 324	1,07
1938	10 877	0,24	3 726	1,43
1944	11 109	0,35	3 484	- 1,12
1945	10 693	- 3,82	3 459	- 0,72
1946	9 523	- 11,59	3 392	- 1,96
1947	8 765	- 8,29	3 399	0,21
1948	8 893	1,45	3 446	1,37
1949	8 892	- 0,01	3 447	0,03
1950	8 925	0,37	3 463	0,46

Sources : Demograficka prirucka, 1982.

TABLEAU 13.- MIGRATIONS INTERNATIONALES

Date	Pays tchèques			Slovaquie		
	Emigration	Immigration	Migration nette	Emigration	Immigration	Migration nette
1920-24	110 689	50 501	- 60 188	138 196	46 156	- 92 040
1925-29	45 416	12 633	- 32 783	66 577	15 019	- 51 558
1930-34	16 962	6 383	- 10 579	30 600	16 723	- 13 877
1935-38	8 978	2 360	- 6 618	23 103	6 449	- 16 654
1939[a]	48 000	70 000	22 000	64 000	20 000	- 44 000
1945-46[a]	2 807 000	80 000	- 2 727 000	64 000	64 000	0
1947-49	7 688[b]	61 341	53 653	5 134[b]	1 919	- 3 215

Notes : a) Estimations ;
b) Seulement l'émigration légale.
Sources : Demograficka prirucka, 1982.

L'émigration massive des pays tchèques après la deuxième guerre mondiale concerne surtout les Allemands. En Tchécoslovaquie en 1930, il y avait 3,3 millions d'habitants de nationalité allemande. Plusieurs d'entre-eux ont émigré vers l'Allemagne avant la fin de la guerre. 2 256 000 Allemands ont été transférés officiellement en accord avec les autorités d'occupation alliées ; à peu près 200 000 sont restés en Tchécoslovaquie. L'émigration des Tchèques et des Slovaques a recommencé aussi après la guerre.

II.- LA SITUATION DEMOGRAPHIQUE DEPUIS 1950

1) L'évolution de la fécondité

Après la transition démographique, les taux bruts ont beaucoup perdu de leur signification et il est préférable de considérer la fécondité et la reproduction (tableau 14). Le niveau de la fécondité fut plus élevé en France que dans les pays tchèques après la deuxième guerre jusqu'au milieu des années soixante-dix. Après 1970 on a introduit des mesures pro-natalistes en Tchécoslovaquie. La Slovaquie a connu une fécondité encore assez élevée après la guerre mais elle s'est approchée de celle ces pays tchèques tout récemment. La baisse de la fécondité est due aux mères âgées ; la fécondité dans les groupes d'âges 15-19 ans est restée élevée. On peut donc prévoir une poursuite de la baisse de la fécondité dans les prochaines années. La structure par âge de la fécondité a subi des changements importants pendant les trois dernières générations (tableau 15). La fécondité est toujours de plus en plus concentrée dans la première moitié de la période de procréation (avant 30 ans). La différence entre les pays tchèques et la Slovaquie est très marquée mais les variations sont similaires à des niveaux différents.

TABLEAU 14.- INDICE SYNTHETIQUE DE FECONDITE (A) ET TAUX NET DE REPRODUCTION (B)

Période	Pays tchèques		Slovaquie		France
	A	B	A	B	A
1950-54	2,69	1,22	3,54	1,52	2,78
1955-59	2,42	1,12	3,33	1,52	2,69
1960-64	2,22	1,03	2,94	1,37	2,82
1965-69	1,95	0,92	2,56	1,20	2,68
1970-74	2,13	1,02	2,50	1,18	2,36
1975-79	2,34	1,12	2,48	1,18	1,86
1980-84	2,01	0,95	2,28	1,08	1,88
1985-88	1,94	0,92	2,19	1,04	1,83

Sources : Demograficka prirucka, 1982 ;
Calculs : Département de démographie, Univ. Charles.

Si le remplacement de la population est encore assuré en Slovaquie, il ne l'est plus dans les pays tchèques (la République Tchèque) depuis le début des années quatre-vingts.

TABLEAU 15.- TAUX DE FECONDITE GENERALE PAR AGE (P. 1 000)

Age de la femme	Année Pays Tchèques						
	1921	1936	1950	1960	1968	1974	1987
15-19	17,6	14,5	50,2	44,0	45,1	57,2	48,7
20-24	132,5	98,0	187,2	184,6	166,1	213,7	178,3
25-29	185,0	104,2	158,3	115,2	99,2	141,5	102,0
30-34	142,3	66,9	97,7	49,3	40,1	60,1	36,5
35-39	89,5	35,8	53,7	19,7	14,0	17,2	11,1
40-44	36,0	12,4	17,2	5,1	2,9	2,6	1,8
45-49	4,1	1,1	1,4	0,3	0,2	0,1	0,1
15-49	91,6	52,6	80,9	57,6	56,3	79,4	52,4

Age de la femme	Slovaquie						
	1921	1937	1951	1960	1968	1974	1980
15-19	37,3	28,7	54,1	50,5	38,6	44,4	48,2
20-24	237,1	150,6	212,8	226,6	192,0	213,3	204,8
25-29	273,4	154,7	198,9	166,9	132,6	155,7	131,1
30-34	204,3	112,7	136,0	98,4	71,1	72,7	56,0
35-39	163,1	76,3	82,7	52,4	32,8	29,2	18,9
40-44	70,3	32,6	33,0	18,5	9,3	7,0	4,3
45-49	12,2	3,7	3,1	1,5	0,7	0,5	0,2
15-49	147,3	86,3	109,1	93,1	69,1	82,8	77,3

Sources : Demograficka prirucka, 1982 ;
Analyses de l'Office statistique tchèque, 1988.

2) *Nuptialité et divortialité*

Les taux bruts de nuptialité et de divortialité donnent l'image générale d'une stabilité de la nuptialité à un niveau relativement élevé (similaire dans les pays tchèques et en Slovaquie) et d'une tendance croissante du nombre relatif des divorces (tableau 16). La stabilité du niveau de la nuptialité est réalisée grâce au nombre croissant des remariages (près d'un quart dans les pays tchèques en 1986). Néanmoins, la Tchécoslovaquie n'a pas suivi la même tendance que les pays de l'Europe de l'Ouest -des mariages de plus en plus tardifs et de moins en moins fréquents. On ne connaît pas la fréquence de la cohabitation juvénile. L'indicateur conjoncturel de primo-nuptialité est resté à un niveau élevé ; il est passé de 0,92 dans les années soixante-dix à 0,85 dans les années quatre-vingts pour les hommes et il est resté presque autour de 0,9 pour les femmes.

Le niveau de divortialité est à peu près deux fois plus élevé dans les pays tchèques qu'en Slovaquie depuis 1975 (tableau 16) mais l'accroissement est plus prononcé en Slovaquie à partir d'un niveau de départ plus bas. La somme des taux de divortialité par durée de mariage s'est accrue d'à peu près 200 à 350 p. 1 000 mariages dans les pays tchèques au cours des 20 dernières années et de 83 à 145 p. 1 000 en Slovaquie. Malgré le niveau croissant de la divortialité, le mariage a conservé son importance en Tchécoslovaquie.

TABLEAU 16.- TAUX BRUTS DE NUPTIALITE (A) ET DE DIVORTIALITE (B) POUR 1 000 HABITANTS

Période	Pays Tchèques		Slovaquie	
	A	B	A	B
1925-29	9,5	0,44	8,7	0,16
1950-54	8,9	1,16	9,4	0,48
1960-64	8,0	1,45	7,4	0,57
1965-69	8,0	1,83	7,3	0,64
1970-74	9,6	2,38	8,6	0,94
1975-79	9,0	2,56	9,1	1,25
1980-84	7,7	2,76	7,9	1,35
1985-88	7,9	2,94	7,4	1,58

Sources : Demograficka prirucka, 1982 ;
Demografie 1987, 1989.

La proportion d'hommes célibataires dans le groupe d'âges 50-54 ans est restée entre 4,9 % et 5,7 % dans les pays tchèques après 1950 et elle a diminué de 9,9% à 3,5% pour les femmes. La situation en Slovaquie était similaire. Entre les deux guerres mondiales la proportion de naissances hors mariage était de 10 % à 13 % dans les pays tchèques et de 7 % à 9 % en Slovaquie. Cette proportion n'a pas dépassé 8 % en Tchécoslovaquie après 1950. Le niveau élevé de la fécondité illégitime était surtout le fait de la population allemande avant 1939. Une augmentation légère au cours des dernières années ne fait pas attendre de changement plus profond.

3) *Mortalité et vieillissement de la population*

L'évolution de la mortalité après 1950 montre une situation typique des pays après la transition démographique et des anciens pays socialistes. La mortalité infantile baisse, notamment si nous la comparons avec la période précédente, surtout avant la deuxième guerre mondiale. L'espérance de vie à la naissance (tableau 17) connaît une évolution différente avec une amélioration lente pour les femmes et une stagnation à un niveau

LA TCHECOSLOVAQUIE/CZECHOSLOVAKIA

assez bas pour les hommes. On peut mentionner pour comparaison que la mortalité infantile était de 7,5 décès pour 1 000 nouveau-nés en France en 1989 et l'espérance de vie 72 ans pour les hommes et 80,1 ans pour les femmes pour la période 1986-88. Cette comparaison n'appelle pas de commentaire : nous considérons que cette différence traduit les différences de situations non seulement sanitaire mais plutôt sociale et culturelle.

TABLEAU 17.- MORTALITE INFANTILE (P. 1 000) (A) ET ESPERANCE DE VIE A LA NAISSANCE (EN ANNEES (B)

Période	Pays Tchèques			Slovaquie		
	A	B H	F	A	B H	F
1950-54	46,8	64,5	69,3	78,7	62,4	66,2
1955-59	25,1	67,2	72,3	40,5	65,9	70,5
1960-64	19,8	67,5	73,4	26,8	68,2	72,9
1965-69	22,1	66,8	73,5	26,0	67,7	73,3
1970-74	19,7	66,6	73,4	24,6	66,8	73,4
1975-79	18,1	67,1	74,2	22,5	66,9	74,1
1980-84	15,2	67,1	74,2	18,6	66,8	74,1
1985-88	12,1	67,4	74,8	14,7	67,2	75,0
1989	10,0	-	-	13,5	-	-

Sources : Demograficka prirucka, 1982 ; Demografie, 1990.

On peut mentionner encore ici deux points. Le niveau de la mortalité mesuré par l'espérance de vie à la naissance après 1960 est presque le même dans le République tchèque et en Slovaquie. Cependant, la structure par âge est différente. La probabilité de décès est plus basse pour les enfants dans les pays tchèques et pour les personnes âgées en Slovaquie. Ce phénomène n'est pas facile à expliquer. Le second point est la différence entre l'espérance de vie des femmes et des hommes ; elle est de plus de 7 ans en Tchécoslovaquie et de plus de 8 ans en France.

L'espérance de vie à 60 ans depuis 1960 confirme la stagnation et même l'aggravation du niveau de la mortalité pour les hommes (tableau 18). Cependant on note une amélioration depuis 1980, plus nette à 80 ans et pour les femmes. La situation de la mortalité apparaît à nouveau meilleure pour les personnes âgées en Slovaquie.

TABLEAU 18.- ESPERANCE DE VIE A 60 ET 80 ANS (EN ANNEES)

Période	Pays Tchèques				Slovaquie			
	Hommes		Femmes		Hommes		Femmes	
	60	80	60	80	60	80	60	80
1949-51	15,0	5,8	16,9	5,7	16,2	6,1	16,9	6,0
1960-61	15,1	5,1	18,3	5,7	16,6	5,6	18,4	5,9
1970	14,1	5,0	18,0	5,7	15,5	5,4	18,4	5,8
1980	14,3	4,6	18,2	5,6	15,3	5,2	19,0	6,0
1988	14,9	5,6	19,3	6,6	15,3	6,1	19,8	7,3

Sources : Demograficka prirucka, 1982 ;
Office statistique - table de mortalité 1988.

Les différences entre les pays tchèques et la Suède sont présentées dans le tableau 19. La population suédoise n'a pas été affectée par les guerres pendant plusieurs générations ; elle est souvent utilisée pour les comparaisons démographiques. En Suède en 1980, l'espérance de vie à la naissance était de 73 ans et 80 ans pour les hommes et les femmes respectivement ; dans les pays tchèques en 1987, elle était de 67,6 ans et 74,8 ans. La surmortalité était considérable chez les hommes dans tous les groupes d'âges sauf 20-24 ans et 25-29 ans. Les pourcentages les plus élevés se trouvent dans les groupes d'âges 0, 50-54, 55-59 et 60-64 ans. La mortalité est élevée pour les hommes dans les pays tchèques dès l'âge de 40 ans. Pour les femmes, la situation est plus nuancée. Dans quelques groupes d'âges, la situation était même meilleure qu'en Suède, surtout à 10-14 ans et de 20 à 34 ans. Néanmoins, la situation globale est peu favorable et presque la même que pour les hommes.

La conséquence de la transition démographique est le vieillissement de la population. Aussi la proportion des personnes âgées croît (tableau 20). La population de la Slovaquie reste plus jeune que celle des pays tchèques.

TABLEAU 19.- SURMORTALITE DANS LES PAYS TCHEQUES EN 1987 SOUS LA CONDITION DES TAUX DE MORTALITE PAR AGE EN SUEDE EN 1980 (EN %)

Age	Hommes	Femmes
0	71,3	83,0
1-4	33,6	21,5
5-9	15,0	5,3
10-14	55,3	- 21,1
15-19	36,3	11,2
20-24	7,5	- 15,9
25-29	0,2	- 13,8
30-34	17,7	- 11,0
35-39	34,3	9,1
40-44	51,1	- 6,3
45-49	56,5	24,3
50-54	76,7	40,9
55-59	76,8	43,2
60-64	73,7	50,0
65-69	49,7	50,6
70-74	61,4	75,4
75-79	43,2	49,6
80-84	29,6	43,8
85	14,6	22,5
Total	48,0	42,1

Sources : Analyses de l'Office statistique 1987 ;
Calculs : Dép. de démographie, Univ. Charles.

TABLEAU 20 - PROPORTION DES PERSONNES AGEES DE 60 ANS OU PLUS (EN %)

Année	Pays Tchèques		Slovaquie	
	Hommes	Femmes	Hommes	Femmes
1950	11,2	13,8	8,7	11,0
1960	12,8	16,8	9,5	12,3
1970	15,6	20,6	12,5	15,2
1980	14,0	19,7	11,6	14,9
1986	14,4	20,5	12,3	16,4
1988	14,4	20,6	12,4	16,6

Sources : Demograficka prirucka, 1982 ;
Demografie, 1987 ;
Office statistique - structure par âge 1988.

La baisse de la mortalité pour les femmes se traduit par un pourcentage plus élevé de femmes âgées. La proportion autour de 20 % montre déjà un vieillissement assez avancé.

4) Mouvement de la population après la deuxième guerre mondiale

Après la deuxième guerre mondiale, jusqu'en 1950, le niveau de la natalité était fort et celui de la mortalité aussi assez élevé ; l'accroissement de la population était contrebalancé par une émigration massive (Allemands). Le taux annuel d'accroissement est devenu positif en 1950 dans les pays tchèques. La deuxième période, jusqu'à la fin des années soixante, est marquée par la baisse de la natalité et de la mortalité. Celle-ci s'est arrêtée autour de l'année soixante et on a enregistré une stagnation ensuite, sauf chez les femmes. Le taux d'accroissement négligeable entre 1965 et 1970 (tableau 21) est encore en partie dû à l'émigration importante après 1968. Les migrations internationales après 1950 ne sont pas bien connues (les chiffres officiels sont basés sur l'émigration officielle et donc largement sous-estimés). On a estimé que 148 887 personnes manquaient en 1970 sur la base du recensement précédent et du mouvement naturel en Tchécoslovaquie ; cela représente à peu près 1 % de la population totale. On ne peut pas exclure les erreurs du recensement mais l'émigration illégale est probablement la cause de cette différence. La troisième période est marquée par l'augmentation de la fécondité pendant les années soixante-dix. Ce découpage en périodes est surtout valable pour les pays tchèques. Ces périodes ne sont pas tellement évidentes en Slovaquie où les évolutions ont été plus régulières. La dernière période a commencé dans les années quatre-vingts ; elle n'est pas encore finie et elle mène à un remplacement déficitaire de la population.

TABLEAU 21.- POPULATION DES PAYS TCHEQUES ET DE SLOVAQUIE (EN MILLIERS)

Année Population moyenne	Pays Tchèques accroissement	%	Slovaquie accroissement	%
1950	8 925		3 463	
1955	9 366	0,96	3 727	1,47
1960	9 660	0,62	3 994	1,38
1965	9 785	0,26	4 374	1,82
1970	9 805	0,04	4 528	0,69
1975	10 062	0,52	4 739	0,91
1980	10 327	0,52	4 984	1,01
1985	10 337	0,02	5 162	0,79
1989	10 362	0,06	5 276	0,55

Sources : Demograficka prirucka, 1982 ;
Pohyb obyvatelstva.

LA TCHECOSLOVAQUIE/CZECHOSLOVAKIA

III.- LE COMPORTEMENT ET LA POLITIQUE DE POPULATION

Le comportement démographique a connu une révolution au cours des derniers siècles. Les familles et les individus planifient maintenant précisément le nombre de leurs enfants. Ils considèrent de plus en plus l'échec de leurs plans comme un désastre et ils utilisent tous les moyens pour l'éviter. La procréation désirée s'est répandue avec les méthodes de contraception ; quelques-unes étaient connues depuis longtemps. Il est bien évident que l'avortement provoqué est considéré comme la première méthode contraceptive en Tchécoslovaquie. L'évolution de la fréquence des avortements est inverse de celle du niveau de la fécondité.

Le nombre relatif d'avortements est assez élevé en Tchécoslovaquie par rapport à d'autres pays. Le taux brut d'avortements est plus élevé seulement en Union Soviétique et le niveau de la Tchécoslovaquie est comparable à celui de quelques pays d'Europe de l'Est. Les avortements provoqués représentent en Tchécoslovaquie à peu près un quart du nombre total des avortements. L'accroissement imprévu du nombre des avortements dans la période récente peut s'expliquer par l'introduction de la méthode moderne d'avortement en 1987 (mini-interruption) et par le fait que toutes les restrictions furent levées (tableau 22).

TABLEAU 22.- TAUX BRUTS D'AVORTEMENTS (A) (POUR 1 000 HABITANTS) ET NOMBRES D'AVORTEMENTS PAR NAISSANCE (B) (POUR 100 NES VIVANTS)

Période	Pays Tchèques		Slovaquie	
	A	B	A	B
1958-59	7,6	54,0	6,1	26,1
1960-64	8,3	57,4	7,2	34,6
1965-69	8,7	60,0	7,5	41,7
1970-74	8,4	49,9	7,7	40,0
1975-79	7,9	44,1	7,8	37,5
1980-84	8,9	63,8	8,4	45,5
1985-88	15,7	85,4	10,2	61,9

Sources : Demograficka prirucka, 1982 ; Demografie, 1986, 1990.

Les mesures plutôt sociales qu'on peut considérer comme une politique de population, ont une grande tradition en Tchécoslovaquie. Déjà en 1918, encore sous l'empire d'Autriche-Hongrie, des subventions furent accordées aux mères après l'accouchement. Cependant, c'est seulement après la deuxième guerre mondiale qu'on peut parler de mesures pro-natalistes. Le congé maternel fut prolongé à 18 semaines en 1948 ; les allocations aux enfants ont été augmentées plus de huit fois depuis 1945. En 1964 le congé maternel payé a été à nouveau prolongé à 22 semaines, pour les mères non mariées (à 26 semaines et à 35 semaines dans le cas d'accouchements multiples). Des mesures complexes ont été adoptées en 1971, qui consistaient en allocations aux enfants : allocations à la naissance de l'enfant et allocations maternelles aux femmes élevant leurs enfants jusqu'à l'âge de deux ans dans le ménage. En 1973, on a institué des prêts à faible intérêts accordés aux jeunes couples mariés avant 30 ans : chaque enfant atteignant l'âge d'un an ouvre droit à déduction d'une part de ce prêt.

DEUX QUESTIONS EN GUISE DE CONCLUSION

Les mesures de la politique démographique ont-elles été efficaces ? L'accroissement du niveau de la fécondité dans les années soixante-dix est incontestable. Néanmoins, la descendance finale n'a pratiquement pas changé pour les générations en cause. Cela donne à penser qu'il n'y a eu que des changements du calendrier. Les projets des familles ne pourraient pas être affectés par les mesures matérielles sauf à en hâter la réalisation. C'est un effet sûr mais très difficile à quantifier. Le retard d'une naissance comporte toujours le risque que cette naissance n'ait jamais lieu.

La deuxième question n'est pas moins discutable. La loi sur l'interruption artificielle de la grossesse pour des raisons sociales, adoptée en 1957, a-t-elle contribué d'une façon importante à la tendance décroissante de la fécondité ? Cette loi est entrée en vigueur au moment où l'évolution de la fécondité était déjà clairement définie. Les avortements clandestins sont devenus légaux, la mortalité maternelle a pratiquement disparu. Ici aussi, on ne peut pas quantifier l'effet de cette loi mais l'évolution de la fécondité donne à penser que cet effet n'a pas été très important. De plus la fréquence des avortements est très élevée en Tchécoslovaquie. Il est nécessaire de répandre la connaissance de différentes méthodes contraceptives dans la population et de développer l'éducation sexuelle.

Hungary/La Hongrie
András KLINGER

I.- POPULATION DEVELOPMENT FROM THE END OF THE PAST CENTURY UNTIL THE 1940S

The beginning of the demographic transition in Hungary is put by the majority of experts at the last decades of the past century when the decline in birth rates, slow in the beginning and constantly accelerating from the start of this century, began. This means that the demographic transition in the classic sense started - similarly to that in the rest of Central-Eastern European countries - later than in most Northern and Western countries.

The birth rate of 40 per thousand at the turn of the century was already somewhat lower than it had been ten or twenty years before but it was still regarded as extra ordinarily high in international comparison. A continuous and significant decline in fertility happened only during the first decades of the present century. Birth rate drops by 10 per cent between 1900 and 1910 and by a further approximately 30 per cent between 1910 and 1930. The live-birth rate of 14 per thousand which had established by the mid-1930s was already not among the high even by international standards.

A similar significant decrease took place in total fertility rate (TFR). Its value over 5.0 measured at the turn of the century fell back by almost one half during thirty years. From the beginning of the 1930s this value stabilizes but it represents already only about 2.5 children per woman. It is characteristic of the mortality conditions in Hungary that at a TFR of 2.47 net reproduction rate drops below 1.0 in the early 1940s (table 1).

TABLE 1.- THE DEVELOPMENT OF TOTAL FERTILITY RATE (TFR) (CALCULATED FOR 1 FEMALE)

Period	TFR	The extent of the change 1901-1905 = 100.0
1901-1905	5.01	100.0
1906-1910	4.79	95.6
1911-1915	4.23	84.4
1916-1920	2.64	52.7
1921-1925	3.44	68.7
1926-1930	3.02	60.3
1931-1935	2.63	52.5
1936-1940	2.47	49.3
1947-1950	2.57	51.3

In international comparison, mortality conditions in Hungary have never belonged to the favourable ones. The paces of improvement in mortality were also changing in the course of this century. Noteworthy is the significant improvement in mortality which happened in the last decade of the past century when during ten years life expectancy at birth increased by about 7 years for both sexes as against the increase by only 2 - 2.5 years during the decade following the turn of the century. Between 1910 and 1920 the extent of mortality improvement decreases further followed by a spectacular rise in life expectancy at birth between 1920 and 1930. By that time however the decline in the fertility level is also high and, consequently, this period is characterized by a parallel decline in both fertility and mortality. Essentially, the situation was the same between 1930 and 1941 with the difference that both the pace of the fertility decline and the mortality improvement slowed down as compared to the decade before (table 2).

TABLE 2.- THE DEVELOPMENT OF LIFE EXPECTANCY AT BIRTH (YEAR)

Year (Yearly average)	Males	Females
1890-1891[a]	29.62	30.38
1900-1901	37.67	38.54
1910-1911	39.53	41.20
1920	40.19	42.23
1930-1931	48.70	51.80
1941	54.95	58.24

a) In the country's pre-World War II area.

During the last one hundred years the country's population development was uneven. Even population development was prevented, during the last decades of the past century, by the high mortality caused by epidemics, at around the turn of the century, by large-scale emigration and, later, by the military and civil casualties suffered in the two World Wars (table 3).

TABLE 3.- LIVE-BIRTH, MORTALITY AND NATURAL INCREASE RATES*

Year (yearly average)	Live births	Mortality	Natural increase
1881-1885	45.0	33.5	11.5
1886-1890	43.7	32.4	11.3
1891-1895	41.7	31.9	9.8
1896-1900	39.9	26.8	13.1
1901-1905	36.9	25.6	11.3
1906-1910	35.8	24.0	11.8
1911-1915	32.1	22.9	9.2
1916-1920	21.8	21.7	0.1
1921-1925	29.4	19.9	9.5
1926-1930	26.0	17.0	9.0
1931-1935	22.4	15.8	6.6
1936-1940	19.9	14.1	5.8
1941-1945	19.4	16.4	3.0
1946-1950	20.4	12.5	7.9

* Rates for the country's present-day area.

The first official Hungarian population census was taken on December 31, 1869 and, at that time, the population in the present-day area of the country was somewhat over 5 million. As a result of high fertility and of the above-mentioned mortality improvement the growth-rate of the population was highest between 1880 and 1910. At the time of the 1910 population census the size of the population was more than 7.6 million, by 52 per cent more than forty years before. In other words, between 1870 and 1910 the yearly average growth-rate of the population was over 1 per cent. Between 1915 and 1918 - as a result of the military casualties and of the significant fall-out in births - the size of the population dropped by 140 thousand persons, i.e. by 1.8 per cent of the population at that time. In 1919-1920 this loss was somewhat moderated by immigration from the neighbouring countries so that at the time of the 1920 population census the country's population size was about 8 million. During the subsequent decades, mainly as a result of the improvement in mortality, the population increased. On the other hand, between 1941 and 1949, because of the human losses suffered during World War II and of emigration, the population declined also in an absolute sense. At the time of the 1949 population census the size of the population was 9.2 million, by 110 thousand less than in 1941 (table 4).

TABLE 4.- THE DEVELOPMENT OF POPULATION SIZE*

Year	Population size
December 31, 1869	5 011 310
December 31, 1880	5 329 191
December 31, 1890	6 009 351
December 31, 1900	6 854 415
December 31, 1910	7 612 114
December 31, 1920	7 986 875
December 31, 1930	8 685 109
January 31, 1941	9 316 074
January 1, 1949	9 204 799

* Figures for the country's present-day area.

In Hungary, emigration became a mass movement during the last decades of the past century and was the most significant at around the turn of the century. Between 1899 and 1913 nearly 2 million people emigrated from the country's pre-World War I area. 98 per cent of the emigrants left for the United States. Between the two World Wars the number of emigrants dropped significantly.

The huge population movement related to World War II affected several hundred thousand people who were deported, POWs or fled from the country. In the framework of the so-called population exchange after the war several hundred thousand people were settled in from the neighbouring countries and, respectively, settled out to other countries.

On the whole, in Hungary the starting period of the demographic transition in the classic sense, the widening of the difference between the demographic rates and the accompanying swift population growth began not only later but were also of a very short duration. During the first decades of the present century, parallel to the improvement in mortality, fertility declined while the rate of popualtion growth slowed down gradually. As against the population increase by more than 50 per cent during the forty years between 1870 and 1910, during the following forty years between 1910 and 1950 the population size of the country increased by only 21 per cent.

HUNGARY/LA HONGRIE

II.- DEVELOPMENT DURING THE LAST FORTY YEARS

1) Fertility development

During the last decades Hungarian fertility has been characterized by great fluctuations and, since long ago, by a level below simple reproduction.

In the mid-1950 the ban on abortions resulted in a 20 per cent rise in fertility while the ensuing liberalization of abortions as well as the swift and significant socio-economic transformation causing basic changes in the life of the families and women, were accompanied by a serious fertility decline. During the eight years between 1954 and 1962 the value of TFR dropped by 40 per cent. As a result of the introduction of the child-care allowance (ChCA)[1], fertility increased in the second half of the 1960s and the measures with population-related aims taken in 1973 appeared to cause the repetition of the wave of births which had taken place twenty years before. Between 1973 and 1975 TFR rises by 22 per cent and, then, falls back by 28 per cent between 1975 and 1983. The increase in TFR registered in 1985 and the fact that it has dropped since then to the 1983 minimum of 1.72 are attributable to the introduction of child-care pay (ChCP)[2]. In 1989 the value of TFR was 1.78, the preliminary data of 1990 show stagnation (table 5).

TABLE 5.- THE DEVELOPMENT OF TOTAL FERTILITY RATE (TFR) AND OF THE RATES OF REPRODUCTION

Year	TFR (per 1 female)	Gross rates of reproduction	Net
1950	2.62	1.259	1.106
1955	2.82	1.354	1.256
1960	2.02	0.975	0.917
1965	1.81	0.875	0.831
1970	1.97	0.953	0.912
1975	2.38	1.157	1.111
1980	1.92	0.937	0.909
1985	1.83	0.892	0.867
1989	1.78	0.852	0.831

After World War II, the calendar year indicator of net reproduction rate dropped below 1.0 in 1958 at a 2.17 value of TFR. With the exception of the four years 1974-1977, the value of the net reproduction rate has been continuously below simple reproduction level already for thirty years.

---

[1] See the chapter Population Policy.

[2] See the chapter Population Policy.

2) Age specific fertility

By the significant decrease in general fertility during this century the fertility of women of different ages were affected differently. Thus, the present fertility of women aged under 20 years is even higher than it was in the 1920s and their fertility in the 1970s was over the respective value registered at the turn of the century. It is in this age-group that the change is the smallest. At present the fertility of women aged 20-24 years is the same as it was in the late 1930s but it is hardly more than the half of their fertility at the turn of the century. After W W II the fertility of women aged over 25 years has already never reached the respective value between the two World Wars. However, two years in the early 1950s form an exception when, because of the severe ban on abortions, the fertility of women of this age-group increased until or over the respective level in the 1930s (table 6).

TABLE 6.- THE DEVELOPMENT OF AGE SPECIFIC FERTILITY

Year	Age groups					
	15-19	20-24	25-25	30-34	35-39	40-49
Years Live births per 1 000 females of the respective age						
1930	40.9	158.5	151.8	110.7	74.8	15.7
1940	41.1	144.9	134.5	95.8	56.5	12.1
1950	51.5	170.7	141.0	89.2	50.8	10.6
1960	52.5	159.2	105.6	52.9	25.0	3.6
1970	50.0	159.3	110.3	51.4	18.4	2.2
1980	68.0	158.6	100.0	40.9	13.7	1.5
1989	40.8	141.8	110.7	43.9	15.3	1.5

In Hungary, the fertility level of the married women have always been determinant of the changes in the birth movement and in fertility. The proportion of the births out-of-wedlock is not significant, especially in international comparison. It is true, however, that the trend is increasing which becomes particularly evident in the 1980s. Until the early 1980s the proportion of birhts out-of-wedlock was lower than between the two World Wars but the present proportion of about 12-13 per cent is already the highest in the course of this century.

The trends of the average age of mothers may be divided into two well-separable periods : there is a definitely decreasing trend lasting with minor intermissions until 1980 and there is a definitely increasing trend in the 1980s (table 7). The pace of the decrease is especially swift in the 1950s, stopped for some years by the ban on abortions. Even so, between 1947 and 1960 the average age declines by almost 2.2 years which represents a significant rejuvenation of women giving birth.

TABLE 7.- AVERAGE AGE OF MOTHERS AT THE TIME OF THE BIRTH OF THEIR CHILDREN

Year	Average age
1947	27.85
1950	27.27
1955	27.07
1960	25.79
1965	25.60
1970	25.45
1975	25.33
1980	24.64
1985	24.99
1988	25.39

On the whole, between 1947 and 1980, the average age of mothers at the birth of their children decreased from 27.85 years to 24.64 years which represents a rejuvenation by 3.2 years during 33 years.

The increase observed in the 1980s may be explained in several ways. In the early 1980s there was still a decrease in fertility in all age-groups but the average age of women giving birth increased already. This was primarily due to first marriages and, within the marriage, the time of births having been put off. From the mid-1980s the increase in the average age of wowmen giving birth accelerated which, in its turn, was already the consequence of the already mentioned changes in age-specific fertility, namely, that the fertility of the young continues to decline while that of the more "aged" groups increases.

In the trend of completed generation fertility there is already no trace of the great fluctuations in TFR by calendar years. The number of the ultimate descendants of the generations shows a basically decreasing tendency and reaches its minimum value of about 1.9 in generations born in the years of World War II. The extent of the decrease in the course of 15 generations is over 15 per cent.

In generations born after World War II the trend stabilizes with a value between 1.90 and 1.93. It is noteworthy that completed generation fertility is the lowest exactly in the generation of high numbers born in 1953-1954, during the ban on abortions while it increases modestly again in the generations of smaller numbers born from the second half of the 1950s on.

As far as the extent of generation reproduction is concerned we are limited to estimates. If in France simple reproduction in the 1950s and now was and, respectively, is assured by an average 2.2 and 2.1 children per woman, the respective Hungarian value must surely be higher because of the higher mortality in Hungary. Thus, none of the generations processed reached this level, lagging behind it by 10-20 per cent.

TABLE 8.- THE AVERAGE NUMBER OF DESCENDANTS PER 1 000 FEMALES BY BIRTH COHORTS

Year of birth	Until the age of				The average number of ultimate descendants
	- 20	- 25	- 30	- 35	
		years			
1930	307	1 205	1 749	1 970	2 075
1935	336	1 169	1 638	1 875	1 972
1940	348	1 078	1 598	1 832	1 915
1945	295	1 083	1 608	1 826	1 891
1950	345	1 182	1 686	1 859	1 934*
1953	326	1 181	1 645	1 833	1 909*
1955	376	1 203	1 653	1 852	1 927*

* Partly estimated data.

The proportion of women having given birth to at least one child proves that in Hungary the proportion of women living through their lives childless, is low and shows a decreasing tendency (table 9).

TABLE 9.- THE FORMATION OF THE PARITY RATIO BY GENERATIONS OF BIRTH

Year of birth	Of 10 000 females those who have given birth to at least				
	1 (R1)	2 (R2)	3 (R3)	4 (R4)	5+(R5+)
			Children		
1935	9 032	6 382	2 263	915	1 126
1940	9 065	6 458	2 048	740	930
1945	9 002	6 757	1 974	624	619
1950	9 045	7 135	2 050	599*	507*
1955	9 142*	7 137*	1 999*		

* Partly estimated data.

The proportion of women having given birth to at least two children, too, reaches its minimum value of about 64 per cent in generation born in the second half of the 1930s and then shows an almost continuous increase towards over 71-72 per cent. Its value is over 70 per cent in generations born from the late 1940s on. Probably, this proportion is also among the high in Europe.

The proportion of women having given birth to at least three children is decreasing continuously and significantly and reaches its minimum value of 19-20 per cent in generations born in the years of World War II and, then, increases modestly over 20 per cent.

Completed fertility of 4 and 5 order births seems to stabilize after a long and significant decrease, in generations born after World War II, with values around 5-6 per cent, though these are, to a certain extent, estimates.

The parity progression ratio a_1 in generations born after World War II proves that a constantly growing proportion of women with one child have given birth to a second child (table 10). The ratio a_2 shows signs of a stabilization in generations born after World war II. Essentially, the same may be said about the value of a_3, though on the basis of the estimated values, its trend is rather modestly decreasing. Besides, it is to be noted that values of a_2 and a_3 have never reached in generations born after World War II the respective values in generations born between the two World Wars. On the other hand, values of a_0 and a_1 have never been so high.

TABLE 10.- PARITY PROGRESSION RATIO BY GENERATIONS OF BIRTH

Year of birth	A0	A1	A2	A3
1935	903	707	355	404
1940	907	712	317	361
1945	900	751	292	306
1950	904	789	287*	292*
1955	914*	781*	280*	

* Partly estimated data.

3) Mortality

The current level of mortality in Hungary is relatively high, when compared either to other developed countries or to the mortality levels of the 1960s. The crude death rate of 13.7 in 1989 is among the highest in the more developed regions, and the highest in Europe.

Gains in life expectancy at birth have been considerable until the mid-1960s. However, after that there was a slowdown in improvement and later a fast deterioration. The life expectancy at birth of men was highest in 1966 (68.07 years) and of women in 1979 (73.56 years).

While the decline of mortality was continuous until the mid-1960s, an increase in the age-specific mortality rates of men of all age groups between 25 and 64 years started, followed in the early 1970s by the increase in age-specific mortality rates of women.

Infant and child mortality declined continuously although the infant mortality rate of 15.7 p. 1000 in 1989 was still much higher than in most of the developed countries.

Although the mortality levels of younger and middle aged adults are alarmingly high, the mortality of the aged population is determinant of the overall mortality levels. Currently about 77 per cent of all deaths occur at ages over 60 years and about 56 per cent at ages over 70 years.

Mortality decline in the aged females population has been continuous. In the aged male population it declined much more slowly, and since the mid-1960s the mortality rates of men in practically all age groups increased.

Until the 1950s and 1960s, gains in life expectancy have been greater in childhood and young adulthood than in the higher ages, because they were achieved primarily through the reduction of infectious and parasitic diseases. The case of death pattern is by now dominated by endogenous and degenerative diseases, as the proportion of the major causes of death affecting older adults has increased. Consistent with the trend in life expectancies, the survival probabilities have also increased mostly at younger ages. While at the beginning of the century the probability of a newborn boy to survive to age 60 was 0.34 and of a newborn girl 0.36, in 1989 the same probabilities were 0.69 and 0.85, respectively. The increase in the probability of a person aged 60 to survive has been much smaller as shown in table 11.

Considering aging and life expectancies from a different perspective, one notes that the age at which the survivors to that age have an average of 10 years to live has changed relatively little during this century : from 65 to 70 among men and from 65 to 73 among women. Another interesting point is to see what proportion of the population does actually survive to that age. The change then is impressive : 28 per cent of men and 29 per cent of women survived to age 65 in 1900 whereas 46.1 per cent of men survived to age 70 and 63.9 per cent of women to age 73 in 1989.

TABLE 11.- SURVIVAL PROBABILITIES IN HIGHER AGES

	1900	1989	1900	1989	1900	1989
	Probability of a man aged 60 to survive to		Probability of a man aged 70 to survive to		Probability of a man aged 80 to survive to	
age 70	0.61	0.69	-	-	-	-
age 80	0.19	0.29	0.32	0.44	-	-
age 90	0.01	0.04	0.02	0.06	0.08	0.14

	1900	1989	1900	1989	1900	1989
	Probability of a woman aged 60 to survive to		Probability of a woman aged 70 to survive to		Probability of a woman aged 80 to survive to	
age 70	0.60	0.83	-	-	-	-
age 80	0.19	0.50	0.32	0.60	-	-
age 90	0.02	0.10	0.03	0.12	0.08	0.20

TABLE 12.- LIFE EXPECTANCIES AT BIRTH AND AT HIGHER AGES

	Life expectancy		
	at birth	at age 60	at age 80
	Men		
1950	59.9	15.8	5.3
1960	65.9	15.6	5.0
1970	66.3	15.2	5.1
1980	65.5	14.6	5.0
1985	65.3	15.1	5.2
1988	66.2	15.1	5.4
	Women		
1950	64.2	17.1	5.6
1960	70.1	17.6	5.5
1970	72.1	18.2	5.7
1980	72.7	18.3	5.9
1985	73.1	19.2	6.1
1988	74.0	19.2	6.4

4) Nuptiality, cohabitation, divorce

Age at marriage and celibacy rates have always been relatively low in Hungary. After a rise between the two World Wars, during the late 1940s, mean age at marriage reached again the level observed in the last century, i.e. 25 years for men and less than 22 years for women, whereas the proportions remaining ultimately single kept increasing after the war. Nevertheless, a certain increase in marriage rates after the war occurred when the postponed marriages were contracted.

TABLE 13.- SELECTED INDICATORS OF NUPTIALITY 1950-1988

	1950	1960	1970	1980	1985	1988
	Men					
Proportion ever marrying[a]	95.5	94.4	96.1	95.7	94.7	93.6
Mean age at first marriage	26.6	25.6	24.7	24.2	27.8	24.3
Total first marriage rate	1.3	1.03	0.99	0.78	0.79	0.73
Proportion divorced remarrying	25.3	23.7	16.8	9.4	-	-
	Women					
Proportion ever marrying[a]	92.7	92.7	94.7	95.9	96.1	95.4
Mean age at first marriage	23.3	22.3	21.6	21.2	24.6	21.5
Total first marriage rate	1.19	1.01	0.97	0.89	0.84	0.75
Proportion divorced remarrying	10.7	10.3	8.4	5.6	-	-
Crude marriage rate	11.4	8.9	9.3	7.5	6.9	6.2
Number of divorces per 1 000 marriages contracted in same year (both sexes)		18.7	23.6	34.6	40.0	36.2
a) Proportion of ever married at age 49 in the birth cohorts of 1900, 1910, 1920, 1930, 1935 and 1938.						

This, undoubtedly, was due to the same timing effect as the increasing birth rate, or rather the upswing of the birth rate was clearly closely related to the increased number of marriages. Cohort perspective data show that there was no real post-war "marriage boom" either. Thus the continuously increasing divorce rates are the only ones which seem to follow a Western pattern.

Between 1950 and 1982 the total first marriage rate was monotonously decreasing for both sexes. Since then a slight increase has been registered. Meanwhile no significant change in the mean age at first marriage has occurred, except for a minor decrease in case of men during the 1950s. It should be noted that the decreasing proportion of ever-marrying is revealed also in a cohort prespective, however, as a consequence of the recently experienced postponement of marriages, actual period data show higher final celibacy rates for both sexes than the ones estimated from the cohort tendencies. In other words, according to the cross-sectional analysis, about 20 per cent of men and 17 per cent of women are expected to remain ultimately single in contrast with the 7 and 6 per cent, which can be estimated on the basis of cohort trends. In addition, consensual unions are very rare among the young which indicates that legal marriage is still favoured by the majority. A moderate rise of cohabitation can only be observed among the divorced.

The decline of the remarriage rates has been even faster, in 1965 still 75 per cent of divorced men and 70 per cent of women married again, but the corresponding figures hardly exceeded 50 per cent in 1986. It means also that the narrow gap of the previous period no longer exists. The remarriage rate of widowed persons has fallen fast following a small increase just after the war and by now has come close to nil.

Due to the predominantly catholic and traditional society, divorce rates were especially low before the Second World War. Following the war, however, an upward trend could be observed which seems to continue up to recent years. While only a little more than 11 per cent of the marriages contracted in 1948 would have ended in divorce, provided that the 1948 divorce conditions had prevailed, this proportion exceeded 45 per cent in 1987.

5) *Population policy during the last decades*

During the last decades, in Hungary, measures with population aims were taken several times. The primary aim of these measures was to try to impact on fertility development. Actually, the severe ban on abortions, introduced in the early 1950s but in force only for few years, belongs to these measures, as it made an effort to stop, by voluntary means, the decline in the number of births following World War II. Nevertheless, it was first in Hungary among the European countries where after the war fertility declined, in 1958, below reproduction level. In the early 1960s the birth rate in Hungary was the lowest even in a world comparison. It became more and more evident that the permanent low level of fertility would result, in the long run, in an unfavourable population situation. It became also evident that it was necessary, to take some stimulating measures, parallel to improving the conditions for accepting to have and rear children.

In 1967, the institution of the child-care allowace (ChCA) was introduced. The aim of the ChCA was to enhance the readiness of earning mothers to give birth to children as - female employment having become practically full - the decisive proportion of births was delivered by them. The aim of ChCA was to make it possible that during the first year of life of the child, which are decisive from the children's bodily and mental development, the mother can rear her child at home. In recognition of the social necessity and usefulness of childrearing mothers were given a certain fixed-amount allowance until the age of 3 of their children. At the time of the introduction of ChCA its amount was almost one quater of the average income of women.

In the late 1960s fertility increased moderately but did not reach simple reproduction level.

The necessity to achieve simple reproduction level was first formulated by the 1973 population policy decision. At the same time a many-sided measure of mainly stimulating character was introduced. During four years 1974-1977 fertility was over reproduction level but it has remained permanently below that level ever since.

By the early 1980s a qualitatively new, never before experienced population situation had developed. The natural increase of the population stopped and a decline in population size began and has continued ever since. The 1990 population census registered a population size by 335 thousand (3.1 per cent) less than the population census ten years earlier.

Among the causes not only the decline in fertility but also the deterioration of mortality conditions played a role.

The new population situation demanded the rethinking of population policy and the widening of its content. It became necessary to work out a population policy concept for a longer perspective, which already includes - besides all the important vital events, i. e. births and deaths etc. - also the whole range of family-related problems.

The long term population policy concept was declared in October 1984. The decision set the basic aim to moderate the process of population decrease, to stop it in the long run and, then, to achieve - at a population structure to become more favourable - a population increase. In order to achieve this aim the decision pointed out - as a task equal in rank - to increase fertility and the number of births, to improve the conditions of mortality and to strengthen the role of the family.

Following that, new measures stimulating the readiness to give birth were introduced. Of them, perhaps the most important is the replacement of the child care allowance (ChCA) by the child care pay (ChCP). The essence of ChCP is that mothers, who rear their small children, receive a pay proportional to their earnings until the age of 1 and from January 1, 1988 on, until the age of 2 of their children. The amount of the pay is 65-75 per cent of the earnings.

Since the introduction of ChCP the fertility of women aged over 25 years has increased moderately but the fertility of younger women continues to be of an unchangingly declining tendency.

In the second half of the 1980s the deterioration in the economic situation became to be felt more and more. The accelerating inflation made valueless the formerly still stimulating financial measures. Population problems were also more and more forced to the background behind the accelerating socio-economic changes. At present, it is also questionable whether the conditions for accepting to have children can be maintained in the future too.

Austria/L'Autriche
Peter FINDL

I. HISTORY

The demographic transition in Austria within its present territorial borders started with a sharp mortality decline after the last great cholera epidemic in 1873. During the preceding decades the mortality rate had fluctuated very strongly due to epidemics and famines on a high level and had followed a slight overall downward trend only. Whereas the mortality rate had averaged at 29 deaths per 1000 population between 1820 and 1875, it fell sharply to 19 deaths per 1000 in the years immediately before World War I.

After a setback during the war years the mortality rate resumed to drop and reached a level of 13 deaths per 1000 population in the 1930s. World War II led to very high mortality rates of the civilian population again. Thereafter, the mortality rate stabilized at a level of 12 to 13 during the following decades.

However, this development of the crude mortality rate did not reflect the true course of the underlying process of mortality. Due to the ageing of population the reduction of the age-standardized mortality rate was much larger than that of the crude rate. In terms of expectation of life there was an increase from 32.7 years for new-born males and 36.2 years for new-born females in 1868/71 to 43.5 (males) and 46.8 years (females) in 1909/12. By 1930/33 life expectancy at birth jumped to 54.5 and 58.5 years, respectively. By 1949/51 it leaped to 61.9 and 67.0 years, respectively (see below table 3).

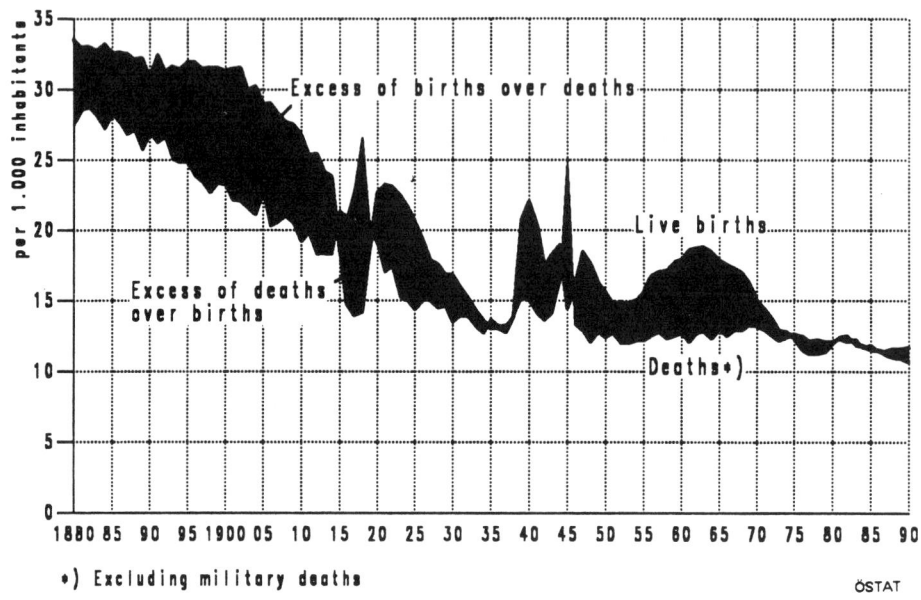

Figure 1.- Birth and Death Rate 1880-1990

Half of this doubling of the average life span was due to a dramatic fall of infant mortality. While around 1870 28% of live-born children had not survived the first year of life, infant mortality fell to 19% in 1909/12 and to 7% in 1950.

When the crude mortality rate dropped sharply after 1873, the crude birth rate started to decline too, but to a much smaller degree (figure 1). Only after the turn of the century the decline accelerated and surpassed the speed of the mortality decline. Therefore, the last quarter of the 19th century was a period of strong and steadily expanding natural increase, followed by a reduction in the years around 1910. Nevertheless the birth surplus remained high until World War I. During the period around 1900 the rate of natural increase culminated in a value of 8 per thousand inhabitants.

This period of strong natural growth was accompanied by high net migration into the territory of today's Austria (table 1). Both components together were responsible for an increase of the population within the present territory of Austria from 4.5 million to 6.65 million between 1869 (the year of the first modern census) and 1910, i.e. by 48% within this 41-year-period. The annual growth rates amounted to 9 or 10 per thousand population. Thus, this period showed the strongest longer prevailing growth of the population history of Austria.

AUSTRIA/L'AUTRICHE

TABLE 1.- POPULATION CHANGE

Period	Population at the begin of the period	Population change	Natural increase	Net migration	Population change	Natural increase	Net migration
	in 1.000				in % of population (col.1)		
1870-1880	4.497,9	465,2	223,5	241,7	10,34	4,97	5,37
1881-1890	4.963,1	454,3	257,1	197,2	9,15	5,18	3,97
1891-1900	5.417,4	586,4	413,1	173,3	10,82	7,63	3,20
1901-1910	6.003,8	644,5	502,6	141,9	10,73	8,37	2,36
1911-1923	6.648,3	-113,6	-128,6	15,0	-1,71	-1,93	0,23
1923-1934	6.534,7	225,5	258,9	-33,4	3,45	3,96	-0,51
1934-1951	6.760,2	173,7	20,6	153,1	2,57	0,30	2,26
1951-1961	6.933,9	139,9	268,9	-129,0	2,02	3,88	-1,86
1961-1971	7.073,8	417,7	340,8	76,9	5,90	4,82	1,09
1971-1981	7.491,5	63,8	-9,9	73,7	0,85	-0,13	0,98
1981-1990	7.555,3	235,6	21,1	214,5	3,12	0,28	2,84

Today's territorial borders of Austria.

Two thirds of the growth between 1869 and 1910 were due to an excess of births over deaths, and for the considerable part of one third, it was due to net migration. In this period, the number of imigrants exceeded the number of emigrants by three quarters of a million, putting Austria - which at that time was the core area of the Austro-Hungarian Empire - into a position of being a distinct immigration country. The development before the turn of the century showed a reverse trend of natural increase and net migration. While the migration surplus had its peak in the 1870s and then continually decreased, the excess of births over deaths showed a strong upward trend; after 1900, both components declined.

The First World War caused not only a loss of war combatants and a high mortality of the civilian population due to famine, but a birth shortage too. Thus, in the census interval between 1910 and 1923, Austria's population decreased by 1.7%. After the War the interrupted trends in mortality and fertility resumed and led to a further reduction in natural population growth. During the Economic Depression the birth rate even sank below the death rate.

However, another turning point of the population history was brought about by an immediate decrease in the traditional immigration flows from the successor states of the Austro-Hungarian Empire into the area of the new republic. Thus, Austria suffered a net emigration between World War I and II.

The decline of births during the first third of the 20th century was more distinct than in other countries. The crude birth rate (table 2) fell from 31 per thousand in 1900 to 13 per thousand in 1935-1937. The total period fertility rate, which amounted to 4.3 around 1880 and to 4.1 children per woman in 1900, decreased even stronger to 1.55 in 1937. The net reproduction rate sank from 1.36 in 1900 to 0.65 in 1937.

TABLE 2.- BIRTH RATE, FERTILITY AND REPRODUCTION

Year	Birth rate	Total period fertility rate	Net reproduction rate
1871	33,6	......	......
1880	33,5	......	......
1900	31,3	4,09	1,36
1910	26,7	......	......
1920	22,7	......	......
1937	12,8	1,55	0,65
1947	18,5	......	......
1951	14,8	2,0189	0,8994
1954	15,0	2,1539	0,9794
1957	17,0	2,5696	1,1736
1960	17,9	2,6931	1,2439
1961	18,6	2,7843	1,2940
1962	18,7	2,7985	1,2998
1963	18,8	2,8188	1,3117
1964	18,5	2,7914	1,3014
1965	17,9	2,7000	1,2600
1966	17,6	2,6598	1,2430
1967	17,3	2,6192	1,2271
1968	17,0	2,5839	1,2114
1969	16,3	2,4857	1,1655
1970	15,0	2,2906	1,0734
1971	14,5	2,1985	1,0305
1972	13,8	2,0840	0,9770
1973	12,9	1,9366	0,9109
1974	12,8	1,9060	0,8972
1975	12,4	1,8256	0,8609
1976	11,6	1,6872	0,7979
1977	11,3	1,6299	0,7722
1978	11,3	1,6034	0,7612
1979	11,4	1,5977	0,7582
1980	12,0	1,6512	0,7844
1981	12,4	1,6732	0,7967
1982	12,5	1,6582	0,7899
1983	11,9	1,5592	0,7429
1984	11,8	1,5221	0,7257
1985	11,6	1,4733	0,7036
1986	11,5	1,4483	0,6921
1987	11,4	1,4285	0,6828
1988	11,6	1,4420	0,6908
1989	11,6	1,4460	0,6924
1990	11,7	1,4549	0,6971

Today's territorial borders of Austria.

The low number of births due to the Economic Depression of the 1930s was increased in a baby boom after Austria's annexation by the German Reich in 1938. This baby boom

AUSTRIA/L'AUTRICHE

did not lead to a high fertility of the generations concerned, but was mainly caused by a "catching up" of births postponed during the years of the Economic Depression.

The census results of 1951 showed a somewhat higher population number than the 1934 census (by 2.6%) due to an influx of refugees during the last war years and the immediate post-war years.

II. TRENDS SINCE 1950

a) Fertility

During the first half of the 1950s fertility remained low. The total period fertility rate was slightly higher than 2.0 children per woman, and the net reproduction rate amounted to 1.0. The subsequent baby boom was characterized by an increase of the birth rate by 27% (1953-1963) and a leap of the total period fertility rate by 35% to 2.82 children per woman. Partially, the baby boom was caused by a rising propensity to marry and a tendency towards early marriage. Nevertheless, fertility within marriage rose too.

The trend towards early marriage and early child-bearing was responsible for a widening gap between period fertility and the fertility of generations. Whereas the total period fertility rate culminated in 2.82 children per woman during the baby boom, the total generation fertility rate reached its top value with 2.45 children per woman for the generations born 1933 to 1935. This value implies a generation net reproduction rate of 1.01 only, whereas the period net reproduction rate culminated in 1.31 (1963).

The decline of births after 1963 dropped the birth rate 40% over the following 15 years. The total period fertility rate went down 43% to 1.60 children per woman, the net reproduction rate fell to 0.76 in 1978.

At the same time the tendency towards early motherhood continued: The mean age of fertility fell between 1963 and 1978 from 27.4 to 26.2 years. The fertility rates of younger age groups started to decline later than the fertility rates of higher age groups.

After a temporary recovery of the birth rate (+10%) and of the total period fertility rate (+5%) during the years 1979 to 1982 the decline of births resumed. In 1987, the total period fertility rate reached with 1.43 children per woman the lowest level in the demographic history of Austria, and the net reproduction rate sank to 0.68. Only the birth rate (11.4 in 1987) was at that time somewhat higher than during the baisse of 1978 according to the fact that large cohorts born during the post-war baby boom had entered the child-bearing age.

Since 1988 a slight upward trend in fertility has occurred. The most recent figures for 1990 show a birth rate of 11.7, a total period fertility rate of 1.45 and a net reproduction rate of 0.70. This trend was accompanied by shifts in the age distribution of fertility. The fertility of young women (below the age of 25 years) is still declining, whereas the fertility in the higher age groups grew considerably.

The decline of births was the consequence of both the strongly reduced marital fertility and of a shrinking number of young married couples due to the declining marriage rates and the trend to later marriage. Non-marital fertility is presently only somewhat lower than during the 1960s and 1970s. According to the much higher number of unmarried persons and to the strongly reduced marital fertility the proportion of illegitimate births related to all live births jumped substantially.

Austria has always been one of those countries with comparatively large proportions of illegitimate births. During the last quarter of the nineteenth century, one out of four children was born out of wedlock. The increase in marriages and the reduction of age at marriage lowered this ratio to 11% in 1965. Since then, the ratio of illegitimate births has been on the increase: In 1990, 24% of all live births and 38% of all first births were illegitimate. About 50% of them are expected to get legitimized by subsequent marriage of the parents according to the legitimization statistics of recent years.

b) *Nuptiality and Divorce*

The post-war baby boom coincided with an increasing propensity to marry, with a declining age at marriage and a decreasing propensity to divorce. During the early 1960s, almost everybody of the younger generations got married. Only 8% of the female generations born in 1936/40 remained single up to the age of 50 years, compared with 25% of the female generations born around 1830.

In the 1970s, however, the trend reversed (table 3). Although the stock of marriages continued to climb up to the present day, the annual number of marriages declined and divorces increased. The total first marriage rate as a period indicator of the propensity of single females to marry fell sharply from around 100% in the early 1960s to 67% during the years 1978 to 1982.

The marriage rates of the 1980s were characterized by some irregularities, which were caused by political measures. In 1987, the number of marriages increased by two thirds after the announcement that the so-called marriage allowance be abolished by 1 January 1988. Similar waves in 1983 and in 1972 were also caused by such fiscal changes, but displayed much smaller amplitudes. Nevertheless, the impact of these marriage booms on the intensity of nuptiality seems to be very small. In each case the boom year was followed by bust years, and in general the booms affected only the timing of marriage, but not the proportion ever married of the generations concerned.

AUSTRIA/L'AUTRICHE

The irregularities of booms and busts in recent years hinder a profound analysis of actual marriage trends. On an average, the total first marriage rate yielded both for 1983-1986 and for 1987-90 a value of 0.66%. Nevertheless, a clear tendency of a rising age at marriage has been observed. Between 1974 and 1990 the median age at first marriage rose for females by three years to 24.3 years and by two years to 26.5 years for men.

TABLE 3.- MARRIAGE AND DIVORCE

Year	Marriage				Divorce	
	Rate per 1000 inhabitants	Total period first marriage rate (females)	Median age at first marriage		Rate per 1000 inhabitants	Total period divorce rate
			female	male		
1928	7,4	...	25,2	27,5	0,8	...
1960	8,3	103,2	21,9	25,4	1,1	13,9
1965	7,8	99,4	22,2	24,7	1,2	14,4
1970	7,1	91,3	21,7	24,4	1,4	18,1
1971	6,4	82,0	21,7	24,4	1,3	17,7
1972	7,6	98,5	21,6	24,5	1,3	17,8
1973	6,5	82,2	21,5	24,4	1,3	17,9
1974	6,5	80,7	21,4	24,4	1,4	19,3
1975	6,1	75,1	21,4	24,4	1,4	19,8
1976	6,0	72,3	21,4	24,5	1,5	20,8
1977	6,0	70,5	21,5	24,5	1,5	22,1
1978	5,9	67,4	21,7	24,5	1,6	23,6
1979	6,0	67,4	21,8	24,6	1,7	25,3
1980	6,2	67,4	21,9	24,6	1,8	26,3
1981	6,3	67,7	22,1	24,7	1,8	26,5
1982	6,3	66,9	22,3	24,9	1,9	28,5
1983	7,4	79,4	22,6	25,1	1,9	29,4
1984	6,1	62,1	22,8	25,3	2,0	29,6
1985	5,9	59,9	23,1	25,5	2,0	30,8
1986	6,1	60,9	23,3	25,7	1,9	29,5
1987	10,1	107,3	23,5	25,8	1,9	29,5
1988	4,7	44,1	23,8	26,0	2,0	29,5
1989	5,6	54,6	24,0	26,2	2,0	30,6
1990	5,9	58,3	24,3	26,5	2,1	32,8

Today's territorial borders of Austria.

The number of divorces started to climb in the 1960s and doubled up to the present day. In 1990, the total period divorce rate is 33%, i.e one out of three of all newly contracted marriages would end in divorce, if the marriage-duration-specific divorce rates were to remain at the levels recorded for this year.

Although non-marital cohabitation has obviously become very common in Austria, the official statistics show still low figures for this phenomenon. Only 5% of all couples irrespective of age and 7% of all men aged 25 to under 30 years (age group with the highest proportion) were recorded by the microcensus as living in consensual unions

(December 1990). Better documented is pre-marital cohabitation: In 1989 and 1990, 45% of all marriage license applications displayed the same address for the bride and for the groom.

c) Mortality

After a sharp decline of mortality in the late 1940s and the 1950s (table 4) some facts indicated that this trend was coming to an end in the 1960s. In the case of women, the decline slowed down noticeably, while male mortality stagnated and in many age groups even increased.

TABLE 4.- EXPECTATION OF LIFE (YEARS)

Period	Male			Female		
	Exact age in years			Exact age in years		
	at birth	1	60	at birth	1	60
1868/71	32,69	45,43	11,87	36,20	47,18	12,08
1879/82	33,43	44,95	12,32	36,70	46,51	12,91
1889/92	35,99	47,99	12,44	38,58	48,85	12,80
1899/1902	40,63	51,71	12,81	43,37	52,68	13,45
1909/12	43,52	53,73	12,94	46,77	55,39	13,97
1930/33	54,5	60,5	14,2	58,5	63,5	15,4
1949/51	61,91	65,90	15,12	66,97	70,09	17,27
1959/61	65,60	67,48	15,25	72,03	73,46	18,67
1970/72	66,58	67,58	15,18	73,69	74,35	19,05
1980/82	69,23	69,31	16,41	76,37	76,22	20,43
1983	69,53	69,48	16,47	76,61	76,39	20,60
1984	70,07	69,97	16,98	77,25	77,03	21,06
1985	70,40	70,33	17,02	77,36	77,07	21,01
1986	71,00	70,85	17,36	77,73	77,41	21,29
1987	71,53	71,31	17,62	78,13	77,82	21,58
1988	72,03	71,66	17,86	78,63	78,22	21,85
1989	72,09	71,75	17,92	78,78	78,38	22,04
1990	72,50	72,11	18,09	79,02	78,59	22,28

1868/71 - 1909/12: Lower Austria, Vienna, Upper Austria, Styria, Carinthia, Salzburg, Tyrol, Vorarlberg.
1930/33-1990: Today's territorial borders.

The 1970s, however, were characterized by a renewed strong increase in life expectancy, which even accelerated during the 1980s. Between 1970/72 and 1980/82, life expectancy at birth rose both for males and for females by 2.7 years, and between 1980/82 and 1990 for males by additional 3.3 years and for females by 2.7 years. In 1990, life expectancy at birth was 72.5 years for males and 79.0 years for females.

Whereas during the 1970s one third of the gain in additional years of life was attributable to the fall of infant mortality, the impact of this persisting phenomenon became smaller

AUSTRIA/L'AUTRICHE

due to the very low level of infant mortality, which was only 7.8 per 1.000 live births in 1990.

On the other side, the remarkable reduction of the mortality of aged people plays an increasingly important role for the life expectancy at birth. In the recent past this reduction was much stronger than in former times, especially for men: Between 1970/72 and 1990, the life expectancy at age 60 rose for men from 15.2 to 18.1 years and for women from 19.1 to 22.3 years. The gain of 2.9 years for men within two decades only was the same as the one which had been achieved before within nine decades (1879/82 to 1970/72). The gain of 3.2 years for women during the last two decades is somewhat less than that which had been achieved during the four preceding decades.

d) *External Migration*

After World War II periods of net emigration alternated with periods of net immigration. During the 1950s, Austria lost 2% of its population (129.000 persons) due to net emigration, which was mainly directed to Germany and Switzerland. In the second half of the 1960s the trend reversed according to the immigration of foreign workers from Yugoslavia and Turkey. For the whole decade 1961-1971, net immigration yielded about 1% of the population (77.000 persons). Almost the same amount of net immigration was recorded for 1971-1981.

TABLE 5.- RECENT POPULATION DEVELOPMENT

Year	End-of-year population	Population change		
		total	by natural increase	by net migration
1980	7,553.326	7.787	-1.570	9.356
1981	7,587.373	34.047	1.249	32.798
1982	7,555.762	-31.611	3.501	-35.112
1983	7,550.967	-4.795	-2.923	-1.872
1984	7,555.630	4.663	768	3.895
1985	7,560.766	5.136	-2.138	7.274
1986	7,569.824	9.058	-107	9.165
1987	7,586.416	16.592	1.596	14.996
1988	7,602.431	16.015	4.789	11.226
1989	7,660.345	57.914	5.352	52.562
1990	7,790.957	130.612	7.502	123.110

In general, immigration and emigration were more or less balanced during the 1980s until 1988 (table 5). In 1989 and 1990, however, a strong economic growth favoured a large immigration wave from Yugoslavia, Turkey and also (and for the first time) from Hungary, Poland and Czechoslovakia. In both years together net immigration amounted to 176.000 persons. This immigration wave was the largest one observed since the 1950s during such a short period. It caused a rise of foreign population to an estimated 482.000 persons by the end of 1990, i.e. 6.2% of total population. A breakdown by nationality is only available for the labour force: Half of all 288.000 employed and unemployed foreigners were Yugoslavs (49%), 22% were Turks, 5% Germans, 5% Poles, 3% Romanians, 3% Hungarians and 2.5% Czechs and Slovaks.

e) Population Growth

During the 1950s population growth was modest. Net emigration lowered the positive impact of the excess of births over deaths on population growth. In the 1960s, both components of population growth worked together into the same direction: the baby boom and the foreign-worker migration yielded together a noticeable population increase by 418.000 persons between the censuses 1961 and 1971 (6% of the population). In the following decade, Austria suffered an excess of deaths over births for several years due to the decline of births, and thus, registered in the census interval 1971-1981 only a small population growth by migration gains. The 1980s again were a period of relatively strong population growth, but this time mainly due to migration gains (1981-1990: +236.000).

f) Ageing of Population

As a consequence of the secular decline of births the proportion of young people has been shrinking and the proportion of old people has been growing since the time of World War I (table 6).

TABLE 6.- AGE STRUCTURE OF THE POPULATION

Year	Under 15 years	15 to under 60	60 and over	Dependency ratios		
				Child	Aged	Total
	in % of total population			per 100 persons aged 15-59		
1869	28,2	63,2	8,6	44,6	13,5	58,1
1880	29,3	61,4	9,3	47,7	15,1	62,8
1890	29,8	60,9	9,2	48,9	15,2	64,1
1900	29,6	61,2	9,1	48,4	14,9	63,3
1910	29,8	60,7	9,4	49,1	15,5	64,6
1923	25,0	64,8	10,1	38,6	15,6	54,2
1934	23,7	64,1	12,3	37,0	19,1	56,1
1951	22,9	61,5	15,6	37,2	25,4	62,7
1961	22,4	59,2	18,4	37,8	31,0	68,9
1971	24,3	55,5	20,1	43,8	36,3	80,1
1981	20,0	60,8	19,2	32,9	31,7	64,6
1990	17,4	62,2	20,4	28,0	32,7	60,7

Today's territorial borders of Austria.

Today the proportion of persons aged 60 and over is 20.4%, that one of persons aged 75 and over is 7.1%. However, the first phase of ageing is already over, because already in

AUSTRIA/L'AUTRICHE

1974 the same proportion of persons over 60 years was observed as today, and last year the proportion of very old people (75 and over) for the first time stopped climbing.

During the last two decades the declining mortality of aged people played an increasing role for the ageing of population and cannot be further neglected. Nevertheless, population projections expect further ageing mainly in connection with the future consequences of the development of births in the past: The next phase of ageing would start shortly before the year 2000, when the large birth cohorts of the years 1939-1944 shall enter the pension age, followed by another phase around 2020, when the first "baby-boomers" of the 1960s become 60 years old.

III. POPULATION AND FAMILY POLICY

From modest beginnings in the late 1940s and the early 1950s, quantitative family policy in Austria has developed since the 1960s into an integrated component of government social policy and of income policy. Also during this period, legal provisions regarding work and social services were substantially improved for the benefit of women bearing and looking after children, particularly for the benefit of gainfully employed pregnant women and mothers. Nevertheless, Austria's birth rate became one of the lowest in the world at that time.

In the early beginnings both population policy and family policy considerations were of importance for the different measures which were established (especially the "Family Burdens Equalization Fund"), but at the beginning of the 1970s this conception underwent a fundamental change. Population policy objectives are rejected today in Austria by the government.

Originally, the Austrian family policy intended a horizontal fiscal redistribution from childless to childcaring households. This conception was also revised in the 1970s. Since that time income independent transfer of payments has taken the place of income dependent tax relief and family policy became therefore an instrument of vertical fiscal redistribution too, favouring lower income families. In addition, a number of use-designated payments and subsidies were created which directly benefitted all potentially entitled claimants.

The largest part of the government expenditures for family welfare has been dedicated to child allowances. In 1991, each child under 18 years of age or, in the case of students, below 25 years of age, is supported with a monthly transfer payment of 1300 AS (186 DM) or 1550 AS (if older than 10 years; 221 DM).

Another important feature of the Austrian family policy are the fiscal and other supportive measures following a birth. Besides a birth allowance of presently 15000 AS (2143 DM), which is payed in four instalments, several subsidies and benefits exist for gainfully employed parents (partially also for self-employed parents and for students). After a fully paid maternity leave of usually two months before and two months after the birth, an unpaid parental leave for the mother or for the father is supported by the state until the completion of the second year of the child's life with a monthly transfer payment of presently 4961 AS (708 DM) or, in the case of lone parents, of 7419 AS (1060 DM). Some additional subsidies from the federal or provincial state are income-dependent or are granted only to housewives. During and shortly after maternity and parental leave the mother or father, respectively, is protected against dismissal from her/his job. As an alternative to the second year of child care leave, the option to work part-time has been created recently.

Institutionalized child care in Austria is limited to the last two or three years before enrolment to the primary school. For younger children places in nurseries or in public or private 'kindergarten' are hardly available. The Austrian school system is organized mainly on a half-day basis, and for the afternoon only relatively few places in child care institutions or whole-day-schools are offered.

Before 1975, legal abortions were performed according to medical indications. Since 1975, abortion has been free of penal sanctions if performed by a physician after proper counselling and within three months of conception. The obvious demographic effect of this law was a sharp reduction of teenage fertility. As a supportive measure against abortion the instrument of a birth allowance (see above) was substantially enlarged, which is given only on condition that a certain number of pre-natal and post-natal medical examinations are performed by a physician. These check-ups proved to be very successful in reducing infant mortality.

Since 1978, the divorce law provides for divorce of long seperated marriages (for six or more years) even without the consent of the other spouse. Presently, about 90% of all divorces were performed by the court with the consent of both spouses.

In 1991, a change in official migration policy appears in outlines. In the past, the government has accepted only the temporary influx of foreign workers due to economic demand, and the immigration of refugees. Being under the spell of the very recent immigration wave due to the open borders to Eastern Europe, favourable economic growth rates and facing the pension problems of tomorrow according to the decline of births, the Minister of the Interior made the proposal to accept an annual net immigration of about 30.000 foreigners to Austria. By this means a regulation of immigration and a selection of immigrants are intended.

La Suisse/Switzerland
Hermann-Michel HAGMANN

I.- UN PEU D'HISTOIRE

1) La Suisse, pays d'émigration !

Quand on connaît l'impact considérable de l'immigration sur l'évolution démographique helvétique, y compris durant la période actuelle, on ne peut qu'être frappé par la relative nouveauté du phénomène.

En effet, jusqu'à la dernière décennie du XIXe siècle, c'est-à-dire il y a à peine un siècle, la Suisse, contrée à faibles ressources, est un pays d'émigration massive. C'est ainsi, par exemple, que le mercenariat couche plus d'un million de Suisses sur les champs de bataille européens, de la fin du moyen âge aux campagnes napoléoniennes. Au XIXe siècle encore, plusieurs crises économiques déterminèrent près de 400.000 Suisses à émigrer.

Néanmoins, la roue allait bientôt tourner. Déjà depuis 1850, l'industrialisation s'accélère. L'immigration étrangère, timidement d'abord, puis avec force, prend de l'ampleur. C'est vers 1890 que se situe le changement fondamental : la Suisse, pays d'émigration chronique, devient une terre d'élection pour des centaines de milliers d'Européens. Le renversement de la balance migratoire atteint son point culminant en 1914 où 600.000 étrangers permanents et environ 90.000 saisonniers forment 17,3% de la population résidante, soit une proportion près de quinze fois supérieure à la moyenne européenne de l'époque (1,2%).

TABLEAU 1.- BILAN MIGRATOIRE, DE 1850 A 1914

Années	Immigration	Emigration	Bilan migratoire
1850/1860	35.000	61.000	- 26.000
1860/1870	25.000	66.000	- 41.000
1870/1880	45.000	68.000	- 23.000
1880/1888	5.000	92.000	- 87.000
1888/1900	127.000	53.000	74.000
1900/1910	131.000	52.000	79.000
1910/1914	41.000	18.000	23.000

Sources : 1. Office fédéral de la statistique.
2. W. Bickel, Bevölkerungsgeschichte der Schweiz, Zurich, Gutenberg, 1947.

Note : Pour les tableaux suivants, sauf précision contraire, l'absence d'indication de source signifie que les données sont tirées des différentes publications de l'Office fédéral de la statistique, avec certains calculs ou certaines adaptations personnels.

TABLEAU 2.- NOMBRE D'ETRANGERS POUR 1000 HABITANTS EN 1910 DANS DIVERS PAYS

Espagne	2	Hongrie	13
Russie	4	Allemagne	17
Italie	9	France	27
Autriche	10	Belgique	31
Hollande	11	Suisse	147

Source : L. Hersch, Les étrangers en Suisse, Revue d'économie politique, Paris, No 1, 1919.

2) La Suisse, pays d'immigration (depuis 1888)

En devenant un pays d'immigration, depuis 1888, la Suisse voit sa croissance démographique s'accélérer. L'effectif global prend les valeurs suivantes :

1800	1.665.000
1820	1.910.000
1850	2.393.000
1888	2.918.000
1900	3.315.000
1914	3.900.000

De 0,5% au milieu du siècle, l'accroissement intercensitaire annuel moyen atteint 1,06% pour 1888-1900 et 1,24% pour 1900-1910. Le tableau 3 détaille le bilan démographique de cette époque.

TABLEAU 3.- BILAN DEMOGRAPHIQUE (EN MOYENNE ANNUELLE).

	Accroissement naturel	Migration nette	Accroissement total
1850/1860	13.410	- 2.430	10.980
1860/1870	18.600	- 4.100	14.500
1870/1880	19.900	- 2.320	17.680
1880/1888	21.640	- 10.900	10.750
1888/1900	26.960	6.180	33.140
1900/1910	35.860	7.920	43.790

3) Fécondité, nuptialité et mortalité.

Le renversement de la balance migratoire, capital pour l'avenir démographique helvétique, ne doit pas occulter toutefois le fait qu'une large part de la croissance (pour les 4/5, de 1888 à 1910, par exemple) est alimentée par l'excédent naturel.

Et pourtant, la fécondité helvétique est plutôt basse, comparée au contexte européen (centre et nord-ouest).

TABLEAU 4.- DESCENDANCE FINALE.

Pays	Génération 1841-1850	Génération 1876-1885
Norvège	4,45	3,47
Suède	4,33	3,21
Angleterre-Galles	4,76	2,79
Belgique	4,43	2,94
France	3,35	2,38
Pays-Bas	5,13	3,82
Allemagne	5,30	3,41
Suisse	4,01	3,00

Source : P. Festy, La fécondité des pays occidentaux de 1870 à 1970, INED, Paris, 1979.

En descendance finale estimée, elle se situe en deuxième position, derrière la France, pour les générations 1841-1850.

La faiblesse de la nuptialité explique pour une part importante cette fécondité relativement basse. Pour l'ensemble des générations féminines nées au XIXe siècle, le célibat définitif ne descend jamais en-dessous de 17%.

TABLEAU 5.- INTENSITE DE LA NUPTIALITE DANS LES GENERATIONS FEMININES DU XIXE SIECLE.

1806/1815	80,8	1856/1865	82,2
1816/1825	79,7	1866/1875	82,3
1826/1835	80,5	1876/1885	82,1
1834/1843	81,7	1887/1896	80,4
1847/1855	82,6	1896/1905	80,8

Seule la Suède présente un score aussi faible, mais elle le compense par une proportion plus grande des naissances hors mariage.

TABLEAU 6.- PROPORTION DE FEMMES MARIEES A 50 ANS DANS LA GENERATION

Pays	1840	1860	1880
Suède	82,7	79,4	77,5
Angleterre-Galles	87,7	84,3	83,6
France	86,7	88,8	89,0
Pays-Bas	86,4	85,1	85,1
Allemagne	89,5	89,3	89,0
Suisse	81,6	82,2	82,2

Source : P. Festy, op. cit.

TABLEAU 7.- NAISSANCES HORS MARIAGE, EN %.

Pays	1866-1875	1896-1905
Suède	10,4	11,5
France	7,4	8,8
Allemagne	8,7	8,7
Autriche	13,2	13,5
Suisse	4,9	4,4
Italie	7,0	5,9

Source : P. Festy, op. cit.

Quant à la mortalité, la Suisse fait plutôt bonne figure :

- face à la France, pour la vie moyenne (tableau 8)

TABLEAU 8.- VIE MOYENNE

	H		F	
Période	France	Suisse	France	Suisse
1877/1881	40,8	40,6	43,4	43,2
1908/1913	48,5	50,7	52,4	53,9

Sources : 1. Annuaire statistique de la France;
2. Office fédéral de la statistique (périodes : 1876/1880 et 1910/1911).

- face à une sélection de pays européens, pour la mortalité infantile (tableau 9).

TABLEAU 9.- MORTALITE INFANTILE (POUR 1000 NAISSANCES VIVANTES)

Pays	vers 1875	vers 1900
Allemagne	261	208
Autriche	256	221
France	172	148
Italie	215	168
Pays-Bas	203	144
Royaume-Uni	149	147
Suède	130	95
Suisse	193	139

Source : J.-C. Chesnais, La transition démographique, INED, Paris, Travaux et documents, cahier No 113, 1986

4) La période 1914-1945

A la forte expansion observée durant les 25 ans de l'avant-guerre vont succéder 25 ans de relative dépression démographique.

Certes, la population résidante progresse, malgré la forte émigration étrangère (tableau 10). Cette donnée est partiellement compensée par le solde migratoire positif provoqué par le retour des Suisses de l'étranger dans les années 30. Mais c'est évidemment l'accroissement naturel qui assure encore un excédent en régression :

1900/1910 : 35.861 (en moyenne annuelle)
1920/1930 : 24.512
1930/1941 : 17.637

En dépit de la très forte diminution de la fécondité, la structure par âge, encore jeune, et la poursuite de la baisse de la mortalité expliquent ce résultat. Pour la vie moyenne, par exemple, voici deux points de repère :

1910/11	50,7/H	53,9/F
1939/44	62,7/H	67,0/F

TABLEAU 10.- POPULATION RESIDANTE SELON L'ORIGINE

Année	Population totale	Suisses	Etrangers
1920	3.880.300	3.477.900	402.400
1930	4.066.400	3.710.900	355.500
1941	4.265.700	4.042.100	223.600
1945	4.412.000	4.220.400	191.600

L'attention doit toutefois se porter sur l'évolution de la fécondité. De 3,89 en 1900, et 3,38 en 1909/12, l'indicateur conjoncturel de fécondité s'affaisse à 2,52 en 1912/22 et à 1,75 en 1937!

Mais dès cette date, le nombre moyen d'enfants par femme se relève : de 1,83 en 1940 à 2,62 en 1946. C'est le début d'une nouvelle période vécue par la population helvétique.

II.- LA PERIODE RECENTE

1) Une croissance sans précédent

Alors que les rares spécialistes des questions de population prédisaient, dans les années 30, un pays en déclin, la Suisse a connu dans les années d'après-guerre une croissance sans précédent: de 4.412.OOO habitants en 1945 (estimation 1.7.45) à plus de 6.750.000 habitants à fin 1990 (estimation 31.12.90), soit 53% d'accroissement. Dans les années 60, par exemple, elle enregistre le taux d'accroissement annuel moyen le plus élevé (1,45%) d'Europe occidentale (tableau 11).

Cette progression n'est cependant pas linéaire. Très rapide dans les années 50 et 60, elle fait place, de 1975 à 1977, à une diminution du nombre d'habitants de 84.000 personnes, suivie d'une reprise plus modérée (+ 0,4% par an) jusqu'à fin 1982. Les années 1983/84/85 subissent un ralentissement passager qui fait place à une nouvelle poussée de 1986 à 1990 (tableau 12).

TABLEAU 11.- TAUX D'ACCROISSEMENT ANNUEL MOYEN, DE 1960 A 1970, EN %

Irlande	0,4	Italie	0,8
Autriche	0,5	Norvège	0,8
Belgique	0,6	Portugal	0,9
Finlande	0,6	Allemagne fédérale	1,0
Royaume Uni	0,6	France	1,0
Danemark	0,7	Espagne	1,1
Grèce	0,7	Pays-Bas	1,3
Suède	0,7	Suisse	1,5

Source : J.-C. Chesnais et A. Sauvy, Progrès économique et accroissement de la population, Population, INED, Paris, No 4-5, 1973.

TABLEAU 12.- EVOLUTION DE LA POPULATION RESIDANTE, DE 1950 A 1990, EN MILLIERS.

Période	Accroissement naturel	Migration nette	Accroissement total
1950/1960	37,4	34,0	71,4
1960/1970	50,6	33,4	84,0
1970/1980	23,1	10,0	13,2
1981	14,0	23,7	37,7
1982	15,7	21,1	36,8
1983	12,9	5,2	18,1
1984	16,1	11,9	28,1
1985	15,1	13,9	28,9
1986	16,2	22,3	38,6
1987	17,0	26,4	43,4
1988	19,7	33,5	53,2
1989	20,3	33,6	53,9
1990	20,4	56,2	76,6

Cette forte croissance a naturellement bénéficié de la reprise rapide de l'immigration étrangère (tableau 13).

TABLEAU 13.- NOMBRE D'ETRANGERS, DE 1950 A 1990

1950	279.000	5,9 (en %)
1960	495.000	11,0
1974	1.065.000	16,8
1979	884.000	14,0
1990	1.100.000	16,4

De 5,9% en 1950, la proportion des étrangers "résidants permanents" atteint 16,8% en 1974, régresse à 14% en 1979, puis retrouve presque le score de 1974 avec 16,4% à fin 1990. A noter que ces chiffres ne comprennent pas :

- 122.000 saisonniers en août 1990 (83.000 en moyenne annuelle),
- 181.000 frontaliers,
- 26.000 fonctionnaires internationaux,
- environ 60.000 demandeurs d'asile (demandes d'asile en suspens),
- les étrangers au bénéfice d'une autorisation de séjour dont la validité est inférieure à une année,
- les étrangers et familles d'étrangers non enregistrés officiellement ...

Environ 130.000 étrangers ont acquis la citoyenneté suisse de 1980 à 1989, avec une tendance à la baisse des naturalisations (9735 en 1980, 6863 en 1989). Quant aux titulaires d'un permis d'établissement, ils représentent plus de 75% des étrangers résidants permanents, soit une forte proportion d'étrangers installés depuis longtemps en Suisse.

Mais le tableau 12 nous indique aussi que l'excédent naturel pèse d'un poids prépondérant dans la croissance démographique helvétique, du moins jusqu'au début des années 1980.

2) Evolution de la fécondité

En présentant quelques dates-clé du nombre de naissances vivantes, le tableau 14 illustre bien les ruptures de l'histoire démographique suisse. Après un premier sommet en 1901, la valeur- plancher est atteinte en 1937. Puis, la remontée est spectaculaire: le point culminant se situe en 1964.

TABLEAU 14.- NAISSANCES VIVANTES : QUELQUES DATES-CLE.

1876	90.786	1951	81.903
1890	78.548	1964	*112.890*
1901	97.028	1970	99.216
1937	62.480	1978	71.375
1946	89.126	1990	83.916

Ces à-coups vont naturellement se retrouver dans l'indicateur conjoncturel de fécondité (tableau 15).

De 1937 à 1946, le nombre moyen d'enfants par femme remonte, légèrement jusqu'en 1940, puis rapidement dès 1941.

La phase de récupération du déficit (années de crise et de guerre) des naissances achevée, l'indice synthétique recule à 2,30 en 1951, pour demeurer à ce niveau jusqu'en 1955.

TABLEAU 15.- INDICATEUR CONJONCTUREL DE FECONDITE

Année	ICF	Année	ICF
1937	1,75	1964	2,67
1938	1,79	1965	2,61
1939	1,81	1966	2,52
1940	1,63	1967	2,41
1941	2,07	1968	2,30
1942	2,29	1969	2,13
1943	2,43	1970	2,10
1944	2,52	1971	2,02
1945	2,61	1972	1,90
1946	2,52	1973	1,80
1947	2,57	1974	1,72
1948	2,54	1975	1,51
1949	2,44	1976	1,54
1950	2,40	1977	1,53
1951	2,30	1978	1,50
1952	2,32	1979	1,52
1953	2,29	1980	1,55
1954	2,28	1981	1,54
1955	2,30	1982	1,55
1956	2,35	1983	1,51
1957	2,41	1984	1,52
1958	2,40	1985	1,51
1959	2,42	1986	1,50
1960	2,44	1987	1,52
1961	2,53	1988	1,57
1962	2,60	1989	1,56
1963	2,67		

Source : J.-P. Sardon, Conseil de l'Europe, Etudes démographiques, No 21, Strasbourg, 1990.

C'est alors que la fécondité du moment connaît une nouvelle croissance qui amène en dix ans l'indicateur conjoncturel à 2,68, valeur proche de celle observée à la veille de la première guerre mondiale. Mais dès 1965, le recul est brutal : 2,10 en 1970, 1,54 en 1976. Contrairement à l'attente de certains, encouragés par les très légères augmentations de 1980 et 1988, aucune véritable reprise ne se manifeste depuis : l'indicateur oscille faiblement entre 1,50 et 1,57. L'année 1990, pour laquelle toutes les données ne sont pas encore disponibles, indique cependant une progression de plus de 2700 naissances, difficile, semble-t-il, à imputer au seul effet de structure provoqué par l'arrivée, encore en légère augmentation, des cohortes nées dans les années 1960.

TABLEAU 16.- NATALITE TRES RECENTE

Année	Total naissances	dont naissances étrangères	naissances étrangères	Solde migratoire étranger
1988	80.345	13.518	16,8	28.000
1989	81.180	14.469	17,8	33.000
1990	83.916	16.430	19,6	60.000

Sources : 1. Office fédéral de la statistique 2. Office fédéral des étrangers

Toutefois, le tableau 16 montre que les naissances étrangères augmentent de près de 2.000 unités, chiffre à mettre en relation avec le solde migratoire, en grande majorité composé d'éléments jeunes. Serait-ce que la fécondité étrangère est supérieure à celle de la population d'origine ? Le tableau 17 est révélateur : si, pour les années 1979/1982, l'indice synthétique de fécondité des étrangères est en moyenne très proche de celui des Suissesses, les différences se creusent par nationalité :

- valeur très basse pour les Françaises et Allemandes, due à une nuptialité très basse,
- valeur plus élevée pour les Italiennes et Espagnoles, provoquée à l'inverse par une forte nuptialité,
- valeur encore plus forte pour les Turques, avec une nuptialité et une fécondité légitime intenses.

TABLEAU 17.-SOMME DES NAISSANCES REDUITES EN 1979/1982

1,54	En tout	
1,53	Suissesses	
1,63	Etrangères	
	dont	
0,71		Allemandes
0,78		Françaises
1,90		Italiennes
1,82		Espagnoles
3,34		Turques

Source : J.-E. Neury, La fécondité en Suisse, vers 1980, Office fédéral de la statistique, Berne, 1984.

Or, la balance migratoire positive de 1990 est alimentée essentiellement par le Portugal, la Yougoslavie et la Turquie. On peut donc risquer une estimation : l'indicateur conjoncturel pourrait atteindre 1,58 en 1990 (estimation personnelle) avec une légère hausse de la fécondité étrangère et une quasi constance de la fécondité helvétique.

L'évolution récente de la fécondité par âge montre que cette stabilité du nombre moyen d'enfants par femme s'obtient par un mouvement de compensation entre la baisse des taux jusqu'à 27 ans et leur relèvement au-delà (tableau 18).

TABLEAU 18.- FECONDITE PAR AGE, EN POUR 1 000

Age	1975	1980	1985	1989
15-19	10,9	7,2	4,6	4,5
20-24	85,7	71,6	57,5	49,1
25	129,7	122,5	116,0	101,2
26	133,3	134,2	126,8	119,4
27	126,7	127,8	132,6	129,5
28	119,4	126,5	129,2	138,5
29	110,6	118,4	125,2	133,2
25-29	123,9	125,9	126,0	124,4
30-34	69,5	77,4	84,8	97,6
35-39	25,6	23,7	25,9	32,1
40-44	6,7	4,7	4,1	4,8
45+	0,5	0,4	0,2	0,2
Age moyen maternité	27,5	27,9	28,3	28,9

Cela se traduit naturellement par un relèvement rapide de l'âge moyen à la maternité (1,4 an de 1975 à 1989), signe d'un remodelage du cycle de vie parental. Ces modifications importantes du calendrier ne doivent pourtant pas nous autoriser à faire l'économie d'une évaluation de l'intensité finale de la fécondité dans les générations concernées.

TABLEAU 19.- DESCENDANCE FINALE SELON LA GENERATION

1901	1,99	1930	2,18
1907	1,97	1935	2,19
1910	2,03	1940	2,09
1914	2,13	1945	1,85
1918	2,25	1950	1,77
1925	2,21	1954	1,70

Sources : 1. Office fédéral de la statistique
2. J.-P. Sardon, op. cit.

Pour les générations plus anciennes, le résultat est connu. Pour la plus récente, la descendance finale peut être estimée à 35 ans, avec une faible marge d'erreur puisque près de 90% des naissances sont déjà présentes (malgré le léger report de calendrier au-delà de 35 ans).

La descendance des générations nées au début de siècle est faible. Il faut attendre les générations des années 1916 à 1935 pour retrouver des valeurs de 2,19 à 2,25 (1918) : ce sont elles qui ont assuré la reprise de la fécondité d'après-guerre.

A partir de la génération 1935, c'est une baisse constante jusqu'à la valeur de 1,70 pour 1954. En vingt ans, les générations helvétiques perdent 0,5 enfant par femme ! Il convient de mettre encore ces chiffres en relation avec l'indicateur conjoncturel de fécondité qui assure le renouvellement théorique de la population, selon la probabilité de survie à l'âge moyen à la maternité (tableau 20).

TABLEAU 20.- NOMBRE D'ENFANTS PAR FEMME NECESSAIRE AU REMPLACEMENT DES GENERATIONS

1910	2,62
1920	2,47
1930	2,31
1941	2,25
1950	2,16
1960	2,12
1970	2,10
1980	2,08

Le constat est frappant : durant ce siècle, aucune génération n'assure son remplacement ! Pour compléter le tableau, faisons une brève incursion dans la nuptialité.

3) Nuptialité et naissances hors mariage

Plus la nuptialité sera intense, plus la descendance finale sera forte, du moins à fécondité légitime constante. Or, ce que l'on pressentait se confirme : après avoir digéré des valeurs exceptionnellement hautes durant lesannées de récupération d'après-guerre, la propension à se marier en Suisse retrouve dans les années 60 une intensité plus conforme à son passé (tableau 21).

Mais dans les années 1970, la chute devient spectaculaire : 42% des hommes et 40% des femmes, en 1976, demeuraient célibataires en valeur du moment. Renversement de calendrier et diminution de l'intensité se combinent alors. Il faut attendre le début des années 80 pour observer une reprise de l'indicateur conjoncturel jusqu'en 1988, avec un léger repli en 1989. L'âge moyen des femmes au premier mariage s'élève, comme attendu, de 24,2 ans (1970) à 26,7 ans (1988).

En dépit du redressement intervenu dans les huit dernières années, la primo-nuptialité demeure à un niveau plutôt faible. Si la propension à se marier ne se modifie pas, cela signifierait un taux de célibat définitif d'environ 30% dans les générations, proportion bien supérieure à celle du XIXe siècle (environ 15 à 20%).

LA SUISSE/SWITZERLAND

TABLEAU 21.- INDICATEUR CONJONCTUREL DE NUPTIALITE

Année	H	F
1950	95	92
1966	86	87
1976	58	60
1978	58	60
1980	64	66
1986	66	68
1987	69	72
1988	72	75
1989	69	73

Dans ces conditions, l'évolution des naissances hors mariage sera essentielle pour l'intensité de la fécondité. Or, l'histoire se confirme pour la Suisse : si la plupart des pays européens complètent leur fécondité légitime par une augmentation rapide des naissances hors mariage, il n'en va pas de même pour la Confédération helvétique (tableau 22).

TABLEAU 22.- NAISSANCES HORS MARIAGE EN %

Pays	1970	1980	1988
Autriche	12,8	17,8	21,0
RF Allemagne	5,5	7,6	10,0
France	6,8	11,4	26,3
Pays-Bas	2,1	4,1	9,9
Norvège	6,9	14,5	33,7
Suède	18,4	39,7	51,0
Royaume-Uni	8,0	11,5	25,1
Italie	2,2	4,3	5,8
Suisse	3,8	4,7	6,1

Source : Evolution démographique récente dans les Etats membres, Conseil de l'Europe, Strasbourg, 1990.

La progression est très faible. Elle s'opère surtout entre 1978 (4,1) et 1982 (5,5). L'évolution récente indique une quasi stagnation :

1984 : 5,7
1985 : 5,6
1986 : 5,7
1987 : 5,9
1988 : 6,1
1989 : 5,9

Même l'Allemagne et les Pays-Bas, à tradition de faible illégitimité, décrochent la Suisse, dont le comportement demeure curieusement "latin". Par conséquent, la faiblesse des naissances hors mariage ne peut compenser l'insuffisance de la seule fécondité légitime pour le renouvellement de la population

4) La mortalité

Les générations de ce siècle ne se renouvellent pas. Et pourtant, la croissance démographique se poursuit, grâce notamment, on l'a vu, à l'immigration. Mais il nous reste à examiner encore l'impact de l'évolution de la mortalité.

En un siècle, les progrès de l'espérance de vie sont considérables :

	H	F
1881/88	43,3	45,7
1988/89	74,0	80,9

Jusqu'au milieu de ce siècle, le recul de la mortalité a touché pour l'essentiel les enfants et les adultes jeunes. La chute de la mortalité infantile est révélatrice (tableau 23).

TABLEAU 23.- MORTALITE INFANTILE EN POUR 1000

Périodes	H	F
1901/1910	138	113
1931/1941	51	41
1958/1963	24,5	18,6
1978/1983	9,5	7,1
1986/1987	7,5	6,1
1987/1988	7,7	5,9
1988/1989	8,0	6,1

A l'examen des derniers chiffres disponibles, il semble qu'une certaine valeur-plancher soit atteinte, même s'il convient de garder à l'esprit les scores japonais (4,8) et suédois (5,8) pour 1988 (sexes réunis).

Mais le résultat d'ensemble de la Suisse est plutôt bon. Comparée à la Suède ou aux Pays-Bas, par exemple, l'espérance de vie helvétique obtient une meilleure progression (tableau 24).

Cette avancée résulte d'un recul sensible de la mortalité aux âges élevés, ce qui vaut à la Suisse d'obtenir le premier rang des pays européens pour l'espérance de vie à 65 ans.

Une telle évolution ne va pas manquer d'influer grandement sur l'avenir démographique : au vieillissement démographique par la base, provoqué par l'effondrement de la fécondité, s'ajoute ainsi depuis plusieurs années un vieillissement, accéléré, par le sommet de la pyramide, dont le terme n'est pas connu.

TABLEAU 24.- ESPERANCE DE VIE A LA NAISSANCE ET A 65 ANS

Pays	Années	0		65	
		H	F	H	F
Suisse	1968/73	70,3	76,2	13,3	16,3
	1986/87	73,8	80,5	15,2	19,3
Suède	1970	71,9	77,0	14,0	16,7
	1987	74,2	80,2	15,0	18,9
Pays-Bas	1970	70,7	76,5	13,6	16,5
	1986/87	73,4	79,9	14,3	19,0
Norvège	1971/72	71,2	76,4	13,2	16,9
	1987	72,8	79,6	14,4	18,5
RF Allemagne	1970	67,4	73,8	12,1	15,2
	1985/87	71,8	78,4	13,8	17,6
Autriche	1970	66,5	73,4	11,7	14,9
	1988	72,0	78,6	14,4	17,7
Belgique	1970	67,8	74,2	12,1	15,3
	1982/83	70,5	77,2	13,1	17,0
France	1970	68,4	75,9	13,1	16,8
	1987	72,0	80,3	15,0	19,4
Royaume-Uni	1970/72	68,8	75,0	12,1	16,0
	1985/87	71,9	77,6	13,4	17,3
Italie	1970	69,0	74,9	13,3	16,1
	1985	72,0	78,6	13,9	17,7

Source : Conseil de l'Europe, op. cit.

III.- PERSPECTIVES ET POLITIQUES

1) Deux scénarios possibles

Pour mieux dessiner le contexte des perspectives, on peut imaginer deux scénarios :

A : un scénario de population décroissante : maintien d'une fécondité basse (1,5 enfant par femme) avec un solde migratoire nul

B : un scénario de population stationnaire selon deux hypothèses :

B1 : reprise de la fécondité jusqu'à la valeur assurant le remplacement des générations

B2 : maintien d'un solde migratoire positif qui compenserait le déficit des naissances. Pour en estimer les incidences, la Commission "Politiques de population" a procédé à diverses simulations. Le tableau 25 reprend les variantes A et B1.

TABLEAU 25.- EVOLUTION DEMOGRAPHIQUE DE LA SUISSE, SELON DEUX VARIANTES.

Variante A	1980	1995	2010	2025	2040
Population résidante (en millions)	6,3	6,4	6,2	5,7	4,9
Indice	100	102	99	90	78
65 ans et + (en %)	13,8	15,6	19,4	24,7	28,2
Variante B1					
Population résidante	6,3	6,6	6,8	6,8	6,7
Indice	100	105	108	108	106
65 ans et +	13,8	15,1	17,8	20,7	20,8

Source : Commission "Politiques de population", Les Suisses vont-ils disparaître ?, Haupt, Berne et Stuttgart, 1985, avec la collaboration de l'Office fédéral de la statistique et de M. Diserens pour les calculs perspectifs.

Le résultat, bien connu du démographe, demande à être clairement explicité pour le politique. Trop souvent encore, certains ont confusément tendance à amalgamer population stationnaire et population décroissante, alors que l'on se trouve en présence de deux schémas fondamentalement différents.

Dans une population stationnaire, la croissance devient nulle et le vieillissement, une fois la structure-limite atteinte, demeure stable (autour de la barre des 20% pour les plus de 65 ans). Dans une population décroissante (ou potentiellement décroissante), après une brève période de répit due à une structure par âge encore favorable, l'effectif diminue chaque année et le vieillissement (là aussi, jusqu'à la structure-limite atteinte) s'accroît bien plus fortement (proche de la barre des 30%).

A terme, une population décroissante n'est à l'évidence pas gérable. Dès lors, quel enseignement peut-on en tirer pour d'éventuelles politiques de population ?

2) *Agir sur la fécondité ou/et sur la migration*

Si l'objectif est d'atteindre une population stationnaire (ou proche de la stationnarité, avec le moins d'oscillations possible dans la structure par âge), le choix de l'action politique peut se synthétiser ainsi :

- agir sur la migration
- agir sur la fécondité
- agir à la fois sur la fécondité et la migration.

a) Agir sur la migration

Pour assurer à terme le renouvellement de la population, le déficit actuel des naissances est d'environ 30.000. Or, un bref retour au tableau 12 nous montre que la migration nette positive couvre largement ce déficit. Le problème ne se règle-t-il pas de lui-même ?

En fait la question ne peut à l'évidence être ainsi simplifiée :

- Les naissances manquantes vont précisément "manquer" à l'économie helvétique, non pas aujourd'hui, mais demain à l'âge adulte; l'apport migratoire actuel s'ajoute au contraire déjà aujourd'hui aux classes d'âge de la population résidante nées en nombre important, notamment durant les années 60, ce qui risque d'aggraver encore un futur déséquilibre : ne risque-t-on pas de subir une "maladie de la structure par âge" qui cumulerait les inconvénients d'une croissance non contrôlée et d'à-coups, dans la structure, délicate à absorber sur le plan de la gestion socio- économique (système éducatif, stabilité du marché de l'emploi, utilisation optimale de l'infrastructure et des équipements collectifs, équilibre financier des régimes de sécurité sociale et des retraites) ?

- Comment seraient trouvés (rappelons par exemple que l'indicateur conjoncturel de fécondité est aujourd'hui de 1,3 en Italie et Espagne, de 1,5 au Portugal et en Grèce, et même de 1,9 en Yougoslavie) et ensuite intégrés les migrants qui devraient arriver en Suisse dans les années 2000 ?

- Est-il bien réaliste, dans le contexte socio-politique (et européen, pourrait-on ajouter, puisque apparaissent clairement les limites d'une société pluri-ethnique) d'émettre une telle proposition ?

- Par ailleurs, sur un plan éthique, on pourrait être en droit de s'interroger sur la légitimité d'une politique qui consisterait à tenter d'"exporter" nos problèmes démographiques.

Si l'on ajoute enfin aux éléments précités la nécessité, à la fois démographique et humanitaire, de favoriser une véritable intégration volontaire des étrangers déjà résidants, il apparaît raisonnable de maintenir l'objectif (devenu théorique ces dernières années...) du Conseil fédéral d'une stabilisation de l'effectif étranger.

b) Agir sur la fécondité

Le thème est immense et dépasse le cadre restreint de la présente communication. Il faut donc se contenter de souligner ici que la question de la population est délicate : elle touche, par exemple, à la légitimité même d'une éventuelle action de l'Etat, puis à son degré hypothétique d'efficacité.

Depuis quelques années, avec d'autres, nous avons lancé le débat, en particulier par la Commission "Politiques de population", débat qui échappe (doit échapper) au seul démographe et qui concerne l'ensemble des acteurs de la vie sociale.

Le scientifique peut toutefois rappeler qu'à la complexité des phénomènes observés doit correspondre un ensemble à la fois multiple et cohérent de réponses adaptées. Voilà pourquoi il paraît vain de proposer une politique étroitement nataliste qui ne pourrait prendre en compte, à elle seule, cette complexité de facteurs interactifs par l'une ou l'autre mesure d'aide financière par exemple. En revanche, on peut légitimement s'interroger sur l'opportunité de la mise en place d'une politique globale de population qui intègre notamment la politique familiale.

Or, si la Suisse, dans plusieurs secteurs de la politique sociale, n'a pas à redouter la comparaison internationale, elle ne dispose pas encore d'une véritable politique familiale, conçue comme un ensemble cohérent. Certes, quelques initiatives ont vu le jour récemment. Sur le plan fédéral, la percée est modeste. Sur la plan des cantons, en revanche, les actions de soutien aux familles (et aux couples) et l'amélioration du cadre d'accueil de l'enfant se multiplient.

Même si l'objectif explicite n'est pas démographique, il rend justice aux familles et peut modifier, peu à peu, favorablement, les conditions de vie socio-économiques et socio-culturelles du couple et de sa procréation.

c) Agir à la fois sur la fécondité et la migration

Agir sur la fécondité ? On pourrait ainsi assister à l'émergence d'un début de consensus, à condition d'agir par petites touches ... dans les communes, dans les régions, dans les entreprises, pour finir par coordonner le tout sur le plan fédéral : le résultat final pourrait bien ressembler à une sorte de politique globale de population, mais... sans le dire.

Et le pragmatisme helvétique pourrait y ajouter un complément d'action sur la migration... toujours sans trop le dire !

LA SUISSE/SWITZERLAND

La gestion du tout, on l'aura deviné, n'ira pas de soi.

3) Gérer le survieillissement

Face aux incertitudes de la fécondité ou de la migration, il y a au moins une certitude sur laquelle le démographe peut s'appuyer : quoiqu'il advienne pour la natalité et la mobilité, nos sociétés européennes sont entraînées dans un processus de vieillissement irréversible. Et la Suisse y est encore plus exposée par sa faible fécondité (malgré le correctif migratoire) et surtout par le fort recul récent de sa mortalité (dont l'impact n'a pas été pris en considération dans le tableau 25, dont les deux variantes avaient retenu une très faible hausse de l'espérance de vie).

De plus, il s'y ajoute un survieillissement considérable. Si les plus de 65 ans passeront d'environ 1 million en 1991 à environ 1,6 million vers 2025, les plus de 80 ans doubleront largement leur nombre pour atteindre vraisemblablement un chiffre supérieur à 500.000 personnes ! Et l'accroissement de l'espérance de vie aux âges élevés devient impressionnant.

Le défi à relever est vaste : de nouveaux rôles et statuts, de nouveaux seuils et âges sont à inventer. Dans ce débat pluri-disciplinaire, la démographie sociale aura sa contribution à apporter : comment définir la vieillesse ?

TABLEAU 26.- PROPORTION DE PERSONNES "AGEES", SELON DEUX CRITERES : AGE ET ESPERANCE DE VIE

Périodes	H		F	
	65 +	esp. de vie = 10	65 +	esp. de vie = 10
1900	5 %	5 %	6 %	6 %
1940	8 %	5 %	9 %	6 %
1990	12 %	7 %	17 %	7 %

Le tableau 26 illustre bien par exemple le relatif arbitraire du découpage traditionnel des classes d'âge. En 1900, la proportion de 5% de la population âgée de 65 ans et plus avait encore une espérance de vie de 10 ans. Aujourd'hui, avec ce dernier critère, le vieillissement masculin serait de 7% au lieu de 12% et le féminin de 7% au lieu de 17% !

Gérer avec la participation de tous les partenaires le survieillissement de nos sociétés, voilà certainement l'enjeu majeur de l'évolution démographique des prochaines décennies.

Bulgaria/La Bulgarie
Kiril DONKOV

Documented demography in Bulgaria has quite a short history. The first census took place in 1880 and the regular collection of vital statistics on population movement started one year later. In this situation it is almost impossible to make any reasonable statement about population reproduction before 1880 (excluding some brief and incomplete historical descriptions). As concerns data accuracy, it became satisfactory only at the turn of the century, because the registration of demographic events in the first decades after the statistics on population movement were introduced, was done by the clergy and was incomplete.

One could discern mainly two periods in the evolution of our population:

a) a period of rapid and systematic drop in fertility and mortality;

b) a period of slow changes characterized by contradicting trends for a certain time. The dividing line between these two periods lies somewhere in the 1960s.

1) *Mortality and fertility during the period of demographic transition*

Let us first consider trends in the intensity of demographic processes, viewed by their gross indicators - fertility rates, mortality rates and rates of natural increase (see Table 1).

The data show that the transition which took place from high to low levels of fertility and mortality is of the classical type, characterized by an overtaking recession of mortality. We must immediately observe that the exact beginning of the transition is questionable owing to the incomplete data for the first decades and no data on earlier periods.

TABLE 1.- BULGARIA. CRUDE BIRTH AND DEATH RATES AND NATURAL INCREASE : 1881-1965 (PER 1000 POPULATION)

Period	Birth rate	Death rate	Natural growth	Period	Birth rate	Death rate	Natural growth
1881-85	36.8	17.8	19.1	1926-30	33.1	17.9	15.2
1886-90	36.0	19.0	17.0	1931-35	29.3	15.5	13.8
1891-95	37.6	27.8	9.8	1936-40	23.2	13.7	9.6
1896-1900	41.0	23.9	17.1	1941-45	22.4	13.4	9.0
1901-05	40.7	22.5	18.2	1946-50	24.8	12.3	12.5
1906-10	42.1	23.8	18.3	1951-55	20.6	9.9	10.7
1911-15	38.6	22.3	16.3	1956-60	18.2	8.7	9.5
1916-20	26.2	23.1	3.5	1961-65	16.4	8.2	8.2
1921-25	39.0	20.8	18.2				

Source: Statistical Yearbooks, CSO

At the turn of the century the level of mortality in Bulgaria was far below 35-40%, and the life expectancy (40.3 years for females and 39.7 for males for the 1909-1912 period) was significantly above the usual pre-transitional level. Therefore the transition to the new model of mortality started on the eve of the 20th century and this led to a rapid growth of the population: up to the First World War the natural growth rate was always above 16 p. 1000, except for the period 1891-1895. If we take into consideration external migration, the population of Bulgaria increased by 434,000 over the 1893-1900 period (i.e. by 15.4 p. 1000 annually on average); for the 1901-1905 period - by 291,000 (15.0 p. 1000); for the period 1906-1910 - by 302,000 (14.4 p. 1000). For the whole period 1893-1910[1] the population growth was 1 027,000 or 32%. In fact the last decades of the 19th century and the first decades of the 20th century were a period of a demographic boom in Bulgaria.

---

[1] Years of population censuses.

The drop in mortality gathered speed between the two wars, and affected above all low and middle ages. Over that period the mortality rate was reduced by almost one-half, while life expectancy rose by 15 years for the female and by 13 years for the male population. After 1950 the drop in mortality slows down and after 1960 (especially for men) this process almost comes to a halt (see Table 2).

TABLE 2.- BULGARIA. LIFE EXPECTANCY AT BIRTH (IN YEARS) : 1909-1971

Period	Males	Females	Period	Males	Females
1909-12	39.7	40.3	1956-57	64.2	67.7
1920-21	40.5	41.5	1960-62	67.8	71.4
1926-27	45.0	45.6	1965-67	68.8	72.7
1933-36	49.2	50.3	1969-71	68.6	73.9
1946-47	53.3	56.4			

Source: Official statistical publications

The very high level of natality persisted up to the middle of the second decade of our century. The local conflicts on the Balkan peninsula and First World War marked the start of a drop in fertility so that, despite the compensatory influence of the post-war period, the natality level in 1921-1925 was lower than in 1906-1910.

One peculiarity of Bulgarian demographic development is that the transition to the new model of fertility took place over a very brief period and at a very high rate: in only 55 years the birth rate decreased more than 2.5 times. That is why the effect of natality changes on the population age structure and the related consequences have been so pronounced.

Periodisation is quite different when we study natality changes among the urban and the rural populations. For the 1908-1912 period (Table 3) natality of the rural population was on average 13 points higher compared to that of the urban population. This indicates that the urban population was already considerably involved in family planning, which can be explained by the considerable differences in living conditions, and the higher cultural standards of the urban population. The first symptoms of a fertility drop in rural areas appeared only after 1920, although the drop was very fast. In the 1940s the rural crude birth rate was still higher than the urban, but the difference did not exceed a few points.

After 1965 (as a result mainly of intensive internal migration during the 1950s) we witness the opposite situation: the rural natality rate fell below the urban rate and the difference is increasingly widening.

TABLE 3.- CRUDE BIRTH RATE (URBAN AND RURAL) : 1908-1975 (PER 1000)

Year	Urban	Rural	Year	Urban	Rural	Year	Urban	Rural
1908	30.7	42.9	1925	28.8	39.0	1955	18.7	20.8
1909	29.8	43.2	1930	23.8	33.4	1960	16.1	18.8
1910	30.8	44.3	1935	19.4	28.3	1965	14.7	15.9
1911	30.2	42.6	1940	16.8	23.7	1970	18.0	14.6
1912	31.0	44.2	1945	21.5	24.8	1975	19.1	13.0
1920	31.7	42.0	1950	24.9	25.3			

Source: Statistical Yearbooks, CSO

The dynamics of some general indicators of fertility are shown in Table 4. In 1890 the average Bulgarian women gave birth to 6.98 children. But data for the following years show a process of progressive drop in fertility. The steepest drop was observed in the period between the two wars: the total fertility rate went down from 5.48 (children) in 1920 to 2.86 in 1946, i.e. almost by half. The decrease continued at a slowing down pace, but the general trend persisted up to 1965.

TABLE 4.- BULGARIA. FERTILITY: 1900-1965

Year	Total Fertility Rate	Gross Reproduction Rate	Net Reproduction Rate
1900	6.98	3.38	1.89
1905	6.85	3.32	1.85
1910	6.27	3.04	1.75
1920	5.48	2.66	1.69
1926	4.87	2.36	1.51
1934	3.51	1.70	1.23
1946	2.86	1.39	1.11
1956	2.31	1.12	1.01
1960	2.32	1.13	1.13
1965	2.08	1.01	0.97

Source: K. Donkov. Basic Characteristics of the Demographic Transition in Bulgaria. Statistics. Vol. 2, Sofia, 1979.

The profound changes in the mode of population reproduction are illustrated more accurately by the evolution of the net reproduction rate. When at the turn of the century the mortality rate was high and corresponding to a life expectancy of about 40 years, the Bulgarian woman had to give birth on average to 3.38 girls, in order to ensure her replacement by 1.89 girls. Owing to the high mortality among children, only a little more than half of the girls born reached maternity age. When mortality decreased the discrepancy between gross and net reproduction rates started to come down, so that in 1965 the net-replacement of one women was realized only by the birth of 1.062 girls (against 0.97 observed).

Since the trends of fertility and mortality have up to now run in parallel, the drop in mortality has largely compensated the decline in fertility and a positive natural population growth has been maintained. But after 1965, when fertility dropped to an extremely low level (net-reproduction rate being below[2] replacement level) the compensation is practically no longer working. This situation may have a quite negative impact on the future population growth.

2) *Recent trends of fertility*

The main trend in the evolution of fertility is downward in spite of some stabilization signs during the 1965-1980 period. Data for 1990 show that the crude birth rate has reached 11.9 p. 1000 - the lowest level in the whole history of the population in this country. The measures to stimulate fertility started in 1968 and 1973, produced two insignificant variations temporarily arresting after the introduction of the demographic measures, the crude birth rates rose by two points, but started to decline only in the following year (Table 5). In 1980 the natality rate fell below its level of 1966. Thus in about 10 years the effect of the two main demographic policy measures was completely exhausted.

The peculiarities in the evolution of urban and rural population derive mainly from the intensive internal migration from the villages towards the towns and cities, with its main part consisting of population in the age group 15-40. The migration flow has increased directly and indirectly the number of births among the urban population, and has thus checked the rapid decline of the fertility rate, which has proceeded at a slower pace compared to the total population of Bulgaria. Moreover, the effect of pro-natalist measures was felt more strongly in the urban areas.

---

[2] The rates in the table are computed from data for the respective calendar year, and do not reflect processes in real cohorts.

TABLE 5- CRUDE BIRTH RATES BY RESIDENCE: 1965-1990 (PER 1000 POPULATION)

Year	Urban	Rural	Total	Year	Urban	Rural	Total
1965	14.7	15.9	15.3	1972	17.0	13.3	15.3
1966	15.5	14.4	14.9	1973	18.4	13.4	16.2
1967	15.9	14.2	15.0	1974	19.8	13.6	17.2
1968	18.0	15.9	16.9	1975	19.1	13.0	16.6
1969	18.7	15.2	17.0	1980	15.7	12.4	14.5
1970	18.0	14.6	16.3	1985	13.8	12.3	13.3
1971	17.4	14.1	15.9	1990	12.1	10.8	11.9

Source: Statistical Yearbooks, CSO

Natality in rural areas has followed a downward trend throughout the postwar period. The growing discrepancy between rates in the rural and urban areas comes from the negative influence of the permanent process of population aging in rural areas. The pro-natalist measures had here only a slight effect in 1968. The reason is that the age structure was profoundly distorted by the strong prevalence of older generations, which cannot be easily influenced by such kind of measures.

One could observe three subperiods in the evolution of total fertility rates: (see Table 6):

- from 1967 to 1972: a first wave-like fluctuation due to the effect of demographic policies; the mean number of live-born children per woman suddenly rose in 1968 (2,17), and then fell back to its initial level in 1972;

- from 1972 to 1980 - the second fluctuation provoked by a reactivation of the demographic policy in 1973. The rise in the total fertility rate was of almost the same magnitude as in the first period, but the time of return to the basic level was 6 instead of 3 years.

- after 1980 - reestablishment of the stable tendency of fertility decline. In 1989 the total fertility rate (TFR) came down to 1.87 children which is far below 2.1 - the theoretical minimum ensuring the simple reproduction.

It is worthwhile stressing that after 1965 the net reproduction rate remained permanently below 1. As a consequence, the intrinsic rate of natural increase (Lotka's coefficient), which is a more realistic indicator of the actual state of the reproduction process, show negative values. In other words we could face depopulation quite soon. One strong evidence of this is the intrinsic rate of natural increase whose value has been rapidly approaching zero in recent years.

BULGARIA/LA BULGARIE

TABLE 6.- FERTILITY AND REPRODUCTION : 1965-1989

Years	TFR	GRR	NRR	Natural Increase Rate (per 1000)	
				On the real population	Intrinsic
1965	2.08	1.01	0.97	7.2	-1.3
1966	2.03	0.98	0.94	6.6	-2.5
1967	2.02	0.98	0.94	6.0	-2.4
1968	2.27	1.10	1.06	8.3	2.2
1969	2.27	1.10	1.06	7.5	2.3
1970	2.17	1.05	1.01	7.3	0.6
1971	2.10	1.02	0.98	6.2	-0.7
1972	2.03	0.98	0.95	5.5	-2.1
1973	2.15	1.04	1.01	6.7	0.3
1974	2.29	1.11	1.07	7.4	2.8
1975	2.22	1.08	1.04	6.3	1.7
1976	2.24	1.09	1.05	6.4	2.0
1980	2.05	0.99	0.97	3.4	-1.5
1985	1.95	0.95	0.92	1.3	-3.3
1989	1.87	0.91	0.89	0.8	-4.1

Source: K. Donkov. Basic Characteristics of the Demographic Transition in Bulgaria. Statistics. Vol. 2, Sofia, 1979.

A comparison of the Bulgarian data with those of other countries indicates that the fall to very low levels of fertility is a general situation. In many cases the total fertility rate (TFR) is below 1.5 even below 1.3 children. Obviously the Bulgarian population follows the development pattern of the European populations with a lag of 10-15 years. The deepening economic crisis, and the parallel intensification of external migration will probably reduce this lag. One proof of this is the abrupt fall of the synthetic measures of fertility over the past two calendar years.

It is important to trace the structural changes in fertility by their determinant factors in the process of fertility decline.

The systematic decline of age-specific fertility rates for the ages above 20 has led to a strong shift of the age curve towards the initial ages, respectively - to a strong decline in the mean age of motherhood (Table 7). Bulgaria is one of the European countries with a very low value for this indicator. The data for 1980 show that the mean age of motherhood in Ireland was 29.6; in Sweden, Finland, Switzerland and the Netherlands -

between 27 and 28 years; in Austria, France, Norway and Greece - between 26 and 27 years. The countries which are closest to Bulgaria (23.9) in this respect are Hungary (24.6 years) and Czechoslovakia (24.9 years).

TABLE 7.- BULGARIA. MEAN AGE AT MOTHERHOOD (IN YEARS) : 1960-1989

Year	Mean age at motherhood	Year	Mean age at motherhood
1960	25.11	1980	23.91
1965	24.89	1985	24.00
1970	24.67	1989	23.98
1975	24.49		

Sources: 1960-1980 - Donkov K. "Fertility and Mortality Conditions and Dynamics in Bulgaria." Nasselenie, Vol.3, Sofia. 1985.; 1985-1989 - Computations from official data of the CSO

In a population which has a low age of procreation (as is the case in Bulgaria) it is very difficult to introduce effective measures aimed at influencing reproductive behavior, because the vast majority of women reach the desired number of children and stop childbearing at a very young age. In the presence of traditions in this sphere it is not realistic to expect any serious achievement of the demographic policy, because it can influence only a limited number of the younger generation. This thesis was supported by our own experience. The pronatalistic measures influenced (and only temporarily) the women below 29 years. The response by the age group 30-34 was hardly felt, and the higher groups were not influenced at all.

Some considerable transformations were observed also in the structure of fertility by the order of live-births (see Table 8).

There is a pronounced trend of a relative increase in the share of first and second births in the TFR, and a decrease in the share of births of third and higher order. This means that the one- and two-child models are becoming ever more established in the attitudes of contemporary Bulgarian families. In fact the birth of a fourth child or of a child of a higher order is an event of low probability. The TFR assumes almost the same values in 1961 and in 1969. Yet in the interval between these two years the share of fourth births in the TFR decreased from 0.10 to 0.07; of fifth births - from 0.06 to 0.03; of births of sixth and higher order - from 0.08 to 0.04.

TABLE 8.- FERTILITY BY ORDER OF LIVE-BORN CHILDREN

Year	Rank of Birth						TFR
	1	2	3	4	5	6+	
1961	0.98	0.83	0.22	0.10	0.06	0.08	2.27
1965	0.94	0.74	0.19	0.09	0.05	0.07	2.08
1970	0.97	0.81	0.25	0.07	0.03	0.04	2.17
1975	0.97	0.92	0.20	0.07	0.03	0.03	2.22
1980	0.97	0.79	0.18	0.06	0.02	0.03	2.05
1985	0.91	0.77	0.17	0.05	0.02	0.03	1.95
1988	0.92	0.79	0.17	0.05	0.02	0.02	1.97

Sources: 1960-1980 - Donkov K. "Fertility and Mortality Conditions and Dinamics in Bulgaria." Nasselenie, Vol.3, Sofia. 1985; 1985-1989 - Computations from CSO' official data.

Fertility data for first marriages indicate that:

- for recent years, the curves describing the coefficients' dynamics tend to stabilize, and for several durations of marriage (e.g. 1, 4, 6, 7, and 8 years) they even tend to rise. But this process cannot be related to changes in family behavior, concerning the final number of children. It is rather a result of structural changes due to births being made up in time.

TABLE 9.- BULGARIA. OFFSPRING REACHED AFTER A CERTAIN DURATION OF A FIRST MARRIAGE (IN %). 1972-1989

Year	Duration of the marriage (in years)						
	0	1	2	3	4	5	10
1972	31.9	45.9	55.4	64.0	72.0	78.2	94.3
1975	29.1	42.6	53.0	62.4	71.2	78.4	94.8
1980	35.1	49.1	60.8	70.3	78.0	83.6	96.4
1985	33.5	47.8	59.3	69.0	77.3	83.9	96.6
1989	34.6	49.2	61.9	72.2	79.6	85.0	97.0

Source: Computations based on official data by the CSO.

- families tend to procreate at ever earlier stages - in the very first years after the first marriage. This is attested too by the growing average number of live-born children from a given marriage after a certain duration of married life (Table 9). For the 1972-1989 period the mean size of offspring reached increases by 2.7 points for the first year of marriage; by 6.5 points for the third year. These data also indicate that family procreation is almost completed at the end of the sixth year of the first marriage. At this duration of marriage 85% of the total offspring were realized in 1989; for 1972 the percentage was 78.2.

3) *Recent mortality trends*

The sixties proved a turning point in mortality evolution. This was the time when the general mortality rate ended its downward trend and started to rise again (see Table 10).

TABLE 10.- EVOLUTION OF THE CRUDE MORTALITY RATE. 1956-1989 (PER 1000)

Period	Mortality Rate	Period	Mortality Rate
1956-1960	8.7	1976-1980	10.6
1961-1965	8.2	1981-1985	10.3
1966-1970	8.9	1986-1989	11.9
1971-1975	9.8		
Source: Statistical Yearbooks, CSO			

The rise in the general mortality rate was largely due to population aging. Nevertheless, a serious contributor to these trends were changes in the age-specific mortality rates which not only did not follow the uniform decline, but increased or were stationary in a great number of age-groups, for a long time. For the 1970-1980 period mortality declined at an insignificant rate, and only at ages 0 to 30 years[3].

For middle-aged adults (30-44 years) the age-specific rates stagnated or grew slowly. An upward tendency is evident for all ages over 45 years, except for women's age groups 65-69 and 70-74.

After 1980 the mortality evolution demonstrates some new features. For males, mortality decreases only in the age group 0-4 years. The previous decrease for ages 5-29 years changes into stagnation, while the rise of mortality for all ages after 30 years is confirmed. For females, mortality rates remain stationary in the ages between 5 and 54.

---

[3] The mortality analyses are made on the basis of five-years intervals.

The declining tendency for the 0-4 years interval is accompanied by a mortality decline in all ages after 55.

The infant mortality trends have been also unfavorable during recent years. The long-lasting and abrupt decline observed up to the early 1980s, has gradually disappeared, and after 1984 infant mortality has maintained an almost constant level. (see Table 11). By 1988 the infant mortality rate was more than 1.5 times higher than in France, Great Britain, Australia, and more than double that of Japan, Switzerland and Sweden.

TABLE 11.- INFANT MORTALITY RATE IN BULGARIA 1965-1990 (PER 1000)

Year	Infant mortality	Year	Infant mortality
1965	30.8	1986	14.6
1970	27.3	1987	14.7
1975	23.1	1988	13.6
1980	20.2	1989	14.4
1985	15.4	1990	15.0*

Source: Statistical Yearbooks, CSO
* According to preliminary data

As a reflection of the evolution of age-specific mortality, the life expectancy of the population increased insignificantly, and even fell during certain periods. In the 1978-80 period life expectancy at birth fell by 0.33 year for males and by 0.36 for females compared with the 1974-76 period. After 1980 a slight rise was restored for females, while for males life expectancy remained close to the level of 1978-1980, which is even lower than in 1965-1967 (see Table 12).

The effects were even more negative for the life expectancies between ages 60 and 85. For males there has been a very clear downward tendency since 1960. Only the most recently computed lifetable registered an insignificant increase by 0.14 and 0.24 year respectively.

For females the declining trend stops in the early 1980s for ages 60 and over, and in the mid 1980s for ages 85 and over. By 1989 the life expectancy increase for these age groups was 0.63 and 0.29 year respectively.

TABLE 12.- BULGARIA. LIFE EXPECTANCY AT AGES 0, 60 AND 85. 1956-1989

Period	Males			Females		
	e0	e60	e85	e0	e60	e85
1956-1957	64.17	16.74	4.99	67.65	18.23	5.42
1960-1962	67.82	16.91	4.90	71.35	18.54	5.17
1965-1967	68.81	16.83	4.69	72.67	18.64	4.89
1974-1976	68.68	16.22	4.22	73.91	19.06	5.31
1978-1980	68.35	15.92	4.33	73.55	18.41	4.68
1984-1986	68.25	15.79	4.29	74.39	18.86	4.33
1985-1987	68.22	15.74	3.67	74.46	18.78	3.88
1986-1988	68.26	15.72	3.65	74.55	18.86	3.89
1987-1989	68.33	15.86	3.89	74.70	19.04	4.17

Source: Statistical publications, CSO.

4) Size and age-structure of the population

By the end of 1989 the population of Bulgaria reached 8,992,000 i. e. over 100 years it has almost tripled in size (see Table 13). Up to 1926 the rate of total increase follows an unevenly rising trend. The highest rate of increase registered (2.17% annually on the average) was between the censuses of 1920 and 1926. From that year on, the rate of increase diminishes and rapidly tends to zero during the last decade. Moreover, for the first time in our demographic development there is a negative growth of the population between two calendar years - a fact which can be explained above all by the intense external migration.

The determinant factors of the uneven population increase were the territorial changes, migrations and changes in the natural movement of the population. The territorial changes which followed the four wars in which Bulgaria was involved after 1887 have led to considerable positive or negative consequences on the country's human resources. The migration which were very intensive during the war periods also significantly affected the numerical changes of the population in both directions. But the most important determinants of the population evolution, of its size and structure, was the radical shift in the mode of population reproduction, a shift from high to low levels of fertility and mortality.

The Bulgarian population has one of the world's fastest rates of aging. The younger generation's share of the total has dropped by half over a 90-year period, while the share of aged people rose 2.4 times in only 55 years (see Table 14). The level of demographic

BULGARIA/LA BULGARIE

aging at the top of the Bulgarian age-pyramid is comparable to that of France, a country which has been experiencing the process of demographic aging for more than 150 years.

TABLE 13.- BULGARIA. NUMBER OF THE POPULATION: 1887-1990

Year*	population	Year	population
1887	3.154	1985	8.949
1900	3.744	1986	8.967
1920	4.847	1987	8.976
1946	7.029	1988	8.987
1956	7.614	1989	8.992
1965	8.228	1990	8.989
1975	8.728		

Sources: Official publications, CSO
* For the 1887-1985 period the data is from the population censuses; after 1985 - from the vital statistics.

TABLE 14.- BULGARIA. POPULATION AGE STRUCTURE: 1900-1989

Years	Age groups		
	0-14	15-59	60+
1900	40.2	51.4	8.4
1920	36,2	55.3	8.5
1934	35.5	56.7	7.8
1946	27.9	62.5	9.6
1965	23.8	62.9	13.3
1975	22.2	61.6	16.2
1985	21.4	60.8	17.8
1989	20.6	60.5	18.9

Sources: 1990-1965 - Donkov, K. Aging of the Bulgarian population and its socio-economic implications. Research Institute in Statistics, Vol. 14, Sofia, 1974; 1975-1989 - Computations from official data of the CSO.

A new feature in the evolution of the population age structure after 1965 has become evident : the diminishing share of the population aged between 15 and 59. This process is a result, on one hand, of the transfer of large generations to the higher age groups and, on the other, of their replacement at the age-pyramid's base by younger generations of smaller size, owing to the persistent fertility decline.

5) *Nuptiality and divorce rate*

Nuptiality was considered as a relatively stable process until very recent years. Indeed, from the turn of the century until the mid 1970s the nuptiality rate (marriages per 1000 people) has been fluctuating within an interval of 8-9%. Only in the periods of postwar compensation did nuptiality exceed 14%, but these are exceptions. But since 1978 the absolute number of marriages started to drop visibly; up to 1989 the absolute number of marriages fell from 75,000 to 63,000, while the nuptiality rate dropped from 8.5 to 7.0% (see Table 15).

TABLE 15.- BULGARIA. MARRIAGES PER 1000 POPULATION. 1965-1989

Year	Nuptiality	Year	Nuptiality
1965	8.0	1982	7.5
1970	8.6	1983	7.5
1975	8.6	1984	7.3
1976	8.4	1985	7.9
1977	8.5	1986	7.3
1978	8.1	1987	7.2
1979	7.9	1988	7.0
1980	7.9	1989	7.0
1981	7.5		
Source: Statistical Yearbooks, CSO			

Several factors brought about these changes:

a) a decline in the number of people of 20 to 29 years by 125,000 for the 1975-1985 period;

b) marriage postponement which is illustrated by the rightward shift of the age-specific nuptiality curve;

c) a certain decline of the age-specific nuptiality rates;

d) an increase of informal marriages. The 1985 census registered 35,000 of them.

The process of a rising divorce rate in a series of Western countries did not spare Bulgaria, although it proceeded at a considerably slower pace. But it would be exaggerated to view the rising divorce rate as an indicator of a crisis in the modern Bulgarian family, or of a disillusionment with marriage as an institution. The fact that many divorced persons re-marry is the most reliable evidence. In our case we rather have a greater freedom of choice in finding a new marriage partner when the existing marriage is a failure.

The data of Table 16 demonstrate a gradual rise in the divorce rate until 1982. The abrupt upsurge in 1983 reflects the nationwide discussion of a new Family Code and the fear of the economic and administrative sanctions it entailed. It is rather the case of a rush to wind up the ongoing divorce suits - a condition repeated in 1985 when the law came actually into force. After 1985 the divorce rate resumed its upward trend, but from a lower initial level. This means that the public adapts itself rapidly to measures that try subjectively to regulate some objective processes.

TABLE 16.- BULGARIA. DIVORCES PER 10,000 POPULATION. 1965-1989

Year	Divorce rate	Year	Divorce rate
1965	10.6	1984	14.8
1970	11.7	1985	16.0
1975	12.6	1986	11.2
1980	14.8	1987	13.0
1981	14.9	1988	13.8
1982	14.9	1989	14.1
1983	16.3		

Source: Statistical Yearbooks, CSO

6) *Demographic prospects*

In 1989 the total fertility rate reached a level far too low to ensure population replacement. At least for the years to come, a quick reversal of the fertility trend is hardly conceivable. On the other hand, for more than two decades now, the age-specific mortality rates have been stalling, and even rising for certain ages. The country's socio-economic situation is such that no decisive changes could be expected there either. A significant increase in the average life expectancy should be possible not earlier than 10 or 15 years from now.

Thus outlined, the existing adverse prerequisites project quite a pessimistic picture about the numbers and structure of the population.

In order to evaluate the future evolution of the Bulgarian population we shall use the long-term projections of the Central Statistical Office for the 1985-2065 period, variants 3, 4, 5 and 6, which outline the possible limits of actual development[4].

TABLE 17.- PROJECTION OF THE BULGARIAN POPULATION: HYPOTHESES OF MORTALITY AND FERTILITY

Years	Average life expectancy at birth (all variants)		TFR			
			Variant 3	Variant 4	Variant 5	Variant 6
	Males	Females				
1985	68.25	74.39	1.96	1.96	1.96	1.96
1990	69.10	75.20	1.94	1.90	1.90	1.88
1995	70.30	76.10	1.92	1.82	1.82	1.80
2000	71.90	77.20	1.90	1.75	1.75	1.72
2005	const.	const.	1.88	const.	1.70	1.64
2010	-	-	1.86	-	1.65	1.56
2015	-	-	1.85	-	const.	1.50
2020	-	-	const.	-	-	const.

The data of Table 18 show the effect of changes in fertility on the population growth in line with the adopted hypotheses. Owing to the inertia of the age structure, the population continues to rise during the first ten years under variants 3, 4 and 5. But after the year 2000 the situation changes radically: in all variants the population begins to decrease, while the magnitude of the negative natural growth rises with the shift from variant 3 to variant 4, 5 and 6.

Over brief periods, the differences in the population numbers between variants have been insignificant. Thus in 1990 the difference between the minimum and the maximum variants is only 17,000 persons. With increasing distance from the initial year, this difference becomes strongly pronounced. By the year 2000 it already reaches 176,000

---

4 The projection have been made in 10 variants through the combining of one hypothesis about mortality changes with 10 hypotheses about changes in fertility. The projection does not take account of the emigration processes after 1988, which are quite intensive.

and by 2065 it should be 2,368,000 persons. In every case the population drops sharply from its initial numbers[5].

TABLE 18.- BULGARIA PROJECTED POPULATION : 1985-2065 (000S)

Year	Variants			
	3	4	5	6
1985	8949	8949	8949	8949
1990	8961	8956	8956	8944
1995	8999	8979	8979	8925
2000	9029	8983	8983	8853
2010	8950	8843	8813	8545
2020	8791	8606	8520	8102
2040	8266	7872	7627	6852
2065	7451	6759	6264	5083

The Bulgarian population will continue to grow older, which will be seen both at the base of the age-pyramid, as well as at its top (Table 19). The relative share of younger generations (from 0 to 14 years of age) will be reduced by 4 to 9 points and reach values between 17 and 12% towards the end of the projected period. The share of the elderly (age 60 or beyond) will increase by 6 to 13 points and establish itself between 24 and 31%.

As a matter of fact, the described trend of the population number and age structure after 2000-2010 shows the limits of some extreme situations. That is why the realization of such a trend is highly improbable. The conclusion that can be made is that the recent evolution of demographic processes in Bulgaria will lead in the near future to a decreasing and aging population.

---

5. One should bear in mind that the data after 2000 have a hypothetic character

TABLE 19.-BULGARIA. POPULATION AGE STRUCTURE: 1985-2065 (IN %)

Year	0-14				Over 60			
	Variants							
	3	4	5	6	3	4	5	6
1985	21.4	21.4	21.4	21.4	17.8	17.8	17.8	17.8
1990	20.3	20.3	20.3	20.3	18.9	18.9	18.9	18.9
1995	19.2	19.1	19.1	18.9	19.4	19.5	19.5	19.6
2000	19.1	18.7	18.7	17.5	19.5	19.7	19.7	19.9
2010	18.5	17.8	17.5	15.7	20.9	21.1	21.2	21.7
2020	17.6	16.7	16.0	14.1	21.7	22.2	22.5	23.8
2040	17.3	15.9	14.7	12.4	23.8	25.1	26.1	29.4
2065	17.1	15.7	14.2	12.0	24.2	26.0	28.1	31.0

7) *Aspects of the demographic policy*

One could speak of a demographic policy in Bulgaria only after the year 1968, when the first legislative act with measures to protect the family and encourage fertility came into force. Five years later the set of pro-natalist measures was considerably widened, while the effect of already existing provisions was reinforced. Ever since, the system of demographic policy has been periodically perfected. Since 1968 a special body has been functioning (subordinate during various periods to the State Council, the Government, or Parliament) and performing programming and consultative work.

The main principles on which the demographic policy was built could be defined as follows:

a) Freedom of the father and mother to decide on their own how many children to have and to solve the problems of their rearing and upbringing;

b) The state shoulders part of the cost of rearing and upbringing the children through a differentiated system of various grants and financial subsidies;

c) Ensured social protection of motherhood during pregnancy and the rearing of children, and creation of the necessary conditions to enable mothers to continue their employment, preserve their qualifications of training and progress of their careers.

BULGARIA/LA BULGARIE

The forms of implementing demographic policies are extremely varied and range from concrete measures to guarantee women the right to choose, all the way to the various forms of money payments, indemnities and paid leave:

- free access to various contraceptive means and methods;

- relative freedom in deciding on abortion[6];

- leave in event of pregnancy, birth and adoption of children;

- paid leave for nursing and tending infants up to a certain specified age;

- non-paid leave for tending a child, with preserved rights of employment under the labour contract;

- protection against release from work;

- monthly family allowances above the labour wages;

- compensation in money for nursing a sick child;

- social and pay privileges for large families (with many children);

- housing credits at advantageous terms;

- credits for everyday needs to newly-weds, which are written off partially or entirely if certain conditions are observed;

- insurance at childbirth before taking employment, or in the event of unemployment, etc.

In all these cases the extra money paid out, the family allowances, grants, paid leaves or credit privileges are differentiated in accordance with the order of the child born into the family.

---

6. Over the past 45 years the policy on abortions in Bulgaria has been rather erratic, often shifting from one extreme to the other. Depending on the legislation in force one could discern : 1946-1951 - a period of complete ban on abortions; 1951-1956 - abortions permitted only by medical indication; 1956-1968 - full freedom of abortions; 1968-1973 - return to strict limitations; and after 1974 - limiting the ban to a definite number of partial cases.

Cyprus/Chypre
Ioanna CHAPPA

I. INTRODUCTION

Cyprus is a small island in the East corner of the Mediterranean Sea, with a population of 698,800 at the end of 1989 and an average density of 75.5 persons per square kilometer.

II. THE PERIOD 1881-1960

The year 1881 seems an appropriate starting point for the description of the development of the Cyprus population because the first census of population was taken in that year. Since then, censuses have been conducted regularly at 10-year intervals up to 1931 and then, with a break due to World War II, in 1946. A census was also taken in 1960 on the establishment of the Republic of Cyprus. Thus the period 1881-1960 can be said to describe the evolution of the population of Cyprus under the British rule as it largely coincides with that period (1878-1960).

1) Population Growth

According to the census results the population of Cyprus totalled 186,173 in April, 1881, more than a century ago. In 10 years time it increased by 12.4% and in twenty years time by 27.3% to reach 237,022 at the beginning of the 20th century. By 1946 it was almost two and a half times larger than in 1881 and by 1960 it had already trebled reaching 573,566. The population (Table 1) had been increasing at an annual rate of growth ranging between 1.1% and 1.5% during the first fifty years up to 1931 and at an accelerated growth rate of 1.7% in the period 1931-1960.

TABLE 1.-POPULATION GROWTH AT CENSUS YEARS

Census date	Population	Index of population growth	Annual growth rate in intercensal period
1881, 4 April	186.173	100.0	
1891, 6 April	209.286	112.4	1.2
1901, 31 March	237.022	127.3	1.3
1911, 2 April	274.108	147.2	1.5
1921, 24 April	310.715	166.9	1.3
1931, 27 April	347.959	186.9	1.1
1946, 10 November	450.114	241.8	1.7
1960 11 December	573.566	308.1	1.7

Source: Demographic Report 1989 (Department of Statistics and Research).

2) Fertility

Administrative data on the number of registered births and deaths are available since the beginning of the 20th century. According to published figures, the crude birth rate fluctuated around 30 per thousand up to 1945, ranging mainly between 26 and 34 with the extreme values of 22.4 recorded in 1942 and 34.7 in 1936. To smooth out some of these fluctuations crude birth rates have been calculated for five-year periods (Table 2).

It should be stressed that civil registration in Cyprus has never been complete. Particularly, at the early stages of introduction of a civil registration system, registration completeness is questionable. It is probable that in an agrarian society such as that of Cyprus at the beginning of the 20th century, births were under-registered so that birth rates could well be of the order of 36 per thousand. In the five-year period 1921-1925 and to some extent in 1926-1930 crude birth rates based on registered events were lower than in previous periods. This might reflect more deficient birth registration in that period, but a genuine lowering of birth rates seems also likely, being in agreement with the lower intercensal growth rate of the period. An increase in births was recorded after World War II. Finally, vital registration became particularly deficient in the period 1955-1960 because of the political situation in the island during the struggle for independence. Vital events and crude rates for that period are estimates. In view of the above, crude birth rates fail to describe accurately the fertility history of the period up to 1960. Other demographic evidence, however, shows that fertility decline must have started around the beginning of the 20th century. There was a further drop in the 1920's and a "baby-boom" in the post World War II period (1945-1950) which was followed by a resumption of the fertility decline.

TABLE 2.- CRUDE BIRTH RATES, CRUDE DEATH RATES AND INFANT MORTALITY RATES

Period	Crude birth rate	Crude death rate	Infant mortality rate
1901-05	29.4	16.0	-
1906-1910	31.4	17.0	-
1911-15	31.6	18.0	-
1916-20	30.0	20.0	138.2
1921-25	26.6	20.0	150.3
1926-30	28.9	15.8	151.8
1931-35	29.8	14.8	141.0
1936-40	31.9	13.5	116.4
1941-45	28.9	12.1	115.2
1946-50	30.6	12.0(E)	67.7
1951-55	26.7	12.0(E)	53.7(E)
1955-60	25.6	11.0(E)	44.2(E)

Source: Calculations based on figures given in "Census of Cyprus, 1946", "Vital and Migration Statistics 1962" and "Mortality in Cyprus, 1985" (Department of Statistics and Research).

The fertility decline is evident in the completed family size of different birth cohorts of women. Ever-married women born in the beginning of the century had born an average of 4.6 children per woman and the mean number of children born to ever-married women of successive birth cohorts declined to reach 3.2 children per woman for ever-married women born between 1935-1939 (Table 3).

Cyprus has undergone some of the phases of demographic transition later than Western European countries but at a faster pace as shown by the rapid transformation of family size. During the first period of fertility decline, the drop of fertility affected mainly the arrival of fifth and higher order births, while later it mainly affected the third and fourth order births. Whereas the parity progression ratio at parity 2 was 0.86 for the 1905-1909 cohort of women, it fell to 0.69 for the 1935-1939 cohort and from 0.81 to 0.54, respectively, at parity 3.

TABLE 3.-MEAN NUMBER OF CHILDREN BORN TO EVER-MARRIED WOMEN

Birth cohort women	Mean number of children ever born
Prior to 1905	4.6
1905-09	4.5
1910-14	4.3
1920-24	4.0
1925-29	3.9
1930-34	3.7
1935-39	3.2

Source: Demographic Survey 1980/81, p. 199 (Department of Statistics and Research).

3)Mortality

Since the beginning of the century, mortality has also been declining. The crude death rate followed a general declining trend except for the period 1916-1925 when the crude death rate had increased. This upsurge in mortality can be explained, in part at least, by the coincidence of the influenza epidemic, which appeared worldwide around 1920, with measles and a particularly serious malaria, as well as by the presence of refugees who had certainly brought with them smallpox and perhaps some other diseases unusual to Cyprus (Jones, p.67).

Infant deaths have been recorded since 1916. However, the under-registration of vital events renders the calculation of infant mortality more problematic as both the numerator and denominator are subject to error. The average infant mortality rate for the period 1916-1920 is rather low (Table 2) and an infant mortality rate of 170, the value recorded in 1920, seems more plausible for the period. Infant mortality rates have also been computed through indirect methods which enable a link between 1950's and more recent periods (Agathangelou). What emerges clearly is the spectacular drop of infant mortality from about 170 infant deaths per thousand live births to about 44 in the period 1956-1960.

The only available life tables during this period put the expectation of life at birth at 57.3 for males and 59.3 for females in 1931/46 and increasing to 63.6 and 68.8 respectively in the period 1948/50.

4) Migration

Migration statistics are available only since 1920. Recorded net migration has mostly been negative during the period, with the exception of 1922 and to a much lesser extent 1930-1931 and 1944-1945. The large positive net migration balance of more than three thousand recorded in 1922, about 1% of the population size, is the result of the Greek evacuation of Smyrna in Turkey. In the period 1921-1930 the implied net migration, obtained by comparing intercensal increase with the natural increase, is positive though the corresponding recorded net migration is negative. This may be partly due to deficient birth registration, but is also explained by the arrival of refugees in considerable numbers in the period 1922-1928 (Census of 1931, p.2, Census of 1946, p.17) not all of whom were recorded.

The refugees have been principally Armenians and Greeks from Asia Minor.

The excess of immigrants over emigrants in 1944-1945 is also understandable in the light of the large numbers of persons who were conveyed to and from the island.

III. THE PERIOD 1960 TO DATE

At the time of Independence in 1960 the population of the new Republic of Cyprus totalled 573 thousand. It was still a fairly youthful population characterised by a population pyramid with a broad base narrowing smoothly to the top. Its median age was 23.1 years, indicative of a population of intermediate age, but the distribution by broad age groups portrayed a still significant young content. The proportion of children below 15 was 36.4% compared to only 6.4% old-aged persons, 65 and over. During the period of 1961-1973 the population grew at an annual rate of 0.8%, clearly a much slower rate than the 1.7% experienced during the post World War II period to Independence. This decline of the rate of growth is attributed to a steady fall in fertility and, at times, heavy emigration.

1) Fertility

The total fertility rate fell from 3.51 in 1961 to 2.54 in 1970 declining gradually to 2.38 by 1973 and dropping further to 2.12 in 1974 (Table 4). In 1975, following the Turkish invasion fertility fell to 2.01 below replacement for the first time in the demographic history of Cyprus. Thereafter there was a reversal in the trend and the total fertility rate increased to reach a peak of 2.50 in 1982, or 2.46 in the period 1982-1985 (averaged over a four-year period to remove any possible effect from the leap-year) Since then, there has been a decrease in the total fertility rate and a resumption of the longer-term declining trend, with a total fertility rate of 2.37 for the period 1986-1989.

TABLE 4.- FERTILITY RATES BY AGE 1960-1989

Year	15-19	20-24	25-29	30-34	35-39	40-45	45-49	TFR
1960	31.8	182.8	210.0	133.0	105.8	32.0	6.6	3.51
1970	18.1	142.1	157.9	111.4	59.1	15.9	3.3	2.54
1975	20.2	133.3	143.5	72.3	26.8	6.1	0.7	2.01
1980	35.6	169.3	169.5	84.9	27.3	4.0	0.4	2.46
1985	34.4	159.5	153.6	91.1	32.8	4.9	0.2	2.38
1986	34.5	162.1	153.0	90.6	33.3	5.9	0.4	2.40
1987	34.1	158.3	149.7	86.4	29.1	5.4	0.2	2.32
1988	36.5	162.3	157.0	85.7	34.9	5.5	0.8	2.41
1989	33.4	154.2	152.3	87.9	33.7	5.9	0.3	2.34

The fertility behaviour within the childbearing ages has also changed over the years. Fertility in the sixties has been of the "late peak" type with maximum fertility in the age-group 25-29 and a significant contribution to total fertility of the age groups above 30 years up to 45 years old. In the seventies there has been a gradual shift towards the "broad peak" type with a plateau of maximum fertility in the ages 20-29.

At the same time there has been a significant drop in the contribution to total fertility of the 35-39 group to about 7% of the total, the contribution of the two higher groups being only minimal. In the eighties fertility shifted further towards the "early peak" type with a contribution of 34% by the 20-24 years old and of 32% by the 25-29 groups in the period 1986-1989.

In the 1980's a slow rise has been recorded in the mean age of women at birth of their children by birth order: For the first child from an average of 23.9 in the period 1980-1983 to 24.4 in the period 1986-1989 and for any child from 26.3 to 26.8 respectively. The increase in the mean age of women at birth of their first child is a direct result of the increase in the age at first marriage as fertility remains in Cyprus almost exclusively within marriage. Extra-marital births though on the rise during the last twenty years account even now for only 0.7% of total births.

2) Nuptiality and Divorce

In Cyprus there exists a prejudice in marrying during leap years as these marriages are believed to be unhappy. Thus marriages follow a four year cycle with a trough in leap years and peaks in the year preceding or succeeding a leap year, since many marriages which would have otherwise been celebrated in leap years are either advanced to the previous year or postponed for the next year. The mean age at first marriage calculated from annual marriage statistics shows a rising trend in the age at first marriage for both females and males. From an average of 22.9 years for the period 1974-1977 the mean age at first marriage of females rose to 23.9 in the period 1986-1989 while the mean age at first marriage of males rose from 25.7 to 26.6, respectively.

Marriage remains almost universal in Cyprus as reflected by the high, though declining, crude marriage rate and the small, though increasing, proportion of those remaining single at the age of 50. The crude marriage rate has been declining in the 1980's from 10.4 in the period 1979-1982 to 9.1 in the period 1986-1989, still high by European standards.

The proportion of never married women in the ages 45-49 has been increasing in recent years from 4.8% in 1960 to 4.9% in 1976 and to 5.4% in 1982. However, celibacy is still far from common. The number of divorces has been increasing but remains low compared to other European countries with a crude divorce rate of 0.6 per thousand population. The same applies to the total divorce rate which shows the proportion of marriages that are expected to end up in divorce which rose to 70 per thousand marriages in 1989 from 42 per thousand in 1980, far below the European experience.

Along with the increase in the number of divorces there has been an increase in the number of remarriages which accounted for 12.2% of all marriages in the period 1986-1989 compared to 7.3% in the period 1975-1978. Cohabitation is not very common in Cyprus, it may precede marriage but does not seem to substitute it.

3) Mortality

The decline in mortality continued in the period from the Independence to date with its main characteristic being a further drop in the infant mortality rate from about 40 per thousand live births in 1960 to about 11 according to the most recent figures. The decline in mortality is also reflected in the increase in the life expectancy at birth which reached 73.9 for males and 78.3 for females in the period 1985-1989 having increased from 70 for males and 72.9 for females in 1973. The increase in life expectancy is in favour of females widening the disparity between the sexes to 4.4 years. It is interesting to note that the decline of mortality during the 1970's and the 1980's is mainly in the ages above sixty years as shown by the expectation of life at the age of 60 which increased for males from 16.5 in 1973 to 19.3 in 1985-1989 and for females from 18.5 to 21.6 respectively.

The decline in mortality at older ages together with the decline of fertility will be contributing to further ageing of the population.

4) Migration

Cyprus has been mainly an emigration country with emigration playing a decisive role in the overall growth and structure of the population. Migration movements are largely affected by the political and economic situation of the country being small in periods of political calm and economic development and large in periods of political upheaval and armed struggle. Emigration recorded its peaks during the period 1960-1961 soon after Independence, in 1964 because of the Intercommunal fighting and during 1974-1976 as a result of the Turkish invasion. In the 1980's the net migration balance turned to positive, though small in magnitude. It is important to stress that emigration is age selective carrying away the younger and early middle age groups (about 80-85% of emigrants both males and females belonged to the under 40 group with peak ages in the 20-29 group). Immigrants on the other hand, who are to a large extent returning migrants are much older than emigrants. Thus emigration had been depleting the reproductive age groups and thus "exported" also part of the "potential natural increase". On the other hand immigrants having a somewhat older age structure than emigrants do not contribute to the same extent to the natural increase.

5) *Population prospects*

Fertility is expected to decline and reach a level below replacement in about fifteen years, or earlier by the year 2000 assuming a more rapid decline. Mortality is also expected to decline further and life expectancy at birth is assumed to reach 80 years for females and 75 years for males in thirty years or so. The net migration balance is assumed to remain positive but of small magnitude based on recent and what can be termed as normal trends.

The present favourable age structure of the population ensures positive population growth beyond the end of the projection period (30 years ahead), even if fertility is assumed to fall below replacement by the year 2000. The numbers and share of the youthful population will be at first increasing because of the favourable age structure of the population and then the share of the youthful population to the total will be declining.

There will be a general rise in the number of the elderly and their share will markedly increase even under the most conservative of assumptions.

The population of working age will also be increasing and ageing as well. The ageing will be more pronounced towards the end of the projection period.

IV. LEGISLATION AND POPULATION POLICIES

Government policy is explicitly stated in the Government Development Plans and population policy has been notably absent from all Government Plans up to the Third Emergency Economic Plan (1979-1981). It was only then that the emerging demographic problems of low fertility, high emigration and slow population growth were considered as contributing to labour shortages, thus affecting adversely the attainment of the objectives of economic planning. The formulation of an appropriate population policy which would reverse the unfavourable demographic trends, curb emigration, encourage the repatriation of Cypriots and contain the downward trend of fertility was amongst the objectives of the 1979-1981 Plan as well as of the subsequent two Development Plans. A series of measures were introduced in the last fifteen years, some of which were considered as having a direct effect on the rate of growth of population, while other measures were viewed more in the context of a general social policy rather than geared to specific population policy objectives.

1) *Measures relating to migration*

With regard to international migration, a tightening of emigration control was imposed soon after the Turkish invasion through the issue of exit permits. This was gradually relaxed as emigration slowed down and economic growth started to recover. A Governmental Service for Overseas Cypriots was formed with the objective of strengthening the links between Cypriots residing abroad and their homeland in order to maintain their Cypriot identity and culture. At some later stage various incentives for the repatriation of Cypriots were introduced. At times of high unemployment, in order to limit emigration, arrangements were made for temporary employment abroad.

2) *Measures relating to fertility*

As far as promoting fertility, various measures were taken which may have an influence on fertility behaviour to a lesser or greater extent:

(a) Those addressed specifically to large sized families (initially with 5 or more children and then extended to families with four or more children) which include free medical care, free education at a time when education was free only up to the 3rd grade of the secondary level, fare subsidies for public transport, priority and special provisions in the government housing schemes.

(b) Income tax reliefs which included progressive deductions from taxable income for parents of children under 16, children attending secondary schools and third level educational institutions in Cyprus or abroad. An additional amount of tax-free income was allowed to working mothers for each child looked after in an approved nursery or attending a kindergarten. For large-sized families with four or more children further deductions of income tax were provided for each child.

(c) Increased marriage and maternity allowances under the Social Insurance law.

(d) Measures which may be thought as contributing to the reduction of the cost of bearing and rearing children, such as the extension of free education up to all grades of the secondary school and relaxation of the criteria for housing and for the provision of free medical care to cover a larger proportion of the population.

(e) Measures aiming at allowing women to combine economic activity with motherhood through the provision of public and communal day-care centres for children of pre-school age with working mothers, expansion of public and private kindergartens and introduction of registered child-minders and other child-care services and more recently the enactment of laws 54/87 and 66/88 for the protection of maternity. This law provides for a mandatory leave of 12 weeks in total, during which maternity allowance is paid, 9 weeks of which must be taken in the period starting two weeks before delivery. In addition during a period of 6 months following confinement the working mother has the right to be absent from work for one hour per day. The rights of seniority, promotion and the right to return to the same work or other equivalent with the same remuneration is also safeguarded.

(f) Child Allowances introduced by laws 314/87, 166/88 and 75/91. With the recent revision of 1991 the monthly tax-free allowance was increased to Ł20 per child and is paid to families with four or more dependent children. The age limit of dependency has been extended beyond 18 to 23 years for unmarried female children and to 25 for unmarried male children, attending a full-time education institution. The family remains entitled to the child allowance as long as there is one dependent child.

To decide freely and responsibly on the number and spacing of children is a fundamental right of the couple. The state cannot therefore interfere with the couple's plans but helps the couple to fulfill its wishes and to exercise its freedom of choice which must exist in practice as well as in theory, since the decision for having children is conditioned by the psychological, social and economic constraints imposed by the organisation of the society. The organisation of modern society has been such that it tends to penalise large families and dissuades many couples from having more children.

The introduction of the child allowance in Cyprus is intended to ensure that the standard of living of the family does not deteriorate with the arrival of additional children. It could also be regarded as a demographic measure designed to reduce the economic constraints that drive a couple to decide to have fewer children than what they would like to, or even as an incentive for some couples to proceed to the fourth child and hence it may be considered as a measure to encourage fertility.

4) Abortion

Abortion had been a criminal offence up to 1974 according to the provisions of the Criminal Code. However, it is common knowledge that many unwanted pregnancies were terminated by medical practitioners in the private sector. This practice was generally accepted by the public and no prosecutions were instituted against the mothers or the medical practitioners themselves.

The law has been amended in 1974 to allow medical termination of pregnancy in cases when pregnancy has been the result of rape, when the continuance of pregnancy would involve risk to the life of the pregnant woman or she would suffer from a mental or psychological injury and when there is substantial risk that if the child were born it would suffer from a serious physical or psychological abnormality.

Thus, the amendment of the law came to legalise what had been the practice under such circumstances. There are no figures available to assess whether the number of abortions have increased since the amendment of the law but it is believed that its effect has not been important.

5) *Marriage and Divorce*

A very recent legislation came into effect in 1989 and 1990 which enables free choice of civil marriage for persons of the Greek community and provides for matters of divorce, judicial separation and family relations of the Greek community to be governed by civil family courts. These were governed until 1990 by the Greek orthodox church. It is difficult to forecast what will be the impact of these changes on the institution of marriage and the incidence of divorce in the future.

Figures for 1990, however, support no change whatsoever, as no civil marriages have been celebrated in lieu of ecclesiastical marriages and petitions for divorce at the newly established family courts were minimal.

Population policies in Cyprus have been mainly of the type of adjusting to consequences of demographic trends and intervention policies have been almost exclusively directed on migration. Intervention policies aiming at promoting fertility have not been explicit and comprehensive but consisted of individual measures taken mainly for social reasons.

To steer demographic behaviour in one or the other direction is not an easy task since Government action cannot go beyond the offering of incentives. As society is changing over the years, legislation and policy measures should be modified to be always in line with the changing attitudes and current life styles in order to be successful.

References

Agathangelou, A. (1985). Mortality in Cyprus, Department of Statistics and Research, Nicosia.

Census reports (various years).

Chappa, I. (1982). Demographic trends in Cyprus, Working paper No.14, UNFPA/ILO Project: Population, Employment Planning and Labour Force Mobility in Cyprus, CYP/77/PO1, Department of Statistics and Research, Nicosia.

Chappa, I. (1987). Population policy issues - Past, present and future, paper presented at the National Workshop on Population and Human Resources Development, Nicosia, April 1987.

Department of Statistics and Research, Demographic Report 1989 (1990).

Jones-St. John, L.W. (1983). The population of Cyprus, Institute of Commonwealth Studies, London

Greece/La Grèce
Georges SIAMPOS

I.- THE POPULATION OF GREECE UP TO THE SECOND WORLD WAR

1) Specific Aspects of the Demographic Evolution in the Past

The demographic situation at present in Greece is the result of the past trends of the components of demographic change, that is, of fertility, mortality and migration, during the hundred year period since the late 19th century. However, as the population change has been greatly affected by the successively liberated and integrated new regions in the country, the demographic situation can better be understood if the demographic evolution is examined since the revolution of 1821.

The process of demographic transition started in Greece in the fourth quarter of the 19th century and it is now in its last phase. The demographic situation, as it is reflected in the population pyramid of ages, although affected by the declining mortality and the waves of emigration, is mainly the result of the fertility decline. The demographic transition in Greece has followed with a time lag the pattern of the western European countries and especially that of Italy among the Mediterranean countries.

Thus, natality (table 1) started its sustained decline in Greece towards the final two decades of the last century, while it was earlier in Italy and much earlier (around the middle of the 19th century) in other western countries.

TABLE 1.- CRUDE BIRTH RATE IN GREECE AND OTHER COUNTRIES, 1821-1940 (PER 1000 INHABITANTS)

Period	Greece	Italy	France	Spain	Portugal	Sweden
1821-1830	40.8	...	31.0	...	...	34.6
1831-1840	52.0	...	29.0	...	...	31.5
1841-1850	52.3	...	27.4	...	...	31.1
1851-1860	49.9	...	26.3	...	...	32.8
1861-1870	50.1	...	26.4	37.9	...	31.4
1871-1880	46.8	36.9	25.4	......	...	30.5
1881-1890	43.6	37.8	23.9	36.2	...	29.1
1891-1900	41.9	35.0	22.1	34.8	...	27.1
1901-1910	39.8	32.7	20.6	34.5	...	25.8
1911-1920	30.7	27.3	17.4	29.8	...	23.1
1921-1924	31.4	29.8	19.8	29.2	33.0	20.3
1925-1929	32.4	26.8	18.4	29.2	31.6	16.3
1930-1934	31.4	23.2	17.0	27.0	29.3	14.4
1935-1939	27.6	...	14.8	21.6	27.2	14.3

Sources:
- Siampos G., "Demographic Evolution of Modern Greece 1821-1985", Athens 1973.
- INSEE,"Annuaire statistique de la France. Resume retrospectif", Paris 1966.
- Kirk M., "Demographic and Social Change in Europe, 1975-2000", (Council of Europe), Liverpool University Press, Liverpool 1981.
- C.I.C.R.E.D., "The population of Italy", "Spain", "Portugal", (1974 World Population Year, U.N.).

The disparities in the crude birth rate between Greece and other European countries can be distinguished into those with the Western European countries and the others with the Mediterranean countries, presenting broader diversities with the former and more similarities with the latter. The higher level of crude birth rate in Greece (relative to those in other western countries), combined with higher mortality rates, resulted in a rather medium level of the rate of natural increase --and has not provoked a population explosion-- throughout the period under consideration, ranging between 12 (or even 10) and 15 per 1000 population. Moreover, migration was always an important component of the population change in Greece; accordingly, the rate of real increase differs from that of natural increase. The evolution of the total population of Greece since the establishment of the State in the newly liberated area of the country (1828) up to the eve of the Second World War (1938) presented its growth together with the population of liberated regions during the 110-year period. In order to make that evolution comparable, the trend of the population density was used instead showing an increase of 245% during the period under consideration. The index shows a somewhat higher increase in the population in Greece as compared with that of selected countries.

Nevertheless, this excess is mainly due to the shrinkage of the base population, because of the casualties of the eight-year war period 1821-28, on the one hand, and the inflow of Greek refugees from Asia Minor and other territories (in 1922-23), on the other hand (See Table 2).

The demographic balance of the period from 1828 to 1938, is the result of both the horizontal and vertical increase of the population in Greece. The liberated and integrated geographic regions, as well as the mass inflow of refugees are two components of the population change, which, when eliminated from the census results, can give the intercensal change due to natural increase and migration effect. The indirect measurement of migration effects is based on the assumption that the population censuses are accurate or, at least, that they have the same degree of inaccuracy. Emigration (to the USA mainly) was very high at the end of the last and the beginning of this century, but its effects were outbalanced by the influx of refugees of 1922 (see Table 3).

TABLE 2.- COMPETITIVE EVOLUTION OF THE POPULATION OF GREECE WITH OTHER COUNTRIES, 1800-1938

Date	Greece	Italy	France	Spain	Portugal	Sweden
1800	100*	100	100	100	100	100
1850	137	145	129	147	115	146
1910	262	204	147	190	197	129
1938	345	233	148	247	255	263

Sources: - National Statistical Service of Greece (N.S.S.G.),"Statistical Year-Book, 1986", Athens 1987.
- INSEE, "Annuaire Statistique de la France. Resume retrospectif 1966, sauf pour la France", La population francaise, Tome I, France Metropolitaine, La Documentation francaise 1955.
- C.I.C.R.E.D., "The Population of Italy", "Spain", "Portugal", (1974 World Population Conference, U.N.).
Note: * For Greece, because of the successive territorial changes during the period under consideration, the population density has been used for the comparative index of the population change in time instead of the absolute size of the population. Also, the base period is that of 1828 (and not of 1800).

TABLE 3.- POPULATION INCREASE DURING THE INTER-CENSAL PERIODS, 1821-1940

Period / Census year	Census population	Intercensal increase				Area km^2
		Total increase	Liberation of new area[1]	Refugees	Natural incr. and migr eff.	
1821-1828 / 1828	753.400	-	753.400		⎫	47.516
1828-1840 / 1840	850.246	96.841	-		⎬ 343.000	47.516
1840-1853 / 1853	1.035.527	185.281	-		⎪	47.516
1853-1861 / 1861	1.096.810	61.283	-		⎭	47.516
1861-1870 / 1870	1.457.896	361.084	+229.516		132.000	50.211
1870-1879 / 1879	1.679.470	221.576	-		222.000	50.211
1879-1889 / 1889	2.187.208	507.738	+344.067		164.000	63.606
1889-1896 / 1896	2.433.806	246.598	-		247.000	63.606
1896-1907 / 1907	2.631.952	198.146	-	26.000	198.000	63.211
1907-1920 / 1920	5.531.474	2.899.522	+2.666.011	50.000	233.000	149.150
1920-1928 / 1928	6.204.684	1.187.724	-514.585	1.260.000 -439.000	367.000	129.281
1928-1940 / 1940	7.344.860	1.140.176	-	26.000	1.110.000	129.281

Sources : - Siampos G., "Demographic Evolution of Modern Greece, 1821-1985", Athens 1973.
- N.S.S.G., "Statistical Yearbook, 1988", Athens 1989.

Note: [1] Geographic regions integrated: 1864, Ionian Islands; 1881, Thessaly; 1912-13, Epiros, Macedonia, Aegean Islands, Crete; 1919, Thrace.

The proportion of the population aged 60 years and over was very low in Greece throughout the 19th century, as a result of the high fertility and high mortality rates. During the 20th century, owing mainly to declining natality and to a lesser degree to declining mortality, as well as the migration movement (emigration at younger ages and return migration at older ages), the ageing became marked, although it was kept at much lower levels than those observed in other European countries (see Table 4).

TABLE 4. GREECE: TOTAL FERTILITY RATE IN COMPARISON WITH OTHER COUNTRIES, 1851-1940 (IN TERMS OF AVERAGE NUMBER OF CHILDREN PER WOMAN)

Period	Greece	Italy	France	Hungary
1851-1855	7.50	...	(3.38)	...
1881-1885	6.20	...	(3.38)	...
1901-1905	5.50	...	2.79	...
1906-1910	5.40	...	2.60	...
1921-1925	4.32	...	2.42	3.52
1926-1930	4.77* / 4.31	3.59	2.30	3.07
1931-1935	4.38* / 4.32	3.17	2.16	2.74
1936-1940	3.88* / 3.73	3.10	2.07	2.55

Sources: - Siampos G., "The Present Demographic Situation in Greece and Future Prospects", (Academy of Athens), Athens University of Economics and Business, Athens 1991.
- Valaoras V., "A Reconstruction of the Demographic History of Modern Greece", Milbank Memorial Fund Quarterly, Vol. 38, No 2, New York, 1960.
- Festy P., "La fecondite des pays occidentaux de 1870 a 1970", INED, Cahier de travaux et documents no 86, Paris, 1979.
- C.I.C.R.E.D., "The Population of Italy", "The Population of Hungary", (1974 World Population Conference, U.N.).
Note: For Greece, the rates of the period 1851-1925 are indirect estimates and the rates of the period 1926- 1940 are in two series, the one of calculated and the other of corrected for under-registration marked with an asterisk(*).

2) *Stages of the Fertility and Mortality Decline*

It might be preferable to follow the evolution of fertility since the middle of the 19th century. In the middle of the century estimated fertility (Table 5) was at very high levels (7.50), much higher than in other European countries. Subsequently, gradually declining, fertility reached lower levels thirty years later (6.20) and much lower (5.50) after twenty years, at the beginning of the 20th century. During the First World War fertility dropped to very low levels and in the inter war period it continued its gradually declining trend (from 4.77 to 3.88).

Mortality, in terms of expectation of life at birth and infant mortality rate, meets some difficulties in its measurement owing to the lack of data. With some corrections of the available data and estimates for the gaps the series of these indicators for the period under consideration has been constructed (see Table 5).

TABLE 5.- GREECE: EVOLUTION OF THE MORTALITY (AS REFLECTED IN LIFE EXPECTANCY AND INFANT MORTALITY), 1861-1940

Period	Life expectancy at birth(1)		Infant Mortality rate(2)
	Male	Female	
1861-1865	29.5	30.3	198
1871-1875	31.4	32.4	196
1881-1885	33.3	34.5	191
1891-1895	35.2	36.6	183
1901-1905	38.1	39.7	173
1911-1915	40.0	42.0	166
1926-1930	45.0	47.5	133
1936-1940	52.9	55.8	109

Sources: (1) Siampos G., "Demographic Evolution of Modern Greece, 1821-1985", Athens 1973.
(2) Valaoras V.,"A Reconstruction of the Demographic History of Modern Greece", The Milbank Memorial Fund Quarterly, April 1960, Vol. 38, No 2, New York.

In the middle of the 19th century mortality was still at very high levels in Greece, reflected in a life expectancy at birth of about 30 years with an excess by less than one year of female over male life expectancy. Gradually increasing life expectancy at birth gained nearly 10 years of life up to the beginning of the 20th century (reaching 38.1 for males and 39.7 years for females). During the first world war the ascending trend was disturbed and it continued its trend during the inter war period, reaching the levels of 45,0 and 47,5 years of life for males and females respectively in 1926-30, and 52.9 and 55.8 for males and females respectively in 1936-40.

In comparison with other European countries, life expectancy in Greece was nearly at the same level as the average of the Southern countries at the beginning of the century, but it had been left behind by 1930, as life expectancy reached the levels of 50.9 and 53.5 in the region of the south, and only 45.0 and 47.5 in Greece for males and females respectively (see Table 5).This observation is obviously due to the consequences of the prolonged 10 year war period, 1912-1922, which ended with the influx of 1.3 million Greek refugees from Asia Minor; (the economic depression, the poor housing conditions for the refugees, the damaged health of a part of the population during the war, and the retardation in the level of living were negative factors for the health of the people during that period). Nevertheless, the improved socio-economic situation during the 12 year peaceful period up to 1940 favoured the health of the population and the life expectancy at birth increased rapidly to 52.9 and 55.8 years for males and females respectively.

3) *The Reproduction of the Population*

TABLE 6.- GREECE: REPLACEMENT RATE - REPLACEMENT OF THE GENERATIONS AT BIRTH, 1850-1900

Generation born around the year	Effective completed fertility rate	Necessary completed fertility rate for the replacement	Proportion of replacement assured
1850	7.45	6.11	123%
1860	6.79	5.91	115%
1870	5.55	5.37	103%
1880	4.55	5.01	91%
1890	3.59	4.69	76%
1900	3.07	4.21	73%
Source: Siampos G., "Recent Demographic Situation in Greece and Future Prospects", (Academy of Athens), Athens University of Economics and Business, Athens 1991.			

In the middle, as well as during the third quarter of the 19th century (table 6) the effective completed fertility rate (estimated when data are lacking) was above the necessary for replacement completed fertility rate, but during the fourth quarter it dropped below replacement level.It is remarkable that, although the completed generation fertility rate dropped below the replacement level, the rate of population growth continued to be at nearly the same level as before. This phenomenon may be attributed to two factors:

- the declining mortality and the increasing survival of the new-born of each generation have built in the population pyramid members of each cohort for longer, as they survive to pass to advanced ages;

- the age distribution, affected by the fertility of the past, was more favourable than it might be according to the current fertility levels.

4) The Demographic Effects of the two World Wars

The involvement of Greece both in the First and the Second World War is characterized by the length of the war period which lasted nearly ten years each, as well as by the high volume of losses.

Regarding the First World War, Greece was initially involved in the Balkan wars in 1912-1913 which ended in defeat in 1922. In the course of the long war period new regions were liberated, resulting in doubling the area and the population, but at the same time the population suffered considerable war casualties, on one hand, and immense mortality among the civilian population, on the other hand. The latter is mainly due to food shortage, caused by the international blockade, and to the influenza epidemic in 1918-1919. There was an influx of 1.3 million Greek refugees from Asia Minor, Eastern Thrace and southern area of Bulgaria in 1922-1923, while about 4 hundred thousand Turks and Bulgarians left the country, according to an agreement of settlement. Such a relatively immense number of refugees was too heavy a burden for the economy of the small country seriously damaged by the long war. However, in spite of all these adverse circumstances, the optimum combination of the national resources together with some international assistance succeeded in changing the desperate situation into a vivid growth both of the population and the economy of the country.

The involvement of Greece in the Second World War started in 1940 and ended in 1949 and brought about an occupation of the country by three armies, a civil war, heavy losses of the population and destruction of the economy and the health of the people. By the end of the Second World War a small region, Dodecanessos, of 2.687 square kilometers and a population of 115,343 inhabitants, was liberated and integrated in 1947, but during the war period (lasting for nearly 10 years) the population fell below its potential by nearly 10 per cent (6 hundred thousand missing persons and about 2,5 hundred thousand never born), owing to war casualties, as well as to high mortality because of the general famine as a result of the food shortage during the occupation and the deterioration of living conditions during that period. Moreover, significant losses occurred because of violent emigrations.

Generally speaking, the demographic losses of those never born in the two war periods are clearly depicted in the population pyramid. The mortality effects, on the other hand, are widely spread on the age scale and are not apparent, although some indications from the sex ratio by age could be detected, but with some reservations as there are also the effects of migration. The registered mortality is not a good source, as it has not full coverage of the phenomenon during that period.

II. THE POST WAR AND RECENT PERIOD

1) The Demographic Growth of Post war Period

The population of Greece, from 7.345.000 inhabitants according to the census of 1940 (taken a few days before the entry of the country into the Second World War), increased to 7.633.000 by the census of 1951, presenting thus a very small increment analysed into the population of Dodecanesos which was integrated in 1947 and a negligible real increase. At the same period the proportion aged "60 years and over" increased from 8.6% to 10.1%.

The total fertility rate, although increased from the low levels to which it had dropped during the war, had not regained its levels of the late inter-war period (3.88), but it reached initially 2.60 in 1950; and then it remained nearly constant varying slightly around 2.30 births per woman throughout the period up to 1965 (see Table 7). The average age of mother at birth presented a gradual decline and the pattern of the age-specific fertility rates shifted towards younger ages.

TABLE 7.- GREECE: TOTAL FERTILITY RATE, 1950-1965 (AVERAGE NUMBER OF BIRTHS PER WOMAN)

Calendar year	Average number of children per woman	Calendar year	Average number of children per woman
1950	2.60	1961	2.19
1956	2.38	1962	2.23
1957	2.32	1963	2.22
1958	2.28	1964	2.31
1959	2.33	1965	2.30
1960	2.28		

Source: Office National de Statistique de la Grèce (O.N.S.G.), "Movement Naturel de la Population de la Grèce", Athenes, 1956-1965, (Annual Volums).

During the same period, mortality increased considerably in the war period, but soon after it started declining again. Life expectancy at birth gained 10.5 years for males and 10.9 years for females in the decade 1940-1950 and also 3.9 for males and 3.7 for females in the decade 1950-1960 - reaching 67.3 years for males and 70.4 years for females. Infant mortality has also made good progress as it dropped from 112 (per 1000 live births) in 1940 to 62 in 1950 and to 50 in 1960.

TABLE 8.- GREECE: EVOLUTION OF MORTALITY, 1949-1965 (IN TERMS OF E0 AND Q0)

Year	1000q0	e0 Males	e0 Females	Year	1000q0	e0 Males	e0 Females
1949	65.0			1959	50.6		
1950	62.0	63.4	66.7	1960	49.7	67.3	70.4
1951	59.7			1961	49.2		
1952	58.6			1962	49.7		
1953	57.5			1963	46.8		
1954	56.4			1964	44.6		
1955	55.5			1965	42.2		
1956	54.8						
1957	53.6						
1958	51.8						

Source: O.N.S.G., "Mouvement Naturel de Statistique de la Population de la Grece", Athenes, 1956-1965, (Annual Volums).
Note: Infant mortality rates adjusted for under-registration.

2) *Recent Evolution of Fertility*

The total period fertility rate fluctuated around 2.30 live births per woman throughout the first thirty years (1950-1980) of the post war period, marking its lowest point in 1961 with 2.19 and its highest in 1968 with 2.56. In the decade of the 1980s total fertility rate fell below replacement level, dropping to 2.09 in 1981 and further gradually declining it reached the very low level of 1.43 in 1989 (see table 9).

It is worth noting that the fertility decline occurred in Greece simultaneously with other Mediterranean countries, Spain and Portugal, with a time lag from Italy. The steady decline of the total fertility rate below replacement level in the 1980s raises the question of the future of the age fertility pattern of women and of the mechanism of changes which leads to the decline of the total fertility rate.

TABLE 9.- GREECE: EVOLUTION OF TOTAL FERTILITY RATE, 1964-1989

Calendar year	Average number of children per woman	Calendar year	Average number of years per woman	Calendar year	Average number of years per woman
1965	2.30	1975	2.37	1985	1.68
1966	2.38	1976	2.39	1986	1.62
1967	2.55	1977	2.27	1987	1.52
1968	2.56	1978	2.27	1988	1.52
1969	2.48	1979	2.26	1989	1.43
1970	2.34	1980	2.23		
1971	2.30	1981	2.09		
1972	2.32	1982	2.02		
1973	2.28	1983	1.94		
1974	2.39	1984	1.82		

Source: O.N.S.G., "Movement Naturel de la Population de la Grece", Athenes, 1965-1989, (Annual Volums).

- The most striking change is the considerable drop of the age-specific fertility rates in the young ages. Thus, the sum of the fertility rates up to the ages of 20 and 25 present a decline (per 10.000) as follows:

	at the age of 20		at the age of 25	
Generation of 1955	465	100	1575	100
Generation of 1960	526	113	1180	75
Generation of 1965	364	78	(920)	58
Generation of 1970	(220)	47		

- Also, since 1981 and from the age of 25 and over there is a declining trend of the age-specific rates with no indication of the point they are to stop their decline:

Age group	Generations	Fertility rates per 10.000 in 1970	Generations	Fertility rates per 10.000 in 1985	Percentage of decrease decrease
20-24	1946-1950	1404	1961-1965	1180	16%
25-29	1941-1945	1430	1956-1960	1025	28%
30-34	1936-1940	937	1951-1955	544	42%
35-39	1931-1935	426	1946-1950	192	55%
40-44	1926-1930	91	1941-1945	44	52%

TABLE 10. GREECE: COMPLETED FERTILITY OF BIRTH COHORTS 1930-1960

Generation	Completed fertility	Generation	Completed fertility
1930	2.19	1945	2.02
1935	2.07	1950	2.03
1940	2.04	1955	2.00
		1960	(1.88)

Sources: Siampos G. and Kotsifakis G., "Fertility by Generations in Greece", in Cohort Fertility in Europe, Population Studies No 21, Council of Europe, Strasbourg 1989.

It seems that through a shifting of the fertility pattern towards younger ages (that is, the increasing of the fertility rates in younger ages counterbalanced the effects of their declining in advanced ages) total fertility rate was kept just above replacement level throughout the post war period up to 1980; and then, in the decade of the 1980s age-specific fertility pattern declined in all ages with a gradually increasing average age of mother at birth and thus the total fertility rate dropped below replacement level following a declining trend (see Table 9).

The question raised at this point is what might be the future fertility level and what might be the degree of replacement? The completed fertility of the generation born in 1955 from the available provisionable data of 1990 shows that even the generation fertility is to drop below replacement level. Also, total fertility rate is already considerably below replacement and, if it is to remain at these levels for long, the generation fertility will be affected, too.

3) Nuptiality

The proportion of the population married steadily increased for both men and women in all age groups throughout the post-war period up to 1981. The same could be observed in the total first marriage rate which presented an ascending trend in the 1960s and the 1970s (when it was 1.04 and 1.15 in 1970 and 1975 respectively). During the 1980s nuptiality presented a decline. The total marriage rate started a descending trend (reaching 0.83 in 1985 and 0.86 in 1989) and the average age at first marriage, which had followed a declining trend during the 1960s and the 1970s, showed an ascending trend, increasing by more than one year of age up to the end of the 1980s (from 22.3 to 23.5).

TABLE 11.- GREECE: PROPORTION OF THE POPULATION MARRIED BY SEX AND AGE GROUPS, 1951-1981

Age	1951	1961	1971	1981
Males				
15-19	1.1	1.0	1.3	1.0
20-24	11.3	11.0	13.3	13.1
25-29	35.8	42.4	48.1	53.3
30-44	78.0	79.2	84.6	86.4
45-54	89.4	91.3	92.2	93.4
Females				
15-19	4.6	5.8	11.0	13.7
20-24	29.5	34.3	46.7	52.1
25-29	59.5	64.6	72.9	77.5
30-44	79.3	81.8	85.8	87.8
45-54	73.1	78.6	81.5	84.7

Source: O.N.S.G., "Recencement de la population de Greece", Athenes 1951, 1961, 1971, 1981.

Perhaps it is in connection with the postponement of marriage that the proportion of extramarital births is increasing - although still very low, it increased in the 1980s as follows:

```
In 1970:   1.1 of total births
 " 1975:   1.3 "  "   "
 " 1980:   1.5 "  "   "
```

```
" 1985:    1.8  "   "   "
" 1989:    2.1  "   "   "
```

The declining nuptiality affected negatively the fertility level, because it had had its bearing on the number of first order births, although it is not the only negative factor. Divorces, on the other side are steadily increasing as the total divorce rate, although still lower than in many other countries, was doubled during the 1970s (increasing from 5.1 to 9.5) and then it increased further in 1980s (reaching 13.1 per 100 marriages in 1988).

4) Recent Mortality Decline and Ageing of the Population

TABLE 12. GREECE: EVOLUTION OF THE MORTALITY (IN TERMS OF LIFE (EXPECTANCY AT BIRTH AND INFANT MORTALITY RATE), 1965-1989

Year	1000q0	Males e0	Females e0	Year	1000q0	Males e0	Females e0	Year	1000q0	Males e0	Females e0
1965	42.2			1974	29.6			1983	14.6		
1966	40.8			1975	27.9			1984	14.2		
1967	39.9			1976	26.0			1985	14.1		
1968	38.9			1977	24.5			1986	12.2	72.6	77.6
1969	37.8			1978	23.0			1987	11.7		
1970	35.9	70.13	73.64	1979	21.7			1988	11.0		
1971	33.6			1980	19.9	72.15	76.55	1989	9.7		
1972	31.9			1981	16.9						
1973	30.6			1982	15.1						

Sources: - O.N.S.G., "Mouvement Naturel de la Population de la Grece", Athenes, 1956-1989, (Annual Volums).
- N.S.S.G., "The Population of Greece in the Second Half of the 20th Century", Athens 1980.
Note: q0, infant mortality rate (per 1000 live births) adjusted for under-registration up to 1980. oe0, life expectancy at birth (in years).

From the 1969-1971 period to 1979-1981 life expectancy at birth increased from 70.1 years to 72.2 for males and from 73.6 years to 76.7 for females. In the years 1984-1987 it was 72.6 for males and 77.6 for females. During the previous decades in the post war period up to the 1970s mortality reduction was mainly due to that of the infants and young adults. It is the decline in the age-specific mortality rates of these two groups that has played an important role in the increase of life expectancy in the past; but at present the mortality rates in the young ages have become so low that no significant gains in life expectancy could be expected from a further reduction of mortality in these ages. Infant mortality, for example, although higher than in many other European countries, has reached very low levels; and this is particularly welcome, but there is still room for a further decline, (see Table 12).

Since the early 1970s the evolution of mortality is mainly due to mortality reduction among the aged population. This aspect of the mortality reduction can be observed in the progress made in life expectancy at the age of 60, as well as, at the age of 85 years old (see Table 13). The change occurred during the 1970s: the progress made in the decade 1970-1980 is much higher than that in each of the two preceding decades, for women both at the age of 60 and the age of 85; and this is also applicable for men at the age of 85, but it is not striking at the age of 60. The observed changes were particularly marked among women. These differentials in the life expectancy reflect the overmortality of males which became more acute during the last decades.

The most important consequence of this change in the evolution of mortality is its effect on the ageing of the population. For measuring these effects, the sex-age population pyramid at certain dates in the period 1951-1985 was calculated on the assumption that mortality was constant on the level of 1950 and the proportion (%) of those of 60 and over to total population was taken, on one hand; and then, the observed proportion (%) of the population aged 60 and over was used, on the other hand (see Table 14).

TABLE 13. GREECE: LIFE EXPECTANCY AT THE AGE OF 60 AND THE AGE OF 85, LIFE TABLES 1950-1980

Period	Males				Females			
	oe60	Gains	oe85	Gains	oe60	Gains	oe85	Gains
1949-1951	16.21		4.31		17.99		4.44	
		+0.67		-0.22		+0.60		+0.06
1959-1961	16.88		4.09		18.59		4.50	
		+0.66		+0.17		+0.74		-0.02
1969-1971	17.54		4.26		19.33		4.48	
		+0.63		+0.69		+1.30		+1.06
1979-1981	18.17		4.95		20.63		5.54	

Source: O.N.S.G., "Mouvement Naturel de la Population de la Grece", Athenes 1956-1989, (Annual Volumes).

A comparison between the two series shows that in 1985, for example, the percentage of population in the age group of 60 years old and over might be 14.8% and not 18.1%; and that the process of ageing, owing to mortality reduction, is particularly significant after 1970, (see Table 14).

TABLE 14.- GREECE: PERCENTAGE OF POPULATION AGED 60 AND OVER, 1950-1985

1950	1955	1960	1965	1970	1975	1980	1985
- At constant mortality level of the year 1950							
9.9	10.4	11.0	12.1	14.1	14.1	14.4	14.7
Currently observed							
9.9	10.8	11.8	13.4	16.0	17.4	16.9	18.1

Source: Siampos G., "Recent Demographic Developments and Future Prospects in Greece", (Academy of Athens), Athens University of Economics and Business, Athens 1991.

5) *Movement of the Population since the Last War*

The summary of the demographic evolution during the post war period 1951-1981 is formulated by means of the series of the aggrregates of the censuses taken and the natural and migration movement in the intercensal periods (see Table 17). Each period is delimited by the census dates and the population change is analysed into its components' intensity:

1951-1961: natality and mortality of medium level and high net emigration (to overseas countries mainly);

1961-1971: natality and mortality of medium level and very high net emigration (to European countries mainly);

1971-1981: declining natality, declining mortality (with increasing crude death rate), and strong return migration (after the energy crisis) from the European countries mainly;

1981-1991: declining natality at very low levels, mortality slightly declining (with slowly increasing crude death rate) and very low return migration with the presence of foreign migrants (Greece, from an emigration country becomes an immigration country).

GREECE/LA GRECE

TABLE 15.- GREECE: MOVEMENT OF THE POPULATION, 1951-1991 (ABSOLUTE NUMBERS IN THOUSAND)

Date of Census	Total Population	Births	Deaths	Natural increase	migration	Net increase
7 April 1951	7,633	1,539	575	964	-211	753
		19.2‰	7.2‰	12.0‰	-2.6‰	9.4‰
19 March 1961	8,389	1,533	694	839	-435	404
		17,8‰	8,1‰	9.7‰	-5.0‰	4.7‰
14 March 1971	8,769	1,446	809	637	+272	909
		15.5‰	8,7‰₀	6.9‰	+2.9‰	9.8‰
5 April 1981	9,740	1,167	907	260	+268	529
		11,7‰	9,1‰	2.6‰	+2.7‰	5.3‰
17 March 1991	10,269					

Source: - Siampos G., "La situation demographique en Grece", a Colloque Franko-Helleniquede Demographic, 18-21/5/1987, Hellenic Societe pour Ettude Demographiques, Athens 1990.
- N.S.S.G., "Mouvement Naturel de la Population de la Grece", Athenes, 1956-1990, (Annual Volumes).

Note: The postenumeration sample surveys showed an overestimation by 0.05% for the census of 1961, an underestimation by 0.42% for the census of 1971, an overestimation by 0.36% for the census of 1981, and probably an overestimation for the census of 1991 (but the results are not available at present).The data for 1991 are provisional.

III. ASPECTS OF THE POPULATION POLICY

Within the frames of the social and economic policies in Greece are elements directly or indirectly related to population. They could be grouped into policy measures related to family, to contraception, to abortion, to divorce and migration.

1) Statutory Economic and Social Support for the Family

The ways in which the State by law and regulation is arranging for assistance to families include family allowances, relief from income tax, support for housing and accommodation costs, and provision for nursery classes, always taking into consideration the number of children.

There are two tiers of family allowances, those paid to employees in the private sector and those paid to employees of the State; and there are also supplementary allowances paid to large families. Family allowances in the private sector were originally established by collective bargaining. The amount of the allowance is calculated according to the number of days worked in the previous year and the number of children (progressively increasing).

The family allowances paid to civil servants are lower than those paid to employees in the private sector; and they are paid to one of the parents (either to father or mother). The amount of these allowances was adjusted in the mid 1980s.

Family allowances according to the number of children are also paid to non working mothers whose husband has joined the army or is in prison, as well as to return migrants or repatriated Greeks (during the first year after their arrival). The amount of these allowances is equal to that paid to wage earners of the lower family income.

Families with many children (five or more), since 1940 have had certain benefits, but no direct money allowance was paid to these families. In 1973 a system of family allowances was established providing for a special allowance to be paid to large families. However, the initial amount of these allowaces was not adjusted to take into account inflation, and thus it resulted in a negligible sum of money (its value became more than 20 times less).

In 1990 a new series of family allowances was introduced, providing that to every mother who bears a third child a monthly family allowance of 37.000 drachmas (which, when proposed as a measure, was nearly equal to the lowest wage in the labour market) is paid for a period of three years, and that to mothers who have already had a third child the same amount of family allowance is paid up to the time the child will complete his third anniversary. An allowance is also paid to every mother who has borne many children (five or more children), according to the number of the unmarried children, and when all are married, the mother is paid a monthly pension equal to four daily wages.

2) *Contraception and Abortion*

There was no statutory control concerning the production and distribution of contraceptives in Greece. In the late 1970s and the early 1980s family planning centers were gradually created providing consultation to young couples and contraceptives were advertised; (condoms were especially advertised against AIDS).

The contraceptive practice in the country had not made wide use of modern methods of contraception. Surveys carried out in the 1960s (Valaoras V., Polychronopoulou A. and Trichopoulos D., "Greece: Post war Abortion Experience", in *Studies in Family Planning*, The Population Council, New York, 1969) showed that at that time the most frequently used methods were coitus interruptus, with 49%, condom, with 22%, induced abortion, with 21%, and others, with 8%.In the 1980s survey showed that contraceptive practice had changed its preference towards modern methods, showing coitus interruption, with 34%, condom, with 28%, induced abortion, with 22% (assumed to be the same), and others, with 16%.

The formal position in the past was that induced abortion was illegal. Abortion was however lawful if performed by a physician for health reasons of the pregnant woman or with the approval of the pregnant woman, if the pregnancy was the result of rape, incest or sexual assault on a girl under 16. In the late 1970s the exception to illegal abortion was extended to include not only the physical health but also the mental and psychological health of the pregnant woman; and in the early 1980s there was a further expansion of the lawful cases of abortion by increasing the lower limit of age for marriage from the 16th to the 18th year of age with the possibility of covering the abortion cost by the government.

3) Divorce

There were nine recognised grounds on which a spouse might seek dissolution of marriage. These include offences by the other partner such as adultery, bigamy, attempted murder, malicious desertion for at least two years and serious impairment of the matrimonial bonds, and also such conditions as the other spouse suffering from mental illness, leprosy, or being incapable of sexual intercourse.

TABLE 16.- GREECE: DIVORCES AND TOTAL DIVORCE RATE (NUMBER OF DIVORCES PER 100 MARRIAGES)

Year	Total divorce	Divorce rate	Year	Total divorce	Divorce rate	Year	Total divorce	Divorce rate
1970	3,492	5.0	1976	3,768	5.0	1982	5,558	8.0
1971	3,675	5.0	1977	4,517	6.5	1983	5,907	8.0
1972	3,395	5.0	1978	4,322	6.0	1984	8,686	12.0
1973	4,075	5.0	1979	4,716	7.0	1985	7,568	11.0
1974	3,631	5.0	1980	6,684	10.0	1986	8,939	13.0
1975	3,726	5.0	1981	6,349	9.0	1987	8,830	13.0
						1988	8,556	12.0

In the late 1970s and the early 1980s new legislation expanded the grounds of divorce by adding to those already in effect, divorce on grounds of mutual consent of the two spouses. It was also provided that married persons who lived apart for more than five years could be declared separated.

Statistics of divorces show a nearly stable number and a nearly constant divorce rate, fluctuating around 5 per 100 marriages in the 1960s and early 1970s; but in the late 1970s it started gradually increasing, reaching 10 in 1980 and nearly 12 (per 100 marriages) from 1984 onwards.

4) Migration

Migration policies on the part of Greece only could not regulate the migratory movement, because migration depends not only on the policy of the country of emigration, but on the policy of the country of immigration, also. In the post war period since 1950 migration policy of Greece -- going beyond the simple tolerance of emigration -- supported in several ways the emigration of the population:

- permission was given to operate in the country the Inter- governmental Committee for European Migration (ICEM) which was partly financed by the Government;

- through bilateral agreements emigration to European countries was facilitated (mainly with the operation in Greece of the German Committee for Migration).

Migration policies of the overseas countries were selective: they preferred skills and experienced workers; and, by nationality, Greeks were among their preference. Most selective were the USA, industralized European countries were less selective, but intended for temporary migrants.

The migration policy of Greece was justified in the 1950s and the 1960s by the existing high unemployment and underemployment of that time and aimed, together with other goals, to strengthen the balance of payments. However, from the beginning of the 1970s these reasons lost their meaning, as in the labour market appeared labour shortages, and the employment of foreign workers started, while the savings of Greeks abroad might be considered enough to secure a satisfactory inflow of foreign exchange. In spite of the new situation created, the migration policy did not change drastically. It was only in 1974 that the government assistance to ICEM was restricted, although the operation of this international organization is continuing. The suspension of the works of the German Committee for Migration, on the other hand, was the result of the migration policy of the F.R. of Germany and not the policy of Greece.

The following measures concerning migration have been taken in the late 1970s and in the 1980s:

- participation of Greece in expenditure on vocational training for Greeks living abroad and their children;

GREECE/LA GRECE

- provision has been made for granting monthly training benefits to children of Greeks working abroad, provided that these children attend regular training programmes in Greece;

- facilities are granted to return migrants allowing them to import goods free of exchange formalities;

- favourable terms for loans enabling migrant workers to acquire a house in Greece, provided that they have deposits in foreign exchange;

- enrolment of Greek migrants' children in apprentice schools in Greece;

- special incentives for labour force mobility from which Greek migrants can also profit.

Population of foreign citizenship has gradually increased from 95.000 in 1970 to 195.000 in 1980 and to 217.000 in 1989, while there is an unknown number of clandestine migrants. Nearly half of the registered foreigners are from the member countries of the Council of Europe, and the rest from other countries (of Eastern Europe, Middle East, North Africa, Philippines, India, Pakistan and others).

L'Albanie/Albania
Piro DISHNICA
Emira GALANXHI

UNE CROISSANCE DEMOGRAPHIQUE RAPIDE

Le premier recensement de la population de l'Albanie a eu lieu au vingtième siècle, au mois du septembre 1923 ; sept autres recensements généraux de la population ont été effectués depuis lors (tableau 1).

L'Albanie est le deuxième pays d'Europe et des Balkans où la population totale compte encore plus d'hommes que de femmes.

Au cours de ce siècle, la population a doublé une première fois entre les recensements de septembre 1923 et d'octobre 1960 et une seconde fois de 1960 à 1989. De 1923 à 1938 la population a augmenté à un taux de croissance annuelle de 1,7 pour cent et pendant les 45 dernières années, l'accroissement naturel a été très élevé, 2,4 pour cent par an[1].

---

[1] Pour la période 1945-1989 la population albanaise est considérée fermée.

TABLEAU 1.- POPULATION DE L'ALBANIE 1923-1989.

Années de recensement	Les deux sexes	Hommes	Femmes
1923 (Septembre)	803,9	-	-
1945 (30.9.45)	1122,0	570,3	551,7
1950 (3.9.50)	1218,9	625,9	593,0
1955 (2.10.55)	1391,5	713,3	678,2
1960 (2.10.60)	1626,3	835,3	791,0
1969 (1.4.69)	2068,1	1062,5	1005,6
1979 (7.1.79)	2590,6	1337,4	1253,2
1989 (2.4.89)	3182,4[2]	1638,9	1543,5

Source : Annuaire Statistique 1990.

Jusqu'en 1950, l'accroissement de la population fut semblable à celui de la période 1923-1938 (tableau 2). A partir de 1950, comme dans tous les pays d'Europe et des Balkans, on observe une accélération de l'accroissement démographique qui dépasse 3 pour cent de 1954 à 1964. Cependant, ce taux est très supérieur à celui des autres pays d'Europe à la même époque : par exemple la population des Balkans (exceptée l'Albanie) s'est accrue au rythme de 1,7 pour cent par an, la population de l'Europe de l'Est de 1.5 à 1.6 pour cent par an et celle des principaux pays de l'Europe de l'Ouest[3] à un taux de 0.7 à 0.8 pour cent. La Turquie est le seul pays dont la croissance fut proche de celle de l'Albanie pendant toute la période de l'après-guerre.

Au cours des années 1970, l'accroissement s'est ralenti et est à peu près stable autour de 2,0 pour cent depuis 1980. Ce taux est encore quatre fois plus élevé que celui de l'ensemble des populations européennes, y compris l'Union Soviétique. Aujourd'hui la population des Balkans s'accroît de 1.3 pour cent par an, - 0.4 point de moins que dans la période susmentionnée -, celle de l'Europe de l'Est de 0,6 pour cent et les principaux pays de l'Europe de l'Ouest de 0.2 pour cent.

Malgré la baisse des taux d'accroissement, l'effectif de la population augmente encore rapidement : de 59000 personnes par an au cours des années 1980, contre 38000 en 1950-1959 et 52 000 en 1960-1969. Cette croissance est principalement le résultat d'une natalité élevée.

---

[2] En Albanie, il y a environ 64 800 personnes (ou 2 pour cent de la population) de nationalité étrangère : Grecs, Macédoniens, Serbes, Monténégrins, etc. Le taux d'accroissement de cette catégorie de la population, pendant les 30 dernières années a été de 1,3 pour cent par an.

[3] Sont inclus l'Autriche, le Royaume Uni, l'Italie, la France, l'Espagne, la R.F. d'Allemagne et la Suisse.

TABLEAU 2.- ALBANIE : TAUX D'ACCROISSEMENT PAR AN (EN POUR CENT)

Années	En %	Années	En %	Années	En %
1923-1938	1,7	1960	3,3		
1945	-	1961	3,3	1976	2,2
1946	-	1962	3,1	1977	2,2
1947	1,2	1963	3,0	1978	2,2
1948	1,6	1964	2,9	1979	2,1
1949	1,7	1965	2,8	1980	2,0
1950	2,7	1966	2,6	1981	2,0
1951	2,2	1967	2,6	1982	2,1
1952	2,3	1968	2,7	1983	2,1
1953	2,5	1969	3,0	1984	2,1
1954	2,9	1970	2,7	1985	2,1
1955	2,9	1971	2,4	1986	2,0
1956	3,0	1972	2,5	1987	2,0
1957	2,9	1973	2,4	1988	2,0
1958	3,0	1974	2,3	1989	1,9
1959	3,3	1975	2,3	1990[a]	2,0

a) au 1.7.1990.
Source: Calculée par les auteurs

Les transformations économiques rapides dans les premières années après la libération et la restructuration de la propriété, notamment dans les zones rurales, ont exercé une influence non négligeable sur le développement des processus démographiques.

1) Natalité

La création d'une structure prioritaire industrielle ramifiée dans les zones urbanisées a rapidement rendu possible le plein emploi et a développé l'émancipation et l'instruction des femmes. Dans les villes et à la campagne, le taux de natalité était resté stable sur une période relativement longue (1947-1969) à des niveaux très élevés (35 pour 1000) pour l'ensemble du pays.

Ensuite, le ralentissement général et la baisse du taux de croissance économique dans la seconde moitié des années 70, puis l'assurance de pensions pour la population rurale et les difficultés d'intégration des nouvelles générations sur le marché du travail ont modifié le climat psychologique et rendu plus difficile d'élever une famille nombreuse. Il en est résulté une baisse de la natalité (tableau 3). Cependant les effectifs de naissances restent élevés car la structure par âge de la population est très favorable à la natalité. Les femmes d'âges les plus féconds (20-39 ans - générations du Baby-boom) étaient plus de trois fois plus nombreuses en 1989 qu'en 1950. Ce phénomène n'interviendra plus à partir de l'an 2000.

TABLEAU 3.- ALBANIE : NAISSANCES VIVANTES POUR 1000 HABITANTS

Années	Taux	Années	Taux	Années	Taux
1938	34,7	1957	39,1	1974	30,6
1939	28,0	1958	41,8	1975	29,4
1940	31,4	1959	41,9	1976	28,7
1941	28,1	1960	43,4	1977	29,3
1942	32,9	1961	41,2	1978	27,5
1945	-	1962	39,3	1979	27,5
1946	26,9	1963	39,1	1980	26,5
1947	35,8	1964	37,8	1981	26,5
1948	36,2	1965	35,2	1982	27,8
1949	39,1	1966	34,0	1983	26,0
1950	38,9	1967	35,3	1984	27,3
1951	38,5	1968	35,6	1985	26,2
1952	35,2	1969	35,3	1986	25,3
1953	40,9	1970	32,5	1987	25,9
1954	40,8	1971	33,3	1988	25,6
1955	44,5	1972	32,8	1989	24,7
1956	41,9	1973	30,4		

A peu près le quart des enfants, naissent pendant le première année du mariage, la moitié, quatre ans après le mariage et le cinquième après 10 ans et plus de mariage (moyenne annuelle pour 1988-1989).

En 1950, 37 pour cent des naissances étaient de rang quatre ou plus (tableau 4) ; cette proportion dépassait 40 pour cent en 1970. Depuis les naissances de ces rangs sont devenues relativement moins nombreuses. Les rangs un et deux représentent 55 pour cent des naissances en 1989, contre 45 pour cent en 1950.

TABLEAU 4.- ALBANIE: NAISSANCES VIVANTES SELON LE RANG DE LA NAISSANCE
(EN POURCENTAGE)

Rang de la naissance	1950	1960	1970	1980	1988	1989
Total	100,0	100,0	100,0	100,0	100,0	100,0
Premier rang	24,7	19,9	20,8	29,1	33,7	35,7
Deuxième rang	19,3	19,5	21,2	24,1	28,1	28,9
Troisième rang	16,5	17,3	17,2	16,3	17,0	16,5
Quatrième rang	12,9	13,9	13,1	10,5	8,7	8,2
Cinquième rang	9,0	10,8	10,1	7,3	4,9	4,3
Sixième rang	6,1	7,5	7,4	5,4	3,2	2,7
Septième rang et +	8,7	10,0	9,8	7,2	4,0	3,4
Inconnus	2,8	1,1	0,4	0,1	0,4	0,3

L'ALBANIE/ALBANIA

2) Fécondité

Depuis les années 1950, l'indice synthétique de fécondité a fortement baissé (tableau 5). La baisse s'est ralentie depuis 1980 et l'indice synthétique est de 3,0 naissances par femme en 1989. La baisse à l'avenir sera sans doute moins rapide que par le passé. La baisse rapide au cours des année 1970 a été parallèle à la baisse de la mortalité infantile (tableau 5) ; les parents atteignaient environ la même taille de famille (enfants survivants) en procréant moins du fait de la baisse de la mortalité. Cependant la mortalité infantile reste encore élevée, notamment en zone rurale. Un autre facteur fait penser que la baisse de la fécondité va se ralentir : le nombre désiré d'enfants à l'enquête 1986 est supérieur de 1 enfant à la fécondité observée (pour les zones urbaines et rurales). Le désir d'avoir des enfants reste donc très fort.

TABLEAU 5.- ALBANIE, FECONDITE ET MORTALITE INFANTILE, 1950-1989.

Années	Indice synthétique de fécondité	Mortalité infantile (pour 1000 naiss.viv)
1950	6,146	121,2
1955	6,982	103,9
1960	6,852	83,0
1970	5,161	97,9
1980	3,617	50,3
1981	3,439	50,6
1982	3,561	41,4
1983	3,246	41,2
1984	3,378	32,4
1985	3,263	30,1
1986	3,107	32,1
1987	3,164	28,2
1988	3,027	25,2
1989	2,956	30,8

Toutefois, l'indice synthétique de fécondité reste encore très supérieur au remplacement des générations. Cependant on peut considérer que les conditions économiques (activité féminine) et le désir de loisirs ont fait baisser la fécondité au-dessous de la taille de famille désirée. L'élévation de l'âge des femmes au mariage, l'élévation du niveau d'instruction des femmes, le désir d'éducation pour les enfants, la surface disponible des appartements (généralement de petite dimension) sont intervenus pour faire baisser la fécondité et la mortalité infantile (instruction des femmes).

Bien que l'avortement soit interdit et que la contraception ne soit pas légalisée, la planification de la famille (régulation des naissances) est généralement admise par tous les couples. Il s'agit donc d'une contraception traditionnelle. Le refus de légaliser la contraception vise à encourager la natalité, en baisse rapide depuis plusieurs années.

3) *Mortalité*

Depuis la seconde guerre mondiale, la mortalité générale et plus particulièrement la mortalité infantile ont baissé rapidement. Du fait de l'accroissement de la population, le nombre des décès a varié dans des limites très étroites : le plus souvent entre 15000 et 18000 depuis 1960 (tableau 6), ce qui confirme le rôle prépondérant des naissances dans l'accroissement démographique (cf. ci-dessus). La mortalité infantile est encore très liée aux facteurs exogènes.

Le niveau de la mortalité infantile en Albanie en 1988 est à peu près le même qu'en URSS (25,4 p. 1000), en Roumanie (25,6 p. 1000) et en Yougoslavie (24,8 p. 1000). La Turquie connaissait un niveau plus élevé (75,6 pour 1000).

La position de l'Albanie pour le taux brut de mortalité (5,4 p. 1000) est parmi les meilleures en Europe en raison de la jeunesse de la structure par âge de la population.

Les taux de mortalité par âge ont connu une baisse rapide de 1960 à 1989 (tableau 7). La baisse a été la plus importante aux âges jeunes, notamment avant 5 ans, mais elle est encore importante jusqu'à 45 ans, principalement pour les femmes car les hommes connaissent une quasi stagnation à 20-24 ans. Les gains se réduisent progressivement ensuite et font place à un accroissement à partir de 70 ans.

Aujourd'hui en Albanie l'espérance de vie pour les deux sexes est de 72,4 ans, environ 20 ans de plus que vers 1950 (tableau 8). L'espérance de vie, a donc augmenté chaque année en moyenne de 6 mois. Cette baisse rapide de la mortalité (plus rapide que dans les autres pays d'Europe à la même époque) est due au niveau élevé de départ. Avec une espérance de vie de 55,2 ans dans les années 1950-1955, l'Albanie était la dernière en Europe et très en retard sur les autres pays (à l'exception de la Yougoslavie avec 58,1 ans). Actuellement l'espérance de vie en Albanie se rapproche du niveau des pays de l'Europe de l'Est et la différence avec les pays de l'Europe de l'Ouest diminue.

Avec les valeurs récentes du mouvement naturel (mortalité et natalité basse, espérance de vie à la naissance supérieure à 65 ans et indice synthétique de fécondité inférieur à 3,0) l'Albanie entre dans la quatrième phase de la transition démographique.

L'ALBANIE/ALBANIA

TABLEAU 6.- DECES ET TAUX DE MORTALITE (POUR 1000)

Année	Décès Total	Décès à moins d'un an Total	pour 100 décès	Taux brut de mortalité	Taux de mortalité infantile
1938	18512	3616	19,5	17,8	100,1
1939	12584	2962	18,5	15,1	103,6
1940	17812	-	-	16,6	-
1941	18297	-	-	16,8	-
1942	15899	2753	17,3	14,3	75,0
1946	17200	2685	15,6	15,2	88,1
1947	21824	4597	21,1	19,1	112,2
1948	18883	4523	24,0	16,2	107,3
1949	14970	4826	32,2	12,7	104,5
1950	17215	5732	33,3	14,2	121,2
1951	18862	5946	31,5	15,2	124,4
1952	19826	4449	22,4	15,6	99,5
1953	17822	5305	29,8	13,7	99,6
1954	17560	5329	30,3	13,1	97,5
1955	20750	6369	30,7	15,1	103,9
1956	16370	4856	29,7	11,5	81,5
1957	17241	4980	28,9	11,8	87,0
1958	14059	4305	30,6	9,3	68,3
1959	15305	4991	32,6	9,8	76,5
1960	16775	5786	34,5	10,4	83,0
1961	15445	5439	35,2	9,3	79,5
1962	18363	6188	33,7	10,7	92,1
1963	17646	6248	35,4	10,0	90,6
1964	15811	5593	35,4	8,7	81,5
1965	16731	5700	34,1	9,0	86,8
1966	16469	5742	33,2	8,6	84,0
1967	16565	5459	33,0	8,4	78,8
1968	16214	5407	33,3	8,0	75,2
1969	15624	5595	35,8	7,5	76,2
1970	19774	6802	34,4	9,3	97,9
1971	17768	6827	38,4	8,1	93,8
1972	18077	6005	33,2	8,1	81,6
1973	18032	6499	36,0	7,9	93,2
1974	16840	5359	31,8	7,2	74,6
1975	16296	4977	30,5	6,8	70,4
1976	16425	5021	30,6	6,7	71,2
1977	17394	4698	27,0	6,9	64,0
1978	16219	4234	26,1	6,3	60,0
1979	17421	4520	25,9	6,7	62,7
1980	16981	3558	21,0	6,4	50,3
1981	18001	3653	20,3	6,6	50,6
1982	16521	3194	19,3	5,9	41,4
1983	17416	3042	17,5	6,1	41,2
1984	16618	2565	15,4	5,7	32,4
1985	17179	2333	13,6	5,8	30,1
1986	17369	2457	14,1	5,8	32,1
1987	17119	2247	13,1	5,6	28,2
1988	17027	2021	11,9	5,4	25,2
1989	18168	2432	13,4	5,7	30,8

TABLEAU 7.- TAUX DE MORTALITE PAR SEXE ET AGE, 1960 ET 1989.

Groupes d'âge	1960			1989		
	HF	H	F	HF	H	F
Moins d'1 an	83,0	78,1	87,9	30,8	33,2	28,3
1-4 ans	12,9	11,4	14,6	3,8	3,8	3,8
5-9 ans	1,8	1,6	2,0	0,8	0,9	0,7
10-14 ans	0,8	1,0	0,7	0,5	0,5	0,4
15-19 ans	0,9	1,1	0,7	0,6	0,8	0,4
20-24 ans	1,3	1,2	1,5	0,9	1,1	0,6
25-29 ans	1,4	1,6	1,3	0,9	1,1	0,7
30-34 ans	2,0	1,9	2,0	0,9	1,1	0,8
35-39 ans	2,2	2,3	2,0	1,2	1,4	1,0
40-44 ans	3,2	3,2	3,2	1,6	1,9	1,4
45-49 ans	3,5	4,5	2,5	2,4	3,0	1,7
50-54 ans	6,7	9,3	4,3	4,7	6,3	2,9
55-59 ans	10,8	14,1	7,7	7,7	10,8	4,4
60-64 ans	16,2	20,6	12,3	13,6	18,8	8,5
65-69 ans	22,9	27,3	19,5	23,9	33,3	15,7
70-74 ans	39,4	46,7	33,6	41,1	56,6	28,3
75-79 ans	53,9	61,2	48,4	77,4	93,7	66,3
80-84 ans	85,4	100,1	75,3	109,4	142,7	90,2
85 ans et +	144,1	156,1	136,7	190,5	235,2	168,4
Tous âges	10,4	10,2	10,8	5,7	6,2	5,1

Source : Annuaires de statistique 1964 et 1990.

TABLEAU 8.- ALBANIE : ESPERANCE DE VIE (e_0), A LA NAISSANCE

Années	Total	Hommes	Femmes
1938	38,3	-	-
1950-1951	53,5	52,6	54,4
1955-1956	57,8	57,2	58,6
1960-1961	64,9	63,7	66,0
1979-1980	69,5	67,0	72,3
1980-1981	70,2	67,7	72,2
1981-1982	70,5	67,8	73,7
1982-1983	71,0	68,4	73,7
1983-1984	71,4	68,5	74,4
1984-1985	71,5	68,7	74,4
1985-1986	71,9	68,7	75,5
1986-1987	72,0	68,8	75,5
1987-1988	72,2	69,4	75,5
1988-1989	72,4	69,6	75,5

Source : Annuaire de statistique 1990.

4) Nuptialité et divorces

Faible avant la guerre, le taux de nuptialité a dépassé 10 pour mille et même 15 pour mille de 1946 à 1952 (tableau 10). Il a baissé ensuite autour de 8 pour mille ou même 7 pour mille avant de connaître une remontée depuis la fin des années 1970, atteignant 9 pour mille au cours des années 1980. L'âge moyen au mariage s'est élevé de 3,5 ans pour les hommes et de 1,8 an pour les femmes de 1955-1959 à 1985-1989 (tableau 9).

TABLEAU 9.- ALBANIE : REPARTITION PAR AGE DES MARIAGES SELON LE SEXE (EN POUR CENT)

Groupes d'âge	Hommes		Femmes	
	1955/1959	1985/1989	1955/1959	1985/1989
Total	100,0	100,0	100,0	100,0
- de 20 ans	11,2	1,2	52,1	20,7
20-24 ans	37,6	29,3	35,3	56,7
25-29 ans	32,5	50,3	7,7	18,1
30-34 ans	10,0	14,1	2,8	3,3
35-39 ans	4,3	3,0	1,1	0,8
40-44 ans	2,0	1,0	0,5	0,2
45-49 ans	1,1	0,5	0,2	0,1
50 ans et +	1,3	0,6	0,3	0,1
Age moyen au mariage (en années)	26,5	30,0	21,2	23,0

La proportion de remariages parmi les mariages féminins a beaucoup diminué. En 1950, sur 100 femmes qui se mariaient 89,7 pour cent étaient célibataires et 11,3 pour cent avaient été mariées au moins une fois. En 1989 cette dernière proportion est seulement 4,6 pour cent. Pendant ces 30 dernières années, le nombre des mariages de femmes veuves a beaucoup diminué, même en nombre absolu, du fait de la baisse de la mortalité. Jusqu'aux années 70 la moitié des femmes divorcées se mariaient avec des hommes célibataires ; aujourd'hui plus de la moitié se marient avec des hommes divorcés.

On n'observe pas en Albanie une montée importante du nombre des divorces au cours des dernières années et l'indice se situe au niveau d'un peu plus de 9 divorces pour 100 mariages au cours des années 1980 (tableau 10). On observe même une baisse par rapport à la décennie 1968-1977. La montée de la fréquence du divorce pendant ces années est une conséquence directe du mouvement - pour "l'émancipation continue de la femme dans la vie sociale en général et son affranchissement des lois patriarcales dans la famille" - qui en 1967 a gagné, le pays tout entier et surtout les zones rurales.

TABLEAU 10.- ALBANIE : MARIAGES ET DIVORCES

Année	Mariages Total	Pour 1 000 habitants	Divorces Total	Pour 1 000 habitants	Divorces pour 100 mariages
1938	5990	5,8	-	-	-
1939	5367	5,1	-	-	-
1940	6576	5,9	-	-	-
1941	6867	6,3	-	-	-
1942	7696	6,9	-	-	-
1946	11207	10,0	713	0,6	6,4
1947	16541	14,4	590	0,5	3,6
1948	17712	15,1	1139	1,0	6,4
1949	11580	9,6	1144	0,9	9,9
1950	12341	10,1	976	0,8	7,9
1951	12550	10,2	1114	0,9	8,9
1952	13077	10,4	1515	1,2	11,6
1953	12647	9,7	1447	1,1	11,4
1954	10760	7,9	981	0,7	9,1
1955	11258	8,0	1057	0,9	9,4
1956	10389	7,2	967	0,7	9,3
1957	11819	7,9	908	0,6	7,7
1958	11931	7,8	849	0,5	7,1
1959	11479	7,2	922	0,6	8,0
1960	12571	7,8	850	0,5	6,8
1961	18723	11,3	1314	0,8	7,0
1962	12838	7,5	1236	0,7	9,6
1963	13128	7,5	1046	0,6	7,9
1964	13021	7,2	1104	0,6	8,5
1965	13921	7,5	1041	0,6	7,5
1966	12968	6,8	1217	0,6	9,4
1967	16853	8,6	1415	0,7	8,4
1968	15845	7,8	1773	0,9	11,2
1969	15322	7,4	1608	0,8	10,5
1970	14449	6,8	1625	0,7	11,2
1971	15300	7,0	1758	0,8	11,5
1972	16159	7,2	1718	0,7	10,6
1973	18481	8,0	1791	0,8	9,7
1974	17148	7,3	1934	0,8	11,3
1975	18729	7,8	1853	0,7	9,9
1976	18593	7,6	1948	0,8	10,5
1977	19934	7,9	2003	0,8	10,0
1978	20464	8,0	1836	0,7	9,0
1979	21355	8,2	1849	0,8	8,7
1980	21729	8,1	2024	0,7	9,3
1981	23301	8,5	2222	0,8	9,5
1982	25157	9,0	2206	0,8	8,8
1983	25607	9,0	2371	0,8	9,3
1984	26397	9,1	2335	0,8	8,8
1985	25271	8,5	2451	0,8	9,7
1986	25718	8,5	2383	0,8	9,3
1987	27370	8,9	2537	0,8	9,3
1988	28174	9,0	2597	0,8	9,2
1989	27655	8,6	2628	0,8	9,5

L'ALBANIE/ALBANIA

A partir de 1968 les jeunes gens et jeunes filles ont rompu nombre d'unions, liées arbitrairement par leurs parents ; de même ont été rompues les fiançailles des enfants qui n'avaient pas l'âge minimum (légal) du mariage (18 ans pour les hommes et 16 ans pour les femmes). Actuellement le quart des divorces ont lieu avant le premier anniversaire de mariage - contre 11,8 pour cent en 1960 - et la moitié des couples rompent leur union sans avoir encore d'enfants (62 pour cent en 1960).

5) La population selon la résidence

Dans sa majeure partie, la population de l'Albanie habite dans les zones rurales. En 1923, 15,9 pour cent et en 1945, 21,3 pour cent de la population était considérée urbaine. La population urbaine a augmenté sans interruption. En 1979, le tiers de la population du pays habitait dans les villes et au 1.7.1990 36,1 pour cent de la population était urbaine. Parallèlement à la croissance naturelle des villes, la migration interne des villages vers les villes ainsi que la création de nouvelles villes ont été très importantes. En 1945, avec une population urbaine de 238800 habitants l'Albanie comptait 24 villes ; en 1989, la population de ces villes était de 918600 habitants , soit 3,8 fois supérieure, et représentait 80 pour cent de la population urbaine du pays. En 1989, on comptait 67 villes, c'est-à-dire qu'en 45 ans 43 villes - mais regroupant seulement 227900 habitants - se sont créées.

Les raisons de cette augmentation sont étroitement liées aux transformations économiques et sociales, à la politique industrielle et à la politique de l'extension du secteur productif et du secteur des services. Pour réaliser ce processus, le recours à la main d'oeuvre venue de la campagne a été indispensable, mais le nombre en a été toujours très contrôlé (migrations de travail uniquement). Pendant les dix dernières années la population urbaine a augmentée de 282000 habitants, dont 177000 sont dus à la croissance naturelle et 105000 aux migrations. Dans ces dernières sont incluses les personnes accompagnant les migrants pour des raisons de travail, ainsi que tous ceux qui changent de domicile en raison du mariage ou pour habiter près de leur proche famille (femmes divorcées qui retournent dans la famille de leurs parents, personnes en retraite qui retournent chez leurs enfants, etc.). En général cette forme spontanée de migration de la population rurale exprime indirectement le désir d'amélioration des conditions économiques et sociales (éducation et niveau de vie). Selon les données statistiques, sur 100 personnes installées dans les villes du pays pendant la période 1979-1989 et venant des zones rurales, 51 pour cent sont des femmes, 20 pour cent sont venus pour le travail, 39 pour cent pour accompagner des travailleurs et 28 pour cent pour se marier.

Tirana, la capitale, représente plus du cinquième de la population urbaine du pays. Actuellement en Albanie on compte 67 villes. Sont considérées comme de grandes villes, Tirana (239400 habitants), Durres (83300), Elbasan (81100), Shkoder (80200), Vlore (72100), Korce (64100), Fier (43800) , Berat (43000), etc. On note une descente de la population des montagnes vers les zones basses la proportion de population vivant au-dessus de 600 mètres d'altitude est passée de 26,6 pour cent en 1960 à 22,3 pour cent en 1989.

6) Les familles et leur composition

Le dernier recensement de la population a dénombré 675 400 familles (tableau 11).

TABLEAU 11.- ALBANIE : NOMBRE ET TAILLE DES FAMILLES

Années de recensement	Nombre de famille en milliers	Personnes par famille		
		Total	Urbaine	Rurale
1923	143,1	5,6	4,9	5,8
1945	196,8	5,7	4,9	6,0
1950	211,6	5,8	4,7	6,1
1955	251,8	5,5	4,9	5,8
1960	279,8	5,8	5,3	6,1
1969	346,6	5,9	5,0	6,1
1979	463,3	5,6	4,6	6,2
1989	675,4	4,7	3,9	5,3

Jusqu'au recensement de 1979, la population s'est accrue plus vite que le nombre des familles. En 1989, pour la première fois, l'accroissement du nombre des familles dépasse celui du nombre de la population. La tendance à une diminution du nombre des personnes par famille, quelle que soit son échelle, a caractérisé non seulement chaque ville du pays, mais aussi tous les villages. Elle représentera aussi la tendance générale, en déterminant un nouveau panorama de la situation de la famille et de sa taille dans les années 90 et au siècle prochain.

TABLEAU 12.- ALBANIE : FAMILLE SELON LA TAILLE

	1955	1950	1960	1969	1979	1989
Familles total	100,0	100,0	100,0	100,0	100,0	100,0
1 personne	8,9	7,4	6,1	3,7	3,3	4,2
2 à 3 personnes	21,2	19,0	16,7	16,1	17,2	23,3
4 à 6 personnes	39,5	41,1	41,3	43,1	46,1	55,2
7 personnes et +	30,4	32,5	35,9	37,1	33,4	17,3

La baisse du nombre moyen de personnes par famille se reflète dans la baisse de la proportion des familles de plus de 7 personnes (tableau 12) qui passe de 37 pour cent en

1969 à 33 pour cent en 1979 et seulement 17 pour cent en 1989. Dans le même temps les familles composées de deux à trois personnes sont passées de 16 pour cent à 23 pour cent et celles composées de 4 à 6 personnes de 43 pour cent à 55 pour cent. L'effectif des familles de moins de quatre personnes a doublé de 1979 à 1989 alors que le nombre de celles composées de 5 personnes et plus a augmenté de seulement 10 pour cent.

TABLEAU 13.- ALBANIE : COMPOSITION DES FAMILLES SELON LES ZONES DE RESIDENCE (EN POUR CENT) (RECENSEMENT DE 1989)

	Familles		Nombre de personnes			
	total	1	2-3	4-6	7-10	11 et +
Tout le pays	100,0	4,2	23,3	55,2	16,0	1,3
Zone Nord-Est	100,0	3,5	16,3	45,8	30,6	3,8
Zone Sud et Sud-Est	100,0	4,2	23,2	60,0	12,2	0,4
Villes	100,0	5,9	31,6	57,2	5,2	0,1
Grandes villes	100,0	6,7	33,1	56,0	4,1	0,1
Tirana	100,0	9,3	39,4	49,6	1,7	0,0
Campagne	100,0	3,0	17,2	53,8	24,0	2,0

La répartition des familles selon la taille et la zone de résidence montre des différences importantes, notamment les familles (ménages) de une personne sont deux fois plus fréquents à Tirana que dans l'ensemble du pays, trois fois plus que dans le nord (tableau 13). La différence est encore plus marquée pour les familles de sept personnes ou plus, et les villes se distinguent nettement de ce point de vue. Dans toutes les villes du pays, le nombre des familles composées d'une seule personne est plus grand que le nombre des familles de 7 membres ou plus. En particulier, pour la capitale, Tirana, qui représente le quart des familles urbaines.

Le recensement de l'année 1989 marque la fin des familles nombreuses et le seuil, où le type de familles composées de 4 à 6 personnes devient prépondérant. La famille nucléaire s'est déjà consolidée dans les zones urbaines où elle représente 87,7 pour cent des familles. Les familles rurales sont pour 75 pour cent des familles nucléaires, proportion observée dans les villes il y a 20 ans.

REFERENCES BIBLIOGRAPHIQUES

Nations Unies.- La population mondiale à la sortie du XXe siècle, Etudes démographiques, n° 111.

Nations Unies- Monographies sur les politiques de population : France.

Bulletin démographique des Nations Unies, n° 28/1989.

Rapport sur la situation démographique en Albanie (natalité, mortalité, nuptialité en 1976, 1983, 1986,1987). Dept.de Démographie, D.S.

Rapport sur les principales caractéristiques démographiques en Albanie dans les années de recensements de 1960, 1979, 1989. Dépt. de Démographie, D.S.

P. Dishnica.- "L'évolution démographique du district du Tirana", analyse et perspectives, Revue *Problèmes Economiques* n° 1, janvier-fevrier-mars 1983, IEE.

Analyse des problèmes actuels de fécondité et de mortalité en Albanie (selon les enquêtes sur ce sujet 1987, Dept. de Démographie, D.S.

Yugoslavia/ La Yougoslavie
Dragana AVRAMOV

I.- INTRODUCTORY COMMENTS

The initiation of the secular fertility decline among heterogeneous populations of present day Yugoslavia occurred within the timespan starting from the end of the 19th century up to the mid-1960s. Indeed, the most striking feature of the current demographic situation derives from the diversified population dynamics. In the last decades of the 20th century Yugoslavia is one of very few European countries faced with two population problems, below replacement fertility, on the one side, and doubling of generations, on the other side. By its ethnic and territorial fertility differentials, Yugoslavia may be compared only to those European countries whose territories extend to the Asian continent. The Yugoslav regions with below replacement fertility are not areas of lowest fertility levels in Europe, but the high fertility region has highest birth rates in Europe and stands at the upper end of the world fertility scale.

Due to the scarcity of data, analysis of the population dynamics of the present day Yugoslav territories cannot encompass the distant past. Historical data about populations that inhabited the present day Yugoslav regions in the 19th century pertain only to some territories and do not enable generalizations for the entire country. The fertility transition among most Yugoslav populations coincided with the military campaigns and struggles for national autonomy under different political and cultural settings. In the last decades of the 19th century the populations lived in two independent kingdoms, those of Serbia and of Monte Negro. Croatia and Slovenia were within the Austro-Hungarian Empire, parts of the present day Voivodina were under direct Hungarian administration, Bosnia and Hercegovina was annexed by Austria-Hungary in 1878, while southern Serbia, Kosovo and Macedonia were under Turkish rule. First population censuses were undertaken in the mid-19th century only in the Kingdom of the Serbs and on the territories of the Austro-Hungarian Empire. However, due to the fact that direct data are available for other regions only as of 1910, relatively reliable assessments about the total population do not go back beyond 1880 (Vogelnik, 1974). After the foundation of the Kingdom of Serbs, Croats and Slovenes in 1918, which encompassed most parts of present day Yugoslavia, two censuses were undertaken - in 1921 and in 1931, and after the Second World War censuses followed in 1948, 1953, 1961, 1971 and 1981.

The research is not only confined by the scarcity of statistical data but also by the impossibility of pursueing longitudinal analysis due to the administrative and territorial changes. Hence, insight into the population dynamics in Yugoslavia, from the onset of the mortality decline in the mid-19th century and the beginning of the fertility transition from the end of the 19th century onward, is not possible by means of precise indicators such as cohort fertility and net reproduction rates. The reconstitution of the population movement during the demographic transition among the populations of present day Yugoslavia, is only partially founded on the historical statistical base, data from censuses and vital statistics, and is partly based on different statistical methods of estimation.

II.- POPULATION DYNAMICS FROM THE END OF THE 19TH TO THE MID-20TH CENTURY

The 50 year period, from 1880, when the population was assessed at 8.9 million, to 1931 when it stood at 14.5 million, is the period of fast population increase and marked regional differences in growth. The regions along the western and northern border, present day Slovenia, Croatia and Voivodina, were at the bottom part of the growth scale in Yugoslavia with intermediate population growth rates. The central and southern parts, present day Monte Negro, Macedonia and Serbia Proper stood out with high growth, while Kosovo and Bosnia and Hercegovina were at the upper end of the scale as their populations more than doubled in half a century (Table 1).

Population decline or stagnation on all Yugoslav territories during the 1919-1921 period indicates the magnitude of direct and indirect demographic losses due to the First World War (Table 2). On territories of greatest war casualties, in Serbia and in Monte Negro, the demographic loss was estimated at 1.2 million people (Djuric, 1924). After the war, in the newly established state, the explosive phase of the demographic transition continued and in the decade between 1921 and 1931 the population of Yugoslavia exhibited highest population growth in this century with the annual rate of 1.5 percent. Voivodina and Slovenia recorded annual population growth under 1 per cent while in Kosovo, Serbia Proper and Bosnia and Hercegovina the annual average growth rate exceeded 2 per cent.

TABLE 1. POPULATION OF YUGOSLAVIA 1880-1931 (000s)

	1880	1910	1921	1931
YUGOSLAVIA	8877	12962	12545	14534
Bosnia & Hercegovina	1158	1898	1890	2324
Monte Negro	(207)	344	311	360
Croatia	2479	3375	3427	3789
Macedonia	(528)	876	809	950
Slovenia	1182	1321	1288	1386
Serbia total	3323	5148	4819	5726
Serbia Proper	1896	3147	2843	3550
Voivodina	1187	1526	1537	1624
Kosovo	(240)	475	439	552
Index				
YUGOSLAVIA	100	146	141	164
Bosnia & Hercegovina	100	164	163	201
Monte Negro	100	166	150	174
Croatia	100	136	138	153
Macedonia	100	166	153	180
Slovenia	100	112	109	117
Serbia total	100	155	145	172
Serbia Proper	100	166	150	187
Voivodina	100	128	129	137
Kosovo	100	198	183	230

Source: Vogelnik (1974)

1) Natality - Fertility

At the turn of the 19th century all Yugoslav territories, with the exception of Slovenia, had similar crude birth rates of approximately 45 per 1000 population. Lower rates in Slovenia may be explained by the "malthusian transition" that occurred earlier through nuptiality control, namely later marriages and traditionally higher singlehood. In the last decades of the 19th and the first decades of the 20th century the Yugoslav populations had uneven fertility decline and the differences in birth rates reached peak levels in the 1920s. The threshold of fertility transition, the 10 per cent decline in crude birth rates, was crossed in Croatia, Voivodina and Serbia Proper in the last decade of the 19th century; in Monte Negro in the 1920s; in Bosnia and Hercegovina, Macedonia and Kosovo in the early 1930s. As the fertility transition started among Yugoslav populations with a time lag of one century in comparison to France, in the 1930s all Yugoslav territories were high fertility regions. With 28 live births per 1000 population in the second half of the 1930s Yugoslavia stood out as a high fertility country. Even the lowest crude birth rate of 20.5 in Voivodina fell in the upper part of the natality scale in Europe. At the time France registered 14.8 live births per 1000 population, England and Wales 14.9, Sweden 14.5, Germany 19.4 (Pressat, 1991).

TABLE 2. AVERAGE ANNUAL POPULATION GROWTH (PER 1000 POPULATION)

	1880-1910	1910-1921	1921-1931
YUGOSLAVIA	13	-3	15
Bosnia & Hercegovina	17	-0.5	21
Monte Negro	17	-9	15
Croatia	10	1	10
Macedonia	17	-7	16
Slovenia	4	-2	8
Serbia total	16	-6	17
Serbia Proper	17	-9	23
Voivodina	8	1	6
Kosovo	23	-7	23
Source: Vogelnik (1974)			

Crude birth rates exhibited a clear downward trend that is observed also for total fertility rate estimates (Table 4). Nevertheless, both indicators show very high fertility of the Yugoslav populations in the first half of the 20th century. Women born between 1869 and 1903 gave birth on average to 5.2 liveborn children. In this cohort highest completed fertility rate of 7 was found in Bosnia and Hercegovina and lowest 4.6 in Serbia Proper (Gacesa, 1989).

2) Mortality

A gradual mortality decline started in the mid-19th century in more developed regions and towards the end of the century in less developed ones. As there are no precise mortality indicators for the end of the 19th and the beginning of the 20th century, the most reliable assessment is judged to be that of Vogelnik (1974). Along the western and northern range, in Slovenia, Croatia, Voivodina and in Serbia Proper mortality stood at around 30 per 1000 population while in Bosnia and Hercegovina, Macedonia, Monte

Negro and Kosovo it ranged around 35 per 1000. The mortality decline in Yugoslavia can be documented by vital statistics data for crude death rates and infant mortality rates as of 1931 while for 1921 only estimates are possible.

TABLE 3.- CRUDE BIRTH RATES (LIVEBIRTHS PER 1000 POPULATION)

	1880-85	1886-90	1891-95	1896-1900	1901-05	1906-10	1926-30	1931-35	1935-39
YUGOSLAVIA	43.2	42.5	42.1	40.4	39.8	39.9	34.2	32.6	27.9
Bosnia & Herceg.	45.0	45.0	45.0	44.0	44.0	44.0	44.3	40.0	37.0
Monte Negro	45.0	45.0	45.0	43.0	43.0	43.0	37.3	31.2	29.4
Croatia	42.9	42.8	41.9	40.7	39.3	39.6	32.6	30.0	25.8
Macedonia	45.0	45.0	45.0	43.0	43.0	43.0	43.1	38.6	34.9
Slovenia	35.1	35.1	34.8	34.8	34.0	31.3	27.8	25.7	22.5
Serbia	45.5	43.5	43.0	39.8	39.0	39.2	34.7	31.6	25.2
Ser.Pro.	45.7	43.2	42.4	39.2	38.0	38.5	35.2	33.5	25.7
Voivodina	45.0	43.7	41.7	39.9	39.9	39.4	25.1	24.4	20.5
Kosovo	45.0	45.0	45.0	43.0	43.0	43.0	43.2	37.6	36.6

Source: Vogelnik, (1974)

TABLE 4.- ESTIMATED TOTAL FERTILITY RATES

	1880	1910	1921	1931
Yugoslavia	5.6	5.3	4.5	4.2

Source: Estimates of Breznik on basis of the assessed total population in 1880 and 1910 by Vogelnik and estimated number of women in the age group 15-49 for 1921 and 1931 by Simeunovic.

While it may be said that the regional differences in fertility levels in the first half of the 20th century coincide with the indicators of overall regional development, such a generalization does not hold true for the mortality levels. In the 1920s and the 1930s regional differences in crude death rates were less marked than in crude birth rates and infant mortality rates were in clear discrepancy with other indicators of demographic and general development. The two most developed regions with lowest birth rates, Voivodina and Croatia, registered the highest infant mortality rates in Yugoslavia (Table 5). In the

1921-1939 period mortality decline evolved at a similar pace as the natality decline, and the rate of natural increase declined by 30 percent (Table 6).

TABLE 5. MORTALITY IN YUGOSLAVIA; CRUDE DEATH RATE (PER 1000 POPULATION)

	1921*	1931	1934	1939
YUGOSLAVIA	20.9	19.8	17.1	14.9
Bosnia & Hercegovina	21.0	20.8	19.0	18.4
Monte Negro	17.0	14.0	13.9	14.0
Croatia	20.0	20.5	17.2	15.8
Macedonia	27.0	22.3	17.9	19.0
Slovenia	17.0	16.9	14.2	14.0
Serbia total	23.0	19.5	16.8	14.0
Serbia Proper	22.0	18.5	15.7	12.6
Voivodina	22.0	20.1	18.1	16.2
Kosovo	27.0	24.6	20.6	17.6

Infant mortality rate (per 1000 live births)

	1931	1934-1937**
YUGOSLAVIA	164.7	143.0
Bosnia & Hercegovina	160.1	139.3
Monte Negro	118.6	122.6
Croatia	203.6	172.4
Macedonia	175.9	137.3
Slovenia	138.3	116.3
Serbia total	149.7	135.8
Serbia Proper	121.6	110.4
Voivodina	208.1	194.8
Kosovo	196.5	161.7

* Estimates Vogelnik, (1974)
** Estimates Simeunovic, (1964)
Source: For 1931, 1934, and 1939 Simeunovic (1964)

TABLE 6. CRUDE BIRTH AND DEATH RATES AND NATURAL INCREASE (PER 1000)

	Live births	Deaths	Natural increase
1921	36.7	20.9	15.8
1925	34.2	18.7	15.5
1930	35.5	19.0	16.5
1935	29.9	16.8	13.1
1939	25.9	14.9	11.0

Source: Simeunovic, (1964)

High fertility and the discrepancy between birth and death rates, during the transition period, was manifested in the first half of the 20th century through the high share of young and the low share of over 60 in the population, together with mentioned regional variations. In the highest population growth decade in this century, between 1921 and 1931 the share of 60 and over population declined in Yugoslavia (Table 7).

TABLE 7. THE SHARE OF THE AGE GROUPS 0-19 AND ABOVE 60 IN THE TOTAL POPULATION

	1921		1931		1989	
age(years)	0-19	60+.	0-19	60+	0-19	60+
YUGOSLAVIA	45.3	8.7	43.7	8.4	30.6	14.3
Bosnia & Hercegovina	50.0	5.6	50.3	5.2	32.3	10.6
Monte Negro	46.4	9.8	46.3	9.8	32.9	12.7
Croatia	43.5	8.8	41.0	9.4	27.0	17.1
Macedonia	48.1	11.1	47.9	9.6	35.2	10.9
Slovenia	42.3	10.4	40.2	10.7	28.6	15.8
Serbia total	45.1	8.9	42.8	8.1	30.7	15.2
Serbia Proper	46.2	8.5	43.7	7.3	26.4	17.2
Voivodina	41.5	9.6	38.6	9.8	26.0	17.5
Kosovo	50.6	9.7	49.8	7.6	48.4	6.7

Source: Simeunovic (1964) for 1921 and 1931 and Vital Statistic SZSfor 1989

3) The demographic impact of the Second World War

The quantification of the demographic effects of the Second World War have been made on the basis of assessments founded on demographic-statistical methods and analysis of historical data from various sources (Breznik, 1985). Due to scarce demographic data, incomplete registration of direct losses, unreliable data on emigration and territorial changes, no fully reliable evidence of direct and indirect war losses of the Yugoslav population, may be found. The assessment made by the Yugoslav government about war victims given immediately after the war was that Yugoslavia lost 1.7 million inhabitants (Federal Statistical Office, 1989). Not only did later assessments of the direct losses differ according to various authors, but there were marked differences in the evaluation of the magnitude of fertility decline prior and during the war and the volume of emigration during and immediately after the war. Assessments about direct losses during the war operations and indirect losses due to low birth rates, emigration and surmortality caused by living conditions during the war fall within the range from 2 million (Lah, 1952, Zerjavic, 1989) to 2.8 - 3.2 million (Vogelnik, 1952). Between these values lie assessments (Breznik and Simeunovic, 1961, Breznik, 1985, Tasic, 1948) that the demographic impact of the Second World War may be measured by the loss of 2.2 to 2.4 million inhabitants.

III.- MAIN FEATURES OF POPULATION DYNAMICS IN THE SECOND HALF OF THE 20TH CENTURY

The direct and indirect demographic war losses were partly compensated for in the early 1950s during the "baby-boom" when the population of Yugoslavia was growing at a high average annual growth rate of 1.4 per cent. Already in the second half of the 1950s a marked slowdown in the population growth may be observed. The average annual growth rate fell by then to 1 per cent and fluctuated around that level until the mid-1970s. In the early 1980s a gradual slowdown in the population growth followed and in the 1980-1988 period the population of Yugoslavia was increasing at the pace of 0.8 per cent per year.

The total population of Yugoslavia was estimated at 23.8 million in 1990 [1]. Over the time span of seven decades between the first census of 1921 in the newly created state until 1990, the population of Yugoslavia has almost doubled, index of growth being 190.

---

[1] In the population censuses of 1971 and 1981 the stock of Yugoslav workers temporarily employed abroad and their dependent family members were included in the count of the total population of Yugoslavia. All subsequent official estimates of the total population by age and sex used by the statistical offices for the calculation of vital rates are based on the definition of the total population of Yugoslavia which includes the stock of migrants abroad regardless of the duration of their stay.

The slowdown in population growth in the second half of the century is an outcome of a clear downward trend in the natural increase due to the declining birth rates (Table 8). Between 1950 and 1990 the natural increase fell by 71 per cent, i.e. from 17.3 to 5.0 per 1000 population.

TABLE 8. POPULATION OF YUGOSLAVIA 1939-1990

	1939	1947	1950	1960	1970	1980	1990
Total population (000s)	15,596	15,679	16,346	18,402	20,371	22,304	23,809
Crude birth rate	25.9	26.7	30.3	23.5	17.8	17.1	14.0
Crude death rate	14.9	12.8	13.0	9.9	8.9	8.8	9.0
Natural increase	11.0	13.9	17.3	13.6	8.9	8.3	5.0

Source: Vital Statistics 1988 and Communication of the Federal Statistical Office of 18, December 1990

In terms of the reproductive behavior of its population in the early 1950s Yugoslavia fell in the group of high fertility European countries with birth rate around 30 per 1000 population and total fertility rate of 3.7. By the 1980s Yugoslavia had intermediate fertility with crude birth rate of 17 and total fertility rate of 2.1. Fertility decline was sharpest in the 1950-1970 period during which the total fertility rate dropped from 3.7 to 2.5 (Table 9). After 1970 fertility continued to decline but at a slower pace and the decline from 2.5 to the replacement level in the next 15 years is only one third of the change that occurred in the preceding 15 years. Between 1980 and 1990 the crude birth rate declined by approximately 7 per cent, i.e. from 17.1 per 1000 population to 14 per 1000 while the total fertility rate declined from 2.12 to 1.99. Net reproduction fluctuated just under 1 in the first half and fell to 0.91 in the second half of the 1980s.

Behind relatively favorable averages of moderate population growth, and birth rates, about cohorts that are being replaced, lie profound imbalances in population development. Regional differences in the average annual population growth in the 1980s fell between the lowest value of 0.1 per cent in Voivodina and the highest of 2.1 per cent in Kosovo. The replacement of the population of Yugoslavia (Table 10) is evolving under circumstances where the fertility level is almost twice the value of generational replacement among the Albanian population in Yugoslavia and 20 per cent below replacement level in populations of Bosnia and Hercegovina, Croatia, Slovenia, Serbia Proper and Voivodina.

TABLE 9. TOTAL FERTILITY RATE

	1950-1955	1955-1960	1960-1965	1965-1970	1970-1975	1975-1980	1980-1985	1985-1990
Bosnia & Hercegovina	4.9	4.1	3.7	3.2	2.6	2.1	2.0	1.8
Monte Negro	4.5	3.8	3.3	2.9	2.6	2.2	2.2	2.0
Croatia	2.7	2.4	2.1	2.1	1.9	1.9	1.9	1.7
Macedonia	5.3	4.5	2.8	2.8	2.7	2.6	2.5	2.2
Slovenia	2.8	2.4	2.3	2.3	2.2	2.2	1.9	1.7
Serbia total	3.2	2.5	2.5	2.5	2.3	2.3	2.2	2.2
Serbia Proper	2.8	2.1	2.0	2.0	1.9	1.9	1.8	1.8
Voivodina	2.6	2.2	2.1	2.1	1.7	1.8	1.8	1.7
Kosovo	7.0	6.4	6.3	6.3	5.5	4.8	4.3	4.0
YUGOSLAVIA	3.7	2.8	2.7	2.5	2.3	2.2	2.1	2.0
EUROPE	2.6	2.6	2.6	2.5	2.2	2.0	1.8	1.7

Source: for Yugoslavia Vital Statistics for Europe World Population Prospects, United Nations 1989

TABLE 10. COHORT FERTILITY

women born in	Yugoslavia	Kosovo	Slovenia
1930-1935	2.5	5.5	2.0
1935-1940	2.4	5.3	2.0 19
40-1945	2.3	5.2	2.0
1945-1950	2.1	4.7	1.9
1950-1955	2.0	3.8	1.8

Source: Gecesa (1989)

In Serbia Proper and in Voivodina the net reproduction rate fell below unity already in 1955, in Croatia in 1957, in Bosnia and Hercegovina in 1977, in Slovenia in 1981 and in Monte Negro in 1984.

Hence, it may be said that the path from the "baby boom" to the "baby bust" was passed in less than a decade by some Yugoslav populations while the "baby boom" of the Albanian populations seems to be a cultural option.

In the early 1950s all Yugoslav regions had high birth rates. Lowest values of around 23 live births per 1000 population were found in Voivodina, Slovenia and Croatia; Serbia Proper had somewhat higher level of 26, while in Monte Negro crude birth rate stood around 33 per 1000. Bosnia and Hercegovina were regions of very high natality with birth rates of almost 40 per 1000 population. Kosovo stood out not only with highest birth rate in comparison to other Yugoslav regions but also by the fact that the birth rate of 46 per 1000 population recorded in 1956 was higher than the peak level in the 19th century. Indicators of population dynamics in Kosovo illustrate that there was an interruption of the fertility transition with the temporary reversal of trends. A new wave of fertility transition with a 10 per cent decline in birth rates may be located in the late 1960s. By 1990 the crude birth rate stood at 14 per 1000 population and the regional differences, if Kosovo is not included, have been reduced. The rates fall between the lowest value of 10.4 in Voivodina and highest of 16.9 in Macedonia. The exception is Kosovo with the birth rate that has been fluctuating around 30 per 1000 for almost a decade and stands at 28 per 1000 in 1990.

Because of the effect the age structure of the population has on crude rates, such as the birth rate, their evolution may not coincide with trends in fertility, as measured by the total fertility rate. Indeed, in the 1950s regions with similar crude birth rates exhibited clear differences in the average number of liveborn children per woman. In the "baby boom" years in Croatia, Slovenia, Voivodina and Serbia Proper the total fertility rate was somewhat below 3, in Monte Negro somewhat above 4, in Bosnia and Hercegovina and in Monte Negro around 5 and in Kosovo 7. The total fertility rate exhibited a clear downward trend in all Yugoslav populations and converged around similar values everywhere except in Kosovo. In 1990 the total fertility rate is between 1.7 and 1.9 in Voivodina, Serbia Proper, Slovenia, Croatia, Bosnia and Hercegovina and Monte Negro. In Macedonia it is just above replacement level while in Kosovo it stands at 4 children per woman (Table 9).

Fertility behavior of the Yugoslav population converged to levels of demographically more developed regions in Europe. However, while it may be said that Yugoslav low fertility regions have the total fertility level similar to France, the regions of intermediate fertility are similar to the level of Poland, the reproductive behavior of the Albanian population of Kosovo cannot be compared to other European populations. Although the population of Kosovo has more demographic similarities with the population of the neighboring Albania than with other parts of Yugoslavia, throughout the 1980s the Albanian women of Kosovo, on average, were giving birth to one child more than women in Albania (Avramov and Penev, 1987).

The marked decline in crude birth rate and total fertility rate corresponded to the gradual decline in the number of live births in all Yugoslav regions except in Kosovo where live births have been continuously increasing. Changes in the distribution of live births by birth order (Table 11) illustrate the motivation to master fertility and the efficacy of birth control. The share of fifth and higher birth order was very high and stood between 20 per cent and 30 percent in 1955 in Kosovo, Bosnia and Hercegovina, Macedonia and Monte Negro. It was around 10 per cent in Croatia, Slovenia, Serbia Proper and Voivodina. Thirty years later, in 1985 fifth and higher birth orders have almost disappeared in Croatia, Slovenia, Serbia Proper and Voivodina, are low in Bosnia and Hercegovina, Monte Negro and Macedonia. Kosovo does not fall in the general trend. The share of fifth and higher birth orders continued to increase until the mid-1960s. On basis of the current share of high birth orders and other indicators such as the birth interval and contraceptive use it may be said that one out of four women in Kosovo has not mastered her fertility.

The share of fourth birth orders has declined by 2 to 3 times in all Yugoslav regions except in Kosovo where it has been fluctuating around similar values during the past three decades. Third birth order changed the least and their share had a clear downward trend only in Serbia Proper and in Voivodina.

Age specific fertility rates indicate a declining trend in all age groups and resulted in the shortening of the individual fertility history. Highest birth rates are in the 20-24 age group in all Yugoslav regions except in Kosovo where the peak fertility level is reached in the 25-29 age group. In most regions fertility declines sharply after the age of 30, except in Kosovo where the threshold is 10 years later but where fertility is high also among women above the age of 40. The mean age of mothers at first birth reached the lowest level of 22 years in the late 1960s and then gradually increased. In most recent years it has been fluctuating around 23.7. From the late 1960s till the late 1970s the mean age of women for all births declined considerably due to the fall of higher order birth orders, but in the 1980s in low fertility regions the average age of mothers started increasing due to the postponement of the first birth.

4) Contraception and abortions

The research about knowledge and use of contraception during the decades of sharpest fertility decline testifies about very low sexual and health culture in Yugoslavia. In 1970 only 74 per cent of married women had elementary knowledge about means and methods of family planning and only half used some type of contraception. Out of those using some means of protection against unwanted pregnancy two thirds resorted to coitus interruptus. One third of women using contraception had one or more unwanted pregnancies (Sentic, 1980). Lack of knowledge and contraceptive inefficacy resulted in the epidemiological magnitude of abortion in Yugoslavia in the second half of the 20th century.

TABLE 11.- LIVE BIRTHS BY BIRTH ORDER

	Year	Total	Birth order				
		(000s)	(per 100 live births)				
			I	II	III	IV	V
YUGOSLAVIA	1955	471	32.2	25.8	16.0	9.8	16.2
	1985	363	43.8	35.7	11.1	4.3	5.1
Bosnia &	1955	110	25.9	21.9	16.6	12.1	23.5
Hercegovina	1985	72	45.5	35.5	12.0	3.8	3.2
Monte Negro	1955	13	24.1	21.9	18.3	13.8	21.9
	1985	10	36.7	33.5	18.1	6.7	5.0
Croatia	1955	88	38.9	27.0	14.7	8.0	11.4
	1985	61	48.0	38.8	9.7	2.2	1.3
Macedonia	1955	48	23.1	22.7	18.7	12.8	22.7
	1985	38	42.1	36.8	12.2	4.7	4.2
Slovenia	1955	32	38.8	27.8	14.9	8.0	10.5
	1985	25	49.1	38.7	9.1	2.1	1.0
Serbia Total	1955	177	34.9	28.4	15.6	8.4	12.7
	1985	154	41.2	34.0	10.9	5.4	8.5
Serbia Proper	1955	105	37.8	30.4	14.9	6.9	10.0
	1985	75	49.1	40.0	7.6	2.0	1.3
Voivodina	1955	36	39.8	30.3	14.8	6.8	8.3
	1985	26	48.9	40.7	7.6	1.6	1.2
Kosovo	1955	36	19.6	19.3	17.4	14.1	29.6
	1985	53	26.4	22.2	17.0	12.2	22.2
Data: Vital statistics SZS 1955 and 1985							

The position of the states towards abortion evolved from the total prohibition of abortion as a criminal act for which both woman and executor were persecuted, in all Yugoslav territories at the onset of the fertility transition. Abortion was legalized on medical grounds only in 1929 and as of 1951 indications were extended also to social considerations. Full liberalization of abortion that may be performed upon simple request of a major of age women until 10 weeks of pregnancy occurred in 1960 and since then access to abortion made it the most widespread means of birth control. According to incomplete registration kept for 1960 and 1966 the number of abortions performed in medical institutions rose from 139 thousand in 1960 to 217 thousand in 1966 (Rasevic, 1990). Reliable data on induced abortion pertain to the 1969-1986 period and point to the magnitude of growth from 253 thousand in 1969 to 389 thousand in 1986. Abortion is clearly not only a corrective for inefficient contraception but rather the prevailing means of limiting family size. Married women account for 90 per cent of abortions and in the 1980s the number of abortions exceeded the number of live births. In 1969 there were 66.2 abortions per 100 live births while in 1986 the ratio stood at 108 abortions per 100 livebirts. The resort to induced abortion differs according to the cultural features of different Yugoslav populations rather than according to levels of economic development. In Serbia Proper there are 218 abortions per 100 live births, in Voivodina 152, in Croatia 91, in Slovenia 87, in Bosnia and Hercegovina and Macedonia 80, in Monte Negro 75 and in Kosovo 22 abortions per 100 live births (Rasevic,1990).

5) *Nuptiality and cohabitation*

The sharpest fertility decline in Yugoslavia coincides with the time when "everybody" married. In Yugoslavia like in most European countries nuptiality rates reached the peak levels in this century in the 1950s and the early 1960s and in this country they fluctuated around the level of 9 marriages per 1000 population until the mid-1970s. The total first marriage rate which indicated the share of women who will ultimately remain single if the conditions of the particular year prevail, fluctuated around very high values in the 1950s, 1960s and 1970s (Table 12).

TABLE 12.- TOTAL FIRST MARRIAGE RATE (PER 1000) AND DIVORCES PER 1000 MARRIAGES

	Marriages	Divorces
1950-55	969	90
1955-60	908	116
1960-65	991	130
1965-70	987	124
1970-75	962	122
1975-80	890	134
1980-85	852	131
1986	811	140
1987	832	140
1988	820	144
1989	817	143
1990	-	130
Data: Vital statistics 1950-1989 and Communication SZS No. 456 for 1990		

YUGOSLAVIA/LA YOUGOSLAVIE

Although it may be said that marriage was a universally accepted institution and a prevailing living arrangement, short term fluctuations in first marriage rates may be observed. Postponement of marriage has not been an outcome of choice between marriage and alternative forms but rather points to the lack of choice for young adults. Changes in the timing of marriage occurred in the socially turbulent years when young adults could not afford the expense of establishing their own household outside their parental home. In the 1980s the Yugoslav populations differed considerably according to all fertility indicators, but all regions exhibited rather high total first marriage rates and low divorce rates.

The recent below replacement level fertility seems to coincide with a gradual decline in the total first marriage rate from 1985 to reach 0.817 in 1989. It is not however possible to establish whether it is the beginning of the disenchantment with the institution and the beginning of the declining nuptiality trend or whether marriage is postponed due to the acute economic crisis and turbulent political transition. The fact that the number of marriages in 1990 declined somewhat in respect to 1989 but that the number of divorces declined considerably may point to the conclusion that the lack of existential security may be causing the postponement of personal decisions which have long term implications for the individual.

The average age of women at marriage has been fluctuating around 24 years during the past three decades. By contrast the average age of men who married in the 1980s increased by 1 year in comparison to the 1950s and now stands at 28 years of age.

The crude divorce rates have been constant in Yugoslavia over the past four decades and have been fluctuating around or just above 1 per 1000 population. One out of 10 marriages has been ending in a divorce. The sharpest increase in divorces occurred in the first post war decade. From the level of 50 divorces per 1000 marriages in the second half of the 1930s the rate doubled in the second half of the 1940s. Throughout the 1950s and the 1960s divorces in Yugoslavia, like in other socialist countries have been higher than in Western Europe (Avramov, 1990). However, from the mid-1960 onward the divorce rate has not changed much and Yugoslavia today has one of the lowest divorce rates in Europe. Although there are no marked changes in divorce levels, the structure of divorces according to duration has been changing. Between the mid-1960s and the mid-1980s the number of divorces after 15 and more years of marriage has doubled while there are hardly any change in divorce levels during the first years of marriage.

No data on cohabitation have yet been gathered and there is no indication that modern unions as alternatives to marriage have any impact on fertility levels in Yugoslavia. In the population censuses the share of non-family households has been constant around 1.5 per cent of all households and furthermore comprised rather senior citizens than young adults. Under conditions of high unemployment that affects mainly young adults, no unemployment benefits for those seeking first employment and chronic apartment shortage, the number of young adults who can leave the parental household without relying on the network of family solidarity, is very small.

In Yugoslavia as a whole out-of-wedlock births do not have a major impact on fertility levels. The share of out-of-wedlock births has been fluctuating around 8 per cent until the early 1980s when a gradual increase occurred. The share of out-of-wedlock births in 1989 stood at 10.5 per cent of all births. The only Yugoslav region where a sharp increase in out-of-wedlock births may be observed, in particular since the mid-1980s, is Slovenia where in 1989 almost one out of four (23.2 per cent) children were born out-of-wedlock. Data on acknowledgement of a child by the father indirectly illustrate the different nature of the out-of-wedlock fertility in different cultural settings. In Slovenia 84 per cent of children born out-of-wedlock were acknowledged by their fathers while in Bosnia and Hercegovina it was the case only for 7 per cent of children born outside matrimony.

TABLE 13. INFANT MORTALITY RATE (PER 1000)

Year	YUGOSLAVIA	Slovenia	Kosovo
1950	118.6	80.6	141.3
1960	87.7	35.1	132.5
1970	55.5	24.5	96.3
1980	31.4	15.3	57.7
1990	20.2	8.9	40.6

Source: Vital statistics 1950-1989 and Communication No. 456 SZS for 1990

TABLE 14. LIFE EXPECTANCY (YEARS) AT CERTAIN AGES IN 1980/81 AND 1988/89

Age	0	1	15	45	65
1980/1981					
Males	67.7	69.0	55.6	27.8	12.9
Females	73.2	74.4	60.9	32.1	15.1
1988/1989					
Males	68.6	69.4	55.9	27.9	13.1
Females	74.5	75.2	61.6	32.7	15.6

Data: Mortality tables SZS

Yugoslavia no longer has features of a high fertility country but it has maintained its demographic specificity in the nuptiality pattern, namely the universality of marriage, low divorce rates, marginality of alternative unions to marriage and low rates of out-of-wedlock births.

6) Mortality and aging

In the second half of the 20th century a marked increase in life expectancy resulted primarily from the declining infant mortality and mortality at early ages. Mortality decline among men in the age group 40-60 was modest and minor above the age of 70. Between 1952 and 1989 the mean life expectancy at birth increased from 59.3 years to 74.5 years for women and from 56.9 to 68.6 years for men with increasing difference in favor of women. In the 1980s the average increase in longevity amounted to 2 months each calendar year for women and 1.3 months for men.

Although infant mortality rate has fallen sharply, with 20 infant deaths per 1000 live births (Table 13) Yugoslavia has one of the highest rates in Europe. Marked regional differences are exhibited in three groups: Slovenia, Croatia and Voivodina stand out with infant mortality of approximately 10 per 1000, Monte Negro, Bosnia and Hercegovina and Serbia Proper have rates between 12 and 17 while Macedonia and Kosovo have extremely high infant mortality of 36 and 40 per 1000 live births respectively.

Changes in the age composition of the population indicate a decline in the share of young and increase in the share of older population in all Yugoslav territories. However, regional differences in the age structure as the outcome of the diversified population dynamics are marked (Table 7).

7) External migration

Ever since its foundation Yugoslavia has traditionally been an emigration country. Nevertheless, migration records are poor and there are no fully reliable data on migratory flows. According to estimates, only partially founded on the data from the population censuses, the migratory balance in the 1948-1953 intercensus period stood at between -20000 and -30000 per year. The negative net migration further increased between the censuses of 1953 and 1961 ranging between -45000 and -50000 per year (Vogelnik, 1974). For the next 1961-1971 intercensus period negative annual migratory balance was estimated at -22000 (Vogelnik, 1974) and for the 1971-1981 period at -6500 (Breznik, 1991). In the first post-war decade emigration was mainly political in nature due to the change of borders, political regime, expatriation of German and Italian nationals and mass departure of Turks in the 1950s. From the mid-1960s after an unsuccessful economic reform a mass exodus of the labor force started. According to the census of 1981 the stock of Yugoslav workers and their family members in Western and Northern Europe stood at 875 thousand people.

Due to the marked difference in wages between Yugoslavia and Western Europe, Yugoslavs have been going abroad as temporary, seasonal or day laborers for decades. However, with the breakdown of the communist regimes in Eastern Europe a new migratory flow is beginning to affect Yugoslavia. Yugoslavia is not only attractive but has become easily accessible to poorer neighbors who can leave their country and return freely and are coming as illegal laborers in growing numbers. Until 1989 between 1 and 2.5 thousand Rumanians crossed the border each year. In 1990 the number of Rumanian tourists rose to 2.1 million (Politika, 21 April 1991). There are no statistical data which would enable to distinguish between tourists and illegal laborers from Eastern Europe, but the growing presence of cheap labor force is observed both in the cities and in the countryside, and tensions are often occurring between local and foreign day laborers.

8) Population policy

If we compare indicators of population growth and fertility levels for Yugoslavia as a whole with the averages for Europe, we may observe that the natural increase is 7.5 times higher in Yugoslavia, the crude birth rate is 25 per cent higher and the total fertility rate is 20 per cent above the average for Europe as a whole. A seemingly logical conclusion may follow, that the demographic parameters are satisfactory and the demographic situation in Yugoslavia favorable. Indeed, that is the evaluation that was made by the Yugoslav government when data for the UN policy bank were given (United Nations, 1987). However, a relatively favorable average results from different fertility levels by ethnicity which in turn cause changes in the ethnic composition and contribute to the increase of social tensions (Avramov, 1991). Hence, series of political initiatives have been taken in order to articulate the general principles and political stands about parenthood as a basic human right codified in the Resolution about family planning (1969) and in the Constitution (1974) and to reconcile these principles with the macro population interests. The need to overcome regional imbalances in the population reproduction was articulated in the development program up to 1985 and in the Resolution on the population development emanated by the Federal Assembly (1989). This Resolution (Sluzbeni glasnik SFRJ, 1989) may be said to be a political answer to the perception of the demographic future determined by the present below replacement fertility, on the one side, and population explosion, on the other side. However, all these documents were only declarative in their nature. They diagnosed the population problems but have never been translated into a consistent system of population policy nor have they been operationalized through policy measures targeted at increasing or decreasing fertility levels according to the regional needs.

9) Population projections

Starting from the general assessment that the turbulent phase of political and economic structural transformation will have a strong impact on demographic parameters in the forthcoming decade, in the latest population projections for Yugoslavia (Futurama

Yugoslavia) the following hypothesis were developed: marked fertility decline will occur, no major improvements in health conditions and hence in mortality levels may be expected and emigration will not increase in the next decade due to the limiting nature of immigration policy in Western Europe.

TABLE 15. PROJECTIONS OF THE RESIDENT POPULATION AND OF THE OFFICIALLY REGISTERED POPULATION (INCLUDING THE STOCK OF MIGRANTS) IN 2001 AND 2021 (000s)

	Resident population		Officially registered population	
	2001	2021	2001	2021
YUGOSLAVIA	23862	24092	24700	24649
Bosnia & Hercegovina	4379	4376	4563	4515
Monte Negro	649	673	669	678
Croatia	4615	4524	4803	4729
Macedonia	2202	2388	2306	2375
Slovenia	2050	2056	2099	2108
Serbia	9964	10072	10258	10242
Serbia Proper	5723	5419	5919	5766
Voivodina	2014	1928	2075	2014
Kosovo	2226	2724	2263	2460
Source: Futurama Yugoslavia, Avramov, (ed.) (1991)				

The population assèssments and projections officially used by the statistical offices include the stock of Yugoslav workers abroad and their family members. Hence, numerous distortions of demographic parameters occur since the total population used as the base for the calculation of vital rates exceeds in number the resident population for which vital events are recorded. For the analysis of social and economic implications of expected demographic changes at the turn of the century we have developed two versions. Thus, the resident population of Yugoslavia would amount to 23.8 million in 2001 while the number of Yugoslavs would exceed 24.7 million in 2001 if the stock of Yugoslavs abroad is taken into account.

References

Avramov, Dâ. (1991) (ed.), Futurama Yugoslavia, Fondazione GiovanniAgnelli Project

Avramov, D. (1991) Population Policy in Multi-ethnic Societies: The Yugoslav Case, in Cliquet, R.L. (ed.) Desirabilities and Possibilities of a Fertility Recovery at Replacement Level in Europe,NIDI CBGS Publications Swets & Zeitlinger B.V. Amsterdam/Lisse

Avramov, D., G. Penev (1987) Demographic Characteristics of EthnicAlbanians in Yugoslavia and of the population of Albania, in PrimoIncontro Demographico della Regione Adriatica IDRA, Universita G.D' Annunzio, Pescara

Breznik, D. (1991) Stanovnistvo Jugoslavije, manuscript

Breznik, D. (1985) Metodoloska pitanja demografskih ocena ratnihgubitaka stanovnistva Jugoslavije i njihove aproksimacije nekim odizloznih metoda, okrugli sto 20-21 juni SANU, Beograd

Breznik, D. i V. Simeunovic (1961) Kretanje stanovnistva Jugoslavije 1921-1961, Socijalna politika br. 7-8

Gacesa, Lj. (1989) Transverzalni i kohortni pristup analizifertiliteta zenskog stanovnistva SFR Jugoslavije u periodu 1950-1987, magistarski rad, Beograd

Lah, I. (1952) Istinski demografski gubici Jugoslavije, Statistickarevija 2-3

Politika, of 21 April 1991

Pressat, R. (1991) La population de la France, Country Report for the European Demographic Conference, Paris 21-25 October

Rasevic, M. (1990) Thirty years of induced abortion in Yugoslavia,paper presented at the WHO, UNFPA, IPPF conference From Abortion to Contraception, Tbilisi, 10-13 October

Savezni zavod za statistiku (1989) Stanovnistvo Jugoslavije 1921-1981, Beograd

Sentic, M. (1980) Kontracepcija i njeni demografski aspekti, inBreznik, D. (urednik) Fertilitet stanovnistva i planiranje porodiceu Jugoslaviji, Centar za demografska istrazivanja, Beograd

Simeunovic V. (1964) Stanovnistvo Jugoslavije i socijalistickihrepublika 1921-1961, Savezni zavod za statistiku, Beograd

Skracene tablice mortaliteta (1980/1981) Savezni zavod za statistiku, Beograd

Sluzbeni list SFRJ br. 27/1989

Tasic, D. (1948) Konacni rezultati popisa stanovnistva od 15. marta1948. kjniga I, Beograd

United Nations (1989) World Population Prospects, 1988, New York.

United Nations (1987) Global Population Policy Database, 1987, NewYork. Vital statistics, various years, Savezni zavod za statistiku,Beograd

Vogelnik, D. (1974) Population Growth and Components of Growth inBreznik. D. (ed.) The Population of Yugoslavia, C.I.C.R.E.D.Series, Demographic Research Center, Belgrade

Vogelnik, D. (1952) Demografski gubici Jugoslavije u drugomsvetskom ratu, Statisticka revija, Beograd br. 1

Zerjavic, V. (1989), Gubici stanovnistva Jugoslavije u drugomsvetskom ratu, Naprijed, Zagreb

Malta/Malte
Reno CAMILLERI

The Maltese archipelago consists of the islands of Malta, Gozo and Comino. The total area is 316 km2 with a population density of 1126 persons per km2 and is, as such, the highest densely populated country in the Mediterranean.

Malta has always been the centre of attraction for the peoples of the Mediterranean littoral. Archeological inverstigations indicate that the first settlers came from nearby Sicily towards the fifth millenium B.C.. Around 800 B.C. a Phoenician type of culture brought the prehistoric period to an end. Then came the Carthaginians who, in turn, were ousted by the Romans. Successive rulers included the Greeks, Arabs, Normans, Angevins, Aragonese, Castilians, the Knights of St John, the French and the British. But notwithstanding the influence that the different cultures and religions have had on Malta, the Maltese are distinguished as a separate nation by their ancient tongue. It is a distinc language with a Semitic structure enhanced by foreign additions and assimilations.

I.- GROWTH PROFILE

Since 1842, when the first population census was taken, there has been a more or less continuous growth of the population except for the 1911-1921 period and the early 1960s. Lack of jobs forced thousands of workers to settle in Australia and North America so that the census held in 1921, showed a small reduction of 111 persons in the total population when compared with the previous census.

In the years following the First World War, the picture was a fairly consistent one of accelerated growth in female population, and a male population fluctuating widely in its rate of increase depending on the emigration flow. After 1948, planned emigration became a major policy of Government, and whole families took up permanent residence abroad so that within a few years the age structure of the population and, as a consequence, the birth rate, were drastically readjusted.

During the intercensal period 1948 to 1957, the population increased by only 13,629 persons of whom, 11,186 were females. The average rate of increase during these years of heavy emigration was less than 0.5 per cent per annum, the corresponding rates for males and females being 0.2 and 0.7 per cent, respectively.

After 1963, the population reversed its long history of almost continuous growth, and began to show a slow declining trend brought about by a renewed spurt in the emigration drive in the wake of the rundown of the British military forces on the island. This emigration drive caused a marked tendency for the birth rate to decline resulting in a reduction of 3,814 persons, that is, 1.2 per cent of the population between 1957 and 1967.

The Maltese population was estimated at 355,910 as at the end of 1990, consisting of 175,782 males and 180,128 females - a sex ratio of 976 males to 1000 females. There has been therefore, an average annual growth of 0.9 per cent during the last decade. A slight easing of the growth rate had been recorded between 1985 and 1987; thereafter a marginal increase in the growth rate from 0.7 to 1.0 per cent was observed. The gross reproduction rate is estimated at unity.

II.- MIGRATION

The potential effect of migration can be easily gauged by tracing briefly the history of the Maltese migratory movement.

Before the 20th century, Maltese emigrants had sought employment in countries bordering on the Mediterranean such as Tunis, Egypt and Algeria and by 1911, around 34,000 Maltese had settled in such places. After the First World War, the 'traditional' countries for Maltese emigrants, Canada, USA and Australia assumed their importance. Since then, Maltese settlements in these countries have been very rapid. By 1921, Australia was already taking more Maltese than any other country. By this time too, the Maltese Government emigration policy was already amply defined, and in the same year, the Department of Emigration was set up to guide Maltese emigrants and provide them with assistance abroad. After the Second World War, efforts to facilitate emigration were intensified.

MALTA/MALTE

Until 1975, the number of returned emigrants was relatively low and most of them re-emigrated within a short time. Since then, however, a new phenomenon has been evident, in that there had been an influx of returnees which was greater than the number of those leaving to settle abroad. A heavy net inflow was observed during the period 1975-1977 when net returnees averaged 1,200 per year. At present, the yearly net migration is about 700.

Although in Malta's case emigration has acted as a safety valve in easing post-war population growth it has disturbed to a marked extent the age structure of the population. It will furthermore affect the sex ratio of the population creating a surplus of women in Malta (and particularly in Gozo). It has been estimated that in the period of heavy emigration around 60 per cent of emigrants were aged 18-34 years. The Fertility Survey Report of 1963 issued by the Central Office of Statistics refers to a sex ratio of three females for every male in the 20-30 age group. The counter-effects of returned migrants are not likely to correct the imbalances referred to, since their number has been relatively small (until 1975) and falls within the older age groups.

III.- DEMOGRAPHIC TRANSITION

Malta's demographic transition has followed closely the pattern of the 'model' founded mainly on European experience. There is, however, one important difference; whereas by the 1930s most of the Western countries had completed the full cycle of their demographic transition and in some cases their fertility levels even fell short of replacement level, Malta had still one of the highest birth rates in Europe. Yet it had later succeeded to accomplish within the following two decades, a chapter of demographic history which most other European countries had taken much longer to write.

The first or early stage of demographic transition persisted right up to the first half of the forties. The crude birth rate averaged 31 per 1000 while the crude death rate averaged 25 per 1000. This situation symptomised a society in which the standard of living was low ; proper medical care (particularly in the prenatal and postnatal stages) was practically non-existent and the level of the most basic social services was extremely poor. In such a state, epidemics like cholera, smallpox and gastroenteritis had, at times, claimed a large number of victims. As will be argued later on, these epidemics were the main cause of fluctuations in the aged segment of the population during the past century particularly around 1865 and 1890.

The 'second' phase of demographic transition may be considered to have coincided with the steep decline in the infant mortality rate recorded after 1942. In that year infant mortality accounted for over a third of live births. The crude birth rate as a result of the post war baby boom, reached 39.9 per 1000 in 1944, the highest rate recorded in the present century.

The 'third' phase, characterized by a decline in the crude birth rate and a constant levelling off of the crude death rate started towards the mid-fifties. There is some evidence to suggest that at that time, public awareness of the acute social and economic problems which the country would have had to face in the future in the absence of any control of population growth, might have been triggered by a fertility survey of the Maltese Islands carried out in 1955. Although the report on the survey did not contain any explicit reference to the introduction of fertility control, yet the overall message was that, given the then broad base to the age pyramid, the population was likely to continue to grow and to reach alarming levels within two decades, unless the fertility level was immediately brought down.

The signs of a decline in fertility which were first visible in the 1950s, continued unabated since then. In the period 1950-1955 Malta still had one of the highest birth rate in Europe. Twenty years later, it could be compared to that of most European countries, while the projected rate for the last quinquennial of the century is expected to be among the lowest in Europe. By 1970, Malta had therefore reached the 'fourth' or last phase of its transition cycle.

The main reason underlying the decline in fertility is more of a sociological rather than economic character. Prior to the 1950s, parents were more inclined to emigrate to alleviate their poor standing rather than restrict the number of their children. The high mortality rate, on the other hand, reflected the lack of medical and welfare facilities. Rising standards of living and education and the development of social services since the late fifties contributed a good deal to lower the birth rate and prolong life. The natural increase in population has been, however, kept to a minimum or offset for a number of years through emigration as already pointed out, so much that during the intercensal years 1958-1967, the population registered a drop of over 5,000 persons. Since 1970, other factors such as the wider availability of contraceptives, the diffusion of education particularly among women, the changing role and status of women in Maltese society could be considered relevant causes of family limitation.

IV.- MARRIAGE

One need not to go beyond the census findings of 1948 in order to assess the changes in the marital status of the population brought about by the periodic upswing or slump in migration and other social and economic factors such as housing and the distribution of income. In 1948, of the population of 15 years and over, 53.5 per cent were married and 7.5 per cent widowed (table 1). The ratio of singles to the total population aged 15 years and over stood at 42.0 per cent and 37.6 per cent for males and females respectively.

MALTA/MALTE

TABLE 1.- PERCENTAGE DISTRIBUTION OF THE POPULATION AGED 15 YEARS AND OVER BY MARITAL STATUS - 1931-1985

	1931		1948		1957		1967		1985	
Status	M	F	M	F	M	F	M	F	M	F
Single	46.2	41.4	42.0	37.6	39.6	37.2	43.2	41.7	34.4	31.4
Married	47.8	48.3	54.9	52.0	55.7	52.5	53.1	48.8	62.5	59.1
Widowed	5.0	10.3	4.1	10.4	4.7	10.3	3.7	9.5	3.1	9.5

During the 1967 census it was established that 53.1 per cent of males and 48.8 per cent of females were married. Moreover, the married segment of the population within the 20-30 age group was also higher than that recorded during the previous census. The 1985 census showed that 62.5 per cent of males and 59.1 per cent of females aged 15 years and over were married, giving an overall ratio of 60.7 per cent of the population aged 15 years and over. The increase in the married portion of the population was mainly reflected in a sharp decline in the number of single persons which dropped to 34.3 per cent and 31.4 per cent in respect of males and females respectively.

One should also make reference to two other important factors. First, there has been a gradual stepping up in the medium age at first marriage of both the bride and bridegroom during the past twenty years. The median age of brides is now 22.5 years compared to 20.5 years while that of bridegrooms has shifted to 25.0 years from 23.5 years during the last two decades. Secondly, births are not only fewer but most of them are being postponed to later years in marriage.

Markedly in sharp contrast to most European countries, the number of marriages has remained high, cohabitation has slightly increased while the proportion of illegitimate births is extremely low by any standard. Divorce remains illegal in Malta while the increase in the number of one-parent families has not been so pronounced as in other countries. Deep family links are a standing characteristic of Maltese society.

V.- THE FALL IN HOUSEHOLD SIZE

The dramatic fall in family size[1] during the past forty years is a salient feature of Maltese demographic history. Whereas the large household consisting of 10 members and over and 7-9 persons represented 19.3 per cent of families in 1948 (table 2), the former are practically non existent in 1985 while the latter accounts for only 2.5 per cent.

---

[1] For the purpose of this note, the 'household' family as distinct from the 'nuclear' one, has been considered.

TABLE 2.- PERCENTAGE DISTRIBUTION OF HOUSEHOLDS BY SIZE

Census Year	Number of persons in household			
	2-3	4-6	7-9	10+
1948	38.3	42.4	16.0	3.3
1957	42.1	38.8	14.9	4.2
1967	42.8	41.2	12.6	3.4
1985	49.6	47.8	2.5	0.1

The shift is discernible in the first instance, in the 4-6 persons households. The number of smaller households (2-3 persons) which in 1948 made up 38.3 per cent now account for 49.8 per cent of all households. Analyses of the 1985 census show that a) the 3 or 4 person households are a common feature of all localities, particularly in those where the population is very old or very young and b) it is difficult to locate the traditional 'big' household so that there is very little correlation between household size and the urban or rural areas of Malta and Gozo or with some other traditional demographic dimension.

Further indication of the fall in the size of the average Maltese family is provided by reference to the mean number of births related to selected marriage cohorts (table 3). Those women who were married during 1912-1923 had an average of 7.38 births; 1924-1935 marriage cohorts produced an average of 6.71 births, while births related to marriages taking place between 1948 and 1960 averaged 3.93 per marriage.

TABLE 3.- MEAN NUMBER OF BIRTHS PER MARRIAGE COHORT - MALTESE ISLANDS

Year of first marriage	Mean Number of live births	Year of first marriage	Mean Number of live births
1915	6.9	1945	5.1
1920	7.1	1950	4.5
1925	6.9	1955	3.7
1930	6.3	1960	3.0
1935	6.1	1965	2.7
1940	6.1	1970	2.4

VI.- CHANGING AGE STRUCTURE

Spanning a period since 1851 one does not notice any marked change in the age composition of the Maltese population prior to the twentieth century. In 1851, 32.4 per cent of Matla's population were in the 0-14 age group. By the turn of the century this segment fluctuated within very narrow margins (table 4). The 15-64 age group and the 65 and over age group retained also more or less their precentage representation hovering around 61 and 7 per cent respectively during a period of fifty years.

MALTA/MALTE

TABLE 4.- PERCENTAGE DISTRIBUTION OF POPULATION BY BROAD AGE GROUPS
1851-1985

Census Year	0-14	15-64	65 years over
1851	324	614	62
1861	329	610	61
1871	296	645	59
1881	307	622	71
1891	329	603	68
1901	341	605	54
1911	336	613	51
1921	318	626	56
1931	321	621	58
1948	349	594	57
1957	374	558	68
1967	298	618	84
1985	241	660	99

At the 1901 census the 0-14 age group represented 34.1 per cent of the enumerated population but this segment has been gradually declining and stood at 24.1 per cent in 1985. The post war baby boom can, however, be read in the data against 1948 and 1957. The difference had been shifted to the older age groups. Whereas the 15-64 age group now accounts for 66 per cent compared to 60.5 per cent in 1901, the most significant upswing could be discerned in the 65 and over age group which hiked to 9.9 per cent from 5.4 per cent in 1901. This was the combined result of natural ageing and migration.

Fifty years ago the expectation of life in Malta was around 43 years for males and around 46 years for females. As the infant mortality rate falls and fertility remains high, the population is constantly becoming younger. With the onset of the 'third phase' of demographic transition, the ageing process became evident.

Ageing - a twentieth century phenomenon

This phenomenon which until recently was regarded as being of particular significance to industrialized countries, is fast becoming a feature of developing countries, including Malta. In the study of this phenomenon, one has to pay attention not only to the proportion of the aged in the population but should consider the elderly in absolute terms as well. The same attention should be focused on the characteristics of the aged such as their need for care, risk of dependence, housing and social environment.

The dependency ratio (table 5) illustrate the burden of the inactive segment of the population upon the active segment. They take into account local conditions, in that education is compulsory up to the age of 16 years so that, those aged 15 are included within the 'young' component, while those aged 61 and over are included within the 'old' segment. Since the ageing factor in Gozo is much higher than in Malta, separate indices have been worked out.

TABLE 5.- DEPENDANCY RATIO (AS A % OF 16-60 AGE GROUP)

	0-15 years	61 + years	0-15 & 61 + years
Maltese isl.	41.9	21.9	63.8
Gozo	39.4	33.0	72.3

VII.- POPULATION PROJECTIONS

Population projections demonstrate that those aged 65 years and over which represent 10.4 per cent in 1990, will go on rising to 12.2 per cent by the end of the century and may reach 14.0 per cent by the year 2010. Those aged 75 years and over who in 1990 accounted for 4.0 per cent of the population are projected to represent 4.8 per cent in the year 2000 and will touch a new level at 6.0 per cent a decade later. The female component will continue to rise from 11.5 per cent in 1990 to 14.0 per cent in the year 2000 to stand at a leval of 16.0 per cent during the following decade.

People in Malta are living longer and are having fewer children although the total fertility rate has not fallen below replacement threshold. As a result there will be fewer workers to support an ever growing number of pensioners. Faced with this trend, Government has to make choices and the main issue will be how to distribute the national output between workers and non- workers without endangering growth.

REFERENCES

Central Office of Statistics, Malta, Population censuses reports.

Cirillo R.- *Social Aspects of Maltese Migration.*

Council of Europe - country reports.

Delia E.P.- *The Determinants of Modern Maltese Migration.*

Department of Labour, Malta, Departemental Reports.

Seers D.- *A Fertility Survey in the Maltese Islands.*

Italy/L'Italie
Antonio GOLINI
Annunziata NOBILE

I.- A HISTORICAL PROFILE FROM 1861 UP TO THE 2ND WORLD WAR

1) General trends of demographic evolution

At the time of the unification of the nation (1861), Italy's demographic regime still showed the characteristic signs of the pre- transitional stage. High levels of mortality (higher than 30 p. 1000) still persisted and during the first half of the 19th century they produce an even slower rhythm of growth than in other European countries, particularly in the north-western area. The Italian population had an annual average growth rate of 5.5 p. 1000 during these fifty years. This was much lower than in the north-western area of Europe and in the European territories of the eastern countries (Table 1). This led to an inevitable loss of demographic weight in the continent as a whole (on the other hand there was significant internal differentiation[1]). This weight fell from 9.7% to 9% in fifty years.

---

[1] In this overall picture, two contrasting situations stand out: the great expansion of the population of Great Britain which was growing at a rate of more than 13 p. 1000 and the slow growth in France, caused by an early decline in natality.

In the second half of the century, as was the case in most of the other European countries, the growth rate increased despite the fact that emigration abroad, which was at a very low level in the years immediately following unification, became more pronounced after 1880 and remained so until the end of the 1920s. In fact, the heavy migratory losses were more than compensated for by the excess of births over deaths. The growth rate continued to grow progressively from the beginning of the 1880s until the end of the 1920s, interrupted only during the period of the 1st World War (Table 2). In the last two decades of the last century, the natural balance grew considerably from the previous average levels of about 7 p. 1000 to over 10 p. 1000.

TABLE 1 - EVOLUTION OF THE POPULATION IN EUROPEAN COUNTRIES FROM 1800 TO 1900

Regions/ Countries	Average annual increase x 1000 inhabitants		% of the European population		
	1800-1850	1850-1900	1800	1850	1900
N.W. Europe	7.3	7.0	47.9	48.5	45.8
Great Britain	13.1	11.5	5.9	8.0	9.4
France	5.2	2.2	14.3	13.1	9.7
S.W. Europe	4.9	5.8	17.7	15.9	14.1
Italy	5.5	6.1	9.7	9.0	8.1
Spain	4.1	4.7	6.4	5.5	4.6
Eastern Europe	7.6	10.6	34.4	35.6	40.0
Europe	7.0	8.2	100.0	100.0	100.0
European population (in millions)			187.7	266.2	400.6

Source: elaboration of data obtained from G. Sundbärg, *Aperçus statistiques internationaux*, Stockholm, 1908.

The determinant factor of this evolutive process was the progressive and marked decline in mortality which began at the start of the 1880s when natality was still maintaining its traditionally high levels. Figure 1 demonstrates very clearly how natality and mortality evolved in different ways. In the first twenty years after unification, mortality fluctuated around 30 p. 1000 - one of the highest figures in the Western Europe. It frequently rose above this figure as a result of recurrent epidemics such as the 1867 cholera epidemic which had devastating effects. In the following years, the decline in mortality picked up speed and became irreversible, interrupted only by the war and the last great epidemic in Italian history - the "Spanish flu" epidemic of 1918-19. On the eve of the 2nd world war, the death rate was below 14 p. 1000 i.e. similar to that of the countries of north- western Europe whose death rate had begun to fall earlier. Natality, however, only began its falling trend towards the end of the century, when the social and cultural pre-conditions which form the basis of Malthusian behaviour slowly began to be established in Italy as well as in other countries. During the 1890s, the rate fell from the initial levels of 37 p. 1000 to below 34 p. 1000 and the fall became more marked during the 1920s. Despite this rapid decline (in 1939 the rate was little more than 23 p. 1000), natality in Italy was still at clearly higher levels than those found in the north-western area countries in the same period.

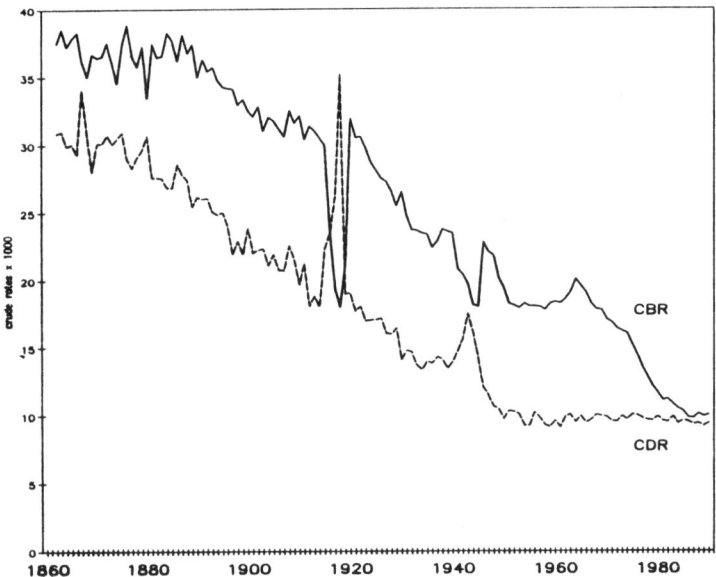

Figure 1.- Evolution of natality and mortality in Italy. 1862-1990

TABLE 2.- EVOLUTION OF THE ITALIAN POPULATION BETWEEN 1861 AND 1941

Periods	Population (*) boundaries at the time	present boundaries	Average annual rates (p. 1000) of total increase	natural increase	net migration	Cumulated net emigration(**)
1861	22182	26328				
1862-71	27304	28151	6.8	7.1	- 0.3	78
1872-81	28953	29791	6.0	7.3	- 1.3	456
1882-91	31161	31992	7.6	10.4	- 2.8	1301
1892-01	33178	34015	6.1	10.6	- 4.5	2769
1902-11	35971	37059	7.5	10.9	- 3.4	3946
1912-21	38483	37890	3.4	5.4	- 2.0	4682
1922-31	41887	41277	8.9	11.3	- 2.4	5625
1932-41	45516	44885	8.5	9.1	- 0.7	5908

(*) De jure population at the end of the period; figures in thousands.
(**) Figures in thousands.
N.B.: the rates have been calculated for the de facto population within present boundaries.
Source: elaboration of data obtained from ISTAT, Sviluppo della popolazione italiana dal 1861 al 1961, Annali di statistica, serie VIII, vol. 17, Roma, 1965, 115.

As a result of all these demographic trends, the Italian population (without taking territorial variations into account) increased by 18.6 million at an average annual rate of

6.7 p. 1000 during the 80 years from 1861-1941 when most of the changes comprising such major demographic transition took place.

The changing trends outlined in this overall picture were not very uniform over the Italian territory as a whole. Towards the end of the 19th century, a dichotomy was already beginning to emerge between the demographic regimes in the north and the south. This dichotomy, caused by the fact that demographic transition began at different times (earlier in the north), was to become clearcut immediately after the 1st world war and even today is still a permanent characteristic of Italian demographic evolution.

2) Stages in the decline in fertility and mortality

The evolution of the total fertility rate confirms that the decline in fertility definitely took hold during the 1890s (Table 3), but it was nevertheless consistently higher than that observed in the countries of north-western Europe where, in addition, the decline had begun earlier on. Basically, these territorial differences mirror difference in nuptiality. In Italy, the frequency of marriage was greater and the mean age at marriage was lower[2]. Legitimate fertility by age at marriage was in fact in line with average European values.

As regards cohort fertility, there was a continuous reduction in the number of offspring which became more marked in the case of the generations born in the 1880s i.e. those generations with their highest fertility period in the years immediately preceding the 1st world war (Table 4). By and large, generation replacement was assured for all those born before 1890. After that, the net rate of reproduction fell to just under 1 i.e. on the threshold of replacement. This slightly deficit reproductive behaviour was largely compensated for by the continued decrease in mortality which meant that the newborn lived longer than their mothers with a resultant increase in the population.

The gradual reduction in mortality is summarized very well by the evolution of life expectancy at birth during the decades beginning at the time of national unification and ending at the start of the 1930s (Table 5). The low figures for the first two periods under consideration (around 31 years) unequivocally show the general economic and social backwardness of a country in which modern factors of transformation and development had not yet surfaced. Survival rates only began to increase significantly during the 1880s. At the end of this decade, life expectancy exceeded 42 years for both sexes. Despite this progress however, Italy was still considerably behind the other western European countries. In the same period, life expectancy at birth had already reached 50 years in the Scandinavian countries and 47 years in France and Belgium. In the years to follow, there was a considerable increase in life expectancy which, at the beginning of the 1930s, rose

---

[2] Up to the beginning of the 20th century, the proportion of women who were still unmarried at 50 years of age was over 20% in most of the countries of northern Europe and the meane age at marriage was between 26 and 27 years of age. In Italy, the proportion of unmarried women fluctuates around 11-12% up to the beginning of the 2nd world war and the mean age at first marriage was under 24 years in the same period.

to around 54 years for men and 56 years for women. The causes for this increase were numerous and complex the most important being the development of better hygiene and sanitary structures.

TABLE 3.- TOTAL FERTILITY RATE IN ITALY AND SOME OTHER EUROPEAN COUNTRIES. 5-YEAR PERIODS FROM 1862 TO 1941

Periods	Italy	France	England and Wales	Sweden
1862-66	5.18	3.50	4.91	4.58
1867-71	4.99	3.50	4.93	4.22
1872-76	5.12	3.42	4.94	4.49
1877-81	5.06	3.45	4.88	4.51
1882-86	5.24	3.38	4.55	4.34
1887-91	5.30	3.12	4.16	4.25
1892-96	5.14	2.97	3.90	4.09
1897-01	4.97	2.90	3.62	4.05
1902-06	4.85	2.79	3.40	3.91
1907-11	4.77	2.60	3.14	3.76
1912-16	4.30	2.25	2.84	3.31
1917-21	3.31	1.65	2.42	2.94
1922-26	3.86	2.42	2.40	2.58
1927-31	3.47	2.30	2.01	2.08
1932-36	3.10	2.16	1.79	1.77
1937-41	3.08	2.07	1.80	1.82

Note: data for Italy are estimates. For France, England and Wales and Sweden, the five-year periods are the following: 1861-65, 1866-70, ..., 1936-40.
Source: Italy: M. Breschi, *La popolazione della Toscana dal 1640 al 1940. Un'ipotesi di ricostruzione*, Serie Ricerche Empiriche n. 17, Dipartimento Statistico, Università di Firenze, 1990. Other countries: J.C. Chesnais, *La transition démographique. Etapes, formes, implications économiques*, INED, Cahier de travaux et documents n. 113, Paris, 1986.

A determinant factor for this evolution was the marked decline in mortality in the first year of life. During the first 30 years following unification, the infant mortality rate was still higher than 200 p. 1000 - although it was falling. Such a level of infant deaths is typical of the demographic trends of pre-modern societies[3]. This regression only began to become noticeable with the start of the new century. This trend continued and by the 1930s the initial rate had been halved.

The reduction of mortality in Italy appears to be linked to the transformation of the nosological framework that started at the beginning of the 20th century which followed in the footsteps of progress already made by the more developed European countries[4].

---

[3] During the same period, the infant mortality rate in most of the north-western European countries had already fallen below 150 p. 1000 and the lowest levels were almost down to 100 p. 1000 in the Scandinavian countries.

[4] Infectious and parasitic diseases and later, diseases of the respiratory and digestive systems - which were responsible for about 60% of all deaths at the beginning of the 1880s - were becoming progressively less

In particular, the gains made in terms of life expectancy between 1900 and 1930 (11 years for men and 13 for women) can be accounted for - to the tune of about 23% - by the reduction in the number of infectious and parasitic diseases which dominated the "traditional" nosological structure.

TABLE 4.- REPLACEMENT OF GENERATIONS AT BIRTH - GENERATIONS 1851-1910

Generations	Total fertility rate	Survival ratio (*)	Net reproduction rate
1861-65	5.11	0.4765	1.18
1866-70	5.04	0.4786	1.17
1871-75	4.91	0.5069	1.21
1876-80	4.65	0.5202	1.18
1881-90	4.07	0.5567	1.10
1891-900	3.32	0.5908	0.96
1901-10	2.96	0.6525	0.94

(*) probability of survival from birth up to the mean age of fertility (30 years). Life tables for the generations of 1862, 1868, 1873, 1878, 1885, 1895, 1905.
Source: for total fertility rate: P. Festy, *La fécondité des pays occidentaux de 1870 à 1970*, INED, Cahier de travaux et documents n. 86, Paris, 1979; for generation life tables : M. Natale, A. Bernassola, *La mortalità per causa nelle regioni italiane. Tavole per contemporanei 1965-66 e per generazioni 1790-1964*, Istituto di Demografia della Facoltà di Scienze Statistiche Demografiche e Attuariali, Università di Roma, 1973.

TABLE 5.- EVOLUTION OF MORTALITY IN ITALY BETWEEN 1862-64 AND 1930-32

Years	Expectation of life at birth		Infant mortality(*)	
	M	F	M	F
1862-64	30.20	31.11	250.9	227.0
1872-76	31.69	32.63	234.2	213.3
1881-82	35.16	35.65	212.4	192.3
1889-90	42.50	43.00	177.8	160.9
1910-12	46.57	47.33	148.5	134.9
1921-22	49.27	50.75	135.6	121.3
1930-32	53.76	56.00	115.3	102.3
% change 1862-64/1930-32	+ 78.0	+ 80.0	- 54.0	- 54.9

(*) Probability of dying (p. 1000) between age 0 and 1.
Source: G. Caselli, *Mortalità e sopravvivenza in Italia dall'unità agli anni '30*, in Società Italiana di Demografia Storica, *Popolazione, società e ambiente. Temi di demografia storica italiana (secc. XVII-XIX)*, Bologna, CLUEB, 1990.

important if compared to diseases of the circulatory system. At the beginning of the 1930s, the first group of diseases accounted for 44% of all causes of death, whilst the proportion of deaths caused by circulatory diseases rose from 6 to 13%.

ITALY/L'ITALIE

3) Emigration abroad

Emigration abroad has always been of significant dimensions in Italy. If we estimate net emigration as the difference between total growth and natural increase, the net migratory deficit over the whole period 1862-1941 involved almost 6 million people (cf. Table 1).

Italy is one of the countries that became involved in the European migratory process late in the day. In fact, it was only from the 1880s on that emigration began to involve large numbers. It then expanded in the twenty years bridging the new century, when migratory losses exceeded 2,600,000 people. The roots of this great movement can mainly be found, in Italy as elsewhere, in the model of national economic growth. As opposed to other countries however, Italian development strategy was exclusively centered on the industrial sector which was moreover concentrated in some north-western areas thus causing an unbalanced utilization of the labour force. Furthermore, the conditions for mass emigration were created, on the one hand by the serious agricultural crisis of the 1880s which further worsened the unemployment situation in the south, and on the other, by the "discovery" of emigration as a real and concrete way of achieving better living conditions.

TABLE 6.- DEPARTURES FROM ITALY ACCORDING TO SOME DESTINATIONS (1876-1940) - PERCENTAGE DISTRIBUTION

Destinations	1876-86	1887-900	1901-14	1919-31	1932-40	1876-940
European countries	62.8	42.7	40.8	50.4	56.2	45.4
- France	29.8	9.9	10.0	37.5	27.7	17.6
- Germany	5.1	7.4	10.1	0.5	10.7	7.2
- Switzerland	7.1	5.8	11.4	6.4	11.2	8.9
Non-European countries	37.2	57.3	59.2	49.6	43.8	54.6
- United States	7.8	17.4	38.6	24.2	18.3	28.2
- Argentina	14.3	15.6	11.4	16.9	11.5	13.6
- Brazil	4.8	19.7	4.7	2.6	2.0	7.4
Total	100.0	100.0	100.0	100.0	100.0	100.0
annual average (thousands)	134.7	269.7	616.3	275.7	59.6	295.2

Source: Elaboration based on the time series published in G. Rosoli (ed.), *Un secolo di emigrazione italiana 1876-1976*, Roma, Centro Studi Emigrazione, 1978, Appendice statistica.

The most important destinations for Italian emigration were initially in Europe, especially France, which took in about 30% of all departures between 1876 and 1886 (Table 6). In the following years and up to the eve of the first world war, the door to the Americas was opened for Italian emigrants as a result of the consolidation of the overseas economies, the expansion of the international labour market, better means of transport, the often unscrupulous activities of middle men who, for financial gain, pushed people to emigrate, and the encouragement of people who had already emigrated thus creating migration chains. In this period, the United States, Argentina and Brazil alone absorbed more than half of the intense emigration flow coming from Italy[5]. When this impetus to emigrate had exhausted itself in the 1930s as a result of the closure of overseas outlets and the fascist anti-migratorian policy, European destinations were once again prevalent.

II.- DEMOGRAPHIC TRENDS AND CHANGES FROM THE SECOND WORLD WAR TO THE PRESENT

1) Evolution during the 1950s and 60s

In the course of the 1950s, the long process by which Italy's demographic regime was moving towards the development model of western societies began to speed up.

Nevertheless, after the second world war, demographically speaking, Italy was still at a less advanced stage of evolution than that of the majority of the industrialized countries, especially in terms of survival. Even though life expectancy at birth (almost 64 years for men and just over 67 for women, cf. Table 7) had increased by nearly ten years since the 1930s, it was still much lower than the thresholds of 69 and 71 years observed by the countries at the top of the league, for example Sweden. These differences in survival conditions were mainly linked to a higher risk of death in the first year of life. In Italy, the number of babies who did not reach their first birthday (66.6 per thousand born in 1951) was more than double that of many northern European countries at that time.

Once the typical post-war recovery mechanisms had worked themselves through, fertility was at significantly lower levels (2.35 children per woman in 1951) than those recorded at the beginning of the 1940s. This was also due to a late but nevertheless rapid adjustment to the situation already prevalent in the rest of the continent. Moreover, in the 1950s, Italian fertility was already among the lowest in Europe[6].

The demographic picture in the following period was dominated by the unexpectedly strong revival of fertility which affected all the countries of Europe - albeit at different times and to different extents. In Italy, this shortlived revival began towards the end of the 1950s at a time when the period fertility index of 2.33 had been more or less stable for about 5 years. It then rose rapidly to peak (2.7) in 1964 when the absolute number of births also peaked at 1,016,000. This evolution of fertility was preceded, in Italy as elsewhere, by a large increase in nuptiality. The period index continued to grow

---

[5] It is worth noting here that a large proportion of emigrants did not leave Italy definitively. This meant that more than a few emigrants returned and in some cases they may have emigrated several times over a period of only a few years. As a result the number of departures does not accurately reflect net emigration.

[6] In the same period, for example, the total fertility rate was around 2.7 in France and 2.2-2.3 in Sweden.

throughout the 1950s until the beginning of the 1960s when the threshold of 1 first marriage per women was exceeded - 1963 saw the record figure of 1.1. This was the result of the combined effect of an increase in both intensity and precocity of marriage in the relevant generations[7].

TABLE 7.- MAIN DEMOGRAPHIC INDICATORS. ITALY, 1951-71

Demographic indicators	1951	1961	1964	1971
Population (thousands)	47516	50624	51906	54137
0-14 years (%)	26.2	24.6	24.3	24.4
65 years and over (%)	8.2	9.5	9.9	11.3
Nuptiality rate	6.9	7.9	8.1	7.5
Total first marriage rate (x 1000 women)	82.5	102.4	109.5	102.8
Average age at first marriage (women)	25.1	24.7	24.3	23.93
Crude birth rate	18.1	18.4	19.7	16.8
Total fertility rate	2.35	2.41	2.70	2.41
Crude death rate	10.1	9.3	9.5	9.7
Infant mortality rate	66.6	40.7	36.1	28.5
Expectation of life at birth				
M	63.7	66.9	...	69.0
F	67.2	72.1	...	74.9
Growth rate *	6.4	7.4	6.4	
Natural increase rate *	8.5	9.5	8.3	
Net migration rate *	-2.1	-2.0	-1.9	

* annual average during the period per 1,000 inhabitants.
Source: elaboration of ISTAT data.

In the period under consideration, mortality continued its downward trend. Between 1951 and 1971, the modernization process in the country was accelerating mainly as a result of a marked increase in industrialization and education. In this period, life expectancy at birth increased by about 6 years for men and almost 8 years for women, reaching levels (69.0 and 74.9 for men and women respectively) similar to those of the European countries with the best survival conditions. These gains were largely produced by the spectacular reduction in infant mortality - the rate fell by at least half (from 66.6 p. 1000 to 28.5 p. 1000) during the same twenty years.

The evolution of fertility and mortality maintained the natural balance at high levels during the period under consideration -consistently over 8 p. 1000 and with an exceptional peak of 9.5 p. 1000 in the three-year period 1961-64. Overall growth was,

---

[7] In the generations born at the end of the 1930s who reached the age of maximum intensity of marriage at the beginning of the 1960s, the proportion of unmarried women falls below 6% and the mean age at first marriage was about one year lower than that observed in generations born only a few years earlier (from 25.33 for the 1934 generation dow to 24.32 for the 1939 generation).

however, held back by a negative migratory balance of considerable size. The consequences of the 2nd world war on the economic fabric of the country had in fact once again encouraged people to emigrate, initially overseas and later within Europe where the markets were more economically dynamic. The migratory deficit therefore remained high (equal to an annual average of about 2 p. 1000) throughout the twenty-year period 1951-71.

2) *Recent developments*

Over the last twenty years, Italy has undergone an extraordinary stage of demographic transformation. The most important factors of this transformation have been the unexpectedly marked reduction in fertility and the increasingly effective control of early death both of which have led to the situation where Italy has become one of the world leaders as regards longevity. The reduction in fertility has been spectacular both as regards the size of the reduction and the very short length of time in which it has occurred. It has only taken just over two decades for the annual number of births to fall by half.

After reaching a post-war peak in 1964 (1,016,000), the figure fell to barely 574,000 in 1990 (Table 8). This is clearly not enough to maintain the present demographic size of the country (57.6 million inhabitants at the beginning of 1990). Given present mortality levels, at least 758,000 births would be required each year to prevent a fall in the population in the medium-long term.

The average number of deaths has been stationary for several years at about 530-540,000. The increase in the percentage of old people with the highest risk of death (the over sixty-fives account for 14.1% today as against 9.9% in 1964) masks the large decrease in deaths in the other age groups, above all in the first year of life. Survival conditions have in fact further improved if compared to the beginning of the 1970s and today a newborn has on average almost 73 or more than 79 years of life ahead of him or her respectively.

After a century during which emigration played a very important role, it has now reached its final stage. Indeed, for the first time in the history of post-unification demography, the migratory balance is in credit and the modest overall increase in population is mainly due to this fact. Indeed, the natural balance has almost reached zero. In the country as a whole it only remains above zero thanks to the contribution from the southern regions. On the other hand, in the north the number of deaths has exceeded the number of births since 1979.

TABLE 8.- ITALIAN DEMOGRAPHIC BALANCE - 1971-1990

Period	Births	Deaths	Natural increase	Net migration	Population change	Population at the end of period
	Average annual figures in thousands					
1971-75	884	533	351	1	352	55589
1976-80	725	549	176	2	178	56479
1981-85	612	545	67	77	145	57202
1986	562	545	17	72	89	57291
1987	560	535	25	83	108	57399
1988	577	538	40	65	105	57505
1989	567	532	36	36	72	57576
1990	574	540	34	129	163	57739
	rates per 1,000 inhabitants					
1971-75	16.1	9.7	6.4	0.01	6.4	-
1976-80	12.9	9.8	3.1	0.04	3.2	-
1981-85	10.7	9.6	1.1	1.4	2.5	-
1986	9.8	9.5	0.3	1.3	1.6	-
1987	9.8	9.3	0.4	1.4	1.9	-
1988	10.1	9.4	0.7	1.1	1.8	-
1989	9.9	9.2	0.6	0.6	1.2	-
1990	10.0	9.4	0.6	2.2	2.8	-

Source: elaboration of ISTAT data.

a) Fertility, marriage and the family

In 1989 the total fertility rate in Italy was at the level of 1.29 (the lowest out of the large populations) and so the Italian population is virtually in rapid decline since this level of fertility is 35% lower than that necessary to maintain zero growth. The uninterrupted decline of the period indexes of fertility which began in 1965 has gone through different stages from those in most other European countries. A slow decline until 1974 then suddenly accelerated to a previously unequalled extent and the TFR fell from 2.31 to the above-mentioned 1.29. The period indexes do however somewhat exaggerate the intensity of the decline. The difference between the cohort fertility measures are much less marked[8] due to the changes produced by the different timings within the family formation process (increase in the mean age at marriage and increase in the mean age of

---

[8] If we compare the complete fertility rate of the generations born half way through the 1940s (about 2.07) with that of women born at the end of the 1950s (estimable as around 1.75), the difference is only 0.32.

childbearing)[9]. This series of delays in producing offspring has provoked a sharp fall in period fertility which appears to be more intense than it actually is.

However, the fact remains that fifteen or so generations (born between 1975 and 1990) were particularly low in number. This is of great demographic importance since it has accentuated the current imbalances in the age structure and has in part prejudiced population growth for the decades to come.

Apart from bearing witness to a real decline in final family size as shown by the the falling trend of marital fertility (Fig. 2), the extent of this fall also reflects recent nuptiality patterns. The evolution of nuptiality has affected general fertility because when it was at a high level, this had a braking effect on the decline in general fertility. However, when nuptiality itself began to decline rapidly, it had the opposite effect.

If we look at the fertility of the most recent marriage cohorts, a falling trend can be seen for second order-specific birth rate in all marriage durations and for first order-specific birth rate in the shorter durations, in particular in duration 1. This would seem to suggest, therefore, that Italian couples also tend to favour the family model with only one child to be produced later on in the marriage.

This changed timing in childbearing and the decline in fertility are interactively linked with the evolution of women's status. This has come about mainly because of their greatly improved level of education and employment. This has contributed to changing couples' family planning strategy. What is more, this strategy is increasingly tending to be inspired by criteria of rationality and "hedonism" which has been encouraged by the lack of any adjustments in government policy as regards taxation, family allowances, housing and work to meet the new needs arising as a result of women's and the Italian family's new situation.

We have already seen how the evolution of fertility is linked to that of nuptiality. In fact, nuptiality plays a fundamental role within the reproductive process since, in Italy in any case, children are almost always born within marriage.

---

[9] The mean age at marriage for women has risen - between 1975 and 1987 - from 24 to 24.7 years. In the same period, the mean age of fertility rose from 27.6 to 28 years.

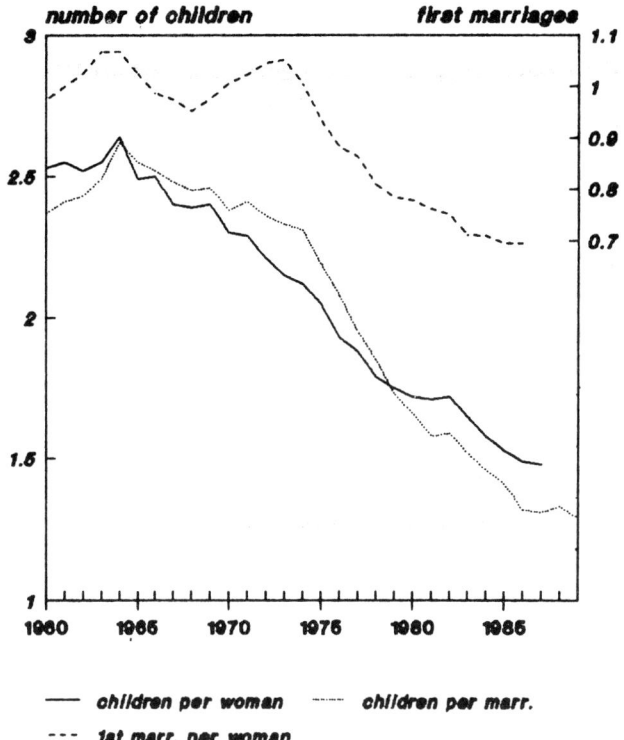

Figure 2- General fertility, marital fertility and nuptiality. Italy, 1960-1989

The nuptiality rates, confirmed by almost a century of values of 7-8 p. 1000, began a rapid decline in the mid 1970s. This decline became more marked precisely at the time when the increasingly numerous contingents of young people born in the years of the baby boom themselves began to reach marriageable age. The recent developments in the nuptiality period indexes (Table 9) shows this very clearly. On the basis of the nuptiality conditions in 1975, 93.4% of women would have married, whilst at a distance of little more than 10 years, this quota fell to 67.3%. It is difficult to say whether this development is the result of genuine and long-lasting changes in social relationships - in particular as regards attitudes to living together as couples - or if the present drop in nuptiality levels is perhaps not the result of changes in the timing of marriage from generation to generation which may also be the result of the difficulties young people encounter in their search for housing and employment.

TABLE 9.- MARRIAGES, DIVORCES, CIVIL MARRIAGES AND NATURAL CHILDREN.
ITALY, 1970-1989

Years	Total first marriage rate (women) %	Total divorce rate %	Civil marriages %	Extra-marital births %
1970	100.7	-	2.3	2.2
1975	93.4	3.1	8.4	2.6
1980	77.8	3.2	12.4	4.3
1985	69.5	4.1	13.9	5.4
1986	69.5	4.3	14.2	5.7
1987	67.3	6.5	14.5	5.8
1988	..	..	16.9	5.8
1989	..	..	16.9	6.1

.. not available
Source: Total first marriage rate: Istituto di Ricerche sulla Polazione, *Secondo rapporto sulla situazione demografica italiana*, Roma, 1988; total divorce rate: A. Monnier, "La conjoncture démographique", *Population*, n. 4-5, 1990; civil marriages and extra-marital births: ISTAT.

The lack of support for the institution of marriage which could also be deduced from the marked fall in nuptiality and which is increasingly affecting many countries in western Europe does not seem to be very widespread in Italy as yet, at least as far as one can tell from the official statistics. Few people favour living together since unmarried couples account for barely 1.2% of the total (1987 estimate). Indirect signs of a change in habits are however emerging from the increase in the number of extra-marital births which rose from 4.3% to 6.1% in the course of the 1980s, even if this figure is not very significant if compared to the exceptionally high figures observed in Sweden (51%) or in Great Britain and France (about 25%).

Furthermore, in Italy, the institution of marriage seems to be less fragile than in other European countries. The percentage of marriages ending in divorce, even if slightly on the increase, is still very low (6.5%) especially if compared with that observed in the Scandinavian countries (more than 40%) or with nearby France (30.8% in 1987).

Family structure has been radically changed by the joint and complex action of all the events under consideration here not to mention by the evolution in mortality. The relationship between population growth and family growth has greatly changed. In more recent years, the speed of family growth has been much more intense than that of the population because of the decline in the average number of family members. Between 1971 and 1987, the population grew by 204,000 people a year whilst families grew by 268,000 units. The reduction in average family size is mostly due to the significant increase in one-member families which currently (1987) account for just under 17% of the total. In more than 50% of cases, these are old people, usually women (72.2%). In fact, in Italy, people of different generations increasingly rarely share the same house. In contrast, cases of families with 3 generations living at the same time have increased. At

ITALY/L'ITALIE

the beginning of the century, only one woman in eight aged 55 years had a living mother aged over 80 years whilst today this is true for one woman in two. As a result, in 50% of cases, the responsibility for one old woman falls upon another slightly younger one.

b) Mortality

As we have already said, improvements in the field of survival have surpassed even our wildest expectations. Following a slackening in the 1960s, gains in life expectancy began to surge ahead again and in the most recent period, for the first time, these gains are slightly better for men than for women. Between 1981 and 1987, life expectancy increased for men from 71.1 to 72.9 years while for women it increased from 77.8 to 79.4 years with an average annual change of 0.4% and 0.3% respectively (Table 10). Italy now enjoys one of the highest levels of life expectancy in the world together with Japan - which holds yet another world record in this field too (75.6 years on average for men and 81.4 years for women in 1987) - and western European countries.

TABLE 10.- EVOLUTION OF MORTALITY. ITALY, 1971-1987

Years	e_0		e_{60}		e_{80}		q_0	
	M	F	M	F	M	F	M	F
1970-72	69.0	74.9	16.7	20.2	5.8	6.7	31.3	25.1
1981	71.1	77.8	17.0	21.4	5.8	7.3	15.6	12.5
1987	72.9	79.4	17.9	22.4	6.2	7.7	10.5	8.7
annual change (%)								
1970-72/1981	0.3	0.4	0.2	0.6	0.0	0.9	-5.0	-5.0
1981/1987	0.4	0.3	0.9	0.8	1.1	0.9	-5.4	-5.1
	100*Fe0/Me0		100*Fe60/Me60		100*Fe80/Me80		100*Mq0/Fq0	
1970-72	108.6		121.0		115.5		124.7	
1981	109.4		125.9		125.9		124.8	
1987	108.9		125.1		124.2		120.7	

q_0: infant mortality rate (p. 1000)
Source : ISTAT

Most of these gains have been achieved thanks to a further, strong reduction in mortality during the first year of life. In 1987 this had fallen to one third of the figure observed at the beginning of the 1970s. However, the extension of the life expectancy is not only linked to the reduction in infant mortality[10]. The most important aspect of the recent evolution of mortality has in fact been the strong reduction in deaths at an advanced age, above all over eighty years of age. Life expectancy at this age has in fact increased for both sexes at a clearly faster rate than that of life expectancy at birth, in particular during the last six years.

The most recent developments seem to have slightly reduced the differences in mortality between the two sexes which are however still marked at all ages and more so as regards old people. Large numbers of men and women survive to sixty years of age (85.1% and 92% respectively according to the 1987 life tables). However, very few men reach the threshold of 80 years of age - 36.1% as opposed to 59.3% of women.

c) Aging

In Italy, at the end of the 20th century, as in all western societies, the aging of the population is the most significant demographic phenomena of the moment. The proportion of old people in the population as a whole has been greatly increasing over the last thirty years (Table 11), mainly as a result of the prolonged weakening of the birth flows which, renewing the population, feed the base of the age pyramid. Furthermore, in more recent years, the evolution of mortality - greater improvement in survival for old people than for other age groups - has also become an important factor of aging.

The rise in the number of over-eighties has increased tremendously, almost doubling in the space of twenty years and now accounting for 15.3% of the elderly population as a whole. What is more, the fact that excess male mortality has become more marked with time means that the over-eighties group is increasingly made up of women. The most recent figures (1990) show that women comprise 67.2% of the total number of the oldest old.

However, as regards the aging process, the speed at which the number of old people increases is just as important as the proportion itself. This is because adjustments to the social and health structures and the social security system must be made in function of the speed of increase.

---

[10] During the 1970s, the reduction in infant mortality contributed to the extent of 69% and 40% (respectively for males and females) to the lengthening of the life expectancy recorded during this period. Furthermore, for women an important contribution (36%) also came from the reduction in mortality over the age of 60 years.

TABLE 11.- SOME ASPECTS OF AGING OF THE ITALIAN POPULATION

Indicators	1971	1981	1990
Population aged 0-19 (ooo)	17076.8	16816.5	14066.5
(%)	31.5	29.7	24.4
Population aged 60 and over (ooo)	9011.9	9850.8	11615.3
(%)	16.6	17.4	20.2
Population aged 80 and over (ooo)	996.0	1247.2	1782.0
(%)	1.8	2.2	3.1
Women per 100 population 80 and over	62.5	67.1	67.2
Oldest old ratio (a)	11.1	12.7	15.3
Aging ratio (b)	52.8	58.6	82.6
Old-age dependency ratio (c)	32.1	33.0	36.4
Annual percentage change rates			
Population aged 0-19		- 0.15	- 2.21
Population aged 60 and over		0.89	2.08
Population aged 60-79		0.71	1.68
Population aged 80 and over		2.27	4.56

Notes: Population at the censuses of 1971 and 1981; ISTAT estimate as at 1 January for 1990.
(a) $100*(P80+/P60+)$; (b) $100*(P60+/P0-19)$; (c) $100*(P60+/P20-59)$.
Source: elaboration on ISTAT data.

This was particularly high during the 1980s, when the over-sixties group increased at an average annual rate of 2.08% (compared with the 0.89% of the previous decade) and the over-eighties group was even increasing at a rate of 4.56%. The most difficult aspect of the aging question is not however so much the growth of the elderly population as a whole but rather the extremely marked growth of the over-eighties segment within it, made up of people who are not always totally self-sufficient and who are, in any case, particularly in need of both health and social services.

d) A new framework for migration

As we have already mentioned, Italy's long migratory experience has reached its final stage. The almost uninterrupted outflow of emigrants over the last century is slowly coming to an end. It reached its peak on the eve of the first world war (900,000 in 1913 alone) and then after the second world war it remained at an annual level of around 300,000 people for many years up to the mid-sixties when it began to fall to reach today's level of about 40,000. The Italian migration model has profoundly changed. Mass movements have been replaced by select migration, for short periods, involving technicians and specialized workers who are often working under international cooperation projects.

There was another important change in the migration scene in the 1980s which broke with a tradition that was centuries old - Italy has progressively become an immigration country. This process began about 20 years ago with the arrival in the large urban centres of Asian and African foreign workers (mainly women going into domestic service) and Tunisians who came to do seasonal work in Sicily (in the fishing sector). Since then, the numbers of foreign immigrants have steadily been increasing. This may seem paradoxical given the fact that unemployment in Italy is still at a very high level. In sample surveys carried out in 1989, more than 2,800,000 Italians said they were looking for work (12% of the labour force). The fact is that the present demand/supply gap for labour which is afflicting the internal market, is mainly of a qualitative and not a quantitative nature. Better levels of education have in fact led to a situation where Italian workers will refuse tiring or unskilled jobs, thus creating opportunities for unskilled workers coming from the developing countries, above all in those sectors of the market where casual - and unregistered - labour is required.

It is extremely difficult to evaluate the number of foreigners in Italy since a large proportion of immigrants are clandestine. As a result, the estimates have a fairly wide range of variation, fluctuating from around 700,000 to over 1,200,000 people[11].

The foreign community is thus beginning to take on significant proportions. The most recent data regarding the numbers of foreigners who took advantage of the 1990 amnesty law to regularize their position and regarding the numbers of sojourn permits issued in the same year (Table 12), show that there are at least 780,000 foreigners legally present in Italy[12] the majority of whom come from non-EEC countries. This group appears to be concentrated in the centre-north of Italy, especially in the Latium and Lombardy regions[13].

---

[11] According to ISTAT (The National Statistics Institute), the number of immigrants in Italy in 1989 was 1,444,000, of whom 963,000 came from non-EEC countries and 60% of whom had not regularized their position; cf. ISTAT, *Gli immigrati presenti in Italia: una stima per il 1989*, a report presented at the Conferenza Nazionale dell'immigrazione, Rome, 4-6 June 1990.

[12] The number of foreigners taking advantage of the amnesty law - non-EEC immigrants only - cannot be added to the number of sojourn permits since these also include most of the former group.

[13] There is also a large number of foreigners in Umbria (estimated according to the number of sojourn permits) if compared with the total population of the region (61 per 1,000 inhabitants). This is largely due to the University for Foreigners being located in Perugia.

ITALY/L'ITALIE

TABLE 12.- TOTAL FOREIGN POPULATION HAVING REGULARIZED OR IN THE PROCESS OF REGULARIZING THEIR POSITION ON THE BASIS OF THE AMNESTY LAW AND SOJOURN PERMITS ISSUED BY THE ITALIAN HOME OFFICE - 1990

Territorial divisions/ regions	Foreign population (*)			Sojourn permits (**)			
	Number	%	p. 1000 inhabitants	Number	%	% non-EEC	p. 1000 inhabitants
Central and Northern Italy	155845	69.3	4.3	624802	80.0	79.5	17.1
Piedmont	12287	5.5	2.8	48000	6.1	80.5	11.0
Lombardy	33959	15.1	3.8	116609	14.9	80.6	13.1
Emilia Romagna	13604	6.0	3.5	44030	5.6	85.4	11.2
Tuscany	14623	6.5	4.1	61346	7.9	78.4	17.2
Umbria	3206	1.4	3.9	50060	6.4	62.3	61.0
Latium	51730	23.0	10.0	197465	25.3	84.2	38.2
Other regions	26526	11.8	2.7	106904	13.7	74.7	11.0
Southern Italy	69092	30.7	3.3	156336	20.0	87.0	7.4
Campania	16803	7.5	2.9	47721	6.1	83.0	8.2
Sicily	33518	14.9	6.5	61523	7.9	91.5	11.9
Other regions	18771	8.3	1.9	47092	6.0	85.3	4.7
ITALY	224937	100.0	3.9	781138	100.0	81.0	13.6

(*) foreigners having regularized or in the process of regularizing their position as at 29 June 1990;
(**) sojourn permits issued by the Italian Home Office by 31 December 1990;
Source : elaboration of Italian Home Office data.

III.- OUTLOOK AND PROBLEMS

Italy is on the doorstep of an important turning point as regards demographic trends given a fertility level well below that necessary to ensure zero population growth - which for reasons of inertia only become apparent after a certain time.

There are three possible scenarios which can reasonably be outlined for the future of the population. They are based on the alternative roads that fertility could take: 1) a further decline (down to 0.97 children per couple); 2) maintenance of present levels; and 3) a revival (up to two children per couple); all of which coupled with a fall in mortality and emigration abroad intentionally taken as zero (in order to better evaluate the "natural" trends only). The three scenarios - see Table 13 - show that Italy is at a turning point which is a prelude to a fall in population and perhaps a large one, over the next fifty years. This is a situation without precedent in the recent history of the country. In fact, the only way to maintain the present (1988) total of 57 million inhabitants would be a steady revival of fertility. A further decline would instead lead to a drastic reduction (of about 19 million), whilst in the case of fertility remaining at current levels, the reduction would be limited to about 12 million.

Another revolutionary transformation concerns expected changes in the age structure of the population which will upset century old equilibria. The over-sixties will probably increase from the present 11.2 million (equal to 19.4% of the population as a whole) to 17.6 million with their percentage weight fluctuating between 31 and 46% depending on the evolution of the other segments of the population.

Particular attention should be paid to the strong growth in the number of people aged 80 and over, the oldest old. At the moment, 1 person in 35 is in this age group whilst in 2038 this figure could become 1 in 11 under the intermediate hypothesis. This is one of the highest proportions foreseen for this date in the whole world. The general aging of the population will thus be accompanied by an intense and rapid aging within the elderly population itself. It is precisely the rapidity of this process that causes the most concern. It will in fact be necessary to adjust the socio-sanitary and other structures in good time to meet the changing needs of the population and the family.

The increase in the over-sixties group is becoming more significant in that it is going hand in hand with the decrease in the other broad age groups, above all the infants and young people group. This latter group has more recently begun to decline and the forecasts under the zero migration hypothesis project a worrying picture. Under the most pessimistic hypothesis, this group could decline to a quarter of its present size and there would therefore be one person under twenty years for every five people aged over sixty.

A steady reduction in the working age population (20-59 years) has also been foreseen - even under the revival of fertility hypothesis. The differential evolution of this population group and the elderly group will alter the required equilibrium between those who work and those who are benefitting from their pensions. The social security system will therefore be under considerable strain.

Another group of problems derives from the fact that the evolution of the working age population will be progressively more differentiated across the territory. It is already the case in the last decade of this century that the population in this age group will decline in the centre-north regions of the country, whilst it will increase, at least initially, in the southern ones. This fact will actively encourage a redistribution of the population across the territory with a possible revival of internal migration flows and - alternatively or at the same time - there will be an increase in foreign immigration.

A moderate revival of fertility up to two children per woman, as projected in hypothesis R, would only serve to limit the decline of the population and to slow down the speed of aging. Also in the case of this hypothesis, the annual number of births would in fact remain well below that of deaths. As a result, a pro-natalist policy aiming at achieving a fertility level to guarantee generation replacement would therefore only serve to slow down the decline in the population and the speed of its aging.

TABLE 13.- ITALIAN POPULATION PROJECTIONS
SITUATION AS AT 1988 AND SCENARIOS IN 2038

Demographic indicators	1988	2038		
		Variant C	Variant D	Variant I
Population (thousands)	57399.1	45113.0	38386.1	57531.5
Popolation by age groups (millions)				
0-19	14790.4	6988.4	3760.6	13539.5
20-59	31451.4	20459.5	16960.4	26327.0
60+	11157.3	17665.0	17665.0	17665.0
80+	1607.0	3964.2	3964.2	3964.2
60+ (%)	19.4	39.2	46.0	30.7
Mean age	37.9	49.1	53.9	43.0
Households (thousands)	20275.8	21033.9	19622.4	23480.6
householder aged 60+ (%)	34.0	53.4	57.2	47.8
mean size of household	2.8	2.1	1.9	2.5
Births (*)	584.4	318.8	152.8	666.0
Deaths (*)	545.8	809.5	804.1	818.6

(*) mean annual number (1983-88 and 2033-2038) in thousands.
Variant C: fertility constant at 1988 levels (TFR = 1.32); mortality: following trends observed between 1981 an 1987; after 1997, stabilization of life expectancy at 75.1 years for men and 81.6 years for women; migration: zero.
Variant D: further decline in fertlity, TFR down to 1; mortality and migration: as Variant C.
Variant I: gradual increase in fertiity, TFR reaching the level of 2 in 2000; mortality and migration as Variant C.
Source: Istituto di Ricerche sulla Popolazione, *Tre scenari per il possibile sviluppo della popolazione delle regioni italiane al 2038*, Roma, 1989.

IV.- ASPECTS OF POPULATION POLICY

Until the advent of fascism, post-unification governments in Italy had all shown very little interest in demographic questions. Although the public administrations realized that the population constituted an endogenous variable to be taken into consideration in the economic and social fields, they had never deemed it necessary to intervene directly in any way to modify or influence demographic trends. There were occasional indirect interventions only in the case of international emigration, which was in fact encouraged in the early decades of the century and then regulated by the establishment of an emigration commissariat which took over the jobs of the private operators and speculators. The population policy put into practice by the fascist regime therefore represents an absolute novelty in the history of the unified nation.

The ultimate goal of this policy, which also had important ideological and political implications, was more intense population growth. With this end in mind, a coordinated series of provisions was introduced with the purpose, on the one hand, of stimulating fertiliy and, on the other, of discouraging emigration. In order to achieve the goal of high fertility, a series of economic incentives were set up (marriage awards and low-cost loans for young couples, birth awards, tax exemptions for large families, and family allowances of increasing value as family size grew). These economic incentives were then accompanied by a series of provisions - more social in nature - to safeguard motherhood (services for pregnant women and babies, protective measures during pregnancy and the post-partum period for women workers). These measures were associated with some repressive provisions aimed at removing the obstacles to high fertility (a bachelor tax, a ban on the propoganda and diffusion of contraceptive methods, and repression of voluntary abortion).

Following this experience which ended with the fall of fascism, the Italian State continued to maintain the official attitude of broad agnosticism held by the post-unification liberal governments, except - once again - when it encouraged emigration (mainly in the 1950s and 60s), amongst others by means of bilateral international agreements aimed at protecting Italian emigrants, especially in terms of social security. A series of pro-birth measures that had been in force during fascist rule survived in any case until the end of the 1960s. In particular, the regulations of the Criminal Code condemning crimes such as the diffusion, propoganda and sale of contraceptive methods, were only repealed in 1971[14]. Voluntary abortion became legal even later on in 1978[15]. Marriage law has also only recently been changed. Following bitter political polemic, in 1970 a law was approved introducing divorce in Italy[16]. What is more, the family law reform introduced in 1975 (Law No. 151) foresaw the raising of the age of consent to 18 years.

However, these amendments to the legislative framework were not all inspired by demographic needs, rather they mirrored new social orientations and the need to adjust the constitutional rights of individuals to the changing situation in the country. As regards the fertility problem, in particular, the legislative innovations aimed to encourage the full enjoyment of a couple's desires concerning the number of children they wanted to have. As well as the above-mentioned provisions, family advice centres were also set up within this framework (1975). Amongst other tasks, these centres were assigned the job of publicizing information on contraceptive methods and distributing them.

---

[14] The judgement of the Constitutional Court of 16 March 1971 declared that Art. 553 of the Criminal Code was unconstitutional. The article dealt with the diffusion, propoganda and sale of contraceptive methods punishable by fines or imprisonment.

[15] Law No. 194, "Regulations for the social protection of motherhood and voluntary interruption of pregnancy" entered into force on 22 May 1978.

[16] Law No. 898 of 1 December 1970.

ITALY/L'ITALIE

Some other formally pro-natalist measures still survive today e.g. family allowances, assistance for working mothers, and tax exemptions for families with dependant children. However, these measures do not really come under the umbrella of population policy either, but they are kept on on the basis of general principles of social justice or as a vaguely social service.

The financial burden of these provisions is minimal and this fact completely frustrates their purpose. Indeed, in Italy, there is a legislative injustice in that couples who want to have a(nother) child are penalized, objectively speaking, in respect of childless couples. Faced with the high financial cost of children, the State does not in fact supply any financial support. Tax deductions and family allowances are both ridiculously low. In any case, family allowances are only granted to families who are actually living below the poverty line. The financial burden for family allowances which started off very low, has slowly been further devalued with time. At the moment, it can be estimated at around 1% of total public spending. A public incentive scheme would have to be of much greater value to eliminate the objective economic penalties which exist today for those who have children. Furthermore, the lack of financial support for couples with children combined, what is more, with the shortage of services allowing parents to work and run the home, have produced an important psychological and cultural effect in that there is a complete lack of interest shown in procreation by the community at large and by the State.

In Italy there is a complete lack of any coordinated social and family policy aimed at achieving general social objectives. There has been a succession of laws and provisions with single, specific aims but if these are placed all together, a clearly anti-natalist leaning is evident.

In the field of migration, legal adjustment to the profound changes that have come about in more recent years has arrived late in the day and has not yet been completed. Faced with large flows of foreign workers, the attitude of the public administration has largely been to let things be. Only in 1986 (with Law No. 943) were any initiatives taken to protect non-EEC workers e.g. granting of rights enjoyed by Italian workers and the setting up of special lists at the employment exchanges. Non-EEC workers were further given the opportunity of remedying an otherwise possibly clandestine position. This first provision, which passed relatively unnoticed, was succeeded in 1990 by a new law (No. 39) which on the one hand eliminated some types of discrimination such as limitations to the number of countries from which refugees would be accepted and special lists at the employment exchanges, and on the other, it offered a new opportunity to clandestine and illegal immigrants to regularize their position by clarifying the criteria for entry and sojourn in the country and introducing the possibility of establishing, year by year, the quota of immigrants to be granted entry into Italy.

Lastly, with the establishment of the VII Cabinet presided over by the Right Honourable Mr. Giulio Andreotti, on 12 April 1991 a new "Minister without _portfolio for Italians abroad and foreign immigration" was nominated. This Minister's remit is to coordinate and promote initiatives regarding the Italian community abroad and foreign immigrants in Italy. The bestowal of the office of Minister without portfolio on the subject of migration to and from Italy without - for now - the addition of an actual Ministry bears witness to the existence of a political desire to give a unified and coordinated orientation to the subject, but it will certainly be rather difficult to transform the desire into concrete results given the resistance that will come from the Ministries already holding some responsibilities for various aspects regarding foreigners (entry and sojourn, work, health, education, quota determination, etc.).

The problem of immigration from developing countries is destined to become more acute with time and not only in Italy, given the marked differences in terms of opportunities for work, earnings and socio- political conditions that exist between the areas of departure and the developed countries of the western area. As far as Europe is concerned, it is therefore necessary to formulate an organic Community migration policy in the framework of which national policies can be harmoniously inserted.

L'Espagne/Spain
Juan Antonio FERNANDEZ CORDON

I. LES GRANDS TRAITS DE L'EVOLUTION DEMOGRAPHIQUE AU XXEME SIECLE.

Pour de nombreux pays développés, la période de forte croissance démographique se situe à la fin du XIXème siècle. En Espagne, par contre, l'accroissement de la population ne s'est intensifié qu'à partir des années 1920 et s'est poursuivi à un rythme élevé jusqu'à la fin des années soixante (voir figure 1).

Le taux de mortalité diminue tout au long du siècle, sauf les pointes de mortalité provoquées par l'épidémie de choléra de 1885, l'épidémie de grippe de 1918 et par la guerre civile de 1936-39 et l'immédiate après-guerre. Jusqu'en 1954, la baisse a été continue et pratiquement linéaire. A partir de cette date, les taux de mortalité diminuent plus lentement du fait que la croissance de l'espérance de vie se ralentit et que le vieillissement de la population s'accentue.

Le rythme de la baisse de la mortalité en Espagne a été différent de celui du reste de ses pays voisins. La diminution de la mortalité dûe aux épidémies, initiée au XVIIIème siècle, n'est vraiment effective qu'à partir de 1900 et la baisse de la mortalité ordinaire, surtout infantile, ne s'intensifie qu'à partir de la première guerre mondiale, début, en Espagne, des grands courants migratoires vers les villes (Nadal, 1986).

Au début du siècle, l'espérance de vie était de 34,8 ans (33,9 ans chez les hommes et 35,7 ans chez les femmes), beaucoup plus faible que celle des autres pays européens, et la mortalité infantile atteignait 186 pour mille.

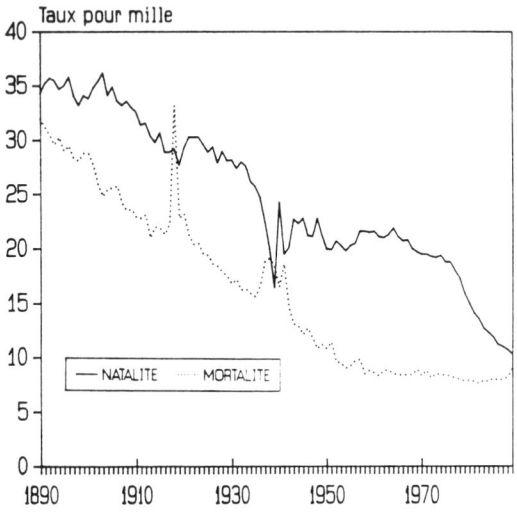

Figure 1.- Accroissement naturel (1890-1989)

Entre 1900 et 1950, l'espérance de vie à la naissance a augmenté de 78%, passant de 34,8 à 62,1 ans, l'espérance de vie à 15 ans est passée de 42,7 à 54,1 ans, soit une augmentation de 26,7% et l'espérance de vie à 65 ans de 9,1 à 12,7 ans, soit un gain de 39,6%. C'est donc la très importante baisse de la mortalité infantile, dont le taux passe de 186 à 77 pour mille, et juvénile, qui explique la progression de l'espérance de vie à la naissance au cours de cette période.

La natalité, mesurée par le taux brut de natalité, suit également une tendance nettement décroissante tout au long du XXème siècle, Auparavant, au cours de la deuxième moitié du XIXème, le taux de natalité avait oscillé, passant de 35,3 pour mille en 1858 à 39,8 pour mille en 1861, pour revenir à 35-36 pour mille aux alentours de 1870 et, avec quelques fluctuations, s'y maintenir jusqu'à la dernière décennie du siècle. C'est au cours des années 1890 que la baisse s'amorce avec netteté. Elle se poursuit sans interruption, mais accompagnée de fluctuations parfois importantes, jusque vers les années 1950-54, où le taux moyen atteint 20,1 pour mille.

La fécondité a connu, entre 1922[1] et 1950-54, une longue période de baisse, coupée par des fluctuations mineures et par la profonde perturbation de la guerre civile de 1936-39.

---

[1] Année à partir de laquelle les données sur les naissances selon l'âge de la mère sont disponibles en Espagne.

L'ESPAGNE/SPAIN

Si l'on fait exception de l'année 1939, très perturbée par la Guerre Civile, l'indice le plus bas est atteint en 1954 avec 2,46 enfants par femme. Après la chute importante de 1936-39 et la modeste reprise de 1940, la fécondité s'élève jusqu'à un maximum de 2,96 en 1945, inférieur toutefois au niveau des premières années de la Guerre Civile.

Le rapprochement avec d'autres pays européens montre des taux systématiquement plus élevés en Espagne, malgré une certaine similitude dans l'évolution. Jusqu'au début des années quarante, la baisse est moins rapide en Espagne, ce qui la distingue de l'Italie, par exemple, dont la fécondité est plus élevée en 1920, mais décroît plus rapidement par la suite. En 1939, l'indice espagnol, le plus bas de la période, est cependant supérieur à celui de la France et de la Suède. La récupération d'après-guerre en Espagne se produit au moment où la fécondité diminue chez ses voisins européens, du fait de la guerre, ce qui accentue les différences. Le baby-boom européen va momentanément rapprocher les fécondités dans la deuxième moitié des années quarante, mais la reprise de la natalité qui se produit en Espagne à partir de 1954, alors que d'autres pays européens connaissent une certaine baisse des taux jusque vers 1960, va de nouveau creuser les écarts.

Le début des années cinquante marque la fin d'une étape de l'évolution démographique en Espagne. L'essentiel de la transition démographique est accompli, en un temps très inférieur à celui de ses voisins du Nord. Désormais son histoire va rejoindre de plus en plus celle du reste des pays européens.

II.-L'EVOLUTION DEMOGRAPHIQUE RECENTE

1) La chute de la fécondité

Après une remontée qui débute en 1954, la fécondité atteint, en 1964, son niveau maximum, pratiquement 3 enfants par femme en moyenne. Une baisse s'amorce alors, d'abord modérée, comme c'est également le cas dans d'autres pays du Sud de l'Europe, puis très intense à partir de 1977 (voir tableau 1 et figure 2).

L'indice synthétique de fécondité est passé de 2,8 enfants par femme en 1976 à 1,38 en 1989[2], soit une baisse de plus de 50% en seulement 13 ans. L'évolution n'a pas été uniforme tout au long de cette période. Après une chute brutale de 1977 à 1981, qui fait passer l'indice en dessous de la valeur de remplacement des générations, la baisse se ralentit au cours des trois années suivantes, pour s'intensifier de nouveau au cours de ces dernières années. En 1989, seule l'Italie a une fécondité inférieure à celle de l'Espagne.

---

[2] Estimation de l'Instituto de Démografia (Institut de démographie du Conseil supérieur de la recherche scientifique espagnol) à partir de données provisoires.

La diminution récente de la fécondité s'accompagne, dans la plupart des pays d'une augmentation de la proportion d'enfants nés hors mariage. C'est également le cas en Espagne, où la proportion est passée de 1,4% en 1970 à 8% en 1985, mais reste encore très inférieure à ce qu'elle est dans d'autres pays européens.

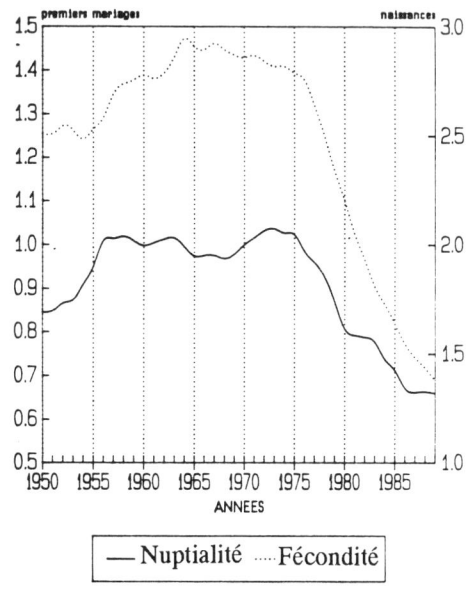

Figure 2.- Nuptialité et fécondité(1950-1989) (somme des événements réduits)

Les écarts géographiques sont importants en ce qui concerne la fécondité, pour laquelle les données sont plus détaillées et plus récentes (Delgado M. y Fernández Cordón J.A., 1989, Gozalvez V., 1989). En 1975, la fécondité allait de 3,27 enfants par femme, dans la communauté de Murcie, à 2,30 dans la communauté des Asturies, aucune région ne se trouvant en dessous du niveau de remplacement des générations. Dès 1985, par contre aucune ne dépasse ce seuil. En 1988, c'est toujours Murcie qui jouit de la fécondité la plus élevée avec un indice synthétique de 1,84, suivie de l'Andalousie et de l'Extrémadoure, avec 1,77. Les niveaux les plus bas se trouvent dans les Asturies et au Pays Basque, autour de 1,09 enfant par femme. L'écart absolu entre les régions a diminué de 1 à 0,75 enfant entre 1975 et 1988, mais il s'est accru en termes relatifs, puisque le niveau moyen a fortement diminué dans cette période. En règle générale, ce sont les régions qui avaient au départ la fécondité la plus faible qui ont enregistré la baisse la plus forte, ce qui entraîne une dispersion géographique relative accrue.

La baisse de la fécondité dans les régions s'explique en Catalogne, Madrid et dans les régions du Nord par la baisse de la fécondité légitime, alors que dans les régions du Centre et en Extrémadoure, Castilla-León et Castilla-la-Mancha, la nuptialité est moins intense et plus tardive. Les régions qui ont les indices de fécondité les plus élevés ont à la fois une forte fécondité légitime et un taux de nuptialité élevé.

TABLEAU 1.: L'EVOLUTION DE LA FECONDITE (1950-1989)

Année	ISF	Année	ISF
1950	2,51	1970	2,85
1951	2,49	1971	2,88
1952	2,57	1972	2,84
1953	2,53	1973	2,81
1954	2,46	1974	2,83
1955	2,54	1975	2,78
1956	2,56	1976	2,78
1957	2,71	1977	2,64
1958	2,74	1978	2,51
1959	2,75	1979	2,33
1960	2,79	1980	2,21
1961	2,75	1981	2,04
1962	2,78	1982	1,94
1963	2,85	1983	1,80
1964	2,98	1984	1,73
1965	2,90	1985	1,64
1966	2,88	1986	1,54
1967	2,94	1987*	1,48
1968	2,89	1988*	1,44
1969	2,87	1989*	1,38

Source: 1950-84: Fernandez Cordon, J.A. (1986); 1975-86: Delgado M. Y Fernandez Cordon J.A. (1989); 1987-89: estimations indirectes à partir de données provisoires.

2) La fécondité des générations

Les études démographiques longitudinales sont très difficiles en Espagne. Les statistiques de naissances ne sont classées selon l'année de naissance de la mère que depuis 1975, ce qui ne donne pas un recul suffisant. On peut cependant estimer les indices longitudinaux à partir des taux par âge, au prix de certains ajustements pour la période antérieure à 1975, puisque le classement par année d'âge n'existe, lui aussi, que depuis cette date. Les considérations qui suivent sont basées sur des estimations indirectes de l'auteur (Fernández Cordón, 1986).

La diminution de la descendance finale est pratiquement linéaire jusqu'à la génération 1916-17 puis s'amortit dans les suivantes, passant de 3,28 enfants par femme dans la génération 1901-02 jusqu'au minimum local de 2,51 de la génération 1923-24.

La fécondité augmente légèrement dans les générations suivantes, jusqu'à 2,67 enfants par femme dans les générations 1935-36, puis diminue sans interruption jusqu'aux générations qui sont actuellement en pleine fécondité. Les dernières générations dont la fécondité est au moins égale au niveau de remplacement sont celles du début des années cinquante. Au delà, les extrapolations deviennent plus hasardeuses, mais on peut estimer, de façon pratiquement certaine, que les femmes nées dans la deuxième moitié des années cinquante auront au total moins de deux enfants en moyenne.

La fécondité des générations espagnoles est assez différente de celle d'autres pays européens. Les femmes espagnoles nées vers 1901-1905 ont eu en moyenne 1 enfant de plus que les françaises, 1,25 enfant de plus que les allemandes et 1,25 enfant de plus que les suédoises. Ces écarts se réduisent progressivement, du fait de la diminution de la descendance finale en Espagne et de son augmentation dans les autres pays. Malgré cette tendance, la génération de moindre fécondité, au cours de la première période, qui est celle de 1923-24 avec 2,51 enfants, se situe encore très au-dessus de l'allemande (1,95) ou de la suèdoise (2,05). Par contre, la fécondité des femmes nées au cours des années vingt est presque identique en France et en Espagne, et cette similitude se maintient par la suite. La géneration de 1942-43 a une descendance finale de 2,5 en Espagne et de 2,6 en France.

Les générations qui ont eu leurs enfants entre 1950 et 1970 atteignent pratiquement la même descendance finale en France et en Espagne. Les différences entre les deux pays, au cours de cette période, doivent donc être attribuées à des divergences dans l'évolution du calendrier.

Les générations ayant subi une mortalité en forte décroissance, l'évolution du taux de reproduction nette ne suit pas celle de la descendance finale. De ce point de vue, on peut distinguer trois groupes de générations. Les générations anciennes (nées avant 1925) sont les véritables porteuses de la transition démographique. La baisse de la mortalité est compensée chez elles par la diminution de la fécondité, ce qui maintient pratiquement invariable le taux net de reproduction. Ces générations anciennes ont dominé la période antérieure à 1950. Les générations nées entre 1925 et la guerre civile sont celles qui ont le plus contribué à la croissance de la population, du fait d'une nuptialité et d'une fécondité élevées et d'une mortalité en baisse. Leur descendance s'est constituée entre 1945 et 1975 environ.

Avec les générations d'après-guerre débute l'étape moderne de la démographie espagnole, dont les effets se font sentir à partir de la seconde moitié des années soixante.

L'ESPAGNE/SPAIN

3) Evolution récente de la nuptialité féminine

La nuptialité des femmes célibataires a été très élevée tout au long de la période 1954-1975, au cours de laquelle la somme annuelle des premiers mariages réduits dépasse souvent l'unité. Cette évolution est attribuable à la fois à l'augmentation de l'intensité et à la diminution continue de l'âge au premier mariage, qui passe de 26,3 en 1954 à 23,2 ans en 1975. A partir de 1976, la nuptialité diminue fortement (voir tableau 2 et graphique 2).

TABLEAU 2. - EVOLUTION DE LA NUPTIALITE (1950-1989)

Année	ISN	Année	ISN
1950	0.845	1971	1.002
1951	0.841	1972	1.015
1952	0.874	1973	1.034
1953	0.863	1974	1.041
1954	0.913	1975	1.047
1955	0.940	1976	0.985
1956	1.025	1977	0.965
1957	1.009	1978	0.928
1958	1.024	1979	0.868
1959	1.009	1980	0.780
1960	0.993	1981	0.779
1961	1.005	1982	0.760
1962	1.012	1983	0.763
1963	1.021	1984	0.701
1964	0.996	1985	0.642
1965	0.968	1986	0.632
1967	0.976	1987	0.660
1968	0.978	1988	0.666
1969	0.964	1989	0.660
1970	0.976		

Source: 1950-1974: Fernandez Cordon, J.A. (1986); 1975-1986: Delgado M.y Fernandez Cordon J.A. (1990); 1987-1989: Estimations indirectes à partir de données provisoires.

Cependant, les données de l'I.N.E. surestiment la baisse des années 1980-85[3], à cause d'un sous-enregistrement des mariages catholiques, qui semble avoir été éliminé à partir

---

[3] Instituto Nacional de Estadistica.

de 1986. Avec les données corrigées (Delgado M. y Fernández Cordón J.A., 1988), la somme des premiers mariages réduits diminue de 25% entre 1975 et 1980, passant de 1,04 à 0,79, se stabilise au cours des trois années suivantes, pour baisser de nouveau fortement jusqu'en 1986, où l'indice atteint 0,66, niveau auquel il demeure constant, d'après les données de 1987 à 1989, qui sont encore provisoires.

La première période de baisse, 1975-1980, résulte sans doute d'une diminution de l'intensité, en partie masquée par un léger rajeunissement du calendrier. La deuxième, beaucoup plus accusée, marque la fin du rajeunissement. La constance de l'indicateur trois années de suite permet de supposer que la baisse de la nuptialité est, pour le moment, arrêtée.

4) Evolution récente de la mortalité

L'espérance de vie atteint 76,5 ans en 1985-86 (73,2 ans chez les hommes et 79,7 ans chez les femmes)[4]. L'augmentation de l'espérance de vie doit encore beaucoup à la réduction de la mortalité infantile, dont le taux a poursuivi la baisse jusqu'à atteindre 8,1 pour mille en 1988, niveau parmi les plus bas du monde.

De nos jours, les gains, qui sont encore importants, bénéficient davantage aux grands âges et aux femmes. L'espérance de vie est passée de 75,6 à 76,5 ans entre 1980 et 1985, soit un gain de presque un an en cinq ans. Les hommes ont gagné 0,7 an et les femmes 1,1 année, l'écart entre eux est maintenant de 6,5 ans. Les données provisoires disponibles montrent que la baisse s'est poursuivie après 1985.

Les différences régionales sont moins bien connues pour la mortalité que pour d'autres phénomènes. On dispose des tables de mortalité de l'ensemble des provinces, pour la période 1976-80 (Devolder, 1986), et celles des communautés autonomes[5], pour les années 1975 et 1980, sans qu'elles aient fait l'objet d'analyse approfondie. En 1976-80, l'espérance de vie des provinces variait de 69,8 ans à 74,5 chez les hommes et de 76,1 à 79,1 ans chez les femmes. Elle était inférieure à la moyenne nationale dans les provinces de la périphérie du Sud, Andalousie et Extrémadoure, et du Nord, Galice, Pays Basque et Cantabria

---

[4] Données provisoires, non publiées, de l'I.N.E.

[5] L'espagne est organisée, politiquement et administrativement, en 17 régions appelées communautés autonomes, qui englobent chacune un nombre variable de provinces. Au total il existe 52 provinces, plus Ceuta et Mélilla.

L'ESPAGNE/SPAIN

5) *La structure par âge*

Au cours de ces dernières années, les indicateurs du vieillissement démographique ont augmenté de façon sensible, quoique la population espagnole se trouve encore parmi les plus jeunes de l'Europe des douze. En 1988, la proportion des 60 ans et plus[6] était de 17,7% et les personnes de 80 ans et plus représentaient 2,6% de la population. Les jeunes de moins de 20 ans constituaient 29,9%. Seule l'Irlande et le Portugal ont, à cette date, une structure par âges plus jeune que l'Espagne.

Un trait de la structure par âges de sa population qui distingue l'Espagne par rapport à la plupart de ses voisins est l'excédent relatif de jeunes nés entre 1965 et 1976, années pendant lesquelles la fécondité était nettement plus élevée en Espagne. Ces jeunes, qui ont entre 15 et 26 ans en 1991, se présentent sur le marché du travail entre le début des années 80 (les plus âgés ont eu 16 ans en 1981) et la fin du siècle (les plus jeunes auront 25 ans en l'an 2001). La reprise économique de la deuxième moitié des années 80 n'a pas bénéficié en Espagne de l'arrivée de classes creuses sur le marché du travail, ce qui explique la moindre incidence des créations d'emploi sur le taux de chômage des jeunes.

6) *Les migrations internes*

Depuis 1960, les migrations internes, constituent une des variables clés dans la dynamique des populations régionales et provinciales, et jouent un rôle considérable dans le rééquilibrage démographique des régions espagnoles.

Les mouvements migratoires internes atteignent un maximum dans la période 1961-70, avec 4,5 millions de migrants, soit une proportion de 14,6 pour mille habitants. Le nombre total de migrants diminue quelque peu au cours des années suivantes, en même temps que les migrations de courte distance, au sein des provinces, s'intensifient, en particulier dans les aires métropolitaines de Bilbao, Valence, Barcelone et Madrid (Olano A., 1989).

Au départ, les trois régions de plus fort développement industriel, Madrid, Catalogne et le Pays Basque, attiraient l'essentiel des migrants, en provenance d'Extrémadoure, des deux Castilles, d'Andalousie et, dans une moindre mesure de Galice. Ce modèle fortement orienté se maintient jusque vers le milieu des années soixante-dix. Dans la deuxième moitié de cette décennie, période de crise économique, les zones d'attraction traditionnelles voient diminuer leur solde migratoire, qui devient même négatif au Pays Basque. Les soldes négatifs des régions d'émigration diminuent également et deviennent positifs dans certaines d'entre elles.

---

[6]Nous utilisons les mêmes groupes d'âges qu'Eurostat, pour faciliter les comparaisons.

Au cours de la période 1981-85, ces tendances se renforcent. Le solde migratoire de la Catalogne devient négatif, alors que ceux de Madrid et de la communauté de Valence ne sont que très légèrement positifs. Dans les régions qui avaient alimenté auparavant le mouvement d'émigration vers les villes, le solde négatif est beaucoup plus faible dans les deux Castilles et en Extrémadoure, et commence à être positif en Andalousie.

La composition par âge des soldes montre cependant que les courants traditionnels n'ont pas disparu. Madrid, la Catalogne et la communauté de Valence reçoivent toujours un flux de migrants jeunes à la recherche d'un emploi, compensé par un mouvement de retours de migrants plus âgés vers leur province d'origine. La crise économique a donc provoqué des retours, qui ont modifié les soldes migratoires, sans que la division traditionnelle entre zones d'émigration et zones d'immigration se soit modifié pour l'essentiel.

7) *Les migrations internationales*

Pendant des siècles, l'Espagne a été un pays d'émigration. Ce n'est que depuis quelques annés que le courant s'est inversé, d'abord sous l'effet du retour de ses émigrants puis par un afflux d'immigrants étrangers.

A partir de la fin des années cinquante s'ouvre une période d'émigration vers l'Europe, d'abord vers la France puis vers la Suisse et finalement vers la République Fédérale Allemande. Ce courant est croissant jusqu'en 1973. A partir de cette date, la crise économique diminue la demande dans les pays d'accueil et provoque même des retours. Les données officielles ont enregistré un million d'émigrants entre 1960 et 1973, mais certaines estimations font état de deux millions de départs avec un solde net proche de un million.

A partir de 1974, le solde migratoire avec le reste de l'Europe est positif pour l'Espagne: les retours dépassent les départs. Entre 1975 et 1985 environ 350.000 émigrants retournent en Espagne ce qui réduit à environ 750.000 le nombre d'espagnols en Europe.

Le retour des émigrés est maintenant pratiquement terminé, mais le solde positif se maintient par l'afflux croissant d'immigrants étrangers, ce qui amorce une situation nouvelle.

La population étrangère en Espagne n'atteint pas encore des proportions importantes. Quoique les données soient incomplètes, on peut estimer le nombre d'étrangers en situation régulière à environ 410.000 (López de Lera, 1991), un peu plus de 1% de la population, mais son rythme de croissance est rapide (8% annuel entre 1981 et 1989). Il faut en outre ajouter les immigrés en situation irrégulière, dont le nombre, bien plus difficile à estimer, serait de 175.000, d'après une récente étude de l'Institut Espagnol d'Emigration (Instituto Español de Emigración, 1990).

L'ESPAGNE/SPAIN

Le contingent le plus important de résidents étrangers en situation régulière est formé de ressortissants d'autres pays de la CEE (environ 58% du total en 1989), dont une part importante de retraités installés dans les zones côtières. Beaucoup de latino-américains, qui arrivent comme étudiants ou réfugiés politiques, finissent par rester et occupent des emplois semi-qualifiés ou qualifiés. Ils représentent 16% de la population étrangère. Les immigrés originaires du Tiers Monde, principalement des Philippines et du Maroc, travaillent surtout dans les services. L'immigration de travailleurs originaires d'Afrique, et surtout du Maghreb, prend actuellement de l'ampleur, leur pourcentage ayant passé de 2,5% en 1981 à 6% en 1989[7].

L'origine des étrangers en situation irrégulière confirme les tendances les plus récentes. Les Africains dépassent 60%, dont plus de la moitié sont Marocains. Il y a 11% de Philipins et 3,5% sont originaires des pays de l'Est.

III. LES TENDANCES FUTURES

1) Les perspectives

Dans la plupart des perspectives de population qui ont été récemment élaborées en Espagne, la mortalité est maintenue constante au niveau de départ, du fait de la faiblesse de ses variations possibles et de son peu d'incidence sur l'évolution de la population totale. L'évolution récente de ce phénomène montre cependant que les gains ont été importants, malgré le haut niveau d'espérance de vie déjà atteint, et portent presque exclusivement sur les grands âges. Si les tendances actuelles se maintiennent, le poids des plus vieux tendra à s'accroître davantage, ce qui posera des problèmes d'attention sanitaire et sociale difficiles et coûteux. La baisse de la mortalité des plus âgés, et surtout des grands vieillards, est à notre avis le phénomène démographique qui risque d'avoir les conséquences les plus lourdes dans l'avenir proche.

La fécondité suit, depuis 1976, une course descendante ininterrompue. L'arrêt de la baisse de la nuptialité, à laquelle la fécondité est très liée, et l'expérience d'autres pays européens où la baisse s'est récemment interrompue, permet de formuler l'hypothèse d'une certaine récupération de la fécondité au cours des prochaines années, dont l'importance ne peut être prévue. Le maintien du niveau de remplacement des générations, un objectif qui suppose une augmentation de plus de 30% de la fécondité actuelle, exigera cependant, sans doute, des politiques actives de soutien de la natalité.

Même si, à long terme, la population peut diminuer, sa croissance va se poursuivre au cours des prochaines années, quel que soit le niveau de la fécondité (De Miguel C. y Agüero I., 1986). Si celle-ci se maintient au niveau de 1,5 enfant par femme, la

---

[7] Annuaires statistiques de l'I.N.E.

population atteindra un maximum de 40 millions vers 2006, avant de décroître. Avec une fécondité de 1,8, un maximum de 42 millions serait atteint vers 2011. Les personnes de 65 ans et plus représentaient en 1981 11,3% de la population (tableau 3). Si la fécondité se maintient au niveau de 1,5 enfants par femme, elles seront 16% en l'an 2001, et il y aura une personne âgé pour chaque jeune de moins de 15 ans, au lieu de deux jeunes par personne âgée en 1981. Il y aura en Espagne en 2001, plus de six millions de personnes du troisième âge et plus de deux millions et demie auront 75 ans et plus. La proportion des personnes de 65 ans et plus augmentera jusqu'à atteindre en 2026 18% ou 20%, selon que la fécondité sera de 1,5 ou de 1,8, mais, en valeur absolue, leur nombre sera multiplié par 2,3, passant de 3,3 millions à 7,4 millions, alors que le groupe des 75 et plus passera de 1,1 à 3,1 millions. Ces estimations ne tiennent pas compte d'une très probable diminution de la mortalité à ces âges.

TABLEAU 3.- ESPAGNE, 1900-1991; EVOLUTION DE LA STRUCTURE PAR AGE

Année	0-14		15-64		65+		Total
	Effectif (en milliers)	%	Effectif (en milliers)	%	Effectif (en milliers)	%	Effectifs (en milliers)
1900	6233	33,5	11396	61,3	968	5,2	18597
1910	6786	34,0	12086	60,5	1106	5,5	19978
1920	6892	32,3	13213	62,0	1217	5,7	21322
1930	7483	31,7	14706	62,2	1440	6,1	23629
1940	7750	29,9	16439	63,5	1691	6,5	25880
1950	7334	26,2	18607	66,5	2022	7,2	27963
1960	8348	27,4	19612	64,4	2505	8,2	30465
1970	9460	28,0	21064	62,3	3290	9,7	33814
1981	9635	25,6	23760	63,2	4221	11,2	37616
1991	7424	19,1	26138	67,3	5303	13,6	38864

Sources: 1900-81: INE. *Anuario estadistico de Espana, 1989*; 1991: AGÜero, I, y OLANO, A. *Proyecciones de la poblacion espanola 1986-2036*, inédit.
* Entre 1900 et 1950: population de fait; entre 1960 et 1981: population de droit; 1991: projection au 1er janvier.

2) *Situation démographique et politiques de population*

Il n'existe pas actuellement en Espagne de politique de population en tant que telle. Un certain nombre de dispositions, dans les domaines de la fiscalité ou de la protection sociale notamment, sont susceptibles d'avoir une incidence spéciale sur la démographie, de façon plus ou moins directe. La question d'un appui direct à la natalité revient périodiquement dans la presse et dans certains débats, et a fait l'objet d'initiatives parlementaires, émanant, en particulier, de l'opposition politique de droite. Une enquête de fécondité de l'I.N.E., qui date de 1985, a montré l'existence d'un désir de maternité non satisfait chez les femmes. Un peu plus de 22% de celles soumises au risque de grossesse renoncent à la maternité, en dépit de leur désir, exprimé sans condition (9%), ou bien sous réserve de certains changements (13%) qui portent essentiellement sur leur situation économique. Ce désir non satisfait est plus important chez les femmes qui ont déjà deux enfants, puisqu'il touche 31% d'entre elles, que chez celles qui en ont moins ou qui en ont davantage.

Ces quelques données montrent qu'une éventuelle politique d'appui à la natalité, qui est un objectif socialement souhaitable dans les conditions actuelles, non seulement n'aurait pas un caractère contraignant mais pourrait contribuer à mieux réaliser les souhaits des femmes et des familles.

L'opinion publique se montre cependant contraire à l'intervention de l'Etat dans le domaine de la natalité. D'après une enquête du CIS[8] de 1988, 20% de la population seulement estime que l'Etat devrait intervenir pour accroître le nombre de naissances, alors qu'en 1985, 33% était favorable à l'intervention. Cette évolution est d'autant plus surprenante qu'entre 1985 et 1988, l'opinion publique a pris davantage conscience du caractère négatif de la baisse de la natalité. Le rejet d'une intervention directe de l'Etat pour la solution de ce problème, dont on est par ailleurs de plus en plus conscient, obéit sans doute à des raisons idéologiques et à une répugnance particulière à voir l'Etat s'immiscer dans le domaine privé par excellence, au moment où le vent tourne de plus en plus du côté du libéralisme.

CONCLUSION

La situation démographique de l'Espagne est très semblable aujourd'hui à celle de ses voisins européens: très faible natalité, espérance de vie très élevée, population vieillissante et pression d'immigrants étrangers qui cherchent à s'établir dans le pays. L'avenir présente également des traits communs: la nécessité d'adapter l'économie, les institutions et les mentalités à une situation de faible ou nulle croissance démographique avec une proportion croissante de personnes âgées. Ces changements sont inévitables, même s'il se produit une certaine reprise de la fécondité au cours des prochaines années, par ailleurs souhaitable pour éviter que la situation démographique ne devienne insoutenable à long terme.

---

[8] Centro de Investigaciones Sociologicas.

RÉFÉRENCES BIBLIOGRAPHIQUES

Centro de Investigaciones Sociólogicas(1989) Problemas sociales: actitudes y opiniones de los españoles ante la natalidad, el aborto y la eutanasia., CIS, Madrid.

Del Campo, S. y Navarro M.(1987) Nuevo análisis de la población española Ariel, Barcelona.

Delgado M. y Fernández Cordón J.A. (1989) "La fecundidad en España desde 1975", Doc. de Trabajo No. 2, Instituto de Demografía, CSIC, Madrid, septiembre 1989.

(1990) "Análisis de las cifras de matrimonios en España desde 1975", Revista de Estadística Española, Vol. 31, no. 121, 1990, p.281-295.

De Miguel C. y Agüero I.(1986) "Evolución demográfica y oferta de trabajo", in Tendencias demográficas y planificación económica, Ministerio de Economía y Hacienda, Madrid.

Devolder B.(1986) "Tablas de mortalidad provinciales 1976- 1980", Documento de trabajo, Centre d'Estudis Demografics, Univ. Autónoma, Barcelona.

Fernández Cordón J.A. (1986) "Análisis longitudinal de la fecundidad en España", in Tendencias demográficas y planificación económica, Ministerio de Economía y Hacienda, Madrid.

(1987) "La fecundidad reciente en España", Revista Economistas, Madrid, Febrero-Marzo, 1987.

Gozalvez Pérez V.(1989) "Crise et contrastes spatiaux de la fécondité espagnole", Espace, Populations, Sociétés.

Instituto Español de Emigración (1990) Mapa de inmigrantes extranjeros en situación irregular, Ministerio de Trabajo y Seguridad Social, Madrid.

López de Lera, D.(1991) "Análisis de la estadística sobre la población extranjera", III Jornadas sobre la Población Española, AGE, Málaga.

Nadal J.(1986) La población española, Siglos XVI al XX., Ariel, Barcelona, 4a. ed.

Olano A.(1989) "Hacia un nuevo modelo de migraciones interiores en la población española", Economistas, Madrid, VII, 39

Le Portugal/Portugal
Maria José CARRILHO y Joao PEIXOTO

I.- L'EVOLUTION HISTORIQUE DE LA POPULATION PORTUGAISE

Jusqu'à la fin du siècle dernier, les sources disponibles sur la démographie portugaise sont insuffisantes. Depuis longtemps, il existe des comptages de la population - dénombrements, listes de foyers et population -, mais dont la qualité est discutable. A partir de la seconde moitié du XIXème siècle et surtout au cours du XXème siècle, les statistiques ont acquis plus de fiabilité. En 1864, le pays a commencé d'effectuer des recensements modernes de la population, utilisant les procédés statistiques recommandés aux Congrès Internationaux d'alors. En 1886, pour la première fois, sont divulguées des statistiques du mouvement naturel. Cependant une analyse approfondie de la population n'est possible qu'après les premières décades de notre siècle.

Le Graphique 1 représente la population totale présente au Portugal continental (excluant les Iles atlantiques et les possessions coloniales des diverses époques), entre 1768 et 1981, et la population résidente sur le territoire actuel (Continent et Iles), entre 1864 et 1981 (voir aussi le Tableau 1). Malgré la diversité des sources - de 1768 à 1861, inclusivement, on a utilisé les dénombrements ou recensements non classiques; après 1864, sont représentés les recensements modernes -, une évolution est décelable. Jusqu'au milieu du XIXème siècle, la croissance démographique est lente; néanmoins, elle n'est pas négligeable. Une réduction significative de la mortalité serait apparue dès le XVIIIème siècle, avec la disparition des crises associées aux conditions de vie très déficientes et aux longs voyages maritimes des Portugais. A partir de la seconde moitié du XIXème siècle, la croissance s'accentue ; une baisse accrue de la mortalité doit être la source principale de l'expansion démographique ; elle a été suffisante pour compenser - comme on le verra - les effets d'une émigration croissante.

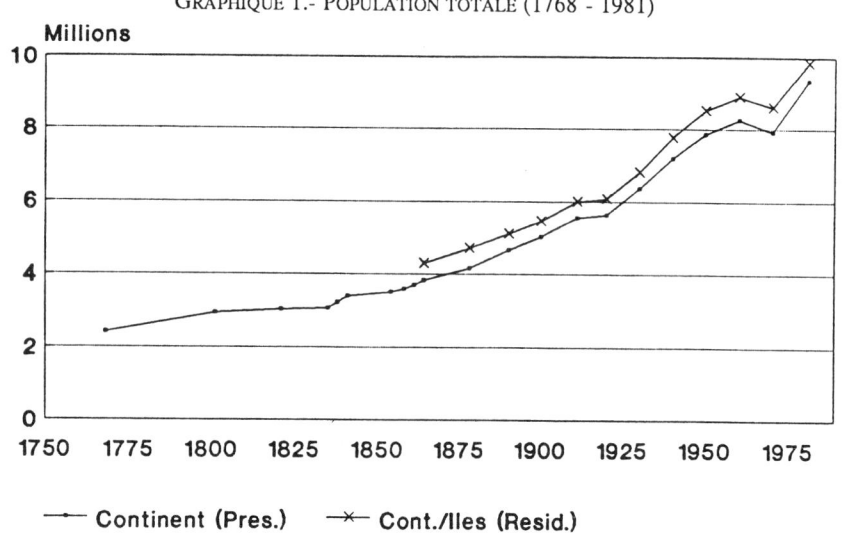

GRAPHIQUE 1.- POPULATION TOTALE (1768 - 1981)

— Continent (Pres.)   —×— Cont./Iles (Resid.)

TABLEAU 1.- POPULATION RESIDENTE ET TAUX DE CROISSANCE ANNUEL MOYEN.

Années	Population résidente	Taux de croissance (%)	Evolution 1864=100
1864	4286995		100
1878	4698984	0.658	110
1890	5102891	0.694	119
1900	5446760	0.654	127
1911	5999146	0.882	140
1920	6080135	0.149	142
1930	6808719	1.138	159
1940	7755423	1.306	181
1950	8510240	0.933	199
1960	8889392	0.437	207
1970	8611110	-0.318	201
1981	9833014	1.303	229

Source: INE, Recensement de la population

A partir de 1864, on enregistre des fluctuations importantes. La première phase de 1864 à 1911 correspond à un accroissement continu de la population. De 1911 à 1920 - seconde phase -, la population augmente à un rythme très lent: c'est le résultat des effets de la Première Guerre Mondiale, de la mortalité due à une épidémie de grippe pneumonique ainsi que du premier grand essor migratoire de l'histoire contemporaine portugaise. La troisième phase, entre 1920 et 1960, est le témoin d'une croissance rapide ; on y remarque deux sous-phases: l'une, de 1920 à 1940, où le rythme d'accroissement s'accentue; l'autre, de 1940 à 1960, où l'accroissement est modéré. La croissance de la population devient négative pendant la période 1960-1970 - quatrième phase; c'est le grand cycle de l'émigration européenne. Enfin, la dernière phase : 1970-1981, enregistre la croissance la plus forte de toute la période analysée. Pourtant, cette dernière période est fortement diversifiée: jusqu'en 1973, on remarque toujours l'exode migratoire; en 1974 et 1975, on assiste à une "explosion démographique" associée au processus de décolonisation - retour des portugais des ex-colonies; en 1976, commence un accroissement démographique constant où le déclin des soldes naturels - résultant de la chute de la fécondité - est compensé par l'inflexion de l'émigration européenne - réduction des départs et accélération du mouvement de retour des émigrants.

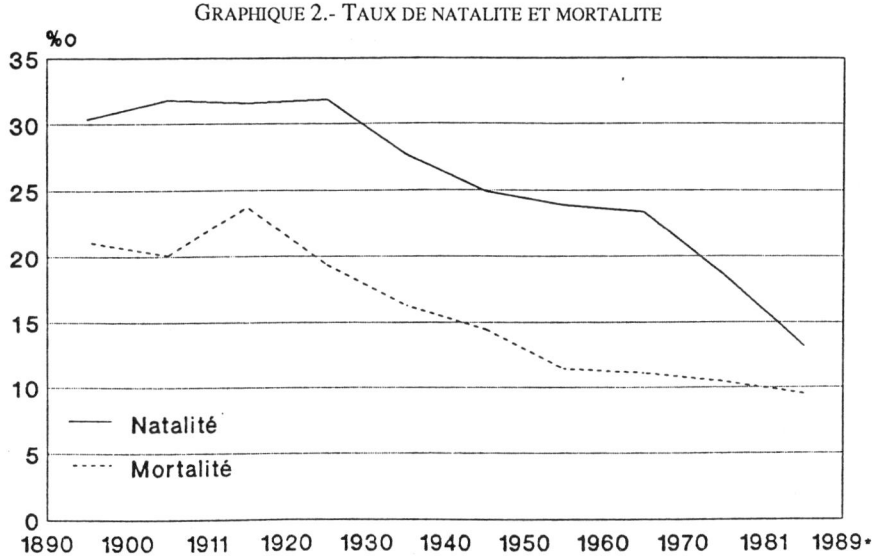

GRAPHIQUE 2.- TAUX DE NATALITE ET MORTALITE

* Evaluation

On peut analyser plus en détail l'évolution des composantes de la croissance de la population portugaise. Sur le Graphique 2, sont représentés les taux bruts de natalité et de mortalité entre 1890 et 1989, par périodes inter-censitaires. Jusqu'aux premières décades de ce siècle, ce sont les seuls indicateurs du mouvement naturel pouvant être calculés directement. Malgré leur limite - liée aux perturbations structurelles - et les imperfections de l'information statistique, les tendances de l'évolution apparaissent bien marquées. En ce qui concerne la mortalité, l'indicateur a enregistré, jusqu'à la moitié des années 20, des oscillations autour de la même valeur: 20‰; l'unique exception a eu lieu pendant la période 1911-20, à cause de la Première Guerre Mondiale et de la grippe pneumonique, en 1918. A partir des années 30 le taux brut de mortalité commence une baisse graduelle, jusqu'en 1960, s'approchant alors des 10‰. Depuis. 1960, sa valeur a diminué très légèrement. Le vieillissement de la population explique cette presque stabilisation: depuis lors, l'amélioration des conditions de vie (comme le démontrent des indicateurs comme le taux de mortalité infantile) se répercute peu sur le taux brut de mortalité. La natalité, de son côté, a connu des oscillations autour de la même valeur - un peu au-dessus des 30‰ - jusqu'à la moitié des années 20. A partir de cette date, tout comme pour la mortalité, commence un déclin, plus intensif jusqu'aux années 40 où le taux atteint 25‰, puis plus lent jusqu'à la moitié des années 60. Dans les années 70 et 80 la baisse a regagné son intensité première, l'indicateur s'approchant aujourd'hui des 11‰. Donc, on a enregistré, au Portugal, de la fin du XIXème siècle jusqu'aux années 60, une longue période de croissance pendant laquelle le solde naturel est élevé et à peu près constant. C'est seulement au cours des vingt dernières années - 1970 à 1989 - que le pays a assisté à une contraction assez rapide des naissances et, aussi, de l'excédent naturel.

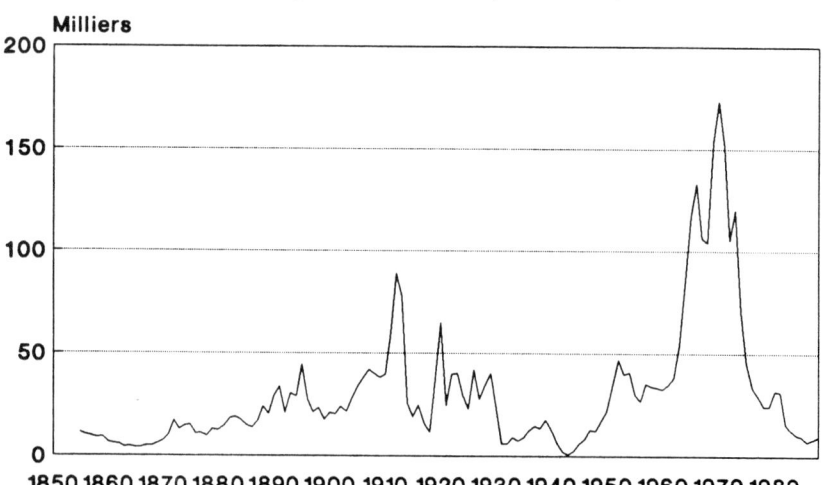

GRAPHIQUE 3.- EMIGRATION (1855 - 1988)

Il est difficile de déterminer, avec rigueur, les pas principaux de la transition démographique au Portugal. D'un côté, les mécanismes de la transition sont tellement variés qu'ils ne permettent pas, sur le plan théorique, d'identification facile. D'un autre côté, la déficience de l'information statistique inhibe une connaissance plus approfondie des variables en cause. Malgré cela, on peut formuler quelques hypothèses. Déjà, au XVIIIème siècle, on trouve quelques signes de la première phase de transition, mais leur présence ne devient marquante qu'à la moitié du XIXème siècle. Comme on l'a vu plus haut, le déclin de la mortalité apparaît déjà au cours du XVIIIème siècle et devient plus important après 1850. La seconde phase de transition a dû commencer à partir de la moitié des années 20 de notre siècle avec une chute décisive de la natalité (celle-ci n'a pas dû beaucoup baisser au cours du XIXème siècle même s'il est probable que ses valeurs antérieures aient été plus élevées - et plus proches d'une fécondité naturelle). Très récemment, le pays est entré dans la phase finale - conclusive - de la transition: le taux brut de natalité rejoint pratiquement le taux de mortalité au cours des années 80. Les moments décisifs des déclins - surtout pour la fécondité - semblent être plus tardifs que dans la plupart des pays européens.

Un accroissement naturel élevé a alimenté, depuis le XIXème siècle, la forte émigration portugaise. Jusqu'en 1955, seule l'émigration légale est représentée (Graphique 3) ; les flux migratoires réels doivent les excéder légèrement. Ensuite on enregistre également les flux clandestins vers la France. D'après ce que l'on sait, l'émigration du territoire portugais est très ancienne; au XVIème siècle, on signalait déjà des sorties vers les différentes colonies - du Brésil à l'Inde, en passant par l'Afrique. Au début, cette "émigration" était de caractère colonisateur puis à partir du XIXème siècle, il apparaît une certaine altération dans le statut des émigrants, qui deviennent travailleurs moins qualifiés. Les données disponibles permettent d'identifier quelques cycles. Jusqu'en 1870, on remarque un flux régulier d'émigration, de dimension amoindrie. De 1870 à 1920, a eu lieu le premier grand mouvement migratoire: il s'agit de déplacements en masse pour le Brésil. Entre 1920 et 1930, les sorties se sont stabilisées à des valeurs élevées. De 1930 à 1950, l'émigration est presque nulle, étant données la crise économique mondiale et les barrières à l'entrée des migrants au Brésil et en Amérique en général. De 1950 à 1973, a eu lieu le second grand essor migratoire de l'histoire contemporaine portugaise; la destination des émigrants est, cette fois, l'Europe de l'après-guerre - et le Portugal fait partie des intenses flux de main-d'oeuvre qui y convergent alors. Après 1973, le flux est de nouveau en extinction - la clôture des marchés internationaux du travail coïncide avec les altérations économiques et politiques au Portugal (situation semblable, d'ailleurs, à celle enregistrée immédiatement après 1930) - et le courant migratoire s'inverse.

Le pays a connu de fortes fluctuations conjoncturelles de l'accroissement global, surtout déterminées par les flux migratoires (Tableau 2). Les plus fortes croissances correspondent aux périodes avec émigration réduite ou immigration (dans ce dernier cas, on trouve les périodes 1930-40 et 1970-1989); les croissances les plus faibles correspondent aux exodes migratoires - dont l'effet se cumule avec le déclin des naissances: 1911-20 (et alors aussi l'augmentation de la mortalité) et 1950-70 (en 1960-70 on a même une diminution absolue de la population totale). La migration nette cumulée enregistre une perte supérieure à 2 millions d'individus sur toute la période - concentrée sur les seules années 1950-70. Cette valeur correspond à environ 1/5 de la population portugaise et reflète la dimension de l'émigration portugaise.

TABLEAU 2.- ACCROISSEMENT DE LA POPULATION LORS DE DIVERSES PERIODES INTERCENSITAIRES (EN MILLIERS)

Période	Accroissement de la population	Accroissement naturel	Migration nette	Migration nette cumulée
1890-00	343.9	488.1	-144.2	-144.2
1900-11	552.4	738.2	-185.8	-330.0
1911-20	80.9	425.6	-344.7	-674.7
1920-30	728.6	804.3	-75.7	-750.4
1930-40	946.7	828.7	118.0	-632.4
1940-50	754.8	847.8	-93.0	-725.4
1950-60	379.2	1088.4	-709.2	-1434.6
1960-70	-226.1	1073.5	-1299.6	-2734.2
1970-81	1169.7	828.7	341.0	-2393.2
1981-89	504.0	290.5	213.5	-2179.7

Source: INE, Recensements de la Population; Statistiques démographiques; 1981-89: Evaluations de la population.

Quelques indices plus fins que les simples taux bruts ont pu être calculés avant 1950. L'indice synthétique de fécondité diminue, entre 1930 et 1950, de 3,8 à 2,8 enfants par femme. On doit remarquer que pendant la Grande Dépression, cette valeur était tombée, par exemple, à 1,6 en Allemagne et 1,7 au Royaume Uni; au Portugal cette implosion n'a pas eu lieu. La mortalité infantile était, jusqu'à 1950, très supérieur à 100‰; elle atteignait même les 150‰ en 1911-20 et 1930-40. L'espérance de vie à la naissance n'était, en 1920, que de 35,8 ans chez les hommes et 40 ans chez les femmes, pour atteindre 55,5 ans et 60,5 ans respectivement en 1950.

II.- LA DEMOGRAPHIE PORTUGAISE APRES 1950

1) Répartition par sexe et âges

L'augmentation de la proportion de personnes de 65 ans et plus et la diminution des jeunes de moins de 15 ans (Tableau 3) caractérisent la période entre 1950 et 1989. La proportion des personnes âgées s'est élevée de 7,0% en 1950 à 13,1% en 1989; en même temps, la part des jeunes a baissé de 29,6% à 20,9%.

TABLEAU 3.- POPULATION PAR GRANDS GROUPES D'AGES (EN %)

Années	0-14 ans	15-64 ans	65 et +
1890	33.1	60.6	6.4
1900	33.7	60.4	5.9
1911	34.3	59.6	6.1
1920	32.6	61.0	6.4
1930	31.9	61.7	6.4
1940	32.0	61.3	6.8
1950	29.6	53.4	7.0
1960	29.2	62.9	8.0
1970	28.5	61.9	9.7
1981	25.5	63.0	11.4
1982	24.7	63.6	11.7
1983	24.2	64.0	11.7
1984	23.8	64.4	11.9
1985	23.3	64.6	12.1
1986	22.7	64.9	12.4
1987	22.1	65.3	12.6
1988	21.5	65.6	12.9
1989	20.9	66.0	13.1

Source: INE; De 1890 à 1950, Population présente; de 1960 à 1991: Population résidente; De 1982 à 1989: Evaluations.

L'accroissement de la proportion de la population âgée entre 1950 et 1970 découle de la chute de la population jeune et aussi de la diminution de la population d'âge actif dû à l'émigration. Depuis 1981, le fort accroissement relatif des personnes âgées est accompagné, seulement, de la diminution des jeunes. Le rapport personnes âgées / jeunes est passé, en cette période, de 24 pour 100 en 1950, à 63 pour 100 en 1989.

Les pyramides par âge pour les années de 1950 et 1989 illustrent bien l'impact des différents phénomènes affectant la structure par âge : fécondité, mortalité et migrations, surtout masculines. Pourtant, la pyramide de 1989 est déjà bien ré-équilibrée par rapport à celles de la période d'émigration, autour de 1970, en raison de la fin de l'émigration et des mouvements de retour. Entre ces dates on assiste aussi au processus de vieillissement de la population portugaise "par le bas" et "par le haut".

La chute accélérée de la fécondité et les flux migratoires sont les facteurs qui expliquent le vieillissement démographique au Portugal. Jusqu'à présent les effets de la baisse de la mortalité sont surtout liés à la mortalité infantile et juvénile.

2) *Fécondité*

Après avoir été stable entre 1950 et les années 70, la fécondité portugaise a commencé son mouvement continu de baisse. L'indice synthétique de fécondité est tombé de 2,8 en 1950, à 1,5 enfants par femme en 1989, soit une réduction de près de moitié. Depuis 1982 la fécondité a glissé au dessous du seuil de renouvellement des générations (Tableau 4).

TABLEAU 4.- INDICE SYNTHETIQUE DE FECONDITE (NOMBRE D'ENFANTS PAR FEMME) ET ESPERANCE DE VIE A LA NAISSANCE (EN ANNEE).

Années	ISF	E0	
		Hommes	Femmes
1920		35.8	40.0
1930	3.8	44.8	49.2
1940	3.1	48.6	52.8
1950	2.8	55.5	60.5
1960	2.9	60.7	66.4
1970	2.8	64.2	70.8
1980	2.2	69.1	76.7
1981	2.1	68.3	75.3
1982	2.1	69.0	76.0
1983	1.9	69.3	75.9
1984	1.9	69.4	76.4
1985	1.7	69.7	76.7
1986	1.6	70.2	77.1
1987	1.6	70.7	77.5
1988	1.5	70.6	77.7
1989	1.5	71.2	78.2

Source: INE

On doit remarquer que la structure par âge de la population a eu un effet favorable sur le nombre de naissances et l'accroissement naturel.

Dans les dernières années, on observe aussi d'importantes modifications des taux de fécondité par âge. Avant les années 1980 on observe un rajeunissement de la fécondité, dû à la baisse de la fécondité des mères âgées (Graphique 4) suivie au cours des années 1980 par la chute de la fécondité des jeunes femmes et le déplacement du mode de 20-24 ans à 25-29 ans.

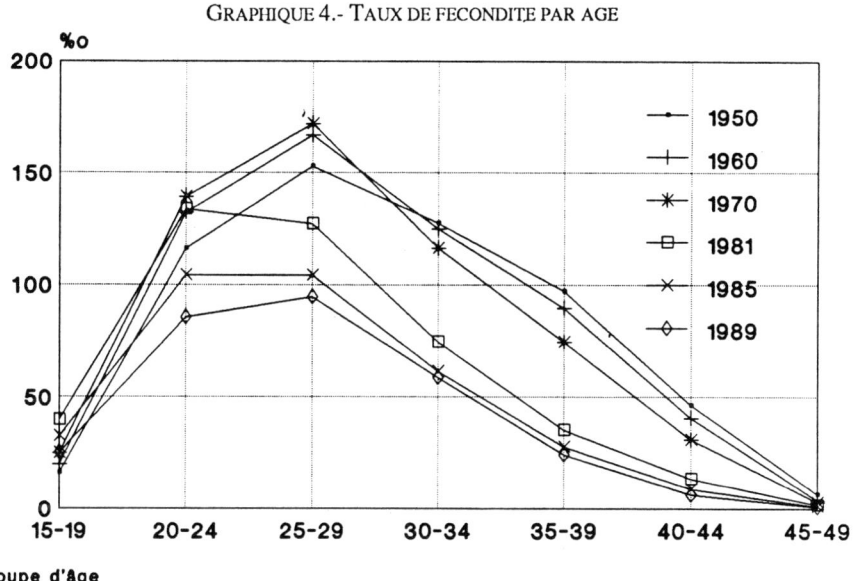

GRAPHIQUE 4.- TAUX DE FECONDITE PAR AGE

L'évolution des rang de naissances depuis 1950, rend compte des changements dans la taille de la famille. Les naissances des rang 5 et suivants accusent une baisse très forte : elles représentaient 24,6% en 1950 contre 4,1% en 1989 (Tableau 5). La part des naissances du premier rang s'accentue: en 1989, elles représentaient plus de la moitié des naissances vivantes totales.

TABLEAU 5.- RÉPARTITION SELON LE RANG DES NAISSANCES ET PROPORTION DE NAISSANCES HORS MARIAGE (EN %)

Années	1ère	2ème	3ème	4ème	5ème et plus	Hors mariage
1950	28.0	21.0	15.6	10.8	24.6	11.8
1955	30.5	20.3	14.4	10.4	24.6	11.0
1960	32.1	21.2	13.9	9.7	23.2	9.5
1965	30.9	21.8	14.1	9.7	23.5	7.8
1970	32.8*	23.8*	13.1*	8.5*	21.9*	7.3
1975	40.1	27.8	11.9	6.2	14.0	7.2
1980	45.4	31.3	11.0	4.8	7.5	9.2
1981	44.2	32.7	11.3	4.8	7.0	9.5
1982	45.1	32.5	11.4	4.7	6.4	10.0
1983	45.5	32.2	11.5	4.7	6.2	10.7
1984	46.4	31.7	11.5	4.7	5.8	11.5
1985	47.1	31.5	11.3	4.6	5.5	12.3
1986	47.8	31.5	11.0	4.5	5.2	12.8
1987	48.3	31.8	10.7	4.4	4.8	13.3
1988	50.0	31.6	10.1	4.1	4.3	13.7
1989	51.0	31.1	9.9	3.9	4.1	14.5

Source: INE, statistiques démographiques

Il est aussi intéressant d'observer l'évolution des naissances hors mariage au Portugal. En 1950, la proportion de naissances hors mariage était de 11,8%, un niveau proche de celui enregistré au milieu des années 80. Aujourd'hui, après un minimum vers 1975, cette valeur est de 14,5%.

Les facteurs explicatifs de l'évolution de ce dernier phénomène se trouvent au niveau régional. Ce sont les districts du Sud du pays, en particulier l'Alentejo, qui enregistrent, depuis longtemps, les plus hauts pourcentages de naissances hors mariage. L'économie agricole et le régime de propriété - latifundia - de ces régions, associés à une moindre importance de la religion et des mariages formels, expliquent cette situation. La crise dans cette région, depuis les années 60, associée à un haut niveau de migrations internes vers la région de Lisbonne, doit être un facteur explicatif de la diminution de la proportion de naissances illégitimes. Toutefois - comme on le verra plus loin -, tout le pays a connu une augmentation de la nuptialité en cette période.

La rapidité du recul, la hausse des naissances hors mariage et le recul de l'âge à la maternité sont les traits les plus marquants de l'évolution récente de la fécondité portugaise.

3) Nuptialité et divortialité

Au cours de la période 1950-81 le taux brut de nuptialité ne cesse d'augmenter (Tableau 6). Cette évolution est accompagnée du rajeunissement de l'âge au mariage. En effet, en 1950, l'âge moyen au premier mariage se situait à 27,0 ans chez les hommes et à 24,8 ans chez les femmes; en 1981, il était tombé à 25,4 ans chez les hommes et à 23,3 ans chez les femmes.

TABLEAU 6. - EVOLUTION DE LA NATALITE, MORTALITE, NUPTIALITE ET DIVORTIALITE
(TAUX EN POUR MILLE)

Période	Taux brut de natalité	Taux brut de mortalité	Taux de mortalité infantile	Taux brut de nuptialité	Taux brut de divortialité
1890-00	30.4	21.1		6.6	
1900-11	31.8	20.1		6.5	
1911-20	31.5	23.7	153.6	6.5	
1920-30	31.8	19.4	132.1	7.3	
1930-40	27.7	16.3	148.7	6.5	
1940-50	24.9	14.5	114.9	7.6	0.0
1950-60	23.9	11.4	90.3	8.0	0.1
1960-70	23.4	11.1	65.2	8.7	0.1
1970-80	18.6	10.4	38.9	9.2	0.4
1981	15.4	9.7	21.8	7.7	0.7
1982	15.2	9.3	19.8	7.4	0.7
1983	14.4	9.6	19.2	7.5	0.8
1984	14.2	9.6	16.7	6.9	0.7
1985	12.8	9.6	17.8	6.7	0.9
1986	12.4	9.4	15.8	6.8	0.8
1987	12.0	9.3	14.2	7.0	0.9
1988	11.9	9.5	13.0	6.9	0.9
1989	11.5	9.3	12.1	7.1	0.9

Source: INE
    De 1890 à 1950 - population présente
    De 1950 à 1981 - population résidente
    De 1982 à 1989 - Evaluations de la population

Au cours des années 80 on observe un recul de la nuptialité et, en 1985, le taux brut a atteint son niveau le plus bas, avec 6,7 mariages pour 1000 habitants. Pourtant, depuis 1986 on assiste à un renversement de tendance ; en 1989, il s'est élevé à 7,1‰.

Les premiers mariages, dans les années 80, ont eu lieu de plus en plus tard. Actuellement, l'âge moyen au premier mariage se situe à 26,1 ans chez les hommes et à 24,1 ans chez les femmes. L'évolution récente, de 1980 à 1989, de la somme des premiers mariages réduits montre aussi le recul de la fréquence des premiers mariages. On observe la même évolution pour l'ensemble des mariages.

L'augmentation de l'âge au mariage, aussi bien que celle de la proportion des nés-vivants hors mariage, a un lien étroit avec l'augmentation de la cohabitation, surtout lorsque celle-ci précède le mariage officiel. Toutefois, le Portugal ne dispose pas encore de données en ce domaine.

Le nombre de divorces (Tableau 6) a été très bas jusqu'en 1974. La forte augmentation enregistrée depuis 1975 reflète la possibilité de dissolution des mariages catholiques. Au cours des années 80, le taux brut de divortialité a augmenté légèrement; il est, en 1989, de 0,9%.

Jamais le refus du mariage en tant qu'institution n'a été aussi fort, les naissances hors mariage aussi nombreuses et les taux de divorce aussi élevés au Portugal.

4) *Mortalité*

La mortalité a régressé de façon très sensible entre 1950 et 1989 (Tableaux 4 et 6).

Entre 1950 et 1989 l'espérance de vie à la naissance s'est élevée de 55,5 ans à 71,2 ans chez les hommes, et de 60,5 à 78,2 ans chez les femmes. On constate que la surmortalité masculine s'est accentuée entre ces deux dates: aujourd'hui les femmes vivent, en moyenne, 7 ans de plus que les hommes, contre 5 ans en 1950. Les accidents de circulation et les maladies cardio-vasculaires sont les principales raisons de cette surmortalité.

Au cours du temps le taux de mortalité infantile a connu une baisse très considérable. On observe que le niveau est tombé de environ 94 ‰, en 1950, à 12,1 ‰, en 1989, soit une réduction de 87% entre ces deux dates.

Les conditions socio-économiques, culturelles, la nutrition et la vaccination sont les facteurs explicatifs du recul de la mortalité infantile. Néanmoins, il y a encore beaucoup à faire, car le niveau actuel est le plus élevé parmi les pays de l'Europe des Douze.

5) *Migrations*

Le panorama migratoire portugais s'est profondément altéré vers le milieu des années 70.

Jusqu'en 1950, comme on l'a vu, l'émigration avait presque exclusivement comme destination l'Amérique, et surtout le Brésil; entre 1950 et 1959, ce continent a encore représenté environ 90% des destinations. Les premières années de la décennie 1960 ont marqué un changement rapide: en 1960-64 le Brésil et l'Amérique ont perdu le rôle principal au profit de la France et l'Europe (avec 47% et 51%, respectivement, des destinations). A partir de 1965, l'émigration européenne est devenue massive: jusqu'en 1974, y ont convergé environ un million de portugais -. soit, environ 80% de l'émigration totale de la période. Ces chiffres représentent des taux migratoires énormes: pour le pays entier ils se sont situés, en 1965-74, entre 10‰ et 20‰ chaque année. La France a été le pays de destination le plus fréquent : de 1960 à 1984, elle a reçu entre 50% et 80% des émigrants. Après 1974, l'émigration a fortement décliné. Dès lors, l'émigration américaine prend la relève, et en 1985-88 elle est de nouveau majoritaire avec les 2/3 des émigrants. Pourtant, les destinations ont changé : le Brésil a pratiquement disparu comme pays de destination et l'Amérique du Nord - surtout les Etats-Unis - a pris la relève. Dans les années 80, on enregistre de nouvelles destinations - l'Australie ou le Moyen-Orient (ce dernier sur un plan surtout cyclique).

L'année 1974 est la date, également, de l'altération radicale du solde migratoire. Non seulement les flux de sorties ont diminué, mais on a aussi enregistré de nombreuses entrées. En 1974 et 1975, le pays a accueilli environ un demi million de Portugais qui résidaient aux ex-colonies, résultat de la décolonisation. A la fin de la décade s'intensifie, également, le retour d'émigrants: ce mouvement, originaire de l'Europe, et que l'on enregistrait déjà dans les années 60, n'a pas cessé, dés lors, d'augmenter. Le flux de retour est devenu, cependant, moins intensif au cours des années 80; un retour en masse a apparemment été remplacé par une plus grande intégration dans le pays de destination.

Le Portugal commence, enfin, à enregistrer quelques signes d'immigration étrangère. Le chiffre des étrangers n'est pas élevé, avec près de 100 000 individus - environ 1% de la population résidente. La plupart a toujours été liée au Portugal: individus originaires d'ex-colonies, brésiliens, descendants d'émigrants portugais. Le chiffre le plus élevé est celui des Africains des anciennes colonies avec environ 42% des étrangers; parmi ceux-ci, le Cap Vert possède, de loin, la communauté la plus importante, avec plus d'un quart du total des étrangers. Les européens - en particulier ceux de la Communauté Européenne - constituent le second groupe, avec presque 30% des étrangers. La clandestinité est assez importante : les estimations donnent un chiffre situé entre 70 000 et 100 000 - valeur proche de celle des immigrants légaux.

TABLEAU 7.- RÉPARTITION DES ÉMIGRANTS PAR PRINCIPAUX PAYS ET CONTINENTS DE DESTINATION (1950-1988) (a)

Années	AMERIQUE				AUTRE
	Brésil	USA	Autres	Total	Total
1950-54	145867	5569			
%	79.6	3.0			
1955-59	91460	10524	37548	139532	6367
%	57.3	6.6	23.5	87.4	4.0
1960-64	58289	15997	39515	113801	6239
%	23.7	6.5	16.1	46.3	2.5
1965-69	14978	50677	54088	119743	14061
%	2.4	8.3	8.8	19.5	2.3
1970-74	5646	43838	57527	107011	5645
%	0.9	7.1	9.3	17.3	0.9
1975-79	3484	39646	32059	75189	7542
%	2.2	25.4	20.5	48.2	4.8
1980-84	963	16271	19443	36677	14873
%	0.9	16.0	19.1	36.0	14.4
1985-88	276	10242	12342	22860	4697
%	0.8	29.8	36.0	66.6	13.7
Total	321130	192836.9	252619.3	768503.7	59252.9
%	15.2	9.1	11.9	36.2	2.8

Années	EUROPE				TOTAL
	France	RFA	Autres	Total	Total
1950-54	1629				183271
%	0.9				100,0 (b)
1955-59	13095	19	644	13758	159657
%	8.2	0.0	0.4	8.6	100,0.0
1960-64	116590	5721	3639	125950	245990
%	47.4	2.3	1.5	51.2	100,0
1965-69	425261	41606	13102	479969	613773
%	69.3	6.8	2.1	78.2	100,0
1970-74	407019	85677	14380	507076	619732
%	65.7	13.8	2.3	81.8	100,0
1975-79	67069	1816	4390	73275	156006
%	43.0	1.8	2.8	47.0	100,0
1980-84	48559	183	1668	50410	101760
%	47.7	0.2	1.6	49.5	100,0
1985-88	5915	107	745	6767	34324
%	17.2	0.3	2.2	19.7	100,0
Total	1085419	135153.3	38578.7	1259150	2115113
%	51.3	6.4	1.8	59.5	100,0(b)

(a) Englobe l'émigration clandestine vers la France
(b) Englobe des destinations ignorées en 1950-54
Source: INE, Statistiques Démographiques et Secretaria de Estado das Comunidades Portuguesas

III.- LES POLITIQUES DE LA POPULATION AU PORTUGAL

1) Famille, Troisième Age et Natalité

Il n'existe pas, au Portugal, une "politique démographique". Il existe de nombreuses mesures politiques avec une incidence démographique, mais certaines sont, seulement, indirectes, car il n'existe pas d'objectifs politiques précis dans ce domaine. Actuellement la politique familiale est dispersée entre plusieurs départements gouvernementaux et politiques sectorielles: aides financières à la famille, équipements sociaux, dégrèvements fiscaux, aide à l'habitat, etc; il existe des tentatives d'harmonisation, avec l'appui de la Direction Générale de la Famille (du Ministère de l'Emploi et de la Sécurité Sociale). La coordination de la politique familiale a déjà été essayée en 1980-83: à ce moment-là, la famille assumait une très grande importance dans la structure gouvernementale - Secrétariat d'Etat de la Famille -, et l'autonomie lui a été conférée face à d'autres politiques sectorielles. En 1988, on a de nouveau reconnu la nécessité d'une politique intégrée, et quelques mesures ponctuelles ont été adoptées: augmentation des allocations familiales et des pensions de retraités; introduction de nouveaux types d'horaires, plus flexibles, pour les familles qui ont des enfants; création de la Commission Nationale pour la Politique du troisième âge entre autres.

Bien que les prestations financières aux familles et au Troisième Age - allocations familiales, pensions de retraités, subsides de naissance, allaitement, mariage, décès, aide aux enfants handicapés - soient régulièrement augmentées, elles se maintiennent, aujourd'hui encore, à de faibles valeurs. Une telle situation est due, en grand partie, à l'histoire politique et institutionnelle du pays: l'Etat-Providence, au Portugal, est relativement récent - avant les altérations politiques internes de 1974 (l'instauration de la démocratie), il n'a pas rencontré une grande expression. Les difficultés économiques du pays ainsi que la crise que les divers Etats-Providence ont connue depuis cette date, n'ont pas permis leur expansion, même tardive.

Il est difficile de croire que l'Etat ait influencé, par ses politiques, les comportements démographiques. Une certaine efficacité a existé, toutefois, dans certains domaines : la natalité ou la divortialité. Néanmoins, les mesures politiques adoptées dans ces domaines n'ont pas visé des objectifs démographiques explicites.

Le planning familial au Portugal, par exemple, a eu une diffusion relativement réduite avant 1974; des raisons culturelles, politiques ou religieuses expliquent cette situation. L'existence et l'accès aux moyens contraceptifs ont été divulgués amplement dès 1974: à ce moment-là, les services médicaux ont été élargis sur tout le territoire portugais; de jeunes médecins ont été placés dans les zones les moins favorisées; et des consultations régulières de planning familial ont été créées. Il est probable que ce phénomène ait contribué à la chute accentuée de la fécondité à la fin des années 70, en conjonction avec les divers changements politiques, sociaux, culturels qui se sont déroulés à cette époque.

L'avortement était complètement interdit jusqu'à très récemment ; sa légalisation a été discutée au niveau politique à partir de 1974. Il a été autorisé seulement très récemment en certaines circonstances exceptionnelles (risques pour la santé de la mère). La réalité de l'avortement clandestin est, pourtant, bien connue au Portugal.

La divortialité est également liée aux politiques de l'Etat. La légalisation du divorce pour les individus mariés par l'Eglise Catholique, en 1975, a clairement contribué à l'augmentation du nombre des divorces. Après une brusque augmentation, la divortialité s'est accrue, dés lors, régulièrement.

2) Politiques migratoires

Pendant de longues années, le Portugal a adopté une politique peu active par rapport à l'émigration. D'un côté, elle contribuait à appauvrir plusieurs régions en éloignant certains de ses éléments les plus actifs; de l'autre, elle garantissait l'envoi de remises financières. Le financement de l'économie nationale par les émigrants est un fait dont l'importance date déjà de la fin du XIXème siècle; au tournant des actuelles années 70, il a constitué un élément décisif de l'équilibre financier du pays. En tous cas, les autorités n'ont pas stimulé l'émigration, et quelques mesures restrictives ont même été adoptées, comme l'exigence de présentation de contrats de travail; l'émigration clandestine a, toutefois, largement dépassé les restrictions. Quelques mesures ponctuelles d'aide aux communautés d'émigrants ont, aussi, toujours existé : avant et après 1974, des accords bilatéraux ont été conclus de façon à protéger les droits sociaux des émigrants, faciliter la réunification familiale, etc. Le retour des émigrants - ou, au moins, le placement de leur épargne - a également été protégé: plusieurs bénéfices financiers ont été créés pour les émigrants. Il existe un département gouvernemental chargé de l'aide aux émigrants et à leur retour: l'Institut d'Aide à l'Emigration et aux Communautés Portugaises du Ministère des Affaires Etrangères.

Par rapport à l'immigration d'étrangers, il n'existe pas encore de politique définie. Jusqu'à présent, le pays n'a pas connu d'importants problèmes de ce genre: le petit nombre d'étrangers et leurs liens avec le Portugal favorisent une bonne tolérance institutionnelle. La plupart des permis de séjour demandés sont accordés et plusieurs séjours irréguliers ont leur régularisation facilitée - s'il existe, dans les deux cas, la garantie de moyens de subsistance. Les naturalisations ainsi que les acquisitions de nationalité ne sont pas très restrictives. La législation qui règle l'acquisition de la nationalité est du type du "droit du sol": les individus nés au Portugal, de parents étrangers, peuvent être portugais si leurs parents résident dans le pays depuis 6 ans, ne sont pas au service de leur Etat et déclarent que c'est leur intention. Il existe, encore, des coopérations bilatérales avec les pays d'origine des immigrants, semblables à celles que le Portugal a souscrites à la position contraire. L'appréciation des demandes de permis de séjour ainsi que l'accompagnement des étrangers sont à la charge d'un département spécifique: le Service des Etrangers et des Frontières du Ministère de l'Administration Interne.

BIBLIOGRAPHIE

Alarcao, A. et J. Pais Morais (1974), La population du Portugal, CICRED

Carrilho, M.J. (1991), "Aspectos demograficos e sociais da populaçao portuguesa no periodo 1864-1981: evoluçao global no Continente português", Estudos Demograficos, 30

Conim, C. (1975/1976), "Algumas consideraçoes sobre a situaçao demografica portuguesa de 1960 a 1975", Revista do Centro de Estudos Demograficos, 22

Evangelista, J. (1970), Um século de populaçao portuguesa, Lisboa, INE / Centro de Estudos Demograficos

Instituto Nacional de Estatistica (INE), Anuarios Demograficos, Estatisticas Demograficas, Recenseamentos Gerais da Populaçao e Folhas de Divulgaçao

Nazareth, J.M. (1985), "A demografia portuguesa no século XX: principais linhas de evoluçao e transformaçao", Analise Social, 87-88-89

(1990), "Le Portugal", in W. Dumon (Ed.), Family policy in EEC countries, Comission of the European Communities

(1991), "Portugal na Europa Comunitaria no final dos anos oitenta", Estudos Demograficos, 30

Neto, M.L. (1971), "Demografia", in J. Serrao (Org.), Dicionario de Historia de Portugal, Vol.I, Lisboa, Iniciativas Editoriais

Serrao, J. (1977), A emigraçao portuguesa. Sondagem historica, Lisboa, Horizonte, 3 ed.

Le Luxembourg/Luxembourg
Jean LANGERS

Le Luxembourg existe dans sa forme territoriale actuelle depuis 1839. Sa superficie est de 2 586 km^2 et les pays limitrophes sont la Belgique, l'Allemagne et la France.

1) Poids des migrations dans l'évolution démographique

Les flux migratoires tant vers l'étranger qu'en provenance de l'étranger ont fortement marqué l'histoire démographique du Luxembourg. Au cours du dernier siècle, de nombreux Luxembourgeois quittent leur pays, souvent poussés par le manque de perspectives qu'offre une économie agricole peu développée. Cette vague d'émigration qui s'est étendue de 1825 à la 1re guerre mondiale, diminue cependant nettement après 1890. On estime qu'entre 1839 et 1891, le nombre de départs s'est élevé à quelque 65 000 personnes, l'immigration étant restée négligeable. Pour l'ensemble de cette période, le taux d'émigration annuel moyen aurait été d'environ 7 p. mille.

L'implantation d'une puissante industrie sidérurgique lors des dernières décennies du 19e siècle engendre une forte demande de main-d'oeuvre qui est satisfaite par la venue de nombreux étrangers (Allemands, puis Italiens). En effet durant cette période, les Luxembourgeois se sont montrés peu enclins à occuper ces emplois.

A partir de cette époque les fluctuations économiques (et les deux guerres mondiales) rythment les flux migratoires. Ainsi la 1re guerre mondiale et la récession survenue au lendemain du conflit ont obligé de nombreux étrangers à retourner dans leurs pays d'origine.

Un fort afflux de travailleurs étrangers caractérise la période suivante (1922 - 1930) marquée par la reprise économique et l'extension de la sidérurgie. Le solde migratoire (+22 300) dépassera largement le solde naturel (+15 000).

La tendance se renverse de nouveau avec la crise mondiale des années trente et la 2e guerre mondiale, les départs devenant largement supérieurs aux arrivées (- 25 000 entre 1930 et 1945).

Depuis la fin de la 2e guerre mondiale, on assiste à une immigration massive entraînant un accroissement pratiquement continu de la population de résidence et ceci malgré l'apparition de soldes naturels très faibles, voire négatifs. La population est passée de 283 000 habitants en 1946 à plus de 380 000 en 1990, les soldes naturel et migratoire ayant été de respectivement 25 000 et 72 000.

I. LA POPULATION DU LUXEMBOURG JUSQU'A LA SECONDE GUERRE MONDIALE

1) Grandes étapes de l'évolution démographique

1839 - 1890 : croissance relativement faible

Avec des taux de natalité généralement compris entre 35 p. mille et 30 p. mille et des taux de mortalité se situant entre 20 p. mille et 25 p. mille, la population du Luxembourg aurait pu connaître des taux d'accroissement annuels moyens légèrement supérieurs à 10 p. mille. Mais un important mouvement d'émigration les a ramenés à environ 4 p. mille.

1890 - 1914 : accélération de la croissance

Un net ralentissement de l'émigration ainsi que l'arrivée de travailleurs étrangers attirés par le développement de la sidérurgie aboutissent à des flux migratoires équilibrés. Durant ces années, la population a donc augmenté au rythme de l'accroissement naturel. Les taux de natalité avoisinent toujours 30 p. mille (avec cependant une tendance à la baisse à partir de 1910) et les taux de mortalité s'élèvent en moyenne à quelque 20 p. mille (aux alentours de 1905 ils tombent durablement au-dessous de ce seuil).

Pour l'ensemble de la période, le taux d'accroissement annuel moyen a atteint donc quelque 1 %.

TABLEAU 1.- EVOLUTION DE LA POPULATION TOTALE

Année	Population	
	en milliers	1840 = 100
1840	171	100
1865	203	119
1891	212	124
1900	235	137
1914	266	156
1922	262	153
1930	300	175
1935	297	174
1940	299	175

1915 - 1922 : Diminution de la population

Par suite du retour de nombreux étrangers dans leur pays d'origine et, à partir de 1916, d'un affaissement de l'accroissement naturel (des soldes négatifs ont même pu être enregistrés en 1917 et 1918), la population a régressé. Le mouvement à la baisse de la natalité amorcé dès 1910 s'est renforcé, les taux devenant inférieurs à 20 p. mille. Les soldes négatifs des deux dernières années du conflit résultent d'une brusque remontée de la mortalité. La récession économique de l'après-guerre ayant incité beaucoup d'étrangers à quitter le pays, la progression du nombre de naissances qui est allée de pair avec un net recul de la mortalité n'a pas entraîné d'augmentation de la population au cours des années 1919-22.

1923 - 1930 : Croissance démographique record

L'arrivée, liée à la reprise économique, d'un grand nombre de travailleurs étrangers, le léger relèvement de la natalité ainsi que la confirmation de la tendance à la baisse de la mortalité sont à l'origine d'une croissance exceptionnelle : + 1,7 % de moyenne annuelle, dont 1 % au titre de l'immigration nette. De 13 % en 1922, la part des étrangers monte à 19 % en 1930.

1931 - 1940 : Période de stagnation

Dès 1931, la crise mondiale entraîne des départs massifs conduisant à une émigration nette qui dépassera 9 000 personnes pour les années 1931 - 1935. Une nouvelle chute de la natalité fait descendre les taux afférents au palier des 15 p. mille. En raison de nouvelles diminutions de la mortalité, les soldes naturels restent positifs, de sorte que la population reste pratiquement stable en dépit des nombreuses sorties d'étrangers.

2) Les étapes de la baisse de la natalité et de la mortalité

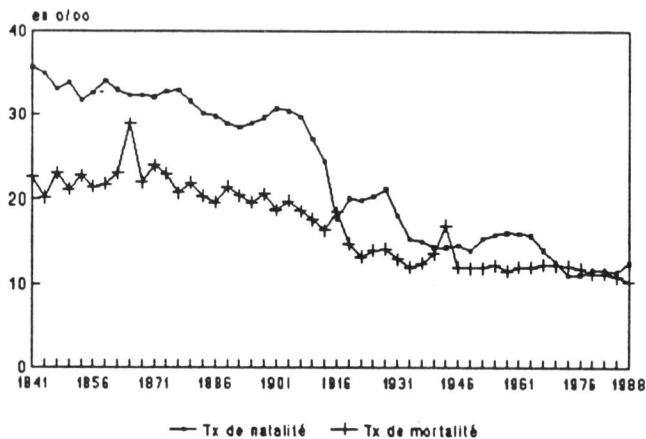

Figure 1.- Taux de natalité et de mortalité (1841-1990)

En considérant les taux de natalité plusieurs phases peuvent être distinguées :

- Jusque vers 1885, ils demeurent supérieurs à 30 p. mille;

- Les vingt années suivantes sont marquées par de légères fluctuations autour de 30 p. mille. Il semble bien que les taux sont devenus inférieurs à 30 p. mille durant les années 1886 à 1889.

- Lors d'une troisième phase, allant jusqu'à la fin de la guerre, la baisse devient manifeste. Entre 1916 et 1919, les taux n'atteignent même plus 20 p. mille.

- Au cours des années vingt, la natalité remonte pour se fixer à un niveau d'environ 21 p. mille.

- C'est probablement la crise de 1930 qui est à l'origine d'une nouvelle régression qui amène les taux à environ 15 p. mille.

A partir de 1871, on peut, pour les années censitaires, calculer le taux de fécondité générale (nombre de naissances rapporté aux effectifs féminins en âge de procréer : 15 à 49 ans).

La chute de la fécondité apparaît clairement. En 1930 l'indicateur retenu n'atteint même plus la moitié des niveaux relevés avant la 1re guerre mondiale.

TABLEAU 2.- EVOLUTION DU TAUX BRUT DE NATALITE

Période	Taux (p. mille)	Période	Taux (p. mille)
1841-1845	35,8	1915 - 1919	18,4
1846-1886	32,5	1920 - 1931	20,6
1887-1908	29,5	1932 - 1940	15,4
1909-1914	26,9		

TABLEAU 3.- EVOLUTION DU TAUX DE FECONDITE GENERALE

Année	Taux (pour 1 000 femmes)	Année	Taux (pour 1 000 femmes)
1871	131,8	1905	127,8
1875	126,6	1907	132,6
1880	135,1	1910	116,8
1885	127,5	1922	74,5
1890	120,6	1930	81,2
1900	126,1	1935	57,9

Les taux de mortalité n'ont, eux, commencé à baisser qu'à partir du début de ce siècle pour se stabiliser durant les années précédant la 2e guerre mondiale.

- L'examen des taux du XIXe siècle ne laisse pas apparaître d'orientation vers la baisse. La plupart du temps, ils sont restés légèrement supérieurs à 20 p. mille avec des pointes (par exemple jusqu'à 40 p. mille en 1866) dues à des épidémies.

- Un premier mouvement de recul a lieu entre 1900 et 1916.

- Après une brève remontée en 1917, 1918 et 1919, due aux privations de la guerre, les taux baissent fortement pour atteindre des niveaux proches de ceux que l'on a pu observer jusqu'à une époque récente.

La baisse de la mortalité infantile a été longue à se dessiner, les premiers signes n'apparaissant que durant la période 1916-1920 (l'accroissement de la mortalité des années 1917-1919 n'a donc affecté que les adultes). A partir de ce moment, la situation s'améliore continuellement. Du début du siècle à l'immédiat avant-guerre, le nombre de décès de moins d'un an pour 1000 naissances vivantes passe de 159 à 71.

TABLEAU 4.- EVOLUTION DES TAUX BRUTS DE MORTALITE

Période	Taux (p. mille)	Période	Taux (p. mille)
1840-1900	22,1	1917-1919	19,2
1901-1909	19,1	1920-1930	13,7
1910-1916	16,8	1931-1940	12,4

TABLEAU 5.- EVOLUTION DU TAUX DE MORTALITE INFANTILE

Période	Taux (p. mille)	Période	Taux (p. mille)
1876-1880	149,3	1921-1925	110,4
1901-1905	158,6	1926-1930	107,6
1906-1910	156,1	1931-1935	85,6
1911-1915	146,1	1936-1940	71,2
1916-1920	127,8		

Les premières indications sur les espérances de vie remontent au début du XXe siècle. Si la hausse des espérances de vie à la naissance survenue durant les quarante premières années peut paraître considérable, des comparaisons internationales montrent que le Luxembourg se classe en médiocre position. Entre les périodes 1901-1905 et 1936-1940, elle a augmenté de 45,4 ans à 58,9 ans chez les hommes et 48,3 ans à 62,7 ans chez les femmes.

TABLEAU 6.- EVOLUTION DE L'ESPERANCE DE VIE A LA NAISSANCE

Période	Hommes	Femmes
1901-1905	45,4	48,3
1911-1915	47,4	51,6
1921-1925	53,6	57,6
1936-1940	58,9	62,7

II. LA POPULATION DU LUXEMBOURG DEPUIS LA DERNIERE GUERRE MONDIALE

Immigration et croissance démographique

Au début des années quatre-vingt-dix, le nombre d'habitants du Grand-Duché dépasse de près d'un tiers celui de l'immédiat après-guerre (+93 000). L'immigration nette n'est pas loin de représenter les trois quarts de cet accroissement, l'excédent des naissances sur les décès étant relativement faible, principalement en raison du nombre réduit des naissances. De 10% en 1947, la part des étrangers a atteint de 27% vers 1990, chiffre encore jamais atteint dans l'histoire démographique luxembourgeoise.

1) L'Après-guerre : Faible reprise de la natalité et baisse sensible de la mortalité

Si le baby-boom des 20 années qui ont suivi la fin de la dernière guerre, a pu être observé également au Luxembourg, il n'en reste pas moins vrai que la remontée de la natalité a été beaucoup plus limitée que dans la plupart des autres pays. Le nombre des naissances a été le plus élevé entre le milieu des années 50 et le milieu des années 60, avec des taux de natalité se situant autour de 16 p. mille. Ce n'est que durant cette période que l'indicateur conjoncturel de fécondité dépasse le seuil de remplacement. Signalons, à titre de comparaison, que, dans l'immédiat après-guerre (1946 - 1949), cet indice avoisine 3 enfants par femme en France alors qu'il n'est que légèrement supérieur à 1,9 au Luxembourg.

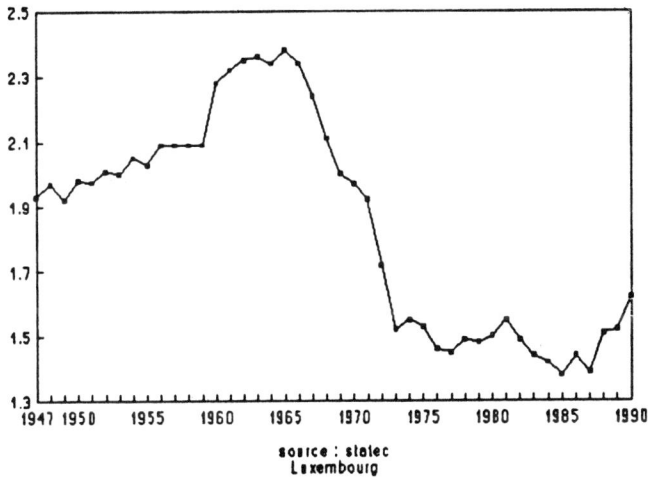

Figure 2.- Indicateur conjoncturel de fécondité (1947-1990)

Durant la période considérée, la mortalité a régressé, l'espérance de vie à la naissance passant de 61,5 ans (1946-49) à 66,0 ans (1960-64) chez les hommes et de 65,6 ans à 72,4 ans chez les femmes.

Même si elle a nettement reculé, la mortalité infantile est restée assez élevée avec des taux moyens d'environ 60 p. mille vers 1946-49 et d'environ 30 p. mille vers 1960-64.

2) Evolution démographique récente

a) Fécondité

La chute de l'indicateur conjoncturel de fécondité débute vers 1968/69, le creux de la vague étant atteint durant les années 1983-87 avec, en moyenne, 1,4 enfant par femme. Un relèvement non négligeable a été enregistré ces deux dernières années, les indicateurs considérés passant de 1,52 en 1989 à 1,62 en 1990. Cette augmentation de la fécondité étant allée de pair avec l'arrivée aux âges à pleine fécondité des classes nombreuses nées entre 1959 et 1965, une importante hausse du nombre de naissances s'en est suivie.

Au Luxembourg, la fécondité est marquée par des différences non négligeables entre autochtones et étrangères, ces dernières représentant à peu près un tiers de la population en âge de procréer. Dans le passé, les niveaux de fécondité des étrangères ont toujours été nettement supérieurs à ceux des Luxembourgeoises. Ainsi par exemple en 1970, les ICF se sont élevés à respectivement 1,88 et 2,37. Celui des femmes luxembourgeoises est même descendu jusqu'à 1,20 en 1976. Mais au cours des vingt dernières années, les deux fécondités se sont sensiblement rapprochées. Suite à un changement de législation accordant automatiquement la nationalité luxembourgeoise à des enfants nés d'un père étranger et d'une mère luxembourgeoise (alors qu'ils étaient considérés auparavant comme étrangers), la fécondité des étrangères était même devenue, à un moment donné, inférieure à celle des Luxembourgeoises. Toutefois en recalculant les taux selon l'ancienne législation, les résultats s'inversent : la fécondité des étrangères redevient plus élevée. Reste que l'écart s'est nettement rétréci. Cela n'a d'ailleurs rien d'étonnant, la majorité des étrangères étant originaires de pays comme l'Italie ou le Portugal où la fécondité a diminué de façon parfois spectaculaire.

TABLEAU 7.- INDICATEUR CONJONCTUREL DE FECONDITE 1964 - 1990

Année	ICF	Année	ICF	Année	ICF
1964	2,34	1973	1,52	1982	1,49
1965	2,38	1974	1,55	1983	1,44
1966	2,34	1975	1,53	1984	1,42
1967	2,24	1976	1,46	1985	1,38
1968	2,11	1977	1,45	1986	1,44
1969	2,00	1978	1,49	1987	1,39
1970	1,97	1979	1,48	1988	1,51
1971	1,92	1980	1,50	1989	1,52
1972	1,72	1981	1,55	1990	1,62

Si la chute de la fécondité a affecté l'ensemble des groupes d'âges, elle a été particulièrement forte aux jeunes âges. Entre 15 et 19 ans, les taux n'atteignent plus que le tiers du niveau de 1965; moins de la moitié dans le groupe d'âges suivant. Le recul a été beaucoup moins important aux âges compris entre 25 et 34 ans où l'on a également enregistré les hausses les plus importantes lors de la récente remontée.

Les changements décrits plus haut aboutissent donc à une élévation de l'âge à la maternité.

TABLEAU 8 : TAUX DE FECONDITE PAR GROUPE D'AGES.

Année	Taux de fécondité (p. mille)					
	15-19	20-24	25-29	30-34	35-39	40-44
1965	32,1	157,1	153,5	84,7	39,2	10,1
1970	27,7	132,1	126,6	64,6	33,1	9,3
1980	16,7	86,0	111,3	62,9	18,6	4,0
1985	10,7	72,6	104,8	66,2	19,3	2,7
1989	11,1	72,4	118,2	76,6	25,3	2,9
Année	1965 = 100,0					
	15-19	20-24	25-29	30-34	35-39	40-44
1965	100,0	100,0	100,0	100,0	100,0	100,0
1970	86,3	84,1	82,5	76,3	84,4	92,1
1980	52,0	54,7	72,5	74,3	47,4	39,6
1985	33,3	46,2	68,3	78,2	49,2	26,7
1989	34,6	46,1	77,0	90,4	64,5	28,7

En ce qui concerne la descendance finale, les données disponibles restent malheureusement fragmentaires et pour le moment, on n'a que des évaluations provisoires pour les groupes de générations (1941-1945) et (1946-1950). Aucune d'entre elles n'a très vraisemblablement atteint le seuil de remplacement, les valeurs moyennes s'élevant à respectivement 1,95 et 1,85. Pour les générations 1951 à 1955 on dispose d'une première estimation donnant un indice de 1,65.

b) Nuptialité et divortialité

Ces 25 dernières années, la nuptialité des célibataires a fortement baissé comme le montrent les chiffres se rapportant à la somme des premiers mariages réduits. En 1986, elle n'est plus que de 0,527 chez les hommes et de 0,528 chez les femmes. Un mouvement vers la hausse a commencé à se dessiner à partir de 1988.

TABLEAU 9.- SOMME DES PREMIERS MARIAGES REDUITS[1]

Année	Hommes	Femmes
1965	0,879	0,948
1970	0,837	0,870
1975	0,852	0,799
1980	0,653	0,661
1985	0,545	0,566
1986	0,527	0,528
1987	0,526	0,555
1988	0,553	0,591
1989	0,571	0,614
1990	0,595	0,653

[1] Les mariages de célibataires sont rapportés à la population totale

Même si des données précises font défaut, tout indique que la cohabitation hors mariage se développe également au Luxembourg. La progression de la part des naissances hors mariage constitue un indice. Avant 1970, elle s'est située en moyenne entre 3 et 4 %, durant les années soixante-dix elle a légèrement augmenté jusqu'à 5 %. Depuis 1980 l'accroissement est quasi continu et le taux de 13 % a été atteint en 1990.

Le nombre de divorces n'a cessé d'augmenter depuis la deuxième moitié des années soixante-dix. Ainsi en 1989, il y a eu 855 divorces pour 2 184 mariages. Cette hausse de la divortialité est attestée par l'évolution de la somme des divorces réduits qui est passée de 0,058 en 1960 à 0,333 en 1987.

c) Mortalité

Tout en se maintenant à des niveaux relativement élevés, la mortalité a continué de baisser durant la période considérée. Chez les hommes, l'espérance de vie à la naissance est passée de 66,5 ans vers 1961-63 à 70,6 ans au cours des années 1985-87, les valeurs ayant été de respectivement 72,2 ans et 77,9 ans chez les femmes.

TABLEAU 10.- ESPERANCE DE VIE A LA NAISSANCE

Période	Hommes	Femmes
1961-63	66,5	72,2
1970-72	67,1	73,4
1980-82	70,0	76,7
1985-87	70,6	77,9

TABLEAU 11.- ESPERANCES DE VIE A 60 ANS ET A 80 ANS

Période	Hommes		Femmes	
	e_{60}	e_{80}	e_{60}	e_{80}
1945-51	15,2	5,0	16,9	5,4
1961-63	15,5	5,4	18,3	6,1
1970-72	15,2	5,4	18,8	6,1
1980-82	16,0	5,5	20,6	6,8
1985-87	16,4	5,4	21,3	6,3

Les niveaux nettement plus élevés de l'espérance de vie à la naissance observés durant les années 1980 s'expliquent en grande partie par un important recul de la mortalité infantile qui a régressé de 30 p. mille à moins de 10 p. mille dans l'intervalle de temps pris en compte.

TABLEAU 12.- TAUX DE MORTALITE INFANTILE

Année	Décès de moins d'un an pour 1 000 naissances	Année	Décès de moins d'un an pour 1 000 naissances
1960	31,5	1979	13,0
1965	24,1	1980	11,6
		1981	14,1
1970	24,8	1982	12,0
1971	22,6	1983	11,2
1972	13,6	1984	11,7
1973	14,9	1985	9,0
1974	13,7	1986	8,0
1975	14,9	1987	9,3
1976	17,8	1988	9,0
1977	10,7	1989	11,7
1978	10,6	1990	7,4

En ce qui concerne maintenant l'évolution de la mortalité aux âges élevés, il ressort des chiffres présentés (couvrant les 40 dernières années) que ce sont surtout les femmes qui ont bénéficié d'une augmentation des espérances de vie. A soixante ans, le gain s'est élevé à 4,4 ans ; il a encore été de près d'une année à 80 ans. Pour le sexe masculin il a été beaucoup plus faible avec 1,2 an et 0,4 an. L'écart entre les deux sexes s'est donc encore creusé.

d) Mouvement de la population depuis 1960

La croissance démographique des 30 années écoulées a eu un profil assez irrégulier : de fortes expansions alternent avec des développements plus modérés. Partant de deux composantes du mouvement de la population (naturel et migratoire), une certaine périodisation devient possible.

TABLEAU 13.- CROISSANCE DEMOGRAPHIQUE 1960 - 1990 (événements en milliers et taux pour 1000)

Date	Population (en milliers)	Moyenne annuelle de la période				
		Naissances	Décès	Accrt. naturel	Migration nette	Accrt. total
1-1-1961	314,9					
		5,2	3,9	1,3	2,0	3,3
		16,0	12,0	4,0	6,2	10,2
1-1-1967	334,8					
		4,6	4,1	0,5	1,0	1,5
		13,7	12,2	1,5	3,0	4,5
1-1-1971	339,8					
		4,0	4,3	-0,3	4,4	4,1
		11,4	12,3	-0,9	12,6	11,7
1-1-1976	360,4					
		4,1	4,1	0	0,7	0,7
		11,3	11,3	0,0	1,9	1,9
1-1-1986	367,2					
		4,5	3,9	0,6	2,2	2,8
		12,1	10,5	1,6	5,9	7,5
1-1-1990	378,4					

1961-1966 : Une natalité relativement élevée dégageant des soldes naturels positifs ainsi qu'une immigration nette importante aboutissent à une croissance annuelle moyenne dépassant 1 %.

1967-1970 : Une natalité en recul, une mortalité en légère hausse réduisent l'accroissement naturel. L'immigration nette connaissant également un ralentissement, l'augmentation annuelle de la population diminue de moitié par rapport à la période précédente.

1971-1975 : Bien que les décès soient devenus plus nombreux que les naissances, le nombre d'habitants s'accroît sensiblement en raison d'un afflux massif d'étrangers.

1976-1985 : Un solde naturel pratiquement nul et une immigration nette peu importante engendrent une croissance peu élevée.

LE LUXEMBOURG/LUXEMBOURG

1986-1990 : Remontée de la natalité, mortalité en baisse, des arrivées de l'étranger en hausse : la croissance démographique reprend.

A noter que durant l'ensemble de la période, le solde migratoire moyen dépassait le solde naturel moyen.

e) Evolution de la structure par âge 1960 - 1990

TABLEAU 14.- STRUCTURE PAR AGE (1960 - 1990) (EN %)

Indice	1960	1966	1970	1975	1980	1985	1990
moins de 20 ans	28,5	30,2	30,6	27,8	26,6	24,5	23,2
20-59 ans	56,6	54,0	53,0	53,8	55,7	57,3	57,9
60 ans et plus	14,9	15,8	16,4	18,4	17,7	18,3	18,9
Indice de dépendance 60 ans +/20-59 ans	26,3	29,3	30,9	34,2	31,8	31,9	32,6
Indice de dépendance (0-19)+(60+)/20-59 ans	76,7	85,2	88,7	85,9	79,5	74,7	72,7

L'évolution de l'indice de jeunesse est largement tributaire de celle du nombre de naissances : hausse de l'indice à la suite de l'accroissement des naissances entre 1956 et 1966, chute, entraînée par le recul de la natalité, à partir de 1975.

Sur l'ensemble de la période, la tendance à l'augmentation de la proportion des personnes âgées de 60 ans et plus est manifeste.

La part de la population en âge de travailler s'est fortement accrue ces vingt dernières années en raison de la venue massive de travailleurs étrangers.

Le rapport entre le groupe des "60 ans et plus" et celui des "20 à 59 ans" fournit une première indication sur la charge représentée par les retraités. Au Luxembourg, la signification de cet indice se rapportant aux seuls résidents est limitée par deux facteurs :

- le groupe des "60 ans et plus" ne comprend pas les personnes qui, quittant le Luxembourg à la fin de leur vie active, reçoivent leurs pensions à l'étranger;

- le groupe des "20 à 59 ans" ne tient pas compte des frontaliers, qui, bien que résidant à l'étranger, cotisent à la Sécurité sociale luxembourgeoise.

L'autre indice de dépendance qui intègre également les jeunes, considérés comme inactifs, a, dans un premier temps, fortement progressé jusqu'à atteindre près de 90 %

vers 1970. Depuis il est en baisse à cause de la diminution du poids des jeunes et de l'augmentation de celui des personnes en âge de travailler.

III. ASPECTS DE LA POLITIQUE DE POPULATION

1) Politique familiale

La politique familiale avant 1970 était plutôt considérée comme un élément composant de la politique sociale. Le côté démographique (natalité) n'était certes pas ignoré mais il ne jouait qu'un rôle mineur. Toutefois, lors de l'introduction des allocations de naissances des arguments démographiques furent avancés.

La forte chute de la natalité dans la population de nationalité luxembourgeoise à partir des années 1970, a cependant amené les gouvernements successifs à s'occuper de façon plus intensive de politique de population. Ainsi, en 1976 et 1989, Monsieur Gérard Calot, directeur de l'INED, fut chargé d'analyser la situation et de proposer des remèdes à la dénatalité.

Les premières mesures en faveur des familles furent prises au cours de la première guerre mondiale avec l'introduction d'indemnités familiales dans la fonction publique (loi du 8 août 1916). Ces dispositions furent alors également appliquées dans la sidérurgie. La généralisation de ce régime pour l'ensemble des salariés n'a eu lieu qu'en 1947. Plus tard, en 1954, une nouvelle mesure législative a étendu le bénéfice de ces allocations aux non salariés.

Une complète uniformisation du système n'a eu lieu qu'en 1964. Le fait que l'on ait mis 50 ans pour y arriver montre bien que les préoccupations natalistes ne dominaient pas.

En matière d'imposition, les premières dispositions remontent à 1927 où un système assez rudimentaire (bonification uniforme pour chaque descendant ou ascendant à charge) de réductions d'impôts fut mis en place. Au cours des années des améliorations y furent apportées et la dernière réforme, entrée en application le 1er janvier 1991, assure de nettes réductions d'impôts aux couples avec enfants.

Après la 2e guerre mondiale, fut créé, en 1947, un système d'allocations de naissance. La législation afférente a été profondément modifiée en 1977 en liant l'attribution de l'allocation à l'obligation de passer un contrôle médical systématique. Par la même occasion, leur montant a été augmenté de 50 %.

La panoplie de mesures en faveur des familles fut complétée, en 1986, par une allocation de rentrée scolaire dont bénéficient les enfants faisant partie d'un groupe familial de deux enfants ou plus.

Toutes ces allocations sont indexées sur le coût de la vie.

Signalons encore les congés de maternité de 4 mois (5 mois en cas d'allaitement) accordés aux femmes occupant un emploi salarié. Ces mesures furent, dans une certaine mesure, étendues aux mères non-salariées auxquelles une allocation forfaitaire est allouée durant cette même période.

2) *Contraception et avortement*

Il n'existe pas de législation spécifique pour les contraceptifs. Ceux qui se prennent par la voie orale sont considérés comme des médicaments et tombent sous la législation générale concernant les médicaments. Un arrêté ministériel de 1963 les classe parmi les spécialités pharmaceutiques qui ne peuvent être délivrées que sur ordonnance médicale. Aux termes d'une loi datant de 1958 toute publicité en faveur des médicaments ayant un effet anticonceptionnel est interdite. Les contraceptifs ne tombant pas sous la législation des médicaments ne sont pas réglementés. Le Gouvernement accorde des subventions importantes au "Planning familial" qui a des centres de consultations dans plusieures localités du pays.

Les dispositions du Code pénal interdisant l'avortement furent abrogées par la loi du 15 novembre 1978 qui stipule que l'interruption volontaire de la grossesse pratiquée dans les douze premières semaines de celle-ci ne sera pas punissable lorsque la poursuite de la grossesse, ou les conditions de vie que pourrait entraîner la naissance, risquent de mettre en danger la santé physique ou psychique de la femme enceinte. Il en sera de même, lorsqu'il existe un risque sérieux que l'enfant à naître sera atteint d'une maladie grave, de malformations physiques ou d'altérations psychiques importantes. Un dernier cas prévu par la loi concerne les grossesses qui sont la conséquence d'un viol.

Il n'existe pas de statistiques sur le nombre annuel d'interruptions pratiquées.

3) *Le divorce*

Cette matière était régie par le "Code Napoléon" et la législation était donc assez proche de celle en vigueur en France. Au Luxembourg, la possibilité du divorce par consentement mutuel avait cependant été maintenue, même si une procédure longue et fastidieuse visait à en limiter l'utilisation. C'était justement pour faciliter l'obtention du divorce par consentement mutuel que la loi du 6 février 1975 a modifié les articles en question du Code civil. Une nouvelle loi, en date du 5 décembre 1978, introduisit la possibilité de demander le divorce après une séparation de fait de 3 ans. Il semble bien que ces lois aient produit leurs effets. A partir de 1976, on a assisté à une montée considérable du nombre de divorces par consentement mutuel qui représentent aujourd'hui environ la moitié de l'ensemble des divorces prononcés par les tribunaux. La part de ceux où une séparation de fait de trois ans est invoquée se situe autour de 10 %.

4) *Immigration et acquisition de la nationalité luxembourgeoise*

Jusqu'en 1972 l'entrée et le séjour des étrangers au Luxembourg étaient réglementés principalement par une loi de 1893 qui fixait les cas dans lesquels l'entrée et l'établissement pouvaient être refusés à un ressortissant étranger et qui énumérait les causes pouvant justifier son expulsion.

Un arrêté grand-ducal, pris en 1934, sur la base d'une loi de 1920, ayant pour objet de limiter l'arrivée d'étrangers sur le territoire du Grand-Duché, a précisé les conditions de l'établissement des étrangers et les soumettait à l'obligation de la carte de séjour. Cette dernière devait être sollicitée par tout étranger qui se proposait de résider au Grand-Duché pendant plus de 3 mois.

La réglementation de l'emploi de travailleurs étrangers remonte, pour l'essentiel, à un arrêté grand-ducal de 1929 fixant les conditions à remplir par les salariés de nationalité étrangère pour l'embauchage. Ce texte plutôt restrictif a été modifié parce que, d'une part, il était entré en contradiction avec la réglementation de la CE sur la libre circulation des travailleurs et parce que, d'autre part, il était dépassé par l'évolution économique caractérisée par des besoins grandissants de main-d'oeuvre.

La situation sur le marché de l'emploi étant devenu le principal facteur d'appréciation concernant l'admission d'un travailleur étranger, il était logique de charger l'Office National du Travail (devenu en 1976 l'Administration nationale de l'emploi) de délivrer le permis de travail remplaçant l'ancienne autorisation d'embauchage accordée à l'employeur.

La quasi-totalité des travailleurs provenant des pays de la CE, c'est la législation communautaire qui de fait régit cette matière. Durant une période transitoire, une réglementation spéciale va rester en vigueur en ce qui concerne les ressortissants portugais.

Les règles relatives à la nationalité luxembourgeoise se sont dégagées au cours du dernier siècle d'un ensemble de dispositions reposant parfois sur des conceptions différentes. Les articles afférentes du code civil s'inspiraient du principe de la filiation, tout en admettant dans certains cas celui de la territorialité, alors que la loi fondamentale des Pays-Bas de 1815 (en vigueur jusqu'en 1839) s'attachait principalement au critère de la territorialité. Cette double empreinte a continué de marquer les textes qui sont venus modifier par la suite les dipositions du code civil.

D'autre part, le régime des naturalisations a fait l'objet de lois particulières.

Actuellement, les conditions et les modalités de l'acquisition de la nationalité luxembourgeoise sont réglées par la loi du 11 décembre 1986 qui a assoupli les conditions d'acquisition de la nationalité par un abaissement significatif de l'âge requis pour présenter la demande de naturalisation ou par la possibilité donnée à un enfant, même né à l'étranger d'opter pour la nationalité luxembourgeoise s'il a accompli sa scolarité obligatoire au Luxembourg. Autre innovation basée sur le principe de l'égalité entre l'homme et la femme au niveau de la transmission de la nationalité : les enfants d'une mère luxembourgeoise et d'un père étranger auront dorénavant la nationalité luxembourgeoise, alors que sous le régime antérieur ils étaient considérés comme étrangers. C'est le caractère rétroactif de cette disposition qui a fait entrer 3 330 enfants mineurs étrangers dans la population luxembourgeoise au 1er janvier 1987.

En s'en tenant aux possibilités les plus courantes, on devient Luxembourgeois :

- par naturalisation : si l'on a atteint l'âge de dix-huit ans et si l'on a résidé dans le Grand-Duché pendant dix ans à condition que pendant les cinq dernières années cette résidence n'ait pas subi d'interruption. La résidence obligatoire est réduite à cinq ans lorsque celui qui sollicite la naturalisation est né sur le sol luxembourgeois ou s'il a eu la qualité de Luxembourgeois et l'a perdue (d'autres cas, sur lesquels nous ne nous étendrons pas ici, existent).

- par option : si l'on est né dans le pays d'un auteur étranger; si l'on est né à l'étranger d'un auteur ayant eu la qualité de Luxembourgeois d'origine; si l'on épouse un Luxembourgeois. La déclaration d'option doit être faite entre l'âge de dix-huit et vingt-cinq ans révolus.

Entre 700 et 1 000 étrangers acquièrent chaque année la nationalité luxembourgeoise.

BIBLIOGRAPHIE

Statistiques : "Statistiques historiques 1839-1989" STATEC Luxembourg 1990.

Etudes :

ALS (Georges) "La population du Luxembourg" STATEC Luxembourg 1975 195 p.

CALOT (Gérard) "La démographie du Luxembourg, passé, présent et avenir" STATEC Luxembourg 1978 165 p.

CALOT (Gérard) et CHESNAIS (Jean-Claude) "L'évolution démographique au Grand-Duché de Luxembourg" STATEC Luxembourg 1991.

Sweden/La Suède
Peter SPRINGFELDT

I.- POPULATION DEVELOPMENT IN A 200-YEAR PERSPECTIVE

Swedish population statistics have a long history with roots in church registers. As early as the 17th century, the local clergy fairly widely began to register births, deaths, and later the number of people in the parish. The Church Law of 1686 made it compulsory for the clergy to keep these records. These registers started being used for statistical purposes when Tabellverket, a national volume of statistical tables, was established in 1749. It is possible though to track some population figures back in time another ten years or so. This means that there is an unbroken series of annual population statistics for a period of time close to two and one-half centuries.

1) The Demographic Transition

The first, pretransitional, phase can be said to cover the period up to 1810. During this period, both the average fertility and death rates show wide variations from year to year (33 births and 27 deaths per 1000 of the population). In some cases the deaths exceed the births, resulting in a temporary population decrease. This happened in the years 1741-43 and is explained by war, failure of the harvest, and famine, in the years 1772-73 (a failed harvest followed by starvation), and in the years 1808-09 (war and dysentery).

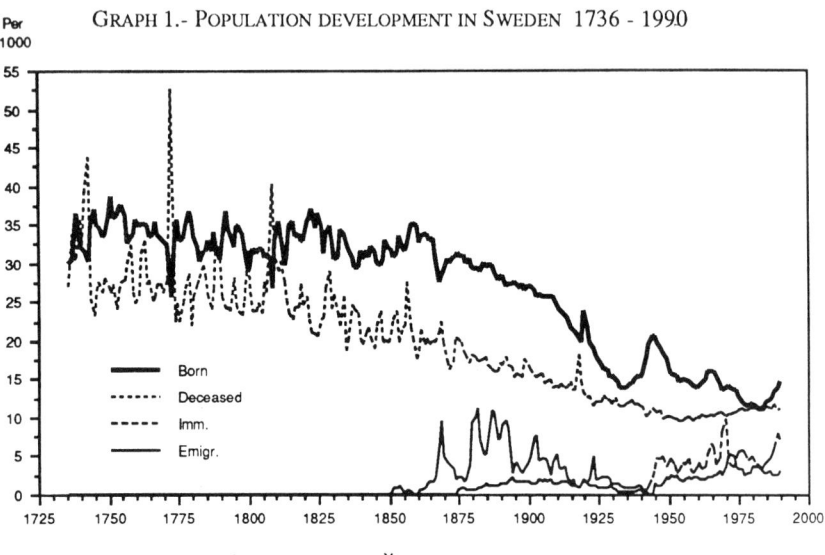

GRAPH 1.- POPULATION DEVELOPMENT IN SWEDEN 1736 - 1990

During the first half of the 18th century, the annual population growth was about 0.7 per cent. At the turn of the century, it had slowed to about 0.5 per cent. The total fertility rate was about 4.5 children per woman for the whole century (4.9 around 1750, see below).

The second phase in the population development, between 1810 and 1870, is the real first demographically transitional phase with a declining death rate. The decline in mortality starts with diminishing death rates for children and women. It is not until about the middle of the century that death risks also starts to fall among adult men . The large earlier annual variations are here replaced by a calmer development, and there is no year when the death rate exceeds the birth rate. The death rate decreases during the period from about 25 to 20, while the birth rate varies between 30 and 35 per 1000 persons. The decline in mortality results in an increase in population growth and at the end of the period this growth is slightly higher than 1 per cent per year.

The period between 1870 and 1930 can be seen as a third phase in the transition. The start of the period can be set at the observation of a slight decrease in the birth rate. From a birth rate of around 30, the rate is decreasing, modestly in the beginning . At the turn of the century, it is 27. The pace of the decrease is then faster and at the end of the period, the birth rate is down to 15. During the same period, the death rate decreases from 20 to 12, resulting in a strong natural population increase. The average total annual increase was 0,8 per cent. The relatively low rate of increase is due to large scale emigration.

The fourth phase, the period after 1930, sometimes called the post-transition stage, is characterized by low and fluctuating fertility, and low and stable mortality. The natural population growth is low. In the 1930s, a period with economic recession, the birth rate was very low. Demographers at that time expected the population growth to halt in the near future. But, the low birth rates of the 1930s were followed by high ones in the 1940s.

2) *Immigration and emigration*

Statistics on immigration and emigration do not have as long a history as that for fertility and mortality. Statistics on emigrants start in 1851 and on immigrants in 1871.

Of course, there was extensive migration in and out of the country in periods prior to these but that migration cannot be observed in any statistical records. A striking example is the dominant role German immigrants played in Swedish trade and culture during the 13th-15th centuries. As regard the international migration that is statistically registered over time, one period above all is quantitatively outstanding: the emigration to North America during the second half of the 19th century and early decades of the 20th century. During the time-period 1880-1930, about 950,000 persons emigrated to North America, that is, 18 per cent of the population size in Sweden at the turn of the century. There were big differences between the emigrant areas of origin in Sweden. In some areas in southern Sweden where the preconditions for reclaiming land were poor and the pressure from rising population heavy, half of the population emigrated. It was above all persons in the age group 15-35 who migrated, especially unmarried men and young families. The age selective migration created substantial problems in the areas from which the migrants left.

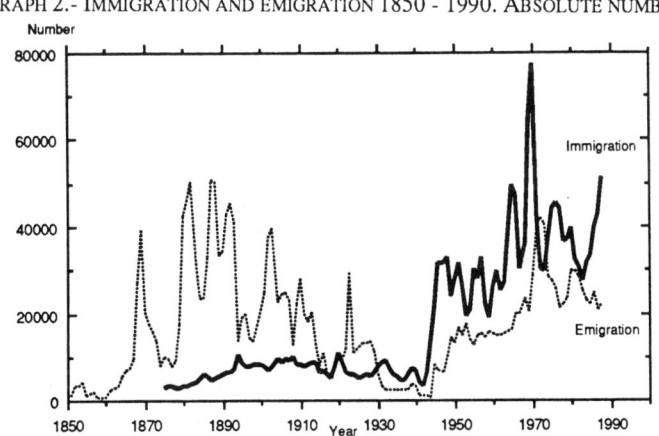

GRAPH 2.- IMMIGRATION AND EMIGRATION 1850 - 1990. ABSOLUTE NUMBERS

It was not only North America that was regarded as a "promised land": about 20 per cent of those who left migrated to other countries. Some moved to neighbouring countries like Denmark or Germany, and a few moved to countries far away, like Argentina. In North America, the Swedish emigrants especially settled in districts similar to the old home district in Sweden, for example, Minnesota. But, for many emigrants the move implied a shift from a rural environment in the old country to an urban one in the new. In 1930, Chicago had, after Stockholm and Gothenburg, the third largest Swedish population.

The extensive emigration also created some immigration. Some emigrants came back to Sweden for a period of time, and then returned to America . Some came back and stayed. But the overwhelming number of emigrants stayed in their new countries.

Until 1930, Sweden was a country of emigration. Since the turn of the century, the prevailing immigration policy was one with many restrictions and regulations. The protectionist policy, aiming to protect both the labour market and the Swedish people from foreign element, was strengthened during the interwar period and the first years of the Second World War. The economic recession during the 1930s led to moderate migration. At the end of the war, Sweden started becoming more "generous" in its policy and the borders were not as closed as previously. In May 1945 the number of foreigners in Sweden was close to 200,000. About half of them were refugees and a majority of them came from neighbouring countries.

3) *Population size and age structure*

During a period of two centuries, 1750-1950, the population of Sweden grew from almost 1.8 million to slightly more than 7 million persons. As was mentioned above, fertility decreased. Measured as the total period fertility rate, it decreased from 4.9 children per women in the beginning of this period to about 1.8 at the end. During the same period, infant mortality decreased from more than 205 children per 1000 births to 46, and the life expectancy at birth increased for women from 36 years to 72 (men from 34 years to 70).

At the same time as the population size increased, changes occurred in where people live, at least at the local level. At the regional level, the inhabitants of Sweden lived in districts that had been settled for a long time, with the exception of the northern half of Sweden which experienced a rising share of the total population in Sweden. But the urbanization on the local level has been pronounced. In 1880, two out of ten Swedes lived in towns or urban areas, fifty years later it was five out of ten, and after a further fifty years, eight out of ten. It should though be remembered that the Swedish definiton of urban area requires only a small population size of 200 persons. But even in an international perspective, the majority of the population live in urban areas. Using a more common international limit for an urban area, that of 2000 persons, yields an urban population of 75 per cent in Sweden. Over half the population live in the country's 15 largest towns and three metropolitan areas.

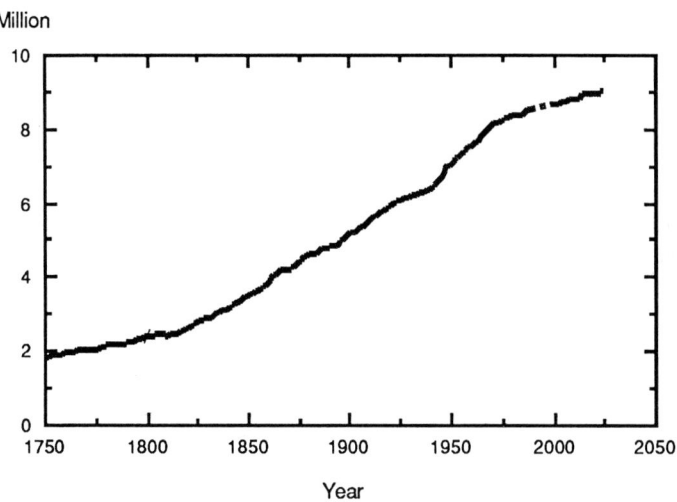

GRAPH 3.- POPULATION SIZE EN SWEDEN 1750 - 1990, AND A PROGNOSIS UPT TO 2025

The age structure of a population and its changes can be seen by calculating an age-dependency ratio. The proportion of young and elderly in the population divided by the population in their working ages. The ratio itself has not changed drastically over the centuries, but the proportion of elderly among the economically dependent parts of the population has exploded over the past 100 years:

TABLE 1.- AGE STRUCTURE

Years of age	1780	1880	1980
- 14	31.7	32.6	19.4
15 - 64	63.2	61.5	64.3
65 +	5.1	5.9	16.3
Age dependency ratio	0.58	0.63	0.56

II. POPULATION DEVELOPMENT AFTER 1950

Characteristics of population trends in Sweden during the period 1950-1990 are fluctuating birth rates, decreasing death rates, an aging population, and, periodically, extensive immigration.

1) *Fertility*

Period fertility was quite high at the beginning of the period, at least compared to the figures 15-20 years earlier, and exceeded what was required for full reproduction. In 1964, the trend of high birth rates was broken, and the total fertility rate fell. The lowest rate was in 1983 at 1.61 and the same picture of "crisis in the population issue" as in the 1930s arose. Different official investigations were initiated to explain the reasons behind low fertility and its consequences for the society. The second part of the 1980s has been characterized by increasing and high fertility. In 1990 the total fertility rate again reached the "magic" level of full reproduction, 2.10.

But to present fertility in Sweden in terms of period measures, yields only a partial picture. To make the picture more complete, cohort fertility must also be studied. In the graph, both period- and cohort fertility can be seen. The x-axis represents figures for the calender year. Cohort fertility for the calender year is given by the birth cohort 27 years earlier.

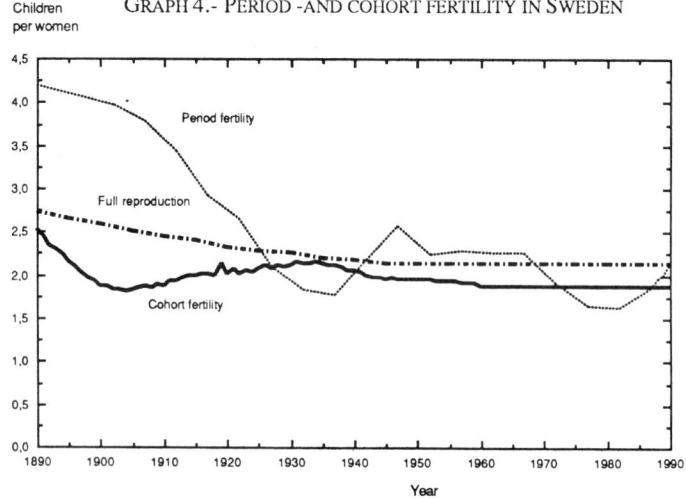

GRAPH 4.- PERIOD -AND COHORT FERTILITY IN SWEDEN

Cohort fertility has been remarkably stable over this century. But, we have seen a slight increase since the period of very low fertility among women born around the turn of the century. Today more women give birth than previously, but they are not having as large families as was more common before. For women born in 1930 onwards the cohort fertility has been around 2. Contemporary norms in Sweden for having children are more homogeneous in all social classes than previously. The dominant norm is quite clearly two children and quite similar for women and men. Almost nine out of ten women have had at least one child, which is an unusually high figure. A hundred years ago childlessness was twice as common.

2) *Nuptiality*

The ways in which families are formed have always been regulated in certain respects and protected by rules. These have been expressed in the form of customs, norms, rules of inheritance, and various laws. The prevailing pattern has changed over the past few decades; many couples now live together without being formally married. They cohabit - a new custom!

This less formal type of family has become common in many countries. What is special about Swedish cohabitation is that this is for many couples comparable to a traditional marriage. This means that many cohabitants have the same mutual relationships as married couples, they share household costs and have children together.

This decreasing importance of marriage has developed over a rather short time. Among women born in the late 1930s, half married after living together with their partner for a year, among women born in the late 1950s, the corresponding figure was only 4 per cent.

Moving together with someone is no longer an irrevocable decision. It has become increasingly common to experience several cohabiting relationships or marriages.

Unmarried cohabitation can only be statistically measured for the whole of the population at census time. The definition of being an unmarried cohabitant at the census is that you have to be registered as living at the same address and in the census form say that you are living together with someone. This definition can in Sweden be seen as rather "strict". Less strict definitions used in some surveys, yield 10-20 percent higher proportions of unmarried cohabitants. The rise of unmarried cohabitation in recent decades has been very rapid, especially among younger couples. In Sweden it surprised many social scientists that the trend of unmarried cohabiting started among daughters in the working class in northern Sweden. It was a common belief that this kind of social innovation would have been started by high educated city people.

TABLE 2.- UNMARRIED COHABITANTS AS A PERCENTAGE OF ALL (MARRIED OR UNMARRIED) COUPLES.
CENSUS DATA.

Age	1975		1980		1985	
	Men	Women	Men	Women	Men	Women
16 - 19	92.1	88.3	91.8	91.0	93.8	93.2
20 - 24	70.8	56.8	80.5	69.3	86.2	77.9
25 - 29	35.5	22.7	50.7	36.9	61.4	48.1
30 - 34	14.6	9.5	25.8	18.0	36.6	27.8
35 - 39	7.6	5.6	13.9	10.2	22.3	17.1
40 - 44	5.5	4.4	8.9	7.3	14.6	11.8
45 - 49	4.6	3.9	6.8	5.9	10.7	9.2
50 - 54	4.0	3.5	5.5	4.8	8.4	7.3
55 - 59	3.2	3.0	4.6	4.0	6.6	5.6
60 - 64	2.8	2.8	3.5	3.3	5.1	3.5
Total	11.2	11.2	14.6	14.7	18.7	18.7

That unmarried cohabition in Sweden is common can also be seen in the development of the proportion of children born to an unmarried mother. Unmarried mother in most cases means a cohabiting unmarried mother. Figures from censuses imply that something like 5 percent of the children are born of mothers who do not live with a male partner. During the 1950s, every tenth child was born to an unmarried mother; today this is true for more than every second child. The regional differences are rather great. In some counties in northern Sweden, 65 per cent of the children are born of unmarried mothers, while it is just 45 per cent in some counties in southern Sweden.

To cohabit without marriage can in many ways be seen as something very similar to a traditional marriage. But there are some signs hinting that this is not the case. One sign was the many older cohabitants who rushed to get married when changes were made in the pension system for women. Those who did not get married before the end of 1989 would end up with poorer pension benefits.

Another sign is that fertility among unmarried cohabitants is lower than among married couples, and that the risk for separation is much higher among unmarried couples than married ones.

The new patterns in Swedish family life will of course change household composition and the living conditions for children. Families with children can be divided into three main categories: traditional families (78 per cent of the children under the age of 18), new families (9 per cent), and single-parent families (13 per cent). During a child´s livecourse, he/she could experience all three categories. According to a big survey, children in Sweden today can, be divided into the following types of families:

- The majority of children live with both their parents in a "traditional" family, and where there are brothers or sisters they are full siblings (78 per cent of all children below the age of 18 years old)
- About one child in ten lives with a single parent, who in most cases is the mother (13 per cent)
- If the single parent cohabits with another person the child will get a "stepfather" or "stepmother" (3 per cent)
- In the new families are more children born - half-brothers and half-sisters - and there are both children who have their two biological parents and children who have a stepmother or a stepfather (5 per cent)
- A small fraction of all children live in families where both parents have children from previous marriages or cohabitations (1 per cent)
- Very few children live in families where there are "my children", "your children" and "our children" (0.3 per cent).

3) *Mortality*

The measure of life expectancy at birth can be seen as an indicator of the health situation and mortality trends in a population at a specific point in time. In Sweden, the life expectancy at birth for women has increased during the period 1948 to 1989 from 71.6 years to 80.1 years. The corresponding figures for men are 69.4 years and 74.2 years. The differences between the sexes have increased; at the beginning of the period it was 2.2 years reaching 5.9 years in the end of the period. This tendency towards a greater difference between the sexes can be seen in most countries in Western Europe.

The greatest increase in life expectancy at birth during this time period can be related to the continuous decrease in infant mortality. It decreased from 19 per thousand births to 6. For other age-groups, the development of mortality has been more varying. A comparison between the death-risks at the end of the 1970s with the risks twenty years earlier illustrates the remarkable decrease in the death-risks of women during this period (see graph 5 a). Among adult men, the death-risks have more or less remained stable, except for middle-aged men for whom even a slight increase occurred. In the beginning of the 1980s, the death risks in a similar way decreased for all ages, and for both sexes (see graph 5b). Analysis of the development during the last part of the 1980s shows a continuation of the decrease, once again similarly for both sexes, except that middle aged men seem to show a stronger reduction than women of the same ages.

GRAPH 5.- A) AND B) CHANGES IN DEATH-RISKS BETWEEN DIFFERENT PERIODS

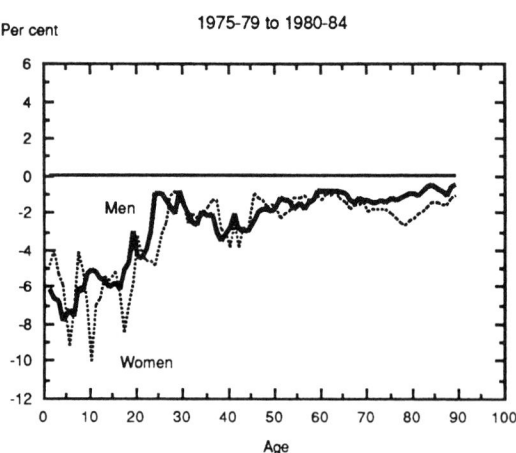

The reduction in mortality since the 1950s has "saved" a lot of lives. The size of the Swedish population in 1988 exceeded by about 1/3 million the size it would have had if the mortality had continued at the same level as in the beginning of the 1950s. The "saved lives" are rather uniformly distributed for men. But, the number of "saved women"

is about three times the number of men and more concentrated in the higher ages. Many of those women are widows, who live alone at the end of their lives. Old-age pensioners account for 40 per cent of all one-person households.

GRAPH 6.- "SAVED LIVES"

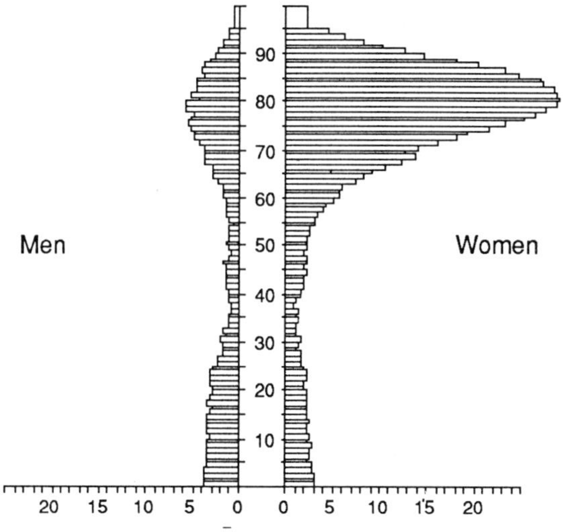

Men   Women

4) Migration

Sweden has over the past forty years shifted from a country with a net emigration to one with a net immigration (see graph 2). Another striking change is that during recent decades the numbers of migrants, in- as well as out- migration, are much more extensive than has previously been the case

Migration of the past 40 years can be grouped into three phenomena. The first one is characterized by labour immigration, the second by emigration of earlier labour immigrants, and the third by immigration of refugees and relatives of previous immigrants.

The great expansion of the Swedish economy after the Second World War called for an increase in the workforce, both in industry and in the rapidly expanding public sector. Workers were recruited from the Nordic countries, mainly Finland, and, through special recruiting campaigns, from southern Europe. The largest group that came to Sweden were Finns, but these campaigns also attracted many persons from southern Europe. At the end of the 1970s, for example, over 70,000 persons from Yugoslavia and Greece were living in Sweden.

To avoid labour-market problems, immigration was restricted in the late 1960s, but this did not mean that immigration to Sweden ceased all at once. Instead, it actually increased for a few years, mainly due to a large increase in the number of the Finns who still could immigrate due to the open Nordic labour market.

When the economic situation changed in Sweden as well as in the immigrant home-countries, many immigrants returned to their places of origin. The first fairly large emigration in Sweden in modern times consisted of Finns moving back to Finland in the 1960s and 1970s. Today only about half of the Finns that came to Sweden in the 1960s and 1970s still live in Sweden. The general pattern among immigrants is that about one out of three has left the country after a period of five years.

TABLE 3.- PROPORTION (%) OF IMMIGRANTS THAT HAVE LEFT SWEDEN (AFTER LENGTH OF STAY IN SWEDEN)

Year of immigration	Number	Proportion that have left Sweden after years				
		1	5	10	15	20
1969	64.503	13	39	45	50	52
1974	37.430	16	33	43	47	
1979	37.025	14	39	41		
1984	31.486	11	25			
1988	21.461	21				

Since the 1970s, labour immigration has practically come to a halt, being replaced by refugees and relatives of previous immigrants. This new type of immigration partly changed the pattern of countries of origin of the immigrants. Political conflicts and wars in countries and cultures far from Sweden are steering for who will come to Sweden. Previously (1970), 10 per cent of the immigrants came from non-European countries; during the second part of the 1980s, the corresponding figure was about 50 per cent (1989).

GRAPH 7.- IMMIGRANTS ACCORDING TO COUNTRY OF ORIGIN 1986-1990.

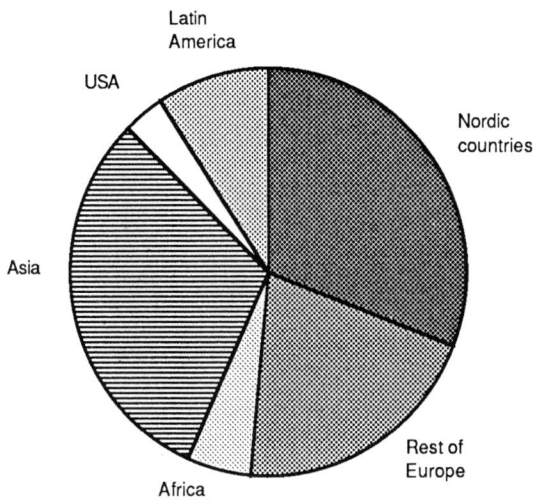

5) *The latest population development and a prognosis*

The population development in recent years in Sweden has been especially linked to rising fertility. Other tendencies include a continuation of declining death risks, a rather strengthening of the family as an institution, and rising immigration until 1989. In December 1989, the rules and regulations for asylum started being implemented more strictly, resulting in a decrease in immigration.

The total fertility rate increased from 1.73 in 1985 to 2.13 in 1990 (Table 4). Figures for the first half of 1991 indicate that this high level is continuing into 1991. The fertility in Sweden is at present one of the highest in Europe. The rise in Swedish fertility can to a great extent be explained by earlier postponements of births for which women are now compensating. A more and more common attitude among young Swedish women and couples is to try to plan their lives in such a way that education and a gainful employment precedes periods of having and raising children. The relatively low birth rates among younger women is a manifestation of the fact that younger generations

TABLE 4.- SOME INDICATORS OF POPULATION DEVELOPMENT IN SWEDEN IN RECENT YEARS

Year	TFR	Births	Deaths	Marriages	Divorces	Immigrants	Emigrants	Pop.
1985	1.73	98500	94000	38300	20000	33100	22000	8358100
1986	1.79	102000	93000	39000	19100	39500	24500	8381500
1987	1.84	104699	93000	41200	18400	42700	20700	8414100
1988	1.96	112000	97000	44200	17700	51100	21500	8458900
1989	2.02	116000	92000	109000	18900	65900	21500	8527000
1990	2.13	124000	95000	40000	19000	60000	25200	8590600

choose to invest in education and worklife first, and children later. During the past 15 years, the mean age of mothers giving birth to their first child has increased by almost two years (1989: 26,2 years of age). This means that the proportion of women at a certain age that has given birth to their first child has decreased (see graph 8). The peak of the curve in the diagram for 20 years-olds shows that women born in the middle of the 1940s had their first child relatively early. More than 23 per cent gave birth to their first child at the age of 20. The corresponding figure for women born in the middle of the 1960s was 6 per cent. Women in the 1950s had their first child successively later. The low proportions of childbearing in young ages results in a great proportion childless women in their thirties who then try to catch up and give birth to their normative two children.

Another central component in the explanation of the fertility increase in Sweden is the reduction in the time elapsing between the children to which a woman gives birth. The fact that the upswing has occurred so rapidly is due to the fact that more second and third children are being born than was previously the case. Childbearing is now more concentrated in time for most women. The faster pace is seen (see graph 9) in the proportion of women who give birth to their second child within 2.5 years of the first (the length of the time period has in part been chosen with regard to the parental allowance specifications). The proportion was previously greatest among young women. (In the graph, they are represented by the women who gave birth to their first child at the age of 20.) A peak of 35 per cent was reached in the early 1960s. During the 1970s, the proportion sank closer to 20 per cent at the same time as the differences between the ages levelled off. From the middle of the 1970s, the pace has increased rapidly. Over 40 per cent of mothers now have their second child within 2.5 years. And the curve is pointing upwards.

GRAPH 8.- PROPORTION OF WOMEN WITH CHILDREN, BY WOMAN´S YEAR OF BIRTH AND AGE

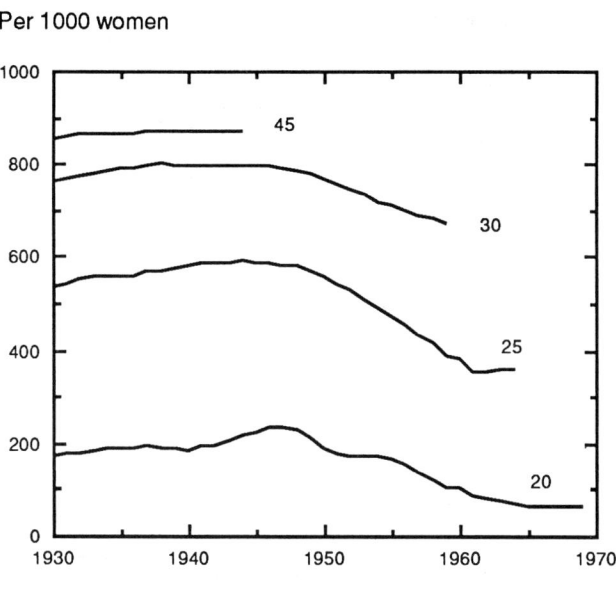

TABLE 5.- EXTRA-MARITAL BIRTHS. PER CENT.

Year	Per cent	Year	Per cent
1900	11.4	1982	42.0
1950	9.8	1983	43.6
1955	10.0	1984	44.6
1960	11.3	1985	46.4
1965	13.8	1986	48.4
1970	18.4	1987	49.9
1975	32.4	1988	50.9
1980	39.7	1989	51.8
1981	41.2		

GRAPH 9.- PROPORTION OF WOMEN WHO GIVE BIRTH TO THEIR SECOND CHILD WITHIN 2.5 YEARS OF THEIR FIRST, BY AGE AT BIRTH OF FIRST CHILD.

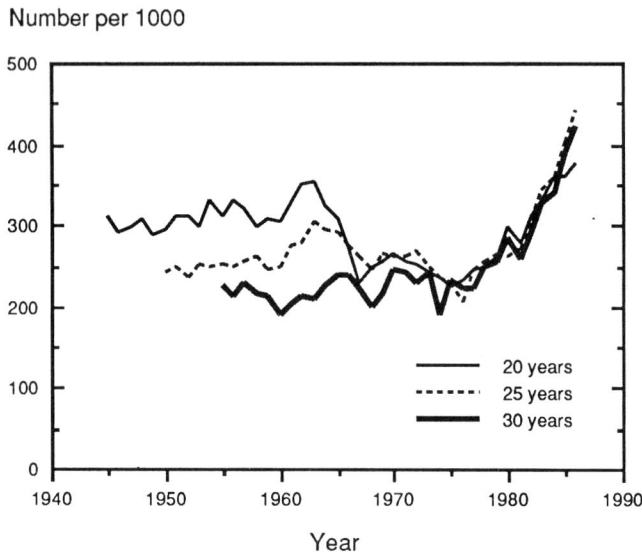

In the field of family, recent years have been characterized by a slight increase in marriages and a small decrease in divorces (Table 4). The changes has been moderate, with one remarkable exception. A new law came into force at the turn of the year 1989/90 stipulating new conditions for widows' pensions This law implied less favourable widow pensions, and after encouragement on the part of the largest trade unions and substantial media attention, many cohabiting couples then married causing a marriage explosion. In 1989, the number of marriages was almost three times as many as in normal years, that is 109,000 compared to 40,000. During December 1989, 64,000 couples got married, compared with normal figures for the previous December of 3,000. Most of the women who married during December were older than brides usually are: their average age was 34 years old compared with 32 years in the corresponding month the previous year.

Mortality has continued to decrease slowly in much the same way as during the 1980s. There might be a slight tendency towards a more similar development of the decrease in the death-risks between the sexes than what was the case in previous years.

SWEDEN/ LA SUEDE

The stricter review of applications for asylum in Sweden has broken the rising immigration of recent years. After the new practices began being applied at the turn of the year 1989/90, the number of immigrants decreased by 10 per cent during the first year. The decrease seems to be continuing. The number of immigrants during the first quarter of 1991 was 33.per cent fewer than during the corresponding period the previous year. Corresponding figures for emigration showed an increase of 17 per cent between 1990 and 1989. Emigration is continuing to increase during 1991, with the first quarter of 1991 showing a further increase of 9 per cent compared with the previous year. This resulted in a decrease in the net surplus of immigrants by over 20 per cent per year.

In the latest population prognosis for Sweden for the years 1990-2025, it is assumed that fertility will fall from its present high level to 1.95 child per woman by 1994. In a long term perspective, it is assumed that the cohort fertility will decline from 2.0 for the cohorts born in the beginning of the 1940s to 1.95 for cohorts born later. Younger women, like the cohort 1960, are assumed to have even fewer children, 1.87 per woman. The motivation for this assumption is that many women in those young cohorts postponed starting families, which will result in more women not giving birth. At the same time, the norm with two children is more widespread, while fewer women have large families:

Women born	Parity					Number of children per women
	0	1	2	3	4 +	
1940	13	16	42	21	8	2.00
1960 (prognosis)	15	15	45	20	5	1.87

In the prognosis, it is assumed that the reduction in mortality is continuing. During the first ten years of the forecast period, it is assumed that the death-risks for most ages will decrease by 1-2 per cent. After the turn of the century, it is assumed, that the death-risks will remain at the level they then have. Those assumptions result in the life expectancy at birth for men rising at the turn of the century by one year to 75.4 years, and for women by one year to 81.7 years of age. The future annual net migration is assumed to be 15,000 per year, which will mean a decrease in relation to previous years.

The result of the prognosis is that the population size in Sweden will pass 9 million in 2003, and at the end of the period will reach 9.5 million. But, the future population will also be an old one. At the turn of the century, 16.9 per cent of the population will be older than 65 years of age, and 5.0 per cent older than 80 years of age. In 2025, the proportions will increase to 20.2 and 5.6 per cent respectively. This is an increase of the present proportions by 2.4 and 1.4 per cent respectively.

If we instead look only at the "growth power" of the initial population itself, assuming the net migration to be zero, the population will grow by 130,000 persons by the turn of the century. Assuming this, the population at the end of the forecast period, the year 2025, will have started its decline. The population size at that time will exceed the present by just 90,000 persons. The proportion of retired persons would in 2025 be 21.8 per cent, and the proportion of very old 6.0 per cent.

III. POPULATION POLICY

Sweden has no politically recognized population policy, although there is an extensive political activity in different fields of politics like family-, housing-, health-, support to refugees etc, all of which directly or indirectly affect the size, age composition, and growth of the population. Political decisions and measures taken can have expected as well as unexpected, desired as well as undesired, effects on fertility, mortality, migration, and other demographic indicators.

During various phases of the development of the population, people and politicians have expressed great concern about the economic and political consequences a new trend might have. Often this concern has been channeled into various typically Swedish committees of inquiry, which have been assigned the investigation of the problem. The earliest examples of commissions of this kind date back more than two hundred years.

At the beginning of the century, the concern over the previous decades' emigration led to a public and political debate on the need in Sweden of a general economic reform and socio-political improvements.

The low birth rate in the early 1930s brought about extensive political activity. The book *Crisis in Population* by Alva and Gunnar Myrdal was much cited in the debate and had great political impact. The general political concern about the population development was used to push through well needed improvements for families with children.

Widespread urbanisation during the 1960s led to the appointment of various regional-political commissions. One result of these was that several government agencies were moved out from Stockholm to the provinces.

The low birth-rates during the 1970s and early 1980s caused new concern about the demographic future of the population. The government appointed a committee to investigate whether a low birth rate might in the long term create problems for economic growth. The results indicated that resources can be released when there are fewer children to be brought up and educated. If these resources are invested, economic growth will not slow down.

In this paper we will briefly describe some political fields that might have a demographic impact on the population.

1) Abortions

The Swedish law on abortion in principle specifies that the woman herself is to decide whether she wants to have an abortion or not, on the condition that the abortion be carried out before the 18th week of the pregnancy and that the abortion is judged not to cause any harm to the woman's health. After the 12th week of pregnancy, a compulsory consultation discussion is required. The present law is from 1975, and at that time replaced a much stricter law. Simultaneously with the new liberal law, a comprehensive campaign was started which was aimed at preventing abortions (information on sexual matters, advisory services on the use of contraceptives, etc). The new law led to an increasing proportion of abortions carried out early in the pregnancy. Today 92 per cent of all abortions are carried out before the 12th week of pregnancy. In the late 1960s, the corresponding figure was only 43 per cent. It is of course very difficult to determine the impact of the new and more liberal abortion law on the birth rate, and to what extent legal abortions would be replaced, by illegal ones. Further, it is hard to know what impact a legal abortion has on a woman's total number of children or if it just affects the point in her life when she has her children.

Since the new abortion law took force, about 30,000 abortions have been carried out annually in Sweden. The number has been rather constant over time and corresponds to about one in four pregnancies being terminated by an abortion (if all pregnancies are seen as births + abortions). Recent years' increase in fertility has been followed by a similar increase in abortions.

2) Family policy

Within the concept of family policy, a spectrum of different political goals and measures can be included. This concept can cover different areas such as housing policy and price policy. In the first area, there are special rent subsidies for families with low incomes, in many cases families with children, and for the latter, the state subsidizes milk since it is an important ingredient in families' daily consumption. But in the public debate, family policy is most often just seen as the monetary support (or reduction in taxes and fees) that goes directly to families with children, and the different measures that are taken which are aimed at facilitating everyday life for families with children and at making it possible for both parents to work outside the home. This is an extremely important political field in Sweden while labor force participation for women is very high. At present, the labor force participation rate for women is 81.4 per cent. This is just 4.2

percentage lower than what men have. The gap between labor force participation of men and women has diminished dramatically. Women with children often work part-time. Of all women with a child under the age of seven, about one-third work full-time and about half work part-time.

Some of the support made directly to families with children, and to no one else, are:

a) CHILD ALLOWANCES

Child allowances were introduced into Swedish family policy in 1948. The principle behind this form of support is that every child is to receive the same monthly economic support regardless of the income of its parents. The child allowance was over a long period of time the same for every parity. But since 1982, the sum is higher for child number three up to child number six. The motivation for the reform was not to stimulate people having more children, but to help families with many children in times of inflation and rising prices for food and daily consumption goods. The allowance is received until the child is 16 years old. If the child continues his/her studies, an additional support can be received for another few years.

In 1990, the child allowance in relation to number of children was:

1 child	560	SEK/month
2 children	1120	-"-
3 children	1960	-"-
4 children	3584	-"-
5 children	5465	-"-
6 children	6944	-"-

b) MATERNITY/PARENTAL LEAVE

Since before World War II, Swedish women working in paid employment have had the right to a paid maternity leave after the arrival of a child. Since then, the right has been extended several times as well as the concept. One of the most important changes was made in 1974 when the rights were extended to men and allowed the parents to share the benefit with paid leave in any way they wish.

At present, the law can be summarized in the following way:
The payment for maternity leave is linked to the concept of sick leave. Normally, the payment is 90 per cent of the salary. To receive this payment as maternity leave, a woman must have been employed for the past 6 months or for at least 12 months during the past two years.

SWEDEN/ LA SUEDE

Women with physically demanding work have the right during the two last months of their pregnancy to perform less strenuous or to receive a special kind of pregnancy allowance in connection with sick leave.

When a child is born, the father has the right to be at home for a total of 10 days with 90 per cent of his salary. Those 10 days are exclusively for the father and are intended to be used after the mother has returned from the hospital.

The mother or father has the right to be home from work during a total period of 450 days. One year is accompanied by sick leave, and the additional 90 days with a lower benefit of the same amount for all parents (60 SEK per day).

Up until the child is 8 years of age, both parents have the right to reduce their working hours by up to 25 per cent. This reduction is followed by a similar reduction in salary.

c) SPECIAL MATERNITY LEAVE

From the birth of the child up until its 12th birthday, both parents have the right to be home when the child is sick. The parent is to receive her or his ordinary sick leave. The right to be home is limited to 60 days per child and year.

Both parents also have the right to come with the child to the day care center or school three days a year. The economic compensation is equal to the ordinary sick leave.

Within the concept of *Swedish family policy*, all kinds of services provided to the child and parents by the state free of charge or with subsidies are included. This encompasses various kinds of health and hospital care, free dental care, free schooling and school-books, etc.

An important goal of Swedish family policy is to provide all children at the age of one and a half year a place in a day-care center. This right will form the basis for the possibility of parents to work outside the home.

3) Citizenship and immigration

The Nordic countries together form an open labour market, which means that the migration among these countries is unrestricted. A person from any Nordic country can come to Sweden and work on the same conditions as a Swede. For non-Nordic citizens, it is necessary to obtain a residence permit to stay in the country and a working permit to work.

In order to become a Swedish citizen it is in principle necessary for a person:

- to have been a resident in Sweden for five years (Nordic citizens two years)
- to be at least 18 years of age (children usually become Swedish citizens when their parents do)
- to have a clean criminal record

During the 1980s, about 20,000 persons annually were naturalized, one fourth of whom were born in Sweden. Those who received Swedish citizenship in the late 1980s may be described as follows:
- One in three was a citizen of a Nordic country; Finnish citizens comprised the largest group
- One in four was a citizen of some other European country; the commonest countries were Poland, Yugoslavia, Greece and Hungary.
- One in four was a citizen of some Asian country, normally from India, Iraq, Lebanon or South Korea
- One in ten was a citizen of some South American country, mainly Chile, Colombia or Uruguay.
- One in ten was a citizen of an African country; the largest group was from Ethiopia

The new Swedes are on average young; half of them are under 25 years of age. Only one in ten was over 50.

During the past few years the Swedish immigration policy partly has been partially reoriented, and the government has decided to build up a system that to a greater extent than before gives those refugees that are in the most need the right to immigrate here. At the same time more aid will be given to refugees in their home countries to assist and help them to create a decent future there. However, it is still too soon to see the results of this new direction in the migration policy.

 Co-Éditions

L'Institut National d'Études Démographiques (INED) publie les résultats de travaux d'intérêt démographique dans plusieurs collections (catalogue sur demande à l'INED) :

The National Institute for Demographic Studies in Paris (INED) publishes in several series a wide variety of works of demographic interest (catalogue available at INED on request):

Un accord particulier avec les éditions John Libbey Eurotext pour la série «Congrès et Colloques», prévoit une co-édition des ouvrages publiés partiellement ou totalement en langue anglaise. Ces ouvrages, signalés par le logo "JL" dans l'extrait du catalogue ci-dessous, sont diffusés par John Libbey.

> Travaux et documents
> Manuels
> Classiques de l'Économie et de la Population
> Données statistiques
> Congrès et Colloques

A special agreement has been signed with John Libbey Eurotext for the series «Congresses and Colloquia», concerning books partly or fully written in English. These editions are identified in the following list by "JL" and are sold directly by John Libbey.

Congrès et Colloques

9 *European population.* En préparation JL
Vol. 2: New dynamics, new analyses.

8 Jean-Louis Rallu et Alain Blum (éds) 300 F JL
European population. Vol. 1: Country analysis. 1991, 450 p.

7 Thérèse Hibert et Louis Roussel (éds) 150 F Ined
La nuptialité. Evolution récente en France et dans les pays développés.
280 p.

6 Denise Pumain (éd.) 300 F JL
Spatial analysis and population dynamics / Analyse spatiale et dynamique des populations. 1991, 458 p.

5 Georges Tapinos, Didier Blanchet, David E. Horlacher (éds) 150 F Ined
Conséquences de la croissance démographique rapide dans les pays en développement. 1991, 368 p.

4 France Prioux (éd.) 150 F Ined
La famille dans les pays développés : permanences et changements.
1990, 316 p.

3 André Chaventré et Derek F. Roberts (éds) 150 F Ined
Approche pluridisciplinaire des isolats humains / Pluridisciplinary approach of human isolates. 1990, 460 p.

2 Catherine Bonvalet et Anne-Marie Fribourg (éds) 130 F Ined
Stratégies résidentielles. Séminaire Ined, Pca, Metlm, 1990, 460 p.

1 Actes du 1er Colloque franco-soviétique de démographie, Paris, oct. 1984. 75 F Ined
La situation démographique en France et en Union soviétique.
1991, 276 p.

BULLETINS DE COMMANDE DES OUVRAGES CONGRÈS ET COLLOQUES

Édités par JOHN LIBBEY EUROTEXT *

Renvoyer à John Libbey Eurotext :
6, rue Blanche, 95120 MONTROUGE, France - Tél. (1) 47 35 85 82

Nom : .... Prénom : ....

ou Raison sociale : ....

Adresse : ....

| Titre : | .... | n° | ...... |

| Titre : | .... | n° | ...... |

*Joindre la somme de .... F * (Ajouter 10% aux prix du catalogue pour couvrir les frais de port), par chèque bancaire ou postal, à l'ordre de John Libbey Eurotext.*

------------✂------------

Édités par l'INED *

Renvoyer à l'INED :
27, rue du Commandeur, 75675 PARIS Cedex 14, France - Tél. (1) 43 20 13 45

Nom : .... Prénom ....

ou Raison sociale : ....

Adresse : ....

| Titre : | .... | n° | ...... |

| Titre : | .... | n° | ...... |

| Titre : | .... | n° | ...... |

*Joindre la somme de .... F * (Ajouter 10% aux prix du catalogue pour couvrir les frais de port), à l'ordre de l'Agent Comptable de l'INED*

☐ par chèque bancaire   ☐ par virement postal CCP PARIS 9061-56H

---

* Les mentions Ined ou JL (John Libbey), ainsi que le prix de chaque ouvrage, sont indiqués ci-avant dans la liste des ouvrages. Les ouvrages édités par l'INED sont en vente en librairie universitaire (PUF).

Achevé d'imprimer par Corlet, Imprimeur, S.A.
14110 Condé-sur-Noireau (France)
N° d'Imprimeur : 2587 - Dépôt légal : octobre 1991
Imprimé en C.E.E.